GRAMMAR OF NEW TESTAMENT GREEK.

GRAMMAR OF
NEW TESTAMENT GREEK

BY

FRIEDRICH BLASS, Dr.Phil., D.Th., Hon. LL.D. Dublin

PROFESSOR OF CLASSICAL PHILOLOGY IN THE UNIVERSITY OF HALLE-WITTENBERG

TRANSLATED BY

HENRY ST. JOHN THACKERAY, M.A.

EXAMINER IN THE EDUCATION DEPARTMENT

WIPF & STOCK · Eugene, Oregon

Wipf and Stock Publishers
199 W 8th Ave, Suite 3
Eugene, OR 97401

Grammar of New Testament Greek
By Blass, Friedrich W. and Thackeray, H. St. J.
ISBN 13: 978-1-60608-140-2
Publication date 11/15/2010
Previously published by Macmillan and Co., 1898

PREFACE TO THE ENGLISH EDITION.

PROFESSOR BLASS'S *Grammatik des Neutestamentlichen Griechisch* appeared in Germany in October, 1896. The present translation reproduces the whole work with the exception of the Preface, which the author considered unsuitable to the English edition, on account of the somewhat personal character given to it by the dedication which he had combined with it. Some points of the Preface, however, are of sufficient general interest to be reproduced here in a summary form.

The author maintains that whereas Hellenistic Greek cannot in comparison with Attic Greek be regarded as a very rich language, it is for all that (except where borrowed literary words and phrases intrude themselves) a pure language, which is governed by regular laws of its own. He applies to it the proverb $\tau\hat{\omega}\nu$ $\kappa\alpha\lambda\hat{\omega}\nu$ $\kappa\alpha\grave{\iota}$ $\tau\grave{o}$ $\mu\epsilon\tau\acute{o}\pi\omega\rho o\nu$ $\kappa\alpha\lambda\acute{o}\nu$.

The present work does not profess to give the elements of Greek grammar, but presupposes some knowledge on the part of the reader. Those who desire to read the Greek Testament after a two months' study of the Greek language are referred to such works as Huddilston's *Essentials of New Testament Greek.*

With regard to textual criticism, a distinguishing feature in the grammar is that whereas earlier grammarians quote the editions of the leading N.T. critics, Professor Blass quotes the MSS., leaving the reader to draw his own conclusions as to the true text in each instance. Whilst admitting that we have now reached something like a new "Textus Receptus" based on the oldest Greek tradition, and acknowledging the services rendered to N.T. criticism by such critics as Lachmann, Tischendorf, Westcott and Hort, and Tregelles, he has to confess that a definite conclusion on this subject has not yet been arrived at.

The only point in reference to matters of 'higher criticism' to which attention has to be called is that the John who wrote the

Apocalypse is distinguished from John the author of the Gospel and Epistles. The first and second Epistles of Peter do not present sufficiently well-marked differences to require a distinction to be drawn between them in a grammar of this kind. The Pauline Epistles are all quoted as the work of St. Paul; the Epistle to the Hebrews is naturally not so quoted. The general position taken up by Professor Blass with regard to questions of authorship is shown by the following words: 'The tradition which has been transmitted to us as to the names of the authors of the N.T. books, in so far as it is unanimous, I hold to be approximately contemporary with those authors; that is to say, the approximation is as close as we can at present look for; and, without claiming to be a prophet, one may assert that, to whatever nearer approximation we may be brought by fortunate discoveries in the future, Luke will remain Luke, and Mark will continue to be Mark.'

The books to which the author expresses his obligations are the grammars of Winer (including the new edition of P. Schmiedel) and Buttmann, Jos. Viteau, *Étude sur le Grec du N.T.*, Paris, 1893, and Burton, *Syntax of the Moods and Tenses in N.T. Greek*, Chicago, 1893. The first-named of these works having grown to such voluminous proportions, the present grammar, written in a smaller compass, may, the author hopes, find a place beside it for such persons as maintain the opinion μέγα βιβλίον μέγα κακόν.

The isolation of the N.T. from other contemporary or nearly contemporary writings is a hindrance to the proper understanding of it, and should by all means be avoided; illustrations are therefore drawn by the writer from the Epistle of Barnabas, the Shepherd of Hermas, the first and the so-called second Epistle of Clement, and the Clementine Homilies.

The translator has merely to add that the references have been to a great extent verified by him, and that the proofs have all passed through the hands of Professor Blass, who has introduced several additions and corrections which are not contained in the original German edition. He has also to express his thanks to the Rev. A. E. Brooke, Fellow of King's College, Cambridge, for kindly looking over the greater part of the translation in MS. and removing some of its imperfections, and to two of his own sisters for welcome assistance in the work of transposing the third of the Indices to suit the new pagination.

H. St. J. T.

May 13, 1898.

CONTENTS.

PART I.

INTRODUCTION, PHONETICS, AND ACCIDENCE.

	PAGE
§ 1. Introduction,	1
§ 2. Elements of the New Testament language,	2
§ 3. Orthography,	6
§ 4. Division of words, accents, breathings, punctuation,	13
§ 5. Elision, crasis, variable final consonants,	18
§ 6. Sporadic sound-changes,	20
§ 7. First and second declensions,	25
§ 8. Third declension,	26
§ 9. Metaplasmus,	28
§ 10. Proper names. Indeclinable nouns,	29
§ 11. Adjectives,	32
§ 12. Numerals,	35
§ 13. Pronouns,	35
§ 14. System of conjugation,	36
§ 15. Augment and reduplication,	37
§ 16. Verbs in -ω. Tense formation,	40
§ 17. Verbs in -ω. New formation of a present tense,	40
§ 18. Verbs in -ω. On the formation of the future,	41
§ 19. Verbs in -ω. First and second aorist,	43
§ 20. Verbs in -ω. Aorist and future of deponent verbs,	44
§ 21. Verbs in -ω. Terminations,	45
§ 22. Contract verbs,	47
§ 23. Verbs in -μι,	48
§ 24. Table of noteworthy verbs,	52
§ 25. Adverbs,	58
§ 26. Particles,	60
§ 27. Word-formation by means of terminations and suffixes,	61
§ 28. Word-formation by composition,	65
§ 29. Proper names,	70

PART II.

SYNTAX.

	PAGE
§ 30. Subject and predicate,	72
§ 31. Agreement,	76

SYNTAX OF THE NOUN.

§ 32. Gender and number,	82
§ 33. The cases. Nominative and vocative,	84
§ 34. The accusative,	87
§ 35. The genitive,	95
§ 36. Continuation: genitive with verbs, etc.,	100
§ 37. Dative,	109
§ 38. Continuation: instrumental and temporal dative,	116
§ 39. The cases with prepositions. Prepositions with the accusative,	121
§ 40. Prepositions with the genitive,	124
§ 41. Prepositions with the dative,	130
§ 42. Prepositions with two cases,	132
§ 43. Prepositions with three cases,	136
§ 44. Syntax of the adjective,	140
§ 45. Numerals,	144
§ 46. The article. I. ὁ, ἡ, τό as pronoun; the article with independent substantives,	145
§ 47. The article. II. The article with adjectives etc.; the article with connected parts of speech,	154

SYNTAX OF THE PRONOUNS.

§ 48. Personal, reflexive, and possessive pronouns,	164
§ 49. Demonstrative pronouns,	170
§ 50. Relative and interrogative pronouns,	172
§ 51. Indefinite pronouns; pronominal words,	177

SYNTAX OF THE VERB.

§ 52. The voices of the verb,	180
§ 53. Active voice,	181
§ 54. Passive voice,	184
§ 55. Middle voice,	185
§ 56. The tenses. Present tense,	187
§ 57. Imperfect and aorist indicative,	190
§ 58. Moods of the present and the aorist,	194

CONTENTS.   ix

		PAGE
§ 59.	The perfect,	198
§ 60.	Pluperfect,	201
§ 61.	Future,	201
§ 62.	Periphrastic conjugation,	202
§ 63.	The moods. Indicative of unreality (and repetition),	205
§ 64.	Conjunctive and future (or present) indicative in principal clauses,	208
§ 65.	Conjunctive and future (or present) indicative in subordinate clauses,	211
§ 66.	Remains of the optative,	219
§ 67.	Imperative,	221
§ 68.	Infinitive,	221
§ 69.	Infinitive and periphrasis with ἵνα,	222
§ 70.	Infinitive and periphrasis with ὅτι,	230
§ 71.	Infinitive with the article,	233
§ 72.	Cases with the infinitive. Nominative and accusative with the infinitive,	237
§ 73.	Participle. (I.) Participle as attribute—representing a substantive —as predicate,	242
§ 74.	Participle. (II.) As an additional clause in the sentence,	247
§ 75.	The negatives,	253
§ 76.	Other adverbs,	257
§ 77.	Particles (conjunctions),	259
§ 78.	Particles (continued),	270
§ 79.	Connection of sentences,	275
§ 80.	Position of words (position of clauses),	287
§ 81.	Ellipse (Brachylogy), pleonasm,	291
§ 82.	Arrangement of words; figures of speech,	295

INDEX.

I.	Index of subjects,	304
II.	Index of Greek words,	312
III.	Index of New Testament passages,	332

CORRIGENDA.

p. 3, line 28, *for* 'of the present day' *read* 'or those which they have reached at the present day
p. 60, line 22, *for* οὐν *read* οὖν.
p. 68, last line, *for* 3 Jo. 2 *read* 3 Jo. 9.
p. 114, line 14, *for* κολλᾶσθαι *read* κολλᾶσθαί.
    line 29, *omit the comma before* τῇ πίστει.
    line 36, *for* 'for which' *read* 'for the dative.'
p. 115, 12 lines from the bottom, *for* πλήγας *read* πληγάς.
    2 lines from the bottom, *for* τινι *read* τινί.
p. 172, line 14, *for* Mt. 24. 23 *read* Mt. 24. 43.
p. 220, note 1, *for* A. 1. 8 *read* A. 1. 20.
p. 232, line 3, *for* H. 13. 8 *read* H. 13. 18.

PART I.

INTRODUCTION: PHONETICS AND ACCIDENCE.

§ 1. INTRODUCTION.

1. The special study of the grammar of New Testament Greek has been for the most part prompted by purely practical needs. In Greek literature as such the writings brought together in the New Testament can claim but a very modest position; and the general grammar of the Greek language can take but very limited notice of the special features which they present. Yet, on the other hand, their contents give them so paramount an importance, that in order to understand them fully, and to restore them to their primitive form, the most exact investigation even of their grammatical peculiarities becomes an absolute necessity.

The New Testament writers represent in general that portion of the population of the Hellenised East, which, while it employed Greek more or less fluently as the language of intercourse and commerce—side by side with the native languages which were by no means superseded—yet remained unfamiliar with the real Hellenic culture and the literature of classical Greek. How far, in this respect, exceptions are to be admitted in the case of Luke and Paul, as also in the case of the author of the Epistle to the Hebrews (Barnabas), it is not easy to decide: at any rate the traces of classical culture even in these writers are next to nothing, whereas in the next generation a Clement of Rome, with his γυναῖκες Δαναΐδες καὶ Δίρκαι and his story of the phœnix,[1] at once displays an entirely different character. Accordingly, the language employed in the N.T. is such as was spoken in the lower circles of society, not such as was written in works of literature. But between these two forms of speech there existed even at that time a very considerable difference. The literary language had always remained dependent in some measure on the old classical masterpieces; and though in the first centuries of Hellenic influence it had followed the development of the living language, and so had parted some distance from those models, yet since the first century before Christ it had kept struggling back to them again with an ever-increasing determination.

[1] Clem. ad Corinth. vi. 2 : xxv.

If, then, the literature of the Alexandrian period must be called Hellenistic, that of the Roman period must be termed Atticistic. But the popular language had gone its own way, and continued to do so until out of ancient Greek there was gradually developed modern Greek, which, however, in its literature—its prose literature in particular—is still very strongly affected by classic influences. The N.T. then shows us an intermediate stage on the road between ancient and modern Greek; on this ground, too, its language is deserving of a special treatment.

2. It is indeed true that for a knowledge of the popular language of the first century after Christ, as of the immediately preceding and succeeding periods, the N.T. is by no means our only source. In the way of literature not much is to be added, certainly nothing which can diminish the supreme importance of the N.T. Undoubtedly the Greek translations of the Old Testament show a great affinity of language, but they are translations, and slavishly literal translations; no one ever spoke so, not even the Jewish translators. Of profane literature, one might perhaps quote the discourses of Epictetus contained in Arrian's commentary as the work most available for our purpose. But the spoken language is found quite pure, purer by far than in the N.T. itself—found, too, in its various gradations, corresponding naturally to the position and education of the speaker—in those private records, the number and importance of which is being perpetually increased by fresh discoveries in Egypt. The language of the N.T. may, therefore, be quite rightly treated in close connection with these. A grammar of the popular language of the period, written on the basis of all these various authorities and remains, would be perhaps, from the grammarian's point of view, more satisfactory than one which was limited to the language of the New Testament.[1] The practical considerations, however, from which we set out, will be constantly imposing such a limitation; for it cannot be of the same importance to us to know what some chance Egyptian writes in a letter or deed of sale, as it is to know what the men of the N.T. have written, however true it may be that in their own day the cultured world drew no distinction between these last and the lower classes of Egyptians and Syrians, and despised them both alike.

§ 2. ELEMENTS OF THE NEW TESTAMENT LANGUAGE.

1. By far the most predominant element in the language of the New Testament is the Greek of common speech which was disseminated in the East by the Macedonian conquest, in the form which it had gradually assumed under the wider development of several centuries. This common speech is in the main a somewhat modified Attic, in which were omitted such Attic peculiarities as appeared too strange to the bulk of the remaining Greeks, such as ττ instead of σσ in θάλαττα etc., and ρρ instead of ρσ in ἄρρην

---

[1] Cf. G. A. Deissmann, Bibelstudien (Marburg, 1895), p. 57 ff.

etc. As a matter of course it is the later Attic, not the older, which lies at the base of it, which explains, to take one example, the absence of any trace of a dual in this language. But as the development extended, the remaining distinctions in the language between duality and plurality were also set aside: not only is πότερος abandoned for τίς, ἑκάτερος for ἕκαστος, and so on, but above all the superlative is abandoned for the comparative: and this is a state of things which we find in the language of the N.T., but by no means in the literary language of a contemporary and later date, which affords no traces of these peculiarities. With this is connected the more limited use of the optative, and many other usages, to be discussed in their place. Another not very considerable portion of the alterations concerns the phonetic forms of declension and conjugation, under which may be classed the extension of the inflexion -α, gen. -ης to words in -ρα, and the transference of 1st aorist terminations to the 2nd aorist. A third and much larger class embraces the uses and combinations of forms and "form-words," in which a similar striving after simplification is unmistakable. Very many usages disappear; the use of the infinitive as the complement of the verb is extended at the expense of that of the participle, the objective accusative at the expense of the genitive and dative; the rules concerning οὐ or μή are as simple as they are intricate for the classical languages. Of quite another order, and concealed by the orthography, which remained the same, are the general changes in the sounds of the language, which even at that time had been carried out in no small measure, though it was not till long afterwards that they reached their later dimensions of the present day. A last class is composed of changes in lexicology—for the most part the substitution of a new expression in place of the usual expression for a thing or an idea, or the approach to such a substitution, the new appearing side by side with the old as its equivalent. This, however, does not as a rule come within the province of grammar, unless the expression be a kind of "form-word," for instance a preposition, or an irregular verb, an instance of this being the present of εἶδον, which in general is no longer ὁρῶ, but βλέπω or θεωρῶ. The Hellenistic language as a whole is in its way not less subject to rules nor less systematic than Attic; but it has certainly not received such a literary cultivation as the latter, because the continuous development of culture never allowed it completely to break away from the older form, which was so exclusively regarded as the standard of what the language should be.[1]

[1] Since the κοινή had such a wide diffusion, from Italy and Gaul to Egypt and Syria, it is *a priori* impossible that it should have been everywhere entirely uniform, and so it is correct to speak also of an Alexandrian dialect (ἡ 'Αλεξανδρέων διάλεκτος) as a special form of it (W.-Schm. § 3, 1, note 4). Of course we are not in a position to make many distinctions in details in this respect; yet even in the N.T. writers certain differences are well-marked, which have nothing to do with a more or less cultivated style, e.g. some writers, and Luke in particular, confuse εἰς and ἐν, whereas the author of the Apocalypse is able to distinguish between these prepositions. Again Hermas, undoubtedly

2. One element of the popular languages of that time, and therefore of the New Testament language, which though not prominent is clearly traceable, is the *Latin* element. The ruling people of Italy intermingled with the population of all the provinces; Roman proper names were widely circulated (as the N.T. at once clearly shows in the names of its authors and the persons addressed); but appellatives (κουστωδία, σουδάριον, κεντυρίων) also found admission, and some phrases, particularly of commercial and legal life, were literally translated (as τὸ ἱκανὸν ποιεῖν, λαμβάνειν = *satisfacere, satis accipere*). In general, however, this influence remains confined to lexicology and phraseology; in a slight degree it affects the formation of words (Ἡρῳδ-ιανοί, Χρηστ-ιανοί), in perhaps a greater degree the syntax (ἐκέλευσεν αὐτὸν ἀπαχθῆναι = *duci eum iussit*), still it is difficult here to determine what is due to native development of the language and what to foreign influence.

3. The national *Hebrew* or *Aramaic* element influenced Greek-writing Jews in a threefold manner. In the first place it is probable that the speaker or writer quite involuntarily and unconsciously rendered a phrase from his mother tongue by an accurately corresponding phrase; again, that the reading and hearing of the Old Testament in the Greek version coloured the writer's style, especially if he desired to write in a solemn and dignified manner (just as profane writers borrowed phrases from the Attic writers for a similar object); third and last, a great part of the N.T. writings (the three first Gospels and the first half of the Acts) is in all probability a direct working over of Hebrew or Aramaic materials. This was not a translation like that executed by the LXX., rendered word for word with the utmost fidelity, and almost without any regard to intelligibility; but it was convenient to adhere to the originals even in expression instead of looking for a form of expression which was good Greek. The Hebraisms and Aramaisms are, then, for the most part of a lexical kind, i.e. they consist in the meaning which is attributed to a word (σκάνδαλον is the rendering of מִכְשׁוֹל in the ethical sense, hence σκανδαλίζειν), or in phrases literally translated (as πρόσωπον λαμβάνειν נָשָׂא פָנִים 'to respect the person,' hence προσωπολήμπτης – λημψία); these expressions, which moreover are not too numerous, must have been current in Jewish, and subsequently in Christian, communities. In the department of grammar the influence of Hebrew is seen especially in a series of peculiarities in the use of prepositions, consisting partly of circumlocutions such as ἀρέσκειν ἐνώπιόν τινος instead of τινί, πρὸ προσώπου τῆς εἰσόδου αὐτοῦ, 'before him,' partly in an extended use of certain prepositions such as ἐν (ἐπί) on the

---

a representative of the unadulterated κοινή, uses often enough the superlative forms in -τατος and -ιστος in elative sense, whereas the forms in -τατος are generally absent from the writers of the N.T., and even those in -ιστος are only very seldom found (see § 11, 3). Such cases must, then, go back to *local* differences within the κοινή, even if we can no longer rightly assign the range of circulation of individual peculiarities.

§ 2. 4.]   ELEMENTS OF THE N.T. LANGUAGE.   5

analogy of the corresponding Hebrew word (בְּ); much is also taken over in the use of the article and the pronouns; to which must be added the periphrasis for the simple tense by means of ἦν etc. with the participle, beside other examples.

4. The literary language has also furnished its contribution to the language of the N.T., if only in the case of a few more cultured writers, especially Luke, Paul, and the author of the Epistle to the Hebrews.[1] A very large number of good classical constructions are indeed found in the N.T., but confined to these particular writers, just as it is only they who occasionally employ a series of words which belonged to the language of literary culture and not to colloquial speech. Persons of some culture had these words and constructions at their disposal when they required them, and would even employ the correct forms of words as alternatives to the vulgar forms of ordinary use. This is shown most distinctly by the speech of Paul before Agrippa (Acts xxvi.), which we may safely regard as reported with comparative accuracy. On this occasion, when Paul had a more distinguished audience than he ever had before, he makes use not only of pure Greek proverbs and modes of speech (πρὸς κέντρον λακτίζειν 14, οὐκ ἔστιν ἐν γωνίᾳ πεπραγμένον τοῦτο 26), but there also appears here the only superlative in -τατος in the whole N.T. (τὴν ἀκριβεστάτην αἵρεσιν 5), and here only ἴσασιν for 'they know' (4), not οἴδασιν; he must therefore have learnt somewhere (? at school), that in order to speak correct Attic Greek one must conjugate ἴσμεν ἴστε ἴσασιν. So also it is not surprising if Paul writes to his pupils and colleagues in a somewhat different, i.e. in a somewhat higher style, than that which he uses in writing to his congregations. It is noteworthy that in the artificial reproduction of the ancient language the same phenomenon repeated itself to a certain degree, which had long before occurred in the reproduction of Homeric language by subsequent poets: namely, that the imitator sometimes misunderstood, and accordingly misused, a phrase. Just as Archilochus on the strength of the Homeric line: τέκνον ἐμόν, γενεῇ μὲν ὑπέρτερός ἐστιν Ἀχιλλεύς, πρεσβύτερος δὲ σύ ἐσσι (Il. xi. 786, Menœtius to Patroclus) employed ὑπέρτερος = νεώτερος (a sense which it never bore)[2]: so in all probability Luke (with or without precedent) used μετὰ τὴν ἄφιξίν μου in A. 20. 29 as equivalent to 'after my departure,' because he had misunderstood μετὰ τὴν ἄπιξιν (correctly 'arrival') τῆς γυναικός in Herodotus, 9, 77 The same writer has ἀπήεσαν, ἐξήεσαν (from the obsolete ἄπειμι, ἔξειμι) with the force of the aorist, ἐκεῖσε, ὁμόσε, in answer to the question Where? and many other instances.

[1] The discrimination between the popular element and the literary element interwoven into it is very minutely worked out in J. Viteau, Étude sur le Grec du N.T.: Le verbe, syntaxe des prépositions, Paris, 1893.
[2] Vide the Scholia to Il. loc. cit. (Archilochus, frag. 28, Bergk.).

§ 3. ORTHOGRAPHY.

1. One portion of the changes in the Greek language that have been alluded to (§ 2, 1) concerned generally the sounds and combinations of these; but in general alterations of this kind it is usual for the spelling not to imitate the new sound off-hand, and certainly not without hesitation, in the case of a word which already had a stereotyped and ordinary spelling. So, in Greek, in the time of the composition of the N.T., there was, as we know from manifold evidence of stone and papyrus, no one fixed orthography in existence, but writers fluctuated between the old historical spelling and a new phonetic manner of writing. The sound-changes, at that time not nearly so great as they afterwards became, had principally to do with the so-called ι adscript in the diphthongs ᾳ, ῃ, ῳ (strictly āι, ηι, ωι with *i* pronounced), which, since about the second century before Christ, had become mute, and with the old diphthong ει, which from about the same period ceased to be distinguished from long ι. But the writing of AI, HI, ΩI, EI did not on that account become obsolete, preserved as they were by their occurrence in all ancient books and literal transcripts of them; only it was no longer known in which cases ā, ē, ō should be furnished with the symbol for ι mute, and in which cases long *i* should be written as EI. Many persons took the drastic measure of omitting the ι mute in all cases, even in the dative, as Strabo[1] attests, in the same way that we also find I as the prevailing spelling for ī (though still not without exceptions) in manuscripts of the period[2]; others considered that in EI as against I they had a convenient means of distinguishing between ī and ĭ, in the same way that ē and ĕ, ō and ŏ were distinguished. So κινεῖs is sometimes ΚΙΝΙC, sometimes ΚΕΙΝΕΙC; and even ΚΕΙΝΙC would be frequently written by any ordinary scribe. It was not until a later date that the historical method of writing was uniformly carried out, and even then not without occasional errors, by learned grammarians, especially Herodian of Alexandria, who taught in Rome under M. Aurelius. This was in keeping with the prevailing impulse of the time, which made for the revival of the old classical language. Since then, in spite of increasing difficulties, this method of spelling has been continuously taught and inculcated in the schools with the help of numerous artificial rules up till the present day.

2. It is impossible therefore to suppose, after what has been stated, that even Luke and Paul could have employed the correct historical spelling in the case of ι mute and ει; for at that time there was nobody in the schools of Antioch and Tarsus who could teach it them, certainly not in the case of ει, though some rules might be formulated at an earlier period with regard to ι mute. We are debarred from all knowledge as to how they actually did

---

[1] Strabo, xiv., p. 648, πολλοὶ γὰρ χωρὶς τοῦ ι γράφουσι τὰς δοτικάς, καὶ ἐκβάλλουσι δὲ τὸ ἔθος φυσικὴν αἰτίαν οὐκ ἔχον.

[2] Papyrus MS. of the poems of Hero(n)das, London, 1891.

§ 3. 2–4.] ORTHOGRAPHY. 7

write, and it is a matter of indifference, provided that one realizes this state of things, and recognizes that e.g. ΔωcιN stood equally well for δῶσιν or δώσειν. The oldest scribes whose work we possess (cent. 4-6) always kept themselves much freer from the influence of the schools than the later, i.e. they frequently wrote phonetically or according to the rule ει = ῑ (so the scribe of B), and indeed ι mute finds no place in MSS. before the seventh century. In our case there can be no question that we should follow the Byzantine school, and consistently employ the historical spelling in the N.T., as well as in the case of all profane writers, and remove all half measures, such as those, for instance, still remaining in Tischendorf, without any regard to the MS. evidence. The recording and weighing of evidence of this kind in the case of individual words, e.g. words in -εια, -ια, is the most unprofitable of tasks that a man can undertake.

3. The ι mute should therefore be supplied, as the correct historical spelling, in the following words, as well as in the well-known cases: μιμνῄσκειν, θνῄσκειν (for -η-ίσκειν), πανταχῇ, πάντῃ, εἰκῇ, κρυφῇ, λάθρᾳ, πεζῇ, (ἀντι)πέρᾳ[1] (old dative forms); ἀθῷος, ζῷον, πατρῷος, ὑπερῷον, ᾠόν, Τρῳάς, Ἡρῴδης (for Ἡρωΐδης, from ἥρως), πρῷρα, σῴζειν (for σω-ΐζειν). In the case of σῴζειν, it is not yet satisfactorily ascertained how far the tenses partook of the ι, since σαόω interposes itself and supplies ἐσώθην (for ἐσαώθην), σωτήρ etc.; in the active we may write σώσω, ἔσωσα, σέσωκα: in the perf. pass. σέσωσμαι appears to be correct, like νενόμισμαι, but σέσωται (A. 4. 9) on the model of ἐσώθην. It is also doubtful whether an ι was ever present in the forms first found in Hellenistic Greek, δῴην, γνῴην (optat.), πατρολῴας, μητρολῴας (Attic δοίην, γνοίην, -λοίας); but since ι is essential to the optative, we may insert it in those instances. As yet there is not sufficient evidence to decide between πρᾶος – πρᾷος, πραότης – πρᾳότης. For ει in place of ῃ vide infra 5.

4. Eι for ῑ is established in MSS. and editions, being found most persistently in Semitic words, especially proper names, where it would never once be without use as an indication of the length of the ι, provided only that it be correctly understood to have this meaning, and not to represent a diphthong, which is fundamentally wrong. We can, if we please, in these cases assist the pronunciation by means of the symbol for a long vowel (ῑ): thus Δαυίδ, Ἀδδί, Ἀχίμ, Βενιαμίν, Ἐλιακίμ, Ἐλισάβετ,[2] Ἰάιρος, Κίς, Λευί(ς), Νεφθαλίμ, Σάπφιρα,[3] Ταβιθά, Χερουβίν; Γεθσημανί,[4] Ἰεριχώ[5]; ἠλί, ῥαββί, ταλιθά,

[1] Certainly in later times the α in (κατ)αντιπερα appears to be short, since it is elided in verse, Maneth. iv. 188.

[2] Ελεισ. always in B, generally ℵ, occasionally CD, see Tisch. on L. 1. 5.

[3] The MSS. (A. 5. 1) vary between ει, ι, υ: there is no doubt of the identity of the name with the Aram. שַׁפִּירָא (pulchra), still it has been Grecised (gen. -ης like μάχαιρα, -ρης, § 7, 1) no doubt in connection with σάπφ(ε)ιρος, in which the ει is quite unjustifiable (Ap. 21. 19, -ιρος BP).

[4] See Kautzsch in W.-Schm. § 5, 13 a (Hebr. שְׁמַנֵי גַּת for גַּת־שְׁמָנִים). The spelling with η at the end as against -ει, -ι has only the very slenderest attestation; even the η of the second syllable must perhaps give way to the α of the western tradition (many authorities in Mt. 26. 36: cp. Mc. 14. 32).

[5] With ει Mt. 20. 29 BCLZ; so always B, frequently ℵ(D).

σαβαχθανῖ. The proper names in -ίας have in most cases ῖ, and therefore no ει (so Μαριαμ, Μαρία), but rightly Ἠλείας, Ἠλίας אֵלִיָּה, Ἰωσείας, -σίας יֹאשִׁיָּהוּ, Ὀζείας, -ίας עֻזִּיָּה, Οὐρείας אוּרִיָּה.[1] Ἐλισαῖος L. 4. 27 אֱלִישָׁע has undoubtedly ῖ, and is also spelt with ει in B (only), just as B has Φαρεισαῖοι (Mc. 7. 1, 3, 5, A. 5. 34 etc.), Γαλειλαία, -αῖος (Mc. 1. 14, 16, Jo. 7. 1, A. 5. 37 etc.), Σεινά (G. 4. 24 f.), Σειών (R. 9. 33 etc.). Σαμάρεια follows the analogy of Ἀντιόχεια, Ἀλεξάνδρεια etc., and must therefore retain ει in our spelling of it,[2] although the inhabitant is called Σαμαρίτης, as the inhabitant of Μαρώνεια is Μαρωνίτης.

5. With regard to **Greek** words and names, the following must be noted for the correct discrimination between ει and ι: οἰκτίρω, not -είρω (cp. οἰκτιρμός, -ιρμῶν, which in B certainly also have ει § 4, 2). Ἰκόνιον, not Εἰκ. (ῖ according to Etym. M. *sub verbo*, which, however, does not agree with the coins, which give ι and ει; the MSS. in A. 13, 51, 14. 1 also read ι). μείγνυμι, ἔμειξα etc., μεῖγμα. τίνω, τείσω, ἔτεισα. φιλόνικος, -νικία (from νίκη). πανοικεί A. 16. 34 (אAB¹C), παμπληθεί L. 23. 18, see § 28, 7. There is considerable fluctuation in the language from the earliest times between -ειᾰ (proparoxyt.) and -ίᾱ; κακοπαθία Ja. 5. 10 (B¹P) is the form attested also for Attic Greek; ὠφέλεια, however (R. 3. 1, Jude 16), already existed in Attic beside ὠφελία. The spelling στρατείας (B) 2 C. 10. 4 cannot be invalidated on the ground that in Attic στρατεία 'campaign' and στρατιά 'army' are interchanged, and the one form stands for the other; ἐπαρχία 'province' A. 25. 1 has for a variant not ἐπαρχεία but ἡ ἐπάρχειος (A, cp. א¹). Ει is produced from ηι according to the later Attic usage (which converted every ηι into ει) in the words λειτουργός, -ία, -εῖν (orig. ληϊτ., then λῃτ.), which were taken over from Attic, and in βούλει (L. 22. 42, the literary word = the colloquial θέλεις § 21, 7), whereas, in other cases η in roots and in terminations (dat. 1st decl., conjunct., 2 sing. pass.) remained as ē, and the use of the future for aor. conj. (§ 65, 2, 5) can on no account be explained by this Attic intermixture of the diphthongs.

6. H in the language of the N.T., and also in the standard MSS., is in general far from being interchanged with ι. Χρηστιανοί (and Χρηστός) rests on a popular interpretation of the word, for in place of the unintelligible Χρῑστός the heathen (from whom the designation of the new sect as Χρηστ. proceeded) substituted the familiar Χρηστός, which had a similar sound; the spelling of the word with η (in the N.T. preserved in every passage by א¹ A. 11. 26, 26. 28, 1 P. 4. 16) was not completely rejected even by the Christians, and

---

[1] W. H. Append. 155. B alone is consistent in reading Οὐρείου Mt. 1. 6 (the others -ίου). In the case of Ἐζεκίας חִזְקִיָּה Mt. 1. 9 f. we have only the witness of D for -ει- in the passage L. 3. 23 ff., which it alters to correspond with Mt. However, is the analogy complete? C. I. Gr. 8613 also has Ἐζεκίας (-χίας) beside Ἰωσείας.

[2] Cp. Herodian, Lentz, p. 279, 34.

maintained its position for a very long time.[1] Κυρήνιος for Quirinius L. 2. 2 may be explained in a similar way (by a connection of it with Κυρήνη), but B and the Latin MSS. have Κυρ(ε)ίνου Cyrino.[2] In L. 14. 13, 21 ἀνάπειρος for ἀνάπηρος is attested by quite preponderating evidence (אABD al.), and is moreover mentioned by Phrynichus the Atticist as a vulgar form.[3] εἶ μήν for ἦ μήν H. 6. 14 (אABD¹) is attested also in the LXX. and in papyri[4]; besides, all this class of variations belongs strictly to the province of correct pronunciation [orthoepy], and not to that of orthography. It is the same with the doubtful γυμνήτης or γυμνίτης (γυμνιτεύομεν 1 C. 4. 11, with η L al., which, according to Dindorf in Steph. Thes., is the correct spelling), and σιμικίνθιον semicinctium A. 19. 12 (all MSS.), with which one might compare the comparatively early occurrence of δινάρια denarii[5] (N.T., however, always has δην.). All uncials have σιρικοῦ sericum[6] Ap. 18. 12. The distinction made between κάμηλος 'camel' and κάμιλος 'rope' (Mt. 19. 24 etc., Suidas), appears to be a later artificiality.

7. At a much earlier time than the interchange of η - ι begins that of αι - ε (η), appearing in passive verbal terminations already in the Hellenistic period, in the middle of a word before a vowel somewhere about the second century A.D., and soon after universally, so that little confidence can be placed in our MSS. as a whole in this respect, though the oldest (D perhaps excepted) are still far more correct in this than in the case of ει - ι. The question, therefore, whether, in obedience to these witnesses, κερέα is to be written for κεραία, ἐξέφνης and the like, should not be raised; the following may be specially noticed: Αἰλαμῖται A. 2. 9 (B correctly)[7]; ἀνάγαιον Mc. 14. 15, L. 22. 12 (on quite overwhelming evidence); ῥαίδη raeda Ap. 18. 13 (all uncials ῥέδη); φαιλόνης paenula (the Greek form: strictly it should be φαινόλης) 2 Tim. 4. 13 (ε all uncials except L); but συκομορέα (A al. -αία) L. 19. 4 (from συκόμορον, formation like μηλέα from μῆλον).

8. The diphthong υι is already from early times limited to the case where it is followed by another vowel, and even then it is contracted in Attic Greek from the fifth century onwards into υ; it reappears, however, in Hellenistic Greek, being frequently indeed

---

[1] See Hermes xxx. 465 ff.

[2] Cp. Dittenberger, Herm. vi. 149. In Joseph. also the majority of the MSS. have -ηνιος: to which add Μάρκος Κυρήνιος C. I. A. iii. 599.

[3] Phryn. in Bk. Anecd. i. 9, 22, ἀναπηρία διὰ τοῦ η τὴν πρωτήν, οὐ διὰ τῆς ει διφθόγγου, ὡς οἱ ἀμαθεῖς (Tisch. ad loc.).

[4] Blass, Ausspr. d. Gr. 33³, 77 (Aegypt. Urk. des Berl. Mus. 543).

[5] Ibid. 37, 94.

[6] Cp. (W.-Schm. § 5, 14) σιρικοποιώς (so for -ός) Neapolitan inscription, Inscr. Gr. It. et Sic. 785, to which siricarium and holosiricum are given as parallel forms in Latin Inscr. (Mommsen).

[7] From Αἰλάμ עֵילָם; see Euseb. Onomast. ed. Larsow-Parthey, p. 22. Yet according to Könneke (sub verbo 13) the LXX. have Αἰλάμ and Ἐλαμῖται side by side.

written (in inscriptions and papyri) νει, *i.e.* ü-i, whereas on the other hand the inflexion -υῖα, -υίης (§ 7, 1) implies that the ι is not pronounced. The uncial MSS. of the N.T. write it throughout; it sometimes occurs in the word-division in B that the first scribe divides υ|ιον[1]; A has occasionally what comes to the same thing, ϋιος. The diphthong ωυ is non-existent (as also in Attic it may be said not to occur); Μωυσῆς is a trisyllable, and consequently to be written Μωϋσῆς.

9. Consonants. Z - σ.—The spelling ζβ, ζμ in place of σβ, σμ is widely disseminated in the Hellenistic and Roman period, in order to indicate the soft sound which σ has in this position only. This ζ, however, is found far more rarely in the middle than at the beginning of a word. In the N.T. the MSS. have Ζμύρνα Ap. 1. 11, 2. 8 (א, Latt. partly; but ζμύρνα has little support, as D Mt. 2. 11, σζμύρνης א Jo. 19. 39); ζβεννύναι 1 Th. 5. 19 (B¹D¹FG).

10. Single and double consonant.—With regard to the writing of a single or double consonant much obscurity prevails in the Roman period. The observance of the old-Greek rule, that ρ, if it passes from the beginning to the middle of a word (through inflexion or composition), preserves the stronger pronunciation of the initial letter by becoming doubled,[2] is even in Attic Greek not quite without exceptions; in the later period the pronunciation itself must have changed, and the stronger initial ρ approximated to the weaker medial ρ, so that even a reduplication with ρ was now tolerated (ῥεραντισμένος § 15, 6). The rule cannot be carried out in the N.T. without doing great violence to the oldest MSS., although, on the other hand, in these also there are still sufficient remnants of the ancient practice to be found: thus all MSS. have ἔρρηξεν L. 9. 42, ἐρρέθη Mt. 5. 21, 27 etc. (always in these words, § 16, 1), see Gregory Tisch. iii. 121; ἄρρωστος always, ἄρρητος 2 C. 12. 4, χειμάρρους Jo. 18. 1 etc.; on the other hand, ἄραφος Jo. 19. 23 (ρρ B), ἐπιράπτει Mc. 2. 21 (ρρ B²KMUΓ), ἀπορίψαντες A. 27. 43 אC etc. But while this matter too belongs to orthography, the spelling ρρ recommends itself as a general principle. παρησία is wrong, since it is assimilated from παν-ρησία (παρησ. B¹ Mc. 8. 32, and passim; also אDL sometimes, see Tisch.)[3]; ἀρραβών (a borrowed Semitic word) has the metrical prosody ‿ ‿ — guaranteed and the doubling of the consonant established in its Semitic form (ἀραβ. 2 C. 1. 22 אAFGL, 5. 5 אDE, E. 1. 14 FG), cp. also Lat. *arrha*.[4]

In the case of the other liquids and all the mutes there are only isolated instances. βαλλάντιον, not βαλάντιον, is shown on quite

---

[1] Tischendorf, N.T. Vat., p. xxviii. 4. There seem to have been people who thought themselves bound, for correctness' sake, to pronounce hü-i-os, mü-i-a, in three syllables; cp. Cramer, Anecd. Oxon. III. 251.

[2] Even the initial ρ in Att. inscr. is occasionally written ρρ ('Εφημ. ἀρχαιολ. 1889, p. 49 ff. β, 20 ἀρτήματα ρρυμοῖς).

[3] Evidence for ρ from inscr. and papyri in W.-Schm. § 5, 26 b.

[4] ἀρραβ. C. I. Gr. ii. 2058, B. 34, ἀραβ. Papyrus Notices and Extr. xviii. 2, 344 (W.-Schm. *ibid.* c); but ρρ Berl. Aeg. Urk. 240, 6.

§ 3. 10–12.]   ORTHOGRAPHY.   11

preponderating MS. evidence to be correct, and the orthography is also vouched for on metrical grounds. Φύγελος 2 Tim. 1. 15 אD etc., -ελλος A : the single letter appears to be the better spelling.[1] In μαμωνᾶς מָמוֹנָא the duplication of the μ has very slender attestation. ἐννενήκοντα, ἔννατος are wrong; γέννημα for living creatures is correct (γεννᾶν, γεννᾶσθαι), for products of the field incorrect, since these are termed γένημα from γίνεσθαι Mt. 26. 29, Mc. 14. 25, L. 12. 18 etc. This rests on quite preponderant evidence, which is confirmed by the papyri.[2] On χύ(ν)νω, κτέννω see § 17. In Ἰωάνης the single ν is attested by the almost universal evidence of B, frequently also by that of D (nearly always in Luke and Acts); the word belongs to the series of Hellenised names (§ 10, 2), which treat the *an* of the Hebrew termination as a variable inflection, whereas the interpretation of Ἰωάννης as from Ἰωαναν-ης (W.-Schm. § 5, 26 c) affords no explanation whatever for the -ης.[3] On the other hand, Ἅννα חַנָּה is correct, and Ἰωάννα (Aram. יוֹחָן, cp. שׁוֹשָׁן Σουσάννα, Μαριαμ = Μαριάμμη of Josephus) is also explicable (L. 8. 3 with ν BD : 24. 10 with ν only DL); the masc. Ἅννας (for חָנָן Hebr., Ἅνανος Joseph.) might be influenced by the analogy of Ἅννα.—Mutes : κράβατος appears to be commended by Lat. *grăbātus*, and the duplication of the β (introduced by the corrector in B) is accordingly incorrect in any case; but for the ττ there is the greatest MS. authority (for which א has κτ; the single τ in B¹ only at Mc. 2. 4). Cp. W.-Schm. § 5, note 52. Ἰόππη is the orthography of the N.T. (1 Macc.); elsewhere Ἰόπη preponderates (W.-Schm. § 5, note 54).

11. **Doubling of the aspirate.**—The aspirate, consisting of Tenuis + Aspiration, in correct writing naturally doubles only the first element, κχ, τθ, πφ; but at all times, in incorrect writing, the two are doubled, χχ, θθ, φφ. So N.T. Ἀφφία for Ἀπφία (§ 6, 7) Philem. 2 D¹; Σάφφιρα A. 5. 1 DE (but σάπφ(ε)ιρος Ap. 21. 19 in all MSS.); εφφαθα or -εθα Mc. 7. 34 nearly all: especially widely extended is Ματθαῖος (in the title to the Gospel אBD); Ματθίας A. 1. 23, 26 B¹D; Ματθάν Mt. 1. 15 B(D); Ματθαθ (-ααθ, -ατ) L. 3. 29 א¹B¹.

12. **Assimilation.**—Much diversity in writing is occasioned in Greek (as also in Latin) at all periods by the adoption or omission of the assimilation of consonants, which clash with each other by reason of their juxtaposition within a word. In the classical period the assimilation is often further extended to independent contiguous words, and many instances of this are still preserved in the oldest MSS. of the Alexandrian period; there are a few remnants of it in the MSS. with which we are commonly dealing, including those of the

---

[1] Φυγέλιος (Gentile noun?), C. I. Gr. ii. 3027 cited by W.-Schm. ibid. d.
[2] Ibid. a; Deissmann, Bibelstudien, 105 f.
[3] The inscription, C. I. Gr. 8613 (under a statue of Hippolytus) has Ἰωάνης; similarly Inscr. Gr. It. et Sic. 1106 (end of fourth century); otherwise -νν- has most support in (later) inscriptions.

N.T.: ἐμ μέσῳ Ap. 1. 13, 2. 1 etc. AC, H. 2. 12 AP, Mt. 18. 2, L. 18. 20 LΔ etc.; σὺμ Μαριάμ L. 2. 5 AE al.; σὺμ πᾶσιν 24. 21 EG al.; ἐγ γαστρί L. 21. 23 A. The later period, on the other hand, in accordance with its character in other matters (cp. §§ 5, 1 ; 28, 8), was rather inclined to isolate words and even the elements of words ; hence in the later papyri the prepositions ἐν and σύν remain without assimilation even in composition, and so also in the old MSS. of the N.T., but this more often happens with σύν than with ἐν, see W. H. App. 149 f., W.-Schm. § 5, 25¹. Ἐξ is everywhere assimilated to the extent that it loses the σ before consonants, both in composition and as a separately-written word; but the Attic and Alexandrian writers went further, and assimilated the guttural, so that ἐγ was written before mediae and liquids, ἐχ before θ and φ. But the MSS. of the N.T. are scarcely acquainted with more than ἐξ and ἐκ; for ἔκγονα 1 Tim. 5. 4 D¹ has ἔγγονα (i.e. *eggona*, not *engona*, Blass, Ausspr. 123³), ἀπεγδύσει B* Col. 2. 11; ἀνέγλιπτος D L. 12. 33. We naturally carry out our rule consistently.

13. Transcription of Semitic words.—In the reproduction of adopted Semitic words (proper names in the main) the MSS. occasionally show an extraordinary amount of divergence, which is partly due to the ignorance of the scribes, partly also, as must be admitted, to corrections on the part of persons who thought themselves better informed. Thus the words on the cross in Mt. 27. 46 run as follows in the different witnesses : ηλει – αηλι (ἀήλι) – ἐλω(ε)ι(μ), λεμα – λημα – λ(ε)ιμα – λαμα, σαβαχθαν(ε)ι – σαβακτανει – ζαφθανει (σαφθ.); in Mc. 15. 34 ελω(ε)ι – ελωη – ηλ(ε)ι, λεμα – λαμ(μ)α – λ(ε)ιμα, σαβαχθ.– σαβακτ.–σιβακθανει–ζα(βα)φθανει. Grammar, however, is not concerned with individual words, but only with the rules for the transcription of foreign sounds, which are the same for the N.T. as for the LXX.² The following are not expressed : א, ה, ח, ע, with some exceptions, where ח is represented by χ, as Ῥαχήλ רָחֵל, Ἀχάζ אָחָז, Χαρράν חָרָן, πάσχα פֶּסְחָא, רְחָב varies between Ῥαχάβ Mt. 1. 5, Ῥαάβ H. 11. 31, Ja. 2. 25 ; and ע by γ, as Γόμορρα עֲמֹרָה, Γάζα עַזָּה; Ἀκελδεμάχ A. 1. 19 is strange for חֲקַל דְּמָא (cp. Σιραχ סִירָא).³—ו and י = ι and υ; the latter (a half-vowel, our *w*, not our *v*) blends with the preceding vowel to form a diphthong : Δαυίδ, Εὔα, Λευίς, Νινευῖται L. 11. 32⁴; cp. with this Σκευᾶς A. 19. 14 if this = Lat. *Scaeva*. כ, פ, ת = χ, φ, θ thus with aspiration, except when two aspirates would stand in adjacent syllables, in which case the Greeks differentiate also in native words; so πάσχα (Joseph. has v. l. φασκα: cp. LXX. פַּשְׁחוּר = Πασχώρ and Φασσούρ), Καφαρναούμ כְּפַר נַחוּם (אBD Mt. 4. 13, 11. 23 etc., later MSS. Καπερν., see

---

[1] παλινγενεσία Mt. 19. 28 אB¹CDE etc., Tit. 3. 5 אACDEFG.
[2] Cp. C. Könneke in Progr. von Stargard, 1885.
[3] Reproduction of the guttural by prefixing α is seen in ἀήλι Mt. 27. 46 (see above) L (Euseb.), Ναθαναήλ נְתַנְאֵל, LXX. Ἀερμών חֶרְמוֹן, Ἀενδωρ עֵין דֹּאר.
[4] Another reading Νινευή (*male* -ευί).

§ 3. 13–14, § 4. 1.]   *DIVISION OF WORDS.*   13

Tisch. on Mt. 4. 13), Κηφᾶς. But ת is also represented by τ, as in σάββατον שַׁבָּת; cp. Ἀστάρτη, likewise admitted into the language at an early date; צָרְפַת becomes, in L. 4. 26, Σάρεπτα in אAB¹CD al., Σαρεφθα B²KLM; there is fluctuation also between Ναζαρεθ, -ρετ, -ρα(θ), where the corresponding Semitic form is uncertain. Γεννησαρεθ, -ρετ in Mt. 14. 34, Mc. 6. 53, L. 5. 1, is incorrect, D in Mt., Mc. correctly Γεννησαρ; in Ἐλισαβέθ, -βέτ the τ corresponds to Semitic ע, אֱלִישֶׁבַע. On the other hand ק, ט are rendered by the tenues κ, τ,[1] while π is almost entirely absent from Semitic words. Sibilants: ס צ שׁ = σ, ז = ζ (with the value of French z), but שְׁבִי Mt. 1. 5 Βοες אB, Βοος C, Βοοζ EKLM al.; אֵזוֹב ὕσσωπος. On Ἄζωτος אַשְׁדּוֹד see § 6, 7.

14. In Latin words it must be noted that *qui* is rendered by κυ: *aquilo* ἀκύλων (§ 28, 3); Κυρίνιος *Quirinius* sup. 6; likewise *quā* by κο: *quadrans* κοδράντης. *U* is ου: κουστωδία Mt. 27. 65, Ῥοῦφος; but also υ: κεντυρίων Mc. 15. 39.[2] On *i* = ε see § 6, 3.

§ 4. DIVISION OF WORDS, ACCENTS, BREATHINGS, PUNCTUATION.

1. In the time of the composition of the N.T. and for long afterwards the **division of words** was not generally practised, although grammarians had much discussion on the subject of the position of accents and breathings, as to what might be regarded as ἐν μέρος τοῦ λόγου and what might not. It is absent from the old MSS., and moreover continues to be imperfect in the later MSS. down to the 15th century. Of course it is the case with Greek as with other languages—the controversy of the grammarians shows it—that the individuality of separate words was not in all cases quite strictly established: words that were originally separate were by degrees blended together in such a way that it is not always perceptible at what point in the development the separation came absolutely to an end. One indication of the fact that the blending has been completed is when the constituent parts can no longer be separated by another word: ὅταν δέ, not ὅτε δ' ἄν is the correct expression, whereas ὅς δ' ἄν is employed; in the N.T. we also have ὡσαύτως δέ Mc. 14. 31, L. 20. 31, R. 8. 26 (on the other hand Homer has ὥς δ' αὔτως, which is still met with in Herodotus and Attic writers)[3]; τὸ δ' αὐτό, τῷ γὰρ αὐτῷ are still retained in the N.T. On the same principle the following e.g. form one word: ὅστις (still separable in Attic), καίπερ, τοίνυν, μέντοι, οὐδέ, οὔτε, οὐδέποτε, οὔπω (the two last separable in Att.), μήτι and μήτιγε, ὡσεί, ὥσπερ, ὡσπερεί, in the N.T.

---
[1] Exception: σαβαχθανί (see above) שְׁבַקְתַּנִי, in which case, however, there is a reverse change by assimilation to -κτανι.
[2] Dittenberger, Hermes vi. 296.
[3] Even as late as Philodem. ῥήτορ. ii. 97, Sudhaus.

also indisputably οὐδείς, μηδείς, where οὐδ' ὑφ' ἑνός can no longer, as in Att., take the place of ὑπ' οὐδενός etc. A second criterion is afforded by the new accent for the combined words: ἐπέκεινα (ὑπερέκεινα) from ἐπ' ἐκεῖνα, οὐδείς from οὐδ' εἷς, ἔκπαλαι (ἔκτοτε) from ἐκ πάλαι (ἐκ τότε); a third by the new signification of the compound: παραχρῆμα is no longer identical with παρὰ χρῆμα, καθόλου is different from καθ' ὅλον, the origin of ἐξαυτῆς in ἐξ αὐτῆς τῆς ὥρας and of ἱνατί in ἵνα τὶ γένηται is obscured. All this, however, by no means affords a universally binding rule, not even the absence of the first indication of blending; for in that case one would have to write e.g. ὅς τις in Attic. So also in the N.T. τουτέστι 'that is' is not proved to be erroneous by the occurrence of a single instance of τοῦτο δέ ἐστι (R. 1. 12), but it certainly does prove that it is not the necessary form. In most cases it looks strange for prepositions before adverbs to appear as separate words, because the independent notion of the preposition is lost: therefore we have ἐπάνω, ὑποκάτω, ἐπαύριον 'to-morrow,' ἀπέναντι, καθάπαξ, ὑπερλίαν, ὑπερ(εκ)περισσῶς[1]; still ἀπ' ἄρτι 'from henceforth' appears to be correct, also ἐφ' ἅπαξ 'once for all,' 'at once,' cf. ἐπὶ τρίς. On καθ' εἷς, κατὰ εἷς see § 51, 5; ὑπερεγώ (Lachm. 2 C. 11. 23) is clearly an impossibility, as the sense is, I (subject) am so more than they (predic.).

2. The system of symbols for reading purposes (**accents, breathings,** etc.), developed by the Alexandrian grammarians, was in the first instance only employed for the text of poetry written in dialect, and was not carried out in ordinary prose till the times of minuscule writing.[2] With regard to **accents**, we have to apply the traditional rules of the old grammarians to the N.T. as to other literature, except in so far as an accentuation is expressly stated to be Attic as opposed to the Hellenistic method, or where we notice in the later form of the language a prosody different from that of the earlier language, which necessitates a different accent. Peculiar to Attic is the accentuation διέτης etc., in N.T. accordingly διετής; also μῶρος for μωρός, ἄχρειος for ἀχρεῖος (whereas ἔρημος, ἕτοιμος, ὅμοιος were the ancient forms, and foreign to the κοινή[3]), ἱμάντος for ἱμάντος with a different prosody, χιλιαδῶν for -άδων, imperat. ἰδέ λαβέ for ἴδε λάβε. On the other hand we are informed by Herodian that ἰχθῦς -ὖν, ὀσφῦς -ὖν were the ordinary, not a peculiarly Attic accentuation. One characteristic of the later language is the shortening of the stem-vowel in words in -μα, as θέμα, πόμα (§ 27, 2), therefore κλίμα, κρίμα also are paroxytone,

[1] Also ὑπερεκπερισσοῦ Ε. 3. 20, 1 Th. 3. 10 (5. 13, v.l. -σῶς) always presents a single idea, and is completely held together by ὑπερ. Cp. § 28, 2.

[2] It is true that Euthalius already used those symbols in his edition of the N.T. writings (W.-Schm. 6, 1, note 1), and they are also found in individual uncials dating from the 7th century (Gregory Tisch. iii. 99 f.); in B they originate from a corrector of the 10th or 11th century.

[3] According to Herodian's words (περὶ μονήρους λέξεως, 938 L.) one would have concluded that ἔρημος, ἕτοιμος were peculiar to late Attic; however, modern Greek also has ἔρημος (romance lang. ermo etc., Dietz, Etymol. Wörterb. d. rom. Spr. I. sub verb.) ἕτοιμος, ὅμοιος, but ἀχρεῖος.

not κλῖμα, κρῖμα; but χρῖσμα is not analogous to these (cp. χριστός), and is even written χρεισμα in B¹ (1 Jo. 2. 20, 27). Also πνῖγος for πνῖγος, ῥῖγος for ῥῖγος are attested as vulgar forms (Lobeck, Phryn. 107), but there is no reason to infer from these that ψύχος is the N.T. form of ψῦχος. Herodian informs us that the shortening of ι and υ before ξ was the general rule, hence we get Φῆλιξ, κῆρυξ, κηρύξαι; but we have no ground whatever for extending this rule to ι and υ before ψ, and B has θλειψις, hence accent θλῖψις; similarly ῥῖψαν (ρειψαν B) from ῥίπτω, whereas the prosody of κύπτω is not established, and the accent of κῦψαι is therefore equally uncertain. Κράζω, κρᾶζον; τρίβω, ἔτριψα etc. (with ει before ψ in B and the Herculanean rolls), therefore συντετρῖφθαι Mc. 5. 4 (συντετρειφθαι B). In σπίλος 'spot' the quantity of the ι is unattested, except indirectly by B, which throughout has σπιλος, ασπιλος, σπιλουν; this proves that it is not σπῖλος. In οἰκτίρμων, οἰκτιρμός, in which B has ει in almost all cases (contrary to all analogy: the words occur in the old dialects), the accent does not enter into the question. Γαζοφυλάκιον, not -εῖον, is the constant form in B, and is also made probable by the analogy of such words as τελώνιον, μυροπώλιον; εἰδώλιον (§ 27, 3) has also better attestation in the N.T. (אAB etc.) than -εῖον. In Latin proper names the quantity of the vowel in Latin is the standard for determining the accent. This is definitely fixed for Mārcus, Prīscus, quārtus; hence Μᾶρκος, Κρῖσπος,[1] Κούαρτος; but Σεκοῦνδος or Σέκουνδος. In spite of everything there remains considerable doubt in the accentuation, since the accents of the MSS. are not altogether decisive; everything connected with the Hebrew proper names is completely uncertain, but there is also much uncertainty in the Greek and Grecised names.

3. The same principle must be followed for determining the **breathing**, yet with somewhat greater deference to the MSS., not so much to the actual symbols employed by them, as to the writing with aspirate or tenuis in the case of the elision of a vowel or in the case of οὐκ, οὐχ. It is established from other sources as well that the rough breathing in the Hellenistic language did not in all cases belong to the same words as in Attic; the MSS. of the N.T. have a place among the witnesses, although to be sure some of these, such as D of the Gospels and Acts, are generally untrustworthy in the matter of tenuis or aspirate, and they are never agreed in the doubtful cases. Smooth for rough breathing is especially strongly attested in Jo. 8. 44 οὐκ ἕστηκεν (אB¹DLX al.), which might be a newly-formed perfect of ἔστην, and not an equivalent for ἕστηκεν 'stands,' see § 23, 6. The rough breathing is abundantly vouched for in certain words that originally began with a digamma: ἐλπίς, ἐλπίζω (ἐφ' ἑλπίδι) A. 2. 26 אCD, R. 8. 20 אB¹D¹FG, 1 C. 9. 10 in the first occasion only FG, in the second only A. R. 4. 18 C¹D¹FG, 5. 2 D¹FG, Tit. 1. 2 D¹ (ἐν FG), 3. 7 καθ' FG (κατα D), A. 26. 6 no attestation. ἀφελπίζοντες DP L. 6. 35 (ἀφελπικῶς

---

[1] B has Κρεισπος, also in some places the equally correct forms Πρεισκα, Πρεισκιλλα.

Herm. Vis. iii. 12. 2 א); there is also one example of this from Attic Greek, another from Hellenistic, the Greek O.T. supplies several.[1] —ἰδεῖν: ἀφίδω Ph. 2. 23 אAB¹D¹FG, ἔφιδε A. 4. 29 ADE, ἐφεῖδεν L. 1. 25 DW°Δ(X), οὐχ ἰδού A. 2. 7 אDE, οὐχ ἰδόντες 1 P. 1. 8 B¹ which also has οὐχ εἶδον G. 1. 19; many examples of ἀφ-, ἐφ-, καθ- in O.T.[2] The form ἴδιος often attested in inscriptions[3] exists in καθ' ἰδίαν Mt. 14. 23 D (ibid. 13 all have κατ'), 17. 19 B¹D, 20. 17 B¹, 24. 3 אB¹, Mc. 4. 34 B¹DΔ, 6. 31 B¹ (not 32); in B¹ again in 9. 28, 13. 3 (elsewhere B also κατ'). Ἐφιορκήσεις Mt. 5. 33 א (widely extended, Phryn. p. 308 Lob., from ἐπίορκ.[4]); but ἔτος (κατ' ἔτος L. 2. 41, Hellenistic often ἔτος) does not appear in the N.T. with the rough breathing. Sporadic instances like οὐκ εὗρον, οὐκ ἕνεκεν, οὐχ ὄψεσθε (Gregory Tisch. iii. 90) must be regarded as clerical errors; ουχ ολιγος, however (where there is no former digamma in question), is not only a good variant reading in nearly all the passages in the N.T. (A. 12. 18 אA, 14. 28 א, 17. 4 B*, 19. 23 אAD, 19. 24 א, 27. 20 A; elsewhere only 15. 2, 17. 12), but is found also in the LXX. and the papyri.[5]

4. A difficult, indeed insoluble, question is that concerning the use of **rough or smooth breathing in Semitic words**, especially proper names. The principle carried out by Westcott and Hort appears to be rational, namely, of representing א and ע by the smooth breathing, ה and ח by the rough, a practice which gives us many strange results: Ἀβελ (ה), Ἀλφαῖος (ח), Εὔα (ה), Ἄννα (ה), and Ἀνανίας (ח), ἀλληλουια (ה), but Ἑβραῖος (ע). The MS. evidence, on the other hand, is deserving of little confidence in itself, and these witnesses are anything but agreed among themselves (Ἡσαΐας – Ἠσ., Ἀβραάμ – Ἀβρ., Ἡλίας – Ἠλ. etc.).[6] Initial י must, when represented by ι, receive the smooth breathing, except where Hellenisation connects the Hebrew with a Greek word with a rough breathing: Ἱεροσόλυμα (but Ἱερουσαλήμ, Ἱεριχώ, in accordance with the rule). Ἡσαΐας has dropped the י (so also Aram. אשעיא).

5. Of the remaining symbols, the familiar signs for **long and short** in unfamiliar words might in many cases be employed with advantage, so ῑ in Semitic words as an equivalent for the ει of the MSS. (§ 3, 4). The **marks of diaeresis**, which from a very early time were made use of to indicate a vowel which began a syllable, especially ι or υ, are necessary or useful in cases where the ι or υ might be combined with a preceding vowel to form a diphthong: Ἀχαΐα, Ἀχαϊκός, Ἑβραϊστί, Πτολεμαΐς, Γάϊος (the last name was still

---

[1] Gregory, p. 91; W.-Schm. § 5, 10 a; A. Thumb, Spir. asper (Strassburg, 1889), p. 65, 71.

[2] Gregory, ibid., Thumb 71.

[3] Thumb, ibid.

[4] Ibid. 72.

[5] Berl. Aeg. Urk. No. 72; W.-H. 143. Elsewhere however, as in No. 2, οὐκ ὀλ. and N.T. ἐπ' ὀλίγα D Mt. 25. 21, 23.

[6] Cp. Gregory, 106 f. Jerome in his explanation of Biblical names avowedly brings א ה ח ע under one head, and never writes h for any of these letters.

§ 4. 5-6.] *BREATHINGS, PUNCTUATION.* 17

a trisyllable in Latin when the literature was at its prime).[1] In Semitic names, moreover, it is often a question what is a diphthong and what is not; the use of the marks of diaeresis in ancient MSS. (as in D Χοροζαΰν, Βηθσαϊδά) and the Latin translation can guide us here, thus Ἰεσσαι *Jessae* (-e), Ἐφραίμ *Ephraem* (-em), also אL in Jo. 11. 54 -εμ),[2] but Καϊν, Ναϊν, Ἡσαΐας, Βηθσαϊδά(ν), although in the case of Καινάν, in spite of the Latin *ai* and of Καϊναν in D, according to the primary Semitic form (קֵינָן) αι appears to be more correct.[3]

On Και(α)φας *Caiphas* it is difficult to make any assertion;[4] on Μωϋσῆς see § 3, 8. The **hypodiastole** may be employed in ὅ, τι for distinction, though ὅ τι may likewise be written (but ὅστις).

6. As regards **punctuation**, it is certain that the writers of the N.T. were acquainted with it, inasmuch as other writers of that time made use of it, not only in MSS., but frequently also in letters and documents; but whether they practised it, no one knows, and certainly not how and where they employed it, since no authentic information has come down to us on the subject. The oldest witnesses (א and B) have some punctuation as early as the first hand;[5] in B the higher point on the line (στιγμή) is, as a rule, employed for the conclusion of an idea, the lower point (ὑποστιγμή viz. AYTON.) where the idea is still left in suspense. One very practical contrivance for reading purposes, which (although often imperfectly executed) meets us e.g. in D of the Gospels and Acts, and in D (Claromont.) of the letters of St. Paul, and which Euthalius about the middle of the 5th century employed in his editions of New Testament writings, is the writing in sense-lines (στίχοι), the line being broken off at every, even the smallest, section in the train of ideas, which required a pause in reading.[6] Later editors are compelled to give their own punctuation, and therewith often enough their own interpretation: this they do very decidedly when they put signs of interrogation (which in the MSS. are not earlier than the 9th century) in place of full stops. Economy in the use of punctuation is not to be commended: the most correct principle appears to be to punctuate wherever a pause is necessary for reading correctly.

[1] As proved by Fr. Allen, *Harvard Studies in Class. Phil.* ii. (Boston, 1891), 71 ff.

[2] נַעֲמָן L. 4. 27 is Ναιμαν (-ας) in אABCDKL, hence X Νεμαν, Latt. (some) *Neman*; but Νεεμαν EFM al. and other Latt.; the remaining Latt. *Naaman*.

[3] Καιναμ or -ναν without the marks of diaer. both B and א; B always Βηθσαιδα(ν), א partly (in three instances) -σαϊδα(ν), partly -σαιδα(ν) (three instances also); Ἡσαιας B mostly (except R. 9. 22, 29, 10. 16, 20), א nine times Ἡσαιας, ten times Ἡσαϊας; but Ναϊν, Καϊν אB constantly.

[4] For Καιαφας D and most Latt. have Καιφας (Καειφ., Κηφ.); Καϊάφας is also found in Josephus. The Semitic spelling is קיפא (not כיפא = Κηφᾶς).

[5] Gregory, 345, 348. Tischendorf, N.T. Vat. xix. ff.

[6] See Gregory, 113 ff.

B

§ 5. ELISION, CRASIS, VARIABLE FINAL CONSONANTS.

1. It is in keeping with the tendency to a greater isolating of individual words, which we have mentioned above (§ 3, 12) as characteristic of the language of the period, that only a very moderate use is made in the N.T., according to the MS. evidence which may here be relied on, of the combination of words by means of the ousting (elision) or blending (crasis) of the concluding vowel (or diphthong) of a word. This tendency was carried so far, that even in compound words the final vowel of the first component part was not elided (τετρα-άρχης in the N.T., in later Greek ὁμο-ούσιος; § 28, 8).[1] In no case does elision take place in noun or verb forms; even in the verse of Menander, 1 C. 15. 33, there is no necessity whatever to write χρήσθ' ὁμιλίαι for χρηστὰ ὁμ. for the sake of the verse, since the writing with elision or in full (*plene*, the regular Latin usage) was always, even in verse, quite a matter for individual opinion with the ancients. The only case where a pronoun suffers elision is τοῦτ' ἔστι or τουτέστι (§ 4, 1); so that it is particles alone which are still coupled together with comparative frequency with other words, though here also the elision might be much more abundant than it is.[2] Ἀλλά, according to Gregory, out of 345 cases where a vowel follows, undergoes elision in 215 (in these statistics it must, however, be remembered that the standard MSS. are far from being always in agreement); before articles, pronouns, and particles it shows a greater tendency to combine than before nouns and verbs. Δέ: δ' ἄν frequently, otherwise combination hardly ever takes place (Ph. 2. 18 δὲ αὐτό ℵBP, δ' αὐτό ACDE al.). Οὐδ' ἄν H. 8. 4, οὐδ' οὐ Mt. 24. 21, H. 13. 5, οὐδ' οὕτως 1 C. 14. 21, οὐδ' ὅτι R. 9. 7; in οὐδ' ἵνα H. 9. 25, C deviates from the rest with οὐδέ; the *scriptio plena* is more widely attested in οὐδ' εἰ A. 19. 2, οὐδ' ἡ H. 9. 18; elsewhere the final vowel remains. Τε, οὔτε, μήτε, ἅμα, ἄρα, ἆρα etc. are not subject to elision. In prepositions, elision very seldom takes place where a proper name follows; even on inscriptions of an earlier time there was a preference for preserving the names independent and recognisable by writing the preposition in full. On the other hand, there was a tendency to elision in the case of current phrases, and where a pronoun followed: ἀπ' ἀρχῆς, ἀπ' ἄρτι, ἀπ' αὐτοῦ, ἀπ' ἐμοῦ, ἐπ' αὐτῷ, κατ' ἐμέ, κατ' (καθ') ἰδίαν, κατ' οἶκον, μετ' ἐμοῦ, παρ' ὧν, ὑφ' ἡμῶν (ὑμῶν), ὑπ' οὐδενός (1 C. 2. 15). Ἀντί undergoes elision only in ἀνθ' ὧν; elision is most frequent with διά (because there were already two vowels adjacent to each other), thus δι' ὑπομονῆς R. 8. 25, δι' ἐσόπτρου 1 C. 13. 12; but with proper names διὰ Ἰησοῦ R. 16. 27, διὰ Ἡσαΐου Mt. 8. 17 (before Ἀβραάμ H. 7. 9 διὰ and δι' are both attested).

2. The use of **crasis** is quite limited in the N.T. In the case of the article, which affords so many instances in Attic Greek, there

---

[1] See Gregory, 113 ff.
[2] Gregory, 93 ff. Zimmer, Zeitschr. f. wiss. Th., 1881, 487 ff.; 1882, 340 ff.

§ 5. 2-4.] *CRASIS, VARIABLE FINAL CONSONANTS* 19

occur only the following in the N.T.: τοὐναντίον 2 C. 2. 7, G. 2. 7, 1 P. 3. 9 (stereotyped as a single word, hence τοὐν. δέ); τοὔνομα 'by name' Mt. 27. 57 (D τὸ ὄνομα); κατὰ ταὐτά (γάρ) L. 6. 23, 26, 17. 30, but even in this phrase (which is equivalent to a single word) there is not wanting strong attestation for τὰ αὐτά.¹ With καί the crasis is constant in κἄν = 'if it be but,' fairly constant in κἂν = 'even if' (but κἂν for καὶ ἐάν 'and if' is only sporadically found); in most places there is preponderating evidence for κἀγώ, κἀμοί, κἀμέ, κἀκεῖνος, κἀκεῖ(θεν).² Thus καί is only blended with the following word, if it be a pronoun or a particle; there appears to be no thought of writing κἄλεγεν and the like.³

3. The **variable** *ν* after *ι* and *ε* at the end of a word became more and more firmly established in Attic Greek in the course of time, as the inscriptions show, and so passed over into the Hellenistic language as the favourite termination, though modern Greek shows us that it subsequently disappeared again. In the standard MSS. of the N.T. it is but seldom wanting, whether a consonant or a vowel follow it, or the word stands at the end of a sentence; the rule that the *ν* should always be inserted before a vowel and always omitted before a consonant is indeed not without a certain *ratio*, and receives a certain amount of early support from the usage of the papyri, but as far as we know the rule was only formulated in the Byzantine era, and the instances where it is broken are quite innumerable.⁴ The *ν* is wanting⁵ occasionally after -ε (L. 1. 3 ἔδοξε אBCD etc., -εν AEKSΛ), and in ἐστίν, somewhat more often after the -σι of the plural (χαλῶσι most MSS. Mc. 2. 4, ἔχουσι L. 16. 29, τιμῶσι twice Jo. 5. 23), most frequently, comparatively speaking, after -σι dat. plur.; πέρυσι 2 C. 8. 10, 9. 2 (D*FG πέρσυ, Dᵇ πέρισυ as elsewhere in MSS.),⁶ and εἴκοσι (12 exx. in N.T.)⁷ remain free from it.

4. The σ of οὕτως is also established, for the most part, in the N.T. before consonants as well as before vowels; οὕτω is only strongly attested in A. 23. 11 (אAB before σε), Ph. 3. 17 (אABD*FG

---

¹ In Acts 15. 27 there is for τὰ αὐτά a v.l. in D ταυτα (as τοῦτο is sometimes read for τὸ αὐτό). 1 Th. 2. 14 A ταυτα (with coronis). Ph. 3. 1 א*FGP ταυτα. 1 P. 5. 9 all MSS. τὰ αὐτά. With conjunction, τὰ γὰρ αὐτά, τὸ δὲ αὐτό

² The statistics are given in Gregory, 96 f.; Zimmer, l.c., 1881, 482. Καὶ ἐάν all MSS. in Mt. 5. 47, 10. 13 etc.; κἂν 'and if' 'Mc.' 16. 18, L. 13. 9 (D καὶ ἐάν), 6. 34 D, Ja. 5. 15; more often 'even if,' as Mt. 26. 35, Jo. 8. 14 (but in 16 only א has κἄν).

³ Nor yet of ἀδελφοί, ἀπεσταλμένοι, which Holwerda conjectures in A. 28. 15, Jo. 1. 24, whereas his proposals in A. 22. 5 κἂν (for καί)... ἐμαρτύρει (B), Mt. 12. 21 κἂν (for καί, = καὶ ἐν), L. 18. 7 κἂν μακροθυμῇ (for καὶ μ - εἶ) are more probable. But D* has κἀπεθύμει in L. 15. 16.

⁴ Kühner-Blass, i. 3, i. 292.

⁵ W. H. 146 ff.; Gregory, 97 ff.

⁶ Hermas, Vis. iii. 10. 3 περσυνῇ א, περισυνῇ as, = περυσινῇ, but ii. 1. 1 πέρυσι twice (once περσι א*).

⁷ Εἴκοσι is generally without ν on Attic inscriptions of the classical period, Hedde Maassen de litt. NT paragogica (Leipsic, 1881), p. 34, also in the MSS. of authors like Strabo, Dionys. Halic., Athen. (even before a vowel), Lobeck, Pathol. ii. 156.

before περιπατ.), H. 12. 21 (א*A before φοβερόν), Ap. 16. 18 (אAB before μέγας). Ἄχρι and μέχρι generally stand, as in Attic, even before a vowel without σ, according to the majority of the MSS., but μέχρις αἵματος H. 12. 4 (-ρι D*), and more frequently μέχρις (ἄχρις) οὗ Mc. 13. 30 (א -ρι, D ἕως), G. 3. 19, 4. 19, H. 3. 13 (ἄχρι M), while in 1 C. 11. 26, 15. 25 etc., the witnesses are divided. Ἀντικρὺς Χίου A. 20. 15 'over against' (a late usage), Att. (κατ)αντικρύ (ἄντικρυς in Attic = 'downright').[1]

§ 6. SPORADIC SOUND-CHANGES.

1. General sound-changes in the language of the N.T. as opposed to Attic Greek do not openly present themselves, or at least are no longer apparent, being concealed by the older orthography, which either remained unaltered or was restored by the scribes (cp. § 3, 1). Of sporadic alterations which influenced the spelling as well as the pronunciation of words, the following are noteworthy:—

A – E (αυ – ευ). For αρ we have ερ in τεσσεράκοντα (Ionic, mod. Gk., also papyri) in all cases according to the earliest evidence; also τέσσερα Jo. 19. 23 אALM, Ap. 4. 6, A. 4. 9 אA etc.; but τέσσαρες, -άρων, -αρσι : τέσσερας never, but in place of it -αρες = accusative (see § 8, 2), so that we must give the regular inflection τέσσαρες, -αρα etc., to the N.T. writers (= Ionic and mod. Gk. -ερες, -ερα etc.).[2] Καθαρίζειν also frequently has ερ in the MSS. (καθαρός never; cp. also μυσερός Clem. ad Cor. i. 14. 1, 30. 1 A) : Mt. 8. 3 ἐκαθερίσθη B*EL al. (ibid. καθαρίσθητι, 2 καθαρίσαι all MSS.), Mc. 1. 42 ἐκαθερίσθη AB*CG al. (41 καθαρίσθητι, 40 καθαρίσαι, 44 καθαρισμοῦ all MSS.); elsewhere more often with -ερ-, especially in A;[3] no possible paradigm results from this, -αρ- must be written throughout. Cp. further Πάτερα for -αρα AC A. 21. 1.—Variation between ια – ιε (να – νε): φιάλη, ὕαλος, as in Attic (Ionic and Hellenistic φιέλη, ὕελος Phryn. Lob. 309), χλιερός Ap. 3. 16 only in א ; vice versa, ἀμφιάζει B in L. 12. 28 for -έζει, -έννυσιν see § 17. The vulgar term πιάζω 'seize' (§ 24, λῃστο- πιαστής Papyr. Berl. Aeg. Mus. 325, 2), is derived from the Doric πιάζω = πιέζω 'press,' but has become differentiated from it (πεπιε- σμένος 'pressed down' L. 6. 38).—α and εν at the close of a word: ἕνεκεν (εἵν.) is Ionic and Hellenistic; the Attic ἕνεκα (§ 40, 6) cannot be tolerated except in A. 26. 21, where all the witnesses have it (speech of Paul before Agrippa, cp. § 1, 4 ; on the other hand in 19. 32 -κα is only in אAB).[4] The Ionic and Hellenistic εἶτεν for εἶτα is only found in Mc. 4. 28 אB*L ; ἔπειτεν nowhere (according to Phrynichus 124, Lob., both words are ἐσχάτως βάρβαρα). For ἀγγαρεύω (a word borrowed from Persian: so spelt in mod. Gk.),

---

[1] Apoc. Petr. 21, 26 (κατ)αντικρὺς ἐκείνου, αὐτῶν, 29 καταντικρὺ τούτων.
[2] Gregory, 80. Buresch, Rh. Mus. xlvi. 217 f.
[3] Gregory, 82. Buresch, 219.
[4] Εἴνεκα Hermas, Vis. iii. 1. 9 א, but 2. 1 εἵνεκεν א, ἕνεκα as, 5. 2 ἕνεκεν א, ἕνεκα as.

§ 6. 1–3.] SPORADIC SOUND-CHANGES. 21

ἔγγαρ. Mt. 5. 41 ℵ, Mc. 15. 21 ℵ*B*. For Δαλματίαν 2 Tim. 4. 10, A Δερμ., C Δελμ.; in Latin also we have *Delm.* side by side with *Dalm.*[1] ΑΥ for ΕΥ: ἐραυνᾶν for ἐρευνᾶν Jo. 5. 39 ℵB*, 7. 52 ℵB*T etc. (ℵB* in general, AC occasionally), an Alexandrianism according to Buresch, Rh. Mus. xlvi. 213 (LXX. ℵA generally, not BC).[2]

2. A - O, E - O. Πατρολώας, μητρολώας (§ 3, 3) were written instead of -αλοίας, from ἁλο(ι)ᾶν 1 Tim. 1. 9 according to ℵADFGL, on the analogy of πατρο-κτόνος etc., when the formation of the words had been forgotten. Inversely, βατταλογεῖν Mt. 6. 7 ℵB was written for βαττολ., cp. βατταρίζω (elsewhere in late writers only the form with o is found); μεσανύκτιον Mc. 13. 35 only B*, L. 11. 5 only D*, in A. 16. 25 and 20. 7 all MSS. μεσον-; cp. μεσαστύλιον Lob. Phryn. 195. Κολοσσαί C. 1. 2 is read by nearly all MSS., but the title is πρὸς Κολασσαεῖς in AB*K(ℵ). Of course the text and the title, which certainly did not originate with the author, should be brought into agreement; in favour of o we have the coins and nearly all the evidence of profane writers (-α- is a v.l. in Xenophon, Anab. i. 2. 6).—E - O : ἐξολοθρεύειν A. 3. 23 ℵB³EP al. (-ε- AB*CD), ὀλοθρεύειν H. 11. 28 (-ε- only ADE), ὀλοθρευτής 1 C. 10. 10 (-ε- D*[FG]). Thus the evidence is overwhelming for the second o, which has arisen from assimilation with the first o (as in ὀβολός for ὀβελός), this is also the popular spelling (mod. Gk. ξολοθρεύω); side by side with it ὄλεθρος remains constant in N.T. Buresch[3] is in favour of ε in the N.T. and the LXX.; in the latter, where the word is extraordinarily frequent, we should write with ε according to ℵA*B*(B^c -o-).—In Ἀπελλῆς A. 18. 24, 19. 1 ℵ* for Ἀπολλῶς (Ἀπολλώνιος D) it must be remembered that the names are originally identical: Ἀπέλλων being Doric for Ἀπόλλων. It appears in fact that in the Acts we should read Ἀπελλῆς (in the α text), whereas Ἀπολλῶς is an interpolation from 1 C. 1. 12 etc.; the scholia also (Cramer, Caten., p. 309) seem to assume a difference with regard to the name between Acts and 1 Corinthians.

3. E - I, I - Y. The Latin *i* in the majority of cases where the vowel was no pure *i*, but inclining to *ĕ*, was represented by the older Greek writers not by ι but by ε: Τέβερις,[4] Τεβέριος, Δομέτιος, Καπετώλιον and others (but Τίτος always with ι), see Dittenberger, Herm. vi. 130 ff. In the N.T. Τιβερίου L. 3. 1 is the traditional spelling, but λέντιον *linteum* Jo. 13. 4 f.,[5] λεγεών *legio* the majority of uncials in Mt. 26. 53 (-ι- ℵ*B*DL), Mc. 5. 9 (-ι- ℵ*B*CDLΔ), 15 (-ι- ℵ*BLΔ, hiat D), L. 8. 30 (-ι- ℵ*B*D*L). In the N.T. the *best* authority thus supports -ιών; both forms occur in inscriptions.[6]

---

[1] De Vit. Onomasticon tot. lat. s.v.

[2] Gregory, 81. W. Schmid, Gtg. Gel. Anz., 1895, 40.

[3] Op. cit. 216 f., cp. also H. Anz. Subsidia ad cognosc. Graecorum serm. vulg. e Pentat. vers. repetita (Diss. phil. Hal. xii.), p. 363. Ὀλοθρεύονται stands side by side with ὄλεθρος also in Clem. Hom. xi. 9.

[4] Hermas, however, has Τίβεριν Vis. i. 1. 2.

[5] Ditt. 144 (Hesych.; λεντιάριος, inscr.).

[6] Ibid. 142 (λεγιών also in Plut. Rom. 13, Otho 12).

The opposite change is seen in Ποτίολοι *Puteoli* (A. 28. 13), the ordinary Greek spelling[1] (similar is the termination of λέντιον; the form λέντεον would have looked unnatural to a Greek). In the Greek word ἁλιεύς it appears that if the termination contains ῖ (-ιεῖ, -εῖς), the preceding ι becomes ε from dissimilation: ἀλεεῖς Mt. 4. 18 f. ℵ*B*C, Mc. 1. 16 AB*L^{corr.}, 17 ℵAB*CLΔ, L. 5. 2 ℵ*ACLQ.—I - Υ: Μυτιλήνη is the older spelling, Μιτυλ. A. 20. 14 that of the later writers; for Τρωγίλιον or -ία (Strab., Stephan. Byzant., Plin.) the MSS. in A. 20. 15 have -υλία, -ύλ(λ)ιον (-ύλιον, -ος MSS. of Ptolem. v. 2. 8).

4. Interchange of short and long vowel (or diphthong).—A - Ω. ἀνάγαιον, ἀνώγαιον (cp. on αι – ε, § 3, 7): the spelling with α has overwhelming authority in Mc. 14. 15, L. 22. 12 (from ἀνά-γῆ; ἀνώγαιον with v.l. ἀνόκαιον in Xenoph. Anab. v. 4. 29).—EI before a vowel easily loses its ι from early times, especially in derivatives ("Αρειος πάγος, but 'Αρεοπαγίτης as in N.T.); hence may be explained ἠχρεώθησαν R. 3. 12 O.T. (ℵAB*D*G, in LXX. ℵA²), whereas ἀχρεῖος does not vary. But there are instances in the simple word as well: τέλεος often in Attic, τέλειος N.T.; πλέον also in N.T. occasionally, L. 3. 13 (-εῖον C), A. 15. 28 (D -εῖον), elsewhere πλεῖον, and always πλείων, πλείονος etc. (Attic also has πλέονος); in the derivatives always πλεονεξία, -εκτεῖν.—N.T. always ἔσω (Homer and tragedians have εἴσω and ἔσω); on the other hand, εἵνεκεν with lengthened vowel (Ionic; εἵνεκα is found in Attic Gk. as well, even in prose) is an alternative for ἕνεκεν in L. 4. 18, O.T. (also LXX. Is. 61. 1; supra p. 20, note 4), A. 28. 20 ℵ*A, 2 C. 3. 10 (most MSS.).— Ο - Ω: πρώιμος (from πρωί) and πρόιμος Ja. 5. 7 (ο ℵAB*P) are comparable with πλώιμος (Att.) and πλόιμος (late writers). For χρε-οφειλέτης L. 7. 41, 16. 5 we should not write χρεωφ. (which has less authority);[2] nor should we replace the correct Στωικός A. 17. 18 by Στοϊκός of ℵAD al.—[Υ - ΟΥ: κολλύριον Ap. 3. 18 ℵBC, -ούριον AP does not belong here, on account of the long υ; the latter form, which is found elsewhere, is certainly of Latin origin.] A peculiar word is ὀμείρομαι or ὀμ., which is equivalent to ἱμείρομαι (ἐπιθυμῶ) in sense, 1 Th. 2. 8 (in O.T. sporadically),[3] but cannot easily be connected with ἵμείρ. (from ἵμερος); but μείρομαι appears to exist in this sense (Nicand. Theriac. 403), cp. (ὀ)δύρομαι, (ὀ)κέλλω, and the like, Kühner, I³, i. 186.

5. Contraction and loss of vowel.—In contraction the Hellenistic language, as appears from its inflections, does not go quite so far as the Attic. Still νεομηνία for Att. νουμηνία in Col. 2. 16 is only attested by BFG (LXX. occasionally): while ἀγαθοεργεῖν (1 Tim. 6. 18; ἀγαθουργῶν A. 14. 17, v.l. ἀγαθοποιῶν) arises from the endeavour to keep the two halves of the compound word recognisable, § 28, 8

---

[1] Ditt. 145.

[2] Herodian, ii. 606 L., has ω and ο; the word is certainly not Attic (the oldest form is χρήστης, then χρεώστης); χρεω-φυλάκιον and the like come from Attic χρέως = χρέος. See further Lobeck, Phryn. 691; W.-Schm. § 16, 5, n. 28.

[3] See W.-H. 152 a, W.-Schm. § 16, 6.

§ 6. 5–7.] SPORADIC SOUND-CHANGES. 23

(always κακοῦργος, ἱερουργεῖν etc.).¹ An entirely new kind of contraction is that of ιει = ιι into ι: ταμεῖον from ταμιεῖον, πεῖν (pīn) from πιεῖν, see § 24, ἐπείκεια B* Acts 24. 4² (so also ὑγεία for ὑγίεια, no instances in N.T.). In νεοσσός, νεοσσία, νεοσσίον contraction never took place, but the ε dropped out in (Ionic and) Hellenistic Gk.: so in N.T. νοσσός L. 2. 24 אBE al., νοσσιά with v.l. νοσσία 13. 34, Mt. 23. 37 (condemned by Phryn. 206, Lob.). In ἐλεινός (Att.) for ἐλεεινός it must be remembered that the spelling ελεινος (Ap. 3. 17 AP, 1 C. 15. 19 FG) may also represent ἐλεῖνος, and moreover, contraction in the N.T. is improbable. The reflexives in Hellenistic Gk. are σεαυτοῦ, ἑαυτοῦ (but ἐμαυτοῦ), § 13, 1; the conjunction 'if' is ἐάν, § 26, 4, a form which is also very largely introduced to express the potential particle (ibid.)

6. **Prothetic vowels.**—The only points to note under this head are that θέλω always stands for ἐθέλω; on the other hand κεῖνος never stands for ἐκεῖνος: similarly χθές is not found, but only ἐχθές (also the prevalent Attic form) Jo. 4. 52 אAB*CD al., A. 7. 28 אB*CD, H. 13. 8 אAC*D*M. On ομείρομαι vide supra 4.

7. **Interchange of consonants.**—The main point under this head is that the Hellenistic language did not adopt the Attic substitution of ττ for σσ or of ρρ for ρσ, though isolated instances of this were continually intruding into it from the literary language, especially as Atticising writers naturally imitated this peculiarity as well as others. In the N.T. for σσ we have: θάλασσα, πράσσω, ταράσσω, ἐκπλήσσομαι (·ττ A. 13. 12 B) περισσός; also κρείσσων Pauline epp. on preponderant evidence (1 C. 7. 38, 11. 17, Ph. 1. 23, only 1 C. 7. 9 -ττ- אBDE), but κρείττων Hebrews (ττ 1. 4, 7. 7, 19, 22, 8. 6 [twice], 9. 23, 11. 16, 35, 40, 12. 24, there is diversity only in 6. 9, where ττ is read by D*K, and 10. 34 σσ אA) and Petrine epp. (1 P. 3. 17; doubtful 2 P. 2. 21). To this corresponds ἥσσων, ἡσσοῦσθαι in St. Paul (1 C. 11. 17, 2 C. 12. 13, 15), but the literary words ἡττᾶσθαι, ἥττημα are read with ττ even in his letters, 2 P. 2. 19 f., R. 11. 12, 1 C. 6. 7; ἐλάσσων Jo. 2. 10, R. 9. 12 O.T.; ἐλάττων H. 7. 7, 1 Tim. 5. 9 (all MSS.; cp. § 2, 4); literary words, ἐλαττονεῖν 2 C. 8. 15 O.T.; ἐλαττοῦν H. 2. 7 (9) O.T., Jo. 3. 30. (ττ is also occasionally found in Hermas: Vis. iii. 7. 6 ἔλαττον; Sim. ix. 27. 4 ἐλάττους; 9. 6 ἐλάττωμα. Similarly σήμερον always takes the place of Att. τήμερον.—With regard to Att. ρρ for ρσ the usage is more evenly divided. Ἄρρην Gospels, Ap. 12. 5 (but ἄρ(ρ)ενα אB, clearly a correction for ἄρσεν), R. 1. 27 [twice] (ρρ א*[C]), G. 3. 28 (ρρ א), 1 C. 6. 9, 1 Tim. 1. 10; but along with θάρσος, θάρσει, θαρσεῖτε, which are constant, we find (in Paul. epp. and Hebr.), θαρρεῖν 2 C. 5. 6, 8, 7. 16, 10. 1, H. 13. 6 (also mod. Gk. θαρρῶ; but Apoc. Petr. 5 θαρσήσαντες παραθαρσύνειν); for

---

¹ Also in R. 13. 3 for τῷ ἀγαθῷ ἔργῳ there is a conjectural reading τῷ ἀγαθοεργῷ, but the antithetical clause ἀλλὰ τῷ κακῷ will not suit this.

² Elsewhere always ἐπιεικής, -ιείκεια. In ἐσθίω, ἐσθίεις the analogy of the other parts of the verb prevented the fusion from taking place; on ἀφεὶς from ἀφίημι see § 23, 7.

the vulgar μακράν, μακρόθεν Lc. and Hebr. give πόρρω(θεν) L. 14. 32, 17. 12, 24. 28, H. 11. 13 (Mt. 15. 8, Mc. 7. 6 O.T.; μακρὰν καὶ πόρρω Barn. 20. 2).—Apart from these, there is hardly anything worthy of note. Fluctuation in the aspiration of consonants: σπ – σφ (also fluctuate in Attic) in σπυρίς, σφυρίς Mt. 15. 37 (σφ- D), 16. 10 (σφ- BD), Mc. 8. 8 (σφ- ℵA*D), 8. 20 (σφ- D), A. 9. 25 (σφ- ℵC, hiat D); σφόγγος D Mc. 15. 36 (not Mt. 27. 48; σφ- is also Attic); στ – σθ: μαστός Ap. 1. 13 BCP, -σθός ℵ, μαζός A (ζ orig.=σδ, so still in N.T. Ἄζωτος A. 8. 40 אשדוד, so L. 11. 27 μαστοί most MSS., -σθοί DFG 23. 29 (D*), but C μαζοί (usage also fluctuates in Attic writers, Kühner I³, i. 157). Φόβηθρα is read L. 21. 11 BD for φόβητρα; this suffix takes the form sometimes of -θρον, sometimes of -τρον, Kühner, ibid. ii. 271. 27. The π in 'Απφία ('Αφφία, see § 3, 11), Philem. 2, is aspirated, as in inscriptions of the regions (Phrygia, Caria) to which Appia belonged, where the name is frequent; but it is very doubtful whether this is the Roman name *Appia.* The Attic πανδοκεῖον, πανδοκεύς (Lob. Phryn. 307) occurs in L. 10. 34 f. in ℵ* or ℵ*D*. In οὐθείς, μηθείς the δ of οὐδ(ὲ), μηδ(ὲ) has united, contrary to rule, with the aspirate of εἷς to form θ (elsewhere θ = τ + aspirate); these forms occur from the latter part of the Attic period onwards, in writers (Aristot.), on inscriptions, and on papyri, and so, too, in the N.T. (and LXX.) occasionally: μηθέν A. 27. 33 ℵAB; οὐθενός L. 22. 35 ABQT al., 2 C. 11. 8 ℵBMP; οὐθέν L. 23. 14 ℵBT, A. 15. 9 BHLP, 19. 27 ℵABHP, 26. 26 ℵB, 1 C. 13. 2 ℵABCD°L (thus this spelling is by no means universal). Still ἐξουθενεῖν is the prevalent form (as also in LXX.; only in Mc. 9. 12 BD have -δενηθῇ). W. Schm. § 5, 27, n. 62 (Herm. Mand. iv. 2. 1 οὐθέν ℵ* Sim. ix. 4. 6; Clem. Cor. i. 33. 1, 45. 7 μηθαμῶς, i.e. μηδὲ ἁμῶς).

8. **Insertion and omission of consonants.**—Λαμβάνω in Hellenistic Gk. retains in all forms and derivatives with the stem ληβ the μ of the present tense: ἐλήμφθην, λῆμψις, προσωπολήμπτης etc., § 24, W.-Schm. § 5, 30. The addition of μ in ἐμπί(μ)πλημι, ἐμπί(μ)πρημι is as variable in Attic as in Hellenistic Gk. (W.-Schm. ibid.); N.T. ἐμπιπλῶν A. 14. 17 (with μ DEP), ἐμπιπρᾶσθαι 28. 6 ℵ* for πιμπρᾶσθαι (πιπρ. A; elsewhere uncertainty about the μ only exists in the case of these compounds with ἐμ-).—Insertion of cons. for euphony (ἀν-δ-ρός, μεσημ-β-ρία) takes place in many Semitic names (Ἔσ-δ-ρας, Μαμ-β-ρῆ), in the N.T. Σαμψών, i.e. Σαμ-π-σών, H. 11. 32 ('Ιστραήλ D L. 2. 32, etc.).—σφυδρόν for σφυρόν A. 3. 7 ℵ*AB*C* is unexplained. μογγιλάλος Mc. 7. 32 has no authority (μογιλάλος = ὁ μόγις λαλῶν, and so with one γ in ℵAB*DGK al.: also LXX. Is. 35. 6: B^corr. is the first to write γγ). The excision of a consonant (accompanied by lengthening of a vowel) appears in γίνομαι, γινώσκω (Ionic and Hellenistic); also noticeable is ἄρκος = ἄρκτος Ap. 13. 2 (all uncials), found also in the LXX. and elsewhere in the late language (W.-Schm. § 5, 31).

§ 7. FIRST AND SECOND DECLENSIONS.

1. Words in -ρᾰ and those in -υῖα, i.e. -ῦα (§ 3, 8) follow the pattern of those in -σσα, -λλα etc., i.e. they take in G.D. ης, ῃ instead of Att. ᾱς, ᾳ. (On the other hand those in -ρᾱ [ἡμέρᾱ], and in true -ια [ἀλήθεια, μίᾰ] retain α throughout the sing.) Σπεῖρα, -ης (A. 10. 1 etc.), μαχαίρῃ (A. 12. 2), πλημμύρης (L. 6. 48), πρῴρης (A. 27. 30), Σάπφειρα, -ῃ (5. 1), συνειδυῖα, -ης (5. 2). Similarly the LXX. and the papyri.[1] Exception: στεῖρα (adj.), στείρᾳ L. 1. 36 all MSS.

2. The inflection ᾱ, G. ᾱς, etc. in proper names is not confined to words where a definite sound (ε, ι, ρ) precedes, any more than it is in Attic. Μάρθα, -ας Jo. 11. 1; Λύδδα, -ας (?) A. 9. 38 (cp. § 10, 5). To this corresponds the inflection of masc. names, N. ᾱς, G. ᾱ (as in Doric etc.), D. ᾳ, A. ᾱν, V. ᾱ: 'Ιούδας, -α (Mc. 6. 3); 'Αγρίππας, -ᾱ (A. 25. 23). Cp. § 10, 1. (On the other hand, -ίας, -ίου: so Ζαχαρίας, -ου L. 1. 40, 3. 2, beside Ἄννα and Καϊάφα; 'Ηλίου, 1. 17 [-α אB], 4. 25, like Att. Καλλίας, -ου.)

3. **Peculiarities.**—Θεά A. 19. 27 occurs in the formula ἡ μεγάλη θεὰ Ἄρτεμις (as in inscriptions); but ibid. 37 ἡ θεός, which is the usual Att. form.—Θεός, voc. θεέ, Mt. 27. 46 is unclassical, occasionally in LXX.; cp. Synt. § 33, 4.

4. **Contracted words** in Decl. I. and II.—Βορρᾶς, G. ᾶ, L. 13. 29, Ap. 21. 13 (Att. and later writers have βορέας and βορρᾶς). The use of contracted words of Decl. II. is very limited: νοῦς and πλοῦς are transferred to Decl. III. (§ 9, 3); χειμάρρου Jo. 18. 1 is no doubt from -ρρος; ὀστοῦν Jo. 19. 36 O.T., but uncontracted ὀστέα L. 24. 39 (D ὀστᾶ); -έων Mt. 23. 27, Eph. 5. 30 T.R., H. 11. 22,[2] like χρυσέων Ap. 2. 1 AC, -έους 4. 4 א, -έας 5. 8 א (cp. Clem. Hom. x. 8 χρυσέους, ἀργυρέους, χρύσεα, ἀργύρεα, χάλκεα; xvii. 3 χάλκεα, χρύσεα), but this uncontracted form is in no passage read by all MSS., and alternates with much more numerous examples of contraction in this adj. (and in the adjectives ἁπλοῦς, διπλοῦς) in Ap. and elsewhere. Cp. W. Schmidt de Joseph. eloc. 491 f. Χρυσᾶν Ap. 1. 13 א*AC is a gross blunder, wrongly formed on the model of χρυσᾶς 1. 12 (?).

5. The so-called Attic second declension is wanting, with the exception of the formula ἵλεώς σοι (v.l. ἵλεος) Mt. 16. 22; cp. ἵλεως v.l. -εος H. 8. 12 (Hermas, Sim. ix. 23. 4; ἵλεων [-εως A] Clem. Cor. i. 2. 3). 'Ανώγεων Mc. 14. 15 (-άγαιον, -ώγαιον are the best attested readings), L. 22. 12 (-άγαιον, -ώγαιον, -αγεον, -ωγεον) is an incorrect form; ἡ ἕως is non-existent, αὐγή taking its place; λαός, ναός stand for λεώς, νεώς; ἡ ἅλων, -ωνος for ἡ ἅλως. Ἡ Κῶς A. 21. 1, acc. Κῶ for Κῶν (like late Attic), is declined in this case after the manner of αἰδώς Decl. III.

---

[1] E.g. ἀρούρης Berlin Pap. 328, ii. 32; 349, 8. Ἰδυίης 327, 15. Εἰδνείης (§ 3, 8) 405, 24.

[2] Ὀστοῦν Ἀττικοί, ὀστέον Ἕλληνες says Moeris; but many examples of the uncontracted form survive in Attic as well. Cp. W.-Schmidt, op. cit. 491.

6. Gender in Decl. II.—'Ο and ἡ ἀλάβαστρος are recorded in Mc. 14. 3 (Att. ὁ ἀλάβαστος Aristoph.). 'Ο ἄψινθος for ἡ Ap. 8. 11 (?) (א omits ὁ). 'Ο βάτος in Mc. 12. 26 has overwhelming authority; ἡ is read in L. 20. 37, A. 7. 35 (Hellenistic, according to Moeris). 'Η ληνός Ap. 14. 19 f. as commonly, but, according to ABCP, τὴν ληνὸν ... τὸν μέγαν (cp. LXX., Gen. 30. 38). 'Ο λίθος in all cases, even of the specially precious species of stones (where Attic has ἡ). 'Η λιμός (as in old dialects, LXX.), L. 15. 14, A. 11. 28 (ὁ L. 4. 25). 'Η στάμνος H. 9. 4 (Attic: ὁ Doric and LXX.). 'Ο ὕαλος for ἡ Ap. 21. 18 (cp. λίθος; ὅ ὕελος Theophrast. de lapid. 49).

§ 8. THIRD DECLENSION.

1. **Accusative singular in α and ν.**—The late-Greek forms in -αν for α (inscriptions, papyri: found quite early in dialects), on the analogy of Decl. I. are frequently found in MSS., Mt. 2. 10 ἀστέραν א*C, Jo. 20. 25 χεῖραν AB, A. 14. 12 Δίαν DEH al., ἄρσεναν Ap. 12. 3 A, εἰκόναν 13. 14 A, μῆναν 22. 2 (Tisch. on H. 6. 19); they do not deserve to be adopted. In words in -ης the accus. in -ην is not unknown to Attic (τριήρην, Δημοσθένην), but occurs only in barytone words [paroxyt. or proparoxyt.]; in the N.T. the following are incredible: ἀσφαλην (?accent) H. 6. 19 ACD, συγγενην R. 16. 11 AB*D*, ἀσεβην R. 4. 5 אD*FG, ὑγιην Jo. 5. 11 א*.—In barytones in -ις with τ δ in the stem, the regular Attic accus. is -ιν, and so too in the N.T. χάριν etc. are the usual forms: but χάριτα A. 24. 27 (-ιν א*EL), 25. 9 A, Jd. 4 AB, Hellenistic according to Moeris (papyri).[1] Cp. κλεῖδα L. 11. 52 (LXX.; D κλεῖν as in Attic and Ap. 3. 7, 20. 1, τὰς κλεῖς in the quotation of Justin, cp. 2).

2. **Accusative plural (assimilation to the nominative plural).**—The old termination (ν)ς in vowel stems (τοὺς βότρῦς, τοὺς βοῦς) has disappeared in Hellenistic Gk., and these words are inflected with ας: Mt. 14. 17 ἰχθύας, Jo. 2. 14 βόας. But κλεῖς – κλεῖν – τὰς κλεῖς, Ap. 1. 18 (κλεῖδας B).—For -ας we have -ες in the MSS. (accus. = nom.: old dialects and late Gk.[2]) in the case of τέσσαρες (§ 6, 1), A. 27. 29 א, Jo. 11. 17 אΔ, Ap. (4. 4), 7. 1 A twice, P once, 9. 14 א (so still more often in LXX.). So also we have by assimilation (like αἱ and τὰς πόλεις, τριήρεις) οἱ and τοὺς βασιλεῖς in Hellenistic Gk., and this accus. plur. is regular in N.T. for all words in -εύς.

3. **Relation of the nominative to the cases** (inflection with or without consonant).—The inflection -ας, -αος = ως, as γῆρας, -ως, κέρας, -ως, has almost disappeared. Γῆρας, dat. γήρει in L. 1. 36 (as in Ionic: so usually in LXX., where also the gen. γήρους occurs, as in Clem. Cor. i. 63. 3; ibid. 10. 7 γήρει, v.l. -ᾳ). Κέρας, τέρας take τ (as in Attic and always in Hellenistic Gk. τέρατα, τεράτων acc. to Moeris): κέρατα Ap. 13. 1, τέρατα Mt. 24. 24. We have only κρέας and plur. κρέα R. 14. 21, 1 C. 8. 13 (other cases wanting).

---

[1] See also Viereck, Sermo Graecus quo senatus populusque R. ... usi sunt (Göttingen, 1888), p. 59.

[2] See especially Buresch, Rh. Mus. xlvi. 218.

§ 8. 3–6.]   *THIRD DECLENSION.*   27

There is most attestation for the consonantal inflection with ν for all cases of the comp. in -ων: exceptions are almost confined to the Acts (πλείους nom. or acc. A. 13. 31, 19. 32, 21. 10, 23. 13, 21, 24. 11, 25. 6, 14: but -νες, -νας 27. 12, 20, 28. 23) and John (μείζω, ℵ -ονα 1. 51, ἐλάσσω 2. 10, μείζω ABE al. -ων, D -ονα 5. 36, πλείους 4. 41, elsewhere Mt. 26. 53 πλείω or -ους).—On the other hand the δ is omitted not only in νήστεις Mt. 15. 22, Mc. 8. 3 (Polyb. and others; like πόλεις, wrongly written νῆστις), but also in ἔρεις (acc.) Tit. 3. 9 ℵ°AD al. (ἔριν ℵ*DE al., but in the middle of words that are clearly plurals), G. 5. 20 (nom. with v.l. ἔρις sing.), 2 C. 12. 20 (ditto), cp. v.l. in 1 C. 3. 3, 1 Tim. 6. 4; side by side with ἔριδες 1 C. 1. 11 all MSS. (ἔρεις acc. in Clem. Cor. i. 35. 5).—Assimilation of the nom. to the oblique cases takes place in Hellenistic Gk. in words in -ίς, -ινος when ιν is substituted for ῖς (ῥίν, Σαλαμίν), and so in N.T., ἡ ὠδίν 1 Th. 5. 3 (ἀκτίν Apoc. Petr. 7).

4. **Open and contracted forms.**—'Ορέων Ap. 6. 15 (Hermas, Sim. ix. 4. 4 etc.; Clem. Cor. i. 10, 7), and χειλέων H. 13. 15 (from LXX. Hos. 14. 3) show the widespread tendency, which is apparently not wholly foreign to Attic, to leave this case uncontracted in words in ος. (But ἐτῶν A. 4. 22, 7. 30 etc.) On the other hand we have πῆχυς, πηχῶν for πήχεων Jo. 21. 8 (-εων A), Ap. 21. 17;[1] ἥμισυς (a *barytone* adj. in υς: βαθύς etc. are never so inflected) has ἡμίσους for -εος Mc. 6. 23 (Apoc. Petr. 27), ἡμίσῃ L. 19. 8 ΓΠ (D²), with the var. lect. ἡμίσ(ε)ια ℵBLQ, τὰ ἡμισυ ΑRΔ(D*). 'Ημίσεια would be a not impossible assimilation to ἡ ἡμίσεια; ἡμίσους and -ση are attested as Hellenistic.[2] 'Υγιής, ὑγιῆ Jo. 5. 11, 15 etc. are Hellenistic (Attic has ὑγιᾶ as well)

5. **Genitive -εος and -εως.** βαθέως L. 24. 1 (on preponderant evidence), and πραέως ℵBKL 1 P. 3. 4 are mistakes of the popular language (see Lobeck, Phr. 247) for -έος (otherwise there is no instance of the gen. of the adj. in -ύς).

6. **Peculiarities.**—'Salt' in Attic is οἱ ἅλες, in N.T. τὸ ἅλας, Mt. 5. 13 twice (ἅλα [cp. τὸ γάλα] ℵ twice, D once), Mc. 9. 50 twice (ἅλα once ℵ*, twice LΔ), L. 14. 34 (ἅλα ℵ*D), no doubt derived from τοὺς ἅλας, and inflected like τέρας: ἅλατι Col. 4. 6. This form is also characteristic of the common language, according to Herodian ii. 716, Lentz. (In Mc. 9. 49 D has ἀλί in a clause from Levit. 2. 13 which is wanting in ℵBLΔ; ibid. 50, acc. ἅλα ℵ*A*BDLΔ, ἅλας ℵ°A²CN al.)—Ναῦς only occurs in A. 27. 41 τὴν ναῦν (literary word = vulgar τὸ πλοῖον).—'Ορνιξ 'a hen' nom. sing. L. 13. 34 (cp. Doric gen. ὄρνιχος);[3] for 'bird' N.T. has ὄρνεον Ap. 18. 2 etc. (also Barn. 10. 4, Clem. 1 Cor. 25. 2, Herm. Sim. ix. 1, 8).— Συγγενής, -εῖς, dat. plur. -εῦσι (like γονεῖς, -εῦσι) Mc. 6. 4 (-έσιν ℵ* [om. ℵ*]AB²CD* al.), L. 2. 44 B*LXΔΛ.[4]

---

[1] On the Hellenistic πηχῶν, Lob. Phryn. 243 f. W. Schmidt, Jos. eloc. 498.

[2] Lob. 247. In dialects and in poetry a neuter plur. in -εια of these words occurs, A. Buttmann, Stud. und Kr. 1862, 194.

[3] Babrius ap. Crusius Philol. 1894, 238 (Athen. 9, 374 D, Herodian i. 44. 7 L.).

[4] Cram. Anecd. Ox. iii. 246.

§ 9. METAPLASMUS.

1. Fluctuation between neuter and masculine in Declension II.—
Δεῖπνος for -ον is only a v.l. in L. 14. 16, Ap. 19. 9 (B), 17. Δεσμός
has plural δεσμά (old) L. 8. 29, A. 16. 26, 20. 23, and δεσμοί (old)
Ph. 1. 13 (without distinction). Ζυγός 'yoke' (in use since Polyb.)
never ζυγόν. Θεμέλιον, plur. -α A. 16. 23 (Hom. LXX.; Herm. Sim.
ix. 14. 6; Attic, according to Moeris), elsewhere ὁ θεμέλιος
1 C. 3. 11 f., 2 Tim. 2. 19, Clem. Cor. i. 33. 3 etc. (strictly sc. λίθος;
Attic). Ὁ νῶτος R. 11. 10 O.T. quot. (class. τὸ νῶτον). Σῖτος, plur.
σῖτα A. 7. 12 HP (Att. and LXX.; σιτία read by אAB etc. does not
suit the sense). Στάδιον has plur. στάδια Jo. 6. 19 א*D, and σταδίους
א^corr. ABL al. : the latter also occurs in L. 24. 13 and Ap. 21. 16
AB al. with v.l. -ίων (both plurs. are Attic).

2. Fluctuation between Declensions I. and II.—Compound substantives with ἄρχειν in their second half are formed with -αρχος in
Attic, in (dialectic and) Hellenistic Gk. more often with -άρχης
(Decl. I.), Kühner, i. 3, i. 502. So in N.T. ἐθνάρχης, πατριάρχης,
πολιτάρχης, τετραάρχης ('Ασιαρχῶν Acts 19. 31), also ἑκατοντάρχης
centurio Mt. 8. 13 (-χῳ א^bUΔ), and in the majority of places in the
Acts; but χιλίαρχος *tribunus* always, ἑκατόνταρχος A. 22. 25 and
often (with much variety of reading about the vowel); στρατοπεδάρχος or -ης 28 16, an addition of the β text (om. אAB).[1]
Δυσεντέριον A. 28. 8 according to Moeris is Hellenistic for -ρία,
Lob. Phryn. 518. Ἦχος, ὁ (in L. 21. 25 τό, see 3), L. 4. 37, A. 2. 2,
H. 12. 19, similarly stands for ἠχή (Moeris).

3. Fluctuation between Declensions II. (I.) and III.—The exx.
of interchange of -ος masc., Decl. II., and -ος neut., Decl. III., have
somewhat increased in number, in comparison with those in the
classical language. The Attic ὁ ἔλεος becomes τὸ ἔλεος in LXX. and
N.T. always (exc. Mt. 9. 13 ἔλεον C³EFG etc.: 12. 7 ἔλεον EG etc.,
23. 23 τὸν ἔλεον CΛΔΠ: H. 4. 16 ἔλεον C^bD^cEL: Tit. 3. 5 τὸν
ἔλεον D^cKL), with gen. ἐλέους, dat. ἐλέει (the original forms, if we
may judge from the old derivative ἐλεεινός, cp. φαεινός from φάος,
and the compound νηλεής). Ὁ ζῆλος is the class. and also the usual
N.T. form; τὸ ζ. (nom. or acc.) 2 C. 9. 2 אB, Ph. 3. 6 א*ABD*FG,
with gen. ζήλους A. 5. 17 only B* (Clem. Cor. i. 6. 1, 2, 9. 1 etc.
τό; 5. 2, 4, 5 etc. ὁ). Ἦχους L. 21. 25 for ἤχου (see 2). Ὁ θάμβος
(ancient) for τό L. 4. 36 D (θ. μέγας), cp. A. 3. 10 θάμβου C. Τὸ
πλοῦτος (nom. or acc. sing.) 2. C. 8. 2 א*BCP, E. 1. 7, 2. 7, 3. 8, 16,
Ph. 4. 19, Col. 1. 27 (also ὁ πλ. א), 2. 2 (neut. א*ABC), is attested on
preponderant or very good evidence; elsewhere (even E. 1. 18)
ὁ πλ., and always gen. πλούτου. Τὸ σκότος (cp. σκοτεινός) is
universally found (earlier ὁ and τό): in H. 12. 18 σκότῳ is a wrong
reading for ζόφῳ. Fluctuation between -ος neut. and -α, -η Decl. I.
is rarer: τὸ δίψος (Attic, which has also ἡ δίψα) 2 C. 11. 27 δίψει
(δίψῃ B*); τὸ νῖκος[2] 1 C. 15. 54 f. O.T. quot., 57, Mt. 12. 20 O.T.

---
[1] On the usage of Josephus cp. W. Schmidt, Jos. elocut. 485 ff.
[2] The usual LXX. form: Lob. Phryn. 647.

§ 9. 3. § 10. 1-2.] *PROPER NAMES. INDECLINABLE* 29

quot., Herm. Mand. xii. 2. 5; ἡ νίκη 1 Jo. 5. 4. **Νοῦς** and **πλοῦς** (the latter A. 27. 9) are declined like βοῦς: gen. νοός, dat. νοΐ, as also in Herm. Sim. ix. 17. 2 (cp. § 7, 4).[1] 'H **ἅλων, -ωνος** Mt. 3. 12, L. 3. 17, for ἡ ἅλως, -ω (cp. § 7, 5). The dat. is formed from Decl. III. in words that in their other cases are neuters of Decl. II.: δάκρυον (Ap. 7. 17, 21. 4) – δάκρυα – **δάκρυσιν** L. 7. 38, 44 (also in Attic occasionally; δάκρυ is an old form occurring in poetry): σάββατον – σάββατα – **σάββασιν** always Mt. 12. 1 etc. Consonantal stem of Decl. III. for -o- stem of Decl. II.: κατήγωρ (on the model of ῥήτωρ) Ap. 12. 10 only in A for κατήγορος (אBCP as elsewhere in N.T.).[2]

§ 10. PROPER NAMES. INDECLINABLE NOUNS.

1. The Hebrew personal names of the O.T., when quoted as such, remain with few exceptions unaltered and indeclinable: 'Αδάμ, 'Αβραάμ, 'Ιακώβ, Φαραώ, Δαυίδ etc. The exceptions are mainly nominatives in הָ֑ ,ר which are represented by the termination -ας and declined according to Decl. I. (gen. -α and -ου, see § 7, 2): 'Ιούδας Mt. 1. 2 f.; Οὐρίας, gen. -ου ibid. 6; 'Εζεκίας, 'Ησαΐας etc. (but 'Αβιά [as LXX.] ibid. 7 nom. acc., L. 1. 5 gen.). Other exceptions are: **Μανασσῆ** Mt. 1. 10 acc., Μανασσῆς nom., cp. inf. 3 (Μανασσῆ nom. אᵇB); 'Ιαννῆς and 'Ιαμβρῆς 2 Tim. 3. 8; **Λευις, -εις** nom. H. 7. 9 אᶜBC*, the remaining MSS. -ι (ει): cp. inf. 2. **Σολομων** is declined either with gen. -ῶνος (therefore nom. -μών), so Mt. 1. 6 -μῶνα (but א* -μών indecl.), 12. 42, and elsewhere: or -ῶντος (like Ξενοφῶν, therefore nom. -μῶν): A. 3. 11 -μῶντος (DE -μῶνος), 5. 12 (-μῶνος BDEP); so also LXX., unless, as usually happens, the word remains indeclinable. **Ιησοῦς** *Josua* H. 4. 8. Μωϋσῆς (so, according to the best evidence, with LXX. and Josephus, instead of Μωσ. of the ordinary MSS.), gen. always -έως as if from -εύς, dat. -εῖ Mt. 17. 4 אBD al. (others -ῆ), Mc. 9. 4 AB³DE etc., ibid. 5 אABCDE etc. (nearly all), and so elsewhere with constant variation in the MSS. between -ει and -η: acc. -έα only in L. 16. 29, elsewhere -ῆν (A. 6. 11, 7. 35, 1 C. 10. 2, H. 3. 3). The latter inflection: -ῆς, -ῆ, -ῇ, -ῆν (cp. inf. 3) is that prevalent in the LXX.[3]

2. The same old Hebrew names, if employed as proper names of other persons of the N.T. period, are far more susceptible to Hellenisation and declension. The Hellenising is carried out: (*a*) by appending -ος; 'Ιάκωβος always, Ἄγαβ-ος A. 11. 28, 21. 10: (*b*) in words that in their Greek pronunciation would end in a vowel, by appending -ς to the nom., -ν to the acc.: so 'Ιησοῦς, 'Ιησοῦν (cp. 1), Λευις (also written -εις; therefore ῑ) Mc. 2. 14 (acc. -ιν, indecl. א*A

---

[1] So also ῥοῦς, gen. ῥοός, in later Greek: cp. W.-Schm. § 8, 11, note 7.

[2] Ibid. § 8, 13: it looks as if the original nom. was taken for a gen.: the late form διάκων for διάκονος is parallel.

[3] In Josephus Niese and Naber write -έος (an impossible inflection; in the MSS. -έως is a strongly attested variant), -εῖ, -ῆν in their text; -έως (with v.l. -έος) is found as early as Diodor. Sic. 34. 1. 3. W.-Schm. § 10, 5.

al.), L. 5. 27 (acc. -ιν, indecl. D), 29 (nom. -ις, indecl. D); to which must be added the nom. in -ας, see 1; for the inflection vide inf. 3: (c) in names in -αν, by the substitution of ς for ν in the nom., so that the inflection follows that of 'Ιούδας : Ἄννας L. 3. 4, A. 4. 6, Jo. 18. 13, 24 חָנָן (Joseph. Ἄναν-ος) : 'Ιωνάθας A. 4. 6 D,[1] a name which in Joseph. is still further Hellenised to 'Ιωνάθης : so N.T. 'Ιωάνης (§ 3, 10) יוֹחָנָן or 'Ιωανάν (L. 3. 27 in the genealogy of Christ), gen. -ου,[2] dat. -ῃ (-ει L. 7. 18, 22 אAB or B*[L], Mt. 11. 4 DΔ, Ap. 1. 1 א*, cp. Μωϋσεῖ), acc. -ην. Josephus also makes Καινας out of Καινάν and Ναθας out of Ναθάν. The common name 'Ιωάνης is also abbreviated into 'Ιωνα (Syr. יַרְבָא) LXX. 2 (4) Kings 25. 23, and so Mt. 16. 17 Σίμων Βαριωνᾶ = Σ. (ὁ υἱὸς) 'Ιωάνου Jo. 1. 42 ('Ιωνᾶ AB³ al., Syr.), 21. 15 ff. ('Ιωνᾶ ACcorr· al., Syr. Sin. יונן, a form which also stands for the prophet Jonah L. 11. 29 etc.); 'Ιωνάν or -άμ (אBΓ, Syr.) is found in L. 3. 30 (in the genealogy of Christ). By a similar abbreviation יוֹסֵף became יוֹסֶה 'Ιωσῆς, gen. -ῆτος (inf. 3) Mc. 6. 3 BDLΔ ('Ιωσήφ א, 'Ιωσῆ AC), 15. 40, 47 (with similar v.l.): cp. the var. lect. to Mt. 13. 55, 27. 56, A. 1. 23, 4. 36; in this name the evidence preponderates for the full Hebrew form without alteration, vide inf. (d) The Hellenisation is carried furthest in Σίμων, -ωνος = Συμεών (this form occurs for Peter in A. 15. 14 in James' speech, 2 P. 1. 1 [Σίμων B] : for others in A. 13. 1, L. 2. 25 etc.): the pure Greek name with a similar sound is substituted for the Hebrew name, after a fashion not unknown to the Jews of the present day, just as 'Ιάσων (A. 17. 5 etc.) is substituted for *Jesus*, and perhaps Κυδίας for Χουζᾶς (L. 8. 3 according to the Latin cod. *l*). On the other hand, the following, though employed in this way, remain unaltered and indeclinable : 'Ιωσήφ generally (vide sup.), Ναθαναήλ (also the names of the angels Μιχαήλ [Μειχ. B] and Γαβριήλ), Μαναήν A. 13. 1. Similarly the woman's name 'Ελισαβέτ : whereas מִרְיָם sometimes remains as Μαριάμ, esp. for the mother of Christ, and sometimes is Hellenised to Μαρία (Μαριάμμη in Joseph.), with great diversity of reading in the MSS. (gen. Μαρίας Mt. 1. 16, 18, 2. 11 etc.; acc. Μαριάμ 1. 20 [-ίαν BL] : in chaps. 27 and 28 the form -ία for the nom. has most support in the case of the other Maries; in L Μαριάμ 1. 27, 30, 34, 37, 39 etc., but τῆς Μαρίας 41, ἡ Μαρία 2. 19 אBD [D has also frequently elsewhere nom. -α, dat. -α i.e. -ᾳ, acc. -αν]; Paul in R. 16. 9 has Μαριάμ, an unknown lady, in ABCP -ίαν).[3] The following are declinable without further addition : Ἄννα חַנָּה (nom. L. 2. 36) and Μάρθα Syr. מַרְתָּא (gen. -ας, see § 7, 2); the following are Hellenised by the addition of α (ᾶ?): 'Ιωαν(ν)α יוֹחָן, Σουσαννα שׁוֹשַׁנָּה (L. 8. 3, 24. 10), and there is a similar addition of η in Σαλώμη שָׁלֹם Mc. 15. 40, 16. 1.

---

[1] 'Ιωνάθας appears already on an Egyptian papyrus of the 3rd cent. B.C., Flinders Petrie Pap. ii., p. 23: 'Απολλώνιον...[παρεπ]ίδημον, ὃς καὶ συριστὶ 'Ιωνάθας [καλεῖται].

[2] 'Ιωάνου in LXX. 2 Chr. 28. 12.   [3] Cp. W.-Schm. § 10, 1, note 1.

§ 10. 3-5.] PROPER NAMES, INDECLINABLES. 31

3. The declension of Hebrew masc. proper names whose stem ends in a long vowel (with the exception of those in -ίας), and of the similar Greek or Graeco-Roman names which are formed by *abbreviation* (§ 29), follows the same pattern on the whole for all vowels, and is consequently known as the "mixed" declension. Three cases (G.D.V.) exhibit the pure stem (those ending in α, η, ω being in our spelling extended by an ι mute); the nom. in all cases has s, the acc. generally ν, but this is often wanting in LXX. and N.T. with the η(ι) and ω stems : Μανασσῆς, acc. -ῆ, vide sup. 1 (so LXX., e.g. 2 (4) Kings 20. 21, 21. 1, 2 Chron. chap. 33) : Λευις, vide sup. 1, 2 : 'Απολλῶς, acc. 'Απολλῶ A. 19. 1 (-ων A²L, 'Απελλῆν ℵ*, § 6, 2), cp. Κῶ acc. § 7, 5, 1 C. 4. 6 (-ων ℵ*AB), Tit. 3. 13 (-ων ℵD^bH, -ωνα FG). Exx. (*a*) Βαραββᾶς, Βαρνάβας, 'Ιούδας, Ζηνᾶς (from Ζηνόδωρος), Σιλᾶς (=Σιλουανός). (*b*) (Μανασσῆς, vide sup.) 'Απελλῆς R. 16. 10, acc. -ῆν (as in A. 19. 1 ℵ, vide sup.). The gen. of *Greek* names of this class, in classical Greek -οῦ, is unrepresented in N.T. (*c*) Λευις, vide sup. 2. (*d*) Ἰησοῦς, -οῦ, -οῦ, -οῦν, -οῦ. (*e*) 'Απολλῶς (from 'Απολλώνιος). In extra-Biblical Greek besides this declension of such names there is found a second, in which there is a similar nom. in -s, but the stem for the remaining cases is extended by the addition of a consonant (usually δ, in Egypt τ), e.g. 'Αππᾶς, -ᾶδος, Ἑρμῆς, -ῆδος : the single N.T. example of this declension is 'Ιωσῆς, -ῆτος, sup. 2.

4. **Roman proper names.**—There need only be noticed *Agrippa* 'Αγρίππας, -α : *Aquila* 'Ακύλας : *Clemēns, Crescēns, Pudēns*, gen. *-ēntis* =(Κλήμης)-εντος Ph. 4. 3, Κρήσκης 2 Tim. 4. 10, Πούδης (-εντος) 21. The *n* of the nom., which was hardly pronounced, is often absent from Latin inscriptions.

5. **Names of places, mountains, rivers.**—In this category it is the usual practice in by far the majority of cases for non-Greek names to remain un-Hellenised and undeclined, with the exception, of course, of prominent place-names, which were already known to the Greeks at an earlier period, such as Τύρος ; Σιδών, -ῶνος ; Ἄζωτος *Asdod* (cp. § 6, 7) A. 8. 40 ; Δαμασκός etc. and (river-name) 'Ιορδάνης, -ου. The Hellenisation is well marked, a new etymology (ἱερός, Σόλυμοι) being given, in the case of Ἱεροσόλυμα, -ων, a form which is employed in the N.T. alongside of Ἱερουσαλήμ (in the latter there is no good reason for writing the rough breathing, § 4, 4 ; Mc. and John (Gosp.) always have Ἱεροσ., and so Mt. exc. in 27. 37 : Ἱερουσ. is always the form in Ap., Hebr., and in Paul, except in the narrative of G. 1. 17 f., 2. 1 : L. gives both forms, but Ἱερουσ. rarely in his Gospel.[1] Other exceptions are : Βηθανία, gen. -ας, acc. -αν Jo. 11. 1, Mc. 11. 12, Jo. 12. 1, Mc. 11. 11 etc. (but Mt. 21. 17, Mc. 11. 1 B* εἰς Βηθανία, L. 19. 29 ℵ*BD* εἰς Βηθφαγῆ καὶ Βηθανία) : Γολγοθα, Mc. 15. 22 τὸν Γολγοθᾶν τόπον (Γολγοθα ACDE al.) : Γόμορρα, -ων Mt. 10. 15 (-ας CDLMP), -ας 2 P. 2. 6, cp. inf. 6 (ἡ Γομόρρα) : Λύδδα, gen. Λύδδης A. 9, 38 B²EHLP, -ας ℵ*B*C, -α indecl. ℵᶜA (which is harsh in the con-

---

[1] LXX. Ἱερουσ., except in 2, 3, 4 Macc. and Job. See W.-Schm. § 10, 3.

nection ἐγγὺς οὔσης Λ. τῇ Ἰόππῃ); elsewhere the acc. is Λύδδα, ibid. 32, 35 (-αν CEHLP), either as neut. plur. or as indecl. (?):[1] Σάρεπτα acc. L. 4. 26 (-ων gen. LXX. Obad. 20): τὸν Σαρωνα (Ἀσσαρ.) 'The plain' שָׁרוֹן; Decl. III. or (with Aramaic -a) indecl. (?): Σόδομα סְדוֹם (therefore Hellenised), -ων Mt. 10. 15, 11. 24, 17. 29, 2 P. 2. 6; -οις Mt. 11. 23 (Mc. 6. 11 Text. Rec., an insertion from Mt.), L. 10. 12 (so earlier in LXX.). On the other hand the following e.g. are unaltered and indecl.: Βηθλεέμ, Βηθφαγῆ, Καφαρναούμ, Αἰνών Jo. 3. 23, Σαλίμ ibid., Σιών; (mountain) Σινᾶ, (brook) Κεδρών Jo. 18. 1 (τοῦ χειμάρρου τοῦ K. correctly AS; other MSS. are corrupt with τῶν Κέδρων, τοῦ Κέδρου; Josephus declines τοῦ Κεδρῶνος). Ἐλαιών, Mount of Olives, as a Greek rendering cannot be indecl.; therefore, as we elsewhere have τὸ ὄρος τῶν ἐλαιῶν, we must also read ὄρος (acc.) τὸ καλούμενον ἐλαιῶν (not Ἐλαιών) L. 19. 29, 21. 37: all MSS. give a wrong inflection in A. 1. 12 τοῦ καλουμένου Ἐλαιῶνος for ἐλαιῶν: cp. § 33, 1.

6. **On the declension of place-names.**—Double declension as in class. Greek is seen in Νέαν πόλιν A. 16. 11; therefore also read Ἱερᾷ πόλει Col. 4. 13. Instances of metaplasmus: Decl. I. fem. sing., Decl. II. neut. plur.—Λύστρα, acc. -αν A. 14. 6, 21, 16. 1, but dat. -οις 14. 8, 16. 2: Θυάτειρα acc. Ap. 1. 11 ℵ, -αν ABC, gen. -ων A. 16. 14, dat. -οις Ap. 2. 18 (B -ρῇ, § 7, 1), 24 (ℵᶜ -ρῇ, B -ραις), cp. Λύδδα, supra 5. Decl. III. and Decl. I. confused.—Σαλαμίν, dat. -ῖνι A. 13. 5, but -ίνῃ ℵAEL, cp. (W.-Schm. § 10, 5) gen. Σαλαμίνης in Suid. Ἐπιφάνιος (cod. A), *Salamina(m)* Latt. ap. Acts ibid. like Justin ii. 7. 7, *Salaminae insulae* xliv. 3. 2, *Salaminam* (cp. the new formations in romance languages, Tarragona, Cartagena, Narbonne).

7. **Gender.**—In place-names the fem. is so much the rule that we have not only ἡ Ἱερουσαλήμ (A. 5. 28 etc.), but even πᾶσα Ἱεροσόλυμα Mt. 2. 3 (on A. 16. 12 Φιλίππους, ἥτις ἐστί ... πόλις, see § 31, 2). The masc. ὁ Σιλωάμ (the spring and the pool) in L. 13. 4, Jo. 9. 7, 11 is explained by the interpretation added in Jo. 9. 7 ἀπεσταλμένος.[2]

8. Of **indeclinable appellatives** there are only a few: (τὸν κορβαν Mt. 27. 6 B*, correctly τὸν κορβανᾶν; indecl. in another sense Mc. 7. 11, where it is introduced as a Hebr. word): μάννα, τό (Ap. 2. 17 τοῦ μ.): πάσχα, τό (L. 2. 41 τοῦ π.): (σαταν gen. for -νᾶ 2 C. 12. 7 ℵᶜ al.; more a proper name than an appellative): σίκερα acc. L. 1. 15 (indecl. in LXX.): ἡ οὐαί Ap. 9. 12, 11. 14 (like ἡ θλῖψις etc.: also used as a subst. elsewhere, LXX. and 1 C. 9. 16, see W.-Gr.).

§ 11. ADJECTIVES.

1. **Adjectives in -ος, -η (-α), -ον and -ος, -ον.**—(a) Compound adj. ἡ ἀργή (ἀργός = ἀ-εργός) 1 Tim. 5. 13, Tit. 1. 12 (Epimenides), Ja.

---

[1] There is a similar fluctuation in Josephus, W.-Schm. ibid.

[2] Josephus has ἡ Σ., sc. πηγή, B. J. v. 12. 2, vi. 8. 5, but μέχρι τοῦ Σ. ii. 16. 2, vi. 7. 2.

§ 11. 1-3.] ADJECTIVES. 33

2. 20 BC* (v.l. νεκρά); Att. ἀργὸς γυνή Phryn. Lob. 104 f. Ἡ αὐτομάτη Mc. 4. 28 (not unclass.). Ἡ παραθαλασσία Mt. 4. 13 (τὴν παραθαλάσσιον D, παρὰ θάλασσαν ℵ*), but ἡ παράλιος L. 6. 17; these compounds in -ιος admit of both forms. (b) Uncompounded adj. Ἡ ἔρημος always (Att. -μος and -μη). Ἡ ἕτοιμος Mt. 25. 10 (A -μαι), -μη 2 C. 9. 5, 1 P. 1. 5 (Att. -μος and -μη). Ἡ αἰώνιος is the usual form as it is in Att.; -ία 2 Th. 2. 16 (-ιον FG), H. 9. 12, often as a v.l. Ἡ βεβαία always (Att. -α and -ος). Ἡ κόσμιος (Att. -ία) 1 Tim. 2. 9 ℵ*AD^corr. al.; v.l. -ίως. Ἡ μάταιος and -ία (as in Att.). Ἡ ὅμοιος ? Ap. 4. 3. Ἡ ὅσιος 1 Tim. 2. 8 (-ία Att. and LXX.). Ἡ οὐράνιος L. 2. 13 (v.l. οὐρανοῦ), A. 26. 19 (Att. -ία). In other cases the N.T. is in agreement with the ordinary grammar.

2. Τὸ συγγενής L. 1. 36 has the fem. ἡ συγγενίς for Att. -ής (Clem. Hom. xii. 8 : Phryn. Lob. 451 ; cp. εὐγενίδων γυναικῶν Clem. Rom. Epit. ii. 144), whereas strictly this fem. only belonged to words in -της, -του, and to those in -εύς (βασιλίς).

3. **Comparison.**—The absorption of the category of duality into that of plurality (cp. §§ 2, 1, and 13, 5), occasioned also the disappearance from the vulgar language of one of the two degrees of comparison, which in the great majority of cases (cp. inf. 5) was the superlative, the functions of which were taken over by the comparative.[1] The single instance of a superl. in -τατος in the N.T. is ἀκριβέστατος A. 26. 5 (in literary language, the speech of Paul before Agrippa, § 2, 4). The remaining superlatives are in -ιστος, and are generally employed in intensive [elative] sense, and in some cases have quite lost their force : ἐλάχιστος *perexiguus* passim[2] (as a true superl., either due to the literary language or corrupt reading in 1 C. 15. 9 : for which ἐλαχιστότερος occurs in E. 3. 8, inf. 4): ἥδιστα 2 C. 12. 9, 15, A. 18. 3 D ('gladly,' 'very gladly'): κράτιστε in the dedication L. 1. 1 : μέγιστος *permagnus* 2 P. 1. 4 : πλεῖστος Mt. 11. 20, 21. 8, cp. § 44, 4 : 1 C. 14. 27 (τὸ πλεῖστον 'at most'):[3] ὡς τάχιστα A. 17. 15 (literary language, a true superl.) : ὕψιστος passim: ἔγγιστα D Mc. 6. 36 (Joseph. passim : Clem. Cor. i. 5. 1). The most frequent superlative which still remains is (μᾶλλον -) μάλιστα (Acts, Pauline epp., 2 Peter : still there are no more than twelve instances in all).[4] Cp. Synt. § 44, 3.

[1] The usage of the Ep. of Barnabas agrees with that of the N.T. On the other hand in Hermas, although his Greek is the unadulterated language of ordinary speech, superlatives in -τατος and -ιστος are quite common with *intensive* [*elative*] sense, while he also uses the comparative for the superlative proper. This (Roman) form of the κοινή thus held the same position in this respect as the Italian of to-day, which does not distinguish between comp. and superl., but has preserved the forms in -*issimo*, etc., in intensive sense.

[2] Hermas, Mand. v. 1. 5 τοῦ ἐλαχίστου ἀψινθίου 'the little bit of wormwood,' in a preceding passage (ibid.) ἀψίνθιον μικρὸν λίαν. A similar use occurs as early as Aeschin. iii. 104.

[3] Herm. Sim. viii. 5. 6, 10. 1, ix. 7. 4 τὸ πλεῖστον μέρος, but viii. 1. 6 τὸ πλεῖον μ.

[4] A popular substitute for μᾶλλον, μάλιστα as also for πλείων and πλεῖστος is supplied by the adjective περισσός ('superabundant,' 'ample') together with its adverb and comparative. τὸ περισσὸν τούτων Mt. 5. 7 = τὸ πλέον τ. (cp.

C

4. Special forms of the comparative.—For comp. of ἀγαθός we never have ἀμείνων, βέλτιον as an adv. only in 2 Tim. 1. 18 (-ίων Herm. Vis. iii. 4. 3, 7. 1); κρείσσων (-ττων, § 6, 7) only in Pauline epp., Hebrews, and Pet. ('more excellent' or 'mightier,' 'of higher standing,' opp. to ἐλάττων H. 7. 7); the vulgar ἀγαθώτερος (Herm. Mand. viii. 9. 1) is never found in the N.T.[1] For comp. of κακός, χείρων 'worse' is frequent; τὸ ἧσσον is opp. to τὸ κρεῖσσον 1 C. 11. 17; ἧσσον adv. 'less' (of degree) 2 C. 12. 15. Ἐλάσσων *deterior* is the opposite to κρείσσων Jo. 2. 10, H. 7. 7, vide supra: or, as in Attic, to μείζων R. 9. 12 O.T. quot.; adv. ἔλαττον 'less' (of number) 1 Tim. 5. 9 (μικρότερος is 'smaller' as in Attic). Τάχιον (Hellenistic, B ταχειον) is the constant form, not θᾶττον (Att.) or -σσον, unless the latter is to be read for ἆσσον in A. 27. 13 (a literary word, cp. in Clem. Cor. i. 65. 1 the juxtaposition of the cultured phrase ὅπως θᾶττον with conj., and the vulgar εἰς τὸ τάχιον with inf.). Ἐλαχιστότερος 'the lowest of all' (see 3) is correctly formed according to the rules of the common language; μειζότερος 3 Jo. 4 shows an obscured sense of the idea of the comp. in μείζων, but is not without analogies in the older language (*e.g.* ἀμεινότερος). Διπλότερον Mt. 23. 15 = *duplo magis* (Appian also has διπλότερα τούτων = διπλάσια τ. Proem. 10), whereas ἁπλούστερος shows the Attic formation of such comparatives.

5. Adjectival comparative (and superlative) of adverbs.—The superl. πρῶτος has been retained where the comp. πρότερος in the sense of 'the first of two' has disappeared, so Jo. 1. 15, 30 πρῶτός μου, A. 1. 1 τὸν πρῶτον λόγον (but πρότερος = 'former,' 'hitherto' survives in E. 4. 22 τὴν προτέραν ἀναστροφήν, cp. Herm. Mand. iv. 3. 1, 3 etc.); the corresponding adv. πρότερον = 'formerly' H. 10. 32, 1 P. 1. 14 τὸ πρότ. (§ 34, 7) in Jo. 6. 62, 9. 8 (ibid. 7. 50, 51 as a wrong reading), G. 4. 13, 1 Tim. 1. 13, whereas the first of two actions is here also denoted by πρῶτον (Mt. 7. 5, 8. 21, L. 14. 28, 31 etc.), except in H. 4. 6, 7. 27 (literary style; in 2 C. 1. 15 πρότερον should apparently be erased with ‍א*). The opposite word ἔσχατος is likewise also used in comp. sense (Mt. 27. 64); while ὕστερος is superl. 1 Tim. 4. 1 (a wrong reading in Mt. 21. 31); the adv. ὕστερον is

---

§ 44, note 3), L. 12. 4 περισσότερόν (περισσόν AD al.) τι = πλέον τι; 12. 48 περισσότερον, D πλέον; cp. Mt. 11. 9 = L. 7. 26, Mc. 12. 40 = L. 20. 47, Clem. Cor. i. 61. 3. The adv. περισσῶς = μᾶλλον Mt. 27. 23, Mc. 10. 26, 15. 14 (-σσοτέρως ENP al.). (In conjunction μᾶλλον περισσότερον [-έρως D] Mc. 7. 36, -έρως μ. 2 C. 7. 13, vide inf., cp. § 44, 5 and pleonasms like εὐθέως παραχρῆμα.) So also the Berlin papyri, 326, ii. 9 εἰ δ' ἔτι περισσὰ γράμματα καταλίπω ('further'), and mod. Greek περισσότερος, adv. -ρον 'more.' In St. Paul, however, περισσοτέρως appears occasionally to have a still stronger force = ὑπερβαλλόντως 2 C. 7. 15, 12. 5, G. 1. 14, cp. A. 26. 11 (περ. μᾶλλον 2 C. 7. 13 (?) = 'still much more,' cp. sup.), while in other passages of his writings it may be replaced by μᾶλλον or μάλιστα, as περισσότερος by πλείων: Ph. 1. 14, 2 C. 1. 12, 1 C. 12. 23 f., 2 C. 10. 8 etc. So also H. 7. 15 περισσότερον (= μᾶλλον) ἔτι κατάδηλον, 2. 1, 13. 19 -ρως, Herm. Mand. iv. 4. 2, Sim. v. 3. 3.

[1] Kühner, i. 3, 1. 565. ἀγαθώτατος is also found in Herm. Vis. i. 2. 3 ('excellent'; as a proper superl. in Diod. Sic. xvi. 85); Herm. Sim. viii. 9 has ἡδύτερος, Kühner, ibid. 555.

common (also in superl. sense, as in Mt. 22. 27, L. 20. 32). Further exx. of comp. of adverbs: ἐξώτερος Mt. 8. 12 etc. (Herm. Sim. ix. 7. 5), ἐσώτερος A. 16. 24, H. 6. 19, κατώτερος E. 4. 9 (of course also in superl. sense); these adjectives are not found in Attic, which however has the corresponding adverbs: ἀνώτερον L. 14. 10, H. 10. 8 (Att. more often -ρω),[1] κατωτέρω Mt. 2. 16 (κάτω perhaps more correctly D), πορρωτέρω (-ρον AB) L. 24. 28, ἐγγύτερον R. 13. 11.

§ 12. NUMERALS.

1. Δύο has gen. δύο, dat. δυσίν (plural inflection): similarly LXX.:[2] δυσίν for δυοῖν is condemned by Phrynichus (Lob. 210).

2. In compounds of δέκα with units, at least from thirteen upwards, δέκα occupies the first place (this practice is more frequent in the later language than in the older: in mod. Gk., except in the case of eleven and twelve, it is universal): (δεκαδύο [Polyb.] A. 19. 7 HLP, 24. 11 same evidence; δεκατέσσαρες Mt. 1. 17, 2 C. 12. 2, G. 2. 1: δεκαπέντε Jo. 11. 18, A. 27. 28, G. 1. 18 (δέκα καὶ πέντε Herm. Vis. ii. 2. 1 ℵ): δεκαοκτώ L. 13. 4 (δέκα καὶ ὁ. ℵ°A al.), 11 (δ. κ. ὁ. AL al.). The ordinals, however, take the reverse order: τεσσαρεσκαιδέκατος A. 27. 27, πεντεκαιδέκατος L. 3. 1 (Ionic and later language: Attic usually τέταρτος καὶ δέκ.). With larger numbers there is a similar order of words, with or (usually) without καί: εἴκοσι τρεῖς 1 C. 10. 8, τεσσεράκοντα καὶ ἕξ Jo. 2. 20.

§ 13. PRONOUNS.

1. **Personal.**—The 3rd pers. is represented by αὐτοῦ: the same form is used for the 3rd pers. possessive. Reflexives: 1st pers. sing. ἐμαυτοῦ, 2nd sing. σεαυτοῦ (not σαυτοῦ), 3rd sing. ἑαυτοῦ (not αὑτοῦ):[3] plural 1st, 2nd, and 3rd pers. ἑαυτῶν (so in Hellenistic Gk., not ἡμῶν α., ὑμῶν α., σφῶν α.; on ὑμῶν αὐτῶν in 1 C. 5. 13 from Deut. 17. 7, see § 48, 10).

2. **Demonstratives.**—Οὗτος, ἐκεῖνος as usually; the intensive ι (οὑτοσ-ί) is unknown, but is employed by Luke (in the Acts) and Paul (Hebrews) in the adv. νυνί = νῦν. Ὅδε is rare and almost confined to the phrase τάδε λέγει: Acts 21. 11, Ap. 2. 1, 8, 12, 18,

---

[1] Quite plebeian are ἔτι ἄνω, ἔτι κάτω for ἀνώτερον, κατώτερον in the apocryphal addition to Mt. 20. 28 in D.

[2] W.-Schm. § 9, 11.

[3] Even in the inscriptions of this period the trisyllabic forms, ἑαυτοῦ etc. supplant the dissyllabic, which in classical times were used alongside of them. In the old edd. of the N.T. the latter still appear pretty frequently, but are now rightly replaced by ἑαυτοῦ or αὐτοῦ (see Synt. § 48, 6), so even in R. 14. 14 δι' ἑαυτοῦ ℵAB, A. 20. 30 ὀπίσω ἑαυτῶν ℵAB. The long α results from the contraction (ἕο αὑτοῦ); in the Hellenistic and Roman period it has occasioned the loss of the υ in pronunciation, whence the spelling ἑατοῦ (just as the ι in ᾳ̃, ᾳ was unpronounced). See Wackernagel in Kuhn's Zeitschr. xxxiii. (N. F. xiii.), p. 2 ff.

3. 1, 7, 14; elsewhere τάδε A. 15. 23 D; τῇδε L. 10. 39; τήνδε Ja. 4. 13 (Clem. Cor. ii. 12. 5 ἥδε is only a conjecture). Cp. Synt. § 49, 1, and inf. 4.

3. **Relatives.**—Ὅς, ἥ, ὅ: ὅστις, ἥτις, ὅ,τι; the latter, however, only in the *nom.* sing. and plur., except that ὅ,τι also appears as acc.: in meaning it becomes confused with ὅς, see Synt. § 50, 1. We have the stereotyped phrase ἕως ὅτου in Luke and John (ἀφ' ὅτου in D L. 13. 25); otherwise there is no instance of these old forms (so we never find ἅσσα, ἅττα for ἅτινα), in the same way that the forms τοῦ, τοῦ (= τίνος, τινός), τῷ, τῷ (= τίνι, τινί) etc. from τίς, τις have become obsolete. Ὅσπερ is only in Mc. 15. 6 אᶜB³C al. ὅνπερ ἠτοῦντο (*male* ὃν παρῃτ. א*AB*; the right reading in DG ὃν ἂν ἠτοῦντο § 63, 7). On the use of ὅς for a demonstrative pron. see Synt. § 46, 2.

4. **Correlative pronouns.**—Ποῖος – τοιοῦτος (τοιόσδε only 2 P. 1. 17 τοιᾶσδε, cp. 2) – οἷος – ὁποῖος. Πόσος – τοσοῦτος – ὅσος. Πηλίκος (G. 6. 11, H. 7. 4) – τηλικοῦτος (2 C. 1. 10, H. 2. 3, Ja. 3. 4, Ap. 16. 18) – ἡλίκος (Col. 2. 1, Ja. 3. 5). To these must be added ποταπός (with similar meaning to ποῖος), Synt. § 50, 6. On the correlative adverbs, see § 25. Τοιοῦτος and τοσοῦτος (τηλικοῦτος) have neut. in -ον and -ο (both forms are also found in Att., though the first is more frequent): with var. lect. Mt. 18. 5, A. 21. 25 β text, H. 7. 22: with -ον only H. 12. 1; on the other hand τηλικοῦτο Herm. Vis. iv. 1. 10 (2. 3 with v.l.).

5. With pronouns and pronominal forms it has also happened that words indicating duality as distinct from plurality have become obsolete (πότερος – τίς; ἑκάτερος – ἕκαστος), with the exception of ἀμφότεροι (the N.T. form, never ἄμφω) and ἕτερος, which, however, already becomes confused with ἄλλος. Cp. Synt. § 51, 6.

§ 14. SYSTEM OF CONJUGATION.

1. The system of the conjugation of the verb is apparently not much altered from its earlier state, since nearly all the classical forms are found in the N.T., the dual, of course, excepted. The voices remain as before: and the tenses are the same, except that in all voices only one future exists: ἔχω, ἕξω (the fut. σχήσω, which is derived from the aorist and related to it in meaning, never occurs); μιμνήσκομαι, μνησθήσομαι (not μεμνήσομαι fut. perf., of which the name 'Attic future' is sufficient indication that it was absent from the Hellenistic language); ἔστην, στήσομαι; ἐστάθην, σταθήσομαι, but not ἑστήξω[1] fut. perf.; φαίνομαι, φανήσομαι, but the form φανοῦμαι, which in Attic was allied to the present as distinguished from φανῆσ. which belonged to ἐφάνην, no longer appears (1 P. 4. 18 is a quotation from LXX. Prov. 11. 31). This certainly destroys the harmonious structure of the system of the tenses, viz. continuous

---

[1] For κεκράξονται L. 19. 40 the better attested reading is κράξουσιν אBL (κράξονται D: κεκράξομαι passim in LXX.). But cp. the aor. ἐκέκραξα A. 24. 21, inf. § 24.

action in present, past, and future time = pres. impf. and fut. of the present (ἕξω, τιμήσομαι pass.): completed action in past and future time = aorist and fut. of the aorist (σχήσω, τιμηθήσομαι): continuity of completed action in present, past, and future time = perf., plupf., and fut. of the perfect (ἑστήξω, βεβλήσομαι pass.). Of the moods, moreover, the optative is clearly on its way to becoming obsolete, being only found in Luke's writings with any frequency, where its presence is due to the influence of the literary language which retained it. Of the future opt. there is no trace, and this tense is, generally speaking, almost confined to the indic., since the use of the fut. infin. is, with few exceptions, limited to the Acts (11. 28, 23. 30, 24. 15, 27. 10: cp. Synt. § 61, 3), and the fut. part. outside the writings of the same author (Gosp. 22. 49, Acts 8. 27, 20. 22, 22. 5, 24. 17) is of quite rare occurrence (Mt. 27. 41 σώσων, but σῶσαι ℵ*, καὶ σώσει D Jo. 6. 64 [?], 1 C. 15. 37, H. 3. 5, 13. 17, 1 P. 3. 13, 2 P. 2. 13 with v.l.), cp. Synt. § 61, 4. Finally, the verbal adjective has practically disappeared, with the exception of forms like δυνατός which have become stereotyped as adjectives; the only exx. are παθητός 'liable to suffering' A. 26. 23, and βλητέον L. 5. 38 (ℵ*D βάλλουσιν): cp. Herm. Vis. iv. 2. 6 αἱρετώτερον.

2. **Periphrastic forms.**—The perf. and pluperf. indic. are not unfrequently represented by a periphrasis (as is also the case in Att.), while for the perf. conjunctive (passive) a periphrasis is a necessity (as in Att. for the most part); the perf. imperat. is expressed periphrastically in L. 12. 35 ἔστωσαν περιεζωσμέναι; on the other hand we have πεφίμωσο Mc. 4. 39. By means of periphrasis the place of the fut. perf. may also be supplied (L. 12. 52, Mt. 16. 19, 18. 18, H. 2. 13); periphrasis has, on the whole, a very wide range in the N.T., see Synt. § 62.

§ 15. AUGMENT AND REDUPLICATION.

1. The **syllabic** augment is wanting as a rule in the pluperf. (as also in other Hellenistic writings, but not in Att.); exceptions are chiefly in the passive (W. Schmidt de Josephi elocut. 438): ἐβέβλητο L. 16. 20, ἐπεγέγραπτο A. 17. 23 (ἦν γεγραμμένον D), συνετέθειντο J. 9. 22, περιεδέδετο 11. 44 (περιδέδ. D*), ἐπεποίθει L. 11. 22 (πέποιθεν D), and many others.

2. The syllabic augment, in places where in Attic it holds an exceptional position instead of (or in addition to) the temporal, has been ill maintained: ὠνοῦμαι, ὠνούμην (Att. ἑων.), ὠθῶ, ὦσα (ἐξέωσεν A. 7. 45 only in ℵ*E; ὦθουν Ev. Petr. 6): in ἀνοίγω, κατάγνυμι it has indeed survived, but through being misunderstood has intruded into the other moods and the fut. (see irreg. verbs, § 24); προορώμην (-ωρ- B³P) A. 2. 25 O.T. quot.: ἑώρων Jo. 6. 2 ℵΓΔ al. is no doubt a wrong reading for ἐθεώρουν (cp. ibid.). On the reduplication in ἑόρακα, vide inf. 6.

3. The augment ἠ- instead of ἐ- (less frequent in Att. than in later writers) is always used with θέλω (Att. ἐθέλω, ἤθελον), never with

βούλομαι (a word adopted from the literary language : but ἠβούλετο Herm. Sim. v. 6. 5); in δύναμαι and μέλλω there is much variation in the MSS. between ἤδυν., ἠμ-, and ἐδυν., ἐμ- (cp. W.-Schm. § 12, 3).

4. Loss of the temporal augment.—The addition of the *temporal* augment was not without exceptions even in Attic Gk. in the case of an initial diphthong of which the first letter was ε or ο. The N.T. has εἶξα G. 2. 5 (as in Att.), οἰκοδομῶ, οἰκοδομήθη אB* Jo. 2. 20, οἰκοδόμησεν B*D A. 7. 47, ἐποικοδόμησεν 1 C. 3. 14 (ἔπωκ. B³C) : on the other hand ᾠκοδόμησεν Mt. 21. 33 all MSS., ᾠκοδόμητο L. 4. 29 (οἰκοδόμηται D), cp. ἐνῴκησεν 2 Tim. 1. 5 (-οί- only D*), κατῴκησεν (-ισεν) Ja. 4. 5 O.T., παρῴκησεν H. 11. 9 etc. W. H. App. 161. Since the original documents of the time show several instances of unaugmented οἰ, and Phrynichus refers to it as a custom of his time (Phryn. Rutherford, 244), it may safely be attributed to the writers; besides ὁ (for οἱ) no longer bore much resemblance to οἰ (which in ordinary pronunciation somewhat inclined to ῡ). Cp. W.-Schm. § 12, 5. Εὐ in older Attic when augmented always became ηυ, in the later Attic (which also used ηι, ει interchangeably) not always;[1] in the N.T. ευ preponderates, but ηυ- also occurs not unfrequently : ηὑρίσκετο H. 11. 5 acc. to אADE, προσηύξαντο A. 8. 15 (-ευ- only B), 20. 36 (-ευ- B*D), ηὐχόμην R. 9. 3 (εὐχ. DEKL).[2] For unaugmented αι the only ex. is 2 Tim. 1. 16 ἐπαισχύνθη (-η- א*K ; interchange of αι = ē and η ?).—The augment is wanting in the case of a single short vowel in ἐληλύθειν (as in Att.: Attic redupl.) : in ἀνέθη for -είθη A. 16. 26, ἀφέθησαν R. 4. 7 O.T. (ε arose from the moods instead of ει = i : similarly LXX.) : in ὄφελον as a particle introducing a wish, cp. § 63, 5 ; other cases appear to be clerical errors : διερμήνευ(σ)εν L. 24. 27 (-η- EHKM al.), διεγείρετο Jo. 6. 18 B al., προορώμην A. 2. 25 O.T.,vide supra 2, ἀνορθώθη L. 13. 13 (-ω- אE al.) etc.

5. Temporal augment η or ει.—In general the N.T. agrees with Attic ; thus it has ἐργάζομαι, ἠργαζόμην A. 18. 3 א*AB*DE, ἠργασάμην Mt. 25. 16 א*B*DL, 26. 10 א*B*D, Mc. 14. 6 א*B*D, L. 19. 16 א*AB*DE* al., H. 11. 33 א*D* (see also R. 7. 8, 15. 18, 2 C. 7. 11, 12. 12 ; B* reads εἰ- only in R. 15. 18, א in all these four passages, DE never) as in Attic, and in the Berlin Egyptian Records 530. 15 συνηργάσαντο (but perf. -ει-, augm. and redupl. being distinguished, see 6).

6. Reduplication.—Initial ρ loses its peculiarity in ῥεραντισμένος H. 10. 22 א*ACD*P for ἐρρ.: περιρεραμμένος Ap. 19. 13 only א* (περιρεραντισμ. אcc), cp. ῥεριμμένοι Mt. 9. 36 D*. (Similar forms in Ionian and late writers, W.-Schm. § 12, 8 : Kühner, I.³ ii. 23). On ρ for ρρ, vide supra § 3, 10. μνηστεύω, μεμνηστευμένη (on the model of μέμνημαι) L. 1. 27, 2. 5 only as a v.l. (Clem. Hom. xiii. 16:

---

[1] In the later Atticism this is purely phonetic, as is shown by the fact that this ευ was also introduced as the augment for αυ : εὔξησα from αὐξάνω. The same ευ appears in inscriptions of the Roman period ; but in the N.T. the only example is D εὔξανε A. 12. 24.

[2] W.-Schm. § 12, 5 b.

§ 15. 6–7.] *AUGMENT AND REDUPLICATION.* 39

Kühner, ibid. 24). εἴργασμαι (from FεFέργ.) as in Att. (augm. η, see 5) Jo. 3. 21, 1 P. 4. 3. Similarly we have ἑόρακα beside ἑώρων: in this case, however, the spelling ἑώρακα is very widely spread both in Att. and in the N.T. (1 C. 9. 1 -o- אB*D^cEFGP, -ω- AB³ al.: Jo. 1. 18 -o- B*EFGHKX, -ω- אAB³CLM al. etc.). εἰλκωμένος is read by nearly all MSS. in L. 16. 20 (as if from ἕλκω).

7. Augment and reduplication in compound verbs and verbs derived from compounds.—Where the simple verb (with initial vowel) has been forgotten, the augment precedes the prepos. (so usu. in Att., but always in N.T.): καθεύδω, ἐκάθευδον; καθίζω, ἐκάθισα, ἐκαθεζόμην, ἐκαθήμην¹; ἠμφιεσμένος. In addition to these N.T. has ἀφία (=ἀφίημι) ἤφιεν Mc. 1. 34, 11. 16 (attested also in Att., but hardly correctly, as an alternative for ἀφίει, ἠφίει), and ἀνοίγω, ἤνοιξα side by side with ἀνέῳξα, ἠνέῳξα, with inf. ἀνεῳχθῆναι L. 3. 21 (ἀνοιχθ. only in D): impf. only (δι)ήνοιγε L. 24. 32, perf. act. in nearly all cases ἀνέῳγα Jo. 1. 52 (ἠνεῳγότα א), 1 C. 16. 9, 2 C. 6. 11. See irreg. verbs, § 24. Thus whereas in this instance the double augm. appears as against the Att. usage, ἀνέχομαι has only the single augm.: ἀνεσχόμην A. 18. 4 (ἤν. DEHLP), ἀνείχεσθε 2 C. 11. 1 (ibid. 4, but BD* ἀνεχ.), cp. Moeris's dictum ἠνέσχετο Ἀττικοί, ἄν. Ἕλληνες; elsewhere, too, in the N.T. there is no instance of doubly augmented forms of this kind.

Verbs derived from compounds (παρασύνθετα) are in general treated like compound verbs in Attic Gk., if the first component part is a prepos.: the same is always the rule in N T., except in the case of προφητεύειν: ἐπροφητεύσαμεν Mt. 7. 22 אB*CLZ, προεφ. B²EGM al., 11. 13 ἐπροφήτευσαν אB*CDG, προεφ. B**EFG al., (with similar division of MSS.) 15. 7, Mc. 7. 6, L. 1. 67, A. 19. 6 (א always ἐπρ. except in Jd. 14 προεπροφήτευσεν: B* ἐπροφ., B³ ἐπροεφ., all others προεφ.).² So also διακονῶ makes διηκόνουν (from διάκονος: does διά form part of the word?), but in Att. ἐδιακόνουν (we even have περισσεύω, περιέσσευον in E Acts 16. 5, a form proscribed by Phrynichus). Verbs formed from compounds of εὖ, when the adverb is followed by a short vowel, have a tendency in the late language to augment this vowel: εὐαγγελίζομαι, εὐηγγελιζόμην (so always): εὐαρεστῶ, εὐηρεστηκέναι H. 11. 5 אDEP (εὐαρ. AKL).³ Verbs compounded of two prepositions tend to a double augmentation: ἀπεκατέστη (ἀποκ. B) Mc. 8. 25, ἀπεκατεστάθη (ἀποκ. DK) Mt. 12. 13: similarly Mc. 3. 5 (ἀποκ. D), L. 6. 10 (parallel forms occur in inscriptions and the papyri); but in H. 12. 4 ἀντεκατέστητε is hardly attested.

---

¹ Ἐκάμμυσαν Mt. 13. 15 O.T., A. 28. 27 O.T., explains itself. Καμμύω from κατ(α)μύω: the verb is proscribed by Phryn. Lob. 339.

² This verb is treated at length in Κόντος κριτικαὶ καὶ γραμμ. παρατηρήσεις (1895), p. 70 ff.: see also W. Schmidt, Joseph. eloc. 442. Παρρησιάζομαι ἐπαρρ. does not come under this head (πᾶν not παρά is imbedded in it).

³ Hermas, Vis. iii. 1. 9 εὐαρεστηκότων א, εὐηρ. *as*: εὐηρέστησαν Sim. viii. 3. 5.

§ 16. VERBS IN -Ω. TENSE FORMATION.

1. Verbs with pure stem.—Φορέω keeps a short vowel in the formation of the tenses (Att. -η-), ἐφορέσαμεν, φορέσομεν 1 C. 15. 49 (φορέσαι Herm. Sim. ix. 16. 3, but perf. πεφορηκότες ibid. 1);[1] inversely (ἐπι)ποθέω makes ἐπεπόθησα 1 P .2. 2 (LXX.; in old and Attic Gk. -εσα preponderates). Cp. ἐρρέθην from stem ῥε- Mt. 5. 21 אLM al., 27 KL al., 31 אLM al., and so elsewhere interchangeably with ἐρρήθην (cp. LXX. and other late writings), but the short vowel is limited in N.T. and other writings to the indic.: where there is no augment the form is always ῥηθείς etc. Πεινᾶν makes πεινάσω, ἐπείνασα (no doubt with ᾰ, not ᾱ) L. 6. 25 etc. (so also LXX.); but διψᾶν, διψήσω. With σ we have λελουσμένοι H. 10. 23 אD*P, but λελουμ. as in Att. in Jo. 13. 10 (-σμ- only E): κέκλεισμαι always (L. 11. 7 etc.), as against Att. -ειμαι (-ημαι): ἐκλείσθην as Att.: cp. irreg. verbs ζώννυμι, κεράννυμι, σῴζω.

2. Verbs with mute stem.—Of verbs in -ζω the following have a guttural character: νυστάζω, ἐνύσταξαν Mt. 25. 8 (Hellen.: Att. -ασα): παίζω, fut. ἐμπαίξω, aor. pass. ἐνεπαίχθην Mc. 10. 34, Mt. 2. 16 etc. (Doric and Hellen.: ἔπαισα etc. Att.); the following is dental: σαλπίζω, σαλπίσω, ἐσάλπισα (1 C. 15. 52, Mt. 6. 2 al.), Hellenistic for -ι(γ)ξα; the following fluctuate: ἁρπάζω, -άσω, ἥρπασα, -άσθην (=Att.), but -άγην Hellenist. 2 C. 12. 2, 4, cp. ἅρπαξ (Att.), ἁρπαγή (old and Att.), ἁρπαγμός (ἁρπάζω Homeric fut.): στηρίζω, -ίσω, -ισα L. 9. 51 BCL al. (-ιξα אAD al.), 22. 32 (-ξ- D al.), Ap. 3. 1 ACP (-ξ- אB), 2 Th. 3. 3 B, A. 15. 32 CE, elsewhere -ξ- (and ἐστήριγμαι, στηριγμός), which was the old inflection: cp. στῆριγξ. Ἁρμόζω (ἡρμοσάμην), σφάζω (ἔσφαξα) are unrepresented in present and imperfect.

3. Verbs with liquid stem.—Verbs in -αίνω, -αίρω take only -ᾱνα, -ᾱρα in the 1st aor. act., without regard to the preceding sound: thus ἐξήρᾱνα (ρ precedes) as in Att., but also ἐλεύκανα (ἐκέρδανα),[2] ἐβάσκᾱνα, ἐσήμᾱνα for Att. -ηνα: ἐπιφᾶναι from -φαίνω L. 1. 79, ἀναφάναντες (male -φανέντες AB*CE al.) A. 21. 3, φάνῃ Ap. 18. 23: ἐξεκάθᾱρα 1 C. 5. 7, 2 Tim. 2. 21 (ἐκάθαρα is also sporadically found in 4th century Attic). Ἆραι (contracted from ἀεῖραι) agrees with Att. Perf. pass. ἐξηραμμένος Mc. 11. 20 (Att. -ασμαι, though -αμμαι is also attested), μεμιαμμένος Tit. 1. 15 (Att. -σμ-), cp. μεμαραμμένος Herm. Vis. iii. 11. 2 א (-ασμ- as), κατῃσχυμμένος Mand. xii. 5. 2.

§ 17. VERBS IN -Ω. NEW FORMATION OF A PRESENT TENSE.

A new present tense is formed out of the perf. (instances of which are forthcoming also at an earlier period: γεγωνέω from γέγωνα): γρηγορεῖν (Phryn. 118) from ἐγρήγορα (the latter never in N.T.:

---

[1] The ε in φορέω is never found elsewhere except in the aorist and future active.

[2] 1 C. 9. 21 אAB al., but אᶜDEKL κερδήσω the regular form elsewhere, cp. Irreg. Verbs, § 24.

§ 17. § 18.]   *NEW PRESENT TENSE.*   41

γρηγ. LXX., never in good writers, N.T. with aor. ἐγρηγόρησα):
στήκω 'stand' from ἕστηκα (used along with the latter word),
Mc. 11. 25 στήκετε (-ητε; στῆτε ℵ), 3. 31 στήκοντες BC* (v.l. στάντες,
ἑστηκότες, ἑστῶτες), 1 C. 16. 13 (imperat. στήκετε), G. 5. 1 (id.),
Ph. 4. 1 (id.), 1 Th. 3. 8 (id.), the only additional forms elsewhere
are στήκει R. 14. 4, and στήκετε indic. Ph. 1. 27 : thus it is almost
confined to Pauline writings, and is mainly found in the imperat.
(for which ἕστατε is the old form, ἑστήκετε is unexampled). The
word (mod. Gk. στέκω : στήκω, Epigr. Kaibel, 970) is thoroughly
plebeian. Other exx. of new present forms are : ἀμφιάζω for -έννυμι
(Hellenist., also LXX.) L. 12. 27, ἀμφιάζει B, -έζει DL (the latter
form, elsewhere unattested, is cited by Cramer, An. Ox. 2. 338,
as κοινόν, and -άζω as δωρικόν), -έννυσι ℵA etc. as all MSS. read in
Mt. 6. 30 :—ἐνδιδύσκω ' put on ' Mc. 15. 17 ℵBC (D ἐνδυδισκ.) for
ἐνδύω: ἐνδιδύσκομαι 'put on oneself' L. 8. 27 ℵ^{ca}A (D -δυδί-) al.
(v.l. aor.), 16. 19 (LXX., Herm. Sim. ix. 13. 5):—κρύβω (Hellenist.,
see Phryn. Lob. 317: formed from the Hellenist. aor. ἐκρύβην, like
ἐγράφην from γράφω: see § 19, 2), L. 1. 24 περιέκρυβεν impf., not
2nd aor.: elsewhere no instances of pres. or impf. in N.T., Ev.
Petr. 16 ἐκρυβόμεθα :—(ἀπο)κτέν(ν)ω for -κτείνω, with extremely uncertain spelling: Mt. 10. 28 -κτεννόντων (-ενόντων E al., -εινόντων B):
Mc. 12. 5 -κτέννοντες, FG al. -ένοντες, B -εννύντες, ℵ^c -ιννύντες, MS
-αίνοντες: L. 12. 4 -εννόντων, -ενόντων DG al., -αιν- M, -ειν- B:
2 C. 3. 6 -έννει, ACDE al. -ένει, B -είνει: Ap. 6. 11 -έννεσθαι, BP
-είνεσθαι: 13. 10 -ένει, -ενει BCP, -είνει ℵ; here Lachm. writes -αίνει
(as he does in 2 C. 3. 6), Tischend. -ενεῖ.[1] The ordinary -είνω has
most support in Mt. 23. 37 (-εννν- CGK, -εν- ℵ), L. 13. 34 (-εννν- AK
al.).   For the spelling with -νν- or -ν- see on χύν(ν)ω:—νίπτω (apparently not earlier than Hellenistic Gk., from νίψω, ἔνιψα) for νίζω:—
χύν(ν)ω for χέω (Hellenist., mod. Gk.: cp. κέχυμαι, ἐχύθην with
ἐπλύθην from πλύνω) everywhere except in Mt. 9. 17 ἐκχεῖται
(probably in an interpolation, cp. D); in Ap. 16. 1 we should write
ἐκχέατε aor. with B instead of -έετε.[2] The best MSS. write the word
with νν: A. 9. 22 ℵB*C, 21. 31 ℵ*AB*D, 22. 20 ℵAB*, Mt. 26. 28
ℵABCD al., similarly 23. 35, Mc. 14. 24, L. 11. 50, 22. 20; in other
writings, however (Lob. Phryn. 726), χύνω is the only recognised
form, and this also has analogy in its favour. Cp. further in the
table of verbs, § 24, βλαστᾶν, γαμίζειν, ὀπτάνεσθαι (under ὁρᾶν).

§ 18. VERBS IN -Ω. ON THE FORMATION OF THE FUTURE.

1. The so-called **Attic future** of verbs in -έω, -άζω etc. disappears,
as the name itself implies, from the Hellenistic language, and accordingly from the N.T.; therefore -έσω, -άσω, not -ῶ -εῖς, -ῶ -ᾷς in N.T.

---

[1] In Acts 3. 1 for ἀνέβαινον A has ἀναίβεννον, C ἀνέβεννον, in L. 10. 31 A καταί-
βεννεν. The spelling -κταίνω has, however, little probability in view of the consistent forms of the fut. -ενῶ and aor. -εινα ; with -ένω one might compare μένω.
(ἀποκτέννω also occurs occasionally in LXX., W.-Schm. § 15 note.)

[2] Herm. Vis. v. 5 συγχύννου ℵ ; in Sim. viii. 2. 7 παραχέειν of as should
perhaps be emended παραχέαι.

Greek are correct (whilst the LXX. still has forms in -ῶ -ᾷς). So in particular καλῶ καλέσω, τελῶ τελέσω (ἀπόλλυμι, ἀπολέσω, ἀπολοῦμαι, § 24). On the other hand, verbs in -ίζω to a great extent form their fut., as in Att., with -ιῶ, particularly (W. H. ii. App., p. 163) in the 3rd pers. plur. act., where the following syllable also begins with a σ: ἐλπιοῦσιν L. 1. 48, ἐδαφιοῦσιν 19. 44 etc. (only in Col. 4. 9 γνωρίσουσιν אᶜBFGP, -ιοῦσιν א*ACDᶜ al., whereas ibid. 7 all MSS. have γνωρίσει, cp. E. 6. 21, Jo. 17. 26). In the LXX. the formation in -ιῶ prevails, and this is accordingly found in O.T. quotations, παροργιῶ R. 10. 19, μετοικιῶ A. 7. 43. Additional exx.: Mt. 25. 32 ἀφορίσει א*LΔ, -ιεῖ אᶜABD al. (-ιοῦσιν 13. 49 all MSS.): βαπτίσει always: Ja. 4. 8 ἐγγιεῖ (-ίσει A): ἐμφανίσω, θερίσω, καθίσω are constant: διακαθαριεῖ Mt. 3. 12, item (L. 3. 17) H. 9. 14 (καθ.): κομιεῖσθε 1 P. 5. 4, κομιεῖται Col. 3. 25 א*ACD* (-ίσεται אᶜBDᶜ al.), E. 6. 8 אᶜDᶜ al. (-ίσεται א*ABD* al.), κομιούμενοι 2 P. 2. 13 (v.l. ἀδικούμενοι): στηρίξω, -ίσω or -ίξω, § 16, 2: φωτιεῖ Ap. 22. 5 אB, -ίσει AP: χαρίσεται R. 8. 32: χρονιεῖ H. 10. 37 O.T. אᶜADᶜ al., -ίσει א*D* (οὐ μὴ χρονίσῃ LXX.ᵉᵈ·): χωρίσω. Since in O.T. quotations the -ιῶ of the LXX. has not been corrupted by scribes into -ίσω, it appears that in original passages of the N.T. the reading -ίσω should in general be preferred.

2. **Future without the characteristic form of the future tense.**— Πίομαι agrees with the Att. form: for ἔδομαι N.T. has φάγομαι, L. 14. 15, 17. 8, Jo. 2. 17 O.T., Ja. 5. 2, Ap. 17. 16 (LXX. has ἔδομαι passim: φάγομαι, ἔφαγον correspond to πίομαι, ἔπιον: Phryn. 327, φάγ. βάρβαρον). In place of the fut. χέω the LXX. and N.T. have χεῶ, χεεῖς etc.; ἐκχεεῖτε Deut. 12. 16, 24 (Clem. Cor. ii. 7. 5 παθεῖται for πείσεται from πάσχω, cp. καθεδοῦμαι).

3. Whereas in Att. many active verbs form a future *middle*, in N.T. the active form is in most cases employed throughout. Ἀκούσομαι occurs in the Acts (exc. in 28. 26 O.T. quot. -ετε) and R. 10. 14 a wrong reading of א*DE al. for -σωσιν אᶜB; but ἀκούσω, Jo. 5. 25 (-ονται AD al.), 28 (item), 10. 16 al. (where there is diversity of reading -σω is preferable, since -σομαι has not been corrupted in the Acts). Ἁμαρτήσω Mt. 18. 21 (Herm. Mand. iv. 1. 1, 2): ἀπαντήσω Mc. 14. 13: ἁρπάσω Jo. 10. 28 (אDLX οὐ μὴ ἁρπάσῃ): βλέψω Acts 28. 26 O.T.: γελάσω L. 6. 21: (γνώσομαι as ordinarily): διώξω Mt. 23. 34 al.:[1] (ἐσθίω, φάγομαι, see 2): ζήσω Jo. 5. 25 אBDL (-ονται A al.), 6. 51 אDL (-εται BC al.), 57 ABC² (-εται ΓΔ al., ζῇ C*D), with diversity of reading ibid. 58 and so *passim*, ζήσομαι all MSS. in Jo. 11. 25, R. 8. 13, ζήσω (1 Th. 5. 10, see § 65, 2) 2 Tim. 2. 11 (συνζήσομεν; -ωμεν CLP is only a corruption): both forms also occur in Att.: (ἀποθανοῦμαι as usual): θαυμάσονται Ap. 17. 8 אB, correctly for N.T. θαυμασθήσονται AP (from θαυμάζομαι = -ω, cp. 13. 3): κλαύσω L. 6. 25, Jo. 16. 20, Ap. 18. 9 (wrongly -ονται אA, though so read in Herm. Vis. iii. 3. 2):

---

[1] Ἐπιορκήσω Mt. 5. 33 is also the Att. form: κατεπιορκησόμενος Demosth. 54. 40 is passive.

κράζω L. 19. 40 אBL, κεκράξονται AR al. as in Att. and LXX., κράξονται D: (λή(μ)ψομαι, ὄψομαι as usual): παίξω Mc. 10. 34: (πεσοῦμαι, πίομαι as usual): ῥεύσω Jo. 7. 38: σπουδάσω 2 P. 1. 15 (-άζω א): συναντήσω (cp. ἄπαντ.: no Attic instance of fut. from συναντῶ) L. 22. 10, A. 20. 22: (τέξομαι, φεύξομαι, χαρήσομαι as usual).[1]

§ 19. VERBS IN -Ω. FIRST AND SECOND AORIST.

1. 1st aorist act. in -σα instead of 2nd aorist.—(ˇΗξα) beside ἤγαγον is seen in ἐπάξας 2 P. 2. 5, ἐπισυνάξαι L. 13. 34, συνάξαντες A. 14. 27 D (found at the least in dialects, LXX., and late writers): ἡμάρτησα side by side with ἥμαρτον R. 5. 14, 16, Mt. 18. 15, Herm. Mand. iv. 3. 6, vi. 2. 7 etc. (Empedocl., LXX., Lob. Phryn. 732): ἐβίωσα 1 P. 4. 2 (the better Att. form is ἐβίων), ἔζησα often takes the place of the last word (Ionic and late, not Att.) A. 26. 5 etc.: ἐβλάστησα Mt. 13. 26, H. 9. 4, causative Ja. 5. 18 as in LXX. Gen. 1. 11 (Empedocl., late writers), never ἔβλαστον: ἔδυσα intrans. for ἔδυν Mc. 1. 32 BD (ἔδυ א A etc.), L. 4. 40 δύσαντος D, δύναντος a few MSS.; δύνοντος most MSS.: ἔκραξα, as in late writers, almost always (ἀνέκραγον L. 23. 18 אBL, Herm. Vis. iii. 8. 9) except A. 24. 21 ἐκέκραξα אABC as LXX.: ἔλειψα (late) A. 6. 2 (κατέλ.), L. 5. 11 D (id.), Mc. 12. 19 א καταλείψῃ for -λ(ε)ίπῃ, elsewhere ἔλιπον.[2] The assimilation to the fut. is everywhere well marked.—A new 2nd aor. **ἀνέθαλον** is formed from ἀναθάλλω Ph. 4. 10 (LXX.), apparently in causative sense (ἀνεθάλετε τὸ ὑπὲρ ἐμοῦ φρονεῖν), unless τοῦ should be read with FG; cp. §§ 24: 71, 2.

2. 2nd aorist passive for 2nd aorist active.—Ἐφύην for ἔφυν, φυέν (συμφυεῖσαι) L. 8. 6 ff., ἐκφυῇ Mt. 24. 32 = Mc. 13. 20 (like ἐρρύην; late). So also παρεισεδύησαν for -υσαν is read by B in Jd. 4.

3. 1st and 2nd aorist (and future) passive.—In the passive voice the substitution of the 2nd aor. for the 1st is a very favourite idiom. ἠγγέλην L. 8. 20 ἀπ. (LXX., and as early as Att.): ἠνοίγην Mc. 7. 35 (-οίχθ. A al.), A. 12. 10 (-χθη EHLP), Ap. 11. 19 (-χθη B), 15. 5 side by side with -χθην (Att. has 1st aor.): fut. -γήσομαι Mt. 7. 7, L. 11. 10 אAC al., ἀνοίγεται BD (as also B in Mt. loc. cit.), but -χθήσομαι L. 11. 9 f. (A)(D)EF al.: ἡρπάγην 2 C. 12. 2, 4 (late) for Att. ἡρπάσθην (so Ap. 12. 5 ACP, but -άγη א, -άχθη B), with fut. -γήσομαι 1 Th. 4. 17: ἐκάην (Hom., Ionic, late writers) Ap. 8. 7, 1 C. 3. 15 (2 P. 3. 10), elsewhere, as in Att., we have the 1st aor. and the fut. formed from it: ἐκρύβην Mt. 5. 14, etc. In these new 2nd aorist forms there was a preference for the medial letters as the final sound of the stem, even though as in the last instance (κρυφ-) the stem strictly had another termination (-φθην Att., -φην poet.): cp. pres. κρύβω § 17: **κατενύγην** Acts 2. 37: **διετάγην** G. 3. 19, ὑπετάγην R. 8. 20, 10. 3 al., προσετάγη Herm. Mand. iv. 1. 10 (this writer also

---

[1] Χαρήσομαι is also to be regarded as Att. fut. of the aorist, as compared with χαιρήσω fut. of the present.
[2] Herm. Sim. viii. 3. 5 has κατέλειψεν along with -ιπεν. Clem. Cor. ii. 5 καταλείψαντας, 10 -λείψωμεν.

has ώρύγη for -χθη, from ορύσσω Sim. ix. 6. 7), ύποταγήσομαι 1 C. 15. 28, H. 12. 9 (Barn. 19. 7), but L. 17. 9 f. διαταχθέντα as in Attic. Ψύχω makes ψυγήσεται Mt. 24. 12 (-χήσεται K ; late writers even say ψύγω, Lob. on Soph. Ajax, p. 373²: cp. έκρύβην – κρύβω). New 1st aorists (for what in Attic is expressed by a different verb) are έτέχθην L. 2. 11, Mt. 2. 2 (Att. έγενόμην) : άπεκτάνθην passim (Att. άπέθανον). A substitute for 2nd aor. is έκλίθην (poet.), the regular form (also κλιθήσομαι) for Att. έκλίνην.

4. On the intermixture of terminations of the 1st and 2nd aor. act. and mid. see § 21, 1.

§ 20. VERBS IN -Ω. AORIST AND FUTURE OF DEPONENT VERBS.

1. **Aorist passive for aorist middle.**—'Εγενήθην (Hellenist., Phryn. 108, LXX.) in addition to έγενόμην: Mt. 6. 10, 9. 29, 15. 28, 26. 42 imperat. γενηθήτω, in O.T. quot. έγενήθη 21. 42; elsewhere only 11. 23 -νήθησαν אBCD, 28. 4 אBC*DL ; Mc. and Jo. (including Epp. and Apoc.) never have this form except in O.T. quotations, so also L. Gosp., but 10. 13 (= Mt. 11. 23) -νήθησαν אBDLΞ, 18. 23 -νήθη אBL : in Acts the only instance is 4. 4 all MSS. -νήθη, but D also has it in 7. 13, 20. 3, 16; it is frequent, however, in the epistles of Paul and Peter, and in Hebrews. Cp. the perfect γεγένημαι (found in Att.) in addition to γέγονα. 'Απεκρίθην (Hellenist., Phryn. 108) is universal, Luke alone uses the Attic form άπεκρινάμην as well, 3. 16 (23. 9, L correctly -νετο), A. 3. 12 (D is different), and always in the indic.; otherwise the latter form is only found with var. lect.: Mt. 27. 12 (D correctly -ετο), Mc. 14. 61 (-ίθη D; -νετο ?), Jo. 5. 17, 19, 12. 23. The corresponding fut. is άποκριθήσομαι. So also ύποκρίνομαι ' dissemble,' ύπεκρίθην, συνυπεκρίθησαν G. 2. 13 (Herm. Sim. ix. 19. 3, as Polyb.), διακρίνομαι ' doubt,' διεκρίθην. 'Απελογήθην L. 21. 14, -ησάμην 12. 11, but Clem. Alex. ii. 35 f. Dd. (quotation) -ηθήτε (Att. άπελογησάμην, but the other aor. too is very old). Again, έγείρομαι only makes ήγέρθην (found in Att.), never ήγρόμην : άναπαύομαι, (έπ)αναπαήσομαι L. 10. 6 אB* (-αύσεται rell.), Ap. 14. 13 אAC (ibid. 6. 11 -αύσονται or -ωνται all MSS., and so elsewhere ; but Herm. Vis. i. 3. 3 א, iii. 9. 1 א έπάην, and καταπαήσεται Pap. Londin. p. 113, line 916 ; έκαυσα, έκάην corresponds to έπαυσα, έπάην). To verbs expressive of emotion, which also in Att. take a passive aorist, belong άγαλλιώμαι (found along with -ιω, § 24), ήγαλλιάθην (-σθην BL) Jo. 5. 35 (but 8. 56 -ασάμην, and so elsewhere): (θαυμάζομαι, late form) έθαυμάσθην Ap. 13. 3 A (-αύμασεν אBP, -αυμαστώθη C), -σθήσομαι 17. 8, cp. § 18, 3 (the act. -άζω occurs in Ap. 17. 7 and regularly elsewhere; έθαυμάσθην in pass. sense 2 Th. 1. 10): θαμβεΐσθαι Mc. 1. 27 έθαμβήθησαν (-βησαν D), θαμβηθέντες A. 3. 11 D, cp. impf. Mc. 10. 24, 32, but θαμβών A. 9. 6 D as in Hom. etc.—Διελέξατο A. 17. 2 אAB (-έχθη DE), 18. 19 אAB (-έχθη EHLP) is a wrong reading for διελέγετο; the Attic διελέχθην stands in Mc. 9. 34. 'Αρνεΐσθαι and

§ 20. 1–2. § 21.]   VERBS IN -Ω. TERMINATIONS.   45

ἀπ- have only the aor. mid. (Att. more often aor. pass.; a corrupt active form ἀπαρνῆσαι occurs in Herm. Sim. i. 5).

2. **The future passive** (i.e. strictly the aoristic fut., see § 14, 1) is found with other verbs similar to those mentioned: (εὐφρανθήσομαι only B for pres. Ap. 11. 16) κοιμηθήσομαι 1 C. 15. 51, μεταμεληθήσομαι H. 7. 21 O.T. quot., φανήσομαι (φανοῦμαι 1 P. 4. 18 O.T. quot.), φοβηθήσομαι H. 13. 6 O.T. On the other hand: γενήσομαι, δυνήσομαι, ἐπιμελήσομαι 1 Tim. 3. 5: πορεύσομαι (L. 11. 5 etc.).

§ 21. VERBS IN -Ω. TERMINATIONS.

1. As early as Attic Greek there is not wanting an intermediate form between the 1st and 2nd aor. act. mid., with the terminations of the 1st aor. but without its σ: εἶπα beside εἶπον, ἤνεγκα beside ἤνεγκον. The Hellenistic language had a tendency to extend this type to numerous aorists which in classical Greek had the terminations of the 2nd aor. throughout: εἷλα, -άμην, εὗρα, -άμην etc. (Kühner I.³ ii. 104). Still this process, by means of which the second aorist was eventually quite superseded, is in the N.T. far from complete. Εἶπα (W. H. App. 164) keeps α unchanged in the forms with τ (as also in Att.): εἴπατε, -άτω, -άτωσαν; also fairly often before μ: ἀπειπάμεθα 2 C. 4. 2, προείπαμεν 1 Th. 4. 6 (-ο- AKL al.); εἶπας Mt. bis, L. semel, Mc. 12. 32 with v.l. -ες ℵ*DEF al., Jo. 4. 17 -ες ℵB*; -αν has preponderant evidence; rarely εἶπα as in A. 26. 15; imperat. εἰπέ and εἰπόν (for accent, Lob. Phr. 348) interchangeably; the part. εἴπας is rare (A. 22. 29 -ών HLP), εἴπασα hardly occurs (in Jo. 11. 28 all MSS. have εἰποῦσα in the first place, BC* have -ασα in the second; -ασα Herm. Vis. iii. 2. 3 ℵ, iv. 3. 7 ℵ*); on the other hand εἰπόντος etc., εἰπεῖν. Ἤνεγκα has α except in the infin. (only 1 P. 2. 5 has ἀνενέγκαι, always -εῖν in Joseph., W. Schm. de Joseph. elocut. 457); imp. Mt. 8. 4 προσένεγκε (-ον BC), παρ- Mc. 14. 36, L. 22. 42 (male vv. ll. -αι L. al., -εῖν AQ al.). Other verbs never have inf. in -αι nor part. -ας, nor yet imperat. 2 sing. in -ον; on the other hand these forms occur: ἔβαλαν A. 16. 37 BD, 21. 27 ℵ*A (ἐπ-), Mc. 14. 46 ℵB (ἐπ-), (ἐξέβαλαν Mc. 12. 8 B, cp. Mt. 13. 48 D, 21. 39 D, Ap. 18. 19 C); εἶδαν Mt. 13. 17 ℵB, L. 10. 24 ℵBC al., Mc. 6. 33 D etc.: εἴδαμεν Mt. 25. 37 B*I, Mc. 2. 12 CD, 9. 38 DN: εἴδατε L. 7. 22 A, Jo. 6. 26 C: εἶδα Ap. 17. 3 A, 6 ℵA; in these instances -ον has far the most support from the MSS. It is otherwise with εἷλον, -λα: εἵλατο 2 Th. 3. 10 (-ετο K), Herm. Sim. v. 6. 6: ἀνείλατε A. 2. 23, -ατο 7. 21 (-ετο P), -αν 10. 39 (-ον HLP): ἐξείλατο 7. 10 (-ετο H), 12. 11 (-ετο P), -άμην 23. 27 (-όμην HLP), but -έσθαι 7. 34 O.T. quot. Εὗρα has only slender attestation: εὑράμενος H. 9. 12 (-ό- D*), -αν L. 8. 35 B*, Mt. 22. 10 D, A. 5. 10 AE, 13. 6 A: -αμεν L. 23. 2 B*L al. Again there is preponderant evidence for ἔπεσα, -αν, -ατε (G. 5. 4): imp. -ατε L. 23. 30 (-ετε ℵ*ABD al.), Ap. 6. 16 (-ετε ℵBC). Ἦλθα Ap. 10. 9 A (-ον ℵBCP), -αμεν A. 27. 5 ℵA, 28. 16 A. 21. 8 B, Mt. 25. 39 D: -αν is often interchanged with -ον: but the imp. ἔλθατε, ἐλθάτω is

attested by the mass of the MSS. All other instances are quite isolated: ἀπέθαναν Mt. 8. 32 א^b, L. 20. 31 B*, Jo. 8. 53 D*: ἔλαβαν, -αμεν, -ατε Jo. 1. 12 and 1 Jo. 2. 27 B*, L. 5. 5 A: ἔπιαν 1 C. 10. 4 D* etc.

2. The (mod. Gk.) extension of the **terminations** -α, -ας etc. to the **imperfect** is rare, and in no case unanimously attested. Εἶχαν Mc. 8. 7 אBDΔ, A. 28. 2 אAB, 8. 10 א, Ap. 9. 8 אA (9 -ον omn.), L. 4. 40 D, Jo. 15. 22, 24 D* (rell. -ον or -οσαν): -αμεν 2 Jo. 5 אA: ἔλεγαν Jo. 11. 56 אD, 9. 10, 11. 36 א*, A. 28. 6 B. According to Buresch, Rh. Mus. 46, 224, these forms should not be recognised in the N.T., since the MSS. supporting them are quite thrown into the shade by the enormous mass of those which support -ον, -ες etc.

3. The (aoristic) termination -αν for -ασι in the 3rd pers. plur. perf. (Alexandrian according to Sext. Emp. adv. gramm. 213) is not frequent either in the LXX. or in the N.T., and in the latter is nowhere unanimously attested, so that its originality is subject to the same doubt with the last exx. (Buresch, p. 205 ff.). The instances are: ἑώρακαν L. 9. 36 BC²LX, Col. 2. 1 א*ABCD*P: τετήρηκαν BDL Jo. 17. 6: ἔγνωκαν ABCD al., ibid. 7 (ἐτήρησαν — ἔγνων א): ἀπέσταλκαν אAB A. 16. 36: εἰσελήλυθαν BP Ja. 5. 4: γέγοναν R. 16. 7 אAB, Ap. 21. 6 א^cA (-α א*BP, Buresch): πέπ(τ)ωκαν 18. 3 AC: εἴρηκαν 19. 3 אAP.

4. The termination -σαν for -ν in the 3rd pers. plur. in Hellenistic and N.T. Greek is constant in the imper. (also in the pass. and mid. as προσευξάσθωσαν Ja. 5. 14); in the impf. (Hellenist., Kn. ii.³ 55) it is found in ἐδολιοῦσαν R. 3. 13 O.T. quot.: also εἴχοσαν Jo. 15. 22, 24 אB al. (εἶχαν D*, εἶχον AD² which makes a very serious ambiguity), παρελάβοσαν 2 Th. 3. 6 א*AD* (-ετε BFG, -ον א^cD^corrE al., somewhat ambiguous). The forms are apparently authentic, since they were hardly current with the scribes, except in contract verbs, where these forms are also found in mod. Gk.; cp. ἐθορυβοῦσαν D A. 17. 5 (κατοικουσαν? D 2. 46; D also has ψηλαφήσαισαν, εὔροισαν in 17. 27, see 5; Herm. Sim. vi. 2. 7 εὐσταθοῦσαν, ix. 9. 5 ἐδοκοῦσαν). Cp. Buresch, 195 ff.

5. The termination -ες for -ας (in perf. and 1st aor.)[1] is not only quite unclassical, but is also only slenderly attested in the N.T.: Ap. 2. 3 κεκοπίακες AC, 4 ἀφῆκες אC: ἐλήλυθες A. 21. 22 B, ἑώρακες Jo. 8. 57 B*, ἔδωκες 17. 7 AB, 8 B, εἴληφες Ap. 11. 17 C etc. (W.-Schm. § 13, 16; Buresch, 219 ff.; εἴωθες Papyr. of Hyperides c. Philipp. col. 4. 20).

6. The rare optative has 3rd sing. of the 1st aor. in αι (also Clem. Cor. i. 33. 1 ἐάσαι), not the better Att. -ειε; and a corresponding 3rd plur. in αιεν: ποιήσαιεν L. 6. 11 BL (-ειεν אA, -ειαν Att. EKM al.: D has quite a different reading): A. 17. 27 ψηλαφήσειαν B al., -ειεν אE, -αισαν and ibid. εὔροισαν D, which may be correct (cp.

---

[1] Apollonius, Synt. i. 10, p. 37: 37, p. 71, attests εἴρηκες, ἔγραψες, γραψέτω for -ας, -άτω as forms about which grammarians were in conflict. Ἀφῆκετε B* Mt. 23. 23.

§ 21. 6-8. § 22. 1-2.] *CONTRACT VERBS.* 47

LXX. αἰνέσαισαν Gen. 49. 8, ἔλθοισαν Deut. 33. 16, W.-Schm. § 13, 14, note 14), since the scribes of D and of its ancestors certainly did not find the optative in the living language.

7. The plupf. of course keeps ει (not ε) in the plur.: πεποιήκεισαν Mc. 15. 7 etc.

8. The 2nd pers. sing. of the pres. and fut. pass. and mid. regularly ends (as also in the older Attic) in -ῃ; the later Attic ει (ῃι and ει interchangeable, § 3, 5) is found only in the word βούλει, borrowed by Luke from the literary language (L. 22. 42 -λῃ FGR al.; cp. Herm. Sim. ix. 11. 9 βούλῃ, v. 5. 5 apparently βούλει), = θέλεις of the popular language. Along with -ῃ, the termination -σαι, esp. frequent in contract verbs in -αω, corresponding to the forms -μαι, -ται as in the perf., is a new formation of the popular language which coincides with the primitive ending, and in mod. Greek has affected verbs of all classes.[1] Ὀδυνᾶσαι L. 16. 25: καυχᾶσαι 1 C. 4. 7, R. 2. 17, 23, 11. 18: also φάγεσαι, πίεσαι L. 17. 8. (Herm. Vis. ii. 4. 1 πλανᾶσαι: Sim. i. 3 χρᾶσαι [Vis. iii. 6. 7 the same form, but corrupt], ix. 2. 6 ἐπισπᾶσαι.) These should be regarded as the regular forms in the N.T., since ὀδυνᾳ, φάγῃ, πίῃ are not represented.[2]

§ 22. CONTRACT VERBS.

1. **Verbs in -άω.**—Ζῆν takes η as in Att., but πεινᾶν, διψᾶν take α for η as in other Hellenist. writings (cp. ἐπείνασα, § 16, 1). (From ζῆν 1 sing. impf. ἔζην R. 7. 9 B for ἔζων.[3]) From χρῶμαι we have χρῆται in 1 Tim. 1. 8 ℵD al., χρήσηται AP, otherwise there is no apposite example; χρᾶσθαι is Hellenistic, cp. Clem. Cor. ii. 6. 5 A, § 21, 7, W.-Schm. § 13, 24.—Confusion of -άω and -έω: ἠρώτουν Mt. 15. 23 ℵABCD, Mc. 4. 10 ℵC, Jo. 4. 31 C (no MS. in 4. 40 [9. 15 X], 12. 21), A. 16. 39 A; no other form of this vb. with ου:—ἐνεβριμοῦντο Mc. 14. 5 ℵC*, -μούμενος Jo. 11. 38 ℵAU:—κοπιοῦσιν Mt. 6. 28 B:— νικοῦντι Ap. 2. 17 AC, 2. 7 A (-οντι B), 15. 2 C:—κατεγέλουν L. 8. 53 D*KX etc. Cp. mod. Gk.; W.-Schm. § 13, 26.—On -ᾶσαι, 2 pers. sing. pass., see § 21, 7.

2. **Verbs in -έω.**—Uncontracted contrary to the rule is ἐδέετο L. 8. 38 (-εῖτο ℵᵃBC²LX, -εείτο AP formed out of -εετο with correction ει written over it), cp. Clem. Hom. iii. 63, κατέρρεε Apoc. Petr. 26, Phryn. 220.—Confusion of -έω and -άω: ἐλεῶντος R. 9. 16 (-οῦντος B³K), ἐλεᾶτε Jd. 22 ℵBC², 23 ℵAB (there is much variety of reading in this verse); but R. 9. 18 ἐλεεῖ ℵA²BD°L al., ἐλεᾷ only in D*(E)FG (otherwise no exx. of such forms from ἐλεῶ: both forms found in

---

[1] Cp. Lob. Phryn. 360.

[2] It is otherwise with verbs in -έω: L. 23. 40 φοβῇ σύ, Herm. Vis. iii. 1. 9 λυπῇ, but 10. 7 αιτισαι, i.e. αἰτεῖσαι ℵ for αἰτεῖς as. From verbs in -όω, ἀπεξενοῦσαι (sic) LXX. 3 Kgs. 14. 6, διαβεβαιοῦσαι Clem. Hom. xvi. 6. χαριεῖσαι, from χαριοῦμαι, occurs as early as 3rd cent. B.C. on an Egyptian papyrus. Grenfell-Hunt, Greek Papyri, series ii. (1897), p. 29.

[3] Ἔζην also occurs in Demosth. 24. 7 nearly all MSS., Eur. Alc. 295 v.l., Phryn. Lob. 457. Cp. σύζηθι, Herm. Mand. iv. 1. 9; Kühner, Gr. I.³ ii. 436.

LXX.:[1] the tenses have η, though ἐάω has ἐάσω):—ἐλλόγα Philem. 18, -ει ℵ°D^corrEKL, -ᾶται R. 5. 13 only ℵ* (and ἐλλογᾶτο A); the Hellenistic vb. elsewhere employs -εῖν.[2]

3. **Verbs in -όω.**—Infin. -οῖν (= όειν) for -οῦν : κατασκηνοῖν Mt. 13. 32 B*D, Mc. 4. 32 B*: ἀποδεκατοῖν H. 7. 5 BD*: φιμοῖν 1 P. 2. 15 ℵ*: but πληροῦν all uncials in L. 9. 31, and it is the constant form in LXX., so that the termination -οῖν is hardly established for the N.T. Cp. W.-Schm. § 13, 25 : Hatzidakis Einl. in d. neugr. Gramm. 193.—The conjunctive is regular in εὐοδῶται 1 C. 16. 2 (-δωθῇ ℵ°ACI al.): on the other hand it takes the indic. form in G. 4. 17 ζηλοῦτε, 1 C. 4. 6 φυσιοῦσθε (just as the sing. of the conj. act. is identical with the indic., and in vbs. in -άω the whole conjunctive).

§ 23. VERBS IN -MI.

1. The conjugation in -μι, which from the beginning of the Greek language gradually gives way to the other conjugation in -ω, and which has eventually entirely disappeared in modern Greek, in spite of many signs of decay is not yet obsolete in the N.T. In vbs. in -νυμι (and in ὄλλυμι), which in Attic and other early writers have already a very strong rival in the forms in -(ν)ύω, the older method of formation has not yet disappeared in the N.T., and is especially the prevalent form (as in Att.) in the *passive*: Mt. 8. 25 ἀπολλύμεθα, 9. 17 ἀπόλλυνται, etc. *Active forms*: δείκνυμι 1 C. 12. 31 (never -ύω in this form), δεικνύεις Jo. 2. 18 (never -υς), δείκνυσιν Mt. 4. 8 (ℵ -νύει), Jo. 5. 20 (-νύει D, but ibid. D -νυσιν for δείξει), cp. ἀμφιέννυσιν § 24; but ἀπολλύει Jo. 12. 25 (v.l. -έσει), ὀμνύει Mt. 23. 20 ff. (from this verb there is no certain form in -μι), ὀμνύουσιν H. 6. 16. Imperf. only in -ω form : ἐζώννυες Jo. 21. 8, (ὑπ)εστρώννυον Mt. 21. 8 (v.l. ἔστρωσαν), Mc. 11. 8 D, L. 19. 36. Imperat. ἀπόλλυε R. 14. 15, ὀμνύετε Ja. 5. 12, σβέννυτε 1 Th. 5. 19. Infin. ὀμνύειν Mt. 26. 74, Mc. 14. 71 (-ύναι BEHL al.), δεικνύειν 16. 21 (-ύναι B). Partic. ἀπολλύων Ap. 9. 11, δεικνύοντος 22. 8 (-ύντος ℵ): but ὑποζωννύντες A. 27. 17, ἀποδεικνύντα 2 Th. 2. 4 (-ύοντα AFG).

2. In **verbs in -άναι**, -έναι, -όναι there are similar transitions to the ω conjugation. Συνίστημι R. 16. 1, συνίστησι 3. 5, 5. 8, 2 C. 10. 8 are a few certain relics of the *active* of these forms in -άναι (undoubtedly from the literary language); elsewhere this verb takes the form of ἱστάνειν (Hellenist.), for which ἱστᾶν (more often than -άνειν in LXX.) is a frequent v.l., occasionally also the plebeian στάνειν (ἀποκαταστάνεις A. 1. 6 D, 17. 15 καταστάνοντες D*, Mc. 9. 12 ἀποκαταστάνει ℵ*D, -τιστάνει B*). Thus : συνιστάνειν 2 C. 3. 1, FG -άναι, BD* -ᾶν: 4. 2 συνιστάντες ℵCD*FG, -ῶντες D°EKL, -άνοντες ABP, a similar division of the MSS. in 6. 4 (-ῶντες is also read by ℵ°): 1 C. 13. 2 μεθιστάνειν ACKL, -άναι ℵBDEFG (this is the only instance where a μι form is strongly supported as a v.l.) : μεθιστάνει

---

[1] W.-Schm. § 13, 26, note 26.
[2] On this confusion of -άω and -έω see Hatzidakis, Einl. in d. neugr. Gr. 128.

§ 23. 2–4.]   VERBS IN -MI.   49

Herm. Vis. i. 3. 4. Πιμπλᾶν stands for πιμπλάναι in A. 14. 17 ἐμπι(μ)πλῶν (LXX.). The *passive* remains unaffected by this change (cp. 1): περιίστασο 2 Tim. 2. 16, Tit. 3. 9, καθίσταται H. 5. 1 etc. ([ἐμ]πίμπρασθαι A. 28. 6, Tisch. -ᾶσθαι), κρέμαται Mt. 22. 40, κρεμάμενος A. 28. 4, G. 3. 13 O.T. quot.: so also δύναμαι, ἐπίσταμαι as usual, except that δύνομαι, -όμεθα, -όμενος are read by B or B* in Mt. 19. 12, 26. 53, Mc. 10. 39, A. 4. 20, 27. 15 (also in the papyri), cp. ἐξεκρέμετο L. 19. 48 אB: and δύνῃ stands for δύνασαι in Mc. 9. 22 f. א (or א^c) BD al., 1. 40 B, L. 16. 2 אBDP (v.l. -ήσῃ), Ap. 2. 2, but -ασαι is read by all MSS. in Mt. 5. 36, L. 5. 12, 6. 42, Jo. 13. 36 (Phryn. 359: still δύνῃ or -ᾳ is already found in Attic poets). Cp. W.-Schm. § 14, 17; both forms are found in Hermas, e.g. δύνῃ Vis. ii. 1. 3, iii. 10. 8, -ασαι iii. 8. 5.—On ἔστην vide infra 4.

3. **Τίθημι, δίδωμι.**—The pres. indic. as in Att.; τιθι, i.e. τίθει, occurs in L. 8. 16 D; παραδίδως is also found L. 22. 4; διδῶ only occurs in Ap. 3. 9 AC¹ (-ωμι BP, δέδωκα א). But in the impf. the forms ἐτίθει, ἐδίδου are already found in Att. and so in N.T.; 3rd plur. ἐτίθουν A. 3. 2, 4. 35 (cp. for Attic, Bekk. Anecd. i. 90), also 8. 17 according to D*EHLP (-εσαν אAD², -οσαν B, -εισαν C), Mc. 6. 56 ADN al. (-εσαν אBLΔ): ἐδίδουν A. 4. 33, 27. 1, Mc. 15. 23, but A. 16. 4 -οσαν (-ουν HLP), Jo. 19. 3 אB; the forms in -ουν are to be preferred. Imperat. τίθει, δίδου as in Att. But δίδωμι in the *passive* goes over to the ω conjugation, the analogy between the two forms being very close: διεδίδετο A. 4. 35 (-οτο B³P), παρεδίδετο 1 C. 11. 23 (-οτο B³LP), and so 2nd aor. mid. ἀπέδετο H. 12. 16 AC, cp. Mt. 21. 33 א*B*CL, Mc. 12. 1 אAB*CKL, L. 20. 9 א*AB*CL; but ἀπέδοσθε A. 5. 8 all MSS.— For pres. conj. see 4.

4. **2nd aorist active and middle.**—Ἔστην is found as an alternative for ἐστάθην, see 6; τίθημι, δίδωμι employ the 2nd aor. only in the mid., while ἐθήκαμεν, -ατε, -αν, ἐδώκαμεν² etc. are the aor. act. forms in use (only L. 1. 2 has a 2nd aor. act. παρέδοσαν, literary language in the preface). From other verbs ἔβην, ἔγνων may be added. The indic. is regular (for the mid. cp. 3). The conj. to ἔδωκα (and δίδωμι) ἔγνων shows great fluctuation (2 sing. δῷς Mt. 5. 25): in the 3rd sing., which through the loss of the ι in pronunciation had become identical with the 1st sing., beside δῷ (διδῷ) and γνῷ we also have the forms δοῖ (διδοῖ), γνοῖ or δῴη (identical with the optat.). This last form, however, is almost confined to the Pauline Epistles, where the scribes often met with the optat., which was not current in their own day, and therefore introduced it occasionally for the conj. (vide infra): E. 1. 17 δῴη most MSS. (δῷ B), 3. 16 δῴη only DEK al., 2 Tim. 2. 25 δῴη א*ACD*P (Jo. 15. 16 δῴη

---

[1] Δίδω Tisch., others διδῶ, cp. ἀποδιδοῦν for -όν A Ap. 22. 2 (παραδίδων א Mt. 26. 46, D Mc. 14. 42, J. 18. 2, 21. 20). In Hermas τιθῶ occurs Vis. i. 1. 3, ii. 1. 2; Clem. Cor. i. 23 ἀποδιδοῖ. Examples from the papyri in W. Schmidt, Gtg. Gel. Anz. 1894, 45.

[2] No inference for an aor. ἔδωσα can be drawn from ἵνα ... δώσῃ Jo. 17. 2 א*AC al. (v.l. -σω, -σει, δῶ etc.): nor yet from Mc. 6. 37 ἀγοράσωμεν ... δώσωμεν (אBD, v.l. -σομεν and δῶμεν), see § 65, 2.

D

EGH al.; ἀποδοίη D* 1 Th. 5. 15). It is more difficult to decide between δῷ, γνῷ and δοῖ, γνοῖ (the latter like ζηλοῖ): still γνῷ has the greater attestation (Jo. 7. 51, 11. 57 [γνοῖ D*], 14. 31, A. 22. 24: whereas γνοῖ has equal or greater authority in its favour in Mc. 5. 43, 9. 30, L. 19. 15); also (ἀπο)δῷ all MSS. in Mt. 18. 30, the same form or δώῃ all MSS. in E. 1. 17, 3. 16, 2 Tim. 2. 25, Jo. 15. 16 (א δώσει), cp. 13. 29 (δοῖ D).—The optat. δῴη is Hellenistic (Phryn. 345 f., Moeris)[1] and in Paul. Epp. R. 15. 5 etc.—Imperat. ἀνάστηθι and ἀνάστα A. 12. 7, E. 5. 14 O.T. quot. (-ήτω, -ητε are constant), ἀνάβα Ap. 4. 1 (-ηθι A), μετάβα Mt. 17. 20 along with μετάβηθι Jo. 7. 3, κατάβηθι Mt. 27. 40 etc., προσανάβηθι L. 14. 10; this verb also has -βάτω, -βᾶτε Mt. 24. 17, 27. 42, Ap. 11. 12 (-ητε B) like τίμα, -ᾶτε.[2]

5. **Perfect active.**—Of the perfects formed after a partial analogy to verbs in -μι, ἕστηκα limits these shorter forms to the infin. Ἑστάναι L. 13. 25, A. 12. 14, 1 C. 10. 12 (no other form: also usu. in the LXX.), and partic. ἑστώς (in most cases: ἑστηκώς is also found), fem. ἑστῶσα 1 C. 7. 26, 2 P. 3. 5, neut. ἑστός Mt. 24. 15 (v.l. -ώς), Ap. 14. 1 (B -ώς), but ἑστηκός (א -ώς) 5. 6. But the indic. remains ἑστήκαμεν etc. (cp. ἐδώκαμεν). On στήκω see § 17. From τέθνηκα we have inf. τεθνάναι A. 14. 19 DEHLP; τεθνηκώς always. Οἶδα, -ας, -ε, -αμεν etc. (Ionic and Hellenist.); only in A. 26. 4 (speech of Paul before Agrippa) ἴσασιν (literary language); ἴστε H. 12. 17 (unless it be imperat.); plupf. ᾔδειν, -εις etc.; moods as in Att.: εἰδῶ, ἴστε Ja. 1. 19, E. 2. 5 (v.l. ἐστε); infin. εἰδέναι, part. εἰδώς.

6. **Remaining tenses of the ordinary verbs in -μι.**—Ἱστάνω in transitive sense has fut. στήσω, aor. ἔστησα, perf. ἔστακα (differentiated from -ηκα; first found in Hyperides) A. 8. 11. Intransitive are ἵσταμαι, fut. στήσομαι and σταθήσομαι, aor. ἔστην and ἐστάθην; both forms in the simple vb. are identical in meaning, as in Ionic and Hellenist.[3] (in Att. ἐστάθην, σταθήσ. have a passive sense). Compounds of ἵσταμαι, e.g. ἀνθίσταμαι, ἀν-, ἀφ-, δι-, ἐξαν-, ἐξ-, ἐφ- etc. take -ην, -ήσομαι in aor. and fut. in intransitive senses; on the other hand the following also take aor. in -θην in passive senses: καθίσταμαι (R. 5. 19), ἀποκαθ. (Mt. 12. 13, Mc. 3. 5 -στη C, Mc. 8. 25 -στη אBCLΔ, L. 6. 10 -στη א*, H. 13. 19), μεθ. (L. 16. 4).[4] The perf. ἕστηκα has present meaning; but in Jo. 8. 44 οὐκ (אB*DLX al.) ἕστηκεν (§ 4, 3) it has true perfect sense 'has stood,' a new formation related to ἔστην (?).—From φημί, except for -μί, -σί, ἔφη (which is at once impf. and aor., as in Att.), no forms are represented in N.T.

---

[1] This -ῴην is found in other Hellenistic writings in *all* optatives in -οίην: Philodem. Rhet. ed. Sudhaus, ii. 52, 144, 169, 285, εὐπορῴη, ποιῴη, ὁμολογῴη, φρονῴη.

[2] Attic poets also have ἀνάστα, κατάβα, but other forms with η; LXX. only has -στα side by side with -στηθι.

[3] There is not sufficient ground for attributing a passive sense to the simple verb σταθῆναι in passages like L. 21. 36 (D ibid. στήσεται).

[4] But also without passive sense ἐπεστάθην D L. 4. 39, 10. 40, Clem. Cor. i. 12. 4; ἀντεστάθην Herm. Mand. xii. 2. 3, παρεστ. Sim. viii. 4. 1.

§ 23. 6-8.]   VERBS IN -ΜΙ.   51

—Τίθημι has, as generally in the Hellenist. language, perf. act. τέθεικα (Jo. 11. 34 : Att. -ηκα), perf. mid. τέθειμαι (συντ.) Jo. 9. 22 (pass. in ἦν τεθειμένος Jo. 19. 41 אB for ἐτέθη;[1] in the parallel passage L. 23. 53 ἦν κείμενος according to the Att. usage, which is adhered to elsewhere in N.T. in the substitution of κεῖσθαι for τεθεῖσθαι).

7. Ἵημι.—Only found in composition with ἀν-, ἀφ-, (παρ-), καθ-, συν-, and in the case of ἀφ-, συν-ίημι (the only compounds in use in the popular language) with the alternative form in -ίω : in -ίετε, -ίεται the two conjugations coincide. Ἀφίημι (so Jo. 14. 27), -ίησι (Mt. 3. 15), -ιέναι (Mc. 2. 7 etc.); on the other hand -ίομεν (so אᶜABCDE) in L. 11. 4 (Mt. 6. 12 D al., but א*B ἀφήκαμεν); 2nd sing. pres. ἀφεῖς (i.e. -ίεις, -iis, cp. § 6, 5, note 2), though in this case there appears in Att. also -ιεις (and τιθεις); impf. ἤφιεν Mc. 1. 34, 11. 16 ; in the passive there is fluctuation between -ίενται, -ίονται, -έωνται (vide infra). Cp. in Hermas ἀφίησιν Mand. x. 3. 3, -ίενται Vis. ii. 2. 4, -ίουσιν iii. 7. 1. In the case of συνίημι there is only one undisputed instance of the conjugation in -μι : A. 7. 25 συνιέναι : elsewhere Mt. 13. 19 συνιέντος, DF -ίοντος : L. 24. 45 συνιέναι, B* συνεῖναι ; also συνίω, except in quotations, is never without var. lect.: Mt. 13. 13 συνίουσι (language influenced by O.T.: -ιωσιν B** cp. D), 2 C. 10. 12 συνίουσιν (-ιᾶσιν אᵃB, -ίσασιν א*), R. 3. 11 συνίων O.T. quot. (Barn. 12. 10 συνίων, but 4. 6, 10. 12 -ιέναι : Herm. Mand. iv. 2. 1, x. 1. 3 συνίω, iv. 2. 2 συνίει, x. 1. 6 συνίουσιν, Sim. ix. 12. 1 σύνιε ; in the LXX. the forms from ἀφίω and συνίω are more established and fairly frequent, W.-Schm. § 14, 16). Ἀνίημι, ἀνιέντες E. 6. 9 ; καθιέμενος A. 10. 11, 11. 5.—Tenses: N.T. has ἀφῆκαν etc. like ἔθηκαν (4 supra), the perf. -εικα never occurs, while συνήκατε Mt. 13. 51, ἀφήκαμεν καὶ ἠκολουθήκαμεν (BCD, al. -ήσαμεν) Mc. 10. 28 may indeed give the impression of being perfects, but are still to be taken as aorists (cp. Mt. 19. 27, L. 18. 28, and with συνήκατε Aristoph. Ach. 101 ξυνήκαθ᾿ ὃ λέγει). The Doric (and Ionic) perf. was ἔωκα, pass. ἔωμαι, and the latter also appears in N.T.: the form ἀφέωνται is to be preferred in Jo. 20. 23 (wrong variants -ίενται, -(ε)ίονται : א* ἀφεθήσεται), 1 Jo. 2. 12, L. 7. 47 f., 5. 20, 23 (also in Mt. 9. 2, 5 against -ίονται D [5 Dא*], -ίενται א[5 אᶜ]B, Mc. 2. 5 [-ίενται B], 9 [-ίε- אB]). On ἀνέθην, ἀφέθην see § 15, 4.

8. Εἰμί.—The transition to the inflection of a deponent vb. (seen in ἔσομαι : in mod. Gk. universally carried out) appears in ἤμην 1st pers. (differentiated from ἦν 3rd pers. Lob. Phryn. 152), from which ἤμεθα is also formed Mt. 23. 30, A. 27. 37, E. 2. 3 אB; in G. 4. 3 ἦμεν in the first instance (all MSS.) with ἤμεθα (אD*FG) following; elsewhere ἦμεν.—The 2nd sing. impf. ἦσθα only occurs in Mt. 26. 69, Mc. 14. 67 (Euseb. quotes the verse with ἦς), elsewhere it is ἦς (the termination -σθα occurs nowhere else) as in Hellenistic Gk. (Phryn. 149). The imperat. has beside ἔστω, ἔστωσαν the vulgar form ἤτω Ja. 5. 12, 1 C. 16. 22 (Herm. Vis. iii. 3. 4, Clem. Cor. i. 48. 5), cp. W.-Schm. § 14, 1. Ἔνι (i.e. strictly ἔνεστι, ἐνί = ἐν : cp. πάρα = πάρεστι) occurs

---

[1] Herm. Sim. ix. 15. 4 has τεθειμένοι in pass. sense, similarly περιτεθειμένα, Clem. Cor. i. 20. 4.

in 1 C. 6. 5, G. 3. 28, Col. 3. 11, Ja. 1. 17, already in the sense of ἐστίν 'there is,' which together with εἰσί has been supplanted by this word, now written εἶναι, in modern Greek. W. Schmidt, Atticism. iii. 121.

9. **Εἶμι.**—In the popular language the verb occurs neither in its simple form nor in composition, ἔρχομαι taking its place, § 24; the compounds only are employed by L. and Hebr. (from the literary language) and not always correctly. Εἰσίασιν H. 9. 6 for Att. εἰσέρχονται (εἰσίασιν is fut. in Att.): εἴσιθι B Acts 9. 6 (-ελθε): εἰσιέναι 3. 3, 20. 7, 4 D, 27. 43: partic. L. 8. 4 (-ελθόντος D), Acts 13. 42, in *aoristic* sense 21. 17 in the β text, so *aoristic* εἰσῄει 21. 18, 26, -εσαν 17. 10, 15. (Clem. Cor. i. 24. 3 ἄπεισι 'departs' [Att. 'will depart'], cp. 54. 2 : Clem. Hom. ii. 1, iii. 63, (ἐπ)εισιών = -ελθών.)

10. **Ἧμαι, κεῖμαι.**—Κάθημαι, κάθῃ A. 23. 3 (cp. δύνῃ, supra 3; so already in Hyperides for -ησαι), imperat. κάθου (already in late Att.) Ja. 2. 3, Mt. 22. 44 etc., and O.T. for -ησο. Imperf. always ἐκαθήμην § 15, 7; fut. καθήσομαι Mt. 19. 28 (-ίσεσθε CD* al.), L. 22. 30 אAB³ al. Cp. § 24.—Κεῖμαι is regular : also used as perf. pass. of τίθημι as in Att., supra 6.

§ 24. TABLE OF NOTEWORTHY VERBS.

(The prefixing of * indicates that the paradigm embraces several stems.)

Ἀγαλλιᾶν active L. 1. 47 (Ap. 19. 7, prob. more correctly -ώμεθα B; 1 P. 1. 8 -ᾶτε only BC*); elsewhere deponent with aor. mid. and pass., § 20. The verb is absent from profane Greek (which has ἀγάλλομαι instead).

Ἀγγέλλειν, ἠγγέλην constant, § 19, 3.

Ἄγειν, aor. ἤγαγον and rarely ἦξα, § 19, 1 ; perf. act. unattested.

(**Ἀγνύναι**) only in composition κατᾶγν. (as in Att.), pres. impf. unattested : aor. κατέαξαν (Att.) Jo. 19. 32 f., but the use of the augm. is incorrectly extended (§ 15, 2) to the fut. κατεάξει Mt. 12. 20, O.T., and aor. conj. pass. κατεαγῶσιν Jo. 19. 31.

***Αἱρεῖν,** aor. εἷλον and -λα, § 21, 1: fut. ἑλῶ (late writers, LXX.) L. 12. 18, 2 Th. 2. 8 (v.l. ἀναλοῖ, vide inf.), Ap. 22. 19 (but αἱρήσομαι Ph. 1. 22).

Ἀκούειν, fut. ἀκούσω and Attic -σομαι, § 18, 3.

Ἀλήθειν for ἀλεῖν (Phryn. p. 151): only pres. attested (aor. ἤλεσα in LXX.: no other form of the aor. is likely to have existed). Cp. νήθειν.

Ἄλλεσθαι, with compounds ἀν-, ἐξ-, ἐφ-, almost confined to Acts: (Jo. 4. 14, 21. 7 D), 1st aor. ἡλάμην (LXX.) A. 14. 10 (Jo. 21. 7 D): 2nd aor. ἐφαλόμενος 19. 16 (also 3. 8 ἐξαλόμ. is better than -λλ- of the MSS.) : both forms occur in Att.

Ἁμαρτάνειν, fut. ἁμαρτήσω, § 18, 3: 1st aor. ἡμάρτησα along with 2nd aor. ἥμαρτον, § 19, 1.

Ἀμφιάζειν, -ιέζειν, -εννύναι : see § 17.

Ἀναλοῦν=ἀναλίσκειν (both Att., -οῦν also in LXX., W.-Schm. § 15): ἀναλοῖ 2 Th. 2. 8 א* Origen (v.l. ἀναλώσει, ἀνελεῖ). Tenses regular : L. 9. 54, G. 5. 15.

(**Ἀντᾶν**) : fut. ἀπαντήσω, συν-, § 18, 3.

Ἀπειλεῖσθαι deponent A. 4. 17, 21 for Att. ἀπειλεῖν (1 P. 2. 23) ; διαπειλεῖσθαι as depon. is also Att.

Ἁρπάζειν: fut. -άσω, § 18, 3: 2nd aor. pass. -γην (and 1st aor. -σθην? as in Att.), § 19, 3.

§ 24.] TABLE OF NOTEWORTHY VERBS. 53

Αὔξειν, αὐξάνειν, both forms Att., but in transit. sense 'increase,' whereas 'grow' is -ομαι. N.T. has -άνω trans. only in 1 C. 3. 6 f., 2 C. 9. 10 (Herm. Vis. iii. 4. 1 αὔξω, i. 1. 6 αὐξήσας). Elsewhere -άνω (and αὔξω: only E. 2. 21, Col. 2. 19) is used = Att. -ομαι A. 6. 7 al.: along with -άνομαι Mt. 13. 32 (אᵇD -ήσῃ), Mc. 4. 8 v.l., Epp. Paul. passim, 1 P. 2. 2.

Βαίνειν: aor. ἔβην, ἀνάβα, -βατε, § 23, 4.

Βαρεῖν: βεβαρημένος old (βεβ. ηὖδεν Plat. Sympos. 203 B) Mt. 26. 43, L. 9. 32 (Mc. 14. 40 var. lect. βεβ., καταβεβ., καταβαρούμενοι, καταβαρυνόμενοι. Βαρύνω is the ordinary Att. word, but in N.T. besides this passage it only occurs as a v.l. in L. 21. 34 DH, 2 C. 5. 4 D*FG). Elsewhere in the pass.: 2 C. 1. 8, 5. 4, 1 Tim. 5. 16, L. 21. 34. Also the compounds ἐπιβαρεῖν, καταβ. in St. Paul (καταβ. Herm. Sim. ix. 28. 6, βαροῦντα Clem. Hom. xi. 16). W. Schmidt, Atticism. iii. 187.

Βασκαίνειν: aor. -ᾶνα,§ 16, 3.

[Βιοῦν]: βιῶσαι 1 P. 4. 2, for Att. -ναι (the only form in which this verb occurs: elsewhere ζῆν, cp. inf.).

Βλαστάνειν: pres. conj. -νῃ Mc. 4. 27 אAC² al., but BC*DLΔ βλαστᾷ from βλαστᾶν, as Herm. Sim. iv. 1 βλαστῶντα (W.-Schm. § 15): a new 1st aor. -ησα occurs, § 19, 1.

Βλέπειν, 'to look,' aor. ἔβλεψα (Acts 3. 4) as in Att.: περιεβλεψάμην Mc. 3. 5, etc. With the meaning 'to see' (for ὁρᾶν, vide inf.) only in pres. and impf., except Acts 28. 26 βλέψετε O.T. quot., see § 18, 3. (Προβλέψασθαι = προϊδέσθαι H. 11. 40, see § 55, 1.)

Βούλεσθαι, § 15, 3: § 21, 7.

Γαμεῖν: also used of the wife (for Att. -εῖσθαι) Mc. 10. 12 (-ηθῇ v.l.), 1 Tim. 5. 11, 14 etc.; elsewhere for the wife N.T. uses -ίζεσθαι (but aor. -ήθην 1 C. 7. 39 = ἐγημάμην Att.), for which γαμίσκονται is read Mc. 12. 25 E al., L. 20. 34 אBL (ἐκγαμίσκ. E al., ἐκγαμίζ. A al., γαμοῦνται D), 35 B (γαμίζ. אD al., ἐκγαμίζ.ᵢA al.). The act. γαμίζειν (ἐκγ.) 'to give to wife': Mt. 24. 38 (γαμ. אD, rell. ἐκγ.), 1 C. 7. 38.—Aor. act. ἐγάμησα Mt. 5. 32 al., Herm. Mand. iv. 4 (so -ήθην, vide supra), for which the Att. form occurs as a v.l., γήμας Mt. 22. 35 אBL, L. 14. 20 (ἔλαβον D), 1 C. 7. 28 γαμήσῃς ... γήμῃ (D*FG γαμῇ).

Γελᾶν, fut. -άσω, § 18, 3.

Γίνεσθαι (never γίγν. as in Att.), aor. ἐγενόμην and -νήθην, § 20.

Γινώσκειν (never γίγν. as in Att.), 2nd aor. conj. γνοῖ and γνῷ, § 23, 4.

Γρηγορεῖν, § 17; cp. ἐγείρειν.

Δεῖσθαι, ἐδέετο, § 22, 2.

Διακονεῖν, διηκόνουν, § 15, 6.

Διδόναι, see § 23, 3 and 4.

Διψᾶν, -ᾷς, § 22, 1; διψήσω, § 16, 1.

Διώκειν, fut. -ξω, § 18, 3.

Δύνασθαι pres., § 23, 2; augm. ἠ- or ἐ-, § 15, 3; fut. δυνήσομαι, § 20, 2; aor. ἠδυνήθην (and ἠδυνάσθην Mt. 17. 16 B, Mc. 7. 24 אB, Epic and Ionic).

Δύειν intrans. 'to set' E. 4. 26 (Homeric: Att. δύομαι, for which δύνω (Xenoph. and others) occurs in L. 4. 40 (δύσαντος D): aor. ἔδυν, ἔδυσα, § 19, 1 (ἐδύησαν, § 19, 2); ἐνδύνοντες 'creeping in' 2 Tim. 3. 6 (cp. Barn. 4. 10). Ἐνδύειν trans. 'to put on' pres. only in Mc. 15. 17 AN, correct reading -διδύσκειν, see § 17: so mid. ἐνδιδύσκεσθαι, see ibid.: but tenses as in Att. -έδυσα, -άμην etc.: similarly ἐκδῦσαι (pres. and impf. unattested).

Ἐγείρειν 'raise up,' 'awake': intrans. ἔγειρε (not -αι aor. mid.), sc. σεαυτόν Mc. 5. 41 etc. (Eurip. Iph. Aul. 624); intrans. -ομαι 'rise' (διεγείρομαι 'awake' intrans.), aor. ἠγέρθην, § 20; perf. ἐγήγερται 'has been raised' 1 C. 15. 4 (late writers; Att. ἐγρήγορα 'I am awake' has become γρηγορῶ, § 17).

ΕΙΔ – οἶδα, § 23, 5: fut. εἰδήσω H. 8. 11 O.T. quot. (Ionic and late = Att. εἴσομαι).

Εἰπεῖν, εἴρηκα etc. see λέγειν.

Ἐλεᾶν - ἐλεεῖν, § 22, 2.

Ἕλκειν, aor. εἵλκυσα as in Att., fut. ἑλκύσω Jo. 12. 32 (Att. ἕλξω).

Ἑλκοῦν: εἱλκωμένος, § 15, 6.

Ἐργάζεσθαι: ἠργαζόμην, ἠργασάμην, εἴργασμαι, § 15, 5 and 6.

***Ἔρχεσθαι**. In Att. for 'to come' ἔρχομαι is used only in the indic., conj. ἴω, inf. ἰέναι etc., impf. ᾖα, ᾔειν: 'will come' = εἶμι. When εἶμι fell out of use (§ 23, 9), ἔρχομαι was employed throughout: ἔρχωμαι, ἠρχόμην etc., fut. ἐλεύσομαι (Epic and Ionic: Phryn. 37). Aor. ἦλθον and perf. ἐλήλυθα as in Att.

***Ἐσθίειν** and **ἔσθειν** (-θειν as early as Hom., Doric and late writers). The former predominates (as also in LXX.), so without var. lect. Mt. 9. 11, 11. 18 f., 12. 1 etc., R. 14. 2 f., 6, 20 etc.; but ἔσθητε L. 22. 30 BD*T, ἔσθων Mc. 1. 6 אBL*Δ, 12. 40 B, L. 7. 33 BD, 34 D, 10. 7 BD (elsewhere even Mc. and L. have ἐσθίειν in all the MSS.). Fut. φάγομαι from aor. ἔφαγον, § 18, 2: 2nd sing. -εσαι, § 21, 7. Pf. βέβρωκα (from the obsolete βιβρώσκω) Jo. 6. 13, aor. pass. βρωθῇ L. 22. 10 D. (The pres. in the popular language was **τρώγω**, so always in S. John, elsewhere only Mt. 24. 38; see also Herm. Sim. v. 3. 7, Barn. 7. 8, 10. 2, 3.)

Ἔχειν, fut. only ἕξω, § 14, 1; similarly ἀνέχεσθαι has only ἀνέξομαι: impf. and aor. ἀνειχ., ἀνεσχ., § 15, 7.

Ζῆν, fut. ζήσω and -ομαι, § 18, 3: aor. ἔζησα A. 26. 5, Herm. Sim. viii. 9. 1, for which in Att. ἐβίων was introduced as a *supplementary* form (cp. sup. βιοῦν): perf. unattested. (Impf. 1st sing. ἔζην, -ων, § 22, 1.)

Ζωννύναι, perf. pass. and mid. περιεζωσμένος (Att. without σ) L. 12. 35 al.

Ἥκειν: 3rd. plur. ἥκασιν Mc. 8. 3 אADN (al. ἥκουσιν, B εἰσίν), cp. Clem. Cor. i. 12. 2. The transition of this verb of perfect meaning to the inflection of the perfect tense is found also in LXX. and other late writings, W.-Schm. § 13, 2: Kühner I. ii.³ 438: W. Schmidt, Jos. elocut. 470.

Ἡσσοῦσθαι, 2 C. 12. 13 א*BD* ἡσσώθητε (Ionic ἐσσοῦσθαι), with v.l. ἡττήθητε (the Attic form [literary lang.] as in 2 P. 2. 19 f. ἥττηται, ἡττῶνται, and even ἥττημα in S. Paul), FG ἠλαττώθητε, cp. Jo. 3. 30 (literary lang.).

(Θάλλειν), aor. ἀνέθαλον, § 19, 1 (no other form attested); ἀναθάλλω (intrans.) Clem. Cor. i. 36. 2.

Θαυμάζειν (-εσθαι depon.), aor. ἐθαύμασα and -άσθην, fut. (θαυμάσομαι), -ασθήσομαι, § 18, 3: § 20, 1.

Θεᾶσθαι, see θεωρεῖν.

Θέλειν not (as in Att.) ἐθέλειν, the ordinary word of the popular language for 'will' (so mod. Gk.): beside it is found βούλεσθαι (literary lang.) without distinction of meaning, rare in the Gospels, and not often in the Epistles, frequent only in the Acts.—Augm. always ἠ-, § 15, 3 (perfect unattested).

***Θεωρεῖν**, generally defective, only pres. and impf. being used, but fut. Jo. 7. 3, aor. Mt. 28. 1, L. 8. 35 D, 23. 48 אBCD al., Jo. 8. 51 (-σει א), Ap. 11. 12; elsewhere the tenses of θεᾶσθαι (pres. impf. wanting) are used: aor. -ασάμην, perf. τεθέαμαι, aor. pass. ἐθεάθην.

Ἱλάσκεσθαι, mid. (Att.) H. 2. 17; ἱλάσθητι 'be merciful' L. 18. 13, cp. ἐξιλασθέν 'expiated' Plat. Legg. 862 C.

Ἱστάνειν (ἱστᾶν), ἱστασθαι, § 23, 2, 4, 5, 6.

Καθαρίζειν 'to cleanse' not καθαίρειν (Jo. 15. 2 D correctly καθαριεῖ, cp. H. 10. 2; κεκαθαρμένων is found in Herm. Sim. ix. 18. 3). In compounds the simpler form is more attested: διακαθᾶραι L. 3. 17 א*B (al. διακαθαριεῖ), ἐκκαθάρατε 1 C. 5. 7, ἐκκαθάρῃ 2 Tim. 2. 21.

Καθέζεσθαι, καθίζειν, καθῆσθαι. In Attic ἐκαθεζόμην aor. = 'I seated myself,' καθίζω 'I seat' trans. and also intrans. 'I seat myself,' which is elsewhere expressed by -ίζομαι: κάθημαι 'I sit' (in perfect sense). In the N.T. 'I set' or 'seat' is καθίζω, aor. -ισα (as in Att.): 'I seated myself' = ἐκάθισα (not mid.), so that the sense of Jo. 19. 13 is extremely doubtful: there is also a perf. κεκάθικεν (intrans.) H. 12. 2 (the present only appears in trans. sense: for fut. vide inf.); aor. ἐκαθέσθην from καθέζομαι (Phryn. 269) only in L. 10. 39 אABC*

§ 24.] TABLE OF NOTEWORTHY VERBS. 55

al., -ίσασα C³DP etc.; 'sit' is κάθημαι (in the majority of cases) and καθέζομαι (rare): ἐκαθέζετο impf. 'sat' ('had seated himself') Jo. 4. 6, 11. 20, for which ἐκάθητο occurs elsewhere, as in Mt. 13. 1; καθεζόμενος = καθήμ. A. 6. 15 (D -ήμενοι) etc.; fut. καθήσομαι Mt. 19. 28 (-ίσεσθε CD* al.), L. 22. 30 אAB³ al. (-ίσεσθε EF, but B* κάθησθε conj., D καθέζησθε) for Attic καθεδοῦμαι. The 2nd pers. of κάθημαι is κάθῃ, § 23, 9 : imperat. κάθου ibid. ('sit' = 'seat thyself' Ja. 2. 3).

Καίειν: aor. and fut. pass. § 19, 3.

Καλεῖν: fut. καλέσω, § 18, 1.

(**Κεραννύναι**), perf. pass. κεκέρασμαι (late; Att. κέκρᾱμαι) Ap. 14. 10.

Κερδαίνειν (pres. and impf. unattested), aor. ἐκέρδησα as if from κερδέω (Ionic and late writers) Mt. 16. 26 and passim; but κερδάνω (§ 16, 3) 1 C. 9. 21 א*ABC al. (אᶜDE al. κερδήσω, as also four times in the same chap. ver. 19, 20, 22); a corresponding fut. pass. κερδηθήσονται occurs 1 P. 3. 1. There is fluctuation also in Josephus between the Attic and the vulgar forms, W. Schmidt, de Jos. elocut. 451, 459.

Κλαίειν, fut. κλαύσω, § 18, 3.

Κλείειν, perf. pass. κέκλεισμαι for -ειμαι, § 16, 1.

Κλίνειν, aor. and fut. pass. ἐκλίθην, κλιθήσομαι, § 19, 3.

Κράζειν, the pres. rare in Attic (which uses κέκραγα instead) is often in N.T., on the other hand κέκραγα is only used in Jo. 1. 15 : fut. κράξω (κεκράξομαι), § 18, 3: aor. ἐκέκραξα (LXX., from κέκραγα) only A. 24. 21 אABC.

Κρίνειν: ἀποκρίνομαι, ὑποκρίνομαι, aor. and fut. § 20, 1.

Κρύβειν, aor. pass. ἐκρύβην, § 19, 3.

(**Κτείνειν**): only in compound ἀποκτείνω and -έν(ν)ω, § 17; aor. pass. ἀπεκτάνθην (late) Mc. 9. 31 al. = Att. ἀπέθανον.

(**Κυεῖν**) ἀποκυεῖ Ja. 1. 15, -ύησεν 1. 18 (from κύω we have ἐκύομεν in LXX., W.-Schm. § 15).

Κυλίειν (already in Att.; older form -ίνδω) Mc. 9. 20, fut. -ίσω Mc. 16. 3, aor. act. ἐκύλισα, perf. pass. κεκύλισμαι as in Att.

Λᾱκεῖν 'to burst': ἐλάκησεν A. 1. 18 (cp. Acts of Thomas, § 33) as in Aristoph. Nub. 410 διαλακήσασα: elsewhere unknown: to be distinguished from λάσκω 'sound' (aor. ἔλᾰκον).

Λαμβάνειν, fut. λήμψομαι, aor. pass. ἐλήμφθην (λῆμψις Ph. 4. 15, ἀνάλημψις L. 9. 51 : προσωπολήμπτης) as in other Hellenistic writings, § 6, 8. (The later MSS. restore the Attic form by omitting the μ.)

(**Λέγειν** 'to collect'): only in συλλέγω, -ξα, ἐκλελεγμένος (Att. usually ἐξειλεγμ.) L. 9. 35.

***Λέγειν** 'to say': Att. λέξω, ἔλεξα etc.; but in N.T. defective (the beginning of this defective state reaches back into Attic times, Miller, Amer. Journ. of Philol. xvi. 162) with only pres. and impf.; the remaining tenses being aor. εἶπον, -α (§ 21, 1), fut. ἐρῶ, perf. εἴρηκα, aor. pass. ἐρρέθην, ῥηθῆναι, § 16, 1, perf. εἴρημαι. (Still λέγειν and εἰπεῖν were felt to be separate verbs, otherwise we should not find these combinations : τοῦτο εἰπὼν λέγει Jo. 21. 19, εἶπεν λέγων L. 12. 25, 20. 2.) But διαλέγομαι, διελέχθην as in Att. (Mc. 9. 34), see § 20, 1.

Λείπειν: (class.) with alternative form λιμπάνειν, διελίμπανεν Acts 8. 24 D, 17. 13 D, ὑπολιμπάνειν 1 P. 2. 21, ἐγκαταλιμπανόμενοι FG Euseb. Chrys. in 2 C. 4. 9 (also LXX.); 1st aor. ἔλειψα occurs occasionally instead of ἔλιπον, § 19, 1.

Λούειν, λέλουμαι, § 16, 1.

(**Μέλειν**) ἐπιμελοῦμαι (LXX.) or -ομαι (both Attic forms) not represented : fut. -ήσομαι, § 20, 2 : μεταμέλομαι (the only Att. form) 2 C. 7. 8, aor. -ήθην (not attested in Att.) Mt. 21. 29 etc., fut. -ηθήσομαι H. 7. 21 O.T. quot.

Μέλλειν: ἔμελλον and ἤμελλον, § 15, 3.

Μιαίνειν: μεμίαμμαι, § 16, 3.

Μνηστεύειν: perf. pass. μεμνήστευμαι v.l., § 15, 6.
Νήθειν 'to spin' for νῆν (Ionic and late), the constant N.T. form, cp. ἀλήθειν.
Νίπτειν for νίζειν, § 17.

(Ξυρεῖν), pres. unattested: aor. mid. ξύρασθαι as if from ξύρειν (not ξυρᾶσθαι pres.) 1 C. 11. 6 and ξυρήσασθαι A. 21. 24 (both forms unattested in Att.), but in Acts D has ξύρωνται, אB*D²EP ξυρήσονται: perf. ἐξύρημαι (Att.) 1 C. 11. 5.

(Οἴγειν) ἀνοίγειν (never -γνύναι): the augment is always in the α in the comp. διανοίγειν, διηνοίχθησαν L. 24. 31, διήνοιγεν 32 etc.; also in the simple vb. constantly in the 2nd aor. pass. ἠνοίγην A. 12. 10 (-χθη E al.), which is a new formation; in the other forms (the impf. is only attested for διαν.) the old syllabic augm. is still strongly represented: 1st aor. act. ἀνέῳξα Jo. 9. 14 (ἠνέῳξεν LX, ἤνοιξεν D), 17 ἤνοιξεν אAD al., BX ἠνέῳξ., KL ἀνέῳξ., similarly ver. 32: in verses 21, 26, 30 B also has ἤνοιξεν, and this form deserves preference (cp. A. 5. 19, 9. 40, 12. 14, 14. 27, Ap. 6. 1, 3 etc.);—perf. (intrans. as in late writers) ἀνέῳγα Jo. 1. 52 (ἠνεῳγότα א), 1 C. 16. 9, 2 C. 6. 11, elsewhere ἀνέῳγμαι as in Att. R. 3. 13 O.T. quot., 2 C. 2. 12 (ἠνεῳγμ. DEP), A. 10. 11 (ἠνε. E), 16. 27: Ap. 4. 1 B, but אAP ἠνε., similarly 10. 1, 8, 19. 11 (3. 8 ἀν. ABC);—1st aor. pass. ἀνεῴχθην Mt. 3. 16 (ἠνε. B), 9. 30 (ἠνε. BD), 27. 52, L. 1. 64 etc.: ἠνεῴχθ. Jo. 9. 10 with preponderant evidence (ἀν. AK al.): Acts 16. 26 ἠνοίχθ. אAE, ἠνεῴχθ. BCD, ἀνε. HLP: there is diversity of reading also in Ap. 20. 12. Infin. ἀνεῳχθῆναι L. 3. 21 (-νοι- only D), cp. supra ἀγνύναι, § 15, 2. On 1st and 2nd aor. (ἠνοίγην) and fut. -γήσομαι (-χθής-) see § 19, 3.

Οἰκτίρειν (so to be spelt for -είρειν), fut. οἰκτιρήσω R. 9. 15 O.T. quot. (late).

('Ολλύναι) ἀπολλ., § 23, 1: fut. ἀπολέσω as also in Herm. Sim. viii. 7. 5 (= Att. ἀπολῶ 1 C. 1. 19 O.T. quot., so nearly always in LXX.): but fut. pass. ἀπολοῦμαι L. 13. 3 etc.

*'Ορᾶν is still more defective than in Attic, since even the pres. and impf. are rare (being confined to the literary language): the popular language replaced them by means of βλέπειν and θεωρεῖν. (Exceptions: ὅρα, ὁρᾶτε, cave, -ete Mt. 8. 4 etc. [but βλέπετε is also used in this sense A. 13. 40 etc.]: also L. 16. 23, 23. 49, A. 8. 23?, H. 11. 27, 1 P. 1. 8, Ja. 2. 24 [Ap. 18. 18, Jo. 6. 2, Mc. 8. 24]: in composition H. 12. 2, A. 2. 25 O.T., R. 1. 20; pres. and impf. are rare also in Hermas: Vis. iii. 2. 4, 8. 9, Mand. vi. 2. 4: Barn. ὁρᾶτε 15. 8). The perf. is still always ἑόρακα (ἑώρ.), § 15, 6: aor. εἶδον (-α, § 21, 1): fut. ὄψομαι: aor. pass. ὤφθην apparui, fut. ὀφθήσομαι (perf. ὦπται Herm. Vis. iii. 1. 2 א). In addition a new present form is created ὀπτάνομαι A. 1. 3 (LXX.; Papyr. Louvre notices et extr. de MSS. xviii. 2, no. 49 according to the facsimile).

Παίζειν, παίξω etc., § 16, 2; § 18, 3.

Παύειν, ἀναπαήσομαι, § 20, 1.

Πείθειν, aor. pass. ἐπείσθην, fut. πεισθήσομαι L. 16. 31 (πιστεύσουσιν D).

Πεινᾶν, -ᾷς etc., § 22, 1: aor. ἐπείνασα, § 16, 1.

Πειράζειν 'to tempt' or 'try any one' (Hom., and late writers) always for Att. πειρᾶν; also for 'to attempt anything' = Att. πειρᾶσθαι A. 24. 6 al. (πειρᾶσθαι A. 26. 21 speech of Paul before Agrippa).

Πιάζειν, Πιέζειν. The latter = 'to press' as in Att. L. 6. 38; the former is confined to the common language = 'to lay hands on' (mod. Gk. πιάνω), aor. ἐπίασα, ἐπιάσθην (John, Acts, once even in St. Paul, Apoc.).

Πιμπλᾶν for -άναι, § 23, 2.

Πίνειν, fut. πίομαι, πίεσαι, § 21, 7; aor. ἔπιον, imper. πίε L. 12. 19 (Att. also πίθι), infin. contracted to πεῖν, πῖν (§ 6, 5) Mt. 27. 34 א*D, Mc. 10. 38 D, 15. 23 D, Jo. 4. 7 א*B*C*DL, cp. ibid. 9, 10 etc. (Anthol. Pal. xi. 140 in verse: papyri in W. Schmidt, Gtg. Gel. Anz. 1895, 40.)

*Πιπράσκειν, in Hellenistic Gk. conjugated in full with the exception of fut. and aor. act. (so impf. act. ἐπίπρασκον A. 2. 45). In Attic it is only in the pass. that the conjugation is fairly complete: the act. has perf. πέπρακα (Mt. 13. 46: D ἐπώλησεν), but in the other tenses πωλεῖν and ἀποδίδοσθαι

§ 24.]   TABLE OF NOTEWORTHY VERBS.   57

are used. The N.T. employs the aorist of the latter of these two verbs (A. 5. 8, 7. 9, H. 12. 16), from the former we have πωλῶ, ἐπώλουν, ἐπώλησα, πωλοῦμαι pass. (all used in Att. as well) : in addition to these πέπραμαι R. 7. 14, ἐπράθην Mt. 18. 25 etc.

Πίπτειν, ἔπεσον, and more frequently ἔπεσα, § 21, 1.

Ποθεῖν, aor. ἐπόθησα, § 16, 1.

'Ραίνειν, ῥαντίζειν. For reduplication, § 15, 6.

'Ρεῖν, fut. ῥεύσω, § 18, 3 (Attic has pres. fut. ῥεύσομαι, aoristic fut. ῥυήσομαι).

'Ρηγνύναι in the pass. Mt. 9. 17, L. 5. 6 A al.: for which ῥήσσειν (-ττειν, late writers) appears in Mt. 9. 17 D, L. 5. 6 אBL, Mc. 2. 22 AΓ al., v.l. ῥήξει ; aor. ἔρρηξα ; the old epic word ῥήσσειν = τύπτειν, cp. the Attic (and LXX.) ῥάττειν 'to dash down' Demosth. 54. 8 is found with the latter meaning in Mc. 9. 18 (ῥάσσει D), L. 9. 42, LXX. Sap. 4. 19 : Hermas, Mand. xi. 3 ῥᾶξαι as). To this word also belongs προσέρηξεν = προσέβαλε L. 6. 48.

'Ρίπτειν and ῥιπτεῖν, Att., in the N.T. the present stem only occurs in A. 22. 23, -ούντων (-όντων DEHL) cp. ἐρ(ρ)ίπτουν Herm. Vis. iii. 5. 5 : perf. ῥέριμμαι, § 15, 6.

'Ρύεσθαι 'to save' (Epic, Ionic, and late writers) with aor. mid. ἐρ(ρ)υσάμην and aor. pass. ἐρ(ρ)ύσθην (late) L. 1. 74 etc.

Σαλπίζειν, σαλπίσω etc., § 16, 2.

Σημαίνειν, ἐσήμᾱνα, § 16, 3.

*Σκοπεῖν, σκέψασθαι in Attic form one verb, since only pres. and impf. of σκοπεῖν are found, and from σκέψ. the forms -πτομαι, ἐσκεπτόμην are absent. In N.T. σκοπεῖν is used as in Att., ἐπισκέπτεσθαι however is also found in the pres. = 'to visit' (H. 2. 6, Ja. 1. 27) ; ἐπισκοπεῖν = 'to take care' H. 12. 15 (ἐπισκέπτεσθαι 'to inspect' Clem. Cor. i. 25. 5 ; συνεσκέπτοντο Ev. Petr. 43).

Σπουδάζειν, fut. -σω, § 18, 3.

Στηρίζειν, tenses, § 16, 2.

Στρωννύειν (not στορενν., which appears first in late scholiasts), § 23, 1.

Σῴζειν (ι adscript, § 3, 3) : like ἐσώθην (ἐσαώθην, σαόω) the perf. σέσωται is still found Acts 4. 9 אA (v.l. -σται), but σεσωσμένοι E. 2. 5 all MSS., and in v. 8 only P has the Att. form -ωμένοι.

Τάσσειν, ἐτάγην, together with ἐτάχθην, § 19, 3.

Τελεῖν, fut. τελέσω, § 18, 1.

Τίκτειν, ἐτέχθην, § 19, 3.

Τυγχάνειν: the Hellenistic perf. is τέτευχα for Att. τετύχηκα, Phryn. 395: so H. 8. 6 τέτευχεν אcBDcE (v.l. τετύχηκεν P, τέτυχε male א*AD*KL, a form which is also occasionally found in the older editions of late writers : Lob. on Phryn. loc. cit.).

*Τύπτειν is defective and completed by means of other verbs as in Attic : τύπτειν, ἔτυπτον, πατάξω, ἐπάταξα (pres. impf. etc. from this stem not found), ἔπαισα (no pres. and impf. found), pass. τύπτομαι, aor. ἐπλήγην (the only form of this verb represented) Ap. 8. 12.

*'Υπάγειν 'to go,' 'depart,' a word of the common language (never in Acts, Paul, or Hebrews ; mod. Gk. πάγω, πηγαίνω), which makes only a present tense (most frequently the pres. imperat.); supplemented by πορεύομαι (which, however, is not defective itself).

Φαίνειν, ἔφᾱνα, § 16, 3 : φανήσομαι (φανοῦμαι), § 20, 2.

(Φαύσκειν LXX.), Φώσκειν (ἐπιφώσκουσα Mt. 28. 1, ἐπέφωσκεν L. 23. 54), an Ionic and Hellenistic verb, only found in composition with δια-, ἐπι-, ὑπο-, and elsewhere only in pres. and impf. (cp. φάος, φῶς) : N.T. has fut. ἐπιφαύσει E. 5. 14 a quotation (διέφαυσε LXX. Gen. 44. 3 ; ὑπόφαυσις Herodot.).

*Φέρειν, ἤνεγκα, -εῖν etc. § 21, 1.

Φθάνειν, aor. ἔφθᾱσα (so and ἔφθην Attic), perf. ἔφθακα (unattested in Att.) 1 Th. 2. 16 BD*. Meaning 'to arrive at,' 'come upon' as in mod. Gk.; 'to anticipate' only in 1 Th. 4. 15 (for which προφθ. is used Mt. 17. 25).

Φοβεῖσθαι, φοβηθήσομαι, § 20, 2.
Φορεῖν, φορέσω etc. § 16, 1.
Φύειν, in act. only H. 12. 15 (O.T. quot.) intransitive (frequently in late writers); elsewhere only aor. ἐφύην, § 19, 2.
Χαίρειν, χαρήσομαι, § 18, 3.
Χύ(ν)νειν for χεῖν, § 17: fut. χεῶ, § 18, 2: aor. ἔχεα as in Att.: pass. κέχυμαι, ἐχύθην also Att.
Ψύχειν, pres. L. 21. 26 ἀπο-: fut. perf. ψυγήσομαι, § 18, 3.
Ὠθεῖν, augment, § 15, 2.
Ὠνεῖσθαι, augment, § 15, 2: aor. ὠνησάμην A. 7. 16 (Att. ἐπριάμην, which is still used in the LXX.).

§ 25. ADVERBS.

1. **Adverbs of manner** formed from adjectives with termination -ως occasionally have a comparative with a corresponding ending in -τέρως: περισσοτέρως 2 C. 1. 12, and constantly in St. Paul, H. 2. 1, 13. 19 (6. 17 -ότερον, but B -οτέρως, 7. 15 -ότερον), Mc. 15. 14 ENP al. (περισσῶς ℵAB al.), 7. 36 D (-ότερον ℵAB al.), cp. for their meaning and usage § 11, 4; σπουδαιοτέρως Ph. 2. 28 (D*FG -ότερον); cp. ἐσχάτως ἔχειν (Polyb.) Mc. 5. 23. Elsewhere such comparative adverbs take -τερον, which is also the predominant termination in Attic, and from -(ί)ων the constant adverbial form is -(ι)ον (βέλτιον etc., Attic has also the adverbial ending -όνως). 'Well' is καλῶς, no longer εὖ (except in E. 6. 3 O.T. quot., A. 15. 29 literary language: εὖ ποιεῖν 'to benefit' anyone, only in Mc. 14. 7); 'better' is κρεῖσσον (1 C. 7. 38). Διπλότερον 'in double measure' Mt. 23. 15 (late).—On ἀνώτερον, κατωτέρω, πορρώτερον (-τέρω) see § 11, 5. We have an instance of a numeral adverb πρώτως in A. 11. 26 ℵBD² (πρῶτον A al., D* reads differently), i.e. 'for the first time,' cp. Clem. Hom. ix. 4 τὸν πρώτως ἀναγκάσαντα, xvi. 20 πρῶτος ἐφθέγξω, ἃ πρώτως ἠκούσαμεν, always used of the first appearance of something. Similarly in Polyb. vi. 5. 10, Diod. Sic. iv. 24 τότε πρώτως etc., Phryn. Lob. 311 f.—An instance of an adverb formed from a participle (according to classical precedent) is φειδομένως 2 C. 9. 6 (Plutarch).

2. In **adverbs of place** the distinction between '*where?*' and '*whither?*' is not always preserved even in classical Gk. (ἔνθα, ἐνταῦθα, ἐνθάδε, ἄνω, κάτω, εἴσω, ἔξω);[1] in the N.T. there is no longer any distinction whatever, in the same way that ἐν and εἰς begin to be confused (§ 39, 3). Ποῦ is 'where?' and 'whither?' (ποῖ has disappeared); to it corresponds οὗ, ὅπου (που indef. is only in H. 2. 6, 4. 4, and in the sense 'about' in R. 4. 19; δήπου H. 2. 16). 'Here' ('hither') is expressed by ἐνθάδε in L. (esp. in Acts) and Jo. 4. 15 f. (nowhere by ἐνταῦθα), but usu. by ὧδε (in Acts only 9. 14, 21), which no longer has its original meaning 'thus' (from ὧς - δε): Att. also occasionally

---

[1] But Attic writers still have beside εἴσω, ἔξω the forms ἔνδον, ἐντός, ἐκτός to express the answer to the question 'where?'; accordingly Phrynichus 127 condemns the use of εἴσω in answer to this question, in spite of the instances that occur in poetry and prose. N.T. never has ἔνδον, and only rarely ἐντός, ἐκτός (the latter most often in St. Paul), which are still correctly used to answer the question 'where?'.

§ 25. 2–5.]   ADVERBS.   59

uses ὧδε = 'hither.'[1] 'There' ('thither') is ἐκεῖ, in scholarly language ἐκεῖσε A. 21. 3, 22. 5 = 'there' (D ἐκεῖ).[2] Cp. ὁμόσε for ὁμοῦ A. 20. 18 D joined with ὄντων; πανταχοῦ 'to every quarter' Mc. 1. 28, ἀλλαχοῦ 'to another place' ibid. 38, Lob. Phryn. 43 f.—The local adverbs in -η are no longer represented except πάντας πανταχῇ (-οῦ HLP) 'everywhere' A. 21. 28; πάντῃ τε καὶ πανταχοῦ 24. 3 appears to mean 'in every way and everywhere.'

3. Adverbs answering the question 'whence?' with termination -θεν: πόθεν (ποθέν nowhere), ὅθεν (ὁπόθεν nowhere), ἔνθεν (opposed to ἐκεῖ, unclass.) Mt. 17. 20 (ἐντεῦθεν C), L. 16. 26 (= Attic ἐντεῦθεν, ἐνθένδε), elsewhere ἐντεῦθεν, which is also used for Attic ἔνθεν in the phrase Jo. 19. 18 ἐντεῦθεν καὶ ἐντεῦθεν = Attic ἔνθεν καὶ ἔνθεν (Ap. 22. 2 ἐντ. καὶ ἐκεῖθεν AB, ἐντ. καὶ ἐντ. some minuscules, ἔνθεν καὶ ℵ*, ἔνθεν add. ℵᶜ). 'Thence' is ἐκεῖθεν; other forms are πάντοθεν (πανταχόθεν Mc. 1. 45 EGU al. as in Attic prose), ἀλλαχόθεν.—The termination -θεν has become stereotyped and meaningless in most cases in the words ἔσωθεν, ἔξωθεν 'within,' 'without,' as is often the case even in Attic Gk. (they have the meaning 'from within,' 'from without' in Mc. 7. 18, 21, 23, L. 11. 7; these forms are *never* used in answer to the question 'whither?'): also in κυκλόθεν Ap. 4. 8 (Att.): and the termination is entirely without force in ἔμπροσθεν, ὄπισθεν, as it is from the earliest times. On the other hand ἄνωθεν = 'from above' (κάτωθεν does not appear); ἀπ' ἄνωθεν ἕως κάτω in Mt. 27. 51 (ἀπ' om. ℵL), Mc. 15. 38 is like ἀπὸ μακρόθεν beside μακρόθεν Mt. 26. 58 (ἀπὸ om. ℵCF al.), Mc. 15. 40, 5. 6 (ἀπὸ om. AKL al.) etc. (also used in conjunction with ἵστασθαι, so that ἀπὸ and -θεν both lose their force), ἐκ παιδιόθεν Mc. 9. 21 (without ἐκ AX al., D ἐκ παιδός), cp. (ἀπ', ἐξ) οὐρανόθεν Homer, Acts 14. 17 (without prep.); later writers are fond of reviving this kind of expression Lob. Phryn. 46. Μακρόθεν first occurs in Hellenistic Gk. (= Attic πόρρωθεν which occurs in L. 17. 12 with ἔστησαν, H. 11. 13), also παιδ(ι)όθεν is first found in late writers (Lob. Phryn. 93); on the other hand the classical ἐγγύθεν is absent from N.T.

4. **Adverbs of time.**—Πότε, ποτέ, ὅτε (ὁπότε only L. 6. 3 AEHK al., ὅτε ℵBCD al.), τότε; besides these (ἄλλοτε is wanting) πάντοτε frequently in St. Paul for ἀεί[3] (mod. Gk. and late writers, cp. Phryn. 103), and occasionally in Mt. Mc. L. (never in Acts), H. 7. 25 (never in Epp. Cath.); ἀεί only occurs in [Mc. 15. 8 ACD al., om. ℵBΔ] A. 7. 51, 2 C. 4. 11, 6. 10 [Tit. 1. 12 quot., H. 3. 10 O.T.], 1 P. 3. 15 (om. A Syr. Euseb.), 2 P. 1. 12.—Πηνίκα etc. do not occur, only ἡνίκα in 2 C. 3. 15 f.

5. The waning of the system of the **correlative adverbs** is seen chiefly in the indefinite adverbs, of which ποτέ alone is in ordinary

---

[1] Hermas frequently has ὧδε κἀκεῖσε 'hither and thither,' Mand. v. 2. 7 etc.

[2] For ἐκεῖ in A. 18. 19 BHLP have αὐτοῦ, which is only found elsewhere in Mt. 26. 36 (om. ℵC*), A. 15. 34 β text (?), 21. 4 (not without var. lect.).

[3] In Hermas the use of ἀεί instead of πάντοτε is one of the indications which mark the forged conclusion of Simonides (Sim. ix. 30–x.).

use (πως only in εἴπως, μήπως : on που [ποθέν] see 2 and 3); also in the indefinite relatives, which become confused with the definite forms (§§ 13, 3 ; 50, 1), and then in some cases (for ὁπόθεν sup. 3, ὁπότε 4) entirely or almost entirely disappear.

6. On compounded adverbs see § 28, 7.

§ 26. PARTICLES.

1. In the use of particles the New Testament language is poor in comparison with the classical, not only because a considerable number of old particles are completely absent, but more especially because many of the remainder are only employed in a limited way. The Syntax will treat of the manner of employment and the combinations of the individual particles; here we merely give a table of those which are represented and those which are absent, together with remarks on the form of some of them.

2. Particles (and conjunctions) or combinations of particles in the N.T.: ἀλλά, ἅμα, ἄν, ἄρα (ἄραγε), ἆρα (ἀράγε), ἄχρι(ς), γάρ, γε, δέ, δή, δήπου (one ex.), διό, διόπερ, διότι, ἐάν, ἐάνπερ, εἰ, εἴπερ, εἶτα, εἴτε, ἐπεί, ἐπειδή, ἐπειδήπερ (one ex.), [ἐπείπερ R. 3. 30 v.l.], ἔπειτα, ἕως, ἤ, [ἦ, more correctly εἶ (see § 3, 6), in εἰ μήν O.T. quot.], ἤδη, ἡνίκα, [ἤπερ v.l. in Jo. 12. 43], ἤτοι, ἵνα, καθά, καθάπερ, καθό, καθότι, καθώς, καί, καίπερ, καίτοι(γε), μέν, μενοῦνγε, μέντοι, [μέχρι(ς), v.l. for μ. οὗ], ὅμως, μή, μηδέ, [μήν only in εἰ μήν, vide sup.], μήτε, μήτι, ναί, νή, ὅμως, ὁπότε (one ex.), ὅπως, ὅταν, ὅτε, ὅτι, οὐ (οὐχί), οὐδέ, οὐκοῦν (one ex.), οὖν, οὔτε, (περ as in Att. prose only in combinations : διόπερ, εἴπερ etc.), πλήν, πρίν, τε, (τοι only in καίτοι, μέντοι etc.), τοιγαροῦν, τοίνυν, ὡς, ὡσάν, ὡσεί, ὥσπερ, ὡσπερεί, ὥστε.[1]

3. The following Attic particles are entirely wanting : ἀτάρ, ἄτε, αὖ, γοῦν, δῆθεν, δῆτα, εἴθε, μά, νή, μήτοι, μῶν, νυν, ὁπόταν, (οὐκουν), οὔτι, οὔτοι, τέως. But the limitation of the rich store of particles began at an early period, as may be shown *e.g.* by the fact that in the Ἀθηναίων Πολιτεία of Aristotle not only all the last-named particles with the exception of ἄτε are absent, but also the following among those enumerated under 2: ἆρα, ἄρα, ἄχρι, γε, δήπου, διόπερ, διότι, ἐάνπερ, εἴπερ, εἴτε, ἐπειδήπερ, (ἐπείπερ), (ἤπερ), ἤτοι, καίτοι, μενοῦνγε, (μέντοι ?), μέχρι, μήτι, ναί, ὅμως, ὁπότε, οὐκοῦν, οὐχί, τοιγαροῦν, τοίνυν.

4. Ἐάν is the Hellenistic form for 'if' (cp. ἑαυτοῦ, σεαυτοῦ), not ἤν or ἄν; ἄν however is found in the MSS. of the N.T. in some few instances, so Jo. 12. 32 B, 13. 20 (ἐάν DEFG al.), 16. 23 BC al., 20. 23 *bis* (ἐάν AD, *semel* א*), Acts 9. 2 אE. This may perhaps be connected with the disproportionately greater encroachment which ἐάν made into the province of ἄν, out of which a kind of interchange of meanings between the two words might easily grow (modern Gk. uses ἐάν and ἄν for 'if'). Ἐάν is found very frequently after

---

[1] Hermas has further καὶ μήν Mand. iv. 1. 8, V. 1. 7 (Barn. 9. 6) and γοῦν (= οὖν, as also in other late writers, see Steph.-Dind. γοῦν), Sim. viii. 8. 2 ; Barnabas has πέρας γέ τοι in 10. 2 and elsewhere.

relatives in the N.T., as in the LXX. and the papyri:[1] Mt. 5. 19 ὃς ἐάν (immediately followed by ὃς δ' ἄν), 8. 19 ὅπου ἐάν, 10. 42 ὃς ἐάν (BD ἄν), 11. 27 ᾧ ἐάν (ἄν D) etc.; in St. John only in 15. 7 (ἄν B), 1 Jo. 3. 22 (B ἄν), 3 Jo. 5.

§ 27. WORD-FORMATION BY MEANS OF TERMINATIONS AND SUFFIXES.

1. The formation of words is naturally carried further in the Hellenistic language than in the classical to meet new requirements, but in all essentials the old patterns are adhered to.

Verbs from noun forms in -ος have termination -όω: ἀναστατοῦν, ἀποδεκατοῦν (in the older lang. δεκατεύειν), ἀνακαινοῦν (class. -ίζειν), ἀφυπνοῦν 'to fall asleep' (-ίζειν in class. Gk. = 'to awake,' -οῦν in Hellenistic Gk. has the same meaning; 'to fall asleep' in the older lang. = καθυπνοῦν, cp. ἐπικαθυπνοῦν Barn. 4. 13), δολιοῦν 'to deceive' (δόλιος) R. 3. 13 O.T. quot., θεμελιοῦν, κεφαλαιοῦν (-λιοῦν אBL) Mc. 12. 4 appears to mean 'to beat on the head' = κολαφίζειν, but is quite unparalleled in this sense (cp. Lob. Phryn. 95), κραταιοῦν, so also σθενοῦν from τὸ σθένος, (ἐν)δυναμοῦν from δύναμις, νεκροῦν, σαροῦν = σαίρειν (from σάρος: Lob. Phryn. 83), χαριτοῦν from χάρις. Verbs in -έω are principally compounds, see § 28, but there is also δυνατεῖν from δυνατός (ἀδυνατεῖν is old). For ἐξουδενίζειν (Plut.) N.T. generally has ἐξουθενεῖν (LXX.), with ·θενοῦν as a v.l. in Mc. 9. 12.—In -ίζειν or (after an ι) -άζειν: ἁγιάζειν (ἅγιος, old form ἁγίζειν), αἰχμαλωτίζειν, ἀναθεματίζειν, ἀνεμίζειν (old form -μοῦν), δογματίζειν, δειγματίζειν, ἐνταφιάζειν, θεατρίζειν, θυσιάζειν for θύειν (θυσία), ἱματίζειν (from ἷμα = εἷμα, not from ἱμάτιον; ἱματισμός appears already in Polyb.), ἰουδαΐζειν, μυκτηρίζειν, νηπιάζειν (Hippocr.), ὀρθρίζειν, πελεκίζειν (Polyb.), σινιάζειν (σινίον 'sieve,' also a late word; old form σάω, then σήθω), (δια)σκορπίζειν (old-Ionic, Phryn. 218), σμυρνίζειν σπλαγχνίζεσθαι from σπλάγχνα רַחֲמִים, συμμορφίζειν, φυλακίζειν from φυλακή 'prison'; in Hermas συνετίζειν from συνετός, Mand. iv. 2. 2, cp. σοφίζειν 'to make wise' (LXX.) 2 Tim. 3. 15.—Verbs in -εύω are likewise formed from the most various stems: (αἰχμαλωτεύω only in 2 Tim. 3. 6 as a v.l. for -τίζω, vide supra; -εύω Diod. Sic.), παγιδεύειν (παγίς), (ἐξ)ολεθρεύειν (LXX. passim): γυμνητεύειν (-ιτεύειν) from γυμνήτης (§ 3, 6), μεσιτεύειν from μεσίτης (Polyb.) 'to be naked,' 'to be a mediator,' so too ἱερατεύειν (like βασιλεύειν, ἡγεμονεύειν): on a similar pattern ἐγκρατεύεσθαι 'to behave as an ἐγκρατής' (Aristot.) like εἰρωνεύεσθαι: so περπερεύεσθαι 1 C. 13. 4, παραβολεύεσθαι Ph. 2. 30 (nowhere else) 'to show oneself παράβολος' ('foolhardy'), ἀναιδεύεσθαι (ἀναιδής) Herm. Vis. iii. 7. 5, ἀκριβεύεσθαι Barn. 2. 10. —In -ύνω we have σκληρύνω (like βαθύνω, μηκύνω). Cp. W.-Schm. § 16, 1. On new present formations like στήκω, γρηγορῶ see § 17.

2. **Verbal substantives** in -μός, denoting an action: ἁγιασμός, βαπτισμός, ἐνταφιασμός (-άζω 1), ὀνειδισμός, παροργισμός, πειρασμός, ῥαντισμός, σαββατισμός (from σαββατίζω, not in N.T.), σωφρονισμός

[1] For exx. see Berl. Aeg. Urk. no. 12. 18, 13. 10, 33. 16, 46. 17 etc.

all from verbs in -ίζω, -άζω, whereas with other verbs the tendency to form such derivatives (ὀδυρμός, ἀρδμός and others in the earlier language) appears to have almost died out; we only have ἀπελεγμός from ἀπελέγχω, ἁρπαγμός from ἁρπάζω: and in Hermas συμφυρμός Vis. ii. 2. 2 א, πλατυσμός Mand. v. 2. 3 (Clem. Cor. 3. 1). But substantives in -μα (generally denoting the result of the action) are formed from verbs of all kinds : ἀγνόημα 'a sin,' αἰτίωμα A. 25. 7 (a strange form instead of the old αἰτίαμα 'an accusation'),[1] ἀνταπόδομα (old form -σις), ἄντλημα 'an *instrument* for drawing water,' a strange form (elsewhere ἀντλητήρ, -τήριον), ἀπαύγασμα, ἀποσκίασμα, βάπτισμα (cp. supra -σμός, which is never used of John's baptism, and of Christian baptism only in Col. 2. 12 א°BD*FG, cp. H. 6. 2 ; the distinction of meaning is preserved : βαπτισμός is the act of immersion, in βάπτισμα the result is included),[2] ἐξέραμα, ἥττημα, θέλημα, ἱεράτευμα (ἱερατεύειν 1), κατάλυμα (Hellenistic for καταγωγεῖον; here also there is a peculiar use of -μα for the *place* of lodging), κατόρθωμα (Polyb.), πρόσκομμα ; Hermas has ματαίωμα 'a vain thing' Mand. ix. 4, μέθυσμα 'an intoxicating drink' vi. 2. 5 etc. (also in Philo, like ἔδεσμα). Abstract nouns, again, take termination -σις, and are mainly formed from stems that end with a vowel (not from verbs in -ζω, where -σμός is used): βίωσις, ἐπιπόθησις, θέλησις H. 2. 4 (elsewhere -ημα), κατάνυξις R. 11. 8 O.T. quot. (κατανύσσειν 'to stupefy' Dan. 10. 9),[3] πεποίθησις (πέποιθα, Phryn. 294 Lob.), πρόσκλισις (Polyb.), πρόσχυσις (ἁμάρτησις Herm. Vis. ii. 2. 5). Nouns in -εία are from verbs in -εύω: ἀρεσκεία (ἄρεσκος, -σκεύομαι, -εία; Polyb.), ἐριθεία (Aristot.), ἱερατεία (-εύω sup. 1), μεθοδεία (-εύειν is Hellenistic from μέθοδος). The termination -μονή occurs in a few instances : πλησμονή (old), new forms πεισμονή from πείθω and ἐπιλησμονή Ja. 1. 25. LXX. Sir. 11. 29, related to ἐπιλήσμων. Without suffix is οἰκοδομή 'edification' or 'a building,' a new word, and strictly speaking incorrectly formed instead of -ία or -ησις, Lob. Phryn. 490 (the formation δομή belongs to a primitive word δέμω, not to οἰκοδομέω) ; but cp. παρασκευή from -άζω and esp. the Attic μισθοφορά.—New nouns to express the doer are formed in -της (no longer in -τωρ, -τήρ): βιαστής, βαπτιστής, γογγυστής, διώκτης, δότης (old form δοτήρ), ἑλληνιστής from -ίζειν 'to speak Greek,' so the Greek-speaking Jew A. 6. 1 etc., εὐαγγελιστής, λυτρωτής, μεριστής, προσκυνητής ; such words, as is shown *e.g.* by Mt. 11. 12 βιάζεται – βιασταί, Jo. 4. 20 ff. προσκυνεῖν – προσκυνηταί, are coined with almost the same facility as verbal forms. With ἐπενδύτης 'an upper garment' Jo. 21. 7 (already in Sophocles) cp. the German 'Ueberzieher' [English 'overcoat'].—In -τήριον (from -τήρ) are ἱλαστήριον (on σωτήριον inf. 6.), ἀκροατήριον.—It is noticeable that words in -μα in the Hellenistic language follow the analogy of those in -σις and -της (-τος) in so far that they, like the latter, now prefer the verbal stem ending in a short vowel and avoid the stem with

---

[1] Αἰτίωσις in Eustathius p. 1422. 21 is compared.
[2] Joseph. Ant. 18. 5. 2 uses βαπτισμός of John's baptism.
[3] Fritzsche, Paul. ad Rom. ii. 558 ff.

a long vowel: δόμα like δόσις δότης, θέμα (already in old Doric) like θέσις θετός, whence ἀνάθεμα = Att. -θημα,[1] so πόμα = Att. πῶμα, κλίμα, κρίμα, even ἀνάστεμα for -στημα[2] (true stem στᾰ), διάστεμα A. 5. 7 D (but κατάστημα Tit. 2. 3).

3. **Substantives from adjectives**: with termination -ότης: ἁγιότης, ἁγνότης (old form ἁγνεία from -εύω), ἀδηλότης, ἀφελότης A. 2. 46 from ἀφελής 'simple,' 'plain,' Hellenistic (elsewhere the subst. is always ἀφέλεια), γυμνότης, ματαιότης, μεγαλειότης; corresponding forms from substantives are θεότης (Lucian), ἀδελφότης (1 and 4 Macc., Dio. Chrys.) in concrete sense 'the brotherhood' 1 P. 2. 17, 5. 9 (Clem. Cor. i. 2. 4; in abstract sense Herm. Mand. x. 1. 4), κυριότης in concrete sense 'principality' (an angelic order) E. 1. 21 (abstract Herm. Sim. v. 6. 1) etc.—With **-σύνη**: from adj. in -μων, with which this formation is specially frequent (σωφροσύνη, μνημοσύνη), ἐλεημοσύνη (already found in Callimachus: in N.T. usu. in concrete sense 'alms'): from adj. in -ος (like δικαιοσύνη, ἀκεραιοσύνη Barn. 10. 4), but with lengthening of the antepenultimate, as in the comparative, when the syllable preceding it is short: ἀγαθωσύνη, ἁγιωσύνη, μεγαλωσύνη; ἱερωσύνη (= ἱερεωσ. from ἱερεω- which is from ἱερεύς) occurs in the older language. With **-ία**: ἐλαφρία, παραφρονία 2 P. 2. 16 (from παράφρων -ονεῖν, cp. εὐδαιμονία).

4. **Substantives from substantives**: The feminine in -ισσα is the correct form corresponding to masculine in -ιξ, Φοῖνιξ Φοίνισσα, but in the later language this becomes an independent suffix (βαλάνισσα from βαλανεύς, βασίλισσα, Γαλάτισσα), so in N.T. Συροφοινίκισσα from Συροφοῖνιξ (Lucian) Mc. 7. 26 (v.l. Συραφ. i.e. Σύρα Φ.: D Φοίνισσα, Latt. Συροφοίνισσα).[3]—Of *Latin* origin are the designations ending in -ιανός derived from proper names, in the N.T. Ἡρῳδιανοί 'adherents of Herod' Mc. 3. 6 etc., and Χρηστιανοί from Χρηστός = Χριστός, the heathen designation for Christians A. 11. 26, 26. 28, 1 P. 4. 16 (on η cp. § 3, 6), formed on the model of *Pompeiani, Caesariani*; in later times this form was frequently employed for the names of sects.[4]—**Diminutives** are, in keeping with the whole character of the N.T., not abundant; some, however, had become popular expressions, such as παιδίον, παιδάριον, παιδίσκη (old), ψιχίον 'bread-crumb' (only in N.T. from ψίξ), πτερύγιον, ὠτίον, ὠτάριον 'ear' (the latter form in Mc. 14. 47 אBC, Jo. 18. 10 אBC*LX) of the part of the body considered as such (Moeris says ὠτίον is Hellenistic for Attic οὖς),[5] whereas οὖς (together with ἀκοή) denotes the organ of hearing regarded as such; St. Luke, therefore, atticises when he uses οὖς for the part of the body (L. 22. 50: ὠτίον

---

[1] Also in the sense of 'votive offering' L. 21. 5 according to אADX (B al. -θήμασι).
[2] Buresch, N. Jahrb. f. kl. Philol. 1891, 539, cod. A LXX.
[3] W.-Schm. § 16, 2 c, who explains it as due to a form Φοινικίς (βασιλίς), and cites for Φοινίκισσα Herodian L. ii. 455. 19 (but see ibid. i. 268. 14, ii. 708. 10).
[4] R. A. Lipsius Ursprung des Christennamens (Jena 1873); Blass, Hermes xxx. 465 ff.
[5] The popular language was fond of denoting the parts of the body by diminutives (Lob. Phryn. 211 f.), so modern Gk. μάτι 'eye' from ὀμμάτιον, αὐτί 'ear' (also σωμάτιον Clem. Hom. v. 1, and as early as Isocrat. Epist. 4, 11).

DK). Denoting smallness: κλινίδιον L. 5. 19, 24, κλινάριον (Lob. Phryn. 180) A. 5. 15 אBCD (v.l. κλινῶν), βιβλαρίδιον Ap. 10. 2, 8 ff. (Herm. Vis. ii. 1. 3 v.l. βιβλιδάριον, cp. λιθαρίδιον late writers), formed from βιβλάρι(ον) + -ίδιον (only here). The following diminutives contain a subjective idea and belong to the special class of ὑποκοριστικά [endearing terms]: κυνάριον Mt. 15. 26 f., Mc. 7. 27 f., ἰχθύδιον Barn. 10. 5, γυναικάριον (also contemptuous) 2 Tim. 3. 6, also probably ὀνάριον Jo. 12. 14 (elsewhere ὄνος): with the subjective sense of love ῥαβδίον Herm. Sim. viii. 2. 9.—Formed with -ειον or -ιον is εἰδωλεῖον or -ιον (§ 4, 2) from εἴδωλον (also LXX.).[1]—With -ών we should not reckon ἐλαιών 'mount of olives,' which should rather be written ἐλαιῶν gen. plur. (with variant form in A. 1. 12), but no doubt ἀφεδρών 'privy' Mt. 15. 17, Mc. 7. 19, cp. κοπρών, περιστερεών, and others.[2]

5. **Adjectives from verbs.**—Πειθός would be formed directly from a verbal stem, did not this word in 1 C. 2. 4 owe its origin to a patent corruption (πειθοῖς written for -οῖ). In -τος (verbal adjectives) there are many instances of compound words (see § 28, 5); an uncompounded word is παθητός 'capable of suffering' A. 26. 23 (Plutarch), in the narrower sense of words in -τός; on the other hand in the more general sense, equivalent to a perf. part. pass., we have σιτιστός Mt. 22. 4 'fattened' (besides compounded words). With the rare suffix -ωλος we have ἁμαρτωλός LXX. N.T. cp. φειδωλός.

6. **Adjectives from nouns (and participles).**—In -ιος σωτήριος (old); from which the substantive τὸ σωτήριον is formed, in LXX. 'a thankoffering,' also in the N.T. L. 3. 6, A. 28. 28 etc. = 'salvation': cp. ἡ ζευκτηρία A. 27. 40 (only here, ζευκτήριος is old). From the LXX., again, is λαὸς περιούσιος Tit. 2. 14 = עַם סְגֻלָּה 'a people of possession,' = ὃς περίεστι, ὃν ὁ θεὸς περιεποιήσατο ἑαυτῷ, cp. Jerome ap. Tisch. ad. loc., W.-Schm. § 16, 3 b. Quite unique in the Greek language is ἐπιούσιος Mt. 6. 11, L. 11. 3 which cannot well be derived from any other source but ἡ ἐπιοῦσα sc. ἡμέρα (A. 16. 11 and elsewhere in Acts), so that its meaning is 'bread for the coming day': see the detailed exposition in W.-Schm. § 16, 3, n. 23.[3] Origen (i. 245) was not acquainted with the word either in literature or in the colloquial language, and it must therefore be an artificial translation of an Aramaic expression. . An obscure word in -ικός is πιστικός Mc. 14. 3, Jo. 12. 3 (νάρδου πιστικῆς), which should perhaps be rendered 'genuine' and be derived from πιστός or πίστις, but may on the other hand have an entirely different origin, W.-Schm. § 16, 3 b. Other forms in -ικός (or -ακός, after ι) are κυριακός (ἡμέρα Ap. 1. 10, δεῖπνον 1 C. 11. 20), σκεύη κεραμικά Ap. 2. 27 with v.l.

---

[1] For -εῖον 'Ἀπολλωνεῖον and the like are quoted as parallels, but even there -ιον is at least in the majority of cases the correct form, 'Ἀπολλώνιον. But μουσεῖον, καπηλεῖον may be compared. In the LXX., e.g. in 1 Esd. 2. 9 AB have -ιον.

[2] For details see Fischer, Vitia lexicorum N.T. 698 ff.

[3] [See also Lightfoot, On a Fresh Revision of the N.T., Appendix. Tr.]

-εικά i.e. 'the vessels of the potter' (κεραμεύς, but the more natural meaning is 'earthen,' so that the word is incorrectly used instead of κεραμεοῦς, Lob. Phryn. 146), σαρκικός = 'belonging to σάρξ,' 'of the nature of σάρξ' (opposed to πνευματικός), in the MSS. occasionally confounded with σάρκινος 'consisting of flesh' (like λίθινος and N.T. ὀστράκινος) 2 C. 3. 3 (-ικός R. 15. 27, 1 C. 9. 11, 2 C. 1. 12 [FG -ίνῃ], 2 C. 10. 4, 1 P. 2. 11, also 1 C. 3. 3 according to ℵ al. [D*FG -ινοι]; in the similar passages R. 7. 14, 1 C. 3. 1, H. 7. 16, while the best tradition is in favour of -ινος, the sense demands -ικός, since there is an antithesis with πνευματικός). In -ινός we have adjectives of time (as in class. Gk. μεσημβρινός): ὀρθρινός[1] L. 24. 22 (ὄρθριαι K²P al., an atticising correction, Lob. Phryn. 51: -ινός also in Herm. Sim. v. 1. 1), πρωϊνός (older form πρώιος, πρῷος), καθημερινός A. 6. 1, Herm. Vis. i. 3. 2 (a similar form μεθημερινός in class. Gk.) 'daily' (from καθ' ἡμέραν = class. καθημέριος), ταχινός 'speedy' (from τάχα, ταχέως) 2 P. 1. 14, 2. 1, Herm. Sim. viii. 9. 4.

§ 28. WORD-FORMATION BY COMPOSITION.

1. A distinction is drawn in Greek between **true composition** (**σύνθεσις**), in which the first of the component parts, if subject to inflection, is represented by the stem alone without inflection, and **improper composition** (**παράθεσις**), i.e. the mere coalescing of words originally separate, without further adaptation than is required for euphony. To the class of parathetic compounds belong all compounds of verbs with prepositions, together with some substantival forms such as Διόσκοροι from Διὸς κόροι, and many adverbs, in the formation of which the later language showed itself as prolific as it did in the production of compound verbs. A third category is formed by the **derivatives** of (true or improper) compounds (**παρασύνθετα**), such as ἱπποτροφεῖν, -ία from ἱπποτρόφος, Διοσκόριον from Διόσκοροι.

2. To enumerate the new (**parathetic**) compounds formed from verb and preposition, together with the verbal substantives and verbal adjectives belonging to them, does not come within the province of the study of grammar.[2] We may also have more than one preposition combined in a word, as in the classical language; special mention may be made of διαπαρατριβαί 1 Tim. 6. 5 'perpetual disputations' (παρατριβή = 'dispute' Polyb.). Adverbs formed by composition or cohesion (incorrectly used as prepositions) are coined more freely by the later than by the classical language (Lob. Phryn. 45 ff.); as a rule they are composed of preposition and adverb, as ὑπεράνω E. 1. 21 etc. (ἐπάνω, ὑποκάτω belong to the earlier period),

---

[1] In the Hellenistic poets the quantity of the ι, which in other words of this class is short, is used indifferently as long or short; cod. B writes -ινος, not -εινος.

[2] Winer, five essays 'de verborum cum praep. compositorum in N.T. usu,' Leips. 1834-43; A. Rieder 'Verbs (and other words) compounded with more than one prep. in the New and Old Test.,' Progr. Gumbinnen, 1876.

E

ἔκπαλαι 2 P. 2. 3, 3. 5 (ἐκ παλαιοῦ in Attic according to Phrynichus); also from prepos. and adj. as ἐκπερισσοῦ (beside ἐκπερισσῶς? as אBCD read in Mc. 14. 31: the word would naturally be forced into an adverbial form), by accumulation ὑπερεκπερισσοῦ (-ῶς), E. 3. 20, 1 Th. 3. 10, 5. 13, cp. (-ῶς) Clem. Cor. i. 20. 11 (§ 4, 1 note), also ὑπερπερισσῶς Mc. 7. 37 (v.l. ὑπερεκπ.), ὑπερλίαν 2 C. 11. 5, 12. 11, ὑπεράγαν Clem. Cor. i. 56. 2; ὑπερέκεινα 2 C. 10. 16 is another new form (prep. and pron.: ἐπέκεινα is old).

3. **True compounds** are in a few cases fundamentally **substantives**, formed in such a way that in front of a substantive, which keeps its ordinary form, there is placed another substantive (or adject.) more nearly defining or restricting its meaning (*e.g.* lion-head, Greek λεοντοκεφαλή an architectural term); so in N.T. Συροφοίνισσα or -ίκισσα § 27, 4 (Λιβυφοίνικες Polyb.): εὐρακύλων a hybrid word from εὖρος and *aquilo* (cp. εὐρόνοτος 'north east'); ψευδοπροφήτης, -δάδελφος, -δαπόστολος, -δοδιδάσκαλος, (ψευδόμαρτυς appears in Attic); σαρδόνυξ (A σαρδιόνυξ) Ap. 21. 20 from σάρδιος and ὄνυξ, ibid. χρυσόλιθος (but χρυσόπρασος in the same verse is an adjective formed from πράσον 'leak,' sc. λίθος); χρεοφειλέτης from χρέος and ὀφειλέτης, but words of this kind (cp. ἱππηλάτης, ἱπποδιώκτης) belong rather to compounds of subst. and verbal stem, vide infra 5; on the other hand οἰκοδεσπότης (cp. Phryn. 373 who condemns the word: derivative οἰκοδεσποτεῖν) does really consist of οἶκος and δεσπότης.—The subst. is defined by a *particle* in συστρατιώτης (class.), συμπρεσβύτερος, συγκληρονόμος: by a verbal stem in ἀρχιερεύς (but the older form is ἀρχιέρεως, *i.e.* ὁ ἄρχων τῶν ἱερέων), ἀρχιτέκτων (which is likewise strictly to be explained as ὁ ἄρχων τῶν τεκτόνων), ἀρχιτελώνης L. 19. 2, ἀρχιποίμην 1 P. 5. 4, ἀρχάγγελος (but in ἀρχισυνάγωγος, ἀρχιτρίκλινος it is clear that the first component still continues to govern the second).[1]

4. There are a great number of **adjectival** forms composed of adjectives (adv., prep., numeral) and substantive (adj.), which express the combined notion of both ideas, such as the peculiar δευτερόπρωτον σάββατον L. 6. 1 (from two numeral adjectives), variously explained, see Tisch. ad loc. and W.-Grimm; an example of the ordinary type (particle and subst.) is ἀνέλεος Ja. 2. 13 (class. ἀνηλεής: the N.T. form due to τὸ ἔλεος § 9, 3), so σκληροτράχηλος (LXX.) A. 7. 51, δίψυχος Ja. 1. 8, 4. 8 (Hermas *pass.*), ἑτερόγλωσσος (Polyb.), δίστομος and μονόφθαλμος already found in classical Gk.; ἰσάγγελος = ἴσος τοῖς ἀγγέλοις, like Homeric ἰσόθεος; especially with a preposition in the first place, in which case the formation of the adj. in -ιος (ἀκρογωνιαῖος is from -α-ιος) is preferred: παραθαλάσσιος (old), ἐπιθανάτιος 1 C. 4. 9 = ἐπὶ θανάτῳ συνειλημμένος (also in Dionys. Halic.), ἐπίγειος and ἐπουράνιος (old), καταχθόνιος (also old); ἐνώπιον (neuter of ἐνώπιος) likewise takes this formation. From these words again neuter substantives are formed. A peculiar compound of elements which are coordinate and simply added together, is νυχθήμερον (late) 2 C. 11.

---

[1] There are also correspondingly formed adjectives, thus in Hermas περίπικρος 'very bitter' Sim. vi. 2. 5, ἀπόκενος 'somewhat empty' Mand. xii. 5. 2.

§ 28. 4–5.]   BY COMPOSITION.   67

25, 'a period of a night and a day,' Kühner i.³ ii. 318 ; note moreover τὸ δωδεκάφυλον A. 26. 7 = αἱ δώδεκα φυλαί (§ 44, 1) ; ὑποπόδιον 'footstool,' ὑπολήνιον (ληνός) the receptacle or vat excavated beneath the winepress, ἀνάγαιον (§§ 3, 7 ; 6, 4); further ἀκροθίνιον H. 7. 4 (old), μεσονύκτιον (Hellenistic, Lob. Phryn. 53; § 6, 2), ἡμιώριον 'half an hour' Ap. 8. 1 (ἡμίωρον AP, cp. ἡμίδραχμον, ἡμιπόδιον etc.; Kühner i.³ ii. 323); προσάββατον, ἡδύοσμον a plant (garden mint). In the femin. we have ἡ καλλιέλαιος and its opposite ἀγριέλαιος (for which, according to Moeris, Attic has κότινος) R. 11. 17, 24, not ἀγριελαία, although ἀγριο- in the later language is also directly compounded with the substantive (supra 3), as in ἀγριοκολοκύνθη ; also ἀκροβυστία, a distorted form of ἀκροποσθία or -ιον (the old word) from πόσθη. Then from adjectives of this kind there was a further creation of abstract substantives, such as σκληροκαρδία 'hardness of heart' (LXX.) related to σκληροκάρδιος (LXX.), and therefore for -καρδι-ία, cp. διπλοκαρδία Barn. 20. 1, and of verbs (cp. 5), amongst which may be specially noticed ὀρθοποδεῖν (ὀρθόπους is old) G. 2. 14 (nowhere else), and ἐγκακεῖν (the word ἐκκακεῖν is a wrong reading, occurring also in Herm. Mand. ix. 8) 'to be slack in anything' Polyb. 4, 19. 10, formed directly from ἐν and κακός, although no word ἔγκακος ever existed; ἐνωτίζεσθαι A. 2. 14 (LXX.) is also certainly formed directly from ἐν and ὦτα, cp. ἐνστερνίζεσθαι Clem. Cor. ii. 1, ἐνστηθίζειν Athanasius.

5. The greater number of compounds, originally adjectival, are formed of substantive (adject., pronoun) or particle and **verbal stem**; from these adjectives there are then formed parasynthetic abstract substantives and verbs. The most ordinary form is : adj. -ος, abstract subst. -ία, verb -έω, like ἱπποτρόφος, ἱπποτροφία, ἱπποτροφέω. So in the N.T. we have ἀγαθοποιός 1 P. 2. 14, ἀγαθοποιία 4. 19 (ἀγαθοποίησις Herm. Mand. viii. 10, Sim. v. 3. 4), ἀγαθοποιεῖν 2. 15 (beside ἀγαθοεργεῖν 1 Tim. 6. 18, ἀγαθουργεῖν with v.l. ἀγαθοποιεῖν A. 14. 17), καλοποιεῖν 2 Th. 3. 13, κακοποιός (and κακοῦργος, both old), κακοποιεῖν (old), εἰρηνοποιός -εῖν, μοσχοποιεῖν only in N.T. (Acts 7. 41) of the image of the golden calf, where the adjectival stem only exists, and only needed to exist, in idea, ἰσχυροποιεῖν (and -ποίησις) Hermas, Vis. i. 3. 2 etc. With other verbal stems there are : κακουχεῖν an old form (from ἔχω: κακοῦχος nowhere), πληροφορεῖν -ία (first[1] in N.T.: -φόρος nowhere), λογομαχεῖν -ία (late, other writers also have -μάχος), λιθοβολεῖν 'to stone' together with λιθάζειν (the old word was λεύειν), λατομεῖν, ἑτεροζυγεῖν 2 C. 6. 14 (ἑτερόζυγος LXX.), ἀνθρωποκτόνος, ἀνθρωπάρεσκος (ἀρέσκω), of uncertain meaning δεξιολάβος Acts 23. 23 (an infantry corps), according to a probably certain conjecture κενεμβατεύειν = -εῖν Col. 2. 18 (κενεμβάτης has to be imagined : the word is formed like ἐμβατεύειν) etc. Where the verbal stem has an active sense the adjectives generally are paroxytone (in the case of a short paenultima) or oxytone (if the paen. is long), whereas in the case of a passive stem (and a short paenultima) the accent is thrown back on to the first part of the word (πρωτότοκος 'firstborn,' whence πρωτοτόκια, cp. εὐαγγέλιον,

---
[1] [πληροφορεῖσθαι occurs in LXX. Ecclesiastes 8. 11. Tr.]

H. 12. 16). But for words of passive meaning the form of the verbal adj. in -τος is preferred to that in -ος; thus in N.T. πατροπαράδοτος 1 P. 1. 18, σητόβρωτος Ja. 5. 2, λιθόστρωτος (Sophocles) Jo. 19. 3, ποταμοφόρητος (-φορεῖν) Ap. 12. 15,[1] εἰδωλόθυτον (like ἱερόθυτον); just as in active words -της (the noun of the agent) may take the place of -ος, χρεοφειλέτης supra 3, καρδιογνώστης Acts 1. 24, 15. 8 Herm. Mand. iv. 3. 4 (nowhere else), προσωπολήμπτης 10. 34 (-τεῖν, -ημψία). From διδάσκειν the compounds are formed with termination -διδάσκαλος: νομοδιδάσκαλος, καλοδιδάσκαλος Tit. 2. 3 (like χοροδιδάσκ. in older Greek), ἑτεροδιδασκαλεῖν? (= ἕτερα διδάσκειν? or = ἑτέροις διδασκάλοις χρῆσθαι?) 1 Tim. 1. 3, 6. 3; from φυλάσσω with -φύλαξ (Hellenistic words): δεσμοφύλαξ A. 16. 23 (γαζοφυλάκιον Mc. 12. 41 etc. LXX., a παρασύνθετον from γαζοφύλαξ); from verbs in -άω, -έω with termin. -ης (1st decl.): πατρολῴας (§ 6, 2) ἀλοᾶν, φρεναπάτης[2] ἀπατᾶν (whence φρεναπατᾶν), πορφυροπώλης πωλεῖν, with fem. -πωλις A. 16. 14; so also ἀρσενοκοίτης (κοιτάζεσθαι, κοίτη) 1 C. 6. 9, 1 Tim. 1. 10, εἰδωλολάτρης (λατρεύειν), whence εἰδωλολατρεῖν Hermas, εἰδωλολατρία N.T. (a more correct form than -εία like λατρεία; B however, except in 1 C. 10. 14, has -λατρεία = -ία), and from ἄρχειν we have words in -άρχης beside those in -αρχος, see § 9, 2. In ὀφθαλμοδουλία E. 6. 6, Col. 3. 22 (B reads with ει, like δουλεία which is formed from δουλεύω) the underlying word is ὀφθαλμόδουλος (which occurs in Const. Apost.), where the formation is dependent on δοῦλος. Occasionally -ής, -ές also appears as a termination: εἰλικρινής (κρίνω), subst. -ίνεια (old), τηλαυγής Mc. 8. 25 (-ῶς; v.l. δηλαυγῶς א* al.), an old poetical word, but also in LXX.: the sense has become weakened to 'clear,' so also in Herm. Sim. vi. 5. 1; γονυπετής (πίπτω, Eurip.), -τεῖν (Polyb.), νουνεχής (cp. inf. 7) from ἔχω (Polyb.), ἱεροπρεπής (Att.). Ἀλεκτοροφωνία 'cock-crowing' (vulgar word, Lob. Phryn. 229 = ἡ ὥρα ἡνίκα ὁ ἀλ. φωνεῖ) is peculiar, there being no conceivable adjective from which it can be derived. In γλωσσόκομον 'a case'[3] Jo. 12. 3, 13. 29 the verb κομεῖν, κομίζειν is concealed; the Atticists require in place of this vulgar form the longer γλωττοκομεῖον Phryn. Lob. 98 (cp. χερνιβεῖον 'a hand-basin').

6. In the older language it frequently happens that in compound words of this kind the verb is given the first place (φερέοικος, δηξίθυμος), in the later language this does not often occur; on compounds in ἀρχι- vide supra 3: ἐθελοθρησκία (-εια B, cp. 5) Col. 2. 23 based on ἐθελόθρησκος (from θρῆσκος) which is not found, cp. ἐθελοδιδάσκαλος Hermas, ἐθελοδουλ(ε)ία Plato, ἐθέλεχθρος Demosth., ἐθελοκακεῖν Hdt., (ἐθελο- expressing spontaneity): φιλόθεος, φιλάγαθος and φίλαυτος (Aristot.), (φιλόπρωτος late language, and) φιλοπρωτεύων[4] 3 Jo. 2 (no-

---

[1] Hesychius also has the phrase ποταμοφόρητον ποιεῖν, s.v. ἀπόερσεν.

[2] I.e. one who deceives his own mind = 'conceited'; the word also occurs on a papyrus of the 2nd cent. B.C. (in rhetorical and artificial prose, Grenfell 'An Alexandrian erotic fragment,' Oxf. 1896, p. 3).

[3] Strictly a case for the mouthpiece of a flute (γλῶττα).

[4] Found already in an Attic inscription of the 1st cent. B.C., Ἐφ. ἀρχαιολ. 1893, 49 ff., l. 30.

forms with μισο- appear in N.T.).—The words compounded with certain pronouns and particles deserve a special mention : αὐτοκατάκριτος Tit. 3. 11 (αὐτόματος and αὐθαίρετος are old); words with ἀ- **privative** for the most part formed in -τος, *e.g.* in N.T. ἀγενεαλόγητος, ἀδιάκριτος, ἀδιάλειπτος,[1] (ἀδύνατος, -εῖν are old), ἀκατάγνωστος, ἀκατακάλυπτος, ἀκατάκριτος, ἀκατάλυτος, ἀκατάπαυστος, (ἀκατάστατος is old, -ασία Polyb.), ἀναπολόγητος, ἀμετανόητος, (ἀνόητος old), ἀνεξερεύνητος, ἀνεξιχνίαστος etc., not however exclusively in a passive sense (*e.g.* those from ἀπολογεῖσθαι, [μετα]νοεῖν) : so also ἄπταιστος Jude 24 (old) is active.[2] The opposite to ἀ- is ἐν- (*e.g.* ἔντιμος = ἐν τιμῇ opposed to ἄτιμος): ἐμπερίτομος is opposed to ἀπερίτμητος in Barn. 9. 6 C and = ἐν περιτομῇ of אG : Paul has ἄνομος - ἔννομος 1 C. 9. 21, § 36, 11.— With εὖ we have: εὐάρεστος (already in Xenoph.), εὐμετάδοτος 'ready to impart' 1 Tim. 6. 18, εὐπρόσδεκτος, εὐπερίστατος H. 12. 1 (nowhere else) probably = ἡ ῥᾳδίως περιισταμένη 'easily surrounding and thereby hindering' a person ; with δυσ- : δυσβάστακτος, δυσερμήνευτος, δυσνόητος. Ἀ(ν)- (and δυσ-) can also be compounded with ordinary adjectives (in classical Gk. ἄναγνος, δύσαγνος), but in the case of εὐπάρεδρος 1 C. 7. 35 we should rather refer the word to παρεδρεύειν than to πάρεδρος ; a compound of adverb and verb is quite inadmissible, therefore εὐδοκεῖν (Hellenistic) must be derived from an imaginary εὔδοκος (δέχομαι), certainly not from δοκεῖν (aorist εὐδόκησα), similarly the old word καραδοκεῖν (N.T. ἀποκαραδοκία) is derived through an imaginary καράδοκος from κάρα and δέχομαι (cp. δοκεύω).[3] Εὐάγγελος (class.) is from εὖ and ἀγγέλλειν ; whence εὐαγγέλιον (as early as Homer) = reward for good news, thanks for a good message, cp. πρωτοτόκια supra 5 ; it is only late writers who employ it for the good news itself ; εὐαγγελίζεσθαι 'to bring good news' is also found in Attic Greek.—Προσφάγιον Jo. 21. 5, which according to Moeris is Hellenistic for Attic ὄψον 'something eaten with bread,' comes from πρός and φαγεῖν ; προσήλυτος however (LXX.) is connected with προσέρχεσθαι (ἔπηλυς, ἐπηλύτης are old).—A special formation is that in -ασία, -εσία, -ισία, -οσία, -υσία, allied to -σις, and not to be confused with abstract nouns from adjectives in -τος (ἀκαταστασία), since the former has the active sense of the verbal substantive : ὁρκωμοσία 'an oath,' ὁροθεσία A. 17. 26 'a setting of bounds' (unless with Hesychius τὰ ὁροθέσια should be read, cp. τὰ ὅρια ; γυμνάσιον, συμπόσιον), δικαιοκρισία 'righteous judgment' R. 2. 5, αἱματεκχυσία H. 9. 22, also παλιγγενεσία (γίνεσθαι) Tit. 3. 5 ; in composition with a preposition this formation appears in the older language, *e.g.* ἀποστασία (προστασία is as early as Attic ; also from a simple verb ὀνομασία).

7. Of compound adverbs, which were not originally derived from adjectives, there are not many instances in the N.T. In -εί there are παμπληθεί L. 23. 18, πανοικεί A. 16. 34, in the cultivated language of Luke, although these particular instances are not Attic;

---
[1] See note 3, p. 68.
[2] But ἀπείραστος Ja. 1. 13 is passive, cf. § 36, 11.
[3] Cp. § 6, 7 πανδοκεύς.

cp. Kühner i.³ ii. 303 (ῐ is probably an incorrect spelling, ἑλληνιστί and the like have ῑ). Ὁμοθυμαδόν is frequent in the Acts (also occurring in R. 15. 6), a classical word. (For adverbs in -δον see Kühner ibid. 307 f.)

8. As is already apparent from the preceding instances, the employment of compound words in the N.T. is fairly large, and is not absent even from the simplest style, although the more elevated style naturally has a larger number of them: for the διπλᾶ (as Aristotle terms the compounds) serve from the earliest times as an embellishment to the speech. In the short letter to Titus the following striking instances occur (verbal compounds and others are neglected): ἀδόκιμος, ἄκαρπος, ἀκατάγνωστος, ἄμαχος, ἀνέγκλητος, ἀνόητος, ἀνομία, ἀνυπότακτος, ἀνωφελής, ἀπειθής, ἀσωτία, ἀφθορία, ἀψευδής; αὐθάδης, αὐτοκατάκριτος; αἰσχροκερδής; εὐάρεστος; γενεαλογία; ἱεροπρεπής; καλοδιδάσκαλος; ματαιολόγος; οἰκουρ(γ)ός, οἰκονόμος; παλιγγενεσία; πειθαρχεῖν; φιλάγαθος, φίλανδρος, φιλανθρωπία, φιλόξενος, φιλότεκνος; φρεναπάτης.—With regard to the manner of the composition, it is further to be noticed that, at least in the case of words compounded with numerals, the numeral undergoes no elision as it does in Attic, but remains intact, in accordance with the effort after a clearer isolation of the words—a tendency which has likewise diminished the number of cases of elision between separate words (§ 5, 1, cp. 3, 12). Thus τετραάρχης, -χεῖν Tisch. in Acts 13. 1 according to א*, L. 3. 1 א*C etc. (Tisch. on L. loc. cit.), τεσσερακονταετής A. 7. 23, 13. 18, ἑκατονταετής R. 4. 19 (which is an old form in dialects, but this is due to Ϝέτος Kühner i.³ ii. 332; Att. -τούτης from -τοέτης); in addition to these, ἀγαθοεργεῖν 1 Tim. 6. 18, ἀλλοτριοεπίσκοπος 1 P. 4. 15 KLP, but אB -τριεπ-; cp. LXX. γραμματοεισαγωγεύς (Deut. 31. 28), μακροημερεύειν, ἀρχιοινοχόος, later ὁμο-ούσιος and the like.

§ 29. PROPER NAMES.

In the proper names of the N.T. the only grammatical point which calls for attention is the class of (hypocoristic) abbreviated names. These abbreviated names have always existed in Greek, and present a great diversity in their formation, see Bechtel-Fick, Griech. Personennamen 26 ff.: -ις, -ιας, -είας, -έας (-ῆς), -υς, -ιλ(λ)ος, -υ(λ)λος, -ων, -ίων etc.; the Hellenistic language, on the other hand, as it meets us in the N.T., has hardly any other form of the abbreviated name than that in -ας, which is employed not only when the full name contains an α, as in Ἀντίπας Ap. 2. 13 from Ἀντίπατρος, but also when there is no such support for it, and the second half of a name containing two stems is completely set aside. These short names were in some cases given at birth, as when a Mantitheus called his son Mantias, a Niceratus Nicias, a Demoteles Demon, but in others the person originally had the full name, but was frequently called by the shorter name, as Menodorus the admiral of Sextus Pompeius is spoken of by the historians sometimes by his full name, sometimes as Menas (W.-Schm. § 16, 9).¹ An instance of this in the N.T. is Σιλουανός, as he is always called in St. Paul (also 1 P. 5. 12), and Σιλᾶς A. 15. 22 etc.: also no doubt Ἀπολλώνιος A. 18. 24 D and Ἀπολλῶς in St. Paul (Ἀπελλῆς א in Acts, see § 6, 2), Ἀμπλίατος R. 16. 8 with v.l. Ἀμπλίας; but Ἐπαφρᾶς Col. 1. 7, 4. 12 (of Colossae) Philem. 23 and Ἐπαφρόδιτος Ph. 2. 25, 4. 18 (of Philippi) cannot be one and the same person, although undoubtedly the one name is an abbreviation of the other. The remaining abbreviations in -ας, in many cases of which the original name is not distinctly recognisable, are: Ἀρτεμᾶς (Ἀρτεμίδωρος, Varro de lingua Lat. viii. 21), Ἑρμᾶς (Ἑρμόδωρος and the like), Ζηνᾶς (Ζηνόδωρος, see Bekk. Anecd. 857), Νυμφᾶς (Νυμφόδ.), Ὀλυμπᾶς (Ὀλυμπιόδωρος), Δημᾶς (Δημήτριος?), Στεφανᾶς (Στεφανηφόρος? or a development of Στέφανος, found in Attic Greek?),² Παρμενᾶς (Παρμένων),³ Πατρόβας (Πατρόβιος), Λουκᾶς (Λουκανός? Λουκίλιος?).⁴ In -ῆς there are Ἀπελλῆς R. 16. 10 (vide supra), and Ἑρμῆς ibid. 14 (which can hardly be merely identical with the name of the god, although at a later period this kind of appellation is also found);⁵ in -ῶς there is only Ἀπολλῶς, vide supra. The name Ἀνδρέας, which has early attestation, is of a genuine old Greek form.

---

¹ See also Crusius, N. Jahrb. für Philol. 1891, p. 385 ff.

² Bechtel-Fick, op. cit. 253 f., regard Στέφανος itself as an abbreviation of Φιλο-στέφανος or of Στεφανο-κλῆς.

³ Ibid. 205 (cp. Παρμενίδης, -ίσκος, -ίων, -μενις etc.).

⁴ Some ancient Latin MSS. translate the title κατὰ Λουκᾶν by *secundum Lucanum*. In Ἀνδρόνικον καὶ Ἰουνίαν R. 16. 7 is commonly found a man's name Ἰουνίας (= *Junianus*?); some of the ancient commentators (see Tisch.) took them to be a married couple like Aquila and Priscilla.

⁵ Ibid. 304 ff.

PART II.

SYNTAX.

§ 30. SUBJECT AND PREDICATE.

1. It has already been noticed (in § 2, 1) that it is in the syntax, *i.e.* in the method of employing and combining the several word-forms and 'form-words' current in the language, that the principal grammatical difference between the classical and the N.T. language undoubtedly lies, just as it is here too that there is the greatest difference between the individual writers of the N.T. It is also on the syntactical side that the language itself has shown the greatest development, and moreover it is here that the antithesis between the artificial writer and the plain narrator of facts or the letter-writer—as also that between the man who has received a pure Greek education and the man whose education has been wholly or preponderantly Hebrew—is most clearly marked. Hence the difference in culture between the individual N.T. writers must make itself felt in their syntax, from the author of the Apocalypse at one extreme to Paul, Luke, and the author of the Epistle to the Hebrews at the other.

2. The two principal kinds of words are the **noun** and the **verb**. The simplest sentence is formed by the combination of these two, where the noun (ὄνομα) represents the subject, *i.e.* the fundamental idea, and the verb (ῥῆμα) represents the predicate, *i.e.* some further statement concerning the subject. If however the predicate is complex, the noun must very soon be called into requisition for this office as well, and will serve sometimes as the principal part of the predicate, sometimes as the complement of the verb. In the former case, where one noun serves the purpose of specifying and defining another noun, the verb is in many cases a mere 'form-word' necessary for the statement of this relation, though like every verb it still presents the two inflections denoting tense and mood. It is therefore only natural that, at least in the case of the commonest tense, the present, and the commonest mood, the indicative, the language should omit the verbal 'form-word' 'to be' as readily intelligible. On the question of the omission or non-omission of the auxiliary verb different languages are divided. In

§ 30. 2-3.] SUBJECT AND PREDICATE. 73

Hebrew the omission is the rule, in Greek it is allowable from the earliest times and occurs also in the N.T., whereas modern Greek has given up this liberty and always inserts the auxiliary verb.

3. **Omission of the auxiliary verb.** By far the most frequent instance of omission, as in the classical language, is that of the commonest form of the pres. indic. of the auxiliary verb, namely the 3rd pers. sing. ἐστίν. Still this omission never grew into a fixed usage of the language, except in the case of a few stereotyped phrases. Such are: δῆλον ὅτι (class.) 1 C. 15. 27, (1 Tim. 6. 7 ??), also with reverse order of words ὅτι ..., δῆλον G. 3. 11 ; τί ἐμοὶ (ἡμῖν) καὶ σοί Mt. 8. 29, Mc. 1. 24, 5. 7, L. 4. 34, 8. 28, Jo. 2. 4 [1] (=Hebr. מַה־לִּי וָלָךְ Judges 11. 12 etc.; there are, however, similar classical phrases);[2] τί πρὸς σέ (ἡμᾶς) Mt. 27. 4, Jo. 21. 22 f., quid hoc ad te (similar classical phrases),[3] cp. τί γάρ μοι 1 C. 5. 12, and many other instances, infra § 50, 7 ; τί (μοι) τὸ ὄφελος 1 C. 15. 32, Ja. 2. 14, 16 (ἀλλὰ τί τούτων ὄφελος αὐτοῖς Demosth. 9. 69); ἔτι μικρόν, καὶ ... Jo. 14. 19, 16. 16 f., 19 (ἔτι μ. ὅσον ὅσον H. 10. 37 O.T., but in LXX. Is. 26. 20 without this ellipse); μακάριος ἀνὴρ ὅς - Ja. 1. 12, R. 4. 8 O.T. (Hebr. אַשְׁרֵי הָאִישׁ), so also μακάριοι οἱ πτωχοί etc. Mt. 5. 3 etc., in this exclamation where the 3rd pers. is used the auxiliary verb is never expressed (it is different with the 2nd pers., Mt. 5. 11, 16. 17, and in a statement of fact, 11. 6 [om. ἐστιν א ab]=L. 7. 23): cp. the classical μακάριός γ' ἀνὴρ ἔχων κ.τ.λ. Aristoph. Ran. 1482. The classes of sentence where this omission is particularly frequent are exclamations (A. 19. 28, 34 μεγάλη ἡ Ἄρτεμις Ἐφεσίων, R. 11. 33 ὡς ἀνεξερεύνητα τὰ κρίματα αὐτοῦ) and questions (L. 4. 36 τίς ὁ λόγος οὗτος ; A. 10. 21 τίς ἡ αἰτία δι' ἥν -; R. 3. 1 τί τὸ περισσὸν τοῦ Ἰουδαίου, ἢ τίς ἡ ὠφέλεια τῆς περιτομῆς ;): but it is also found not infrequently in statements of fact, Mc. 14. 36 πάντα δυνατά σοι, H. 9. 16 f. ὅπου διαθήκη, θάνατον ἀνάγκη φέρεσθαι τοῦ διαθεμένου· διαθήκη γὰρ ἐπὶ νεκροῖς βεβαία, 1 C. 10. 13 and 2 C. 1. 18 πιστὸς ὁ θεός, 1 Th. 5. 24 πιστὸς ὁ καλῶν ὑμᾶς (with ἐστίν in 2 Th. 3. 3, but the verb is wanting in FG al.), πιστὸς ὁ λόγος 1 Tim. 1. 15, 3. 1, 4. 9, 2 Tim. 2. 11, Tit. 3. 8. Another class of expression where (as in classical Greek) the omission is common consists of impersonal phrases ; ἀνάγκη H. 9. 16 (vide supra), 9. 23, R. 13. 5 ? (with ἐστί Mt. 18. 7 but om. BL), ὥρα R. 13. 11, ἐξόν A. 2. 29, 2 C. 12. 4, ἀδύνατον H. 6. 4, 18, 10. 4, 11. 6, εἰ δυνατόν (as we say 'if possible') Mt. 24. 24, Mc. 13. 22, R. 12. 18 (G. 4. 15 vide infra), but with ἐστίν Mt. 26. 39, Mc. 14. 35. Κεφάλαιον δὲ H. 8. 1 is classical. The verb may also be omitted even when it is not a

---

[1] Nonnus in his metrical paraphrase presents a very noteworthy various reading: τί ἐμοί, γύναι, ἠὲ σοὶ αὐτῇ ; = τί ἐμοὶ ἢ σοὶ γύναι ; ('What is this to me or to you?' cp. the following words οὔπω ἥκει ἡ ὥρα μου). Cp. τί δὲ σοὶ ταῦτα Aristoph. Lysistr. 514.

[2] Kühner, Gr. ii. 364 (Herodot. 5. 33 σοὶ δὲ καὶ τούτοισι τοῖς πρήγμασι τί ἐστι ; Demosth. 29. 36 τί τῷ νόμῳ καὶ τῇ βασάνῳ ;).

[3] Οὐδὲν πρὸς τὸν Διόνυσον ; Dem. 18. 21 οὐδέν ἐστι δήπου πρὸς ἐμέ.

mere copula: 1 C. 15. 40 καὶ σώματα ἐπουράνια (sc. ἐστίν 'there are') καὶ σ. ἐπίγεια. Other forms of εἰμί are omitted: εἰσίν with μακάριοι vide supra, R. 11. 16 εἰ δὲ ἡ ἀπαρχὴ ἁγία, καὶ τὸ φύραμα, καὶ εἰ ἡ ῥίζα ἁγία, καὶ οἱ κλάδοι, cp. R. 4. 14, 1 C. 16. 9, H. 2. 11 etc. Εἰμί, ἐσμέν, εἶ are not often omitted, and the omission is even more rare when ἐγώ, ἡμεῖς, or σύ are not inserted; Mc. 12. 26 = A. 7. 32 O.T. ἐγὼ ὁ θεὸς Ἀβραὰμ κ.τ.λ. (but LXX. has εἰμί here, though it is absent from the original Hebrew, and so Mt. 22. 32; also some MSS. in Mc. and Acts), Jo. 14. 11, 2 C. 10. 7; without a pronoun 2 C. 11. 6 εἰ δὲ καὶ ἰδιώτης τῷ λόγῳ (sc. εἰμί which D*E introduce, St. Paul has been speaking of himself just before in verse 5),[1] Ap. 15. 4 ὅτι μόνος ὅσιος (sc. εἶ), Ph. 3. 15. *Ἦν 3rd sing. is *always* omitted in the phrase ᾧ (ᾗ) ὄνομα L. 1. 26 f., 2. 25, 8. 41, 24. 13 (D ὀνόματι), 18 (ὀνόματι אB al.), A. 13. 6 (D is different), or οὗ τὸ ὄνομα Mc. 14. 32 (ᾧ C), or in the still more Hebraic (cp. 1 Kings 1. 1 etc.) καὶ τὸ ὄνομα αὐτῆς (αὐτοῦ) L. 1. 5, 27; parenthetically ὄνομα αὐτῷ (Demosth. 32. 11 Ἀριστοφῶν ὄνομα αὐτῷ) Jo. 1. 6 (with ἦν inserted א*D*), 3. 1 (א* ὀνόματι, as Luke has elsewhere in his Gospel and almost always in the Acts [class.], cp. §§ 33, 2; 38, 2; Xenophon Mem. 3, 11. 1 writes ᾗ ὄνομα ἦν); in these phrases it makes no difference whether ἦν is to be supplied (with persons) or ἐστίν (with place-names). Ἔσται (or ἐστί) is omitted in 1 P. 4. 17, 1 C. 15. 21, cp. 22. Ἧι only occasionally in St. Paul (2 C. 8. 11, 13). Εἴη is commonly omitted in formulas expressing a wish, such as ἵλεώς σοι (sc. ὁ θεὸς εἴη) Mt. 16. 22, εἰρήνη ὑμῖν etc., as in classical Greek (ἵλαος Soph. O.C. 1477; cp. LXX. 2 Kings 20. 20) and in Hebrew (שָׁלוֹם לְךָ); in doxologies such as εὐλογητὸς ὁ θεός (2 C. 1. 3 etc.) = Hebr. בָּרוּךְ אֱלֹהִים (Ps. 66. 20 etc.) we may supply either 'is' (cp. R. 1. 25 ὅς ἐστιν εὐλ. κ.τ.λ., 2 C. 11. 31 ὁ ὢν εὐλογ., 1 P. 4. 11 ᾧ ἐστιν [ἐστιν om. A] ἡ δόξα, Buttmann p. 120) or 'be' (Winer, who compares 1 Kings 10. 9 γένοιτο εὐλ., Job 1. 21 εἴη εὐλ.); the former, however, appears to be the sense in which the N.T. writers understood the phrase. Ἔστω is omitted in μηδὲν σοὶ καὶ τῷ δικαίῳ ἐκείνῳ Mt. 27. 19 (cp. for the formula what is said above), in χάρις τῷ θεῷ (class.) 2 C. 8. 16, 9. 15, (R. 6. 17); see further H. 13. 4, 5 τίμιος ὁ γάμος κ.τ.λ., R. 12. 19 ff., Col. 4. 6. On the omission of εἶναι and ὤν cp. §§ 34, 5; 73, 4 and 5; 74, 2. The present or imperf. (aor. and fut.) of εἶναι (γίνεσθαι, παρεῖναι, παραγίν.) may, after Hebrew precedent, be omitted after ἰδού = הִנֵּה, which can stand by itself for the verbal predicate, though it may also be introduced in addition to the predicate, Mt. 3. 17 (17. 5) καὶ ἰδοὺ φωνὴ (sc. ἐγένετο) ἐκ τῶν οὐρανῶν λέγουσα (but the same phrase occurs without ἰδού A. 10. 15), L. 5. 18 καὶ ἰδοὺ ἄνδρες φέροντες κ.τ.λ. (sc. ἦσαν, παρῆσαν as in 13. 1), cp. 5. 12, A. 13. 11 καὶ νῦν ἰδοὺ χεὶρ κυρίου ἐπὶ σέ, 8. 36. On the more extended use of the ellipse of the verb vide infra § 81.

---

[1] On R. 1. 15 οὕτως τὸ κατ' ἐμὲ πρόθυμος (so more correctly than -ον) sc. εἰμί (ὀφειλέτης εἰμί precedes), see § 42, 2.

4. **Absence of the subject.** On the absence of the subject, where it is not contained in the verb or in the context, the following remarks may be made for the N.T. usage. The so-called **impersonal verbs** expressing meteorological phenomena are almost entirely wanting. Βρέχει (the vulgar word for ὕει, which nowhere appears) is personal in Mt. 5. 45, sc. ὁ θεός (LXX. Gen. 2. 5, but ὁ θεὸς ὕει is also a classical phrase), impersonal in Ja. 5. 17, L. 17. 29 (Ap. 11. 6 ἵνα μὴ ὑετὸς βρέχῃ, in the Vulgate simply *pluat*) ; βροντᾷ,[1] ἀστράπτει etc. are nowhere found (ἡ ἀστραπὴ ἀστράπτουσα L. 17. 24; the verb is used = 'to shine' as in class. Greek ibid. 24. 4, cp. περιαστράπτειν A. 9. 3, 22. 6 'to shine round about'). Equally uncommon in the N.T. are the classical expressions in which the agent is readily supplied from the verb in the person to whom some particular task belongs (*e.g.* ἐκήρυξε sc. ὁ κῆρυξ): σαλπίσει 1 C. 15. 52 'the trumpet shall sound' (Winer compares the German 'es läutet'; in any case ὁ σαλπιγκτής cannot be understood, the most that can be supplied is ἡ.σάλπιγξ). Peculiar phrases are τρίτην ταύτην ἡμέραν ἄγει ('it is,' as ἄγω ἡμέραν is used) L. 24. 21, and ἀπέχει 'it is enough' Mc. 14. 41 (Anacreontea 28. 31 ; but D has ἀπ. τὸ τέλος, the matter has received its completion). Somewhat more frequent is the impersonal passive, like Latin *itur* 'one goes,' but this usage was never developed to any great extent in Greek : Mt. 7. 2 ἐν ᾧ μέτρῳ μετρεῖτε μετρηθήσεται ὑμῖν (= Mc. 4. 24, L. 6. 38), L. 6. 38 δίδοτε καὶ δοθήσεται ὑμῖν (cp. Mt. 7. 7, Mc. 4. 25), where the writer passes at once to the 3rd pers. plur. act. with equivalent meaning μέτρον ... δώσουσιν : 1 P. 4. 6 νεκροῖς εὐηγγελίσθη, R. 10. 10, 1 C. 15. 42 f. σπείρεται ἐν φθορᾷ, ἐγείρεται ἐν ἀφθαρσίᾳ κ.τ.λ., Herm. Mand. iii. 3 ἐπιστεύθη τῷ λόγῳ μου. But ἐρρέθη ὅτι Mt. 5. 21 does not come under this head, since the question 'What was said ?' finds its answer in the ὅτι clause ; in the same way πρέπει, πρέπον ἐστί, δεῖ, ἔξεστι, ἐξόν (ἐστι), ἐγένετο, ἀνέβη ἐπὶ τὴν καρδίαν αὐτοῦ (A. 7. 23)[2] followed by an infinitive are not instances of the loss of the subject. The use of the 3rd pers. plur. act. without a subject is occasioned by the indefiniteness of the agent, but the subject may also, if one likes, be denoted by οἱ ἄνθρωποι, as in L. 6. 31 καθὼς θέλετε ἵνα ποιῶσιν ὑμῖν οἱ ἄνθρ. = 'that *one* should do unto you.' The instances of omission in this case are not very many : Mt. 7. 16 συλλέγουσιν, Mc. 10. 13 προσέφερον, L. 17. 23 ἐροῦσιν, 12. 20, Jo. 15. 6, 20. 2, A. 3. 2, Ap. 12. 6 (1 C. 10. 20).—In the formulas of citation such as λέγει 2 C. 6. 2, G. 3. 16 etc., φησίν 1 C. 6. 16, H. 8. 5, εἴρηκε H. 4. 4, ὁ θεός is to be understood ('*He* says'); in 2 C. 10. 10 φησίν (אDE etc., ? 'one says') appears to be a wrong reading for φασίν (B), unless perhaps a τις has dropped out (but cp. Clem. Hom. xi. 9 ad init.).

---

[1] Βροντὴ γέγονεν take its place in Jo. 12. 29.
[2] Used impersonally in Herm. Mand. iv. 1, μὴ ἀναβαινέτω σου ἐπὶ τὴν καρδίαν περὶ γυναικὸς ἀλλοτρίας (Hebr. עַל־לֵב עָלָה).

§ 31. AGREEMENT.

1. The arrangement (σύνταξις) of the different parts of the sentence, primarily of subject and predicate, involves a mutual assimilation, inasmuch as the individual nouns and verbs are not represented by a single abstract radical form, but only appear in certain definite and distinctive forms, and these forms cannot differ from each other in different parts of the sentence, where they refer to the same thing or person. In addition to its application in the case of subject and predicate, this law of **agreement** holds good also for nouns which are bound up together into a smaller whole within the sentence, one noun more nearly defining the other (the attribute, apposition). The individual forms [or inflections] to which nouns and verbs are subject express the following ideas: (*a*) one of the three genders, since there are nouns which possess different forms for these genders (adjectives), or which at least draw a distinction between the masculine and feminine genders (designations of persons such as βασιλεύς – βασίλισσα); (*b*) one of the two numbers (the dual no longer existing in the N.T.)—this applies equally to nouns and verbs; (*c*) one of the five cases (nouns); (*d*) one of the three persons in the case of the verb, while the noun is for the 1st and 2nd persons represented by a certain class of words—the pronouns. Any combination of words where the agreement in any of these respects is not adhered to is strictly proscribed as a solecism, except in some definite cases where the language admits of the violation of the law of agreement.

2. **Want of agreement in gender.**—Instances of an adjectival predicate in neuter sing. agreeing with a feminine subject are: Mt. 6. 34 ἀρκετὸν τῇ ἡμέρᾳ ἡ κακία αὐτῆς, 2 C. 2. 6 ἱκανὸν τῷ τοιούτῳ ἡ ἐπιτιμία αὕτη, A. 12. 3 D ἰδὼν ὅτι **ἀρεστόν** ἐστιν τοῖς Ἰουδαίοις ἡ ἐπιχείρησις αὐτοῦ. The third instance is, however, uncertain, since the text in D may be due to corrupt conflation of different readings. In the other two instances it appears better to regard ἀρκετόν and ἱκανόν as imitations of the Latin *satis* (cp. L. 22. 38 ἰδοὺ μάχαιραι ὧδε δύο – ἱκανόν ἐστιν, Herm. Vis. iii. 9. 3 τὸ ἀρκετὸν τῆς τροφῆς *satis cibi*; on the other hand the predicate is ἀρκετός in 1 P. 4. 3) than to compare the classical usage in general propositions such as οὐκ ἀγαθὸν πολυκοιρανίη; in instances like the last the word 'thing' must be supplied, and a comparison is drawn between the *general* idea contained in the subject and other things of a different character. Καλὸν τὸ ἅλας Mc. 9. 50, L. 14. 34 'salt is a good thing' would also in classical Greek be expressed by something like χρήσιμον οἱ ἅλες; but there is an absence in the N.T. of analogous instances of this use with a masculine or feminine subject, just as the fuller classical forms of this neuter predicate—μάταιόν τι, **χρῆμα** σοφόν—are also wanting. Still we find τι 'something (special),' οὐδέν 'nothing' *i.e.* 'nothing worth' used as neuter predicates to a masc. or fem. subject: G. 6. 3 εἰ δοκεῖ τις εἶναί τι μηδὲν ὤν (as in

class. Greek; beside this we have εἶναί τις A. 5. 36, cp. 8. 9 = 'a great man'). Further instances are τί ὁ Πέτρος ἐγένετο (τί εἴη ταῦτα), see § 50, 7; 1 C. 11. 5 (the woman who is unveiled) ἕν ἐστι καὶ τὸ αὐτὸ τῇ ἐξυρημένῃ, Mt. 6. 25 = L. 12. 23 ἡ ψυχὴ πλεῖόν ἐστι τῆς τροφῆς: in general assertions of this kind μία καὶ ἡ αὐτή, πλείων would be impossible. But in particular statements the pronoun is brought into agreement with the noun: R. 11. 5 τίς ἡ πρόσληψις εἰ μή— (German would use the neuter 'was'), E. 1. 18 τίς ἐστιν ἡ ἐλπὶς τῆς κλήσεως αὐτοῦ, 1 C. 3. 17 (ὁ ναὸς τοῦ θεοῦ) οἵτινές ἐστε ὑμεῖς (but in 1 C. 6. 11 ταῦτά [sc. κλέπται κ.τ.λ.] τινες ἦτε = τοιοῦτοι, which would not have been sufficiently clear, while οὗτοι would have been impossible; Herm. Sim. ix. 5. 3 τί ἐστιν [is the meaning of] ἡ οἰκοδομή). If the pronoun is the subject, in this case also there is agreement, which is contrary to German usage: Mt. 22. 38 αὕτη ἐστὶν ἡ μεγάλη ἐντολή, Ph. 1. 28 ἥτις (i.e. resistance, τὸ ἀντικεῖσθαι) ἐστὶν αὐτοῖς ἔνδειξις ἀπωλείας, cp. E. 3. 13, A. 16. 12 Φιλίππους ἥτις ἐστὶ πόλις. But in assimilation of this sort Latin goes a step further than Greek: see 1 P. 2. 19 f. τοῦτο χάρις, εἰ - ὑποφέρει τις—ἀλλ' εἰ - ὑπομενεῖτε, τοῦτο χάρις παρὰ θεῷ, where the Greek regards the two ideas of 'grace' and 'endurance' as too distinct to admit of being merged into one, while the Latin translation has **haec** *est gratia* (Buttmann, p. 112). In interpretations by means of a relative sentence (as in 1 C. 3. 17 οἵτινες quoted above) the prevalent form elsewhere for the relative is the neut. sing. (which in that passage would be intolerable: ὅ ἐστιν ὑμεῖς), even though neither the explanatory word nor the word explained has this gender: Mt. 27. 33 τόπον λεγόμενον Γολγ., ὅ (ὅς A al.) ἐστιν κρανίου τόπος (the repetition of λεγόμενος either before or after τόπος is rightly omitted by א*D), Mc. 15. 22 Γολγ. τόπον, ὅ ἐστιν μεθερμηνευόμενον κρ. τ., 3. 17 Βοανηργές, ὅ ἐστιν υἱοὶ βροντῆς, Jo. 1. 42[1] etc.; Mc. 12. 42 λεπτὰ δύο, ὅ ἐστιν κοδράντης; Col. 3. 14 τὴν ἀγάπην, ὅ (v.l. ὅς, ἥτις) ἐστιν σύνδεσμος τῆς τελειότητος[2] (Barn. 15. 8 ἀρχήν ..., ὅ ἐστιν ἄλλου κόσμου **ἀρχήν**); cp. Mc. 15. 16 τῆς αὐλῆς, ὅ ἐστιν πραιτώριον; E. 6. 17 τὴν μάχαιραν -, ὅ ἐστιν ῥῆμα θεοῦ; in the Apocalypse alone is there assimilation of the relative to the subject or predic.: 4. 5 λαμπάδες, ἅ (v.l. αἵ) εἰσιν τὰ πνεύματα 5. 6, 8. This phrase ὅ ἐστι has become as much a stereotyped formula as the equivalent τοῦτ' ἔστι (τουτέστι) in Mt. 27. 46 ἠλί – τοῦτ' ἔστι Θεέ μου κ.τ.λ., H. 2. 14 τὸν τὸ κράτος ἔχοντα τοῦ θανάτου, τουτέστι τὸν διάβολον, 7. 5, 9. 11 etc. But all these instances represent not so much a classical as a Hellenistic usage. (Τί ἐστι ταῦτα is common to N.T. and classical Greek § 50, 7). On πρώτη πάντων Mc. 12. 28 see § 36, 12; on want of agreement in the constructio ad sensum vide infra 4; on the construction

---

[1] Jo. 19. 17 τὸν λεγόμενον Κρανίου τόπον, ὅ (al. ὅς) λέγεται Ἑβραϊστὶ Γολγοθᾶ is badly corrupted; we should read with LX, vulg. al. Κρ. τ., Ἑβρ. δὲ Γ.

[2] Since this is a case not of interpretation but description, ὅς would be more correct, cp. Col. 3. 5 τὴν πλεονεξίαν, ἥτις ἐστὶν εἰδωλολατρία, where ὅ ἐστι 'that is to say' would be more in place than in verse 14, cp. the v.l. in E. 5. 5. The reading ὅ (BDEFG) for ὅς in Col. 2. 10 is entirely wrong; in 2. 17 ὅ (BFG) for ἅ is harsh.

where the subject of the sentence is composed of several words, or in the case of an attribute to several nouns vide infra 5.

3. Want of agreement in number; neuter plurals with singular verb. Probably there is no more striking peculiarity in the whole of Greek syntax than the rule that where the subject is a neuter plural the verb still remains in the singular. This rule, which in Attic is never broken, is however not without exceptions in Homer and in the Hellenistic language, and modern Greek has gone back completely and exclusively to the use of the plural verb in this instance as in others. In the N.T. (as in the LXX.) there is great fluctuation, and very often this fluctuation extends to the readings of the MSS. in individual passages: while in the Shepherd of Hermas the plural is found in the majority of cases. Of neuter words which denote persons: τέκνα is used with plural verb in Mt. 10. 21 (sing. BΔ) = Mc. 13. 12 (sing. B), but with sing. verb in 1 Jo. 3. 10, R. 9. 8: ἔθνη with plur. verb Mt. 6. 32 (sing. EG al.), 12. 21 O.T., 25. 32 (sing. AE al.), L. 12. 30 (sing. AD al.), Acts 4. 25 O.T., 11. 1 (sing. D*), 13. 48, R. 2. 14 (sing. D^{c}E), 15. 27, 1 C. 10. 20 ? (om. τὰ ἔθνη BDEF al., sing. KL), G. 3. 8 O.T., 2 Tim. 4. 17 (sing. KL), Ap. 11. 18 (sing. א*), 15. 4, 18. 3, 23, 21. 24, Clem. Cor. i. 59. 4 (with sing. verb all MSS. in R. 9. 30, E. 4. 17); but with δαιμόνια the sing. verb preponderates, L. 4. 41 (plur. אC), 8. 2, 30 (plur. CF, also D with another reading, cp. 31 f.), 35 (plur. א^c), 38 (in verse 33 εἰσῆλθον has overwhelming evidence, -εν SU), 10. 17: the plur. is found in Ja. 2. 19; πνεύματα uses both constructions, a plur. verb in Mc. 1. 27, 3. 11 (v.l. sing.), 5. 13 (sing. B), A. 8. 7 ? Ap. 4. 5 ? 16. 14 (v.l. with sing. partially introduced), a sing. verb in L. 8. 2 κατοικεῖ, 10. 20 (v.l. δαιμόνια), 1 C. 14. 32 (v.l. πνεῦμα). Other neuter words besides these appear with plural verb: Mt. 6. 28 τὰ κρίνα πῶς αὐξάνουσιν (but with sing. verb in the corresponding words in L. 12. 37), Jo. 19. 31 has first ἵνα μὴ μείνῃ τὰ σώματα, followed by ἵνα κατεαγῶσιν αὐτῶν τὰ σκέλη, Jo. 10. 8 οὐκ ἤκουσαν (-σεν L) αὐτῶν τὰ πρόβατα. In the verses preceding the last passage quoted a sing. verb is used with πρόβατα, ibid. 3 ἀκούει, 4 ἀκολουθεῖ, with the additional words ὅτι οἴδασιν τὴν φωνὴν αὐτοῦ (because οἶδε would have been ambiguous) and further on another plural in verse 5; in the subsequent verses, 10 has ἔχωσι where πρόβατα must be regarded as the subject, in 12 ἐστιν is read by אABLX, εἰσιν by DΓ al., and so on with constant interchange up till 16 (in 27 and the following verse there are conflicting readings). On the whole, the singular verb certainly is more frequently used with words which have not a personal meaning (the singular is not excluded even by the insertion of a numeral, ἐὰν γένηται – ἑκατὸν πρόβατα Mt. 18. 12), and is uniformly employed with abstract words (exceptions are τὰ ῥήματα ταῦτα with ἐφάνησαν L. 24. 11, and perhaps ἔργα with δύνανται [v.l. -αται] 1 Tim. 5. 25) and with pronouns such as ταῦτα and ἅ (Ap. 1. 19 ἅ εἰσιν καὶ ἅ μέλλει γενέσθαι; Clem. Cor. i. 42. 2 ἐγένοντο ἀμφότερα, cp. 27. 6 πάντα). In 1 C. 10. 11 there are two readings: ταῦτα δὲ τυπικῶς συνέβαινεν and – τύποι συνέβαινον, cp. verse 6 ταῦτα δὲ τύποι ἡμῶν

§ 31. 3-5.]   AGREEMENT.   79

ἐγενήθησαν, the verb taking its number from the noun which forms the predicate, as it does also in classical Greek as well as in Latin (Kühner, Gr. ii.² 67).[1]

4. The so-called **constructio ad sensum** is very widespread in Greek from early times, though without being subject to any rules; the same construction appears in the N.T. It affects both number and gender. The instances mainly consist of the collective words which embrace in a singular noun the idea of a plurality of persons: masculine words like ὄχλος, λαός, feminines like στρατιά, οἰκία, neuters like πλῆθος, σπέρμα (with plur. verb in Herm. Vis. ii. 2. 2). Instances of this construction, where a masculine plural conforming to the sense only appears in a clause appended to the main clause, do not give serious offence even in English: *e.g.* 1 C. 16. 15 οἴδατε τὴν οἰκίαν Στεφανᾶ, ὅτι – ἔταξαν ἑαυτούς (ἔταξεν ἑαυτήν is unnatural), Jo. 6. 2 ἠκολούθει ὄχλος πολύς, ὅτι ἐθεώρουν. The following are rather harsher constructions: L. 2. 13 πλῆθος στρατιᾶς οὐρανίου (= ἀγγέλων), αἰνούντων τὸν θεὸν καὶ λεγόντων, A. 21. 35 ἠκολούθει τὸ πλῆθος τοῦ λαοῦ, κράζοντες Αἶρε αὐτόν (κρᾶζον DHLP) cp. 3. 11. And this want of agreement in number is not excluded even where the singular and plural words are directly connected: A. 6. 11 πολύς τε ὄχλος τῶν ἱερέων ὑπήκουον (-εν AE) τῇ πίστει, 25. 24 ἅπαν τὸ πλῆθος τῶν Ἰουδαίων ἐνέτυχόν (BH -έν) μοι –, βοῶντες κ.τ.λ., Mt. 21. 8 ὁ πλεῖστος ὄχλος ἔστρωσαν, Jo. 7. 49 ὁ ὄχλος οὗτος ὁ μὴ γινώσκων τὸν νόμον ἐπάρατοί εἰσιν. The following also are closely allied to ὄχλος etc.: τὰ ἔθνη 'the heathen,' E. 4. 17 f. τὰ ἔθνη περιπατεῖ –, ἐσκοτωμένοι κ.τ.λ. (1 C. 12. 2 is not an instance of this), αἱ ἐκκλησίαι G. 1. 22 f. (which is followed by μόνον δὲ ἀκούοντες ἦσαν), and names of places: L. 10. 13 Τύρῳ καὶ Σιδῶνι – καθήμενοι, though here the other reading -ναι (DEG al.), since the towns are regarded as wholes (as in Mt. 11. 21 ff.), appears preferable. Cp. § 48, 5 (use of the personal pron. αὐτοῦ and the relative).

5. If the subject consists of **several coordinate words connected by καί**, the common predicate must, according to German feeling, stand in the plural in conformity with the sense, and of course if one of the subject words is ἐγώ, this plural predicate must be the plural of the 1st person: L. 2. 48 ὁ πατήρ σου κἀγὼ ὀδυνώμενοι ἐζητοῦμέν σε, Jo. 10. 30, 1 C. 9. 6. An additional modifying word, referring to the subject, as ὀδυνώμενοι in the passage quoted, will, if declinable, likewise fall into the plural, and into the masculine plural in a case where the subject consists of a combination of masc. and fem. words (Joseph and Mary in that passage). This is always the case if the predicate follows the subject; on the other hand, if it precedes the subject, it is rather the custom for the verb to stand in the singular, and to correspond in form to the subject immediately following it: again, if the verb is interposed between the different subjects, it is made to correspond to the subject which has preceded it, and can only take the number of that subject. Instances of the singular

---

[1] On the stereotyped use of the sing. ἰδού, ἴδε, ἄγε see § 33, 2 note.

verb occupying the first place : A. 11. 24 σωθήσῃ σὺ καὶ ὁ οἶκός σου, where the first word is the main subject 'thou together with thy whole house,' similarly Jo. 2. 2 ἐκλήθη δὲ καὶ Ἰησοῦς καὶ οἱ μαθηταὶ αὐτοῦ, and, so far as the participle at the head of the sentence is concerned, A. 5. 29 ἀποκριθεὶς δὲ Πέτρος καὶ οἱ ἀπόστολοι εἶπαν (cp. verse 21); but the singular verb is also used where the subjects are placed on an equality: Jo. 18. 25 ἠκολούθει δὲ τῷ 'Ι. Σίμων Πέτρος καὶ ἄλλος μαθητής (cp. 20. 3, A. 26. 30; so without exception where the subject words are not persons, as in Mt. 5. 18 ὁ οὐρανὸς καὶ ἡ γῆ); L. 2. 33 ἦν δὲ ὁ πατὴρ αὐτοῦ καὶ ἡ μήτηρ θαυμάζοντες, Mt. 17. 3 ὤφθη (אBD : al. -ησαν) – Μωϋσῆς καὶ Ἠλίας συλλαλοῦντες. From the last two instances it follows that where the predicate is divided, that part of it which precedes the subject is in the singular, the part which follows it is in the plural (so in the passage A. 5. 29 quoted above). In the following instances there is a special reason for the plural verb : Mc. 10. 35 προσπορεύονται αὐτῷ Ἰάκωβος καὶ Ἰωάνης οἱ υἱοὶ Ζεβεδαίου (the pair of brothers who from the first were thought of together), Jo. 21. 2 ἦσαν ὁμοῦ Σίμων Πέτρος καὶ κ.τ.λ., L. 23. 12 ἐγένοντο φίλοι ὅ τε Ἡρῴδης καὶ ὁ Πιλᾶτος, A. 5. 24 ὡς δὲ ἤκουσαν – ὅ τε στρατηγὸς – καὶ οἱ ἀρχιερεῖς (the plural has already been used before of the same persons in verse 21; cp. 1. 13, 4. 27). Accordingly in default of any reason of this kind, where the readings differ, the singular appears to deserve the preference, as in L. 8. 19, A. 17. 14; we even have ἀκούσας δὲ Βαρνάβας καὶ Παῦλος the reading of D in Acts 14. 14, cp. 13. 46 D. Instances of interposition of the predicate are L. 8. 22 αὐτὸς ἀνέβη εἰς πλοῖον καὶ οἱ μαθ. αὐτοῦ, Jo. 4. 36 etc.—For adjectives and participles qualifying several words cp. L. 10. 1 εἰς πᾶσαν πόλιν καὶ τόπον, 1 Th. 5. 23, on the other hand δῶρα καὶ θυσίαι μὴ δυνάμεναι H. 9. 9 (ibid. 3. 6 βεβαίαν is an interpolation from verse 14).—The singular verb is regularly used, if the two subjects instead of being connected by καὶ are separated by ἤ: Mt. 5. 18 ἰῶτα ἓν ἢ μία κεραία οὐ μὴ παρέλθῃ, 12. 25, 18. 8, E. 5. 5 (especially if the verb precedes as in 1 C. 14. 24); G. 1. 8 ἐὰν ἡμεῖς ἢ ἄγγελος ἐξ οὐρανοῦ εὐαγγελίζηται (it would be impossible to include the two subjects in -ζώμεθα). An exception is Ja. 2. 15 ἐὰν ἀδελφὸς ἢ ἀδελφὴ γυμνοὶ ὑπάρχωσιν (occasioned by the adjective, the singular of which, γυμνός or γυμνή, would have been harsh).

6. Solecisms (in the Apocalypse). In distinction from all other New Testament writings, and in particular from those of the Apostle St. John, the Apocalypse exhibits a multitude of the most remarkable solecisms, which depend in the main upon the neglect of the laws of agreement. Thus we have in 1. 5 ἀπὸ Ἰησοῦ Χρ., ὁ **μάρτυς** ὁ **πιστός**, ὁ πρωτότοκος τῶν νεκρῶν καὶ ὁ **ἄρχων** τῶν βασιλέων τῆς γῆς, τῷ ἀγαπῶντι ἡμᾶς κ.τ.λ. (the datives on account of αὐτῷ in verse 6 according to Winer), 11. 4 οὗτοί εἰσιν αἱ δύο ἐλαῖαι καὶ αἱ δύο λυχνίαι αἱ ἐνώπιον τοῦ κυρίου τῆς γῆς ἑστῶτες (א*ABC ; ἑστῶσαι א^{cc}P), 12. 5 καὶ ἔτεκεν **υἱὸν ἄρσεν** (AP; ἄρρενα אB, ἄρσενα P), ὃς μέλλει κ.τ.λ. (the correction -ενα is no improvement; a better alteration would be to strike out υἱόν), 14. 19 ἔβαλεν εἰς τὴν ληνὸν τοῦ θυμοῦ τοῦ θεοῦ **τὸν μέγαν** (τὴν

§ 31. 6.] AGREEMENT. 81

μεγάλην א). Cp. 2. 20 (nom. in apposition with acc.), 3. 12 (nom. for gen.), 6. 1 (the same, as a v.l.), 7. 4 (nom. for acc.), 8. 9 (for gen.), 9. 14 (for dat.), 14. 12 (for gen., which א reads), 20. 2 (for acc.): 7. 9 (ὄχλος ... ἑστῶτες ... περιβεβλημένους; the acc. is dependent on εἶδον which stands at the beginning of the verse, the nom. on καὶ ἰδού which follows εἶδον, Winer), 5. 11f. (λέγοντες following φωνὴν ἀγγέλων and ἦν ὁ ἀριθμὸς αὐτῶν μυριάδες κ.τ.λ.; similar anacolutha with λέγων or -οντες in 4. 1, 11. 15, 14. 7: and with v.l. 11. 1, 19. 6), 21. 9 with v.l. It has even been fixed as a rule for this writer that an appositional phrase following a noun in any case stands in the nominative, although scribes have shown a strong inclination to correct these solecisms.[1] The isolated cases of anacoluthon of this kind which appear in other writings of the N.T. should be regarded either as excusable or as due to a corrupt text. Jo. 1. 14 ὁ λόγος σὰρξ ἐγένετο – καὶ ἐθεασάμεθα τὴν δόξαν αὐτοῦ – **πλήρης** (-ρη D) χάριτος καὶ ἀληθείας. In this passage the word in question is one which to a remarkably great extent, both in the N.T. and also in papyrus documents, appears as indeclinable: thus A. 6. 5 ἄνδρα πλήρης (-ρη BC[2]) πίστεως, 3 πλήρεις (-ρης AEHP) πνεύματος, 19. 28 γενόμενοι πλήρεις (-ρης AEL) θυμοῦ, Mc. 8. 19 κοφίνους πλήρεις (-ρης AFGM) κλασμάτων, 2 Jo. 8 μισθὸν πλήρη (-ρης L); the only passages where it is declined in all MSS. (no genitive following it) are Mt. 14. 20, 15. 37 (-εις), Mc. 4. 28 a v.l. (-ρη), 6. 43 a v.l. (-ρεις); cp. Papyr. Berol. no. 13. 8 ἅπερ ἀπέσχαμεν πλήρης, 81. 27 ἃς παραδώσω πλήρης, 270. 9, 373. 13, 21; Grenfell-Hunt, Pap. ii., p. 107 διὰ τὸ πλήρη[s a]ὐτὸν ἀπεσχηκέναι, 118 (perhaps also 117, where πλήρη is given at the end of a line).[2]—In Philipp. 2. 1 εἴ τις παράκλησις –, εἴ τι παραμύθιον –, εἴ τις κοινωνία –, εἴ τις σπλάγχνα καὶ οἰκτιρμοί, εἴ τι ('if it avails ought,' cp. § 31, 2) ought to be, as it seems, written throughout.—Ja. 3. 8 τὴν γλῶσσαν οὐδεὶς δύναται δαμάσαι, ἀκατάσχετον κακόν, **μεστὴ** ἰοῦ (Tisch. puts a colon after δαμ., making the following clause independent, sc. ἐστίν).—L. 24. 47 κηρυχθῆναι μετάνοιαν – ἀρξάμενοι (-ένων D correctly, -ενον AC³FH al.) and A. 10. 37 οἴδατε τὸ γενόμενον ῥῆμα καθ' ὅλης τῆς Ἰουδαίας, ἀρξάμενος ἀπὸ τῆς Γαλιλ. (ἀρξ. γὰρ AD, which is no improvement; -ενον correctly LP; but the whole clause ἀρξ. ἀ. τ. Γ. is perhaps taken from L. 23. 5). For other instances cp. § 81.

[1] Nestle, Philol. Sacra 7, Einführung in das Griech. N.T. 90 f. Akin to this is what may be called the indeclinable use of λέγων or λέγοντες in the LXX. = לֵאמֹר : Gen. 15. 1, 22. 30, 38. 13, 45. 16 etc., Winer. On the practice of many translators of putting words in apposition with any of the oblique cases in the nominative, see Nestle, Philol. Sacra 7. (Nestle also conjectures in Ap. 1. 4 πνευμάτων τὰ ἐνώπιον τοῦ θρόνου in place of the readings τῶν, ἅ, ἅ ἐστιν or εἰσιν, just as in 5. 13 א alone has preserved the true reading τὸ instead of ὃ or ὅ ἐστιν. In 2. 13 he reads ἐν ταῖς ἡμέραις Ἀντίπα ὁ μάρτυς μου ... ὅς.)

[2] "Πλήρης is also used indeclinably in the LXX., e.g. Num. 7. 13 F, 19 א, 20 BN*, Job 21. 24 all MSS., Sir. 19. 23 B*. Cp. the phrase 'eine Arbeit voller Fehler.'" (E. Nestle.)

SYNTAX OF THE NOUN.

§ 32. GENDER AND NUMBER.

1. The **neuter** of the adjective or participle is occasionally used with reference to persons, not only in phrases like τὸ γεννώμενον L. 1. 35 'that which is to be born,' cp. τὸ τέκνον, but also as in Jo. 17. 2 – πάσης σαρκός, ἵνα πᾶν ὃ δέδωκας αὐτῷ, δώσει αὐτοῖς, where men are first comprised under the collective name σάρξ, then under the neuter πᾶν, and finally (in αὐτοῖς) the usual mode of designation appears. Cp. Jo. 6. 37 (a similar instance), 1 Jo. 5. 4 (πᾶν τό; πᾶς ὁ has been previously used in verse 1); further H. 7. 7 τὸ ἔλαττον ὑπὸ τοῦ κρείττονος εὐλογεῖται, for ὁ ἐλάττων or οἱ ἐλάττονες, in order to represent the thought in a more abstract and so in a more general form. A similar collective use of the neut. sing. appears in classical Greek (Kühner ii.² 13). Elsewhere the neut. plur. is used: 1 C. 1. 27 f. τὰ μωρὰ τοῦ κόσμου – τὰ ἀσθενῆ τ. κ. – τὰ ἰσχυρά, where the sing. would have been wrong because of the idea of unity which it would imply—since the μωροί etc. do not form a definite section—and moreover with the masculine the emphasis would not have lain so strongly upon the abstract quality of foolishness etc. Cp. further G. 3. 22 τὰ πάντα, which is not so strong as τοὺς πάντας, which might also have stood, πάντα Jo. 12. 32 ℵ*D. (In classical Greek τὰ φεύγοντα Xenoph. Anab. 7, 3. 11 ap. Winer; πάντα τὰ συμβεβιασμένα Dem. 8. 41.)

2. The **feminine** appears to stand in place of the neuter, in consequence of a literal rendering from the Hebrew, in the O.T. quotation Mt. 21. 42 = Mc. 12. 11 παρὰ κυρίου ἐγένετο αὕτη καί ἐστιν θαυμαστή, from Ps. 118. 23 = Hebr. זאת 'this.'

3. The so-called **collective** use of the **masc. sing.** (on the neuter sing. vide supra 1) is found in R. 3. 1 τί τὸ περισσὸν τοῦ Ἰουδαίου; i.e. 'What advantage has the Jew as Jew?' (which every individual Jew has *ipso facto*); cp. 2. 17-29, where the individual has already been selected as the representative of the community. We have just the same use with names of nations and rank, 'the soldier,' 'the Jew'; Latin *miles, Romanus* etc.; in classical Greek it is less common (Thucyd. 6. 78 τὸν Συρακόσιον, τῷ Ἀθηναίῳ). Other instances are Mt. 12. 35 ὁ ἀγαθὸς ἄνθρωπος, R. 13. 8 τὸ ἀγαθὸν ἔργον, 1 P. 4. 18 ὁ δίκαιος – ὁ ἀσεβής, R. 14. 1 τὸν ἀσθενοῦντα. But in Ja. 2. 6 τὸν πτωχόν refers to the example of verse 2: also in 5. 6 a single instance is thought of in τὸν δίκαιον, while 1 C. 6. 5 διακρῖναι ἀνὰ μέσον τοῦ ἀδελφοῦ αὐτοῦ is an incorrect expression, which is easily intelligible (since ἀνὰ μέσον of course presupposes more persons than one), for τοῦ ἀδ. α. καὶ τοῦ ἑτέρου ἀδελφοῦ (on account of verse 1 τολμᾷ τις ... κρίνεσθαι, where the language refers primarily to the plaintiff). Cp. lxx. Gen. 23. 15, Winer § 27, 1.

§ 32. 4–5.] GENDER AND NUMBER. 83

4. Of another character is the use of the sing. of objects, which belong *individually* to several persons, where several persons are spoken of, as we also say 'they shook their heads' [die Köpfe] or 'they shook their head' [den Kopf], *i.e.* everyone his own head, where the insertion of 'everyone' would be quite superfluous. In Greek, including N.T. Greek, the plural is usual in such cases; but deviations from this are permitted in classical as in N.T. Greek: A. 25. 24 ἵνα ξυρήσωνται τὴν κεφαλήν (Vulg. *capita*), L. 1. 66 ἔθεντο πάντες ἐν τῇ καρδίᾳ (DL ταῖς καρδίαις) αὐτῶν, Mc. 8. 17 πεπωρωμένην ἔχετε τὴν καρδίαν ὑμῶν, E. 6. 14 περιζωσάμενοι τὴν ὀσφὺν ὑμῶν, Ap. 6. 11 ἐδόθη αὐτοῖς στολὴ λευκή (but ἐσθής in L. 24. 4 is collective 'raiment,' as is usual with this word [ἐσθήσεσιν ACL al.]). The sing. is always used in the Hebraic periphrastic expressions ἀπὸ προσώπου τῶν πατέρων A. 7. 45, κατὰ πρόσωπον πάντων L. 2. 31, διὰ στόματος πάντων A. 3. 18 (21); also διὰ χειρὸς is used with a plural word as in A. 2. 23, but here we have also the conceivable use of διὰ τῶν χειρῶν with a singular; ἐκ τῆς χ. αὐτῶν Jo. 10. 39.

5. The **plural** is used with reference to a **single person** by a generalising mode of expression in Mt. 2. 20 τεθνήκασιν οἱ ζητοῦντες τὴν ψυχὴν τοῦ παιδίου, namely Herod (verse 19); the plural implies the thought, there is nothing more to fear, since with Herod's death all are dead who etc. More peculiar is the use of the plural in the case of a certain group of substantives. This is partly due to the influence of Hebrew; thus αἰῶνες is used in H. 1. 2, 11. 3, 1 Tim. 1. 17 (?) for 'the world,' in L. 1. 33 and often for 'eternity' (esp. in the phrase εἰς τοὺς αἰῶνας τῶν αἰώνων G. 1. 5 etc.) = עוֹלָמִים: οὐρανοί = שָׁמַיִם, but in most writers this plural is only used of heaven in the figurative sense as the seat of God (beside the sing. which is used in the same sense), whereas in the literal sense of the word the sing. prevails, except where, in accordance with the Jewish conception, several heavens are distinguished (E. 4. 10 ὑπεράνω πάντων τῶν οὐρ., cp. 1. 10, Col. 1. 16, 20, H. 1. 10 O.T., 4. 14, 7. 26, 2 P. 3. 5, 7, 10, 12, 13; also probably αἱ δυνάμεις τῶν οὐρανῶν Mt. 24. 29 = Mc. 13. 25 = Lc. 21. 26). Thus we always have ἡ βασιλεία τῶν οὐρανῶν Mt. 3. 2 etc., ὁ πατὴρ ὑμῶν ὁ ἐν (τοῖς) οὐρ. 5. 16 etc.; similarly in Luke 10. 20 τὰ ὀνόματα ὑμῶν ἐγγέγραπται ἐν τοῖς οὐρ. (τῷ οὐρανῷ D), 12. 23 θησαυρὸν ἐν τοῖς οὐρ., A. 2. 34, 7. 56; in Paul 2 C. 5. 1, E. 3. 15, 6. 9 (א οὐρανῷ), Ph. 3. 20, Col. 1. 5, 4. 1 (οὐρανῷ א*ABC), 1 Th. 1. 10; 1 P. 1. 4 (οὐρανῷ א); (John never has the plural; also in the Apoc. it only occurs in 12. 12); in Mt. the passage 24. 31 ἀπ' ἄκρων οὐρανῶν ἕως ἄκρων αὐτῶν runs counter to the rule given above (Mc. 13. 27 has the sing. here), but not 3. 16 f., cp. Mc. 1. 10 f. εἶδεν σχιζομένους τοὺς οὐρανούς –, καὶ φωνὴ ἐκ τῶν οὐρανῶν (L. 3. 21 f. has the sing., but cp. A. 7. 56). Further οἰκτιρμοί = רַחֲמִים in Paul, R. 12. 1 etc.; the sing. only occurs in Col. 3. 12 (plur. K); cp. infra 6. The following plurals agree with the classical use: ἀνατολαί, δυσμαί east and west Mt. 2. 1, 8. 11 etc., but only in the formula ἀπὸ (ἕως) ἀνατολῶν, δυσμῶν, on the other

hand we have ἐν τῇ ἀνατολῇ Mt. 2. 2, 9; ἀπὸ ἀνατολῆς (B-ῶν) is also found beside ἀπὸ δυσμῶν Ap. 21. 13, ἀ. ἀνατολῆς (A -ῶν) ἡλίου 7. 2, 16. 12 (δυσμή never occurs, as in class. Greek δυσμαί is practically the only form). Always ἐκ δεξιῶν, ἐξ ἀριστερῶν or εὐωνύμων; ἐν τοῖς δεξιοῖς Mc. 16. 5, εἰς τὰ δεξιὰ **μέρη** Jo. 21. 6; beside these we have ἐν δεξιᾷ R. 8. 34, E. 1. 20 etc., sc. χειρί (classical use is similar). Cp. τὰ μέρη 'the region' Mt. 2. 22 etc., ἐπέκεινα beyond A. 7. 43 (a wrong reading from the LXX.; it should be ἐπὶ τὰ μέρη). Τὰ ἅγια, τὰ ἅγια τῶν ἁγίων parts of the temple (or tabernacle) H. 9. 2 f. are used as well as τὸ ἅγιον in verse 1 (τὰ ἅγια τ. ἁγίων in LXX. 1 Kings 8. 6). Πύλαι (class.) is only so used in πύλαι "Αιδου Mt. 16. 18 (LXX. Sap. Sal. 16. 23; class.), elsewhere the sing. is used for one gate; similarly θύρα for one door (class. often θύραι), cp. αἱ θύραι **πᾶσαι** A. 16. 26, so that Jo. 20. 19 f. θυρῶν, and perhaps also A. 5. 19, 23, 21. 30 are to be understood of several doors; the plural is used in the expression ἐπὶ θύραις Mt. 24. 33, Mc. 13. 29, cp. Ja. 5. 9 πρὸ τῶν θυρῶν figuratively, πρὸ τῆς θύρας A. 12. 6 literally (but ibid. 5. 23 πρὸ τῶν θυρῶν in a similar connection). Κόλποι (class.) is used in L. 16. 23 ἐν τοῖς κόλποις (τῷ κόλπῳ D) αὐτοῦ ('Αβραάμ), the sing. in verse 22. (Ἱμάτια means 'clothes' including ἱμάτιον and χιτών; but is used inaccurately = ἱμάτιον in Jo. 13. 4, 19. 23, also probably in A. 18. 6). The use of ἀργύρια for 'pieces of money' Mt. 26. 15 is not usual in classical Greek; ὀψώνια 'wages' L. 3. 14 etc. is Hellenistic. Αἵματα (in classical poets) Ap. 18. 24 B (but אACP read αἷμα) is blood shed by several martyrs; Jo. 1. 13 οὐκ ἐξ αἱμάτων is used of the substance from which a man is begotten (Eurip. Ion 693, Winer). The names of feasts are as in classical Greek (Διονύσια, Παναθήναια) in the plural: ἐγκαίνια, γενέσια (τὰ ἄζυμα in Mc. 14. 1 τὸ πάσχα καὶ τὰ ἄζυμα, but D omits καὶ τὰ ἄζ.; strictly ἡ ἑορτὴ τῶν ἀζύμων or αἱ ἡμέραι τ. ἀζ.); also γάμοι 'a marriage-feast' Mt. 22. 2, Lc. 12. 36 etc. (classical): but the sing. is used in Mt. 22. 8 etc. Διαθῆκαι E. 2. 12, R. 9. 4 אCK (ἡ διαθήκη BDE al., as always elsewhere; cp. the classical συνθῆκαι).

6. The plural of **abstract expressions** is found in Greek in a manner that appears strange to us, not only in poets, but also not infrequently in an elevated prose style, being used to indicate the individual concrete manifestations of the abstract quality. In the N.T. the epistolary style occasionally presents a similar usage: 2 C. 12. 10 ἔρις (v.l. ἔρεις, cp. § 8, 3), ζῆλος (v.l. ζῆλοι), θυμοί, ἐριθεῖαι, καταλαλιαί, ψιθυρισμοί, φυσιώσεις, ἀκαταστασίαι cp. G. 5. 20, τὰς πορνείας 1 C. 7. 2, ὑποκρίσεις, φθόνους, καταλαλιάς 1 P. 2. 1 cp. 4. 3, προσωπολημψίαις Ja. 2. 1, αἰσχύνας Jd. 13; also θανάτοις 'mortal dangers' 2 C. 11. 23 (μνῆμαι Herm. Sim. vi. 5. 3).

§ 33. THE CASES—NOMINATIVE AND VOCATIVE.

1. The **nominative** as the case of the name (ὀνομαστική = nominativus) appears to stand occasionally, where a proper name is introduced, without regard to the construction, in place of the case

§ 33. 1–3.] *NOMINATIVE AND VOCATIVE.* 85

which is strictly required. Thus Jo. 13. 13 φωνεῖτέ με ὁ διδάσκαλος καὶ κύριος, but here the nom. has mainly a vocative character, vide inf. 4: Ap. 9. 11 ὄνομα ἔχει (ὅν. ἔχει is omitted by the Latin Vulgate and may be supplied from the preceding words) Ἀπολλύων. Cp. Xenoph. Oecon. 6. 14 τοὺς ἔχοντας τὸ σεμνὸν ὄνομα τοῦτο τὸ καλός τε κἀγαθός (other instances in Lobeck, Phryn. 517. 1). But elsewhere the name is regularly assimilated to the case: Mt. 1. 21, 25 καλέσεις τὸ ὄνομα αὐτοῦ Ἰησοῦν, Mc. 3. 16 ἐπέθηκεν ὄνομα τῷ Σίμωνι Πέτρον (only Δ and the Latin versions have Πέτρος): and without exception in the phrase ὀνόματι 'by name' *e.g.* A. 27. 1 ἑκατοντάρχῃ ὀνόματι Ἰουλίῳ: cp. infra 2. It is accordingly incredible that the Mount of Olives should be translated by ὁ Ἐλαιών and that this word should be used as indeclinable in L. 19. 29, 21. 37 ὄρος (acc.) τὸ καλούμενον ἐλαιῶν, but we must write ἐλαιῶν (τὸ ὄρος τῶν ἐλ. in L. 19, 37 etc.), and in the single passage where we distinctly have the other form, A. 1. 12 (ὄρους τοῦ καλουμένου) ἐλαιῶνος we must correct the text to ἐλαιῶν (as also in Joseph. Ant. Jud. 7, 9. 2), see § 10, 5.

2. The nominative occasionally stands in a parenthesis interrupting the construction: thus Jo. 1. 6 ἐγένετο ἄνθρωπος – , Ἰωάνης ὄνομα αὐτῷ (ἦν is read before ὄν. by ℵ*D*), cp. 3. 1 (where ℵ* has Νικόδημος ὀνόματι; there is a more detailed expression introduced by ἦν δὲ in 18. 10; cp. also Ap. 6. 8, 8. 11, 9. 11; a similar classical use, § 30, 2); for this elsewhere with a more normal adjustment to the construction ᾧ ὄνομα – (often in Lc., but in Acts only at 13. 6; οὗ τὸ ὄν. with v.l. ᾧ ὄν. Mc. 14. 32) or ὀνόματι (Luke, Gospel and Acts) is used. The instances in statements of time are more striking: L. 9. 28 ἐγένετο δὲ μετὰ τοὺς λόγους τούτους, ὡσεὶ ἡμέραι ὀκτώ, καὶ παραλαβὼν κ.τ.λ., Mt. 15. 32 ὅτι ἤδη ἡμέραι (ἡμέρας ℵ) τρεῖς προσμένουσίν μοι. So also we may accordingly interpret A. 5. 7 ἐγένετο δέ, ὡς ὡρῶν τριῶν διάστημα, καὶ ἡ γυνὴ κ.τ.λ., and perhaps too (as Bengel and Winer) L. 13. 16 ἣν ἔδησεν ὁ Σατανᾶς, ἰδοὺ δέκα καὶ ὀκτὼ ἔτη.[1]

3. The **double nominative** (nom. of the subject and nom. of the predicate) is found in the N.T. as in Attic, except that occasionally in place of the second nominative εἰς with the accusative is used after a Hebrew model (as it is also used instead of the second accusative with corresponding active verbs, § 34, 5). This construction appears with εἶναι (more precisely with the fut. ἔσομαι, which has a certain relation to γίνομαι) and γίνεσθαι, but chiefly in quotations: ἔσονται εἰς σάρκα μίαν Mt. 19. 5 O.T. = Hebr. ל, ἐγενήθη εἰς κεφαλὴν γωνίας 21. 42 O.T., ἔσται τὰ σκολιὰ εἰς εὐθείας L. 3. 5 O.T., 2 C. 6. 18 O.T.; seldom except in quotations, as in L. 13. 19 ἐγένετο εἰς (om. εἰς D) δένδρον, Jo. 16. 20 ἡ λύπη ὑμῶν εἰς χαρὰν

---

[1] The use of the nom. with ἰδού, ἴδε (ἴδε ὁ ἀμνὸς τοῦ θεοῦ Jo. 1. 29 etc.) can only appear irregular, if one recalls the original meaning of the words. Already in Attic writers ἰδού (with this accent) has become a particle = *ecce*, and ἰδέ at any rate has become stereotyped like ἄγε and φέρε, so that it is joined with a plural word (Mt. 26. 65 etc.; ἄγε οἱ λέγοντες Ja. 4. 13, cp. 5. 1).

γενήσεται (=μεταστραφήσεται, with which the use of εἰς is not remarkable), Ap. 8. 11 (with 16. 19 ἐγένετο εἰς τρία μέρη cp. διαιρεῖν εἰς: with 1 Th. 3. 5 εἰς κενὸν γένηται ὁ κόπος ἡμῶν cp. the Attic εἰς κέρδος τι δρᾶν). The combination λογίζεσθαι (passive) εἰς is also not Attic, being taken from LXX. Gen. 15. 6 ἐλογίσθη αὐτῷ εἰς δικαιοσύνην; in addition to its use in that quotation we have εἰς οὐδὲν λογισθῆναι A. 19. 27 (the same combination in Is. 40. 17), τὰ τέκνα λογίζεται εἰς σπέρμα R. 9. 8, cp. 2. 26 (for nothing, for a seed; cp. class. οὐδὲν εἶναι, τὸ μηδὲν εἶναι); from this use comes the phrase ἐμοὶ εἰς ἐλάχιστόν ἐστι 1 C. 4. 3.

4. The language has created a special case for **address**, namely the **vocative**; this is limited, it is true, to the singular, and even there is not in all cases distinguished in form from the nominative. This case appears also in the N.T. (ἀδελφέ L. 6. 42, πάτερ Mt. 6. 9), but generally without the accompaniment which it usually has in Attic, namely the interjection ὦ. In most cases where this ὦ is found in the N.T. it expresses emotion: Mt. 15. 28 ὦ (om. D) γύναι, μεγάλη σου ἡ πίστις (γύναι in L. 22. 57, Jo. 2. 4, 4. 21 etc.), 17. 17 (=Mc. 9. 19, L. 9. 41) ὦ γενεὰ ἄπιστος (on the nom. vide infra), L. 24. 25, A. 13. 10 ὦ πλήρης (cp. inf.) κ.τ.λ. (R. 11. 33 ὦ βάθος πλούτου is not an address, but an exclamation, for which purpose ὦ [in this case also written ὤ] is likewise used in Attic), G. 3. 1, 1 Tim. 6. 20. With a less degree of emotion: ὦ ἄνθρωπε R. 2. 1, 3, 9. 20, Ja. 2. 20 (ἄνθρωπε without ὦ in L. 12. 14, 22. 58, 60); it is found without any sense of emotion in the Attic manner only in the Acts: ὦ Θεόφιλε 1. 1 (in L. 1. 3 κράτιστε Θεόφιλε, as the author of the work περὶ ὕψους has the address Ποστούμιε φίλτατε; on the other hand Dionysius of Halicarnassus in the work περὶ τῶν ἀρχ. ῥητόρων has ὦ κράτιστε Ἀμμαῖε; in any case Θεόφιλε without either ὦ or κράτιστε would be much too bald), 18. 14 ὦ (ἄνδρες) Ἰουδαῖοι (Gallio is speaking), 27. 21 ὦ ἄνδρες (while ἄνδρες ἀδελφοί, ἄνδρες Ἀθηναῖοι etc. are used even in this book without ὦ, and even the simple ἄνδρες 7. 26, 14. 15 etc., 27. 10, 25), ὦ βασιλεῦ according to the witnesses supporting the β text in A. 26. 13 (7).— From the earliest times (the practice is as old as Homer) the **nominative** has a tendency to usurp the place of the vocative. In the N.T. this occurs in two instances: on the one hand, with adjectives standing without a substantive or with a substantive whose vocative is not distinguishable from the nomin.: Mt. 17. 17, Mc. 9. 19, L. 9. 41 ὦ γενεὰ ἄπιστος (but D in Mc. and Lc. has ἄπιστε), A. 13. 10 ὦ πλήρης (with which may be compared ὦ δυστυχής in Menander); ἄφρων L. 12. 20 (a variant -ον has little support), 1 C. 15. 36 (ditto);[1]—on the other hand, where the article is introduced, which must naturally be followed by the nominative. The latter use of the nom. for voc. is also found already in Attic, e.g. Aristoph. Acharn. 242 πρόϊθ' εἰς τὸ πρόσθεν ὀλίγον ἡ κανηφόρος, i.e. you (who are) the basket bearer, Ran. 521 ὁ παῖς (you there,

---

[1] Even πατήρ is read by BD in Jo. 17. 21, and by AB in verses 24, 25, θυγάτηρ AB¹D etc. Jo. 12. 15 O.T., L. 8. 48 BKL, Mt. 9. 22 DGL, Mc. 5. 34 BD.

§ 33. 4. § 34. 1.] NOMINATIVE AND VOCATIVE. 87

the lad I mean) ἀκολούθει; in prose σὺ ὁ πρεσβύτατος, ὦ ἄνδρες οἱ παρόντες, οἱ οἰκέται, Πρόξενε καὶ οἱ ἄλλοι οἱ παρόντες (Xen. Anab. i. 5. 16), and esp. with participles, one half of which do not form a vocative at all.[1] And so in the N.T. we have L. 8. 54 ἡ παῖς ἐγείρου, Mc. 5. 41, 9. 25, L. 12. 32 μὴ φοβοῦ, τὸ μικρὸν ποίμνιον, 11. 39 ὑμεῖς οἱ Φαρισαῖοι,[2] R. 14. 4 σὺ ... ὁ κρίνων, Col. 3. 8 ff. αἱ γυναῖκες – οἱ ἄνδρες – τὰ τέκνα etc. = ὑμεῖς μὲν αἱ γυν.—ὑμεῖς δὲ οἱ ἄνδρες, Ap. 18. 20 οὐρανὲ καὶ οἱ ἅγιοι κ.τ.λ.[3] In all these instances we have not so much a simple address as a more definite indication of the person addressed. But the N.T. (and the LXX.) have extended this usage still further; in particular (ὦ) θεέ is not common (only in Mt. 27. 46 in a translation; also rare in LXX.), the phrase ὁ θεός being used instead, L. 18. 11, H. 1. 8 O.T., 10. 7 O.T. etc., κύριε ὁ θεός Ap. 15. 3, and so also ὁ πατήρ Mt. 11. 26, R. 8. 15, ὁ δεσπότης Ap. 6. 10, ὁ κύριός μου καὶ ὁ θεός μου Jo. 20. 28 (ὁ διδάσκαλος καὶ ὁ κύριος 13. 13, vide supra 1); further ὁ βασιλεύς Ap. 15. 3, Mt. 27. 29 (BD al. βασιλεῦ), Mc. 15. 18 (here אBD al. βασιλεῦ), Jo. 19. 3 (βασιλεῦ א), since this βασ. τῶν Ἰουδαίων is not a correct title, but a special designation, whereas the mode of addressing king Agrippa in A. 26. 7 etc. is and must be βασιλεῦ.

§ 34. THE ACCUSATIVE.

1. The use of the accusative **as the complement of transitive verbs**, which is the most ordinary function of this case, in the N.T. gives occasion only for a few special remarks, since in the first place transitives and intransitives are not so sharply distinguished in N.T. Greek as in older Greek, and again other cases besides the accusative offer rival claims to be used as the complement of the verb. The following verbs occasionally appear as transitives. **Μένειν** 'to await,' A. 20. 5, 23 (ὑπομένειν 1 C. 13. 7 etc., also in the sense of 'to await the help of God,' Clem. Cor. i. 34. 8, a quotation, for which LXX. uses the dat.; περιμένειν A. 1. 4, ἀναμένειν 1 Th. 1. 10). **Φεύγειν** 'to avoid' (opposed to διώκειν 'to strive after' anything), 1 C. 6. 18, 1 Tim. 6. 11, 2 Tim. 2. 22 (with Hebraic construction φ. ἀπό in the same sense 1 C. 10. 14); 'to flee before,' 'to escape,' only in H. 11. 34, ἔφυγον στόματα μαχαίρης as in class. Greek, elsewhere φ. ἀπό as in Mt. 3. 7 φυγεῖν ἀπὸ τῆς μελλούσης ὀργῆς (which in class. Greek is only used of places, φεύγειν ἀπὸ τῆς Σκύλλης Xen. Mem. ii. 6. 31, cp. Herm. Mand. xi. 14 φεύγει ἀπ' αὐτοῦ 'from him'); ἐκφεύγειν trans. in L. 21. 36 etc.; ἀποφ. 2 P. 2. 20 (ibid 1. 4 with genit. ? see § 36, 9). **Φυλάσσεσθαι** 'to shun,' trans. as in classical Greek, A. 21. 25 etc., as well as with ἀπό L. 12. 15

---

[1] Krüger, Gramm. § 45, 2. Kühner, Gr. ii.² 41 ff.

[2] So also L. 6. 25 οὐαὶ ὑμῖν, οἱ ἐμπεπλησμένοι, is regular, since οἱ ἐμπ. is equivalent to a vocative.

[3] Without the article we have A. 7. 42 O.T. οἶκος Ἰσραήλ = (ὑμεῖς) ὁ οἶκ. Ἰ. (see on the omission of the article § 46, 9).

(Xenoph. Cyr. ii. 3. 9), cp. φυλάττειν ἑαυτὸν ἀπὸ 1 Jo. 5. 21.[1] Φοβεῖσθαι 'to fear,' usually transitive, takes ἀπό after Hebrew usage in Mt. 10. 28. Θαρρεῖν is only intrans. (in classical Greek also trans.). Θαυμάζειν, usually intrans., is trans. in L. 7. 9 ἐθαύμασεν αὐτόν (om. αὐτ. D), A. 7. 31 τὸ ὅραμα (om. τὸ ὅρ. A). Jd. 16. Αἰσχύνεσθαι is intrans. (with ἀπό in 1 Jo. 2. 28), but ἐπαισχύν. is transitive, cp. ἐντρέπεσθαι infra 2. Ἐλεεῖν (οἰκτίρειν R. 9. 15 O.T.) trans. Κλαίειν mostly intrans., trans. in Mt. 2. 18 O.T. (LXX. is different), L. 23. 28 according to D (in the other MSS. it takes ἐπί with accus.). Πενθεῖν is trans. only in 2 C. 12. 21 (and in L. 23. 28 according to D). Κόπτεσθαι 'to bewail' is trans. in L. 8. 52 (class.), and takes ἐπί with acc. in Ap. 1. 7, 18. 9. Εὐδοκεῖν 'to take pleasure in' is trans. only in Mt. 12. 18 O.T. in א*B (al. εἰς, ἐν), H. 10. 6, 8 O.T. (the LXX. here has ἠθέλησας, elsewhere however it uses εὐδ. transitively *e.g.* Ps. 51. 18). (Ἀπορεῖσθαί τι occurs in A. 25. 20 אABHP, CEL insert εἰς; nowhere else in the N.T. is the accus. found after ἀπ. or διαπ. [occasionally in classical Greek after ἀπ.], which take ἐν or περί, both of which constructions occur in Herm. Sim. viii. 3. 1). Καυχᾶσθαι 'to boast,' mainly intrans., is trans. in 2 C. 9. 2, 11. 30 (with acc. of the thing). Βλασφημεῖν is often transitive (a late use, not Attic), εἴς τινα the Attic construction is found in Mc. 3. 29 (om. εἰς D), L. 12. 10.[2] (Ὑβρίζειν is only used transitively.) Ὀμνύναι is no longer used with accusative of that by which one swears, except in Ja. 5. 12; elsewhere it takes ἐν (εἰς) = Hebr. בְּ Mt. 5. 34 etc., or (as is found as early as class. Greek) κατά τινος H. 6. 13, 16; but ὁρκίζειν τινά (ἐνορκ.) still keeps this accus. Mc. 5. 7, A. 19. 13, 1 Th. 5. 27 (ἐξορκίζω [D ὁρκ.] σε κατὰ with genit. Mt. 26. 63, Herm. Sim. ix. 10. 5). Θριαμβεύειν 'to triumph' is used transitively = 'to lead in triumph' in Col. 2. 15, and somewhat differently in 2 C. 2. 14 ('to cause to go in triumph as a victor'; the use in the first passage may be paralleled by Plutarch Comp. Thes. et. Rom. 4). Μαθητεύειν (a late word) is intrans., 'to be a disciple,' in Mt. 27. 57 v.l., but the passive ἐμαθητεύθη is read by אCD: trans., 'to make a disciple,' in A. 14. 21, Mt. 13. 52 (pass.), 28. 19. Ἐμπορεύεσθαι, a middle verb, is intrans. in Ja. 4. 13 : trans. 'to deceive' in 2 P. 2. 3 (so ἐμπολᾶν Soph. Ant. 1050). Ἱερουργεῖν (a late word) τὸ εὐαγγέλιον (like θυσίαν) occurs in R. 15. 16.[3] Ὑστερεῖν in the sense of 'to be wanting' (without a case in Jo. 2. 3, cp. Dioscor. 5. 86), is trans. in Mc. 10. 21 ἕν σε ὑστερεῖ אBC al. (σοι AD al.), cp. LXX. Ps. 22. 1 (else-

---

[1] In L. 12. 15 (ὁρᾶτε καὶ φυλάσσεσθε ἀπὸ) the words καὶ φυλ. are wanting in the Syriac version, and this same sense of 'to beware of' already belongs to ὁρᾶν = βλέπειν ἀπό, Mc. 8. 15 ὁρᾶτε (om. D, these two verbs cannot stand together) βλέπετε ἀπό, 12. 38 (on the other hand βλέπ. is also used transitively 'to look at' Mc. 13. 9, 1 C. 1. 26 etc., and perhaps Ph. 3. 2 unless here it = φυλάσσεσθε). We also have προσέχειν ἀπό Mt. 16. 6 (ὁρᾶτε καὶ προσέχετε ἀπό, where ὁρᾶτε καὶ is wanting in the Latin witnesses).

[2] 2 P. 2. 12 ἐν οἷς ἀγνοοῦσιν βλασφημοῦντες 'railing at those things in which they know nothing' (the idea is expressed more intelligibly in Jd. 10).

[3] Ἰλάσκεσθαι ἁμαρτίας H. 2. 17 is noticeable on account of the object, since the classical use is (ἐξ)ιλάσκ. θεόν 'to dispose Him to mercy towards one.' But a similar use (= *expiare*) is also found in LXX. and Philo.

§ 34. 1-2.] *ACCUSATIVE.* 89

where the LXX. also has the dat. Buttm. 147; § 37, 3). The following are transitive in virtue of their *composition* with κατά (as in class. Greek): καταβραβεύειν Col. 2. 18, καταγωνίζεσθαι H. 11. 33, κατασοφίζεσθαι A. 7. 19 ('to get the better of' etc.) : with διά (class.) διαπορεύεσθαι, διέρχεσθαι, διαπλεῖν in Lc., Acts, and Hebr. (in one sentence we have beside this the construction with διά and the genit., H. 11. 29 διέβησαν τὴν θάλασσαν ὡς διὰ ξηρᾶς γῆς) : with παρά παρέρχεσθαι (including Mc. 6. 48) : with περί περιέρχεσθαι τὰς οἰκίας 1 Tim. 5. 13 (class.), περιστῆναί τινα A. 25. 7 (class.), περιάγειν (also intrans. § 53, 1) Mt. 9. 35, 23. 15, Mc. 6. 6 (with v.l. ἐν in Mt. 4. 23) : with πρό προέρχεσθαι Lc. 22. 47 (D προῆγεν), = class. προηγεῖσθαί τινι; cp. Lat. *praeire aliquem*;[1] with ὑπέρ ὑπερέχειν Ph. 4. 7 (cp. § 36, 8).

2. **Verbs with variable construction.** Εὖ (καλῶς) ποιεῖν in Attic take the accus. in all cases, similarly κακῶς (πολλὰ κακὰ) ποιεῖν τινα and the like ; but in L. 6. 27 we have καλῶς ποιεῖτε τοῖς –, Mc. 14. 7 εὖ ποιεῖν with dat. (this is wanting in א*) : for the use of these verbs with the accus. cp. infra 4. But ὠφελεῖν and βλάπτειν (a rare word) take τινα in the N.T. as in Attic (λυσιτελεῖν τινι as in Att., but only in L. 17. 2 where D has συμφέρει); similarly κακῶς λέγειν τινα, but only in A. 23. 5 O.T., for which elsewhere κακολογεῖν τινα is used in A. 19. 9 etc., like εὐλογεῖν, besides which we further have καλῶς εἴπωσιν ὑμᾶς, but only in L. 6. 26 (D ὑμῖν). (The simple λέγειν with accus. of the person = 'to allude to anyone in one's speech,' is found in Jo. 1. 15 [a v.l.], 8. 27 [a v.l.], Ph. 3. 18, as in classical Greek.) The following verbs of cognate meaning take the accusative : ἐπηρεάζειν (Att. with dat.) τινα Mt. 5. 44, L. 6. 28, 1 P. 3. 16 : λυμαίνεσθαί τινα A. 8. 3 (Att. τινά and τινί): λοιδορεῖν τινα Jo. 9. 28, A. 23. 4 (as in Att.) : ὀνειδίζειν (Att. τινί) τινά Mt. 5. 11 etc. (in 27. 44 αὐτῷ is a wrong reading for αὐτόν) : μέμφεσθαι αὐτούς H. 8. 8 א*AD*al., αὐτοῖς אᶜBDᶜal. (the latter is the Attic use): καταρᾶσθαι (Att. with dat.) with accus. in (Mt. 5. 44 [D* ὑμῖν]), Mc. 11. 21, L. 6. 28 (ὑμῖν EHL al. Justin Ap. i. 15), Ja. 3. 9 (cp. supra 1 βλασφημεῖν, ὑβρίζειν, with which verbs this whole class, with the exception of εὖ ποιεῖν etc., appears to have been brought into uniformity). Ἐντρέπεσθαί τινα is 'to be afraid of anyone' (Polyb. and Acts ; the earlier use with τινος = 'to trouble oneself about'), cp. ἐπαισχύνεσθαι supra 1 ; βασκαίνειν τινά 'to envy,' 'bewitch,' G. 3. 1 (in Attic it perhaps also takes τινί like φθονεῖν?); προσκυνεῖν τινα (Att.) occurs in Mt. 4. 10 O.T., L. 4. 8 O.T., 24. 52 (om. D), Jo. 4. 22 bis, 23 (αὐτῷ א*; in the same verse all MSS. have τῷ πατρί), 9. 38 D : elsewhere with τινί (a late use, Lobeck Phryn. 463) or absolute (πρ. ἐνώπιόν τινος L. 4. 7); γονυπετεῖν (Polyb.) τινα Mt. 17. 14 (D omits αὐτόν), Mc. 10. 17 : without a case in Mc. 1. 40, with ἔμπροσθεν Mt. 27. 29 (the dat. αὐτῷ in the former passage has very slight support) ; εὐαγγελίζεσθαι in Attic has accus. of the thing, dat. of the person : so also in L. 1. 19, 2. 10,

---

[1] Προηγούμενοι ἀλλήλους R. 12. 10 'to prefer' = Ph. 2. 3 ἀλλήλους ἡγούμενοι ὑπερέχοντας ἑαυτῶν (cp. also 1 Th. 5. 13) ; not elsewhere in this sense, but cp. προκρίνειν. The acc. of course depends on ἡγ., not on πρό.

1 C. 15. 1 f. etc.: but it is also found with accus. of the person L. 3. 18 εὐηγγελίζετο τὸν λαόν and frequently in Luke and Acts, also G. 1. 9 (ibid. 8 with dat.), 1 P. 1. 12;[1] παραινεῖν (only in Luke, from the literary language) has accus. instead of the classical dat. A. 27. 22 (construction like that of παρακαλεῖν)[2]; χρῆσθαι takes acc. in 1 C. 7. 31 οἱ χρώμενοι τὸν κόσμον ℵ*ABDFG, dat. according to ℵᶜDᶜᵒʳʳEK etc. as in 9. 12, 18 etc. (cp. Buttm. p. 157); πεινᾶν and διψᾶν take accus. τὴν δικαιοσύνην Mt. 5. 6 (class. gen.), elsewhere they are used without a case.

3. The so-called accusative of the **inner object** or of **content**, found with intransitive and passive verbs and generally with any verb, is used in the N.T. practically in the same way as in the classical language (there being a special reason for its being kept, as the Hebrew had a similar usage). This accusative, whether it be that of a substantive which is radically connected with the verb or of one connected only in sense, in most cases requires, in order to have any *raison d'être* at all, to be more nearly defined by means of an adjective or a genitive, whereas the dative of verbal substantives when similarly used does not need this nearer definition, see § 38, 3. This is also occasionally omitted with the accusative, if the substantive has a more concrete meaning, as in Mt. 13. 30 (according to the correct reading of D Origen etc.) δήσατε (αὐτὰ) δεσμάς (ℵBC etc. read εἰς δ.) 'into bundles,' which is a quite different use from Mt. 12. 29 δήσῃ τὸν ἰσχυρόν (acc. of the outer object), but at the same time is not entirely similar to the possible phrase δεῖν δέσιν, since the acc. δεσμάς denotes an external result or product of the action (cp. οἰκοδομεῖν οἰκίαν L. 6. 48, ποιεῖν ποίημα, γράφειν γράμματα); an object of this kind may then become the subject to a passive verb (G. 1. 11). A similar instance is L. 2. 8 φυλάσσοντες φυλακάς of 'watch duty,' 'sentry duty' (so in Xenoph. Anab. 2. 6. 10 etc.; also in LXX.), where φυλακή expresses a definite objective kind of φυλάσσειν, and by no means expresses merely the abstract idea of the verb; so ἰδεῖν ὅραμα A. 11. 5, 16. 10 (passively ὅραμα ὤφθη 16. 9).[3] But in other cases we have Mt. 2. 10 ἐχάρησαν χαρὰν **μεγάλην σφόδρα**, Mc. 4. 41 ἐφοβήθησαν φόβον **μέγαν**, Ap. 16. 9 ἐκαυματίσθησαν καῦμα **μέγα**, 1 P. 3. 14 τὸν φόβον αὐτῶν ('fear of them') μὴ φοβηθῆτε, Col. 2. 19 αὔξει ('grows') τὴν αὔξησιν τοῦ θεοῦ. This closer defining of the noun is also not absent where the verb stands in a relative sentence: Jo. 17. 26 ἡ ἀγάπη ἣν ἠγάπησάς με (ᾗ according to D), Mc. 10. 38 τὸ βάπτισμα ὃ ἐγὼ βαπτίζομαι βαπτισθῆναι, Herm. Mand. vii. 1 ὁ φόβος ὃν δεῖ σε φοβηθῆναι. To the same class of accusative belong the cases where, in place of the substantive with the word which more closely defines it, the latter word occurs alone, either in the gender of the substantive,

---

[1] But not with a double acc.; in A. 13. 32 τὴν ... ἐπαγγελίαν should be taken with the following clause.

[2] Διδάσκειν with dat. instead of acc. in Ap. 2. 14 rests on a reading which is quite uncertain.

[3] But ἁμαρτάνοντα ἁμαρτίαν 1 Jo. 5. 16 *is* more closely defined by μὴ πρὸς θάνατον: cp. the following words ἔστιν ('there is') ἁμαρτία πρὸς θ.

which must then be supplied, as in L. 12. 47 f. δαρήσεται πολλάς, ὀλίγας sc. πληγάς, or more commonly in the neuter: L. 5. 33 νηστεύουσιν πυκνά (=πυκνὰς νηστείας), 2 C. 13. 1 τρίτον τοῦτο ἔρχομαι ('for the third time'), Ph. 1. 6 πεποιθὼς αὐτὸ τοῦτο ('having this confidence'), 2. 18, 1 C. 9. 25 πάντα ἐγκρατεύεται (but in Herm. Mand. viii. 2 ἐγκρ. τὸ πονηρόν is an instance of a true objective acc., being opposed to ποιεῖν τὸ π.: ibid. 2-12 the verb is also used with ἀπό, genit., and inf.; cp. νηστεύειν τὸν κόσμον in the Λόγια 'Ιησοῦ from Oxyrhynchus), 10. 33 πάντα πᾶσιν ἀρέσκω, 11. 2 πάντα μου μέμνησθε which is still more adverbial 'in everything,' 'in every respect'; τὸ δ' αὐτὸ Ph. 2. 18, Mt. 27. 44 'in like manner' (on which is modelled the concise phrase in 2 C. 6. 13 τὴν αὐτὴν ἀντιμισθίαν 'in like manner in return,' Fritzsche); μηδὲν διακρινόμενος A. 10. 20, cp. 11. 12; 2 C. 12. 11 οὐδὲν ὑστέρησα,[1] cp. 11. 5, Mt. 19. 20 τί ὑστερῶ; ('wherein am I still backward?' whereas τίνος ὑστ. = 'what do I lack?'), 2 C. 12. 13 τί ἐστιν ὃ ἡσσώθητε (similar sense); R. 6. 10 ὃ γὰρ ἀπέθανεν, τῇ ἁμαρτίᾳ ἀπέθανεν – ὃ δὲ ζῇ, ζῇ τῷ θεῷ, G. 2. 20 ὃ νῦν ζῶ ἐν σαρκί, ἐν πίστει ζῶ (the death that He died, the life that He liveth, or else=in that He died and liveth). Still the use of these neuters in the N.T. is far less extensive than in the classical language.

4. A **double accusative** is found mainly with a number of verbs which can take both a personal object as well as (in another relation) an object of the thing. Thus **διδάσκειν** with ἀποστασίαν πάντας τοὺς – A. 21. 21, cp. Mc. 6. 34 αὐτοὺς πολλά (where however πολλά is rather to be regarded as acc. of the inner object), Jo. 14. 26 ὑμᾶς πάντα, also H. 5. 12 τοῦ διδάσκειν ὑμᾶς τινὰ (not τίνα) τὰ στοιχεῖα κ.τ.λ. (thus the examples with this verb are not many): **ἀναμιμνῄσκειν** 1 C. 4. 17, **ὑπομιμν.** Jo. 14. 26. But **κρύπτειν** τινά τι is not represented, the phrase used being τι ἀπό (Hebr. מִן) τινος, Mt. 11. 25 (ἀπ)έκρυψας ταῦτα ἀπὸ σοφῶν (Herm. Sim. ix. 11. 9) or the still more Hebraistic κρύψατε ἡμᾶς ἀπὸ προσώπου τοῦ – Ap. 6. 16 (passively κεκρυμμένον ἀπ' αὐτῶν L. 18. 34 [as incidentally also in Homer Odyss. 23. 110 κεκρυμμένα ἀπ' ἄλλων], ἐκρύβη ἀπὸ ὀφθαλμῶν σου 19. 42). **Αἰτεῖν** τινά τι Mt. 6. 8 (D is different), Mc. 6. 22 f. etc., besides which παρά may be used of the person (class.) Jo. 4. 9, A. 9. 2 (the middle verb: this never takes double acc.), or ἀπό Mt. 20. 20 BD (v.l. παρ'), 1 Jo. 5. 15 אB (similar v.l.): **ἐρωτᾶν** (ask a question) τινά τι Mt. 21. 24, Mc. 4. 10. (The following are not found with double acc.: **ἀφαιρεῖν, -εῖσθαι**, the person being introduced by ἀπό L. 16. 3, or placed in the gen. [ibid. D; L. 10. 42 etc.], as also in classical Greek: and **ἀποστερεῖν** [the thing is placed in the gen. in 1 Tim. 6. 5, but there is a v.l.]. **Ποιεῖν** τινά τι 'to do something with' occurs in Mt. 27. 22 τί (accus. of the predicate) ποιήσω 'Ιησοῦν, cp. Herm. Sim. i. 4 τί ποιήσεις τὸν ἀγρόν, A. 12. 18 τί ὁ Πέτρος ἐγένετο what was become of P.: Mc. 15. 12 is similar to the passage of Matthew, but D reads τῷ βασιλεῖ=what shall I *do to*? cp. supra 2; with the same meaning we have the construction τι τινί

---

[1] The reading οὐδὲν (אBP οὐδενὸς) χρείαν ἔχω Ap. 3. 17 can hardly be right.

Mt. 21. 40, L. 20. 15, A. 9. 13, Herm. Sim. v. 2. 2, ix. 11. 8: also A. 16. 28 μηδὲν πράξῃς [in place of ποιήσῃς] σεαυτῷ κακόν. In Attic the acc. must be used in all cases in this sense, supra 2, whereas ποιεῖν τινί τι 'to do something for anyone,' as in Mc. 7. 12, 10. 36, is also correct Attic Greek. Instead of ποιεῖν τί τινι we also have π. τι ἔν τινι or εἴς τινα, Mt. 17. 12 [om. ἐν ℵD al.], L. 21. 31, Jo. 15. 21 [ὑμῖν AD² al.]; cp. καλὸν ἔργον ἠργάσατο ἐν ἐμοί Mc. 14. 6, εἰς ἐμέ Mt. 26. 10 [Attic has ἐργ. with double acc.]; οὕτως γένηται ἐν ἐμοί 1 C. 9. 15, cp. L. 21. 31 [Buttm. p. 130]). The double acc. is also found after verbs of *putting on* and *putting off*: ἐνδιδύσκειν, ἐκδιδ. τινά τι Mt. 27. 31, Mc. 15. 17, 20, L. 15. 22; hence we have also in the N.T. (not class.) περιβάλλειν τινά τι L. 23. 11 AD al. (om. αὐτὸν ℵB al.), Jo. 19. 2 (but not with περιτιθέναι which takes τινί τι Mt. 27. 28, nor with περιβάλλειν when used in other connections, see L. 19. 43). Also with χρίειν: H. 1. 9 O.T. τινα ἔλαιον, a Hebraic use (but in Ap. 3. 18 the acc. κολλύριον must certainly be taken in connection with ἀγοράσαι, not with ἐγχρῖσαι). With *causative verbs* this use is more developed than in classical Greek: ποτίζειν τινὰ ποτήριον Mc. 9. 41, γάλα 1 C. 3. 2, 'to make to drink,' cp. Plat. Phaedr. 247 E (so also ψωμίζω in the LXX., 'to make to eat': in 1 C. 13. 3 with the acc. of the thing only, cp. Winer, § 32, note 4), φορτίζειν 'to make to carry' L. 11. 46, ὁρκίζειν and ἐνορκ. (strictly 'to make to swear by,' Hdt. ἐξορκοῦν τινα τὸ Στυγὸς ὕδωρ 6. 74) 'to adjure by' Mc. 5. 7 etc., vide supra 1.—In addition there are the instances, few in number, where the acc. of the inner and of the outer object are found together: Jo. 17. 26 ἡ ἀγάπη ἣν (ᾗ according to D) ἠγάπησάς με, E. 2. 4 τὴν ἀγ. ἣν ἠγάπησεν ἡμᾶς, L. 4. 35 μηδὲν βλάψας αὐτόν, G. 5. 2 ὑμᾶς οὐδὲν ὠφελήσει, 4. 12, A. 25. 10, Mt. 27. 44, Mc. 6. 34 (supra).

5. A different class of **double accusative** is that where one acc. is the acc. of the predicate, the construction corresponding to that of intransitive and passive verbs with a double nominative. This class is used after verbs of *making* (ποιεῖν αὐτὸν βασιλέα Jo. 6. 15, cp. supra 4, ὃν ἔθηκεν κληρονόμον H. 1. 2, τίς με κατέστησεν κριτήν L. 12. 14): *having* and *taking* (A. 13. 5 εἶχον Ἰωάννην ὑπηρέτην, Ja. 5. 10 ὑπόδειγμα λάβετε τοὺς προφήτας): *designating, calling* (Jo. 10. 35 ἐκείνους εἶπε θεούς, 15. 15, Mc. 10. 18 τί με λέγεις ἀγαθόν; L. 1. 59 ἐκάλουν αὐτὸ Ζαχαρίαν: in Hebraic style 1. 13, 31 καλέσεις τὸ ὄνομα αὐτοῦ Ἰωάννην, Ἰησοῦν, cp. the passive ἐκλήθη τὸ ὄν. α. Ἰησοῦς 2. 21, Buttm. p. 132):[1] *confessing*, ὁμολογεῖν αὐτὸν Χριστόν Jo. 9. 22 (with εἶναι D), 1 Jo. 4. 2 (acc. and inf. B), 2 Jo. 7: *regarding*, (Ph. 3. 7 ταῦτα ἥγημαι ζημίαν, ibid. 8 with εἶναι introduced, which is elsewhere always wanting with ἡγεῖσθαι, whereas vice versâ νομίζειν and ὑπολαμβάνειν do not appear with a double acc.; A. 20. 24 ποιοῦμαι τὴν ψυχὴν τιμίαν, but there is a v.l. in which ποιοῦμαι is replaced by ἔχω, for which in this sense [= Lat. *habere*] cp. L. 14. 18 ἔχε με παρῃτημένον, Ph. 2. 29: ἔχειν with ὡς Mt. 14. 5, 21. 26, like ἡγεῖσθαι ὡς 2 Th. 3. 15, Clem.

---

[1] The dat. is used with ἐπικαλεῖν ὄνομα in Mt. 10. 25 B*, cp. § 37, 7.

§ 34. 5-6.]　　　ACCUSATIVE.　　　93

Cor. ii. 5. 6, Herm. Vis. i. 1. 7):[1] *proving* (συνιστάναι G. 2. 18, but ἑαυτοὺς ὡς θεοῦ διάκονοι 2 C. 6. 4; on 2 C. 7. 11 see § 36, 2 note), (*feigning*, ὑποκρινομένους ἑαυτοὺς δικαίους L. 20. 20 D). Beside these double accusatives we occasionally find εἰς prefixed to the predicate, showing Hebrew influence (cp. § 33, 3), A. 13. 22 ἤγειρεν αὐτοῖς τὸν Δαυὶδ εἰς βασιλέα, 47 O.T., 7. 21; Mt. 21. 46 εἰς προφήτην (ὡς πρ. CD al.) αὐτὸν εἶχον (more frequent in LXX.; Clem. Cor. i. 42. 4 καθίστανον εἰς ἐπισκόπους); the inserted ὡς (other instances given above) may also be a Hebraism, cp. ἐλογίσθημεν ὡς R. 8. 36 O.T. (Hebr. ל).—One may refer to this class of double acc. L. 9. 14 κατακλίνατε αὐτοὺς κλισίας ἀνὰ πεντήκοντα, cp. Mc. 6. 39; again Mt. 13. 30 δεῖν αὐτὰ δεσμάς, supra 3; and the classical διαιρεῖν τι δύο μέρη, Kühner ii.[2] 278 f.

6. The **passives** of the verbs specified in 4 (with which verbs when used in the passive the person and not the thing usually becomes the subject) occasionally appear with the object of the thing: 2 Th. 2. 15 τὰς παραδόσεις ἃς ἐδιδάχθητε, 1 C. 12. 13 ἓν πνεῦμα ἐποτίσθημεν (of course ἐνδεδυμένος, περιβεβλημένος also take this object, but they are middle and not passive);[2] we further have (formed after the classical πείθειν τινά τι) πεπείσμεθα τὰ κρείσσονα H. 6. 9, and Ph. 3. 8 τὰ πάντα ἐζημιώθην, Mt. 16. 26 τὴν ψυχὴν αὐτοῦ ζημιωθῇ (cp. Mc. 8. 36, L. 9. 25), opposed to κερδαίνειν, and formed on the model of ζημιοῦν τινα ζημίαν, but with a further derivative sense of the verb = to lose.[3] Since moreover the person who is expressed by the dative after the active verb may become the subject to the passive verb (cp. § 54, 3), such passives may also appear with the acc. of the thing: πεπίστευμαι τὸ εὐαγγέλιον G. 2. 7, οἰκονομίαν πεπίστευμαι 1 C. 9. 17, R. 3. 2, τὴν ἅλυσιν περίκειμαι A. 28. 20 (active περιτιθέναι τινί τι), H. 5. 2 (also L. 17. 2 according to d λίθον μυλικὸν περιέκειτο: Herm. Vis. v. 1, Sim. vi. 2. 5). Finally we have (formed after δεῖν αὐτοῦ πόδας Mt. 22. 13) δεδεμένος τοὺς πόδας Jo. 11. 44, διεφθαρμένοι τὸν νοῦν 1 Tim. 6. 5, ῥεραντισμένοι τὰς καρδίας, λελουμένοι τὸ σῶμα H. 10. 22 f., according to a general usage of the Greek language, which is employed with still greater freedom especially by St. Paul: κατηχούμενος τὸν λόγον G. 6. 6 'he who is instructed *in* the gospel,' cp. A. 18. 25, 21. 24, L. 1. 4?, while with the active verb the person is the object, never the thing; πεπληρωμένοι καρπὸν δικαιοσύνης Ph. 1. 11, cp. Col. 1. 9, 'with the fruit' (a Hebraism, Exod. 31. 3 ἐνέπλησα αὐτὸν πνεῦμα σοφίας); τὴν αὐτὴν εἰκόνα μεταμορφούμεθα 2 C. 3. 18 'into the same image'; (on τὴν αὐτὴν ἀντιμισθίαν πλατύνθητε ibid. 6. 13 cp. supra 4, and for τὸν αὐτὸν τρόπον infra 7; ἀναφανέντες τὴν Κύπρον A. 21. 3 is a wrong reading for ἀναφάναντες).

---

[1] Hermas also has (Sim. viii. 3, 4) γνώσῃ αὐτοὺς πάντας τοὺς κ.τ.λ. 'recognise them to be those who' etc.
[2] Instead of the acc. with περιβάλλεσθαι the Apocalypse has ἐν with dat. in 3. 5, 4. 4 (here AP omit ἐν); so too Mt. 11. 8, L. 7. 25 ἠμφιεσμένον ἐν μαλακοῖς.
[3] Hdt. 7. 37 is wrongly adduced as a parallel: τὴν ψυχήν τινος (his son's) ζημιοῦσθαι (to lose as a punishment): the MSS. have τῇ ψυχῇ.

7. The **accusative of reference** with adjectives and the like has a very limited use in the N.T., since this function is mostly taken over by the dative, § 38, 2. Mt. 27. 57 τοὖνομα 'by name' (class.; elsewhere ὀνόματι): Jo. 6. 10 τὸν ἀριθμὸν ὡς πεντακισχίλιοι: H. 2. 17 πιστὸς ἀρχιερεὺς τὰ πρὸς τὸν θεόν. But this same phrase τὰ πρὸς τὸν θεόν R. 15. 17, together with the phrases R. 12. 18 τὸ ἐξ ὑμῶν – εἰρηνεύοντες, 9. 5 τὸ κατὰ σάρκα and 16. 19 τὸ ἐφ᾽ ὑμῖν as a v.l., τὸ καθ᾽ εἷς 12. 5, has already become an **adverbial accusative**, similar to ἐνεκοπτόμην τὰ πολλά (v.l. πολλάκις) R. 15. 22, τὸ πλεῖστον (at most) τρεῖς 1 C. 14. 27, τὸ πρότερον, τὸ πρῶτον cp. § 11, 5; in τὸ καθ᾽ ἡμέραν 'daily' L. 19. 47, 11. 3, A. 17. 11, 28 D, 19. 9 D the article is meaningless, cp. τὸ πρωΐ 5. 21 D, τὸ δειλινόν 'in the afternoon' 3. 1 D (infra 8); τὸ λοιπόν and λοιπόν 'for the rest,' 'now,' 'already' Mt. 26. 45 = Mc. 14. 41 (in both passages a v.l. without τὸ), A. 27. 20 (λ.), 2 C. 13. 11 (λ.), E. 6. 10 τὸ λ. (אAB τοῦ λοιποῦ 'henceforth,' see § 36, 13), and frequently in the Pauline Epp., also H. 10. 13 (also Attic); τὸ νῦν ἔχον A. 24. 25 'for the present' (Lucian and others); τὸ τέλος 'finally' 1 P. 3. 8, τὴν ἀρχήν 'from the beginning,' 'at all' Jo. 8. 25. Again, the phrases ὃν τρόπον Mt. 23. 37 and *passim*, τὸν ὅμοιον τρόπον Jd. 7 come under the head of accusative of the inner object (besides which we have the dat. Ph. 1. 18 παντὶ τρόπῳ, § 38, 3, and καθ᾽ ὃν τρ. A. 15. 11, 27. 25, cp. R. 3. 2, 2 Th. 2. 3).

8. **Accusative of extension in space and time**: L. 22. 41 ἀπεσπάσθη ἀπ᾽ αὐτῶν ὡσεὶ λίθου βολήν, 2. 44, Jo. 6. 19, answering the question How far? where the acc. may be regarded as a kind of object of the thing; Jo. 2. 12 ἔμειναν οὐ πολλὰς ἡμέρας, answering the question How long? (to be similarly explained, cp. the dat. § 38, 5); as to Mt. 20. 2 συμφωνεῖν ἐκ δηναρίου ('at a denarius') τὴν ἡμέραν, 'a day,' 'per day,' vide § 36, 8. Further, νύκτα καὶ ἡμέραν 'day and night' Mc. 4. 27, L. 2. 37, A. 26. 7; τὰς ἡμέρας – τὰς νύκτας L. 21. 37 'during the days, the nights'; ἡμέραν ἐξ ἡμέρας 2 P. 2. 8 is classical. This accusative appears to go beyond its own department in the phrases τὸ δειλινόν, τὸ πρωΐ (see 7), where the question asked is When? (cp. μέσον ἡμέρας LXX. Dan Sus. 7);[2] as it does moreover in its use with ὥρα (occurring in classical Greek): Jo. 4. 52 ἐχθὲς ὥραν ἑβδόμην, Ap. 3. 3 ποίαν ὥραν, A. 10. 30 (and verse 3 with v.l. περὶ ὥραν ἐνάτην as in verse 9), cp. Aesch. Eum. 159 ὥραν οὐδενὸς κοινήν, Eurip. Bacch. 722 τὴν τεταγμένην ὥραν, Aristot. Ἀθ. Πολιτ. cap. 30 ad fin. τὴν ὥραν τὴν προρρηθεῖσαν, Demosth. 54. 4 etc. (= εἰς ὥραν, 'at the hour,' ἐπὶ τ. ὥραν A. 3. 1), although the N.T. has also ποίᾳ ὥρᾳ and similar phrases, for which and for the encroachment of the dat. on the functions of the accus. see § 38, 4 and 5. A peculiar idiom is found in A. 27. 33 τεσσαρεσκαιδεκάτην σήμερον ἡμέραν, *i.e.* 'it is to-day the 14th day since' etc., 'to-day is the

---

[1] Ὁδὸν θαλάσσης Mt. 4. 15 O.T. is a literal rendering of the Hebr. דֶּרֶךְ = *versus*, which appears elsewhere in the LXX., *e.g.* Deut. 11. 30.

[2] Cp. also LXX. τὴν μεσημβρίαν Gen. 43. 16, τὸ πρωΐ Ex. 7. 15. See Sophocles Lexic. p. 44.

14th day in succession that,' cp. Demosth. τρίτον ἔτος τουτί, 'it is now the third year that.'—In answer to the question How far distant ? beside the accus. (L. 24. 13 ἀπέχουσαν σταδίους ἑξήκοντα ἀπὸ 'Ιερουσ., cp. A. 1. 12), we find also ἀπό with the genitive, probably a Latinism (a millibus passuum duobus, Caes. B. G. 2. 7): Jo. 11. 18 ἦν Βηθανία ἐγγὺς τῶν Ἱερ., ὡς ἀπὸ σταδίων δεκαπέντε, cp. 21. 8, Ap. 14. 20, Herm. Vis. iv. 1. 5 (Diod., Plut. etc.).

§ 35. THE GENITIVE.

1. By far the most extensive use of the **genitive** is that by which it defines a **noun** more closely after the manner of an adjective, and like an adjective either as attribute or predicate; in the latter case the genitive is said to be dependent on εἶναι (γίνεσθαι etc.). The kind of relation which exists between the genitive and its noun can only be decided by the sense and context: in the N.T. this is often purely a matter of theological interpretation, which cannot form part of the teaching of a grammatical work. The place of the noun, which is defined by the genitive, may also be taken by a pronoun and more especially by the article. We select here only the points that are worthy of note.

2. **Genitive of origin and membership.**—As in the classical language, the genitive is used where a particular person is indicated by the mention of his father, Ἰάκωβον τὸν τοῦ Ζεβεδαίου Mt. 4. 21 etc., a use in which the introduction of υἱός is perfectly admissible, Ἰωάνην τὸν Ζαχαρίου υἱόν L. 3. 2; in the case of the sons of Zebedee, if named together, υἱοί (almost) always appears, Mt. 26. 37, 27. 56, Mc. 10. 35, L. 5. 10, only in Jo. 21. 2 ABL al. read οἱ τοῦ Z., while οἱ υἱοὶ Z. is read by אDE; where υἱός is omitted the introduction of one article, contrary to the usual classical practice, causes the insertion of the article with the other noun as well, thus Δαυὶδ τὸν τοῦ Ἰεσσαί A. 13. 22 O.T., cp. § 46, 10 (but without an article Ἰούδαν Σίμωνος Ἰσκαριώτου Jo. 6. 71 etc., similarly in Greek style Σώπατρος Πύρρου Βεροιαῖος A. 20. 4). Indication of the mother by her son's name: Mc. 15. 40 (cp. Mt. 27. 56) Μαρία ἡ Ἰακώβου τοῦ μικροῦ καὶ Ἰωσῆτος μήτηρ, whence in verse 47 M. ἡ Ἰωσῆτος, 15. 1 M. ἡ Ἰακώβου as in L. 24. 10 (the article with the gen. is in this case neglected except in Mt. 27. 56 ἡ τοῦ Ἰακ. – μήτηρ). Of the wife by her husband's name (this is also classical): Mt. 1. 6 τῆς τοῦ Οὐρίου, Jo. 19. 25 Μαριὰμ ἡ τοῦ Κλωπᾶ.[1] Whether in the case of the apostle called Ἰούδας Ἰακώβου L. 1. 16, A. 1. 13, υἱός or in accordance with Jd. 1 ἀδελφός is to be supplied (the latter is grammatically admissible: cp. Τιμοκράτης ὁ Μητροδώρου sc. ἀδ. Alciphron Ep. ii. 2) is a question which need not be discussed here. Membership in a family (including a family of slaves): τῶν Χλόης 1 C. 1. 11, τοὺς (sc. brethren, Christians) ἐκ τῶν (sc. slaves) Ἀριστοβούλου, Ναρκίσσου R. 16. 10 f. Υἱός occurs in a metaphorical sense

---

[1] The v.l. in A. 7. 13 Ἐμμὼρ τοῦ Συχέμ (DH: al. ἐν Σ. or τοῦ ἐν Σ.) is explained in accordance with Gen. 33. 19 as Ἐ. πατρός Σ., which in any case is wrong.

(a common Hebraism) : 1 Th. 5. 5 υἱοὶ φωτός ἐστε καὶ υἱοὶ ἡμέρας; hence with omission of υἱός, the genitive being also used predicatively, οὐκ ἐσμὲν νυκτὸς οὐδὲ σκότους 1 Th. 5. 6, ἡμέρας ὄντες 8, cp. H. 10. 39 οὐκ ἐσμὲν ὑποστολῆς – ἀλλὰ πίστεως. Possession or discipleship: οἱ τοῦ Χριστοῦ 1 C. 15. 23; as predicate, A. 27. 36 τοῦ θεοῦ οὗ εἰμι, R. 8. 9 οὗτος οὐκ ἔστιν αὐτοῦ (Χρ.), 1 C. 1. 12, 3. 4 ἐγὼ μέν εἰμι Παύλου etc., 6. 19 οὐκ ἐστὲ ἑαυτῶν ('do not belong to yourselves,' cp. 20), 3. 21 πάντα ὑμῶν ἐστι (= ὑμέτερα, cp. § 48, 7); L. 20. 14; A. 1. 7 οὐχ ὑμῶν ἐστι γνῶναι 'does not belong to you,' 'is not your concern,' 2 P. 1. 20 προφητεία ἰδίας ἐπιλύσεως οὐ γίνεται; H. 5. 14 τελείων ἐστὶν ἡ στερεὰ τροφή; Herm. Sim. viii. 7. 6 ἡ ζωὴ πάντων ἐστὶ τῶν –, cp. A. 10. 36 after the removal of the interpolated κύριος, A. 20. 3 (Thuc. 1. 113).—The use of ἐν, εἰς with the genitive of the house of anyone is not found in the New Testament, nor yet the phrases ἐν, εἰς Ἀίδου (as in Clem. Cor. i. 4. 11), instead of which we have ἐν τῷ ᾅδῃ L. 16. 22, εἰς ᾅδην A. 2. 27 O.T. (ᾅδου EP and some MSS. of the LXX.), 31 (ᾅδου ACDEP).

3. **Objective genitive.** Noteworthy instances are Mt. 24. 6 ἀκοαὶ πολέμων 'rumours of wars': A. 4. 9 εὐεργεσία ἀνθρώπου 'to a man': R. 10. 2 ζῆλος θεοῦ 'concerning God' (Jo. 2. 17 O.T. ὁ ζ. τοῦ οἴκου σου): Jo. 7. 13, 20. 19 διὰ τὸν φόβον τῶν Ἰουδαίων 'fear of the Jews.' Further instances: Mt. 13. 18 τὴν παραβολὴν τοῦ σπείροντος (cp. 36) about, of: 1 C. 1. 6 τὸ μαρτύριον τοῦ Χριστοῦ, 1. 18 ὁ λόγος ὁ τοῦ σταυροῦ, Mt. 4 23 etc. τὸ εὐαγγέλιον τῆς βασιλείας, Mc. 1. 1 τὸ εὐαγγ. Ἰησοῦ Χρ.; phrases similar to the last are frequent in St. Paul (besides this use we have εὐαγγ. θεοῦ in R. 1. 1 and elsewhere, denoting the author, the meaning being there explained by περὶ τοῦ υἱοῦ αὐτοῦ in verse 3; τὸ εὐαγγ. μου R. 2. 16, 16. 25, cp. 2 C. 4. 3, 2 Tim. 2. 8, denoting the preacher; and τὸ εὐαγγ. τῆς ἀκροβυστίας G. 2. 7 = 'among,' 'to,' similar to the use of εὐαγγελίζεσθαί τινα; but εὐαγγ. Ματθαίου etc. would be presumptuous and false, as if the individual evangelist had a special gospel proceeding from himself, therefore κατὰ Μ. etc. is used, *i.e.* according to Matthew's presentation of it). Other objective genitives are πίστις Ἰησοῦ Χρ. R. 3. 22 etc., for which we also have π. εἰς τὸν κύριον Ἰ. Χρ. A. 20. 21 etc. and ἐν Χρ. Ἰ. 1 Tim. 3. 13 etc.: ὑπακοὴ τοῦ Χρ., τῆς πίστεως, τ. ἀληθείας 2 C. 10. 5, R. 1. 5, 1 P. 1. 22 etc., whereas ἀγάπη τοῦ θεοῦ can be both subjective and objective, but in δικαιοσύνη τ. θ. and δικ. τῆς πίστεως the gen. indicates the author and the cause respectively, hence ἡ ἐκ θ. δικ. Ph. 3. 9, ἡ ἐκ πίστεως δ. R. 9. 30, also διὰ πίστεως Ph. 3. 9. In R. 2. 7 ὑπομονὴ ἔργου ἀγαθοῦ 'endurance in' is also a kind of objective genitive; on the other hand 1 Th. 1. 3 τῆς ὑπομονῆς τῆς ἐλπίδος is parallel with the phrases τοῦ ἔργου τῆς πίστεως and τοῦ κόπου τῆς ἀγάπης, and is rather to be regarded as subjective, expressing patient hope in conjunction with active faith (cp. G. 5. 6) and labouring love.

4. The genitive of **the whole** or **partitive genitive** has not altogether died out, although its place has been taken to a great extent by the periphrasis with ἐξ (ἀπό, ἐν). Mt. 5. 29 f. ἓν τῶν μελῶν σου, 6. 29

§ 35. 4.]   GENITIVE.   97

ἐν τούτων, 10. 42 ἕνα τῶν μικρῶν τούτων etc.; but 10. 29, 18. 12 ἐν ἐξ αὐτῶν, 26. 21 εἷς ἐξ ὑμῶν etc.: in Mt. 6. 27, 7. 9, L. 11. 5, 12. 25 and elsewhere τίς ἐξ ὑμῶν; and, generally speaking, in the case of τίς the gen. appears more frequently with ἐξ than without it (Mt. 22. 28 has τίνος τῶν ἑπτά, but τῶν ἑπτά appears not to be genuine: Mc. 12. 23 τίνος αὐτῶν, here also the gen. is wanting in Δck: L. 7. 42 τίς αὐτῶν, but αὐτ. is omitted by D etc.: 14. 5 τίνος ὑμῶν, D ἐξ ὑμῶν: 20. 33 τίνος αὐτῶν, but αὐτ. om. ℵ*e ff,[2] so that the only certain instances of the simple gen. remaining are A. 7. 52, H. 1. 5, 13). With τις, however, the reverse is the case, the simple gen. preponderating (except in John); with ἕκαστος it is found exclusively; but πᾶς ἐξ ὑμῶν L. 14. 33. This use of ἐξ can hardly be called classical (although μόνος ἐξ ἁπάντων and similar phrases occur),[1] still it is more classical than that of ἀπό in Mt. 27. 21 τίνα ἀπὸ τῶν δύο; the use of ἐν also has classical precedent, Ja. 5. 13, 14, 19, 1 C. 15. 12 τις ἐν ὑμῖν, A. 5. 34 τις ἐν τῷ συνεδρίῳ (D ἐκ τοῦ συνεδρίου); cp. on the periphrasis for the partitive gen. with verbs, § 36, 1. This gen. is used predicatively in ὦν ἐστιν Ὑμέναιος 1 Tim. 1. 20, A. 23. 6: with ἐκ Jo. 18. 17, L. 22. 58, 1 C. 12. 15 f. (Clem. Cor. ii. 14. 1, 18. 1). The following is noticeable: τὰ αὐτὰ τῶν παθημάτων 1 P. 5. 9 (strictly incorrect).—The employment of the partitive gen. or a periphrasis for it as subject or object of the sentence is peculiar: Jo. 16. 17 εἶπον ἐκ τῶν μαθητῶν αὐτοῦ (some of his disciples) πρὸς ἀλλήλους, 7. 40 ἐκ τοῦ ὄχλου ἀκούσαντες – ἔλεγον,[2] παραγενομένων ἐκ τῆς πόλεως L. 8. 35 D (some men of the town), A. 21. 16 συνῆλθον δὲ καὶ (ἐκ add. E) τῶν μαθητῶν ἀπὸ Καισαρείας,[3] 19. 33 ἐκ τοῦ ὄχλου (sc. τινές), Ap. 11. 9, L. 21. 16 θανατώσουσιν ἐξ ὑμῶν (sc. τινάς), 11. 49, Mt. 23. 34, Ap. 2. 10, 2 Jo. 4; it even takes the place of a dative in Jo. 3. 25 ἐγένετο ζήτησις ἐκ τῶν μαθητῶν Ἰωάνου μετὰ Ἰουδαίου (-ων) 'on the part of some of the disciples,' cp. A. 15. 2. This form of expression is due to Hebrew influence (מִן), although in isolated cases the genitive is also so used in Attic (Xenoph. Anab. 3, 5. 16: Hellen. 4, 2. 20).—To the class of partitive genitives belongs also the gen. of the country, added to define the particular place intended, and always with the article (§ 46, 11): Ναζαρὲθ τῆς Γαλιλαίας Mt. 21. 11, Mc. 1. 9, Κανᾶ τῆς Γαλ. Jo. 2. 1, Ταρσὸς τῆς Κιλικίας A. 22. 3, with πόλις 21. 39, 16. 12 ἥτις (Φίλιπποι) ἐστὶν πρώτης (as should be read) μερίδος τῆς Μακεδονίας πόλις. As a definition of time: ὀψὲ σαββάτων Mt. 28. 1 'late on the Sabbath' (which in accordance with the next clause and Mc. 16. 1 must be equivalent to 'after the Sabbath'), δὶς τοῦ σαββάτου 'twice in the week' L. 18. 12. A further instance may be noticed: L. 19. 8 τὰ ἡμίσεια (τὰ ἥμισυ AR[D]) τῶν ὑπαρχόντων with classical assimilation to the gen. instead of τὸ ἥμισυ (Kühner ii.[2] 299, ἡ ἡμίσεια τῆς γῆς);

---

[1] Μόνος in the N.T. is never more nearly defined by a reference to the whole of which it is a part.

[2] Πολλοί is an interpolation of ΓΔΛ al.

[3] Here however τινες τῶν may have dropped out after μαθητῶν, since a second article is required.

G

elsewhere we have ἥμισυ καιροῦ Ap. 12. 14 (cp. 11. 9, 11 without a genitive), ἕως ἡμίσους τῆς βασιλείας Mc. 6. 23, like τὸ δέκατον (sc. μέρος) τῆς πόλεως Ap. 11. 13.

5. A nearer definition of any kind by means of **quality, direction, aim** etc. is expressed by the genitive in a long series of phrases, some of which obviously take their origin from Hebrew (in which language the adjective is but slightly developed): μισθοῦ τῆς ἀδικίας A. 1. 18, μ. ἀδ. 2 P. 2. 15, ὁ οἰκονόμος τῆς ἀδικίας L. 16. 8, τοῦ μαμωνᾶ τῆς ἀδ. 9, ὁ κριτὴς τ. ἀδ. 18. 6 = ὁ ἄδικος (cp. 16. 11 ἐν τῷ ἀδίκῳ μαμωνᾷ): καρδία πονηρὰ ἀπιστίας H. 3. 12, ῥήματα βλασφημίας A. 6. 11 א*D with v.l. βλάσφημα, cp. Ap. 13. 1, 17. 3, χολὴ πικρίας A. 8. 23, ῥίζα πικρίας H. 12. 15 cp. LXX. Deut. 29. 18,[1] A. 9. 15 σκεῦος ἐκλογῆς = ἐκλεκτόν (in R. 9. 22 f. σκεύη ὀργῆς, σκ. ἐλέους are different, being equivalent to persons who bear the wrath or the mercy), οἱ λόγοι τῆς χάριτος L. 4. 22, πάθη ἀτιμίας R. 1. 26, ὁ οἶνος τοῦ θυμοῦ Ap. 14. 10 etc. (where there is no equivalent adjective which could replace the gen.), τὸ σῶμα τῆς ἁμαρτίας R. 6. 6, τὸ σ. τοῦ θανάτου 7. 24 (cp. θνητὸν σ. 6. 12, 8. 11), τ. σ. τῆς ταπεινώσεως ἡμῶν and τ. σ. τῆς δόξης αὐτοῦ Ph. 3. 21, τ. σ. τῆς σαρκός Col. 1. 22, 2. 11 etc. The reverse order of words *e.g.* ἐπὶ πλούτου ἀδηλότητι = ἀδήλῳ πλούτῳ 1 Tim. 6. 17 (ἐν καινότητι ζωῆς R. 6. 4 = ἐν καινῇ ζωῇ, but cp. 7. 6) may be paralleled from the classical language (W. § 34, 3). Further noticeable instances are ἡμέρα ὀργῆς, σωτηρίας, ἐπισκοπῆς etc. after Hebrew models R. 2. 5, 2 C. 6. 2 O.T., 1 P. 2. 12, also ἀναδείξεως L. 1. 80, in which there is nothing remarkable but the Hebraic substitution of ἡμέρα for χρόνος (οἱ χρόνοι τῆς αἱρέσεως Aeschin. 2. 58): ἀνάστασις ζωῆς and κρίσεως '*to* life' etc. Jo. 5. 29 (ἀ. εἰς ζωήν LXX. 2 Macc. 7. 14): ὁδὸς ἐθνῶν Mt. 10. 5, ὁδὸν (a kind of preposition like דֶּרֶךְ, § 34, 8, note 1) θαλάσσης 4. 15 O.T.: instances with the meaning *to*, as ἡ θύρα τῶν προβάτων Jo. 10. 7, πίστεως A. 14. 27 (but θ. τοῦ λόγου Col. 4. 3 = a door by which the word enters), μετοικεσία Βαβυλῶνος Mt. 1. 11 f., ἡ διασπορὰ τῶν Ἑλλήνων Jo. 7. 35: with the meaning *among* (*from*), κίνδυνοι ποταμῶν, λῃστῶν 2 C. 11. 26, followed by ἐξ ἐθνῶν, ἐν θαλάσσῃ, etc.—To the gen. of **content** belongs among other instances Jo. 21. 8 τὸ δίκτυον τῶν ἰχθύων (like class. πλοῖα σίτου); to the gen. of **apposition** (Kühner Gr. ii.² 226 d), *i.e.* where the genitive takes the place of a word in apposition with another, 2 C. 5. 5 τὸν ἀρραβῶνα τοῦ πνεύματος ('which consists in' etc.), R. 4. 11 σημεῖον περιτομῆς (περιτομήν AC*), Jo. 2. 2 τοῦ ναοῦ τοῦ σώματος αὐτοῦ, E. 4. 9 τὰ κατώτερα [μέρη] τῆς γῆς (not partitive, see Win. § 59, 8, but perhaps gen. of the thing compared) etc.; also 2 P. 2. 6 πόλεις Σοδόμων καὶ Γομόρρας like Ἰλίου πόλιν Hom. Il. 5, 642 etc. (this construction occurs here only in the N.T., since πόλεως Θυατείρων A. 16. 14 is the gen. of πόλις Θυάτειρα, like πόλει Ἰόππῃ 11. 5; cp. also 2 C. 11. 32 τὴν πόλιν Δαμασκηνῶν, Ap. 3. 12, 18. 10, 21, 21. 2, 10).—On the gen.

---

[1] Μή τίς ἐστιν ἐν ὑμῖν ῥίζα ἄνω φύουσα ἐν χολῇ καὶ πικρίᾳ; but ῥίζα πικρίας is read by cod. AF, and ἐνοχλῇ for ἐν χ. by B*AF*, and this was the reading followed by the author of the Ep. to the Hebrews.

[§ 35. 5–6.] GENITIVE.

with adjectives and participles used substantivally see § 47, 1.—
The gen. is used predicatively (supra 2 and 4), denoting **quality**,
in Mc. 5. 42 ἦν ἐτῶν δώδεκα, L. 2. 42 ὅτε ἐγένετο ἐτῶν δώδεκα (D is
different),[1] H. 12. 11 πᾶσα παιδεία οὐ δοκεῖ χαρᾶς εἶναι, ἀλλὰ λύπης.

6. As in classical Greek, there is nothing to prevent **two genitives**
of different meaning from being connected with a single substantive:
2 C. 5. 1 ἡ ἐπίγειος ἡμῶν οἰκία τοῦ σκήνους, possessive gen. and gen.
of apposition, Ph. 2. 30 τὸ ὑμῶν (subjective) ὑστέρημα τῆς πρός με
λειτουργίας (objective), Ap. 7. 17, 2 P. 3. 2 τῆς τῶν ἀποστόλων ὑμῶν
('apostles sent *to* you') ἐντολῆς τοῦ κυρίου καὶ σωτῆρος (closely with
ἀποστ. 'sent from etc. to').[2] In most cases, however, if several
genitives stand together, one of them is dependent on the other,
a practice through which writers, especially St. Paul, are occasionally
brought to a really burdensome accumulation of words: 2 C. 4. 5
τὸν φωτισμὸν τοῦ εὐαγγελίου ('which proceeds from the gospel') τῆς
δόξης (content) τοῦ Χριστοῦ, E. 1. 6 εἰς ἔπαινον δόξης (a single idea,
cp. Ph. 1. 17 εἰς δόξαν καὶ ἔπαινον) τῆς χάριτος αὐτοῦ,[3] 4. 13 εἰς μέτρον
ἡλικίας τοῦ πληρώματος τοῦ Χριστοῦ, 1. 18, 19, Col. 2. 12, 1 Th. 1. 3
τῆς ὑπομονῆς τῆς ἐλπίδος (supra 3) τοῦ κυρίου ἡμῶν;[4] Ap. 14. 8 ἐκ
τοῦ οἴνου τοῦ θυμοῦ (supra 5) τῆς πορνείας αὐτῆς, unless τοῦ θυμοῦ
should be removed from this passage and from 18. 3 (with Griesbach)
as an interpolation from 14. 10, 16. 19 τὸ ποτήριον τοῦ οἴνου τοῦ
θυμοῦ τῆς ὀργῆς αὐτοῦ (αὐτοῦ om. ℵ), 19. 15 τὴν ληνὸν τοῦ οἴνου τοῦ
θυμοῦ τῆς ὀργῆς τοῦ θεοῦ. The last genitive of the series is usually
a possessive (Buttm. 136). In order that some clue may be left for
the understanding of the construction, it is necessary (and also in
conformity with Hebrew precedent) that the governing genitive
should always stand before the dependent genitive, while in the
case where two genitives are dependent on a *single* noun, one is
placed before and the other after the noun, see the instances given
above (Buttm. 135 f.). It has further been maintained (ibid. p.
294 f.), that in a case where a genitive without the article dependent
on a preposition governs another genitive, the former must always
occupy the first place: in the same way that a word in *any* case
without an article usually, though not always (Mt. 13. 33 εἰς ἀλεύρου
σάτα τρία) precedes the genitive which it governs. Exceptions
however must be admitted in the former case as well; Mt. 24. 31

---

[1] Here also belongs Ap. 21. 17 ἐμέτρησεν τὸ τεῖχος αὐτῆς ἑκατὸν – πηχῶν, =
'amounting to 100 cubits,' cp. ibid. 16.

[2] However, there is so much obscurity and harshness in this passage that
one is justified in supposing some corruption of the text (τῆς <διὰ> τῶν ἀποστ. ?
cp. the Syriac).

[3] DE read τῆς δόξης, which would necessitate the rendering 'the praise of
the glory of His grace'; cp. l. 12 εἰς ἔπ. (τῆς add. A) δόξης αὐτοῦ, 14 εἰς ἔπ. τῆς
(τῆς om. ℵ) δόξης αὐτοῦ.

[4] Here further, the possessive ὑμῶν is dependent on the first of the two genitives in each case ἔργου, κόπου, ὑπομονῆς, according to the prescribed rule (see
below in the text); but the Western and Syriac MSS. put this ὑμῶν after πίστεως,
and some of these also make the sentence much smoother by reading the acc.
τὸ ἔργον – τὸν κόπον – τὴν ὑπομονήν.

μετὰ σάλπιγγος φωνῆς μεγάλης, if the reading is correct,[1] means 'with a loud trumpet-sound' (cp. H. 12. 19, Ap. 1. 10, 4. 1, 8. 13), and 2 C. 3. 18 ἀπὸ κυρίου πνεύματος 'from the spirit of the Lord,' cp. verse 17.[2] Also βαπτισμῶν διδαχῆς H. 6. 2 (unless B is right in reading διδαχήν) can only mean 'teaching of baptisms.'

§ 36. CONTINUATION: GENITIVE WITH VERBS, ETC.

1. The genitive is used in Greek in connection with **verbs** in a series of instances where the **partitive** meaning is obvious. In the N.T. this partitive genitive with verbs is replaced, even more frequently than in the other cases mentioned (§ 35, 4), by a periphrasis with a preposition (or the use of another case). It is true that μεταλαμβάνειν 'to partake of' always has the gen. (A. 2. 46, 27. 33 f., 2 Tim. 2. 6, H. 6. 7, 12. 10; the verb has a different meaning in the combination καιρὸν μεταλαβών A. 24. 25 = Polyb. 2, 16. 25 = 'to get [an opportunity] later'); so also μετέχειν in 1 C. 9. 12, 10. 21, H. 2. 14, 5. 13, 7. 13, though μετ. ἐκ is found as well in 1 C. 10. 17, and just as these constructions with the gen. are limited to Luke, Paul, and Hebrews, so κοινωνεῖν τινος only appears in H. 2. 14, while Paul, Peter, and John say κοινωνεῖν τινι (using the dat. not only of the person as in classical Greek, but also of the thing as in R. 15. 27 τοῖς πνευματικοῖς αὐτῶν ἐκοινώνησαν τὰ ἔθνη, cp. 1 Tim. 5. 22, 1 P. 4. 13, 2 Jo. 11; R. 12. 13 holds an intermediate position), or else κοινωνεῖν τινι (person) ἔν τινι G. 6. 6, or εἰς λόγον δόσεως καὶ λήμψεως Ph. 4. 15. Μεταδιδόναι never has the genitive, but the accusative, if it is the whole which is imparted R. 1. 11, 1 Th. 2. 8 (the classical usage is analogous), elsewhere only the dat. of the person; μετεῖναι is unrepresented; ὁ ἔχων μέρος ἐν—(of the thing) occurs in Ap. 20. 6. But the greater number of the constructions which come under this head—to take of, to bring, eat, drink of etc.—have been lost to the genitive, and are expressed by ἐκ or ἀπό: L. 20. 10 ἀπὸ τοῦ καρποῦ δώσουσιν,[3] Mc. 12. 2 ἵνα λάβῃ ἀπὸ τῶν καρπῶν (only in A. 27. 36 do we have προσελάβοντο τροφῆς [with many var. lect.], like γενέσθαι, vide infra; beside which ibid. 33 μηδὲν προσλαβόμενοι is correctly used to indicate not the whole but the part), Jo. 21. 10 ἐνέγκατε ἀπὸ τῶν ὀψαρίων, 1 C. 11. 28 ἐκ τοῦ ἄρτου ἐσθιέτω, Jo. 4. 14 ὃς ἂν πίῃ ἐκ τοῦ ὕδατος (as well as ἐσθίειν τι, where the object consists of the whole, Mc. 1. 6 ἐσθίων ἀκρίδας καὶ μέλι ἄγριον, like Aristoph. Eq. 604 ἤσθιον δὲ τοὺς παγούρους; 1 C. 8. 10 τὰ εἰδωλόθυτα ἐσθίειν, cp. 7, Ap. 2. 14, 20, i.e.

---

[1] Φωνῆς is wanting in אL etc., D al. have σ. καὶ φων. μεγ.

[2] The Vulgate has *a domino spiritu* (Tertullian indeed reads *a domino spirituum*). There might also appear to be an irregular order of words in the reading given by Origen (in Matt. tom. xiv. 14) in 1 C. 2. 4: οὐκ ἐν πειθοῖ σοφίας λόγων, ἀλλ' ἐν ἀποδείξει πνεύματος δυνάμεως. But cp. with the last words πνεῦμα τῆς πίστεως 2 C. 4. 13, πν. σοφίας καὶ ἀποκαλύψεως E. 1. 17 etc.

[3] The use with the simple gen. in Ap. 2. 17 τῷ νικοῦντι δώσω αὐτῷ τοῦ (so AC; τὸ B, ἐκ τοῦ א) μάννα τοῦ κεκρυμμένου is not authentic.

meat which comes from sacrifices; 1 C. 10. 18 οἱ ἐσθίοντες τὰς θυσίας, which they consume in common).[1] Of verbs of cognate meaning to these, **χορτάζειν** 'to satisfy' (vulgar word for κορεννύναι, see Athenaeus iii. 99 E) has the genitive Mc. 8. 4, the passive -άζεσθαι only has ἀπό, ἐκ L. 15. 16,[2] 16. 21, Ap. 19. 21, **κορέννυσθαι** (literary language) has the gen. A. 27. 38; **γεύεσθαι** has the gen. in γεύεσθαι θανάτου Mt. 16. 28 etc., H. 2. 9, τοῦ δείπνου L. 14. 24, μηδενὸς A. 23. 14, τῆς δωρεᾶς H. 6. 4: on the other hand the acc. in Jo. 2. 9 τὸ ὕδωρ, H. 6. 5 θεοῦ ῥῆμα, not a classical but most probably a popular usage. The phrase ἐγώ σου **ὀναίμην** Philem. 20 (the word only occurs here)[3] is derived from the literary language; **ἀπολαύειν** is unrepresented; **φείδομαι** always has the gen., but is limited to Luke (A. 20. 29), Paul (R. 8. 32 and passim) and 2 Peter (2. 4 f.).

2. Closely related to a partitive genitive is the gen. with verbs of **touching** and **seizing**. Of this we have the following N.T. instances: **ἅπτεσθαι** Mt. 8. 4 and frequently in the Gospels (in John only in 20. 17 besides 1 Jo. 5. 18; in the Epistles besides the last passage quoted only in 1 C. 7. 4, 2 C. 6. 17 O.T.; never in Acts), **καθάπτειν** A. 28. 3, **θιγγάνειν** (literary language) H. 11. 28, 12. 20; **ἐπιλαμβάνεσθαι** Mt. 14. 31, Mc. 8. 23, Luke passim, 1 Tim. 6. 12, 19, H. 2. 16, 8. 9 O.T., 'to lay hold on any one (anything)': also with the *part* expressed in the gen., Mc. 8. 23 ἐπιλαβόμενος τῆς χειρὸς τοῦ τυφλοῦ,[4] so that the correct construction is in all cases the gen.;[5] on the other hand, κρατεῖν 'to seize,' 'to hold' (Hellenistic) has the whole in the accus. as in Mt. 14. 3 κρατήσας τὸν Ἰωάνην, and the gen. is confined to the part which one seizes on, Mt. 9. 25 ἐκράτησε τῆς χειρὸς (τὴν χεῖρα D) αὐτῆς, Mc. 1. 31 (not D), 5. 41 (τὴν χεῖρα D), L. 8. 54 (κρατεῖν τινὰ τινός is not found except in Mc. 9. 27 according to A al., where אBD read as in the other passages): in metaphorical sense, 'to hold fast to,' 'lay hold on,' with gen. (probably due to the use of κρατεῖν 'to get the mastery of' with gen. in the literary language) H. 4. 14, 6. 18. Luke also says **πιάσας** (vulgar word = λαβών) αὐτὸν τῆς χειρός A. 3. 7, like λαβὼν Πολυξένην χερός Eurip. Hec. 523. In addition to these we have

---

[1] Still in many places a classical writer would have employed the gen. where the acc. occurs in the N.T., as in Jo. 6. 53 ἐὰν μὴ φάγητε τὴν σάρκα τοῦ υἱοῦ τοῦ ἀνθ. καὶ πίητε αὐτοῦ τὸ αἷμα, cp. the use of the acc. in 54, 56, 57 with τρώγειν, a verb which in the N.T., as in classical Greek, never takes the gen., but which a classical writer would not have used in this connection.

[2] There is a v.l. in APQ al. γεμίσαι τὴν κοιλίαν αὐτοῦ ἀπό, cp. infra 4.

[3] Οὕτως ὀναίμην τῶν τέκνων Aristoph. Thesm. 469; on the other hand, apart from these combinations with the gen. of the person, the use of ἀπό with this verb is found as early as Plato, Charmid. 175 E ἀπὸ τῆς σωφροσύνης.

[4] The reading of D λαβόμενος τὴν χεῖρα τοῦ τ. is neither in the style of classical (Plato Parmen. ad init. τῆς χειρός) nor N.T. Greek (which never has the middle λαμβάνεσθαι).

[5] It is only in appearance that ἐπιλαμβ. seems to be used with accus. as well: in A. 9. 27 (cp. 16. 19, 18. 17) ἐπιλαβόμενος αὐτὸν ἤγαγεν, the αὐτόν is dependent on ἤγαγεν, and αὐτοῦ must be supplied with ἐπιλαβ. (L. 23. 26 ἐπιλαβόμενοι Σίμωνά τινα אBCDLX must be a wrong reading instead of Σίμωνός τινος AP al.).

with the gen.: ἔχεσθαι (met.) H. 6. 9 τὰ κρείσσονα καὶ ἐχόμενα σωτηρίας ('connected with,' 'leading to salvation') and ἀντέχεσθαι (met.) Mt. 6. 24, L. 16. 13 τοῦ ἑνὸς ἀνθέξεται 'to attach oneself to,' 'hold to,' Tit. 1. 9 (similar meaning), 1 Th. 5. 14 ἀντέχεσθε τῶν ἀσθενῶν ('to assist'), like ἀντιλαμβάνεσθαι (met.) L. 1. 54, A. 20. 35 ('to assist,' as in LXX. and Hellenist. Greek; but in οἱ τῆς εὐεργεσίας ἀντιλαμβανόμενοι 1 Tim. 6. 2 'to attain,' 'to partake of').

3. The gen. with verbs of **attaining** (cp. ἀντιλαμβάνεσθαι supra 2 ad fin.) only remains in some isolated instances in the more cultured writers. Τυγχάνειν τινός L. 20. 35 (τυχεῖν is absent in Latin MSS.), A. 24. 3, 26. 22, 27. 3, 2 Tim. 2. 10, H. 8. 6, 11. 35, ἐπιτυγχάνειν τινος H. 6. 15, 11. 33, but in R. 11. 7 τοῦτο οὐκ ἐπέτυχεν is read by all the standard MSS. (so οὐδέν Herm. Mand. ix. 5, but τῆς πράξεως x. 2. 4, cp. on the classical use of the neut. pron. or adj. Kühner ii.[2] 301, note 9). Λαγχάνειν takes the gen. only in appearance in L. 1. 9 (τοῦ θυμιᾶσαι = θυμ., § 71, 3), the acc. in A. 1. 17, 2 P. 1. 1 (which is also more frequent in classical Greek than the gen.); κληρονομεῖν only the acc. Mt. 5. 5 etc. (Hellenistic, Phrynich. p. 129; Attic has the gen.); ἐφικνεῖσθαι is followed by a preposition 2 C. 10. 13 f.—Verbs of **desiring** and **striving after**: ἐπιθυμεῖν takes the gen. in A. 20. 33, 1 Tim. 3. 1, but the acc. in Mt. 5. 28 in BDE etc.[1] (αὐτῆς is hardly attested, *the case is wanting in* א* *and some fathers*), elsewhere it takes the inf. or is used absolutely; ὀρέγεσθαι with gen. 1 Tim. 3. 1, 6. 10, H. 11. 16, as also ὁμείρεσθαι (= ἱμείρ.) 1 Th. 2. 8; ἐπιποθεῖν is transitive as in classical Greek, so also contrary to classical usage are πεινᾶν, διψᾶν, § 34, 2.

4. The genitive after '**to be full**,' '**to fill**' has been better preserved. Πιμπλάναι, ἐμπιπλάναι (the former only in Gospels and Acts, the latter also in R. 15. 24) always take the gen., Mt. 22. 10, L. 1. 53 etc.; πληροῦν takes a gen., L. 2. 40 πληρούμενον σοφίας (-ίᾳ א^cBL, vide inf.), A. 2. 28 O.T. (with acc. for v.l. as also in the LXX.), 5. 28, 13. 52, R. 15. 13 (BFG πληροφορῆσαι ἐν [ἐν om. FG] πάσῃ χαρᾷ, vide inf.), 15. 14, 2 Tim. 1. 4: and also ἐκ (partitive, supra 1) Jo. 12. 3 (B ἐπλήσθη): the pass. takes the dat. R. 1. 29, 2 C. 7. 4, cp. § 38, 1, or ἐν E. 5. 18, but Col. 2. 10 ἐν αὐτῷ (Χριστῷ) πεπληρωμένοι[2] is different: cp. also for the active R. 15. 13 supra: with the acc. (supra § 34, 6) Ph. 1. 11, cp. Col. 1. 9: γέμειν with gen. Mt. 23. 27 and passim, also Ap. 4. 6, 8 etc. (ibid. 17. 3 γέμοντα [γέμον] ὀνόματα βλασφημίας is a solecism); so γεμίζειν Mc. 15. 36 (πλήσας D), Jo. 2. 7, 6. 13 ?,[3] Ap. 15. 8, with ἐκ L. 15. 16 v.l. (cp. supra 1), Ap. 8. 5, cp. πληροῦν supra. Under this head may also be brought βάπτειν τὸ

---

[1] So frequently in LXX.: Exod. 20. 17 οὐκ ἐπιθυμήσεις τὴν γυναῖκα κ.τ.λ., Deut. 5. 21 etc. (Winer), Herm. Vis. i. 1. 4, Sim. ix. 9. 7 (with gen. Sim. ix. 13. 8).

[2] Probably 'fulfilled' = 'perfect,' cp. 4. 12 τέλειοι καὶ πεπληροφορημένοι (D^cE al. πεπληρωμένοι) ἐν παντὶ θελήματι τοῦ θεοῦ.

[3] Ἐγέμισαν δώδεκα κοφίνους κλασμάτων ἐκ τῶν πέντε ἄρτων κ.τ.λ.; we might correct κοφ. κλασμάτων as in L. 9. 17, cp. also κόφινον κοπρίων L. 13. 8 D.

§ 36. 4–6.]   *GENITIVE WITH VERBS, ETC.*   103

ἄκρον τοῦ δακτύλου ὕδατος (ὕδατι ℵ) L. 16. 24,[1] and perhaps περισσεύειν ἄρτων L. 15. 17 (Lucian, not class.), cp. λείπεσθαί τινος infra 9.

5. Of verbs denoting **perception,** αἰσθάνεσθαι only appears once (L. 9. 45) and there with the acc. of the thing (αὐτό, 'to understand' = συνιέναι; on the classical use of αἰσθ. τι see Kühner ii.[2] 309); with πυνθάνεσθαι Mt. 2. 4 [not D], Jo. 4. 52 [not B] the person is expressed by παρά, with συνιέναι it is nowhere expressed. Thus the only remaining verb which takes the gen. is ἀκούειν (ἐπακούειν 2 C. 6. 2 O.T. takes the gen.: also ἐπακροᾶσθαι A. 16. 25; ὑπακούειν takes the dative). With this verb the person, whose speech one hears, regularly stands in the gen. (as in classical Greek), while the thing, concerning which one hears tell, stands in the acc. (as does also the person in a similar case, as in E. 4. 21 ἠκούσατε αὐτόν). It is not an essential difference that the person may also be introduced by παρά Jo. 1. 41 and passim (classical), and occasionally by ἀπό (unclassical, A. 9. 13, 1 Jo. 1. 5) or, with Hebrew phraseology, ἀπὸ (διά, ἐκ) τοῦ στόματός τινος L. 22. 71, A. 1. 4 D, 22. 14. But there remains some common ground for the use of genitive and accusative. 'To hear a sound' in classical Greek is ἀκούειν φωνῆς, βοῆς etc.; but in the N.T. we have both ἀκ. φωνῆς and φωνήν, the former being used in St. John's Gospel in the sense of 'to obey' (5. 25, 28, 10. 3, 16 etc.), the latter in the sense of mere perception (3. 8, 5. 37), while in the Acts and the Apocalypse both constructions occur indiscriminately with the latter meaning: acc. A. 9. 4, 22. 9, 14, 26. 14 (gen. E), Ap. 1. 10, 4. 1 etc. (also 2 P. 1. 18); gen. A. 9. 7, 11. 7 (acc. D), 22. 7, Ap. 14. 13, 16. 1, 21. 3 (3. 20 'to obey'), as also H. 3. 7, 15 O.T., 12. 19. 'To hear words' admits of both constructions in classical Greek also; the N.T. generally uses the acc., but the gen. in Jo. 7. 40, 12. 47, 19. 13 (with v.l., cp. 8). The following are used correctly, στεναγμοῦ A. 7. 34, συμφωνίας καὶ χορῶν L. 15. 25; the following are doubtful, τὴν σοφίαν Σαλομῶνος Mt. 12. 42, L. 11. 31, τὴν βλασφημίαν Mt. 26. 65, τῆς βλασφημίας Mc. 14. 64 (acc. ADG), τὸν ἀσπασμόν L. 1. 41; λέγοντα(ς) Ap. 5. 13 is wrong (λαλοῦντας A. 2. 6 D).—It is probably only in appearance that the verb takes a double gen. in passages like A. 22. 1 ἀκούσατέ μου τῆς πρὸς ὑμᾶς ἀπολογίας (Jo. 12. 47 al.; Herm. Mand. xii. 5, cp. μου τὰς ἐντολάς Sim. ix. 23. 2), since μου belongs to ἀπολογίας, the pronoun being similarly placed in Jo. 9. 6 ἐπέχρισεν αὐτοῦ τὸν πηλὸν ἐπὶ τοὺς ὀφθαλμούς.—Ὀσφραίνεσθαι appears nowhere, and ὄζειν is not found with a case that more nearly defines it (the gen. with the latter verb is of course of a different character to the gen. with the former); but on the analogy of ὄζειν, πνεῖν, ἐμπνεῖν τινος 'to smell of something' we have in A. 9. 1 ἐμπνέων ἀπειλῆς καὶ φόνου (LXX. Jos. 10. 40 πᾶν ἐμπνέον ζωῆς).

6. **To remember, to forget.** Μιμνῄσκεσθαι H. 2. 6 O.T., 13. 3) together with its aorist and perfect always takes the gen. (on

---

[1] The LXX. uses ἀπό Levit. 14. 16 (Buttm. 148); the classical instances of βάπτεσθαί τινος (Arat. 650 etc., Buttm. ibid.) are formed on the analogy of λούεσθαί τινος in Homer.

1 C. 11. 2 f. see § 34, 3); also μνημονεύειν for the most part, but the acc. in Mt. 16. 9 (D is different), Jo. 15. 20 א (τὸν λόγον), D (τοὺς λόγους) instead of τοῦ λόγου (gen. in 16. 4 [om. א°D], 21), 1 Th. 2. 9, 2 Tim. 2. 8, Ap. 18. 5 (Herm. Vis. i. 3. 3, ii. 1. 3): with περί ('to make mention') H. 11. 22 (15 gen.): classical usage corresponds to this, both cases being used; ἀναμιμνήσκειν and -εσθαι take acc., Mc. 14. 72, 1 C. 4. 17, 2 C. 7. 15, H. 10. 32 (class. acc. and more often gen.); ὑπομιμνήσκειν and -εσθαι take acc. in Jo. 14. 26, 3 Jo. 10 (2 Tim. 2. 14 ταῦτα ὑπομίμνῃσκε is different, the acc. being that of the inner object), gen. in L. 22. 61, and περί 2 P. 1. 12. Ἐπιλανθάνεσθαι with gen. only occurs in H. 6. 10, 13. 2 (acc. א*), 16; similarly ἐκλανθ. ibid. 12. 5; ἐπιλανθ. takes acc. in Ph. 3. 14 (as occasionally in classical Greek).

7. There are but few remaining instances of the genitive with verbs expressing **emotion**. The cause of the emotion (after ὀργίζεσθαι, θαυμάζειν, ἐλεεῖν etc.) never stands in the gen.; the Hebraic verb σπλαγχνίζεσθαι=ἐλεεῖν (from σπλάγχνα = רַחֲמִים) probably only appears to be followed by the gen. of the person pitied in Mt. 18. 27 [1] (elsewhere it takes ἐπί τινα or ἐπί τινι, περί τινος). Ἀνέχεσθαι 'to bear with,' however, takes the gen. throughout in the N.T. as elsewhere, ὑμῶν Mt. 17. 17 etc. Μέλει takes the gen. in 1 C. 9. 9, but DEFG read περὶ τῶν βοῶν, which is also the construction in Mt. 22. 16 = Mc. 12. 4, Jo. 10. 13, 12. 6, 1 P. 5. 7 (not unclassical); in A. 18. 17 οὐδὲν τούτων τῷ Γαλλίωνι ἔμελεν the construction is probably personal as often in classical Greek (οὐδέν being nominative and τούτων partitive). Still we have ἐπιμελεῖσθαί τινος L. 10. 34 f., 1 Tim. 3. 5; ἀμελεῖν τινος 1 Tim. 4. 14, H. 2. 3, 8. 9 O.T.; προνοεῖσθαι 1 Tim. 5. 8; μεριμνᾶν Mt. 6. 34 with ἑαυτῆς אB etc., τὰ ἑαυτῆς EK, perhaps ἑαυτῇ should be read from the Lat. sibi (τὰ περὶ ὑμῶν Ph. 2. 20, ὑπέρ τινος 1 C. 12. 25).

8. The following verbs of **ruling (excelling)** take the genitive: ἄρχειν Mc. 10. 42, R. 15. 12 O.T., κυριεύειν L. 22. 25, R. 6. 9 etc., κατακυριεύειν Mt. 20. 25, Mc. 10. 42 etc. (for κατεξουσιάζειν ibid. vide inf. 10), αὐθεντεῖν 1 Tim. 2. 12, ἡγεμονεύειν, τετραρχεῖν, ἀνθυπατεύειν L. 2. 2, 3. 1, A. 18. 12 (v.l.), καταδυναστεύειν Ja. 2. 6 א°BC al., but ὑμᾶς is read by א*A like καταβραβεύειν τινά etc., § 34, 1; on κρατεῖν vide supra 2. But βασιλεύειν no longer governs the genitive, except in Mt. 2. 22 τῆς Ἰουδαίας אB (the rest read ἐπὶ τῆς Ἰ. as often in the LXX.), elsewhere (ἐπὶ τῆς γῆς Ap. 5. 10 = 'on earth') it takes ἐπί τινα L. 1. 33, 19. 14, 27, R. 5. 14, after Hebrew precedent (מָלַךְ עַל). On ἡττᾶσθαι see § 37, 4. Verbs denoting excellence: ὑπερβάλλειν τινός E. 3. 19 (so Plat. Gorg. 475 B, the usual classical construction is the acc. or absolute, as in N.T. 2 C. 3. 10, 9. 19), ὑπερέχειν τινός Ph. 2. 3, but τινά (also classical) 4. 7. Here also, therefore, we only find remnants of the old usage; especially is this the case with the gen. of the thing after verbs of **accusing** etc., of which the only

---

[1] Σπλαγχνισθεὶς δὲ ὁ κύριος τοῦ δούλου ἐκείνου 'the lord of that slave.'

§ 36. 8-9.]   *GENITIVE WITH VERBS, ETC.*   105

instance which can be adduced is ἐγκαλεῖσθαι στάσεως A. 19. 40, and this is contrary to Attic usage (ἐγκαλεῖν τινί τι, but τινί τινος in Plutarch Aristid. 10), elsewhere ἐγκ. and κρίνεσθαι (pass.) take περί τινος A. 23. 29, 6 etc. (Attic); for the dat. instead of gen. of the punishment see § 37, 2.—The gen. of **price** is still used with verbs of buying and selling, thus Mt. 10. 29 ἀσσαρίου πωλεῖται 26. 9, A. 5. 8 etc.; also συμφωνεῖν (to agree) δηναρίου Mt. 20. 13, but ἐκ δην. τὴν ἡμέραν ibid. 2,[1] cp. for the same periphrasis for this gen. ἀγοράζειν ἐκ Mt. 27. 7, κτᾶσθαι ἐκ A. 1. 18; see further L. 16. 9 (on the use of ἐν see § 41, 1); a kindred use is ἀξιοῦν (καταξιοῦν) τινος 2 Th. 1. 5, 11, 1 Tim. 5. 17, H. 3. 3, 10. 29; but 'to exchange for' is expressed by ἀλλάξαι τι ἐν R. 1. 23 (after the LXX. Ps. 105. 20), cp. 25 μεταλλάσσειν ἐν, 26 μεταλλ. εἰς (unclassical, although the gen. with μετ. is also absent from classical Greek; in Plat. Tim. 19 A μετ. εἰς means 'to bring over to another place').

9. Of verbs which contain the idea of **separation**, the following are found with the gen.: ἀπαλλοτριοῦν E. 2. 12, 4. 18, ἀποστερεῖσθαι 1 Tim. 6. 5, with v.l. ἀπεστραμμένων ἀπό (D*), cp. 2 Tim. 4. 4, ἀστοχεῖν 1 Tim. 1. 6 (with περί τι 6. 21, 2 Tim. 2. 18), διαφέρειν 'to differ' Mt. 6. 26 etc., κωλύειν τινά τινος 'to hinder from' (Xenoph. Polyb.) A. 27. 43 (elsewhere κ. τινα, κ. τι, also after Hebrew example κωλύειν τι ἀπό τινος L. 6. 29, 'to refuse,' as in LXX. Gen. 23. 6), λείπεσθαι 'to lack' Ja. 1. 5, 2. 15 (ἐν μηδενί 1. 4 'in no respect'), cp. περισσεύειν τινός, supra 4, παύεσθαι 1 P. 4. 1 πέπαυται ἁμαρτίας (ibid. 3. 10 O.T. παύειν τινὰ ἀπό; ἀναπαύεσθαι ἐκ as in class. Greek Ap. 14. 13, κατέπαυσεν [intrans.] ἀπό H. 4. 4 O.T., 10) ἄρχεσθαί τινος does not occur. ὑστερεῖν 'to be inferior to' (cp. ὕστερος) 2 C. 11. 5, 12. 11: 'to lack' L. 22. 35: in the same sense ὑστερεῖσθαι R. 3. 23 (with ἐν 1 C. 1. 7, cp. supra λείπεσθαι: ὑστερεῖν ἀπό 'to remain alienated from ' = 'to lose' H. 12. 15 [LXX. Eccl. 6. 2], cp. ἀνυστέρητος ἀπό Herm. Mand. ix. 4); ἀπέχεσθαι 'to abstain' A. 15. 29, 1 Tim. 4. 3, 1 P. 2. 11 (in A. 15. 20 the reading varies between the simple gen. and ἀπό; with ἀπό 1 Th. 4. 3, 5. 22): ἀπέχειν 'to be distant' L. 7. 6 ℵ*D (v.l. with ἀπό, as in 24. 13 etc.); χρῄζειν Mt. 6. 32, L. 11. 8 (ὅσων, ὅσον ℵ°DE al.), 12. 30, R. 16. 2, 2 C. 3. 1. To these may be added δεῖσθαί τινος 'to ask' Mt. 9. 38, Luke passim (for which πρός τινα is used in A. 8. 24, cp. εὔχομαι πρὸς 2 C. 13. 7, λέγω πρός), 2 C. 8. 4, G. 4. 12; προσδεῖσθαι 'to need' only in A. 17. 25. Quite peculiar is the use of the gen. in οὐ βραδύνει κύριος τῆς ἐπαγγελίας 2 P. 3. 9, 'hesitates and refrains from accomplishing it.' But in other cases separation is expressed by ἀπό or ἐξ (classical Greek uses the simple gen. as well): with χωρίζειν, λύειν, λυτροῦν, ἐλευθεροῦν, ῥύεσθαι, σῴζειν, καθαρίζειν, λούειν; with μεθιστάναι L. 16. 4 there are

---

[1] Unless this ἐκ has a distributive meaning, as in Attic inscriptions (Meisterhans' Grammar of Attic Inscriptions, p. 173. 2); κριθῶν ... πραθεισῶν ἐκ τριῶν δραχμῶν τὸν μέδιμνον ἕκαστον, where an apparently irregular acc. is added in the same way as in Mt. τὴν ἡμέραν. The same inscr. has elsewhere: πραθέντων ἐξ δραχμῶν τοῦ μεδίμνου ἑκάστου; of course ἐξ ἐξ could not well be said. In another instance: ἐξ ὀκτὼ ὀβολῶν τὸν στατῆρα, the acc. likewise has no governing verb ('eight oboli being reckoned for each stater').

variant readings (ἐκ τῆς οἰκονομίας אBD, LX with ἀπό, APR al. with the simple gen.).[1]

10. The following **compound verbs** take the gen. on the strength of the preposition : ἐκπίπτειν in metaphorical sense (not in the literal) G. 5. 4, 2 P. 3. 17; the remaining instances are all compounds of κατά (with the meaning 'against' or 'down over'; on the other hand, with the meaning 'down,' they take the acc., § 34, 1): καταγελᾶν Mt. 9. 24 (D* αὐτόν), Mc. 5. 40, L. 8. 53; καταγινώσκειν 1 Jo. 3. 20 f. (καταδικάζειν τινός is classical, in the N.T. it only takes the acc., Mt. 12. 7, also Ja. 5. 6); κατακαυχᾶσθαι 'to boast oneself against' R. 11. 18, Ja. 2. 13 (κατακρίνειν always takes the acc.; in Attic τινός); καταλαλεῖν Ja. 4. 11, 1 P. 2. 12 (Clem. Hom. xvi. 8, xix. 7 also has καταλέγειν τινός 'to revile'); καταμαρτυρεῖν Mt. 26. 62 etc.; καταναρκᾶν, a Pauline word, 'to be burdensome to' 2 C. 11. 8, 12. 13; καταστρηνιᾶν 'to wax wanton against' 1 Tim. 5. 11; καταφρονεῖν Mt. 6. 24 etc.; καταχεῖν 'to pour over' takes the gen. in Mc. 14. 3 according to אBC al., other MSS. have κατά or ἐπί with gen.: in Mt. 26. 7 it takes ἐπί τινος or ἐπί τι; κατεξουσιάζειν (cp. supra 8) Mt. 20. 25 = Mc. 10. 42; κατηγορεῖν passim.

11. The use of the gen. as the **complement of adjectives and adverbs** is also, as contrasted with classical usage, very limited. The following instances occur: **κοινωνός**, συγκοιν. τινος (gen. of the thing) 2 C. 1. 7, 1 P. 5. 1, R. 11. 17 (also with the gen. of the person, 'the companion of someone,' H. 10. 33, also 1 C. 10. 18, 20 ; beside which we have κοινωνοὶ τῷ Σίμωνι L. 5. 10 [gen. D], cp. § 37, 3 and κοινωνεῖν, supra 1); [not κοινός τινος, nor ἴδιος; Clem. Cor. i. 7. 7 has ἀλλότριοι τοῦ θεοῦ]; **μέτοχος** H. 3. 1, 14, 6. 4, 12. 8 (= 'a companion of someone' 1. 9 O.T.; cp. E. 5. 7 ?); σύμμορφος τῆς εἰκόνος R. 8. 29, i.e. 'a bearer of the image,' cp. § 37, 6 for the dat. (in συνεργός τινος and similar cases with a personal gen. the adjective has become a substantive, cp. ibid.); **ξένος** τινός 'estranged from a thing,' E. 2. 12 (Plat. Apol. 17 D; with dat. Clem. Cor. i. 1. 1); **ἀπείραστος** κακῶν 'untempted by,' Ja. 1. 13 (so in classical Greek ἀπείρατός τινος, ἄγευστος κακῶν etc., Kühner ii.[2] p. 344 f.); in **ἄνομος** θεοῦ – **ἔννομος** Χριστοῦ 1 C. 9. 21 the gen. is dependent on νόμος (a peculiar and bold use, cp. § 28, 6); but ἄσπιλος is followed by ἀπό (ἐκ CP) Ja. 1. 27, as also ἀθῷος Mt. 27. 24, καθαρός A. 20. 26 (Demosth. 59. 78), cp. καθαρίζειν ἀπό supra 9; μεστός τινος Mt. 23. 28 etc., **πλήρης** L. 4. 1 etc. (κενός and ἐνδεής are never found with gen., κ. ἀπό Herm. Mand. v. 7, xi. 4), cp. 'to fill' supra 4 ; **ἄξιος, ἀνάξιος** Mt. 3. 8, 1 C. 6. 2, etc., cp. gen. of price supra 8; **ἔνοχος** θανάτου Mt. 26. 66, Mc. 14. 64, αἰωνίου ἁμαρτήματος (ἁμαρτίας, κρίσεως) Mc. 3. 29, etc. (as well as the use with the dat., modelled on ἐνέχεσθαί τινι, Mt. 5. 21 f., which is the commoner classical construction ; ibid. 22 we also have ἔνοχος εἰς τὴν γέενναν); **ὅμοιος** with gen. only in Jo. 8. 55 אCLX ὑμῶν, but ὑμῖν is read by ABD etc., cp. 9. 9, 1 Jo. 3. 2 and elsewhere in N.T. (the gen. is also classical but rare); ἀκόλουθα τούτων Herm. Mand. viii. 4. 10

---

[1] The reading in A. 19. 27 καθαιρεῖσθαι τῆς μεγαλειότητος (אABE), instead of ἡ μεγαλειότης αὐτῆς or αὐτῆς ἡ μεγ., seems to be impossible.

(classical). Adverbs: ἐγγύς with gen. Jo. 11. 18, R. 10. 8 O.T., H. 6. 8, 8. 13 etc., with dat. (rarely in classical, more often in late Greek) only A. 9. 38 ἐγγὺς οὔσης τῆς Λύδδας τῇ Ἰόππῃ (therefore with good reason), 27. 8 (the text of the passage is not quite certain); πλησίον Jo. 4. 5, cp. L. 10. 29, 36 and ὁ πλησίον σου Mt. 5. 43 etc.; ἐντός L. 17. 21,[1] ἐκτός 1 C. 6. 18 etc.; ἔξω Mt. 21. 39 etc. (not ἔσω, ἔσωθεν, since 2 C. 4. 16 ὁ ἔσω ἡμῶν *sc.* ἄνθρωπος should be taken like the preceding ὁ ἔξω ἡμῶν ἄ. in the sense of 'our' etc.); ἐπάνω Mt. 5. 14 etc., ὑπεράνω E. 4. 10, ὑποκάτω Mc. 6. 11 etc. (not ἄνω, κάτω); ἔμπροσθεν Mt. 5. 16 etc., ὄπισθεν Mt. 15. 23, L. 23. 26, ὀπίσω Mt. 3. 11 etc.; πέραν Mt. 4. 25 etc.; [ἐπέκεινα A. 7. 43 is a wrong reading]; in addition to these χωρίς μέχρι ἕως etc., see § 40, 6 ff. Prepositions.
—The class of adjectives in -ικός, formed from verbs and taking the gen., which is so large in Attic Greek (παρασκευαστικός τινος and the like, Kühner ii.[2], p. 315) is entirely absent (διδακτικός 1 Tim. 3. 2, 2 Tim. 2. 24, but without case). We occasionally find verbal adjectives in -τός (in the sense of a perf. part. pass.) taking the gen., as also indeed the perf. part. pass. in its ordinary form, still this is due to the participle becoming a sort of substantive. Like ἀπόστολος Ἰησοῦ (=ὃν ἀπέσταλκεν Ἰησοῦς) one may also say ἐκλεκτοὶ θεοῦ R. 8. 33, Mt. 24. 31 etc.; ἀγαπητοὶ θεοῦ R. 1. 7; cp. ὁ ἀγαπητός μου 16. 5 etc., οἱ ἀγαπητοὶ ἡμῶν A. 15. 25 (cp. Attic ὁ ἐρώμενός τινος); διδακτοὶ θεοῦ Jo. 6. 45 O.T., cp. 1 C. 2. 13 οὐκ ἐν διδακτοῖς ἀνθρωπίνης σοφίας λόγοις, ἀλλ' ἐν διδακτοῖς πνεύματος (classical parallels in Kühner, p. 322, *e.g.* Soph. El. 343), where, if λόγοις be not spurious, διδακτός has kept its adjectival character; εὐλογημένοι τοῦ πατρός Mt. 25. 34; γεννητοὶ γυναικῶν Mt. 11. 11, L. 7. 28 (LXX. Job 14. 1); in κλητοὶ Ἰησοῦ, however, in R. 1. 6 the gen. is rather a gen. of the possessor, since the Person who gives the call is God rather than Jesus (Winer, § 30, 4).[2] A peculiar use is τὸ εἰθισμένον (D ἔθος) τοῦ νόμου L. 2. 27.

12. The genitive of comparison with the **comparative** (and with what remains of the superlative, cp. § 11, 3 ff.) is found as in the classical language; and along with it (though this is much the rarer construction of the two, as it is in the earlier language)[3] is used the analytical expression with ἤ, particularly when the gen. could not well be employed or would not be sufficiently explicit (*e.g.* with an adj., φιλήδονοι μᾶλλον ἢ φιλόθεοι 2 Tim. 3. 4, with a statement of time R. 13. 11, with an infinitive Mt. 19. 24, A. 20. 35 etc., with a gen. ὑμῶν μᾶλλον ἢ τοῦ θεοῦ A. 4. 19, also with a dat. as in Mt. 10. 15,

---

[1] But in Mt. 23. 25 τὸ ἔσωθεν τοῦ ποτηρίου, 26 τὸ ἐντὸς τ. π. - τὸ ἐκτὸς αὐτοῦ the genitive denotes the whole, as in L. 11. 39.

[2] The gen. in δέσμιος τοῦ Χριστοῦ E. 3. 1 (Paul has similar phrases elsewhere) is also equivalent to a gen. with a substantive, see on this phrase Winer § 30, 2, Buttm. p. 147 (E. 4. 1 has ὁ δέσμιος ἐν κυρίῳ).

[3] O. Schwab, Hist. Syntax d. Gr. Comparation (Würzburg, 1894), ii. 92, reckons that the use of the gen. or ἤ after the comparative is in poetry in the proportion of 18:1, in Attic prose writers in the proportion of 5.5:1; in any later period the use of the former construction is more than three times greater than that of the latter.

A. 5. 29); it is seldom found without some such occasion for it (Jo. 3. 19 ἠγάπησαν μᾶλλον τὸ σκότος ἢ τὸ φῶς, 4. 1 πλείονας μαθητὰς ποιεῖ ἢ Ἰωάνης 1 Jo. 4. 4, 1 C. 14. 5).[1] In addition to this periphrasis there is the periphrasis by means of a preposition: **παρά τινα** (cp. classical passages like Thuc. i. 23. 3, which however are not entirely similar, so that the prep. could not be replaced by ἤ;[2] but in modern Greek παρά or ἀπό is the regular means of expressing comparison) L. 3. 13 πλέον παρὰ τὸ διατεταγμένον (18. 14 μᾶλλον παρ' ἐκεῖνον D, without μ. אBL, other MSS. have the corrupt reading ἢ γὰρ ἐκεῖνος), Hebr. passim, 1. 4 διαφορώτερον παρ' αὐτούς, 3. 3, 9. 23, 11. 4, 12. 24, Herm. Vis. iii. 12. 1, Sim. ix. 18. 2 (=more than, without a comparative, § 43, 4); and **ὑπέρ τινα** (as in the case of παρά, classical Greek only shows the beginnings of this use), L. 16. 8 φρονιμώτεροι ὑπέρ, Jo. 12. 43 μᾶλλον ὑπέρ (ἤπερ ABD al. is corrupt) H. 4. 12, A. 20. 35 v.l. (Herm. Mand. v. 6 has ὑπέρ with the elative; with comparative in elative sense ὑπὲρ πᾶσαν ἁμαρτίαν ἀνομωτέρους Barn. 5. 9; also LXX. e.g. Judges 11. 25, see Winer). The word 'than' is omitted after πλείων and ἐλάσσων before numerical statements (in Attic πλεῖν ἑξακοσίους Aristoph. Av. 1251; Lobeck Phryn. 410 f.;[3] Lat. plus quingentos): A. 4. 22 ἐτῶν πλειόνων τεσσεράκοντα, 23. 13, 21, 24. 11, 25. 6, 1 Tim. 5. 9 χήρα μὴ ἔλαττον ἐτῶν ἑξήκοντα;[4] also L. 9. 13 according to א* οὐκ εἰσὶν ἡμῖν **πλείονες** (other readings are πλεῖον ἤ, πλέον ἤ, with stereotyped πλέον, cp. Kühner ii.² 847 f.) ἄρτοι πέντε, Mt. 26. 53 πλείους (אᶜAC al.; πλείω א*BD) δώδεκα (אBDL; ἢ δ. AC al.) λεγιῶνας (אᶜBD al.; -νων א*AC al.) ἀγγέλων; instead of πλείων we also have **ἐπάνω** (vulgar) Mc. 14. 5 πραθῆναι ἐπάνω δηναρίων τριακοσίων, 1 C. 15. 6 ἐπάνω πεντακοσίοις ἀδελφοῖς.— Instances of looser employment of the genitive: Mt. 5. 20 ἐὰν μὴ περισσεύσῃ ἡ δικαιοσύνη ὑμῶν πλεῖον τῶν...Φαρισαίων (=than that of the Ph., yours is more in comparison with the Ph.); Jo. 5. 36 ἐγὼ ἔχω τὴν μαρτυρίαν μείζω τοῦ Ἰωάνου, where it is ambiguous whether the meaning is 'than John had,' or 'than that given by John': in the latter sense, however, μείζω ἤ (B al. read μείζων) τοῦ Ἰ. would be better. As περισσός and -ότερος have come to be used for πλείων (§ 11, 4), περισσός also takes the gen.: Mt. 5. 37 τὸ περισσὸν τούτων, E. 3. 20 ὑπερεκπερισσοῦ ὧν κ.τ.λ.—A stereotyped use of the neut. πάντων to intensify the superlative appears in Mc. 12. 28 ποία ἐστὶν ἐντολὴ πρώτη **πάντων** (πασῶν is only read by M*al., but D it. omit πάντων), cp. Thuc. iv. 52. 3, Win. § 27, 6.

13. Local and temporal genitive. There are a few remains of a local gen.: L. 5. 19 ποίας (sc. ὁδοῦ, 'by which way') εἰσενέγκωσιν,

---

[1] In 1 Tim. 1. 4 ἐκζητήσεις παρέχουσιν μᾶλλον ἢ οἰκοδομίαν θεοῦ the gen. would not have been in place, especially as μᾶλλον ἤ virtually has in this passage the force of a negative.

[2] For precise details on παρά see Schwab ii. 108 f., 152 f., on ὑπέρ 109 f., on prepositions generally 149 ff.

[3] For details see Schwab 84 ff.

[4] The next word is γεγονυῖα, which some commentators attach to the following ἑνὸς ἀνδρὸς γυνή; still even if it is connected with the preceding words, the usage remains the same, in spite of the Attic εἴκοσιν ἔτη γεγονώς, cp. § 34, 8.

19. 4 ἐκείνης (D ἐκείνῃ) ἤμελλεν διέρχεσθαι, which are incorrect, since the gen. in classical Greek denotes the whole area within which something goes on, just as the corresponding temporal gen. denotes the whole period of time within which something happens.[1] Of this temporal use the N.T. has the following examples: χειμῶνος Mt. 24. 20 = Mc. 13. 18 'during the winter': ἡμέρας Ap. 21. 25 'during the day,' 'in the day,' with v.l. ἡμ. καὶ νυκτός, cp. Mc. 5. 5, L. 18. 7, A. 9. 24 etc. 'in the day as well as by night,' beside which we have νύκτα καὶ ἡμέραν 'all day and night long,' § 34, 8 (but Jo. 11. 9 ἐάν τις περιπατῇ ἐν τῇ ἡμέρᾳ 'by day,' cp. § 38. 4; διὰ τῆς ἡμέρας 'in the course of this day,' L. 9. 37 D): νυκτός Mt. 2. 14 etc., τῆς ν. L. 2. 8 ('in this night'), for which we have διὰ νυκτός A. 5. 19 (v.l. διὰ τ. ν.), 16. 9, 17. 10, 23. 31, like *per noctem*; τεσσεράκοντα ἡμερῶν D* A. 1. 3 for δι' ἡμ. τεσσ. of ℵB etc. and with equivalent sense ('during' *i.e.* 'at intervals in that time,' see § 42, 1); ἡμέρας μέσης A. 26. 13, μέσης νυκτός Mt. 25. 6, μεσονυκτίου, ἀλεκτοροφωνίας Mc. 13. 35 (μεσονύκτιον ℵBC al., cp. § 34, 8), ὄρθρου βαθέως L. 24. 1 (all these denoting a space of time, 'the middle part of the day' etc., not 'a moment of time'), τοῦ λοιποῦ (*sc.* χρόνου) G. 6. 17, E. 6. 10 ℵ*AB 'henceforth' (classical; a stereotyped phrase). With an adverb: δὶς τοῦ σαββάτου L. 18. 12 ('twice in the week'), ἅπαξ τοῦ ἐνιαυτοῦ H. 9. 7, as in classical Greek.

§ 37. DATIVE.

1. In the use of the Greek dative a distinction must be made between the pure dative, which expresses the person more remotely concerned, the instrumental dative (and dative of accompaniment), and, thirdly, the local dative. Still this triple division cannot be applied with absolute clearness and certainty to all the existing usages. The functions of this case were in large measure, more so than those of the accusative and genitive, usurped by different prepositions, particularly ἐν and εἰς; connected with this and with the disappearance of the use of the dative after prepositions, is the subsequent loss of the dative in modern Greek and the substitution for it of εἰς with the accusative. In the N.T., however, the case is still very largely employed.

On the use of the dative as the *necessary* complement of the verb the following points may be noted. **To give, to promise** etc.: there is hardly any tendency to supplant the dat. (δεδομένον ἐν..., § 41, 2; Herm. Vis. i. 4. 8 εἰς τὸ θηρίον ἐμαυτὸν ἔδωκα; iii. 11. 3 παρεδώκατε ἑαυτοὺς εἰς τὰς ἀκηδίας is different, where εἰς expresses the result, as in the N.T., R. 1. 24 etc. [although the dat. is found beside εἰς in E. 4. 19]; παραδ. εἰς συνέδρια Mt. 10. 17 etc. is also justifiable). **To do good** etc., **to be profitable, to injure**: dat. and acc. see § 34, 1 and 4;

---

[1] In classical Greek these must have been expressed by ποίᾳ, ἐκείνῃ, cp. Xenoph. Anab. iii. 4. 37 χωρίον ὑπερδέξιον, ᾗ ἔμελλον οἱ Ἕλληνες παριέναι (therefore D is right in 19. 4, but in the other passage the whole of the evidence supports the gen.).

ἐν is also used in place of the dat., ibid. 4 : **συμφέρειν** always takes the dat., Mt. 5. 29 etc. **To serve** (δουλεύειν λατρεύειν διακονεῖν ὑπηρετεῖν) always takes the dat.; also δουλοῦν 'to make a servant' 1 C. 9. 19; on δουλοῦσθαι pass. vide infra 4 ; προσκυνεῖν etc. take dat. and acc. § 34, 1 ; προσκ. ἐνώπιόν τινος L. 4. 7, Ap. 15. 4 is Hebraic, § 40, 7 ; so also ἀρέσκειν (elsewhere with τινί, like ἀρκεῖν and the adjectives ἀρεστός, ἀρκετός, ἱκανός etc.) ἐνώπιόν τινος A. 6. 5, ἀρεστὸς ἐνώπ. τινος 1 Jo. 3. 22. **To show, to reveal** take dat. always (φαίνειν 'to give light' Ap. 21. 23 [with ἐν אc], ἐπιφαίνειν L. 1. 79), as also 'to seem' (δοκεῖν, φαίνεσθαι); on φανεροῦν ἐν and the like see § 41, 2. **To say to** is expressed, as in classical Greek, by τινί or πρός τινα ; **εὔχεσθαι** takes dat. A. 26. 29, and πρός τινα 2 C. 13. 7, **προσεύχεσθαι** dat. only, Mt. 6. 6, 1 C. 11. 13. **To write, to announce** take dat.; more striking and isolated cases of the dat. with verbs of speaking are : **ἀπολογεῖσθαι** τῷ δήμῳ A. 19. 33, so 2 C. 12. 19 (Lucian, Plut.) 'before or in the presence of anyone,' **ἀποτάσσεσθαι** 'to say farewell' Mc. 6. 46 etc. (Hellenistic, Phryn. Lob. 23 f.); **καυχᾶσθαι** 'to boast of before' 2 C. 7. 14, 9. 2 ; **ὁμολογεῖν** τινι H. 13. 15, τῷ ὀνόματι αὐτοῦ 'to praise,' like ἐξομολογεῖσθαι, ἀνθομολ., R. 14. 11 O.T., Mt. 11. 25, L. 2. 38, 10. 21 (so also αἰνεῖτε τῷ θεῷ Ap. 19. 5, like LXX. Jerem. 20. 13 etc., Buttm. 153 note); 'to confess before anyone,' 'to anyone' A. 24. 14, Mt. 7. 23 (='to promise' A. 7. 17, with v.l. ὤμοσεν and ἐπηγγείλατο D ; Mt. 14. 7 ; on ὁμολ. ἐν see § 41, 2); **ψεύδεσθαί** τινι A. 5. 4 (LXX.; ibid. 3 τινα 'to deceive,' as in classical Greek). **To blame** etc.: ἐπιτιμᾶν, ἐγκαλεῖν take dat. (ἐγκ. κατά τινος R. 8. 33), καταρᾶσθαι and μέμφεσθαι take the dat. as a doubtful v.l., § 34, 2 ; ibid. on παραινεῖν εὐαγγελίζεσθαι ; ἐπιτάσσειν προστάσσειν διαστέλλεσθαι etc. take dat.; also κελεύειν Ev. Petr. 47. 49, Herm. Sim. viii. 2. 8.—**Πείθεσθαι**, ὑπακούειν, ἀπιστεῖν, ἀπειθεῖν take the usual dat.; but **πεποιθέναι** 'to trust in' besides the dat. (as in Ph. 1. 14) more often takes ἔν τινι, ἐπί τινι or τινα, εἴς τινα, and so **πιστεύειν**: with τινι passim, even in the sense 'to believe in,' as in A. 5. 14, 18. 8 τῷ κυρίῳ; with prep. 'to believe in' : ἔν τινι only in Mc. 1. 15 πιστεύετε ἐν τῷ εὐαγγελίῳ,[1] ἐπί τινι 1 Tim. 1. 16, L. 24. 25 (πιστ. om. D), Mt. 27. 42 EF al. (אBL ἐπ' αὐτόν, AD αὐτῷ), R. 9. 33 al. O.T., ἐπί τινα A. 9. 42 etc., εἴς τινα, εἰς τὸ ὄνομά τινος etc., which is the commonest construction. Cp. Buttmann, p. 150 f.[2]—**To be angry** (also ἐμβριμᾶσθαι Mt. 9. 30 etc.; μετριοπαθεῖν τινι H. 5. 2 ; on μέμφεσθαι, § 34. 2), **to envy** take the usual dat.; also **to thank, to owe** etc.—The **adjectives** belonging to these verbs are subjoined : ὠφέλιμος Tit. 3. 8 (σύμφορον or σύμφερον is used substantivally with a gen., 1 C. 7. 35, 10. 33; σωτήριός τινι Tit. 2. 11), ἀρεστός ἀρκετός ἱκανός vide supra; φανερός A. 7. 13, 1 Tim. 4. 15 (v.l. with ἐν), ἐμφανής A. 10. 40, R. 10. 20 O.T., ὑπήκοος A. 7. 39, πιστὸς τῷ κυρίῳ A. 16. 15, cp. H. 3. 2

---

[1] Jo. 3. 15 is different, where if ἐν αὐτῷ (B) is correct it must be taken in connection with ἔχῃ ζωήν.

[2] Ἐλπίζειν τινί 'to hope in anyone' (instead of ἐπί τινα or τινι or εἴς τινα ; τῇ τύχῃ ἐλπίσας Thuc. 3. 97) occurs only in Mt. 12. 21 in a quotation from Is. 42. 4, where LXX. has ἐπὶ τῷ ; ἐν τῷ is read by D al.; cp. § 5, 2, note 3.

§ 37. 1-3.]   DATIVE.   111

(1 P. 1. 21 εἰς θεόν AB, but א^c al. read πιστεύοντας; generally absolute), ἀπειθής A. 26. 19 etc. (ἄπιστος absolute), ἐναντίος Mc. 6. 48 etc. (with πρός τι A. 26. 9); to these may be added the substantive ὀφειλέτης εἰμί τινι R. 1. 14, 8. 12 (with gen. 15. 27 etc.).

2. The dative is used in a *looser manner* (as in classical Greek) with various verbs to denote the person whose **interest** is affected (dativus commodi et incommodi). **Μαρτυρεῖν** τινι 'for anyone' L. 4. 22 etc., also 'against anyone' Mt. 23. 31 μαρτυρεῖτε ἑαυτοῖς. Ἀναπληροῦται αὐτοῖς (D al. ἐπ' αὐτοῖς) ἡ προφητεία L. 18. 31 (D has περί with gen.). Ἔκρινα ἐμαυτῷ τοῦτο 2 C. 2. 1 'for myself,' cp. Herm. Mand. xii. 4. 6 σεαυτῷ κέκρικας τοῦ μὴ δύνασθαι τὰς ἐντολὰς ταύτας φυλαχθῆναι. Also μὴ **μεριμνᾶτε** τῇ ψυχῇ ὑμῶν - τῷ σώματι ὑμῶν Mt. 6. 25 (L. 12. 22), 'for the life—for the body' (other constructions in § 36, 7); and most probably Ap. 8. 4 ταῖς προσευχαῖς, cp. 3 (Winer, § 31, 6). The peculiar Pauline employment of the dat. in the following passages is not quite the same as in the last instances: R. 6. 10 ὃ ἀπέθανεν, τῇ ἁμαρτίᾳ ἀπέθανεν, ὃ δὲ ζῇ, ζῇ τῷ θεῷ, then in verse 11 νεκροὺς μὲν τῇ ἁμ., ζῶντας δὲ τῷ θεῷ, 14. 7 f. οὐδεὶς ἑαυτῷ ζῇ, καὶ οὐδεὶς ἑαυτῷ ἀποθνῄσκει· ἐάν τε γὰρ ζῶμεν, τῷ κυρίῳ ζῶμεν, ἐάν τε ἀποθνῄσκωμεν, τῷ κ. ἀποθνῄσκομεν, from which the conclusion is drawn that in every case τοῦ κυρίου ἐσμέν; cp. further 6. 2, 7. 4 ἐθανατώθητε τῷ νόμῳ - εἰς τὸ γενέσθαι ὑμᾶς ἑτέρῳ κ.τ.λ., 2 C. 5. 15, G. 2. 19, 1 P. 2. 24; the dative therefore expresses the possessor, cp. the dat. with γίνεσθαι infra 3. Further instances: 2 C. 5. 13 εἴτε γὰρ ἐξέστημεν, θεῷ ('it concerns God alone'), εἴτε σωφρονοῦμεν, ὑμῖν ('in your interest'): R. 14. 4 τῷ ἰδίῳ κυρίῳ στήκει ἢ πίπτει, ὁ φρονῶν τὴν ἡμέραν κυρίῳ φρονεῖ· καὶ ὁ ἐσθίων κυρίῳ ἐσθίει· εὐχαριστεῖ γὰρ τῷ θεῷ κ.τ.λ. *i.e.* eating etc. is a matter in which God is concerned, which takes place for Him (for His honour). Cp. also the O.T. quotation ibid. 11 ἐμοὶ κάμψει πᾶν γόνυ, with which may be connected the use of προσκυνεῖν τινι (§ 34, 1). A peculiar use is that in Mc. 10. 33 κατακρινοῦσιν αὐτὸν θανάτῳ (-ου D*) = Mt. 20. 18 (here read by CD al., εἰς θάνατον א, B *omits* the noun), according to Winer, § 31, 1 = 'to sentence to death,' cp. instances from late writers like Diod. Sic. in Lob. Phryn. 475, 2 P. 2. 6 (σταυρῷ Clem. Hom. Epit. i. 145); it may be influenced by the analogy of θανάτῳ ζημιοῦν and the Latin *capite damnare*.

3. The dat. with εἶναι, γίνεσθαι (ὑπάρχειν in Acts and 2 P. 1. 8) denotes the possessor, so that it corresponds to 'to have' or 'get' with an altered construction: οὐκ ἦν αὐτοῖς τόπος 'they had no room' L. 2. 7, ἐγίνετο πάσῃ ψυχῇ φόβος 'all experienced and continued to feel a fright' A. 2. 43, a common construction, as also in classical Greek, used where the possessor is previously known and the emphasis is laid not on him but on the thing which falls to his lot (on the other hand with a gen. αὕτη ἡ οἰκία Σωκράτους ἐστίν 'the house [which is previously known] belongs to Socrates,' cp. R. 14. 8 etc.); but we also have R. 7. 3 ἐὰν γένηται ἀνδρὶ ἑτέρῳ, 4 εἰς τὸ γενέσθαι ὑμᾶς ἑτέρῳ (a Hebraism, modelled on הָיָה לְאִישׁ,

LXX. Lev. 22. 12 etc.), A. 2. 39 ὑμῖν ἐστιν ἡ ἐπαγγελία, due no doubt to ἐπαγγέλλεσθαί τινι, L. 12. 10 ἃ ἡτοίμασας, τίνι ἔσται (sc. ἡτοιμασμένα ?, but D has τίνος). Correctly in A. 21. 23 εἰσὶν ἡμῖν δώδεκα ἄνδρες 'we have here'; Mt. 19. 27 τί ἔσται ἡμῖν. On the model of ἔστιν συνήθεια ὑμῖν Jo. 18. 39 we have also κατὰ τὸ εἰωθὸς αὐτῷ L. 4. 16 (αὐτῷ om. D), A. 17. 2 (ὁ Παῦλος D)?[1] Of time: A. 24. 11 οὐ πλείους εἰσί μοι ἡμέραι δώδεκα ἀφ' ἧς. Also with the meaning 'to happen' Mt. 16. 22 οὐ μὴ ἔσται σοι τοῦτο, L. 1. 45, cp. the dat. with συμβαίνει Mc. 10. 32 etc., and with ellipse of the verb L. 1. 43 πόθεν μοι τοῦτο. The opposite meaning appears in ἕν σοι λείπει L. 18. 22, Tit. 3. 12 (Polyb. 10, 18, 8), cp. the use with ὑστερεῖν, a v.l. in Mc. 10. 21, § 34, 1.—The relation expressed is different, if ἐστί with the dat. only forms a part of the predicate: the idea of possession is then at any rate not in all cases apparent. A. 9. 15 σκεῦος ἐκλογῆς ἐστί μοι οὗτος means 'I have in him' etc.; but 1 C. 1. 18 ὁ λόγος τοῦ σταυροῦ τοῖς μὲν ἀπολλυμένοις μωρία ἐστίν = 'is folly to them,' 'passes for folly with them,' cp. 2. 14 f., Mt. 18. 17; also with the meaning 'it redounds to his' etc., 1 C. 11. 14 f. ἀτιμία αὐτῷ ἐστι (='he gets dishonour therefrom'), whereas 14. 22 εἰς σημεῖόν εἰσιν τοῖς κ.τ.λ. means 'are there for,' 'serve for' (cp. Ja. 5. 3).—With adjectives: καλόν σοί ἐστιν 'is good for thee' Mt. 18. 8 etc. (='thou derivest profit therefrom'), A. 19. 31 ὄντες αὐτῷ φίλοι 'who had Paul for a friend' (φίλος in itself as a substantive regularly takes the gen.: οὐκ εἶ φίλος τοῦ Καίσαρος Jo. 19. 12; similarly ἐχθρός), ἦσαν κοινωνοὶ τῷ Σίμωνι L. 5. 10, 'S. had them for partners' (D ἦσαν δὲ κ. αὐτοῦ, cp. H. 10. 33). With an adverb: ὁσίως ... ὑμῖν ἐγενήθημεν 1 Th. 2. 10 (§ 76, 1); οὐαί μοί ἐστιν 1. C. 9. 16, elsewhere frequently οὐαί τινι without a verb, Mt. 11. 21 etc.: in the Apocalypse it takes an acc. in 8. 13 אB, 12. 12 אACP, cp. Latin vae me and mihi; Buttm. p. 134. —The following are equivalent to datives with εἶναι: 1 C. 7. 28 θλῖψιν τῇ σαρκὶ ('for the flesh'; with ἐν D*FG) ἔξουσιν; 2. C. 2. 13 οὐκ ἔσχηκα ἄνεσιν τῷ πνεύματί μου (with ellipse of the verb G. 5. 13); in conjunction with another dat. 2 C. 12. 7 ἐδόθη μοι σκόλοψ τῇ σαρκί; further instances occur with εὑρίσκειν, Mt. 11. 29 εὑρήσετε ἀνάπαυσιν ταῖς ψυχαῖς ὑμῶν, R. 7. 10, 21, 2 C. 12. 20, Ap. 20. 11; with κινεῖν στάσεις A. 24. 5; with ἀγοράζειν ἀγρὸν εἰς ταφήν Mt. 27. 7 (as one might say ἔστιν ἐνταῦθα ταφὴ τοῖς ξένοις); with an adjective, μονογενὴς τῇ μητρί L. 7. 12 (cp. LXX. Win. § 31, 3).

4. Not far removed from the use of the dat. with εἶναι is its use with the perfect **passive** = ὑπό with a gen.: πέπρακταί μοι τοῦτο 'I **have** done this'; so in N.T. L. 23. 15.[2] The other N.T. instances, however, of the dat. with passive verbs are connected with the particular sense in which the verb is used. In classical Greek we have φαίνεσθαί τινι 'to appear' corresponding to φαίνειν τινί 'to shine,' 'give light' (supra 1), and so in the N.T. in addition to

---

[1] Has this strange usage of Luke arisen from Plat. Rep. ii. 359 E συλλόγου γενομένου **τοῖς ποιμέσιν** (with γενομ.) **εἰωθότος**? Cp. § 2, 4.

[2] D has οὐδὲν ἄξιον θανάτου πεπραγμένον ἐστὶν ἐν αὐτῷ, c invenimus in illo. Perhaps the right reading is ἐστὶν ἐν αὐτῷ without πεπρ., cp. A. 25. 5.

[§ 37. 4-6.] *DATIVE.* 113

φαίνεσθαι, φανερούσθαι we have also ὀπτάνεσθαί τινι (aor. ὀφθῆναι) 'to appear' with the same construction (ὄφθητί μοι is found already in Eurip. Bacch. 914; Hebr. נִרְאָה with אֶל or לְ, Syr. אתחזי with לְ), A. 1. 3 and *passim*, not to be explained as equivalent to ὀφθῆναι ὑπό τινος (in A. 7. 26 ὤφθη αὐτοῖς is rather *supervenit* than *apparuit*). Cp. § 54, 4. So too θεαθῆναι τοῖς ἀνθρώποις Mt. 6. 1, 23. 5, and more frequently γνωσθῆναι 'to become known,' A. 9. 24 etc., § 54, 4 [1] (but ἔγνωσται ὑπ' αὐτοῦ 1 C. 8. 3, 'has been recognised by God,' cp. G. 4. 9), εὑρεθῆναι only in R. 10. 20 O.T. (there is a v.l with ἐν, but the Hebrew in Isaiah 65. 1 has לְ).[2] We have further γαμεῖσθαί τινι of the woman (as in Att.) 1 C. 7. 39 (but cp. § 24 γαμεῖν), μνηστεύεσθαί τινι Mt. 1. 18, and πείθεσθαι as in Attic; Ja. 3. 7 δαμάζεται καὶ δεδάμασται τῇ φύσει τῇ ἀνθρωπίνῃ is ambiguous (δαμῆναί τινι is Homeric, but here the dat. is rather instrumental), in 2 P. 2. 19 ᾧ τις ἥττηται, τούτῳ καὶ δεδούλωται (δουλοῦν τινι) the relative most probably means 'whereby,' since ἡττᾶν in Hellenistic Greek is an active verb and may form an ordinary passive.[3] On συνεφωνήθη A. 5. 9 vide infra 6, page 114, note 1.

5. To the dative expressing the weakest connection, the so-called ethic dative, may be referred Ap. 2. 5 (cp. 16) ἔρχομαί σοι, unless rather the dative, as in Mt. 21. 5 O.T. ἔρχεταί σοι, is an incorrect rendering of the Hebrew לָךְ. Cp. Buttm. 155 f. Another Hebraism is ἀστεῖος τῷ θεῷ A. 7. 20, like LXX. Jonah 3. 3 πόλις μεγάλη τῷ θεῷ (לֵאלֹהִים), i.e. 'very great,' whereas 2 P. 3. 14 ἄσπιλοι καὶ ἀμώμητοι αὐτῷ (God) εὑρεθῆναι probably rather contains the dat. denoting possession, cp. supra 3;[4] Barn. 8. 4 μεγάλοι τῷ θεῷ 'for God,' 'in God's sight.' Another case of assimilation to Hebrew is seen in the fact that the classical use of dat. μοι in addresses (ὦ τέκνον μοι, ὦ Πρώταρχέ μοι) has disappeared and its place been taken by the gen.: τέκνον μου 2 Tim. 2. 1, τέκνα μου G. 4. 19, τεκνία μου 1 Jo. 2. 1 (in 3. 18 as a v.l., אAB al. read without μου, which is the ordinary usage; with παιδία the pronoun never occurs), πάτερ ἡμῶν Mt. 6. 9 (elsewhere πάτερ without pron., as the LXX. also translates the Hebr. אָבִי, Gen. 22. 7 etc.).

6. **Dative of community.**—This dative, which is related to the instrumental dat. (= dat. of accompaniment or association), is

---

[1] With A. 7. 13 ἀνεγνωρίσθη Ἰωσὴφ τοῖς ἀδελφοῖς αὐτοῦ, cp. γνωρίζειν τί τινι 2. 28.

[2] The dat. with εὑρίσκεσθαι in R. 7. 10 etc. is of another character, cp. supra 3 ad fin.; on 2 P. 3. 14 vide infra 5.

[3] Ja. 3. 18 καρπὸς ... σπείρεται τοῖς ποιοῦσιν εἰρήνην is an instance of dat. commodi; cp. 1 P. 5. 9, L. 18. 31 (supra 2).—There are clear instances of the dat. governed by the passive as such in the Clementine Homilies, *e.g.* iii. 68 θεῷ ἐστύγηται, ix. 21 δαίμοσιν ἀκούεται, xix. 23 ἠτύχηται τοῖς ταπεινοῖς.

[4] A comparison, however, of E. 1. 4 εἶναι ἡμᾶς ... ἀμώμους κατενώπιον αὐτοῦ, Col. 1. 22 παραστῆσαι ὑμᾶς ... ἀμώμους καὶ ἀνεγκλήτους κατ. αὐτ., makes it possible to interpret the dat. as equivalent to this periphrasis, which frequently takes the place of the correct dative, 1 Jo. 3. 22 τὰ ἀρεστὰ ἐνώπιον αὐτοῦ.

H

frequently found with ἀκολουθεῖν (συνακ.; with συνέπεσθαι only in A. 20. 4, with ἕπεσθαι nowhere), beside the Hebraic ἀκ. ὀπίσω τινός Mt. 10. 38, Mc. 8. 34 v.l. (μετά τινος, also classical, occurs in Ap. 6. 8, 14. 13; but in L. 9. 49 μεθ' ἡμῶν is not 'us' but 'with us'); with διαλέγεσθαι (also πρός τινα as in class. Greek); ὁμιλεῖν A. 24. 26 'to converse' (πρός τινα L. 24. 14); κρίνεσθαι 'to dispute' Mt. 5. 40 (μετά τινος 1 C. 6. 6, cp. 7, like πολεμεῖν, πόλεμον ποιεῖν μετά τινος Ap. 11. 7, 12. 7 al., Hebr. עִם, cp. § 42, 3; φίλοι μετ' ἀλλήλων L. 23. 12); διακρίνεσθαι (same meaning) Jd. 9 (πρός τινα A. 11. 2, classical; cp. μάχεσθαι πρός Jo. 6. 52); διακατελέγχεσθαι A. 18. 28; διαλλάττεσθαι Mt. 5. 24, and more frequently καταλλάσσειν τινά τινι and καταλλάσσεσθαί τινι; διαβάλλεσθαί (pass.) τινι 'to be calumniated to someone' L. 16. 1, μειγνύναι Ap. 15. 2 (with ἐν 8. 7, with μετά Mt. 27. 34, L. 13. 1); κολλᾶσθαι (προσκολλ.) τινι L. 15. 15 etc.; χρῆσθαι A. 27. 3, 17, 1 C. (a v.l. in 7. 31, see § 34, 2), 9. 12, 15, 2 C. 1. 17, 3. 12, 1 Tim. 1. 8, 5. 23, καταχρῆσθαι 1 C. 9. 18 (συγχρ. Jo. 4. 9 in an interpolated clause); κοινωνεῖν R. 12. 13 al.; ἑτεροζυγεῖν ἀπίστοις (from ἑτερόζυγος Levit. 19. 19, used of beasts of different kinds in a team) 2 C. 6. 14 'to be in unequal fellowship' (like συζυγ. τινί, Win. § 31, 10 Rem. 4); ὁμοιοῦν ὁμοιοῦσθαι Mt. 6. 8 etc.; ὁμοιάζειν 23. 27 (intrans., v.l. παρομ.), like ὅμοιος vide infra; ἐγγίζειν L. 7. 12 etc. (also with εἰς 18. 35 [τῇ Ἱερ. some cursives and Epiphanius], on account of the indeclinable Ἱεριχώ? as in 19. 29, Mt. 21. 1, Mc. 11. 1, though we also have εἰς τὴν κώμην L. 24, 28; with ἐπὶ 10. 9). The verbs compounded with σύν which govern a dative are very numerous, such as συγκαθῆσθαι A. 26. 30 (with μετὰ in Mc. 14. 54, but D has καθήμενος), συγκακοπαθεῖν 2 Tim. 1. 8, συγκακουχεῖσθαι H. 11. 25, συγκατατίθεσθαι L. 23. 51, ὁ λόγος οὐκ ὠφέλησεν ἐκείνους μὴ συγκεκερασμένος (-ους is a wrong reading), τῇ πίστει (instrum.) τοῖς ἀκούσασιν H. 4. 2, etc. (some few also take μετά as συλλαλεῖν in Mt. 17. 3, A. 25. 12, but dat. in Mc. 9. 4 etc., πρὸς ἀλλήλους L. 4. 36; συμφωνεῖν μετά Mt. 20. 2, but dat. in 13 and elsewhere);[1] a peculiar and unclassical instance is συνέρχεσθαί τινι A. 1. 21 etc., 'to go with someone.'—Of adjectives the following deserve special mention : ὅμοιος (with gen.? § 36, 11),[2] ὁ αὐτός (ἐν καὶ τὸ αὐτό) only in 1 C. 11. 5; ἴσος Mt. 20. 12 etc. (for which we have a periphrasis with ὡς καί in A. 11. 17; ὁ αὐτός with καθὼς καί 1 Th. 2. 14, or with οἷος Ph. 1. 30);[3] of compounds with σύν we have σύμμορφός τινι Ph. 3. 21 (gen. of the thing possessed in R. 8. 29 τῆς εἰκόνος, see § 36, 11; for classical parallels Matthiae Gr. 864), σύμφυτος τῷ ὁμοιώματι τοῦ θανάτου αὐτοῦ R. 6. 5; but the remaining compounds of σύν are made into substantives (like φίλος etc.) and take a gen.,

---

[1] There is a peculiar use in A. 5. 9 συνεφωνήθη ὑμῖν convenit inter vos; cp. a late author quoted by Stobaeus, Flor. 39, 32 συνεφώνησε τοῖς δήμοις, 'the communities agreed.'

[2] Besides expressing the similar person or thing, the dat. may also express the possessor of the similar thing (Homer κόμαι Χαρίτεσσιν ὁμοῖαι): Ap. 9. 10 ἔχουσιν οὐρὰς ὁμοίας σκορπίοις, 13. 11; similarly τοῖς ἰσότιμον ἡμῖν πίστιν λαχοῦσιν 2 P. 1. 1, Buttm. p. 154.

[3] In a quotation in R. 9. 29 we have ὡς Γόμορρα ἂν ὡμοιώθημεν.

§ 37. 6–7.]   *DATIVE.*   115

συγγενής συγκληρονόμος σύμβουλος συμμέτοχος (E. 5. 7) συναιχμάλωτος συνεργός σύντροφος. Substantives take no share in these constructions with the dat. (as they occasionally do in classical Greek, Kühner Gr. II.² 372 f.), *e.g.* R. 15. 26 κοινωνίαν ποιήσασθαι εἰς τοὺς πτωχούς, 2 C. 9. 13, τίς κοινωνία φωτὶ (has the light; φωτὸς D*) πρὸς σκότος 2 C. 6. 14, κοινωνίαν ἔχητε μεθ' ἡμῶν 1 Jo. 1. 3, 6, 7. The adverb ἅμα takes the dat. only in Mt. 13. 29 ἅμα αὐτοῖς τὸν σῖτον (but D ἅμα καὶ τ. σ. σὺν αὐτοῖς, cp. ἅμα σύν 1 Th. 4. 17, 5. 10); on ἐγγύς see § 36, 11.

7. A great number of verbs (and adjectives) compounded with other **prepositions** besides σύν govern the dative, while the sentence may also be completed by the use of a preposition; in general there is this distinction made (as occasionally in classical Greek and in Latin), that the preposition is used where the verb has its literal meaning, and the dative where it has a figurative sense. Thus the following compounds of **ἐν** regularly take a preposition : ἐμβαίνειν, ἐμβιβάζειν, ἐμβάλλειν, ἐμβάπτειν, ἐμπίπτειν; the following regularly take the dative : ἐγκαλεῖν (supra 1), ἐμμαίνεσθαι (A. 26. 11), ἐμπαίζειν, ἐντυγχάνειν ('to entreat'; with πρός in Herm. Sim. ii. 8), but we also have ἐμβλέπειν τινί (person) = βλ. εἰς τινα; the following take sometimes the dat., sometimes a preposition : ἐγκεντρίζειν R. 11. 24 εἰς καλλιέλαιον, τῇ ἰδίᾳ ἐλαίᾳ, ἐμμένειν with dat. in A. 14. 22, G. 3. 10 O.T. ℵ*B (with ἐν al. and LXX.), with ἐν H. 8. 9 O.T., ἐμπτύειν. Compounds of **εἰς** take a preposition only (εἰσέρχεσθαι εἰς etc.); with ἐπί cp. the following exx.: **ἐπιβάλλειν** ἐπὶ ἱματίῳ (-ιον) Mt. 9. 16, L. 5. 36; similarly ἐπιβάλλειν τὰς χεῖρας takes ἐπί, except in A. 4. 3 where it has the dat. (D is different); **ἐπιτιθέναι** τὴν χεῖρά τινι and ἐπί τινα occur: elsewhere the prep. preponderates where this verb is used in the literal sense, as in ἐπὶ τοὺς ὤμους Mt. 23. 4 (Jo. 19 2 τῇ κεφαλῇ, but A has ἐπὶ τὴν κεφαλήν; L. 23. 26 αὐτῷ τὸν σταυρόν), and the dat. with the figurative sense, ὄνομα Mc. 3. 16 f., cp. ἐπικαλεῖν τινι ὄνομα (the classical ἐπονομάζειν is similarly used) Mt. 10. 25 B* and Buttm. p. 132, βάρος A. 15. 28, πληγάς 16. 23; ἐπιτίθεσθαι 'to lay hands on' 18. 10, with the idea of presenting 28. 10¹ (the prep. only occurs in Ap. 22. 18 ἐάν τις ἐπιθῇ ἐπ' αὐτά ['adds to'], ἐπιθήσει ὁ θεὸς ἐπ' αὐτὸν τὰς πληγας); ἐφίστασθαι takes dat. and ἐπί, etc. Compounds of **παρά** : παρατιθέναι τινί is used (not so much 'beside anyone' as 'for anyone'), and παρατίθεσθαι 'to commend' takes the same construction; παρεδρεύειν (v.l. προσ.) τῷ θυσιαστηρίῳ (fig.) 1 C. 9. 13, and from this is derived the use with the adj. τὸ εὐπάρεδρον (v.l. εὐπρόσ.) τῷ κυρίῳ 7. 35, which is more striking because this adj. takes the place of a substantive (Kühner II.² 372 f.); also with dat. παρέχειν, παριστάναι, παρίστασθαι (even in the literal sense *e.g.* A. 1. 10, 9. 39); παρεῖναι usually takes a prep. (πρὸς ὑμᾶς 2 C. 11. 8), but the dat. where the verb is used metaphorically 2 P. 1. 9 (and 8 according to A); παραμένειν τινί (Dᵉal. συμπ.) Ph. 1. 25 (also the adj. παράμονός τινι [dat. of thing] Herm. Sim. ix. 23. 3). With **περί** we have: περιτιθέναι with dat., περιβάλλειν L. 19. 43 (on περιβ. τινά τι

---
¹ The Syriac inserts *in navi* (apparently an addition of the β text).

see § 34, 4), περικείμενον ἡμῖν νέφος μαρτύρων H. 12. 1, but with the literal sense of the verb περὶ τὸν τράχηλον Mc. 9. 42, L. 17. 2, περιπίπτειν εἰς τόπον A. 27. 41, but λῃσταῖς, πειρασμοῖς L. 10. 30, Ja. 1. 2, περιπείρειν ἑαυτὸν ὀδύναις 1 Tim. 6. 10. With **πρός**: **προστιθέναι** ἐπί τι is used where the verb has the literal sense Mt. 6. 27, L. 12. 25, ἐπί τινι to add to something L. 3. 20,[1] but the person for whom the addition is made stands in the dat. Mt. 6. 33 etc., H. 12. 19; **προσέρχεσθαι** regularly takes the dat. of the person, also θρόνῳ, ὄρει H. 4. 16, 12. 18, 22 ; the following also take the dat. προσέχειν (e.g. ἑαυτῷ), προσκαρτερεῖν, προσκλίνεσθαι (fig.); and with the literal sense προσπίπτειν (Mt. 7. 25 etc.; only in Mc. 7. 25 πρὸς τοὺς πόδας αὐτοῦ), προσφέρειν (πρὸς τὸν—H. 5. 7, here plainly in figurative sense); προσκυλίειν λίθον τῇ θύρᾳ Mt. 27. 60 (A has ἐπί, so ἐπὶ τὴν θ. Mc. 15. 46); **προσφωνεῖν** τινι Mt. 11. 16, A. 22. 2 (D omits αὐτοῖς) etc., or transitively with τινά 'to summon' L. 6. 13 (D ἐφώνησεν), A. 11. 2 D (L. 23. 20 D αὐτούς, אB αὐτοῖς, absolute verb A al.). —With compounds of **ἀντί** the dat. is the prevailing construction (ἀνθίστασθαι, ἀντιλέγειν, ἀντικεῖσθαι, ἀντιπίπτειν etc.; rarely πρός τινα, as ἀνταγωνίζεσθαι πρὸς H. 12. 4), and the same holds good of compounds of **ὑπό**, with which prep. as with ἀντί the literal meaning becomes obliterated (ὑποτάσσειν τινί, only in quotations do we have ὑπὸ τοὺς πόδας or ὑποκάτω τῶν ποδῶν 1 C. 15. 27, H. 2. 8; ὑποτίθεσθαι 1 Tim. 4. 6 'to advise'; ὑπάρχειν, ὑπακούειν); with **ἀνά** we have ἀνατίθεσθαι (προσανατ.) τινί 'to lay a case before someone' A. 25. 14 etc.—A substantive is also found with a dat. (cp. supra 6) in 2 C. 11. 28 ἡ ἐπίστασίς μοι ἡ καθ' ἡμέραν א*BFG, but the text can hardly be correct (אcD al. μου, Latt. *in me*).

§ 38. CONTINUATION: INSTRUMENTAL AND TEMPORAL DATIVE.

1. The dative as the **instrumental** case is found in the N.T. as in classical Greek, but this use is considerably limited by the employment of the periphrasis with ἐν. The latter usage is by no means foreign to the Greek language (Kühner Gr. ii.[2], 403 f.); for the N.T. writers, however, it is the Hebrew בְּ which has set the example of this construction,[2] and for this reason the frequency with which it occurs differs with the individual writers: in the second half of the Acts (13-28) the usage is rare and never a prominent feature,[3] while

---

[1] 'To add to the community' is expressed in A. 2. 47 by τῇ ἐκκλησίᾳ EP (D ἐν τῇ ἐ.), the other MSS. make the verb absolute as it is in 41 and in 5. 14; with the same meaning in 11. 24 we have τῷ κυρίῳ, which however B*, no doubt rightly, omits; 'to be gathered to his fathers' is expressed by πρός in 13. 36.

[2] In modern Greek, in which the dative is wanting, the instrumental case is expressed by μετά (μέ), this use of ἐν having disappeared.

[3] A. 13. 29 δικαιοῦσθαι ἐν, for which see below in the text; 26. 29 καὶ ἐν ὀλίγῳ καὶ ἐν μεγάλῳ, which in the mouth of Paul (the ἐν ὀλίγῳ of Agrippa in 28 is different) apparently should be taken to mean 'by little, by much,' *i.e.* 'easily, with difficulty.' Moreover the instances in the first half of the Acts are not numerous.

§ 38. 1-2.] *INSTRUMENTAL AND TEMPORAL DATIVE.* 117

the reverse is the case in the Apocalypse.—Examples: with the sword, by the sword (to strike, to perish etc.) ἐν μαχαίρῃ or ῥομφαίᾳ Mt. 26. 52, L. 22. 49, Ap. 2. 16, 6. 8, 13. 10, 19. 21, ἐν φόνῳ μαχαίρης H. 11. 37, μαχαίρῃ without ἐν A. 12. 2, στόματι μαχαίρης L. 21. 24. To season with salt: ἅλατι Col. 4. 6, ἁλίζειν πυρί (ἁλί) Mc. 9. 50 modelled on O.T., but ἐν τίνι ἁλισθήσεται τὸ ἅλας Mt. 5. 13, Mc. 9. 50, L. 14. 34. To consume with fire etc. is ἐν πυρί¹ in Ap. 14. 10, 16. 8, 17. 16 (without ἐν אBP), 18. 8 (for merely 'to burn with fire' even the Apocalypse uses πυρὶ καίεσθαι, 8. 8, 21. 8), πυρὶ in Mt. 3. 12, L. 3. 17. 'To baptize with' is usually expressed by ἐν ὕδατι or ἐν πνεύματι; Luke however has ὕδατι in 3. 16 (with ἐν in D, in the same passage all MSS. have ἐν πνεύματι in the opposing clause), A. 1. 5 (but ἐν πνεύματι ibid.), 11. 16 (with ἐν πν.; but χρίειν πνεύματι 10. 38). With δικαιοῦν δικαιοῦσθαι the dat. is found as in R. 3. 28 πίστει, but also ἐν, ἐν νόμῳ G. 5. 4, A. 13. 39, ἐν τῷ αἵματι τοῦ χρ. R. 5. 9 (ἐκ πίστεως 5. 1 etc.). On the use of ἐν to denote the personal agent, which cannot be expressed by the dat., see § 41, 1; on the Hebraic periphrases for the person with χείρ and στόμα § 40, 9. Μετρεῖν ἔν τινι and τινι are used for 'to measure by' Mt. 7. 2, Mc. 4. 24, 2 C. 10. 12² (ἐν), L. 6. 38 (dat.); also 'to measure with,' Ap. 11. 1, 21. 16 (ἐν) καλάμῳ. The N.T. also has μεθύσκεσθαι οἴνῳ (E. 5. 18, like LXX. Prov. 4. 17), not οἴνου the Attic construction;³ similarly πληροῦν τινι or ἔν τινι, **with** anything (the dat. is occasionally used in classical Greek, in Eurip. Bacch. 18 with πλήρης, in Herc. Fur. 372 and Aesch. Sept. 464 with πληροῦν), besides the gen. for which see § 36, 4; cp. also ὑπερπερισσεύομαι τῇ χαρᾷ (ἐν τ. χ. B) 2 C. 7. 4.

2. The instrumental dative is moreover used to denote the **cause** or **occasion**: R. 11. 20 τῇ ἀπιστίᾳ ἐξεκλάσθησαν, 'on account of their unbelief,' 30 ἠλεήθητε τῇ τούτων ἀπειθείᾳ, 31 ἠπείθησαν τῷ ὑμετέρῳ ἐλέει, 'because God wished to have mercy on you,'⁴ 4. 20 οὐ διεκρίθη τῇ ἀπιστίᾳ, ἀλλ' ἐνεδυναμώθη τῇ πίστει, 1 C. 8. 7 etc.; see also A. 15. 1 περιτέμνεσθαι τῷ ἔθει τῷ Μωϋσέως, '**after,' 'in accordance with'** (the β text has a different and more ordinary expression); it also denotes the part, attribute etc., **in respect of** which anything takes place, 1 C. 14. 20 μὴ παιδία γίνεσθε ταῖς φρεσίν, ἀλλὰ τῇ κακίᾳ νηπιάζετε, ταῖς δὲ φρεσὶν τέλειοι γίνεσθε, Ph. 2. 7 σχήματι εὑρεθεὶς ὡς ἄνθρωπος, 3. 5 περιτομῇ ὀκταήμερος, 'eight days old at circumcision,' 'circumcised on the eighth day'; so φύσει 'by nature,' G. 2. 15 etc., τῷ γένει 'by extraction,' A. 4. 36 etc.; ἀπερίτμητοι τῇ καρδίᾳ A. 7. 51, ἀδύνατος τοῖς ποσίν 14. 8, ἐστερεοῦντο τῇ πίστει καὶ ἐπερίσσευον τῷ ἀριθμῷ 16. 5,

---

¹ An accidental coincidence with the Homeric ἐν πυρὶ καίειν Il. xxiv. 38.

² Here the phrase is ἐν ἑαυτοῖς 'by themselves,' where it is true that in classical Greek the dative could not stand: still no more could ἐν, the phrase would be πρὸς ἑαυτούς.

³ Yet even classical Greek has μεθύειν ἔρωτι; and Lucian de dea Syr. 22 μεθύσασα ἑαυτὴν οἴνῳ. The Apocalypse has ἐκ: 17. 2, 6.

⁴ [The words τῷ ὑμ. ἐλ. may also be taken with the following clause; see Sanday-Headlam and Gifford ad loc. Tr.]

ὀνόματι 'by name' (§ 33, 2), τῷ μήκει ποδῶν ἑκατόν Herm. Vis. iv. 1. 6,[1] etc. etc. The usage of the N.T. language in this respect may be said to be constant, since the alternative use of the accusative which in the classical language is widely prevalent[2] is almost entirely unrepresented (cp. § 34, 7). The cause may, of course, be also expressed by means of a preposition (*e.g.* by ἐν in ἐν τούτῳ A. 24. 16, Jo. 16. 30 'on this account,' § 41, 1); this is especially the case with **verbs expressing emotion** (classical Greek uses the simple dat. and acc. as well): χαίρειν ἐπί τινι Mt. 18. 3 etc., ἐν τούτῳ L. 10. 20 (R. 12. 12 τῇ ἐλπίδι is different, not 'rejoicing over the hope,' but 'in virtue of hope,' 'in hope,') and so ἀγαλλιᾶσθαι, εὐφραίνεσθαι are used with ἐν or ἐπί; εὐδοκεῖν ἐν (εἰς 2 P. 1. 17, Mt. 12. 18 O.T. [ἐν D; acc. ℵ*B], cp. H. 10. 6, 8 O.T., § 34, 1), which in **cultured style** is expressed by εὐαρεστεῖται τοιαύταις θυσίαις H. 13. 16 (Diodor. 3, 55. 9 etc.); θαυμάζειν ἐπί τινι L. 4. 22 etc., περί τινος 2. 18[3] (on θ. τινά, τι see § 34, 1), so ἐκπλήσσεσθαι ἐπί τινι, but 1 P. 4. 12 μὴ ξενίζεσθε τῇ κ.τ.λ. (ibid. 4 with ἐν), καυχᾶσθαι ἐν or ἐπί (for the acc. § 34, 1), συλλυπεῖσθαι ἐπί Mc. 3. 5 (but after ὀργίζεσθαι Ap. 12. 17, μακροθυμεῖν Mt. 28. 26 etc., ἐπί [εἰς, πρός] is used with the person with whom one is angry or long-suffering).

3. This dative further expresses the **accompanying circumstances**, the **manner and style** of an action: 1 C. 10. 30 χάριτι μετέχω, 'with thanks,' 11. 5 προσευχομένη ἀκατακαλύπτῳ τῇ κεφαλῇ (Herm. Sim. ix. 20. 3 γυμνοῖς ποσίν, Vis. v. 1 εἰσῆλθεν ἀνήρ ... σχήματι ποιμενικῷ), H. 6. 17 ἐμεσίτευσεν ὅρκῳ. An alternative for the dat. is μετά τινος: Mt. 26. 72 ἠρνήσατο μεθ' ὅρκου (Xenoph. Cyr. ii. 3. 12 σὺν θεῶν ὅρκῳ λέγω), cp. H. 7. 20 f. οὐ χωρὶς ὁρκωμοσίας – μεθ' ὁρκ.; μετὰ βίας A. 5. 26, 24. 7 (class. βίᾳ, πρὸς βίαν), μετὰ φωνῆς μεγάλης L. 17. 15 (μετὰ σπουδῆς καὶ κραυγῆς πολλῆς Aeschin. 2. 10), etc. In Mc. 14. 65 ῥαπίσμασιν αὐτὸν ἔλαβον is quite a vulgarism, which at present can only be paralleled from a papyrus of the first century A.D. (an argument to Demosth. Midias), where we find (αὐτὸν) κονδύλοις ἔλαβεν.[4] Accompanying (military) forces in classical Greek are expressed by the dat., in the N.T. by ἐν, ἐν δέκα χιλιάσιν ἀπαντᾶν L. 14. 31, cp. Jd. 14, A. 7. 14 (also (εἰσ)έρχεσθαι ἐν αἵματι 'with' H. 9. 25, 1 Jo. 5. 6; ἐν ῥάβδῳ ἔλθω 1 C. 4. 21, 2 C. 10. 14 etc.); ἐν also denotes manner in ἐν τάχει, ἐν ἐκτενείᾳ etc., see § 41, 1. We have παντὶ τρόπῳ, εἴτε προφάσει εἴτε ἀληθείᾳ Ph. 1. 18 (ποίοις τρόποις Herm. Mand. xii. 3. 1), but elsewhere ὃν τρόπον etc., § 34, 7 (ἐν παντὶ τρ.,

---

[1] 2 C. 7. 11 συνεστήσατε ἑαυτοὺς ἁγνοὺς εἶναι (ἐν add. D^bEKLP, cp. ἁγ. ἐν τῇ σαρκί Clem. Cor. i. 38, 2) τῷ πράγματι is very harsh; perhaps εἶναι is a corruption of ἐν, cp. § 34, 5.

[2] The dative is employed in classical Greek if a contrast is made or is present to the mind of the writer, φύσει – νόμῳ, λόγῳ – ἔργῳ; Xen. Mem. ii. 1. 31 τοῖς σώμασιν ἀδύνατοι – ταῖς ψυχαῖς ἀνόητοι; on the other hand in Anab. i. 4. 11 for πόλις Θάψακος ὀνόματι, ὄνομα is correctly restored from the MSS. (cp. §§ 33, 2; 34, 7).

[3] Ap. 13. 3 ἐθαύμασεν ὀπίσω τοῦ θηρίου is very strange, a pregnant construction for ἐθ. ἐπὶ τῷ θ. καὶ ἐπορεύθη ὀπ. αὐτοῦ, see W.-Gr.

[4] See Fleçkeis. Jahrb. f. class. Philol. 1892, p. 29, 33.

§ 38. 3-4.] *INSTRUMENTAL AND TEMPORAL DATIVE.* 119

with a v.l. [male] τόπῳ 2 Th. 3. 16). A usage almost peculiar to the N.T. (and the LXX.) is the dat. ὁδῷ etc. with πορεύεσθαι, περιπατεῖν, στοιχεῖν, in the N.T. always in metaphorical sense (L. 10. 31 κατέβαινεν ἐν τῇ ὁδῷ ἐκείνῃ, B without ἐν), in the LXX. also in the literal, cp. Ja. 2. 25 (class. ἄδικον ὁδὸν ἰόντων Thuc. iii. 64. 4; but Hebr. הָלַךְ לְדַרְכּוֹ Gen. 19. 2, and so Thuc. ii. 96. 1 ἐπορεύετο τῇ ὁδῷ ἣν αὐτὸς ἐποιήσατο 'by means of the way'; literal sense): A.14.16 πορεύεσθαι ταῖς ὁδοῖς αὐτῶν, Jd. 11, R. 4. 12 στοιχεῖν τοῖς ἴχνεσιν (Clem. Hom. x. 15 τῷ ὑμῶν στοιχεῖτε παραδείγματι); further developments are τοῖς ἔθεσιν περιπατεῖν A. 21. 21, κώμοις καὶ μέθαις R. 13. 13, πνεύματι G. 5. 16, πορεύεσθαι τῷ φόβῳ τοῦ κυρίου A. 9. 31 (the acc. is found with the literal sense of the word in τὴν ὁδὸν αὐτοῦ A. 8. 39; with the metaphorical sense we have πορ. ἐν 1 P. 4. 3, περιπατεῖν ἐν 2 C. 4. 2 etc., κατὰ σάρκα R. 8. 4), Buttm. p. 160. Further (ibid 159 f.) verbal substantives used with their cognate verbs or with verbs of similar meaning stand in the dative—the usage is an imitation of the Hebrew infinitive absolute like מוֹת יָמוּת and is consequently found already in the LXX.—whereas the analogous classical phrases such as γάμῳ γαμεῖν ('in true wedlock'), φυγῇ φεύγειν ('to flee with all speed') are only accidentally similar to these. The N.T instances are: (ἀκοῇ ἀκούειν Mt. 13. 14 etc. O.T.), ἐπιθυμίᾳ ἐπεθύμησα L. 22. 15, χαρᾷ χαίρει Jo. 3. 29,[1] ἐνυπνίοις ἐνυπνιάζεσθαι A. 2. 17 O.T., ἀπειλῇ (om. אABD al.) ἀπειλησώμεθα 4. 17, παραγγελίᾳ παρηγγείλαμεν 5. 28, ἀναθέματι ἀνεθεματίσαμεν 23. 12, προσευχῇ προσηύξατο Ja. 5. 17; with which belong ὅρκῳ ὤμοσεν A. 2. 30, θανάτῳ τελευτάτω Mc. 7. 10 O.T., cp. Herm. Sim. viii. 7. 3 (ἀποκτεῖναι ἐν θανάτῳ Ap. 2. 23; 6. 8 is a different use). Cp. on the similar constructions with the acc. § 34, 3; this dative of manner intensifies the verb in so far as it indicates that the action is to be understood as taking place in the fullest sense.

4. While there is no trace of a **local** dative in the N.T.[2] (as is also the case on the whole in Attic prose), the analogous **temporal** dative, answering the question When?, is still fairly frequent: it may of course be further elucidated by the insertion, common also in Attic, of the preposition ἐν. Since the dat. denotes the point of time, not the period of time, while ἐν can have both these meanings, it is quite possible to express 'in the day,' 'in the night' by ἐν (τῇ) ἡμέρᾳ, νυκτί, Jo. 11. 9, A. 18. 9, 1 Th. 5. 2, but the genitive must be used instead of the simple dat., § 36, 13 (τῷ θέρει in Herm. Sim. iv. 3 for 'in summer' is incorrect, ibid. 5 we have ἐν τ. θ. ἐκείνῳ); on the other

---

[1] On the other hand we have Mt. 2. 10 ἐχάρησαν χαρὰν μεγάλην σφόδρα, with a closer defining of the noun, which also may be said to be the *raison d'être* of the added verbal substantive; such closer definition is, speaking generally, never found with the dat. in the N.T., though Hermas has Sim. ix. 18. 3 πονηρευομένους ποικίλαις πονηρίαις, 1. 2 ἴσχυσας τῇ ἰσχύι σου. With Jo. 18. 32 σημαίνων ποίῳ θανάτῳ ἤμελλεν ἀποθνῄσκειν should be compared 21. 19 σημαίνων ποίῳ θανάτῳ δοξάσει τὸν θεόν: it is evident that in the first passage the cognate verb is by no means obligatory, but might be replaced by another verb.

[2] But in Herm. Vis. iv. 3. 7 we have ποίῳ τόπῳ ἀπῆλθεν, probably through the dat. and εἰς having become interchangeable, § 37, 1 and 2.

hand in a statement about a definite day or a definite night, the simple dative is no less correct than the dat. with ἐν. In the N.T. we always have τῇ τρίτῃ ἡμέρᾳ Mt. 16. 21 (D reads otherwise), 17. 23 (ditto), L. 9. 22 (ditto), 24. 7, 46; τῇ πρώτῃ ἡμ. τῶν ἀζύμων Mc. 14. 12, τῇ ἡμ. τῇ ὀγδόῃ A. 7. 8 (with ἐν L. 1. 59, but DL omit ἐν), τακτῇ ἡμ. 12. 21, ποίᾳ ἡμ. (v.l. ὥρᾳ) Mt. 24. 42, ᾗ ἡμ. L. 17. 29 f. (30 D is different), τῇ ἡμ. τῶν σαββάτων L. 13. 14, 16, A. 13. 14, 16. 13, cp. inf. τοῖς σάββασιν, but with ἐν L. 4. 13, the readings vary in 14. 5; τῇ ἐσχάτῃ ἡμ. Jo. 12. 48, with ἐν 7. 37, 11. 24, with var. lect. 6. 39 f., 44, 54; so τῇ μιᾷ σαββάτων (cp. for this Mc. 16. 2[1], 9, Jo. 20. 1; with ἐν A. 20. 7); with ἐκείνῃ and ταύτῃ ἐν is usually inserted, but Jo. 20. 19 has τῇ ἡμ. ἐκ.; and the pronouns are used with νυκτί without ἐν in L. 12. 20, 17. 34, A. 12. 6, 27. 23; always τῇ ἐπιούσῃ or ἐχομένῃ ἡμ. (νυκτί), but confined to Acts, e.g. 7. 26, 21. 26; also τῇ ἑξῆς 21. 1 etc. (but with ἐν L. 7. 11, where D omits ἐν and there is a strongly supported reading ἐν τῷ ἑξῆς; the readings vary in 9. 37), τῇ ἐπιφωσκούσῃ κ.τ.λ. Mt. 28. 1 (ἡμέρᾳ καὶ ἡμέρᾳ 'every day' 2 C. 4. 16 after the Hebrew יוֹם וָיוֹם, = καθ' ἑκάστην ἡμ. H. 3. 13). Further instances are: τετάρτῃ **φυλακῇ** τῆς νυκτός Mt. 14. 25, τῇ ἑσπερινῇ φ. τ. ν. D in L. 12. 38, elsewhere in the same verse this word takes ἐν even in D; ποίᾳ φ. Mt. 24. 43; ᾗ οὐ δοκεῖτε **ὥρᾳ** 44, ποίᾳ ὥρᾳ L. 12. 39, τῇ ὥρᾳ τοῦ θυμιάματος 1. 10, τῇ ἐνάτῃ ὥ. Mc. 15. 34, αὐτῇ τῇ ὥ. L. 2. 38 etc. (αὐτῇ τῇ νυκτί Herm. Vis. iii. 1. 2, 10. 7), as well as ἐν αὐτ. τ. ὥ. L. 12. 12 etc. (ἐν also occurs with ἐκείνῃ Mt. 26. 55 etc., and as a v.l. in Jo. 4. 53); μιᾷ ὥ. Ap. 8. 10, 16, 19, cp. on the alternative use of the acc. § 34, 8. The simple dat. is not used in the case of ἔτος, but ἐν (L. 3. 1); ἔτεσιν τεσσαράκοντα - ᾠκοδομήθη Jo. 2. 20 is a different use of the dative, for which we have also ἐν (om. ℵ) τρισὶν ἡμέραις in the same verse and in 19 (ἐν om. B), answering the question In how long a time?, where in classical Greek ἐν is the ordinary construction.[2] With names of feasts we have Mc. 6. 21 τοῖς γενεσίοις αὐτοῦ, Mt. 14. 6[3]; frequently τοῖς σάββασιν, 'on the Sabbath,' Mt. 12. 1 etc., as well as ἐν τοῖς σ. L. 4. 31 al., also τῷ σαββάτῳ L. 6. 9, σαββάτῳ Mt. 24. 20 (ἐν σ. EF al., D σαββάτου § 36, 13), Jo. 5. 16 D, 7. 22 B (al. ἐν σ., as all mss. read in 23 *bis*), τῷ ἐχομένῳ σ. A. 13. 44 (ἐν σ. δευτεροπρώτῳ L. 6. 1, ἐν ἑτέρῳ σ. 6. 6); **κατὰ** πᾶν σάββατον A. 13. 27 and elsewhere. **Τῇ ἑορτῇ** τοῦ πάσχα L. 2. 41 (with ἐν D); elsewhere ἐν τῇ ἑ. (κατὰ ἑορτήν 'every feast' Mt. 27. 15 etc.). Ἑτέραις γενεαῖς E. 3. 5, ἰδίᾳ γενεᾷ A. 13. 36; with ἐν 14. 16. **Καιροῖς** ἰδίοις 1 Tim. 6. 15. Τῇ θλίψει ὑπομένοντες R. 12. 12, 'in tribulation,' is probably only due to assimilation with the neighbouring datives in the same passage.

---

[1] Λίαν πρωὶ τῇ μιᾷ τ. σ., but ACE al. read τῆς μιᾶς and D μιᾶς, which could be explained as partitive.

[2] Ἐν τρισὶν ἡμ. occurs also in Mt. 27. 40, διὰ τριῶν ἡμ. in 26. 61, Mc. 14. 58.

[3] In Mt. the mss. are divided between γενεσίοις δὲ γενομένοις ℵBDL al., and γενεσίων δὲ γενομένων CK (cp. Mc. 6. 2) or ἀγομένων EG al.; the dative would represent an unusual combination of the absolute use of the participle and the temporal dative, and is best attributed to scribes who interpolated it from Mc.

5. An unclassical use is that of the dative to denote **duration of time**, instead of the accusative. But this use is only guaranteed for transitive verbs, and, in a few instances, for passives: whereas, in the case of intransitive verbs (also with a passive in Ap. 20. 3; and a transitive verb in Mc. 2. 19 ὅσον χρόνον, L. 13. 8 τοῦτο τὸ ἔτος, A. 13. 18 ὡς τεσσερακονταετῆ χρόνον, ibid. 21), the accusative still remains: A. 8. 11 ἱκανῷ χρόνῳ ἐξεστακέναι αὐτούς 'a long time,' L. 8. 29 πολλοῖς χρόνοις συνηρπάκει αὐτόν, R. 16. 25 χρ. αἰωνίοις σεσιγημένου (but ἀπεδήμησεν χρόνους ἱκανούς L. 20. 9, and corresponding phrases occur elsewhere with intrans. verbs); in L. 8. 27 the readings are divided between χρόνῳ ἱκ. and ἐκ (ἀπὸ) χρόνων ἱκ. (οὐκ ἐνεδύσατο ἱμάτιον), in Jo. 14. 9 between τοσούτῳ χρόνῳ (μεθ' ὑμῶν εἰμι) אDLQ and τοσοῦτον χρ. AB al., as in A. 28. 12 between ἡμέραις τρισίν and ἡμέρας τρεῖς (ἐπεμείναμεν). A further instance is ὡς ἔτεσιν τετρακοσίοις καὶ πεντήκοντα ἔδωκεν κριτάς A. 13. 20,[1] 'throughout 450 years' (ibid. 18, 21 the accusative, vide supra). The reason for the employment of the dative appears to be that the accusative was regarded as the direct object, and therefore the writer did not like to place another object beside it.[2]

§ 39. THE CASES WITH PREPOSITIONS. PREPOSITIONS WITH THE ACCUSATIVE.

1. The remaining ideas which complete the meaning of verbs and nouns are expressed not by a case alone, but with the help of a preposition: a practice which in the course of the history of the language became more and more adopted in opposition to the employment of the simple case. The N.T. still preserves the whole collection of the old prepositions proper of the Greek language, with the exception of ἀμφί, but along with these the employment of prepositions not strictly so called was further developed. **Prepositions proper** may be divided into: I. Those that take **one** case: 1. with acc. ἀνά, εἰς: 2. with gen. ἀντί, ἀπό, ἐξ ἐκ, πρό: 3. with dat. ἐν, σύν. II. With **two** cases, *i.e.* with acc. and gen.: διά, κατά, μετά, περί, ὑπέρ, ὑπό. III. With **three** cases: ἐπί, παρά, πρός. A simplification is seen in the fact that μετά, περί, ὑπό are relegated from Class III. to Class II., while ἀνά (as already happens in classical prose) is relegated from II. (dat. and accus.) to I. (the loss being on the side of the dative); moreover πρός is now not far from being confined to the construction of I. 1. **Quasi-Prepositions** all take the genitive, and are strictly adverbs or cases of a noun which received the character of prepositions only at a later period, but in N.T. times resemble the regular prepositions in that they

---

[1] The passage is seriously corrupted in most of the MSS., as the statement of time has become attached to the preceding clause (19), where also there is a transitive verb.

[2] In Josephus, however, there is no perceptible difference between the dative and accusative denoting duration of time, W. Schmidt de Jos. elocut. 382 f. (except that διατρίβειν and μένειν always take the accusative).

never or hardly ever stand without their case : ἕνεκεν, χάριν 'on account of,' χωρίς, ἄνευ, ἄτερ, πλήν 'except,' μέχρι, ἄχρι, ἕως 'unto' (these last are also conjunctions), ἔμπροσθεν, ἐνώπιον, ἐναντίον etc. 'before,' ὀπίσω 'behind,' ἐπάνω, 'upon,' ὑποκάτω 'beneath,' μεταξύ 'between.' Naturally no hard and fast line can be drawn between preposition and adverb in these cases.

2. Of prepositions with the accusative, ἀνά, which has already become rare in Attic prose, has well-nigh disappeared in the N.T. Ἀνὰ μέσον (with gen.) 'between' Mt. 13. 25 etc. (Polyb. etc., LXX.: modern Gr. ἀνάμεσα) = ἐν μέσῳ (L. 8. 7 al.), cp. § 40, 8; ἀνὰ μέρος 'in turn' 1 C. 14. 27 (Polyb.); elsewhere it is distributive 'apiece,' ἔλαβον ἀνὰ δηνάριον Mt. 20. 9 etc., ἀνὰ πτέρυγας ἕξ Ap. 4. 8, or 'at the rate of,' Mc. 6. 40 κλισίαι ἀνὰ ἑκατόν A al. (as in L. 9. 14), but with κατά אBD (κατά being an equivalent for ἀνά in all the above-mentioned uses); stereotyped as an adverb (like κατά, § 51, 5) Ap. 21. 21 ἀνὰ εἷς ἕκαστος τῶν πυλώνων = καθ' εἷς (Herm. Sim. ix. 2. 3, see § 45, 3).

3. **Εἰς** not only maintained its own place in the language, but also absorbed the kindred preposition ἐν; many instances of this absorption appear already in the N.T., although, if we take the practice of the N.T. as a whole, ἐν is considerably more than a match for εἰς. The classical position, namely that ἐν with the dative answers the question 'where?,' εἰς with accusative the question 'whither?,' had from early times been simplified in some dialects by ἐν taking to itself (like the Latin *in*) both cases and both functions; but the popular Hellenistic language went in the other direction and reduced everything to **εἰς with accusative, representing 'where?' and 'whither?'** From this intermixture, which meets us also in the LXX. and in Egyptian private records,[1] no *writer of narrative* in the N.T. is free, with the exception of Matthew: not even Luke in the Acts, where on the contrary most of the examples are found; John has less of it than the others. Passages: Mc. 1. 9 ἐβαπτίσθη εἰς τὸν Ἰορδάνην (ἐν 1. 5, Mt. 3. 6), 1. 39 κηρύσσων εἰς τὰς συναγωγάς (ἐν ταῖς συναγωγαῖς EF al.), 2. 1 εἰς οἶκόν ἐστιν AC al. (ἐν οἴκῳ אBDL), 10. 10 (ἐν AC al. εἰσελθόντος εἰς Syr. Sin.), 13. 3 καθημένου εἰς τὸ ὄρος (καθίζειν εἰς 2 Th. 2. 4 is correct classical Greek), 13. 9, 16 ὁ εἰς τὸν ἀγρόν (ἐν Mt. 24. 18), L. 4. 23 γενόμενα ('done') εἰς τὴν (אB, εἰς DL, ἐν τῇ al.) Καφαρναούμ (1. 44 is also unclassical, ἐγένετο ἡ φωνὴ εἰς τὰ ὦτά μου, cp. γενέσθαι εἰς Ἱερ. A. 20. 16, 21. 17, 25. 15; correctly ἐν 13. 5), 9. 61, 11. 7 εἰς τὴν κοίτην εἰσίν (ἐν D), 21. 37 (?), A. 2. 5 εἰς Ἱερ. κατοικοῦντες (ἐν אᶜBCDE; correctly H. 11. 9 παρῴκησεν εἰς γῆν, Mt. 2. 23, 4. 13, cp. Thuc. ii. 102. 6 κατοικισθεὶς εἰς τόπους). 2. 17 O.T. cp. 31 ἐγκαταλείψεις τὴν ψυχήν μου εἰς ᾅδην, 39 τοῖς εἰς μακράν (class. τοῖς μακρὰν [sc. ὁδόν] ἀποικοῦσιν), 7. 4. 12, 8. 20, 23 (v.l.), 40 εὑρέθη εἰς Ἄζωτον, 9. 21 (ἐν all MSS. except אA), 11. 25 D, 14. 25 (ἐν BCD), 17. 13 D, 18. 21 D, 19. 22 (ἐν D), 21. 13,

---

[1] So in the Egyptian records of the Berlin Museum, vol. ii. 385 εἰς Ἀλεξάνδρειάν ἐστι, 423 κινδυνεύσαντος εἰς θάλασσαν; Kaibel Epigr. 134 (written at Athens in imperial times) εἰς τύμβον κεῖμαι.

§ 39. 3–4.]   WITH ACCUSATIVE.   123

23. 11 bis, 25. 4, 26. 20, Jo. 1. 18 ὁ ὢν εἰς τὸν κόλπον τοῦ πατρός, 17. 23 ἵνα ὦσιν τετελειωμένοι εἰς (τὸ) ἕν, cp. 1 Jo. 5. 8 οἱ τρεῖς εἰς τὸ ἕν εἰσιν. But ἔστη εἰς τὸ μέσον Jo. 20. 19, 26 is classical (Xenophon Cyr. iv. 1. 1), cp. 21. 4 (v.l. ἐπί).[1] On the other hand, the Epistles and—what is still more striking—the Apocalypse—show at least in the local signification a correct discrimination between εἰς and ἐν, except in (1 Jo. 5. 8, see above, and) 1 P. 5. 12 (a postscript to the letter written in the apostle's own hand) τὴν χάριν – εἰς ἣν στῆτε (ἑστήκατε KLP), which certainly cannot mean 'put yourself into it,' but 'stand fast therein.'[2] Εἰς for ἐν is frequent in Hermas, Vis. i. 2. 2 ἔχουσα βιβλίον εἰς τὰς χεῖρας, ii. 4. 3, Sim. i. 2 etc.; see also Clem. Cor. ii. 8. 2 (19. 4 ?), Clem. Hom. xii. 10. It thus appears that at that time this use of εἰς was still a provincialism, although even so the fact that several authors do not share in it is remarkable. On the reverse interchange, ἐν for εἰς, see § 41, 1.

4. Under the head of **intermixture of εἰς and ἐν** may be also reckoned L. 1. 20 πληρωθήσονται εἰς τὸν καιρὸν αὐτῶν (correctly with ἐν Mt. 21. 41, 2 Th. 2. 6), whereas L. 13. 9 κἂν ποιήσῃ καρπὸν εἰς τὸ μέλλον has classical parallels (so ἐς ὕστερον Hdt. 5. 74); correct are also A. 13. 42 εἰς τὸ μεταξὺ σάββατον, 2 C. 13. 2 εἰς τὸ πάλιν (cp. classical εἰσαῦθις); the remaining temporal uses of εἰς are still more completely in agreement with classical Greek.—A. 7. 53 ἐλάβετε τὸν νόμον εἰς διαταγὰς ἀγγέλων = ἐν διαταγαῖς (cp. Mt. 9. 34 and other passages).—After the Hebrew לֵךְ לְשָׁלוֹם, Mc. 5. 34 and Lc. 7. 50, 8. 48 say ὕπαγε εἰς εἰρήνην (so also LXX. 1 Sam. 1. 17 etc.): but the sense seems to be better given by Ja. 2. 16 ὑπάγετε ἐν εἰρήνῃ (so D in both passages of Luke). In other instances the caprice of the writer in his choice of εἰς or ἐν is not surprising, since Hebrew had only the one preposition בְּ, and classical Greek had in most of these cases none at all. Thus πιστεύειν εἰς alternates with πιστ. ἐν (Mc. 1. 15) and πιστ. ἐπί, in addition to which the correct classical π. τινί appears, § 37, 1; there is a corresponding interchange of prepositions with the subst. πίστις (ἡ ἐν Χρ., ἡ εἰς Χρ., beside the objective genitive), and with πεποιθέναι,[3] which also has the simple dative: see for this verb and for ἐλπίζειν § 37, 2; further, with ὀμνύναι (which in classical Greek takes accus., § 34, 1) in Mt. 5. 35 ἐν and εἰς are found side by side; with εὐδοκεῖν 'to have pleasure' ἐν is frequent, εἰς occurs in Mt. 12. 18 O.T. (ὃν simply ℵ*B, ἐν ᾧ D) and 2 P. 1. 17. The rendering of the Hebrew בְּשֵׁם is especially variable: τῷ σῷ ὀνόματι (instrumental dative)[4] Mt. 7. 22, εἰς ὄνομα

---

[1] Ὕπαγε νίψαι εἰς τὴν κολυμβήθραν 9. 7 is supported by parallels from profane writers; νίψαι however appears not to be genuine (Lachm.; om. A al., cp. 11).

[2] 1 P. 3. 20 εἰς ἣν (κιβωτὸν) ὀλίγοι διεσώθησαν is 'into which few escaped,' cp. 2 Tim. 4. 18 (LXX. Gen. 19. 19).

[3] Similarly θαρρῶ ἐν 'confide in' 2 C. 7. 16: but εἰς 10. 1 = θρασύς εἰμι 'toward you.'

[4] The simple dative is further found in (Mt. 12. 21, see § 37, 1, note 2), Mc. 9. 38 AX al. (rell. ἐν), Ja. 5. 10 AKL (rell. ἐν).

προφήτου 10. 41, εἰς τὸ ἐμὸν ὄνομα 18. 20 (28. 19), ἐπὶ τῷ ὀνόματί μου 18. 5, ἐν ὀνόματι κυρίου 21. 9. Again 'to do to anyone' is ποιεῖν (ἐργάζεσθαι) τι ἔν τινι, εἴς τινα, τινί (Att. τινά), see § 34, 4 (beside ποιεῖν ἐλεημοσύνας εἰς A. 24. 17 there is an alternative ποιεῖν ἔλεος μετά [Hebr. עִם] τινος L. 10. 37). With the verb 'to announce,' if the communication is made to several persons, either εἰς or ἐν is admissible in Attic Greek (εἰπεῖν εἰς τὸν δῆμον, ἐν τῷ δήμῳ); so also in N.T. κηρύσσειν εἰς Mc. 13. 10 (ἐν D), 14. 9,[1] L. 24. 47, 1 Th. 2. 9 (ὑμῖν א*), ἐν 2 C. 1. 19, G. 2. 2, εὐαγγελίζεσθαι εἰς 1 P. 1. 25, ἐν G. 1. 16.

5. In place of a nominative (or accusative in the respective passages) **εἰς** is found with the accusative, after a Hebrew pattern, **with εἶναι, γίνεσθαι, λογίζεσθαι,** § 33, 3 : for the sense 'to represent as,' 'reckon as' see § 34, 5. But in G. 3. 14 ἵνα εἰς τὰ ἔθνη ἡ εὐλογία τοῦ Ἀβραὰμ γένηται the simple case would be the dative, cp. § 37, 3, or in classical Greek the genitive; cp. ἐγγίζειν εἰς for τινί, § 37, 6 (in modern Greek εἰς is the usual circumlocution for the lost dative, cp. ibid. 1).—Εἰς for ἐπί or πρός: Jo. 4. 5 ἔρχεται εἰς πόλιν κ.τ.λ. 'comes to' not 'into,' 11. 31, 38 ὑπάγει (ἔρχεται) εἰς (D 11. 38 ἐπὶ) τὸ μνημεῖον, 20. 3 (in 8 εἰς is correct); in accordance with which some would support the reading of DHP in Mc. 3. 7 ἀνεχώρησεν εἰς (instead of πρὸς) τὴν θάλασσαν (similarly in 2. 13 Tisch. reads ἐξῆλθεν εἰς τὴν θάλ. with א*, for παρά, and in 7. 31 with אBD al.).[2] Even Matthew in 12. 41 μετενόησαν εἰς τὸ κήρυγμα Ἰωνᾶ has an instance of εἰς for πρός, cp. Hdt. 3. 52 πρὸς τοῦτο τὸ κήρυγμα οὔτις οἱ διαλέγεσθαι ἤθελε ('in consequence of').

§ 40. PREPOSITIONS WITH THE GENITIVE.

1. **Ἀντί** is one of the prepositions that are dying out, being represented by some twenty instances in the whole N.T. Ἀνθ' ὧν 'for the reason that' = 'because' L. 1. 20, 19. 44, A. 12. 23, 2 Th. 2. 10, classical, also in LXX. 2 Kings 22. 17 = תַּחַת אֲשֶׁר; 'for this' = 'therefore' L. 12. 3, ἀντὶ τούτου E. 5. 31 O.T. (ἕνεκεν τούτου LXX. and Mt. 19. 6, Mc. 10. 7, עַל־כֵּן).—Equivalent to a genitive of price (similarly classical Greek) H. 12. 16 ἀντὶ βρώσεως μιᾶς ἀπέδοτο τὰ πρωτοτόκια.—In a peculiar sense, Jo. 1. 16, χάριν ἀντὶ χάριτος ἐλάβομεν, cp. class. γῆν πρὸ γῆς ἐλαύνεσθαι 'from one land to another,' and frequently ἐλπίσιν ἐξ ἐλπίδων and the like.

2. **Ἀπό** has still maintained its place in modern Greek, while it has taken over the uses of ἐξ, which disappears; in the N.T. this mixture has already begun, although (with regard to the frequency with which either is employed) ἐξ still holds its own fairly easily

---

[1] This passage might indeed be a case of εἰς for ἐν: ὅπου ἐὰν κηρυχθῇ τὸ εὐαγγέλιον εἰς ὅλον τὸν κόσμον, λαληθήσεται κ.τ.λ.

[2] Another incorrect use is δότε δακτύλιον εἰς τὴν χεῖρα L. 15. 22, class. περί, see Plato Rep. ii. 359 E; also in the same passage ὑποδήματα εἰς τοὺς πόδας (class. dat., Odyss. 15. 368).

§ 40. 2–3.]   *WITH GENITIVE.*   125

against ἀπό (as ἐν does against εἰς, § 39, 3). Instances of mixture: ἀπελθεῖν (ἐξ- EHLP) ἀπό (om. HLP) τῆς πόλεως A. 16. 39, which means not 'to depart from the neighbourhood of the city' (where ἀπό is right), but 'to go out of the city,' 13. 50, 'Mc.' 16. 9 ἀφ' (παρ' C*DL) ἧς ἐξεβεβλήκει ἑπτὰ δαιμόνια, H. 11. 15 ἀφ' ἧς (πατρίδος) ἐξέβησαν. However in most cases in a connection of this kind ἐξ and ἀπό are still correctly distinguished.—Also the **partitive** ἐξ, which itself is scarcely classical (§ 35, 4), is occasionally represented by the still more unclassical ἀπό, Mt. 27. 21 τίνα ἀπὸ τῶν δύο (= class. πότερον τούτοιν), and both are used promiscuously in place of the classical genitive in phrases like 'to eat of,' 'to take of,' etc., § 36, 1. Contrary to *Attic* usage is τινὰς τῶν ἀπὸ τῆς ἐκκλησίας A. 12. 1 'those belonging to the community' (not those who came from the community), cp. 6. 9, 15. 5, whereas in A. 10. 45, 11. 2, Tit. 1. 10 we have οἱ ἐκ περιτομῆς correctly (οἱ ἐκ τῆς διατριβῆς ταύτης Aeschin. 1. 54); still Hellenistic writers like Plutarch have similar phrases.[1] Again, ἐξ would be the correct preposition to express **extraction** from a place; but N.T. has ἦν ὁ Φίλιππος ἀπὸ Βηθσαϊδά, ἐκ τῆς πόλεως Ἀνδρέου Jo. 1. 44, cp. 45,[2] Mt. 21. 11, A. 10. 38, and so always, unless as in L. 2. 4 (ἐκ πόλεως Ναζ.), πόλις is added as well; ἀπό is also regularly used of a person's country except in John, A. 6. 9, 21. 27, 23. 34, 24. 18 (but in classical Greek, Isocr. 4. 82 etc. τοὺς ἐκ τῆς Ἀσίας).[3] See also Acts 2. 5. **Material**: ἔνδυμα ἀπὸ τριχῶν Mt. 3. 4. 'After,' 'out of': ἐδυναμώθησαν ἀπὸ ἀσθενείας H. 11. 34 (classical Greek has λευκὸν ἦμαρ εἰσιδεῖν ἐκ χείματος).

3. Ἀπό has supplanted ὑπό in the sense of 'on account of,' 'for' (of things which occasion or hinder some result by their magnitude): ἀπὸ τῆς λύπης κοιμωμένους L. 22. 45, Mt. 13. 44, 14. 26, A. 20. 9, 12. 14 ἀπὸ τῆς χαρᾶς οὐκ ἤνοιξεν, 22. 11, L. 19. 3, (24. 41), Jo. 21. 6, Herm. Vis. iii. 11. 2; cp. ἐξ infra 4. Also ὑπό with a **passive** verb or a verb of **passive** meaning is often replaced by ἀπό, although in this instance the MSS. commonly exhibit much diversity in their readings. A. 2. 22 ἀποδεδειγμένον ἀπὸ τοῦ θεοῦ, 4. 36 ἐπικληθεὶς Βαρναβᾶς ἀπὸ (D ὑπὸ) τῶν ἀποστόλων, Mt. 16. 21 πολλὰ παθεῖν ἀπὸ (D ὑπὸ) τῶν κ.τ.λ. (in the parallel passage Mc. 8. 31 ἀπό is only read by AX al., the rest have ὑπό: in L. 17. 25 ἀπό is read by all).—Ἀπό further encroaches upon the province of παρά with the genitive: ἀκούειν ἀπό A. 9. 13, 1 Jo. 1. 5; μανθάνειν ἀπό G. 3. 2, Col. 1. 7; παραλαμβάνειν ἀπό 1 C. 11. 23 (παρὰ DE, ἀπολαμβ. ἀπό followed by the same verb with παρά Herm. Vis. v. 7) etc.; also in the phrase 'to come from a person': ἀπὸ Ἰακώβου G. 2. 12, ἀπὸ θεοῦ Jo. 13. 3, 16. 30 (ἐκ 8. 42, παρά 16. 27, cp. § 43, 5).—The use of the old **genitive of separation** (§ 36, 9) is far more restricted in the N.T. than in

---

[1] So Plut. Caes. 35 οἱ ἀπὸ βουλῆς, members of the senate.
[2] But in 1. 47 ἐκ Ναζ. δύναταί τι ἀγαθὸν εἶναι; cp. 4. 22 ἡ σωτηρία ἐκ τῶν Ἰουδαίων ἐστίν.
[3] Ἀπό is found already in Homer and poetry: ἀπὸ Σπάρτης Hdt. 8. 114, Soph. El. 691.

the classical language through the employment of ἀπό (ἐξ): so regularly with ἐλευθεροῦν, λύειν, χωρίζειν etc., also with ὑστερεῖν (ibid.). Much more remarkable, however, is the ἀπό, which in imitation of the Hebrew מִן, מִפְּנֵי = 'for,' is employed with verbs meaning 'to hide,' 'to be on one's guard,' 'to fear' (similarly in the LXX., Buttm. p. 278). See on κρύπτειν τι ἀπό τινος § 34, 4; φεύγειν, φυλάσσειν and -εσθαι, φοβεῖσθαι, αἰσχύνεσθαι ἀπό τινος § 34, 1; to which must be added προσέχειν ἑαυτῷ or still more abbreviated προσέχειν (sc. τὸν νοῦν 'to have a care for oneself' = 'to beware'), ἀπό τινος L. 12. 1, Mt. 7. 15 etc.; in a similar sense ὁρᾶν, βλέπειν ἀπό Mc. 8. 15, 12. 38. Τηρεῖν and διατηρεῖν, however, take ἐξ (equally unclassical): ἐξ (ἀφ' D) ὧν διατηροῦντες ἑαυτούς A. 15. 29, Jo. 17. 25, Ap. 3. 10. In these instances also the idea of separation or alienation is expressed by ἀπό, as it is in many expressions, especially in St. Paul, which cannot be directly paralleled from the classical language: R. 9. 3 ἀνάθεμα εἶναι ἀπὸ τοῦ Χρ., 2 C. 11. 3 μὴ φθαρῇ τὰ νοήματα ὑμῶν ἀπὸ τῆς ἁπλότητος τῆς ἐν Χρ., 2 Th. 2. 2, Col. 2. 20 ἀπεθάνετε ἀπὸ τῶν στοιχείων τοῦ κόσμου, similarly with καταργεῖσθαι R. 7. 6, G. 5. 4; also μετανοεῖν ἀπό in A. 8. 22, cp. H. 6. 1, ἐκ Ap. 2. 21 etc.; δικαιοῦν, θεραπεύειν, λούειν ἀπό approach still more nearly to λύειν etc.[1] Cp. in Hermas and other writings: διαφθαρῆναι ἀπό Sim. iv. 7, ἀποτυφλοῦσθαι ἀπό Mand. v. 2. 7, κολοβὸς ἀπό Sim. ix. 26. 8, κενὸς ἀπό Sim. ix. 19. 2, ἔρημος ἀπό Clem. Cor. ii. 2. 3, λιποτακτεῖν ἀπό i. 21. 4, ἀργεῖν ἀπό 33. 1.— On the use of ἀπό in reckoning distance (ἀπὸ σταδίων δεκαπέντε) see § 34, 8.—On ἀπὸ προσώπου τινός infra 9.

4. On the largely employed ἐξ, ἐκ there is little to remark. It takes the place of the subjective genitive 2 C. 9. 2 τὸ ἐξ ὑμῶν ζῆλος (without ἐξ ℵBCP), cp. 8. 7 τῇ ἐξ ὑμῶν ἐν ἡμῖν (?) ἀγάπῃ. For its **partitive** use cp. § 35, 4, § 36, 1; with 'to fill' ibid. 4 (§ 38, 1). In place of a genitive of price: ἠγόρασαν ἐξ αὐτῶν (the 30 pieces of silver) τὸν ἀγρόν Mt. 27. 7, § 36. 8. In a peculiar sense: τοὺς νικῶντας ἐκ τοῦ θηρίου (probably = τηρήσαντας ἑαυτοὺς ἐκ..., supra 3) Ap. 15. 2. Denoting the cause like ἀπό, and classical ὑπό, supra 3: Ap. 16. 10 ἐμασῶντο τὰς γλώσσας αὐτῶν ἐκ τοῦ πόνου, cp. 11, 21: this book with the Gospel and the first Epistle of St. John makes proportionally the largest use of ἐξ, of any of the N.T. books. With attraction ἐξ for ἐν see § 76, 4.

5. Πρό is not represented by very many examples, most of which = 'before' of time; 'before' of place only in Acts (5. 23, v.l.) 12. 6 (v.l. πρὸς in D), 14, 14. 13, Ja. 5. 9 (elsewhere ἔμπροσθεν, vide infra 7); of preference πρὸ πάντων Ja. 5. 12, 1 P. 4. 8. On the Hebraistic πρὸ προσώπου τινός infra 9. In a peculiar usage: Jo. 12. 1 πρὸ ἓξ ἡμερῶν τοῦ πάσχα '6 days before the passover,' cp. Lat. *ante diem tertium Calendas* (so also other writers under the Empire,

---

[1] But H. 5. 7 εἰσακουσθεὶς ἀπὸ τῆς εὐλαβείας cannot be so taken 'heard (and freed) from his fear,' especially as εὐλαβ. 12. 28 rather denotes the fear of God (cp. εὐλαβεῖσθαι 11. 7, εὐλαβής A. 2. 5 etc.); therefore render 'on account of his piety,' cp. p. 125.

§ 40. 5–7.] WITH GENITIVE.

see Kühner Gr. II.² 288, W. Schmidt de Josephi elocut. 513, and cp. μετά § 42, 3, and ἀπό in the reckoning of distance supra 3).

6. Quasi-prepositions with genitive. 'For the sake of' is ἕνεκεν, also εἵνεκεν § 6, 4, ἕνεκα A. 26. 21 (Attic, § 6, 1) in Paul's speech before Agrippa, also L. 6. 22 (-εν D al.), Mt. 19. 8 O.T. אBLZ (LXX. -εν), A. 19. 32 אAB, Mc. 13. 9 B. Not frequent (some 20 instances, including quotations); it denotes the cause or motive which is given for an action, so regularly ἕνεκεν ἐμοῦ in the Gospels, elsewhere it is hardly distinguishable from διά with accus., see § 42, 1; its position (which in Attic is quite unrestricted) is always before the genitive except in the case of an interrogative (τίνος ἕνεκεν A. 19. 32) or a relative sentence (οὗ εἵνεκεν L. 4. 18 O.T.). Χάριν is still rarer (almost always placed after the word).—'**Except**,' '**without**,' is usually **χωρίς**; ἄνευ (also Attic) only appears in Mt. 10. 29, 1 P. 3. 1, 4. 9; ἄτερ (poetical: in prose not before imperial times) only in L. 22. 6, 35 (often in Hermas, e.g. Sim. v. 4. 5; Barn. 2. 6 C, but ἄνευ א); πλήν (Attic) A. 8. 1, 15. 28, 27. 22, Mc. 12. 32, 'Jo.' 8. 10. The position of these words (as also of those that follow) is always before the case, except in one ex. οὗ χωρίς H. 12. 4, § 80, 4; χ. as adverb (often in Attic) only appears in Jo. 20. 7.—'**Unto**' is **ἄχρι(s)**, **μέχρι(s)** as in Attic (on the s see § 5, 4), the former in Lc., Acts, Paul, Hebrews, Ap., Mt. 24. 38: the latter in Mt. 11. 23, 13. 30 (ἕως BD), 28. 15 (א*D ἕως), Mc. 13. 30 (ἕως D), and sporadically in Lc., Acts, Paul, Hebrews; both are also used as conjunctions (in an intermediate stage with the interposition of a relative, ἄχρι οὗ, μ. οὗ; Herm. Vis. iv. 1. 9 μ. ὅτε א*, μ. ὅτου א^c as), see § 65, 10; 78, 3; **ἕως** is also employed in this sense, originally a conjunction throughout (its use as a prep. appears in Hellenistic Gk. and the LXX.), Mt. 1. 17 ἀπὸ Ἀβραὰμ ἕως Δαυίδ, ἕως τοῦ Χριστοῦ etc. (often in Mt., also in Mc., Lc., Acts, rare in Paul and James; in Hebr. only in quotations; John uses none of the three words); here also we have ἕως οὗ, ἕως ὅτου. Ἕως is moreover readily joined with an adverb: ἕως πότε, ἀπὸ ἄνωθεν ἕως κάτω, ἕως ἄρτι, ἕως σήμερον, on the other hand ἄχρι (μέχρι) τοῦ νῦν, τῆς σήμερον (although Thuc. 7. 83 has μέχρι ὀψέ). It occasionally has the meaning 'within': A. 19. 26 D ἕως Ἐφέσου, 23. 23 (β text) ἕως ἑκατόν. Herm. Mand. iv. 1. 5 ἄχρι τῆς ἀγνοίας οὐχ ἁμαρτάνει means 'as long as he does not know' (ἄχρις ἂν ἀγνοῇ = ἄ. ἂν γνῷ 'until').

7. 'Before' (in local sense, rarely πρό, supra 5) is expressed by **ἔμπροσθεν, ἐναντίον** (ἔναντι, κατέναντι, ἀπέναντι), **ἐνώπιον** (κατενώπιον). Of these expressions ἔμπροσθεν and ἐναντίον with the genitive are also classical, and in the case of ἐναντίον the construction with the genitive is also the predominant use of the word, whereas ἔμπροσθεν is more frequently adverbial; ἀπέναντι is Hellenistic (Polyb.); ἐνώπιον (ἐν-ώπ. before the eyes: τὰ ἐνώπια is as old as Homer), κατενώπιον (κατένωπα or κατ' ἐνῶπα Hom.), ἔναντι[1] (ἔναντα Hom.), κατέναντι (κατέναντα in poetry) all take their origin from the LXX.

---

[1] Ἔναντι occurs in inscriptions in translations of Roman senatus consulta, Viereck Sermo graecus Senat. Rom. (Gtg. 1888) p. 16, 66.

and are foreign to profane authors even at a later date than the N.T.,[1] while the N.T. on the other hand has not got ἀντικρύ(ς) (except in A. 20. 15 ἀ. Χίου) καταντ. ἀπαντ. The expressions serve as a rendering for the Hebrew לִפְנֵי, לְעֵינֵי, also for נֶגֶד, and ἔμπροσθεν and ἐναντίον also frequently stand in the N.T. in places where classical Greek would express itself in a simpler manner. Thus Mt. 7. 6 μὴ βάλητε τοὺς μαργαρίτας ὑμῶν ἔμπροσθεν τῶν χοίρων = class. μὴ προβάλητε τ. μ. τοῖς χοίροις. Ἔμπροσθεν is also apparently used of time = πρό (so in class. Greek), in Jo. 1. 15, 30 (or of precedence = has obtained the precedence of me ?); in adverbial sense only in L. 19. 4, 28, Ph. 3. 14, Ap. 4. 6; it is employed by wellnigh all writers (not Pet., James, Jude, Hebr.), most frequently by Mt. Ἐναντίον occurs in Mc. 2. 12 ACD (al. ἔμπρ.), L. 1. 8 אAC al. (ἔναντι BDE al.), 20. 26, 24. 19 (ἐνώπιον D), A. 7. 10 (ἔναντι א), 8. 32 O.T.; ἔναντι is further used in 8. 21 (ἐνώπιον EHLP); κατέναντι ἀπέν. (where the readings often vary) Mt. 21. 2, 27. 24 etc., A. 3. 16, 17. 7, R. 3. 18 O.T., 4. 17 (adverb L. 19. 30); ἐνώπιον is frequent in Luke (in the first half of the Acts; in the second half it is only found in 19. 9, 19, 27. 35) and in the Apocalypse: in John only in 20. 30, 1 Jo. 3. 22, 3 Jo. 6: in Mt. and Mc. never (κατενώπ. in a few passages of Paul and in Jude).—'Before' in the strictly local sense is generally expressed by ἔμπροσθεν alone (the word has only this sense in the Apoc.): ἔμπρ. τοῦ βήματος A. 18. 17, τῶν ποδῶν Ap. 19. 10 (B ἐνώπιον), 22. 8 (A πρό), although the author of the Apoc. also says ἐνώπιον τοῦ θρόνου; similarly 'before anyone' is ἔμπροσθεν Jo. 3. 28, 10. 4 (ἐνώπιον L. 1. 76 אB); ἔμπρ. ἐναντίον ἐνώπιον express 'before anyone' = before the eyes of anyone, also pleasing in anyone's eyes = 'to anyone,' A. 6. 5 ἤρεσεν ἐνώπιον τοῦ πλήθους = τῷ πλήθει, 1 Jo. 3. 22 τὰ ἀρεστὰ ἐνώπιον αὐτοῦ; ἁμαρτάνειν ἐνώπ. τινος = εἰς τινα L. 15. 18, 21 (1 Sam. 7. 6), or τινί, LXX. Judges 11. 27, Buttm. p. 150; so a genitive or dative is often replaced by this circumlocution, Mt. 18. 24 οὐκ ἔστιν θέλημα ἔμπροσθεν τοῦ πατρός μου, where ἔμπρ. might be omitted, 11. 26, L. 15. 10 χαρὰ γίνεται ἐνώπιον τῶν ἀγγέλων = τῶν ἀγγέλων or τοῖς ἀγγέλοις, 24. 11 ἐφάνησαν ἐνώπιον αὐτῶν ὡσεὶ λῆρος = αὐτοῖς, etc. Similar is H. 4. 13 ἀφανὴς ἐνώπιον αὐτοῦ, 13. 21; but in the second half of the Acts it is only used = class. ἐναντίον. Κατέναντι, ἀπέναντι mean 'over against' = class. καταντικρύ, Mt. 21. 2, Mc. 12. 41 etc.; but are also commonly used = 'before' like ἐναντίον, ἐνώπιον, e.g. with τοῦ ὄχλου Mt. 27. 24; a peculiar usage is ἀπέναντι τῶν δογμάτων 'contrary to' A. 17. 7 (ἐναντία τοῖς δόγμασιν or τῶν δογμάτων in classical Greek).

8. The opposite of ἔμπροσθεν in the local sense is ὄπισθεν 'behind,' occurring with genitive only in Mt. 15. 23, Lc. 23. 26, rarely also as an adverb; on the other hand ὀπίσω (in the older language the

---

[1] Cp. Deissmann, Neue Bibelstudien (Marburg, 1897), p. 40 f., who gives instances from the papyri of an adverbial use of ἐνώπιον, in the sense of 'in person,' Latin *coram*; see also Grenfell-Hunt, Pap. ii. 112.

§ 40. 8–9.] WITH GENITIVE. 129

opposite of πρόσω, for which Attic had πόρρω 'far off,' the latter form occurring occasionally in N.T.) is found fairly often, usually as a preposition, more rarely as an adverb. The prepositional use of ὀπίσω, which is foreign to profane writers, takes its origin from the LXX. (Hebr. אַחֲרֵי): ἔρχεσθαι ὀπίσω τινός 'to follow' (also ἀκολουθεῖν ὀπ. τιν., instead of the dative, see § 37, 6), ἀπέστησε λαὸν ὀπίσω αὐτοῦ A. 5. 37, cp. 20. 30; even θαυμάζειν ὀπίσω Ap. 13. 3 (§ 38, 2, note 2). Somewhat different is ἔρχεσθαι ὀπ. τ. Mt. 3. 11 etc., 'to come after (or behind) anyone,' in the Baptist's utterance about Christ.—The compounds, found already in Attic Greek, ἐπ-άνω 'above' and ὑπο-κάτω 'underneath' (used also in Attic with the genitive), have a weakened force in the N.T. = 'upon,' 'under': Mt. 5. 14 πόλις ἐπάνω ὄρους κειμένη = Att. ἐπ' ὄρους, L. 8. 16 ὑποκάτω κλίνης τίθησιν = Att. ὑπὸ κλίνην; ἐπάνω only is used adverbially, and this word is also joined with numerals = 'more than,' without affecting the case, § 36, 12 (before an adverb Mt. 2. 9 ἐπάνω οὗ ἦν τὸ παιδίον, but D here has τοῦ παιδίου).—'**Between**' is expressed by μεταξύ (Att.) Mt. 18. 15 etc. (rare); this word is also used adverbially in Jo. 4. 31 ἐν τῷ μ. = 'meanwhile,' but in the common language[1] = 'afterwards,' A. 13. 42 εἰς τὸ μεταξὺ σάββατον, cp. 23. 24 an addition of the β text, Barn. 13. 5, Clem. Cor. i. 44. 2. Beside μεταξύ we have ἀνὰ μέσον, see § 39, 2 : ἐν μέσῳ (ἐμμέσῳ) with genitive 'among,' 'between,' Mt. 10. 16 (B εἰς μέσον), L. 10. 3 (μέσον D, vide infra), 8. 7 (μέσον D), 21. 22 etc. = Hebrew בְּתוֹךְ and classical ἐν or εἰς, since 'where?' and 'whither?' are not distinguished in this instance (εἰς μέσον never occurs except as a var. lect. in Mt. 10. 16 vide supra, 14. 24 D for μέσον; but of course we have εἰς τὸ μέσον without a subsequent case). Other equivalents are μέσος adjective Jo. 1. 26, L. 22. 55 BL (v.l. ἐν μέσῳ, μετ') or μέσον adverb (cp. modern Greek μέσα), Ph. 2. 15 τέκνα θεοῦ μέσον γενεᾶς σκολιᾶς, L. 10. 3 D, vide supra (adj. or adv. in Mt. 14. 24, L. 8. 7 D). To these must be added ἐκ μέσου with gen. = מִתּוֹךְ Mt. 13. 49 etc. = class. ἐξ; διὰ μέσου with gen. (בְּתוֹךְ) L. 4. 30 διελθὼν διὰ μέσου αὐτῶν = διά, (see also § 42, 1).

9. To express a prepositional idea by a circumlocution, the substantives **πρόσωπον, χείρ, στόμα** are employed with the genitive, similarly to μέσον, in constructions modelled on the Hebrew. Ἀπὸ προσώπου τινός = ἀπό or παρά with gen. after verbs signifying 'to come' or 'to go,' A. 3. 19, 5. 41 : = the N.T. ἀπό (supra 3) after 'to drive out,' 'to hide,' 'to fly' A. 7. 45, Ap. 6. 16, 12. 14, 20. 11, = מִפְּנֵי. Πρὸ προσώπου Mt. 11. 10 O.T. (לִפְנֵי), so L. 1. 76 (אB ἐνώπιον), 9. 52, even (in A. 13. 24, a sermon of Paul) πρὸ προσώπου τῆς εἰσόδου αὐτοῦ 'before (in advance of) him.' Κατὰ πρόσωπον = coram is also a recognised usage in profane writers, and in this sense is correctly employed in A. 25. 16 (without a gen.); elsewhere as in 3. 13 κατὰ πρόσωπον Πιλάτου, L. 2. 31 κατὰ πρ. πάντων τῶν λαῶν it corresponds

---

[1] In this sense it is found in Plut. Moral. 240 B and Josephus.

to the Hebr. בְּכַף ; similarly εἰς πρ. τινος 2 C. 8. 24 (εἰς πρ. without case, and with εἰς in place of ἐν, Herm. Vis. iii. 6. 3).—Χείρ: εἰς χεῖράς (בְּיַד) τινος παραδιδόναι, 'into anyone's power,' 'to anyone' Mt. 26. 45 etc., L. 23. 46, Jo. 13. 8, H. 10. 31 (ἐμπεσεῖν εἰς χ. θεοῦ, cp. Polyb. 8, 20. 8 ὑπὸ τὰς τῶν ἐχθρῶν χ. πίπτειν; ὑποχείριος); for which is substituted ἐν τῇ χ. δέδωκεν (ἐν for εἰς, § 41, 1) in Jo. 3. 35. Ἐν (σὺν ABCDE) χειρὶ ἀγγέλου A. 7. 35 (cp. G. 3. 19) בְּיַד, 'through,' 'by means of.' Ἐκ χειρός τινος 'out of the power of anyone' (מִיַּד) L. 1. 71, A. 12. 11 ἐξείλατό με ἐκ χ. Ἡρῴδου, cp. in classical Gk. Aesch. 3. 256 ἐκ τῶν χειρῶν ἐξελέσθαι τῶν Φιλίππου (here used as a stronger and more vivid expression), etc. Διὰ χειρός, διὰ τῶν χειρῶν = διά 'through,' 'by means of' Mc. 6. 2 and frequently in Acts (2. 23, 5. 12 etc.), of actions; διὰ στόματος, on the other hand, is used of speeches which God puts into the mouth of anyone, L. 1. 70, A. 1. 16 etc. Further, for λόγοι οἱ ἀπό τινος or τινος the fuller and more vivid οἱ ἐκπορευόμενοι ἐκ (διὰ) στόμ. τινος is used in Mt. 4. 4 O.T. = LXX. Deut. 8. 3, L. 4. 22 etc.; for ἀκούειν τινός we have ἀκ. ἐκ (ἀπὸ, διὰ) τοῦ στ. τινός L. 22. 71, A. 1. 4 D, E. 4. 29 etc.; cp. L. 11. 54 θηρεῦσαί τι ἐκ τ. στ. αὐτοῦ, a word from him; ἐπὶ στόματος 'on the assertion of' Mt. 18. 16, and many similar exx.; στόμα was moreover utilized in classical Greek to coin many expressions of this kind. Ἐκ στόματος can also mean 'out of the jaws,' 2 Tim. 4. 17. —On ὁδόν as preposition (*versus*) Mt. 4. 15 see § 34, 8, note 1.

§ 41. PREPOSITIONS WITH THE DATIVE.

1. Ἐν is the commonest of all prepositions in the N.T., notwithstanding the fact that some writers (§ 39, 3) occasionally employ εἰς instead of it. (The reverse change, namely, the misuse of ἐν for εἰς, can only be safely asserted to take place in a very few cases in the N.T. Thus ἐν μέσῳ is used in answer to the question 'whither?', § 40, 8; compare also εἰσῆλθε διαλογισμὸς ἐν αὐτοῖς L. 9. 46 'came into them,' 'into their hearts' [see next verse]: κατέβαινεν ἐν τῇ κολυμβήθρᾳ in a spurious verse Jo. 5. 4 [Herm. Sim. i. 6 ἀπέλθῃς ἐν τῇ πόλει σου, Clem. Hom. i. 7, xiv. 6]. But ἐξῆλθεν ὁ λόγος ἐν τῇ Ἰουδαίᾳ L. 7. 17 [cp. 1 Th. 1. 8] means 'was spread abroad in J.'; in Ap. 11. 11 εἰσῆλθεν ἐν αὐτοῖς is only read by A, αὐτοῖς CP, εἰς αὐτούς אB; classical authors can use ἐν with τιθέναι and ἱστάναι, and with this may be compared διδόναι ['to lay'] ἐν τῇ χειρί τινος Jo. 3. 35 [§ 40, 9; Clem. Cor. i. 55. 5 παρέδωκεν Ὀλοφέρνην ἐν χειρὶ θηλείας], or ἐν τῇ καρδίᾳ 2 C. 1. 22, 8. 16; no conclusive evidence can be drawn from the metaphorical usage in L. 1. 17 ἐν φρονήσει δικαίων, with the meaning 'so that they have the wisdom'; καλεῖν ἐν εἰρήνῃ and similar phrases).—The use of ἐν receives its chief extension through the imitation of Hebrew constructions with בְּ. Under this head comes its instrumental employment, § 38, 1; also its use to indicate the personal agent: ἐν τῷ ἄρχοντι (through) τῶν δαιμονίων

ἐκβάλλει τὰ δαιμόνια Mt. 12. 24 (9. 24), κρίνειν τὴν οἰκουμένην ἐν ἀνδρί A. 17. 31 (1 C. 6. 2).[1] In the same way no doubt is to be explained its use to express the motive : A. 7. 29 ἔφυγεν Μωϋσῆς ἐν τῷ λόγῳ τούτῳ 'on account of' (DE have another reading ἐφυγάδευσεν Μωϋσῆν ἐν 'with'): Mt. 6. 7 ἐν τῇ πολυλογίᾳ αὐτῶν εἰσακουσθήσονται : ἐν τούτῳ 'on this account' A. 24. 16, Jo. 16. 30 : ἐν ᾧ 'since,' 'because' H. 2. 18, or 'on which account' 6. 17; to the same category belongs the use of ἐν with verbs expressing emotion, e.g. χαίρειν, § 38, 2. Another instance of instrumental ἐν is Ap. 5. 9 ἠγόρασας ἐν τῷ αἵματί σου, cp. A. 20. 28 ; this phrase ἐν τῷ αἵματι (τοῦ Χρ.) is found in various connections in the Pauline Epistles and Acts (R. 3. 25, 5. 9 etc.), where the very indefinite and colourless meaning of ἐν does not help to determine the sense more accurately. On ἐνδεδυμένος ἐν and similar phrases see § 34, 6, note 2 ; on ἐν of accompaniment (with 'army' etc.) § 38, 3. Of manner (vide ibid.): ἐν τάχει (class.) L. 18. 8 etc., κρίνειν ἐν δικαιοσύνῃ = δικαίως A. 17. 31, Ap. 19. 11, ἐν πάσῃ ἀσφαλείᾳ = ἀσφαλέστατα A. 5. 23, ἐν (πάσῃ) παρρησίᾳ 'freely,' 'openly' etc. Again ἄνθρωπος ἐν πνεύματι ἀκαθάρτῳ Mc. 1. 23, 5. 2 must mean 'with an unclean spirit' = ἔχων πνεῦμα ἀκάθ. (3. 30 etc.), although a passage like R. 8. 9 ὑμεῖς δὲ οὐκ ἐστὲ ἐν σαρκὶ ἀλλ' **ἐν πνεύματι**, εἴπερ πνεῦμα θεοῦ **οἰκεῖ ἐν ὑμῖν**· εἰ δέ τις πνεῦμα Χριστοῦ **οὐκ ἔχει** κ.τ.λ. is calculated to show the constant fluctuation of the meanings of ἐν and of the conceptions of the relation between man and spirit. Another phrase with an extremely indefinite meaning is ἐν Χριστῷ (κυρίῳ), which is attached again and again in the Pauline Epistles to very different ideas.

2. Occasionally ἐν appears to stand **for the ordinary dative proper.** 1 C. 14. 11 ἔσομαι τῷ λαλοῦντι ('for the speaker') βάρβαρος, καὶ ὁ λαλῶν **ἐν ἐμοὶ** βάρβαρος 'for me,' instead of ἐμοί, which Paul avoided because it might have been taken with λαλῶν. Cp. G. 1. 16 ἀποκαλύψαι τὸν υἱὸν αὐτοῦ ἐν ἐμοί 'to me' ('in me,' i.e. 'in my spirit' would be an unnatural phrase); in 2 C. 4. 3 ἐν τοῖς ἀπολλυμένοις ἐστὶ κεκαλυμμένον 'for' is a better rendering than 'among'; 2 C. 8. 1 τὴν χάριν τὴν δεδομένην ἐν ταῖς ἐκκλησίαις τῆς Μακ., cp. A. 4. 12 where D omits the ἐν ; but 1 Jo. 4. 9 ἐν τούτῳ ἐφανερώθη ἡ ἀγάπη τοῦ θεοῦ ἐν ἡμῖν means 'towards us,' and is like ποιεῖν ἔν τινι, γίνεσθαι ἔν τινι, where moreover either the dative or εἰς can stand, § 34, 4.— Ἐν has the meaning of 'in' or 'by' with μανθάνειν 1 C. 4. 6, γινώσκειν L. 24. 35 etc. (likewise classical); but we also find γιν. ἐκ L. 6. 44 etc., κατὰ τί 1. 18. For 'to swear by' ὀμνύναι ἐν see § 34, 1 (instead of the accus.); for ὁμολογεῖν ἔν τινι 'to profess allegiance to anyone' (a Syriac expression) Mt. 10. 32, L. 12. 8, for which an accus. or two accusatives may be used, see § 34, 5. Ἐν μυστηρίῳ λαλοῦμεν σοφίαν 1 C. 2. 7 = 'as a mystery' (so in classical Greek). On ἐν in temporal sense see § 38, 4.

---

[1] In R. 11. 12 ἐν Ἠλίᾳ λέγει ἡ γραφή might be interpreted in the same way, 'by Elias,' cp. ἐν τῷ Ὡσηέ 9. 25, ἐν Δαυίδ H. 4. 7, ἐν ἑτέρῳ προφήτῃ λέγει Barn. 6. 14. But others class these with ἐν τῷ νόμῳ and the like.

3. Σύν in classical Attic is limited to the sense of 'including,' whereas 'with' is expressed by μετά; but the Ionic dialect and afterwards the Hellenistic language kept the old word σύν in addition to μετά, and it is consequently found in the N.T., although very unequally employed by the different authors, and only occurring with any frequency in Luke (Gospel and Acts) and Paul, while it is unrepresented in the Apocalypse and the Epistles of John, and almost unrepresented in his Gospel.[1] There is scarcely anything noteworthy in the way in which it is employed. Σὺν πᾶσι τούτοις is 'beside all this'. (LXX., Josephus, see W.-Gr.) L. 24. 21. On ἅμα and σύν see § 37, 6.

§ 42. PREPOSITIONS WITH TWO CASES.

1. **Διά with accusative**, local 'through' (poetical) only in L. 17. 11 διήρχετο διὰ μέσον (אBL, D omits διά, § 40, 8; A al. διὰ μέσου) Σαμαρείας καὶ Γαλιλαίας, an inadmissible reading; elsewhere 'on account of,' denoting not only motive and author, but also (what in classical Greek is expressed by ἕνεκα) aim,[2] so that the modern Greek meaning 'for' is already almost in existence: Mc. 2. 27 τὸ σάββατον διὰ τὸν ἄνθρωπον ἐγένετο καὶ οὐχ ὁ ἄνθρ. διὰ τὸ σάββατον, Jo. 11. 42, 12. 30, 1 C. 11. 9 etc.—**With genitive** 'through' of place, time, and agent as in classical Greek. The temporal διά also expresses an interval of time that has elapsed: δι' ἐτῶν πλειόνων 'after several years' A. 24. 17, G. 2. 1; and further (not classical) the period of time within which something takes place: A. 1. 3 δι' ἡμερῶν τεσσεράκοντα ὀπτανόμενος αὐτοῖς '**during** forty days' (not continuously, but at intervals, as was already noticed by the Scholiast following Chrysostom), διὰ νυκτός *per noctem* 'at night' (class. νυκτός, νύκτωρ), 5. 19 etc.; L. 9. 37 D διὰ τῆς ἡμέρας 'in the course of the day.' Instead of the agent, the author may also be denoted by διά (as in Aeschylus Agam. 1486 διαὶ Διὸς παναιτίου πανεργέτα): R. 11. 36 ἐξ αὐτοῦ (source) καὶ δι' αὐτοῦ (the Creator) καὶ εἰς αὐτὸν τὰ πάντα, cp. H. 2. 10 δι' ὃν (God) τὰ πάντα καὶ δι' οὗ τὰ π., 1 C. 1. 9, G. 1. 1 [3] (but the use is different in 1 C. 8. 6 εἷς θεὸς ὁ πατήρ, ἐξ οὗ τὰ πάντα καὶ ἡμεῖς εἰς αὐτόν, καὶ εἷς κύριος Ἰ. Χ., δι' οὗ [ὃν B] τὰ πάντα καὶ ἡμεῖς δι' αὐτοῦ, cp. Jo. 1. 3; Mt. 1. 22 τὸ ῥηθὲν ὑπὸ κυρίου **διὰ** τοῦ προφήτου, etc.).
—Indicating **mode and manner**, διὰ λόγου 'by way of speech,' 'orally' A. 15. 27; also the circumstances in which a man is placed in doing anything: R. 2. 27 ὁ διὰ γράμματος καὶ περιτομῆς παραβάτης νόμου, 'who has the written statute withal,' 14. 20 διὰ προσκόμματος ἐσθίειν

---

[1] See Tycho Mommsen's book, Beiträge zu d. Lehre v. d. gr. Präpositionen (Berlin, 1895), where on page 395 the statistics of σύν and μετά in the N.T. are concisely given. In John σύν occurs in 12. 2, 18. 1, 21. 3 (μετά very frequently); in Paul it is absent from 2 Th., 1 and 2 Tim., Tit., Philem.; as it is also from Hebr. and 1 Pet. [For the distinction between σύν and μετά see also Westcott's note on Jo. 1. 2. Tr.]

[2] Cp. Hatzidakis Einl. in d. ngr. Gramm. 212 f.

[3] It stands for ὑπό with a passive verb in Herm. Sim. ix. 14. 5, Vis. iii. 13. 3.

[§ 42. 1–3.] WITH TWO CASES. 133

'with offence,' διὰ πολλῶν δακρύων 2 C. 2. 4 : also undoubtedly δι' ἀσθενείας (not -ένειαν) εὐηγγελισάμην ὑμῖν G. 4. 13 'in sickness,' as the Vulgate *per* (not *propter*) *infirmitatem*.[1]—In a peculiar use in an urgent petition = 'by' (Attic πρός τινος) : R. 12. 1 παρακαλῶ ὑμᾶς διὰ τῶν οἰκτιρμῶν τοῦ θεοῦ 15. 30, 1 C. 1. 10 and elsewhere in the Pauline Epp. (cp. κατά τινος infra 2).

2. **Κατά with accusative** occurs frequently and in various senses, but in general these agree with the classical uses. As the use of κατά with accus. as a circumlocution for a genitive occurs frequently in the Hellenistic language (ἡ κατὰ τὸν ἥλιον πορεία 'the course of the sun'), so in the N.T. one may adduce : A. 18. 15 νόμου τοῦ καθ' ὑμᾶς 'the law in force with you, your law,' cp. 26. 3, 17. 28, E. 1. 15 τὴν καθ' ὑμᾶς πίστιν, A. 16. 39 D τὰ καθ' ὑμᾶς = τὸ ὑμέτερον πρᾶγμα, and R. 1. 15 τὸ κατ' ἐμὲ πρόθυμον = ἡ ἐμὴ προθυμία ? (but it is better to take τὸ κατ' ἐμέ as *quod in me est*, and then read πρόθυμος with the Latin authorities and supply εἰμί, § 30, 3 ; cp. τὸ κατὰ σάρκα 9. 5 and other phrases, § 34, 7).—The distributive κατά has become stereotyped as an adverb (cp. ἀνά, § 39, 2) in καθ' εἷς, see § 51, 5.—In the headings to the Gospels κατὰ Ματθαῖον etc. the author of this particular form of the Gospel is denoted by κατά, cp. § 35, 3 ; with this is compared (W.-Gr.) ἡ παλαιὰ διαθήκη κατὰ τοὺς ἑβδομήκοντα, and 2 Macc. 2. 13 τοῖς ὑπομνηματισμοῖς τοῖς κατὰ Νεεμίαν, which perhaps means 'which bear the name of N.'

With the genitive the instances are far less numerous ; κατά τινος most often means 'against someone' in a hostile sense, and indeed in the Hellenistic language it also takes the place of Attic ἐπί τινα (ἐστιν and the like) : Mt. 12. 30 ὁ μὴ ὢν μετ' ἐμοῦ κατ' ἐμοῦ ἐστιν (Demosth. 19. 339 ἐπὶ τὴν πόλιν ἐστίν, but Polyb. 10, 8. 5 κατὰ τῆς πόλεως ὑπελάμβανον εἶναι), whereas the Attic κατά 'against' is used after verbs of speaking, witnessing etc.—Rarely in local sense : κατὰ τοῦ κρημνοῦ Mt. 8. 32 etc. 'down from ' ; κατὰ κεφαλῆς ἔχων 1 C. 11. 4, opposed to ἀκατακαλύπτῳ τῇ κεφαλῇ ('hanging down over the head,' 'on the head') ; 'throughout ' A. 9. 31 καθ' ὅλης τῆς Ἰουδαίας, 10. 37, L. 4. 14, 23. 5 (Hellenistic, Polyb. 3, 19. 7 διεσπάρησαν κατὰ τῆς νήσου), in this sense always with ὅλος and confined to Luke's Gospel and Acts (with accus. οἱ ὄντες κατὰ τὴν Ἰουδαίαν A. 11. 1, it means simply 'in'). A peculiar use is ἡ κατὰ βάθους πτωχεία 2 C. 8. 2 'deep' or 'profound poverty' (Strabo 9, p. 419 ἄντρον κοῖλον κατὰ βάθους, W.-Gr.).—For its use with ὀμνύναι, (ἐξ)ορκίζειν Mt. 26. 63, H. 6. 13, 16, see § 34, 1 (κατὰ τοῦ κυρίου ἠρώτησα 'entreated by the Lord' Herm. Vis. iii. 2. 3).

3. **Μετά with accusative** in local sense 'after,' 'behind' only occurs in H. 9. 3 μετὰ τὸ δεύτερον καταπέτασμα (answering to πρό, an unclassical use) ; elsewhere it always has temporal sense 'after.' Οὐ μετὰ πολλὰς ταύτας ἡμέρας A. 1. 5 is 'not many days after to-day,' cp. πρό, § 40, 5.—**Μετά with genitive** has to itself (and not in com-

---

[1] [Still no Greek MS. has the genitive in this passage. See Lightfoot ad loc. Tr.]

mon with σύν) the meaning of 'among,' 'amid,' μετὰ τῶν νεκρῶν L. 24. 5, μετὰ ἀνόμων ἐλογίσθη (Mc. 15. 28) L. 22. 37, O.T. (Hebr. את, LXX. ἐν), as in classical poets; in the sense of 'with' it is interchanged with σύν, § 41, 3, but with this limitation that with expressions which imply mutual participation, such as πολεμεῖν, εἰρηνεύειν, συμφωνεῖν, φίλος, λαλεῖν (Mc. 6. 50 etc.) and others (§ 37, 6), μετά τινος and not σύν τινι is used in place of or by the side of the simple dative (Hebr. עם, class. dative or πρός); it is likewise the only preposition used to express accompanying circumstances, μετὰ φόβου etc., § 3, 3 (class.), and in the sense of 'to' (Hebraic) in ποιεῖν ἔλεος μετά τινος L. 10. 37, cp. 1. 58 (Herm. Sim. v. 1. 1 even has περὶ πάντων ὧν ἐποίησε μετ' ἐμοῦ 'to me,' which differs from the use of the phrase in A. 14. 27 where μετά = 'with'). On the whole the use of μετά far outweighs that of σύν (the number of instances of the former word is nearly three times that of the latter), though in individual books σύν has equally strong or even stronger attestation (in Acts).

4. Περί **with accusative** (not very frequent) is used in local and temporal sense for 'about'; so οἱ περὶ αὐτόν Mc. 4. 10, L. 22. 49 = 'his disciples'; but οἱ περὶ Παῦλον A. 13. 13, as is the case with similar phrases in the literary language, includes Paul; we even have πρὸς τὰς περὶ Μάρθαν καὶ Μαρίαν Jo. 11. 19 A al. (as often in later writers) to denote Martha and Mary only, but the phrase can hardly be considered genuine;[1] it has a further use, which is also classical, to denote the object of the action or of the pains expended (not the subject of speech or thought, which is περί τινος), with ἐπιθυμίαι Mc. 4. 19 (om. D), with περισπᾶσθαι, τυρβάζεσθαι L. 10. 40 f., with ἐργάται A. 19. 25. Paul, *who only began to use* **περί τινα** *at the time of writing the Philippian epistle*, uses it generally for 'concerning' (something like Plato's πονηρὸν περὶ τὸ σῶμα, 'injurious with regard to'): Ph. 2. 23 τὰ περὶ ἐμέ, 1 Tim. 1. 19 περὶ τὴν πίστιν ἐναυάγησαν, 6. 4, 21, 2 Tim. 2. 18, 3. 8, Tit. 2. 7 (τὰ περὶ τὸν πύργον Herm. Vis. iii. 3. 1).

Περί **with genitive** (extremely common) most often in such phrases as 'to speak,' 'know,' 'have a care' etc., 'concerning' or 'about'; at the beginning of a sentence or paragraph 'as concerning' 1 C. 7. 1 etc. (class.); also 'on account of' (class.) with κρίνεσθαι, ἐγκαλεῖν, εὐχαριστεῖν, ἐρωτᾶν (entreat), δεῖσθαι, προσεύχεσθαι, πρόφασιν (an excuse) ἔχειν, αἰνεῖν etc., in which cases it often passes over to the meaning of 'for' and becomes confused with ὑπέρ: Jo. 17. 9 οὐ περὶ τοῦ κόσμου ἐρωτῶ, ἀλλὰ περὶ ὧν δέδωκάς μοι. It is used as absolutely equivalent to ὑπέρ in Mt. 26. 28 τὸ περὶ (D ὑπὲρ) πολλῶν ἐκχυνόμενον (in Mc. 14. 24 περί is only read by A al.), 1 C. 1. 13 ἐσταυρώθη περὶ ὑμῶν only BD* (al. ὑπὲρ), A. 26. 1 περὶ (אAC al.; ὑπὲρ BLP) σεαυτοῦ λέγειν, G. 1. 4 (ὑπὲρ א°B), H. 5. 3 καθὼς περὶ ἑαυτοῦ, οὕτως καὶ περὶ τοῦ λαοῦ προσφέρειν περί (ὑπὲρ C°D° al. as in ver. 1) ἁμαρτιῶν, cp. 10. 6, 8 O.T., 18, 26, 13. 11, 1 P. 3. 18, Mc. 1. 44, L. 5. 14.

---

[1] Πρὸς τὴν M. καὶ M. אBC*L al., similarly without τὴν D; ἵνα παραμυθήσωνται τὴν M. καὶ τὴν M. Syr. Sin.

With verbs expressing emotion: Mt. 9. 36 ἐσπλαγχνίσθη περὶ αὐτῶν (i.e. τῶν ὄχλων; elsewhere the verb has ἐπί τινα or ἐπί τινι, §§ 36, 7; 43, 1 and 3), Mt. 20. 24 and Mc. 10. 41 ἀγανακτεῖν περί τινος, 'concerning anyone' (classical Greek has περὶ τῶν πραχθέντων Plat. Ep. vii. 349 D), L. 2. 18 θαυμάζειν περί ('concerning a thing'), all these constructions hardly classical; περὶ πάντων εὐοδοῦσθαι 'in every respect' 3 Jo. 2. Ποιῆσαι περὶ αὐτοῦ ('to do with him') L. 2. 27 also appears to be an incorrect phrase (περὶ αὐτόν would be better, vide supra, N.T. says αὐτῷ or ἐν αὐτῷ); λαγχάνειν ('to draw lots') περί τινος Jo. 19. 24 may be compared with the classical μάχεσθαι περί τινος.

5. **Ὑπέρ with accusative** (not frequent) 'above,' denotes superiority (no longer found in local sense); hence it is used with the comparative, § 36, 12; it is used adverbially in the Pauline epistles ὑπὲρ λίαν (or ὑπερλίαν §§ 4, 1; 28, 2) 2 C. 11. 5, 12. 11 ὑπὲρ ἐκ περισσοῦ or ὑπερεκπ. 1 Th. 3. 10, E. 3. 20, similarly or ὑπὲρ ἐκπερισσῶς (BD*FG) 1 Th. 5. 13; or it stands by itself 2 C. 11. 23 διάκονοι Χριστοῦ εἰσιν; ὑπὲρ (to a higher degree) ἐγὼ (διάκ. Χρ. εἰμι), cp. the classical words ὑπέρλαμπρος, ὑπερεξακισχίλιοι ([Demosth.] 59. 89), whereas in the N.T. it is impossible *in all cases* to carry out the compounding of the two words into one.—**Ὑπέρ with genitive** 'for,' opposed to κατά τινος Mc. 9. 40 etc., is much limited in its use by the substitution of περί (supra 4), while the reverse change (λέγειν ὑπέρ 'to speak about') which is common in Attic and Hellenistic Greek (as also in the LXX.), is found more rarely and is almost confined to Paul: Jo. 1. 30 ὑπὲρ (περὶ א°A al.) οὗ εἶπον, 2 C. 8. 23 εἴτε ὑπὲρ Τίτου ('as concerning,') 12. 8 ὑπὲρ τούτου παρεκάλεσα ('on this account,' 'on behalf of this,' cp. supra 4 περί), 2 Th. 2. 1, καυχᾶσθαι ὑπέρ often in Paul, also φυσιοῦσθαι ὑπέρ, φρονεῖν ὑπέρ (in Ph. 1. 7 'to think upon,' in 4. 10 'to care for'). Also the object to be attained may be introduced by ὑπέρ, 2 C. 1. 6 ὑπὲρ τῆς ὑμῶν παρακλήσεως ('to'); so also Ph. 2. 13 ὑπὲρ (< οὗ >?) τῆς εὐδοκίας (God's; C adds αὐτοῦ) πάντα ποιεῖτε (the first words are not to be taken with the preceding clause).

6. **Ὑπό with accusative** (not very frequent; in John only in 1. 49 of his Gospel, never in the Apocalypse[1]) '**under**,' answering the questions 'where?' and 'whither?' (the old local use of ὑπό τινος and ὑπό τινι has become merged in ὑπό τι), is used in literal and metaphorical sense; in temporal sense only in A. 5. 21 ὑπὸ τὸν ὄρθρον, *sub, circa* (class.).[2]—**Ὑπό with genitive** '**by**,' denoting the agent, is used with passive verbs and verbs of passive meaning like πληγὰς λαμβάνειν 2 C. 11. 24;[3] in some instances its place is taken by ἀπό, § 40, 3; see also διά, supra 1.

[1] The Apoc. has ὑποκάτω (§ 40, 8) instead, which is also found in John's Gospel 1. 51.
[2] Herm. often uses ὑπὸ χεῖρα in a peculiar way 'continually,' Vis. iii. 10. 7, v. 5. 5, Mand. iv. 3. 6.
[3] Herm. has the peculiar phrases in Sim. ix. 1. 2 ὑπὸ παρθένου ἑώρακας and ὑπὸ ἀγγέλου βλέπεις 'under the guidance of'—'the angel makes you to see,' cp. Ap. 6. 8 ἀποκτεῖναι ἐν ... καὶ ὑπὸ τῶν θηρίων = ποιεῖν ἀποθανεῖν ὑπὸ κ.τ.λ.

§ 43. PREPOSITIONS WITH THREE CASES.

1. **Ἐπί** is the single preposition the use of which with all three cases is *largely* represented. The case, however, which it takes with far the most frequency is the **accusative**. This is used not only, as in classical Greek, in answer to the question Whither? (including such constructions as that with στῆναι, where εἰς may take the place of ἐπί, § 39, 3), but also not infrequently as a substitute for genitive or dative, in answer to the question Where?: Mt. 9. 2 (Mc. 2. 14, L. 5. 27) καθήμενος ἐπὶ τὸ τελώνιον, Mc. 4. 38 ἐπὶ τὸ προσκεφάλαιον (D ἐπὶ προσκεφαλαίου) καθεύδων, L. 2. 25 πνεῦμα ἅγιον ἦν ἐπ' αὐτόν, cp. 40 (where D has ἐν αὐτῷ), Jo. 1. 32 ἔμεινεν ἐπ' αὐτόν (33), A. 1. 15 ἐπὶ τὸ αὐτό 'together' (so fairly often in Acts, and occasionally in Paul and elsewhere, used with εἶναι etc.; LXX. Joseph.), 2 C. 3. 15 ἐπὶ τὴν καρδίαν αὐτῶν κεῖται, A. 21. 35 ἐγένετο ἐπὶ τοὺς ἀναβαθμούς, cp. γίνεσθαι εἰς § 39, 3 (but ἐπί τινος L. 22. 40), Mt. 14. 25 περιπατῶν ἐπὶ τὴν θάλασσαν אB al., gen. CD al., 26 gen. אBCD al., acc. EFG al.; 28 f. all MSS. ἐπὶ τὰ ὕδατα; in Mc. 6. 48 f., Jo. 6. 19 the gen. is used, which in the passage of John some would understand as in 21. 1 in the sense of 'by the sea,' although we should not use such an expression, but 'on the shore.' Moreover with the metaphorical senses of ἐπί the accusative is more widely prevalent than it strictly should be : not only do we have καθιστάναι δικαστὴν ἐφ' ὑμᾶς (direction whither?) L. 12. 14, but also βασιλεύσει ἐπὶ τὸν οἶκον Ἰακώβ 1. 33 (Hebraic, cp. inf. 2, § 36, 8), ἐπὶ ὀλίγα ἦς πιστός, ἐπὶ πολλῶν σε καταστήσω Mt. 25. 21, σπλαγχίζομαι ἐπὶ τὸν ὄχλον 15. 32, Mc. 8. 2, cp. Herm. Mand. iv. 3. 5, Sim. ix. 24. 2 (which in Attic must at least have been ἐπὶ τῷ ...), μὴ κλαίετε ἐπ' ἐμέ L. 23. 28, ἐλπίζειν, πιστεύειν[1], πίστις, πεποιθέναι ἐπί τινα or ἐπί τινι, § 37, 1 alternating with εἰς τινα (ἔν τινι), Mc. 9. 12 f. γέγραπται ἐπὶ τὸν υἱὸν τοῦ ἀνθρώπου 'concerning' (Att. prefers ἐπί τινι). The following further instances may be noticed : A. 4. 22 ὁ ἄνθρωπος ἐφ' ὃν γεγόνει τὸ σημεῖον 'upon' (class. εἰς ὅν, Hdt. i. 114, or περὶ ὅν; cp. also ἐπί τινος infra 2): 10. 35 πεσὼν ἐπὶ τοὺς πόδας προσεκύνησεν, = Att. προσπεσὼν αὐτῷ (Jo. 11. 32 has πρὸς with v.l. εἰς, Mc. 5. 22 πρός). In temporal senses : A. 3. 1 ἐπὶ τὴν ὥραν τῆς προσευχῆς, 4. 5 (L. 10. 35) ἐπὶ τὴν αὔριον, more frequently expressed by τῇ ἐπ-αύριον, denoting the coincidence of an action with a particular time, for which classical Greek uses εἰς (ἐσαύριον); it further denotes duration of time as in classical Greek : ἐφ' ἡμέρας πλείους A. 13. 31 etc.

2. **Ἐπί with genitive** in the majority of cases means 'upon' (answering the question Where?), as in ἐπὶ τῆς γῆς, ἐπὶ κλίνης, καθήμενος ἐπὶ τοῦ ἅρματος, ἐπὶ τοῦ ἵππου etc., but also in answer to the question Whither?, the reverse interchange of meanings taking place with ἐπί with the accus. as was noticed above in 1 : Mc. 4. 26

---

[1] Ἐπίστευσαν ἐπὶ τὸν κύριον A. 9. 42, 11. 17 etc. might be compared with ἐπέστρεψαν ἐπὶ τὸν κ. 9. 35, 11. 21 etc. (direction whither), but we also have τοὺς πιστεύοντας ἐπὶ σέ A. 22. 19 etc., where this explanation is unsuitable.

βάλῃ τὸν σπόρον ἐπὶ τῆς γῆς, 9. 20 πεσὼν ἐπὶ τῆς γῆς (accus. in Mt. 10. 29, 34), Mt. 26. 12 etc.; a further meaning is 'by,' ἐπὶ τῆς ὁδοῦ Mt. 21. 19, ἐπὶ τῆς θαλάσσης Jo. 21. 1 etc. (For the strengthened form ἐπάνω 'upon' see § 40, 8.) With persons it means 'before,' Mc. 13. 9 ἐπὶ ἡγεμόνων σταθήσεσθε, A. 25. 9 κρίνεσθαι ἐπ' ἐμοῦ (ibid. 10 ἐπὶ τοῦ βήματος Καίσαρος ἑστὼς 'before,' but in 17 καθίσας ἐπὶ τ. β. 'upon'), Mt. 28. 14 with ἀκουσθῇ (BD ὑπό), 1 Tim. 5. 19 ἐπὶ μαρτύρων (ἐπὶ στόματος μαρτ. 2 C. 13. 1, Hebr. עַל־פִּי), cp. infra 3, 2 C. 7. 14 ἐπὶ Τίτου (v.l. πρὸς Τίτον). In metaphorical sense of 'over,' of authority and oversight (Attic), it is used not only with εἶναι, but also with καθιστάναι (supra 1), A. 8. 27, R. 9. 5, Mt. 24. 45 etc.; also with βασιλεύειν (cp. supra 1, § 36, 8) Mt. 2. 22 CD al. (אB have the simple genitive). 'To do to anyone,' 'to say of anyone': Jo. 6. 2 ἃ ἐποίει ἐπὶ τῶν ἀσθενούντων, G. 3. 16 οὐ λέγει ... ὡς ἐπὶ πολλῶν κ.τ.λ. (as in Plato Charm. 155 D, W.-Gr.); ἐπ' ἀληθείας 'in accordance with the truth' Mc. 12. 14 etc. (Demosth. 18. 17 etc.); frequently of contemporaneousness (classical) ἐπὶ Ἀβιάθαρ ἀρχιερέως Mc. 2. 26, Mt. 1. 11, H. 7. 11 and elsewhere; Paul uses ἐπὶ τῶν προσευχῶν μου meaning 'in,' E. 1. 16 etc.; a Hebraistic use is ἐπ' ἐσχάτου τῶν ἡμερῶν H. 1. 1, cp. 1 P. 1. 20, 2 P. 3. 3, Jude 18, and cp. § 47, 2.

3. **Ἐπί with dative.**—When the preposition has a local sense the genitive and accusative have the preponderance, and a sharp distinction between its use with those cases and with the dative cannot be drawn. Answering the question Where? we have ἐπὶ θύραις, ἐπὶ τῇ θύρᾳ (classical) 'before the door' Mt. 24. 33, A. 5. 9 etc. (but in Ap. 3. 20 the accus.): ἐπὶ πίνακι 'upon' ('upon' in classical Greek is generally ἐπί τινος, Buttm. p. 289) Mt. 14. 8, 11, Mc. 6. 25, 28: ἐκαθέζετο ἐπὶ τῇ πηγῇ Jo. 4. 6, cp. 5. 2, 'at' or 'by': ἐπὶ ταύτῃ τῇ πέτρᾳ (accus. in D) οἰκοδομήσω Mt. 16. 18 (but 7. 24 ff. accus.): with ἐπιβάλλειν ἐπικεῖσθαι ἐπιπίπτειν Mt. 9. 16, Jo. 11. 38 (without ἐπ' א*, cp. § 37, 7), A. 8. 16 (accus. D*, which is on the whole far the more frequent construction): ἐφ' ἵπποις Ap. 19. 14 (elsewhere always expressed by genit.). The dative also intervenes in the metaphorical sense 'to set over' (as in classical authors) Mt. 24. 47. Most frequently ἐπί τινι denotes the **ground** or **reason**, especially with verbs expressing emotion, such as θαυμάζειν, χαίρειν, λυπεῖσθαι, μετανοεῖν, see § 38, 2 (for the accus. supra 1); also with εὐχαριστεῖν, δοξάζειν τὸν θεόν, κρίνεσθαι (A. 26. 6); καλεῖν ἐπὶ 'to call after' L. 1. 59; ζῆν ἐπί Mt. 4. 4 O.T.; ἀρκεῖσθαι ἐπί 3 Jo. 10; ἐφ' ᾧ 'for the reason that,' 'because' R. 5. 12, 2 C. 5. 4; under this head may be brought πεποιθέναι, πιστεύειν, ἐλπίζειν ἐπί τινι, § 37, 1 (beside ἐπί τινα, supra 1, and other constructions), παρρησιάζεσθαι ἐπὶ τῷ κυρίῳ A. 14. 3, unless the last instance is to be connected with the common ἐπί (like ἐν τῷ ὀνόματί τινος, § 39, 4.—Expressing **addition** to (classical): L. 3. 20, 16. 26 ἐπὶ (ἐν אBL) πᾶσι τούτοις, cp. E. 6. 16 (ἐν אBP), Col. 3. 14, H. 8. 1 (for which we have accus. in Ph. 2. 27 λύπην ἐπὶ λύπην). Expressing a **condition** (classical): ἐπ' ἐλπίδι R. 8. 20, 1 C. 9. 10, Tit. 1. 2 (a different use in A. 2. 26 O.T., 4. 8, 5. 2, where it rather indicates the reason); cp. H. 8. 6, 9. 10, 15, 17; also καλεῖν ἐπ'

ἐλευθερίᾳ G. 5. 13, οὐκ ἐπ' ἀκαθαρσίᾳ ἀλλ' ἐν ἁγιασμῷ 1 Th. 4. 7 : denoting rather **aim**, ἐπ' ἔργοις ἀγαθοῖς E. 2. 10, cp. ἐφ' ᾧ καὶ κατελήμφθην Ph. 3. 12 (4. 10 is similar, but the expression is hardly formed correctly; cp. infra); of **result** 2 Tim. 2. 14 (beside an ἐπί with accus., where however there is a var. lect.). '**At**' or '**to anything**'; 1 C. 14. 16, E. 4. 26, Ph. 1. 3, 2. 17, 1 Th. 3. 7, H. 11. 4, Jo. 4. 27 ἐπὶ τούτῳ (better ἐν ℵ*D); H. 9. 26 ἐπὶ συντελείᾳ τοῦ αἰῶνος; ἐφ' ᾧ ἐφρονεῖτε 'whereon ye thought' Ph. 4. 10; with persons 'against' (cp. accus. supra 1) L. 12. 52 (beside an accusative), Ap. 10. 11, 'concerning' (cp. accus. supra 1) γεγραμμένα Jo. 12. 16 (D περὶ αὐτοῦ), 'in the case of' A. 5. 35 ; ἐπὶ δυσὶ μάρτυσιν ἀποθνήσκει H. 10. 28 = Hebr. עַל־פִּי, cp. supra 2 'if two witnesses are there,' denoting condition or reason.

4. **Παρά with accusative**, mostly in local sense 'by,' 'beside,' is used indiscriminately to answer the questions Where? (strictly παρά τινι) and Whither? (a distinction which is already becoming lost in the classical language, through the encroachment of παρά with the accus.; in the N.T. the local παρά τινι has almost disappeared, vide infra 6). It is not, as it frequently is in classical Greek, joined with personal names (though παρὰ τοὺς πόδας τινός is common); πρός τινα takes its place, infra 7.—In metaphorical sense (classical) 'contrary to,' as opposed to κατά 'according to,' R. 1. 26, 11. 24 παρὰ φύσιν opposed to κατὰ φ.; κατὰ δύναμιν ... παρὰ δύν. ('beyond') 2 C. 8. 3 (v.l. ὑπέρ); 'other than' G. 1. 8 f., also with ἄλλος 1 C. 3. 11 (class.); often 'more than,' both with a comparative, § 36, 12, and also without one : ἐλάτρευσαν τῇ κτίσει παρὰ τὸν κτίσαντα R. 1. 25, 12. 3, 14. 5, L. 13. 2, 4, Herm. Mand. x. 1. 2 (in classical Greek only 'in comparison with,' but this easily leads to the other usage). It denotes also (as in class. Greek) that in consequence of which something is or is not : 2 C. 11. 24 τεσσαράκοντα παρὰ μίαν, i.e. minus one, παρά τι 'almost' L. 5. 7 D, Herm. Sim. ix. 19. 3, οὐ παρὰ τοῦτο οὐκ ἔστιν ἐκ τοῦ σώματος 1 C. 12. 15 f. 'that is no reason for its not being' etc.— In Mt. and Mc. it is only found in local sense, in the Johannine writings (including the Apocalypse) and in the Catholic Epistles the use with accusative is entirely absent.

5. **Παρά with genitive** 'from the side of,' only with persons (so classical Greek), with verbs of coming, hearing, receiving etc. (ἀπό sometimes incorrectly takes its place, § 40, 3) ; it is also rightly used in τοῖς λελαλημένοις παρὰ κυρίου L. 1. 45 (since God did not speak Himself, but the angel who was commissioned by Him, W.-Gr.); but in A. 22. 30 παρά is found with κατηγορεῖσθαι, but only in HLP, the other MSS. reading ὑπό. It occurs without a verb in Mc. 3. 21 οἱ παρ' αὐτοῦ 'His kinsfolk' (LXX. Dan. Sus. 33), but there are several variants (the phrase in classical Greek could only mean the persons sent out by someone): δαπανήσασα τὰ παρ' (παρ' om. D) ἑαυτῆς 5. 26 is good classical Greek; Lc. 10. 7, Ph. 4. 18 etc.

6. **Παρά with dative** is '**by**,' '**beside**,' answering the question Where ? and with the exception of Jo. 19. 25 παρὰ τῷ σταυρῷ is only used of persons (so preponderantly in classical Greek), and more-

over not of immediate neighbourhood [1] (thus not καθῆσθαι παρά, but μετά Ap. 3. 21, σύν A. 8. 31, or πρός Mt. 26. 55 CD), but 'in the house of anyone' as in Jo. 1. 40: or 'amongst a people' as in Ap. 2. 13. The word is further used in a figurative sense : L. 1. 30 εὗρες χάριν παρὰ τῷ θεῷ, Mt. 19. 26 δυνατόν, ἀδύνατον παρά τινι, especially with the meaning 'in the opinion of anyone' (classical) R. 12. 16 (11. 25, where AB have ἐν) φρόνιμοι παρ' ἑαυτοῖς, 1 C. 3. 19 μωρία παρὰ τῷ θεῷ; also A. 26. 8 ἄπιστον κρίνεται παρ' ὑμῖν (Mt. 21. 25 διελογίζοντο παρ' ἑαυτοῖς, but ἐν BL al., as in 16. 8 etc.).—The dative is the rarest of the cases after παρά (on account of its clashing with πρός, vide 7), still nearly all writers use it.[2]

7. **Πρός with accusative** is abundantly used with verbs of coming, sending, bringing, saying etc. = 'to' (a person); often also with the verb 'to be' = 'with' or 'at,' taking the place of παρά τινι, Mt. 13. 56 πρὸς ἡμᾶς εἰσιν, 26. 18 πρὸς σὲ ποιῶ τὸ πάσχα, 26. 55 as a v.l., Mc. 6. 3 etc. (Herm. Mand. xi. 9 etc.); also for παρά τινα (cp. supra 4), ἔθαψαν πρὸς τὸν ἄνδρα αὐτῆς A. 5. 10, εἰσῆλθες πρὸς ἄνδρας 11. 3, *i.e.* 'into their house,' and therefore expressed in Attic by παρά.[3] Also of places and things: Mt. 21. 1 πρὸς (v.l. εἰς) τὸ ὄρος, Mc. 11. 1, L. 19. 29: πρὸς τὴν θύραν Mc. 1. 33, 2. 2, 11. 4 (L. 16. 20), answering the questions Whither? and Where? (in the latter case we have correctly πρὸς τῇ θύρᾳ Jo. 18. 16, πρὸ τῶν θυρῶν A. 5. 23, ἐπὶ θύραις Mt. 24. 33): Mc. 3. 7 πρὸς τὴν θάλασσαν (v.l. εἰς, cp. § 39, 5),[4] L. 12. 3 πρὸς τὸ οὖς λαλεῖν. As in classical Greek we also have θερμαίνεσθαι πρὸς τὸ φῶς ('turning towards') Mc. 14. 54 (L. 22. 56).—In temporal sense it is used of approximation (class.) : πρὸς ἑσπέραν ἐστίν L. 24. 29 (πρ. ἑ. κέκλικεν ἡ ἡμέρα D); and with the meaning 'for a certain time' (and no longer) πρὸς καιρόν, ὥραν, ὀλίγας ἡμέρας, τὸ παρόν,[5] L. 8. 13, Jo. 5. 35, H. 12. 10 f. etc.—To express hostile and friendly relations, with μάχεσθαι, εἰρήνην ἔχειν, ἀσύμφωνος (A. 28. 25), ἤπιος etc.; relevance to, τί πρὸς ἡμᾶς; 'what is it to us?' (so classical Greek, § 30, 3) Mt. 27. 4, Jo. 21. 22; Mc. 12. 12 πρὸς αὐτοὺς τὴν παραβολὴν εἶπεν = of them, cp. 10. 5, Mt. 19. 8, L. 12. 41, 18. 1, 20. 19 etc.; with ἀγαθός, ὠφέλιμος, δυνατός and other adjectives ('to,' 'for') E. 4. 29, 1 Tim. 4. 8, 2 C. 10. 4, in which cases it may also denote destination, aim, or result, as in L. 14. 32, 19. 42 τὰ πρὸς εἰρήνην, Jo. 4. 35 λευκαὶ πρὸς θερισμόν, 11. 4 πρὸς θάνατον (1 Jo. 5. 16 f.), A. 3. 10 ὁ πρὸς τὴν ἐλεημοσύνην καθήμενος, Jo. 13. 28 πρὸς τί εἶπεν 'for what intent.' 'In accordance with' (class.) πρὸς τὸ συμφέρον 1 C. 12. 7, πρὸς ἃ ἔπραξεν 2 C. 5. 10, L. 12. 47, Herm. Mand. xi. 3. 'In comparison with' (class.) ἄξια πρὸς R. 8. 18.

---

[1] L. 9. 47 has ἔστησεν αὐτὸ παρ' ἑαυτῷ, but D ἑαυτόν.

[2] All except the author of the Ep. to the Hebrews.

[3] Confusion with παρά τινι also takes place in Mc. 9. 31 ἐκράτησαν πρὸς ἑαυτούς, 11. 31 (L. 20. 5) διελογίζοντο πρὸς ἑαυτούς, cp. Mt. 21. 25 παρ' ἑαυτοῖς, supra 6.

[4] L. 24. 50 ἐξήγαγεν αὐτοὺς ἕως (om. D) πρὸς (εἰς AX al.) Βηθανίαν, 'as far as to B.,' 'within view of B.,' for that they entered into the place is not to be thought of ; εἰς is wrong.

[5] Classical (Thuc. ii. 22. 1, iii. 40. 7 ; Plato, Leg. v. 736 A).

8. **Πρός with genitive** only occurs in A. 27. 34 (literary language) τοῦτο πρὸς τῆς ὑμετέρας σωτηρίας ὑπάρχει ('on the side of,' 'advantageous to,' 'for,' as in Thuc. iii. 59. 1 οὐ πρὸς τῆς ὑμετέρας δόξης τάδε).
—**Πρός with dative**, in local sense 'by,' 'at' (classical) is very rare, since the accusative takes its place (cp. supra 7): Mc. 5. 11 πρὸς τῷ ὄρει, L. 19. 37 (D accusative), Jo. 18. 16, 20. 11 (with v.l. accus.), 12, Ap. 1. 13.

§ 44. SYNTAX OF THE ADJECTIVE.

1. The adjective may take over the functions of a substantive not only in the masculine and neuter, to denote persons and things (where these ordinary ideas readily suggest themselves), but also in the feminine: in this case there is a more or less obvious ellipse of some well-known substantive, which is sufficiently indicated by the feminine gender, the sense, and the context. The rule which applies to adjectives holds good also for pronouns and participles, as also for adverbial (or prepositional) expressions with the article. In the following phrases **γῆ** must be understood: ἡ ξηρά (Xenoph., LXX.) Mt. 23. 15 (τὴν θάλασσαν καὶ τ. ξ.), H. 11. 29 (אAD*E with γῆς), ἡ περίχωρος (Plut.) Mt. 3. 5 etc., ἡ ὀρεινή L. 1. 30 (or *sc.* χώρα), ἡ ἔρημος; in ἐκ τῆς ὑπὸ τὸν οὐρανὸν εἰς τὴν ὑπ' οὐρ. L. 17. 24 it is better to supply μερίδος; in ἐξ ἐναντίας αὐτοῦ Mc. 15. 39 (D ἐκεῖ), Tit. 2. 8 (class.) the ellipse is quite obscure.—Ellipse of **ἡμέρα**: τῇ ἐπιούσῃ A. 16. 11, 20. 15, 21. 18 (with ἡμ. 7. 26), τῇ ἐχομένῃ, τῇ ἑτέρᾳ 20. 16, L. 13. 33 (τῇ ἐχ. ἡμ. A. 21. 26), elsewhere in Acts (and Luke's Gospel) τῇ ἑξῆς; τῇ (ἐπ)αύριον occurs also in Mt. 27. 62 (Mc., Jo., Ja.); σήμερον καὶ αὔριον καὶ τῇ τρίτῃ L. 13. 32 (elsewhere τῇ τρ. ἡμ.); εἰς τὴν αὔριον... πρὸ μιᾶς Herm. Sim. vi. 5. 3 (Clem. Hom. ix. 1); ἡ ἑβδόμη 'the Sabbath' H. 4. 4, τῇ μιᾷ τῶν σαββάτων A. 20. 7 etc., μέχρι τῆς σήμερον Mt. 11. 23 etc. (elsewhere with ἡμ.); also with ἀφ' ἧς 2 P. 3. 4 ('since') ἡμ. may be supplied, cp. A. 24. 11 (Col. 1. 6, 9), but in L. 7. 45 there can only be an ellipse of ὥρας,[1] as there is in ἐξαυτῆς 'immediately' (§ 4. 1); there is the same ellipse in (ἡ) πρωΐα, ὀψία Mt., Mc., Jo., Herm. (not classical), (ἡ) τετράμηνος Jo. 4. 35, τρίμ. H. 11. 23, cp. ἡ τρίμηνος Hdt. ii. 124. **Ὁδός** is elided in L. 19. 4 ἐκείνης, 5. 19 ποίας (a stereotyped phrase; § 36, 13), εἰς εὐθείας L. 3. 5 O.T. (but ὁδούς occurs soon after). Further instances are: ἐν τῇ ἑλληνικῇ (ἑλληνίδι א) *sc.* **γλώσσῃ** Ap. 9. 11, τῇ πνεούσῃ *sc.* **αὔρᾳ** A. 27. 40 (ἀργυρίου μυριάδας πέντε *sc.* **δραχμῶν** A. 19. 19), ἐπὶ τῇ προβατικῇ *sc.* **πύλῃ** Jo. 5. 2, ἡ δεξιά, ἀριστερά *sc.* **χείρ** Mt. 6. 3 etc., ἐν δεξιᾷ R. 8. 34 etc. 'on the right hand,' unless this should be read ἐνδέξια (classical; N.T. elsewhere has ἐκ δεξιῶν, εἰς τὰ δεξιὰ μέρη Jo. 21. 6, Hermas has also δεξιά, εὐώνυμα for 'to right' or 'left' Sim. ix. 12. 8), δαρήσεται πολλάς... ὀλίγας *sc.* **πληγάς** L. 12. 47 (§ 34, 3; class.), cp. 2 C. 11. 24. The following have become stereotyped: ἀπὸ μιᾶς L. 14. 28 'with

---

[1] It was a stereotyped formula, cp. Herm. Sim. viii. 1. 4 ἀφ' ἧς πάντα ἴδῃς 'as soon as,' 'after that'; 6. 6.

§ 44. 1-3.] THE ADJECTIVE. 141

one mind or voice' (ἀπὸ μιᾶς ὑσπλαγίδος Aristoph. Lysistr. 1000);[1] κατὰ μόνας 'alone' (Thuc. i. 32. 5 etc.) Mc. 4. 10, L. 9. 18 (LXX.; Herm. Mand. xi. 8); frequently κατ' ἰδίαν, ἰδίᾳ 1 C. 12. 11, δημοσίᾳ 'openly' *in publico* (with a different meaning in Attic) A. 16. 37 etc.
—Similar instances of ellipse are found also with the other genders: τῷ πνέοντι sc. ἀνέμῳ A. 27. 15 β text, πρόϊμον καὶ ὄψιμον sc. ὑετόν Ja. 5. 7 with the reading of (א)B, τὸ τρίτον, τέταρτον, δέκατον sc. μέρος Apoc. (not classical), τὸ διοπετές sc. ἄγαλμα A. 19. 35, ποτήριον ψυχροῦ sc. ὕδατος Mt. 10. 42, cp. Ja. 3. 11 (Winer, § 64, 5), ἐν λευκοῖς sc. ἱματίοις Jo. 20. 12 (Herm. Vis. iv. 2. 1), cp. Mt. 11. 8, Ap. 18. 12, 16.
—The opposite procedure to an ellipse takes place when Luke (according to classical precedent) inserts an ἀνήρ with a substantive denoting a person: ἀ. προφήτης L. 24. 19, φονεύς A. 3. 14, ἀνδρὶ Ἰουδαίῳ 10. 28, and in addresses ἄνδρες Γαλιλαῖοι, Ἀθηναῖοι, ἀδελφοί etc., A. 1. 16 and elsewhere.

2. The use of an **adjectival instead of an adverbial expression** in the case of certain ideas that are annexed to the predicate is found in the N.T. as in the classical language, but rarely : the instances are mainly in Luke's writings. Δευτεραῖοι ἤλθομεν 'on the second day' A. 28. 13, cp. πεμπταῖοι 20. 6 D for ἄχρι ἡμερῶν πέντε of the other MSS. Γενόμεναι ὀρθριναὶ ἐπὶ τὸ μνημεῖον L. 24. 22 (ὀρθρινὸς ἐλήλυθας Herm. Sim. v. 1. 1). Αὐτομάτη ἠνοίγη A. 12. 19, Mc. 4. 28. Ἐπιστῇ αἰφνίδιος L. 21. 34 ; also ἑκών, ἄκων, πρῶτος 'first of all' (R. 10. 19); ἀνάστηθι ὀρθός A. 14. 10, τοῦτο ἀληθὲς εἴρηκας (אE ἀληθῶς[2]) Jo. 4. 18 (like Demosth. 7. 43 τοῦτό γ' ἀληθῆ [other MS. ἀληθὲς] λέγουσι). There is a certain amount of mixture of **μόνος** and the adverb **μόνον**, just as in the classical language the one use borders closely on the other : Mc. 6. 8 μηδὲν εἰ μὴ ῥάβδον μόνον (μόνην D), A. 11. 19 μηδενὶ εἰ μὴ μόνον (μόνοις D) Ἰουδαίοις, 1 Jo. 5. 6 οὐκ ἐν τῷ ὕδατι μόνον (B μόνῳ). If the word 'alone' refers without any doubt to a verb (or else to a predicative idea like ἀκροαταί Ja. 1. 22, ἀργαί 1 Tim. 5. 13), then μόνον is the only possible expression ; but it is also not contrary to Greek idiom to say (H. 12. 26) σείσω οὐ μόνον τὴν γῆν, ἀλλὰ καὶ τὸν οὐρανόν 'I am not contented with earth-shaking only,' 2 Tim. 4. 8 οὐ μόνον δὲ ἐμοί, ἀλλὰ καὶ πᾶσιν (to limit the gift to one would be too little). For the reverse use of adverb for adj. see § 76, 1.

3. On the coincidence in meaning of the **comparative** and **superlative** and the reason for it, we have already spoken in § 11, 3 ; the two degrees are in no way differentiated, as they are in modern Greek or in French, by the addition of the article for the superlative, but are indistinguishable :[3] see 1 C. 13. 13 πίστις ἐλπὶς ἀγάπη, τὰ τρία ταῦτα· μείζων δὲ τούτων ἡ ἀγάπη. The form which has remained in ordinary use is in nearly all cases that of the comparative ; πρῶτος

---

[1] Strictly of runners in a race, who rush off together at the fall of the single rope (ὕσπληγξ, ὑσπλαγίς).

[2] Less classical is λέγω ὑμῖν ἀληθῶς L. 9. 27, 12. 44, 21. 3 = ἀμήν (which D reads in 12. 44 and Cyprian in 21. 3.

[3] Barnabas agrees with the N.T. use, e.g. 12. 2 ὑψηλότερος πάντων.

and ἔσχατος are the only exceptions to this (§ 11, 5). Now whereas the superlative in classical Greek is used not only where there is a definite comparison made of several things, but often in what may be called an absolute sense, equivalent to our 'very,' while the classical comparative occasionally corresponds to an English positive (θᾶττον = 'quickly'), so the New Testament comparative may have an ambiguous meaning: Jo. 13. 27 ὃ ποιεῖς ποίησον τάχιον (Luther 'bald' [A.V. 'quickly']; but it may also mean 'as quickly as possible'; cp. 1 Tim. 3. 14, where there is a v.l. ἐν τάχει; in H. 13. 19 probably 'more quickly,' 23 ἐὰν τάχιον ἔρχηται 'if he comes soon'; in A. 17. 15 we have ὡς τάχιστα from the literary language, but D reads ἐν τάχει).[1] Also ἆσσον, μᾶλλον, ἄμεινον etc., similarly νεώτερος or -ρον (καινότερον) can in the classical language be rendered in many cases by the positive (although we also use similar phrases such as 'come nearer,' 'it is better to ...'); in the N.T. cp. (besides πρεσβύτερος used as the designation of a Jewish or Christian official) A. 17. 21 λέγειν τι ἢ ἀκούειν καινότερον (Kühner ii.[2] 848),[2] whereas ἆσσον παρελέγοντο τὴν Κρήτην 27. 13 (if θᾶσσον be not the right reading) must mean 'as near as possible'; so in any case 24. 22 ἀκριβέστερον εἰδώς = ἀκριβέστατα, 25. 10 κάλλιον ἐπιγινώσκεις = ἄριστα, and 2 Tim. 1. 18 should be similarly explained βέλτιον σὺ γινώσκεις (not 'thou knowest better than I,' which can certainly not be right).[3] In A. 17. 22 ὡς δεισιδαιμονεστέρους ὑμᾶς θεωρῶ, it is doubtful whether the comp. has its classical sense of 'unusually (too) god-fearing' or means 'very god-fearing'; but σπουδαιότερος 2 C. 8. 17 can only mean 'very zealous'; and frequently there is a corresponding use of the English comparative, the standard of comparison being readily supplied, 2 C. 7. 7 ὥστε με μᾶλλον χαρῆναι 'still more.' In Hermas, on the other hand, the elative sense is regularly expressed by the superlative, ἀγαθώτατος, σεμνότατος etc., while in other cases he also uses comparative and superlative interchangeably (Mand. viii. 4. πάντων πονηρότατα needs correction); Sim. ix. 10. 7 is noticeable, ἦσαν δὲ ἱλαρώτεραι, which appears to be used in elative sense, and therefore to need correction, but the Latin has *hilares satis.*—Οἱ πλείονες may mean 'the greater number,' as in 1 C. 15. 6 ἐξ ὧν οἱ πλείους μένουσιν, 10. 5, but also 'others,' 'more,' 9. 19 ἵνα τοὺς πλείονας κερδήσω ; (τ. πλ. αὐτῶν Origen), 2 C. 2. 6, 4. 15, 9. 2, Ph. 1. 14 as opposed to the person or persons who have

---

[1] Cp. Clem. Hom. i. 14 τάχιόν σε καταλήψομαι, 'as quickly as possible,' xi. 13 τάχιον ἐπιλανθάνεσθε ('forthwith'); in a quite different sense ix. 23 ὡς τάχιον εἶπον = φθάσας, *modo*, 'just before.' For the superlative or elative sense cp. also Papyr. Berl. Aeg. Urk. 417, 451, 615. Cp. **πυκνότερον** A. 24. 26 where it is ambiguous ('very often' or 'so much the oftener'); Clem. Cor. ii. 17. 3 probably 'as often as possible,' Clem. Hom. Ep. ad Jac. 9 πυκνότερον ... ὡς δύνασθε (in the weaker sense ibid. iv. 2, viii. 7), similarly συνεχέστερον iii. 69.

[2] Hermas, Vis. iii. 10. 3 λίαν πρεσβυτέρα, 5 ὅλη νεωτέρα 'very old,' 'quite youthful,' Sim. ix. 11. 5.

[3] The passage adduced by Winer, Luscian Piscat. 20 ἄμεινον σὺ οἶσθα ταῦτα, ὦ Φιλοσοφία, is different, so far as the meaning of the comp. is concerned: the goddess did actually know better than Lucian.

§ 44. 3–5.]   THE ADJECTIVE.   143

hitherto been considered; cp. ταῦτα εἰπὼν καὶ τὰ τούτων πλείονα Clem. Hom. Ep. ad Jac. 17 (so A. 2. 40 ἑτέροις τε λόγοις πλείοσιν?).[1] —On the remnants of the superlative see § 11, 3 (especially for μάλιστα and μᾶλλον); on the forms of expression to introduce the object compared (gen., ἤ, παρά or ὑπέρ) § 36, 12.

4. The **positive** may also be used with the meaning of a comparative (or superlative): this occasionally takes place in the classical language, but it is mainly due to the example of the Semitic language, which has no degrees of comparison at all. Οἱ πολλοί are the many as opposed to the few, *i.e.* the majority, in classical Greek and Mt. 24. 12, frequently in Mc. (Gregory-Tisch. 128) 6. 2 BL (v.l. without οἱ), 9. 26 ℵABLΔ (same v.l.), cp. 12. 37 infra; in St. Paul τῶν πολλῶν 1 C. 10. 33 is opposed to ἐμαυτοῦ, and is therefore parallel to the same writer's use of οἱ πλείονες elsewhere; πλεῖστος is also found in this sense: Mt. 21. 8 ὁ πλεῖστος ὄχλος[2] = ὁ πολὺς ὄ. of Mc. 12. 37 (αἱ πλεῖσται δυνάμεις αὐτοῦ Mt. 11. 20 'his numerous miracles,' cp. τὰ πολλὰ γράμματα A. 26. 24). A further example is (Buttm. p. 73) Mt. 22. 36 ποία ἐντολὴ μεγάλη ἐν τῷ νόμῳ 'the greatest,' cp. 5. 19. With the idea of comparison more clearly marked (by the addition of a gen.), we have τὰ ἅγια τῶν ἁγίων H. 9. 2 f. (LXX.), a use which is by no means unclassical (κακὰ κακῶν, Kühner ii.[2] 20). In the case where the comparison is introduced by ὑπέρ or παρά (§ 36, 12), on the analogy of the Semitic construction, the adjective may be either positive or comparative: L. 13. 2 ἁμαρτωλοὶ παρὰ πάντας (where a comparative was wanting, cp. δεδικαιωμένος παρὰ 18. 14 ℵBL; frequent in LXX., *e.g.* μέγας παρὰ, πραΰς παρὰ Ex. 18. 11, Num. 12. 3). The positive may however also be used with ἤ: Mt. 18. 8 f, Mc. 9. 43, 45 καλόν ἐστιν ... ἤ (LXX. Gen. 49. 12 λευκοὶ ἤ); similarly where there is no adjective (and μᾶλλον is therefore to be supplied) L. 15. 7 χαρὰ ἔσται ... ἤ, 1 C. 14. 19 θέλω ... ἤ, Lc. 17. 2 λυσιτελεῖ ... ἤ, for which there are classical parallels.[3]

5. The comparative is heightened, as in classical Greek, by the addition of πολύ or πολλῷ: 2 C. 8. 22, Jo. 4. 41; occasionally too by the accumulation of several comparatives: Ph. 1. 23 πολλῷ γὰρ μᾶλλον κρεῖσσον (Clem. Cor. i. 48. 6 ὅσῳ δοκεῖ μᾶλλον μείζων εἶναι is merely pleonastic, like Herm. Sim. ix. 28. 4 μᾶλλον ἐνδοξότεροι), 2 C. 7. 13 περισσοτέρως μᾶλλον ἐχάρημεν, Mc. 7. 36 μᾶλλον περισσότερον (-οτέρως D) ἐκήρυσσον, cp. § 11, 3, note 4. The same accumulation appears in classical Greek, Schwab Syntax der Comparation iii. 59 ff. But in ἥδιστα μᾶλλον 2 C. 12. 9 the words should not be taken together: the sense being 'Gladly (superl. with elative force, and a stereotyped phrase) will I rather glory in my weaknesses.'

---

[1] Classical Greek had the same use: τὸν πλείονα χρόνον ' a longer time' (than at present), πλείονες λόγοι, τὸν πλείω λόγον (Soph. Tr. 731) 'further speech.' Cp. Kühn. ii. 549; E. Tournier, Rev. de philol. 1877, 253; O. Schwab, Syntax der Comparation ii. 178.

[2] Plato, Leg. 700 C.

[3] Kühner ii.[2] 841 (so Herodotus ix. 26 fin. δίκαιόν ἐστιν ... ἤ).

§ 45. NUMERALS.

1. The first day of the month or of the week is expressed in the LXX. and in the N.T. not by πρώτη but by μία, whereas for the higher numbers the ordinal is used, δευτέρα and so on: of course the day being a single day (in the case of δευτέρα 'the second' etc.) does not admit of being expressed by a plural, while all other numbers but εἶς must necessarily be plurals. Thus εἰς μίαν σαββάτων 'on Sunday' Mt. 28. 1, ἐν μιᾷ τοῦ μηνὸς τοῦ δευτέρου Num. 1. 1. This is not a classical,[1] but undoubtedly a Hebrew idiom (Gesenius-Kautzsch, § 134, 4), with this difference that in Hebrew the later days of the month are also denoted by cardinal numbers. This N.T. usage (found also in A. 20. 7, 1 C. 16. 2, Mc. 16. 2) is violated in 'Mc.' 16. 9 πρώτῃ σαββάτου, for which Eusebius however quotes τῇ μιᾷ.

2. Εἶς already begins now and again to pass from the sense of a numeral (**one** as opposed to several) into that of the indefinite article; the latter development, which has analogies in the German and Romance languages, appears completely carried out in modern Greek. The Hebrew אֶחָד, moreover, afforded a precedent to the N.T. writers. In Mt. 8. 19 προσελθὼν εἶς γραμματεύς, 26. 69 μία παιδίσκη, Ap. 8. 13 ἤκουσα ἑνὸς ἀετοῦ etc., εἶς = the classical τις; and similarly we find εἶς with the gen. (or ἐξ): L. 15. 15 ἑνὶ τῶν πολιτῶν, Ap. 7. 13 εἶς ἐκ (ἐκ om. ℵ) τῶν πρεσβυτέρων;[2] it is used in conjunction with τις (classical) εἶς τις ἐξ αὐτῶν L. 22. 50, still in such a way that εἶς forms a contrast to the remaining body (Jo. 11. 49, a v.l. in Mc. 14. 47, 51). Another unclassical use is that of ὁ εἶς ... ὁ ἕτερος for ὁ μὲν (ἕτερος) ... ὁ δὲ (ἕτερος), Mt. 6. 24, L. 7. 41 τὸν ἕνα – τὸν δὲ ἕνα Barn. 7. 6, 17), εἶς ... καὶ εἶς ..., Mt. 27. 38, L. 18. 10 D (Herm. Mand. vi. 2. 1; on the model of Heb. אֶחָד, e.g. in Ex. 17. 12), Mc. 4. 8, 20, cp. Mt. 13. 8, 23 (§ 46, 2) etc., though even classical writers repeatedly employ εἶς when dividing a multitude (or a duality) into its component parts, Hyperid. cont. Athenogenes § 14 f. ὁ εἶς νόμος ... ἕτερος ν. κ.τ.λ., Xenoph. Cyrop. i. 2. 4 τέτταρα ... ἓν μὲν ... ἓν δὲ ... ἄλλο ... ἄλλο; Demosth. xviii. 215 τρία ... ἓν μὲν ... ἕτερον δὲ ... τρίτον δὲ, Arist. Rhet. ii. 20 f., 1393 A, 27 εἴδη δύο, ἓν μὲν – ἓν δὲ, (where the full meaning of the numeral is preserved), cp. Ap. 17. 10 ἑπτά ... οἱ πέντε ... ὁ εἶς ... ὁ ἄλλος. See § 46, 2. Lastly, a quite unclassical but Semitic usage is that of εἶς τὸν ἕνα for ἀλλήλους 1 Th. 5. 11 (1 C. 4. 6 εἶς ὑπὲρ τοῦ ἑνὸς κατὰ τοῦ ἑτέρου is different:

---

[1] Εἶς καὶ εἰκοστός, τριακοστός (the regular form even in Attic inscriptions) is essentially different, since this is only a case of the formation of the ordinal being imperfectly carried out, as in the Latin *unus et vicesimus*.

[2] This use of εἶς is found already in Attic writers, ἑνὶ τῶν πολιτῶν Hyperid. Lycophr. 13, τῶν ἑταίρων εἶς Aesch. c. Ctesiph. 89, although there is always the implied meaning 'belonging to this definite number (or class),' so that the εἶς has a force which is quite absent from it in Luke loc. cit. The instances adduced for the weakened sense of εἶς from Plato and Xenophon (e.g. Plat. Leg. ix. 855 D) are quite irrelevant, since the εἶς is there a true numeral.

the sense being, every individual on behalf of the one against the other, fully expressed εἶς ὑπὲρ τοῦ ἑ. κ. τ. ἑτ. καὶ ἕτερος ὑπ. τ. ἑνὸς [the opposite person to the previous ἑνὸς] κ. τ. ἑτ.).

3. 'Ανὰ and κατὰ with a numeral have a **distributive** sense as in classical Greek: Mc. 6. 40 κατὰ (v.l. ἀνὰ as in L. 9. 14) ἑκατὸν καὶ κατὰ πεντήκοντα (Herm. Sim. ix. 2. 3 ἀνὰ δύο παρθένοι, cp. § 39, 2); besides this we have after the Semitic manner[1] δύο δύο Mc. 6. 7 (ἀνὰ δύο D as in L. 10. 1), just as for κατὰ συμπόσια, κ. πρασιάς Mc. 6. 39 f. has συμπόσια συμπόσια, πρασιαὶ πρασιαί (Herm. Sim. viii. 2. 8 τάγματα τάγματα, 4. 2).[2] On ἀνὰ εἷς ἕκαστος, εἷς καθ' εἷς and the like, see § 51, 4.

4. 2 P. 2. 5 ὄγδοον Νῶε ἐφύλαξεν, 'Noah with seven others,' is correct classical Greek (though ὄγδ. αὐτὸν would be more usual).— Mt. 18. 22 ἕως ἑβδομηκοντάκις ἑπτά is peculiar for 'seventy times seven times': D* alone reads ἑβδ. ἑπτάκις.—'Now for the third time' is τρίτον τοῦτο (§ 34, 3), like Herod. v. 76 τέταρτον τοῦτο (W.); 'for the third time' is (τὸ) τρίτον Mc. 14. 41 etc., ἐκ τρίτου Mt. 26. 44, cp. A. 10. 15.

§ 46. THE ARTICLE. I. 'Ο, ἡ, τό, as pronoun; the article with independent substantives.

1. The article ὁ, ἡ, τό, which had long since been developed out of the old demonstrative pronoun, retains on the whole in the N.T. all its former usages, and amongst them to a certain extent its use as a **pronoun** ('this one,' 'he'). There is here, however, a confusion (found also in other Hellenistic writings, and indeed in the classical period, Kühner ii.[2] 779 f.) between the forms of the ἄρθρον προτακτικόν ὁ, ἡ, τό and those of the ἄρθρον ὑποτακτικόν ὅς, ἥ, ὅ, since the latter are employed as demonstratives instead of relatives.

2. 'Ο μὲν – ὁ δὲ, 'the one – the other.' This use is no longer very frequent in the N.T., and usually takes the form of ὃς μὲν – ὃς δὲ (neut. ὃ μὲν ... ὃ δὲ, plur. ἃ μὲν, οἷς μὲν, οὓς μὲν etc.); moreover the (Semitic) use of εἷς encroaches upon it, § 45, 2, though the latter is not everywhere synonymous with it, and can form no plural. Thus ὁ μὲν – ὁ δὲ refers either to persons already familiar, the one – the other, this one—that one, or is quite indefinite, one – another; on the other hand it does not serve as a means of differentiating a number of persons or things when they are introduced for the first time; hence, whereas Luke can say (23. 33) τοὺς κακούργους, ὃν μὲν – ὃν δὲ, the phrase in Mt. 27. 38 is δύο λῃσταί, εἷς – καὶ εἷς (class. εἷς μὲν – ἕτερος δὲ), cp. § 45, 2. Other instances of ὃς μὲν – ὃς δὲ: Mt. 13. 4 (ἃ μὲν – ἄλλα δὲ [D ἃ δὲ]; similar freedom as to the sequence in the clauses is frequent elsewhere, cp. Kühner ii.[2] 508 note), 13. 8, 16. 14, 21. 35, 22. 5 (ὃς אBC*L, οἱ D), 25. 15, 26. 67 (οἱ δὲ alone, 'but others'),

---

[1] LXX. Gen. 7. 3, 9. From classical Greek Winer adduces Aesch. Pers. 981 μυρία μυρία πεμπαστάν, i.e. τὸν κατὰ μυρίους ἀριθμοῦντα.

[2] A mixed construction ἀνὰ δύο δύο occurs in the Gospel of Peter 35.

28. 17 (ditto),[1] Mc. 4. 4, 12. 5, L. 8. 5, Jo. 7. 12, A. 14. 4, 17. 18 (τινὲς ... οἱ δέ), 32, 27. 44, 28. 24, R. 9. 21, 14. 2 (ὃς μὲν – ὁ [ὃς FG] δὲ ἀσθενῶν), 5, 1 C. 11. 21, 12. 8, 28, 2 C. 2. 16 ('the latter' – 'the former,') Ph. 1. 16 (ditto), 2 Tim. 2. 20, Jd. 22. On the other hand the only instances of ὁ μὲν – ὁ δέ are: 1 C. 7. 7 ὁ μὲν οὕτως ὁ δὲ οὕτως (ὃς אᶜKL), E. 4. 11 τοὺς μὲν – τοὺς δὲ all MSS.; also in H. 7. 20 f., 23 f., 12. 10 we have οἱ μὲν – ὁ δέ, referring to **definite** persons (in 7. 20 f. the priests under the old system – Jesus), who are indicated in this way instead of by a repetition of the names, a case in which ὅς is never used: Mt. 13. 23 also appears to be an instance, ὃς δή (D has τότε for ὃς δή) καρποφορεῖ καὶ ποιεῖ ὁ μὲν ἑκατόν, ὁ δὲ ἑξήκοντα, ὁ δὲ τριάκοντα, but the verse = verse 8, where ὅ is neuter, and it should therefore probably be so taken here as well, cp. Mc. 4. 20 ἐν τριάκοντα κ.τ.λ. (where it is quite wrong to write ἐν).

3. Ὁ δέ 'but he,' ἡ δέ, οἱ δέ (only in the nominative) used in continuing a narrative, are common in all historical writings (least often in St. John);[2] the use of ὁ μὲν οὖν 'he then,' without a δέ strictly corresponding to the μέν, is confined to the Acts. Ὁ δέ, ὁ μὲν οὖν show a special tendency to take a participle after them, which gives rise occasionally to ambiguity. For instance, in A. 8. 4 οἱ μὲν οὖν διασπαρέντες means 'they therefore that were scattered,' since in order to separate οἱ from διασπαρέντες it would be necessary for the subject referred to to have been mentioned just before, whereas here it is a long way off (verse 1); but in 1. 6 οἱ μὲν οὖν συνελθόντες it is ambiguous whether the meaning is 'they therefore who were come together' or 'they therefore, when they were come together.' The demonstrative ὁ (ὅς) no longer appears in connection with other particles: there is no trace of καὶ ὅς, καὶ τόν in the continuation of a narrative, nor of τὸν καὶ τόν 'such and such a one,' or πρὸ τοῦ 'formerly' etc.

4. Ὁ, ἡ, τό used as the **article** with **appellatives** has as in classical Greek a double import: it is either **individual** or **generic**, *i.e.* it either calls special attention to one definite individual out of a class, ὁ ἄνθρωπος = οὗτος ὁ ἄνθρωπος, or it contrasts the whole class as such with other classes, οἱ ἄνθρωποι opposed to τὰ ἄλλα ζῷα (or to ὁ θεός). The latter use is also derived from the demonstrative sense: 'these persons,' to wit 'men.' This sense of the article was known by grammarians in early times (Apollonius Dyscolus) as the '**anaphoric**' sense, because there is a reference back (ἀναφορά) to something already familiar or supposed to be familiar: ὁ δοῦλός σου is 'your slave' (the particular slave whom you know I mean, or the one whom you have), but δοῦλός σου is 'a slave of yours.' If therefore an individual who is not yet familiar is introduced for the first

---

[1] In these last two passages there is no partition indicated at the beginning of the sentence, but it is only through the οἱ δέ that it becomes apparent that the preceding statement was not applicable to the whole body. Cp. Winer, § 17, 2, who compares passages from classical authors.

[2] Jo. 5. 11 ὁ δὲ ἀπεκρίθη אC*GKL al., ἀπεκρ. alone C³DEF al., a peculiar reading ὃς δὲ ἀπ. AB, as in Mc. 15. 23 ὃς δὲ אB. Cp. § 79, 4.

time, or if the whole class (though familiar) is not embraced, but only an undefined part of it, then no article need be used, as *e.g.* in the case of a predicate : for in ὑμεῖς μάρτυρες τούτων there is no ἀναφορά to particular well-known witnesses, nor is the whole class embraced : this is the ordinary rule for expressing a predicate (exceptions are given in § 47, 3).

5. The use of the **individual** article, in cases where it is used at all, is generally speaking obligatory, at least according to classical usage it is so : the necessity for its use is not removed by the insertion of a demonstrative or a possessive : οὗτος ὁ ἄνθρωπος, ἡ ἐμὴ οἰκία. The **generic** article may be far more readily dispensed with, especially in the case where the genus is represented by only a single specimen. With **natural objects** : we have ὁ ἥλιος, ἡ σελήνη, but also ἡλίου δὲ (τοῦ δὲ ἡ. D) ἀνατείλαντος Mt. 13. 6, L. 21. 5 ἔσονται σημεῖα ἐν ἡλίῳ καὶ σελήνῃ καὶ ἄστροις, followed by a contrasted statement καὶ ἐπὶ τῆς γῆς 'here on earth': A. 27. 20 μήτε δὲ ἡλίου μήτε ἄστρων ἐπιφαινόντων, 'neither sun nor stars shining,' 1 C. 15. 41 ἄλλη δόξα ἡλίου, καὶ ἄλλη δόξα σελήνης, καὶ ἄλλη δόξα ἀστέρων, Ap. 7. 2, 16. 12 ἀπὸ ἀνατολῆς ἡλίου, 22. 5 οὐκ ἔχουσιν χρείαν φωτὸς λύχνου καὶ φωτὸς ἡλίου (cp. 21. 23 with art.). In a certain number of these examples the omission or insertion of the article was obviously a matter of choice ; but in A. 27. 20 the meaning appears to be intensified by the omission 'neither any sun,' and with 1 C. 15. 41 verse 39 must be compared, ἄλλη μὲν (σὰρξ) ἀνθρώπων, ἄλλη δὲ κτηνῶν etc., and the reason for the absence of the article might be in both passages that the reference is not so much to the species taken as a whole, or to the uniquely existing sun, as to the distinctive characteristic of the species or of the individual object in the respective passages. Cp. 2 C. 11. 26 κινδύνοις ἐκ γένους (**my** kindred, *i.e.* Jews), καὶ ἐξ ἐθνῶν (elsewhere usually τὰ ἔθνη, vide infra), κ. ἐν θαλάσσῃ ; the article would here be wrong. Further instances of the absence of the art. with θάλασσα : Mt. 4. 15 O.T. ὁδὸν θαλάσσης, A. 10. 6, 12 παρὰ θάλασσαν (after a preposition or a substantive equivalent to a prep., § 40, 9), L. 21. 25 ἤχους θαλάσσης, Ja. 1. 6 κλύδωνι θαλάσσης, Jd. 13 κύματα ἄγρια θαλ. (part of the predicate, and also due to the distinctive character of the sea being the point of the comparison). With γῆ 'earth' the cases of omission of the art. are mainly after a preposition (though even here the cases of insertion far preponderate) : ἐπὶ γῆς Mt. 28. 18 (with τῆς BD), L. 2. 14, 1 C. 8. 5, E. 3. 15, H. 12. 25, 8. 4 (in all these instances except the last in conjunction with ἐν οὐρανοῖς (-ῷ) or ἀπ' οὐρανῶν or ἐν ὑψίστοις), ἐκ γῆς 1 C. 15. 47 (opposed to ἐξ οὐρ.), cp. also ἀπὸ ἄκρου γῆς ἕως ἄκρου οὐρανοῦ Mc. 13. 27. Besides these we have A. 17. 24 οὐρανοῦ καὶ γῆς κύριος, 2 P. (3. 5 οὐρανοὶ ... καὶ γῆ 'a *new* heaven,' similarly 13), 3. 10 οὐρανοὶ (with οἱ ABC)...στοιχεῖα... γῆ (with ἡ CP), cp. 12. Among these instances, in 1 C. 15. 47 the omission was no doubt obligatory, since ἐκ γῆς is 'earthy' (the essential property of earth is referred to). Οὐρανός (-οί) with a preposition frequently stands without an article (often there is a diversity of reading in the MSS.); the omission is obligatory in Mt. 21. 25 f. ἐξ οὐρανοῦ ... ἐξ ἀνθρώπων

='of heavenly' or 'human origin'; so in Mc. 11. 30 f., L. 20. 4 f. Omission of art. where there is no prep. occurs in A. 3. 21, 17. 24 (for 2 P. 3. 5, 12 vide supra). Κόσμος: ἐν κόσμῳ 1 C. 8. 4, 14. 10, Ph. 2. 15 etc. (v.l. in 2 P. 1. 4); of *one* world as opposed to another 2 P. 1. 5 (see above on γῇ); κόσμου forming part of the anarthrous predicate R. 4. 13, 11. 12, 20; the omission is regular in all writers in the *formula* ἀπὸ καταβολῆς (ἀρχῆς, κτίσεως) κόσμου Mt. 25. 34 etc., cp. ἀπ' ἀρχῆς κτίσεως Mc. 10. 6, 13. 19, 2 P. 3. 4; other instances 2 C. 5. 19, G. 6. 14.—The points of the compass, only found in connection with prepositions, never have the article: κατὰ μεσημβρίαν A. 8. 26, ἀπὸ ἀνατολῶν Mt. 2. 1, 8. 11 etc., ἀπὸ δυσμῶν L. 12. 54, ἀπὸ βορρᾶ καὶ νότου 13. 29 (so in other writers); also βασίλισσα νότου Mt. 12. 42 of more definite *regions* in the south, but ἐν τῇ ἀνατολῇ is used in the same sense in Mt. 2. 2, 9.

6. Another class of Being, unique of Its kind, is expressed by θεός, κύριος (=יהוה, but also Christ), and these words come near being proper names; it is not surprising that the article is frequently dropped. This happens especially after a preposition (ἀπὸ θεοῦ Jo. 3. 2, ἐν κυρίῳ passim), or when the word is in the genitive and dependent on an anarthrous noun (particularly a predicate), *e.g.* Mt. 27. 20 ὅτι θεοῦ εἰμι υἱός, L. 3. 2 ἐγένετο ῥῆμα θεοῦ (subject), although we also have εἰ υἱὸς εἶ τοῦ θεοῦ Mt. 4. 3, υἱὲ τοῦ θεοῦ 8. 29, and the usage depends more on a natural tendency to assimilation and abbreviation than on any hard and fast rule. So also υἱὲ διαβόλου A. 13. 10 (διαβ. elsewhere takes an art., as does σατανᾶς except in [Mc. 3. 23 '*one* Satan'] L. 22. 3). On Χριστός vide infra 10. —Under the head of the generic article must also be classed plurals like ἄνθρωποι, νεκροί, ἔθνη; here too it is especially after a preposition and in a few phrases besides that we occasionally have noticeable instances of the omission of the art.: ἐκ νεκρῶν ἐγερθῇ Mt. 17. 9, and so regularly (except in E. 5. 14 O.T., Col. 2. 12 BDEFG, 1 Th. 1. 10 [om. τῶν ACK]), whereas we have ἠγέρθη ἀπὸ τῶν ν. Mt. 14. 2 etc.; ἀνάστασιν νεκρῶν A. 17. 32, 23. 6 etc.; in 1 C. 15. 15 f, 29, 32 the article could not stand, because it is the idea and not the complete number which is in question (verse 52 is different); 1 P. 4. 5 κρῖναι ζῶντας καὶ νεκρούς = all, whether dead or living, cp. 6.—Not infrequently ἔθνη, 'the heathen' is without an art.: after Hebr. גוֹיִם in A. 4. 25 O.T., R. 15. 12 O.T.; ἐξ ἐθνῶν A. 15. 14, G. 2. 15, ἐν ἔθνεσιν 1 Tim. 3. 16, σὺν ἔθ. A. 4. 27; in the gen. πλοῦτος ἐθνῶν, ἐθν. ἀπόστολος R. 11. 12 f. (predic.); also R. 3. 29 f. ἢ Ἰουδαίων (as such) ὁ θεὸς μόνον; οὐχὶ καὶ ἐθνῶν; ναὶ καὶ ἐθνῶν, εἴπερ εἷς ὁ θεός, ὃς δικαιώσει περιτομὴν (as such, or in some individual instances not specified) ἐκ πίστεως καὶ ἀκροβυστίαν διὰ τῆς (anaphoric) πίστεως.

7. The **individual** article could scarcely be expected in formulas like ἀπ' ἀγροῦ, ἐν ἀγρῷ, εἰς ἀγρόν, since there is no question of a definite field (Mt. 13. 24 ἐν τῷ ἀγρῷ αὐτοῦ); if however we also find ἐν τῷ ἀ. etc. without reference to a definite field (Mt. 13. 44, like τὰ κρίνα τοῦ ἀγροῦ 6. 28), the art. must then be regarded as generic (as we say 'the country'). Ἐν ἀγορᾷ L. 7. 32 = ἐν ταῖς ἀγοραῖς (ταῖς om.

§ 46. 7.] THE ARTICLE. 149

CEF al.) in Mt. 11. 16 etc.; ἀπ' ἀγορᾶς Mc. 7. 4 a formula; similarly ἐπὶ θύραις Mt. 24. 33; of time πρὸς ἑσπέραν L. 24. 29, ἕως ἑσπέρας A. 28. 23, μέχρι μεσονυκτίου 20. 7 (κατὰ τὸ μεσ. 16. 25), διὰ νυκτὸς with v.l. διὰ τῆς ν. A. 5. 19, 16. 9 etc. (the art. denoting the particular night), πρὸ καιροῦ = πρὶν καιρὸν εἶναι Mt. 8. 29, ἐν καιρῷ = ὅταν καιρὸς ᾖ 24. 45, ἄχρι καιροῦ L. 4. 13, A. 13. 11, πρὸς καιρόν L. 8. 13, κατὰ κ. R. 5. 6 ('at the right time'; 'in its due time'), παρὰ καιρὸν ἡλικίας H. 11. 11 (so also in classical Greek without art.); ἀπ' (ἐξ) ἀρχῆς, ἐν ἀρχῇ (class.); but ἐν καιρῷ ἐσχάτῳ 1 P. 1. 5, ἐν ἐσχάταις ἡμέραις 2. Tim. 3. 1, Ja. 5. 3 (used along with ἐπ' ἐσχάτου or -ων τῶν ἡμερῶν, § 47, 2) come under the same class as ἀπὸ πρώτης ἡμέρας A. 20. 18, Ph. 1. 5 (אABP insert τῆς), ἀπὸ ἕκτης ὥρας Mt. 27. 45, ἕως ὥρας ἐνάτης Mc. 15. 33 (cp. Herm. Vis. iii. 1. 2, Sim. ix. 11. 7), ἕως τρίτου οὐρανοῦ 2 C. 12. 2, πρώτην φυλακὴν καὶ δευτέραν A. 12. 10, πρώτης (the reading -τη of the MSS. is corrupt) μερίδος τῆς Μακ. πόλις 16. 12, and are explained by a usage of the older language, according to which the art. may be omitted with ordinal numbers, Kühner ii.² 551, and not merely in phrases like ἐσχάτη ὥρα ἐστίν 1 Jo. 2. 18. The usage of the language is however regulated with still greater precision: in statements about the hour the art. is used only either anaphorically as in Mt. 27. 46, cp. 45, or where there is an ellipse of ὥρα as in Mt. 20. 6 (in 9 it is anaphoric), or where a further definition is introduced as in A. 3. 1 τὴν ὥραν τῆς προσευχῆς τὴν ἐνάτην; with ἡμέρα, on the other hand, it is only absent in the case of more indefinite expressions, but is used with more definite statements, thus τῇ τρίτῃ ἡμέρᾳ always, and in Jo. 6. 39 ff. ἐν τῇ ἐσχάτῃ ἡμέρᾳ. —Θάνατος very frequently appears without an art., where German inserts one: ἕως θανάτου Mt. 26. 38, ἔνοχος θανάτου, ἄξιον θανάτου, παραδιδόναι εἰς θάνατον, γεύεσθαι θανάτου; the art. is used either of the actual death of a definite person (1 C. 11. 26), or (but this is almost confined to John's Gospel, Paul, and Apoc.) of death in the abstract, cp. 8. inf., Jo. 5. 24 μεταβέβηκεν ἐκ τοῦ θ. εἰς τὴν ζωήν,[1] or where death is half personified (Ap. 13. 3, 12), besides the case where assimilation to a noun in connection with it requires the article: τὸ ἀπόκριμα τοῦ θ. 2 C. 1. 9 (ἡ πληγὴ τοῦ θ. αὐτοῦ Ap. 13. 3, 12 is anaphoric).—Πνεῦμα: τὸ ἅγιον πν. is used sometimes to a certain extent personally, and then with the article, sometimes for the godlike spirit moving in man, and then without an art., unless there is 'anaphora' as in A. 2. 4, 8. 18, cp. 17; in 10. 44 ἐπέπεσεν τὸ πν. τὸ ἅγ. ἐπὶ πάντας there is a reference to the well-known fact of the outpouring, but this instance also approximates to the first usage. Omission is also occasioned by the presence of a preposition or by assimilation: ἐν πν. ἁγίῳ, ἐν δυνάμει πνεύματος ἁγίου.—3 Jo. 6 ἐνώπιον ἐκκλησίας, 1 C. 14. 4 ἐκκλησίαν οἰκοδομεῖ scarcely need explanation ('a congregation'); in H. 12. 7 τίς γὰρ υἱός, ὃν οὐ παιδεύει πατήρ, we might expect to have ὁ π. 'his father,' as in 1 Tim. 2. 12 after γυναικί to have τοῦ ἀνδρός 'her husband' (so 1 C. 11. 3 κεφαλὴ γυναικὸς ὁ ἀνήρ; in E. 5. 23 the art. goes with

---

[1] On incidental cases of omission of the art. cp. 8.

γυναικὸς), but the relation is neglected ('**whom** a father does not chastise'; see also § 82, 2 note), cp. Herm. Sim. ix. 28. 4 ἵνα δοῦλος κύριον ἴδιον ἀρνήσηται. Πατήρ is used of God in Jo. 1. 14 δόξαν ὡς μονογενοῦς παρὰ πατρός (a kind of assimilation to μονογ.), also in the formula ἀπὸ θεοῦ πατρὸς ἡμῶν R. 1. 7 etc.; πιστῷ κτίστῃ 1 P. 4. 19, with v.l. ὡς π. κτ., is at any rate agreeable to the sense. Σὺν γυναιξὶν A. 1. 14 is a regular formula, cp. 21. 5 σὺν γ. καὶ τέκνοις (classical Greek has the same phrase; so we say 'with women and children'); further, ἐπὶ πρόσωπον πίπτειν L. 5. 12 etc., κατὰ πρ. 2 C. 10. 7[1]; cp. 9.

8. With **abstract words** the article is very frequently absent in Greek, where it is used in German; the more abstract the sense in which such a word is used, the less liable is it to take any article other than the generic. Hence in some passages the question is rather to account for the presence of the art. than for its absence; *e.g.* Col. 3. 5 πορνείαν ἀκαθαρσίαν πάθος ἐπιθυμίαν ... καὶ **τὴν** πλεονεξίαν, ἥτις ἐστὶν εἰδωλολατρία 'and that principal vice, covetousness' etc.; the additional clause ἥτις κ.τ.λ. entails the use of the article. In 1 C. 14. 20 μὴ παιδία γίνεσθε ταῖς φρεσίν, ἀλλὰ τῇ κακίᾳ νηπιάζετε, τῇ κ. is due to ταῖς φρεσίν. Cp. further H. 1. 14 **εἰς διακονίαν** ἀποστελλόμενα διὰ τοὺς μέλλοντας κληρονομεῖν **σωτηρίαν** (2. 3, 5. 9, 6. 9, 9. 28, 11. 7; with art. only in 2. 10 τὸν ἀρχηγὸν **τῆς** σωτηρίας **αὐτῶν**). In 1 C. 13. 13 νυνὶ δὲ μένει πίστις ἐλπὶς ἀγάπη ... μείζων δὲ τούτων ἡ ἀγάπη the art. is anaphoric (so also in the German; cp. verses 4 and 3, R. 13. 10 and 9; R. 12. 7 εἴτε διακονίαν, ἐν τῇ διακονίᾳ· εἴτε ὁ διδάσκων, ἐν τῇ διδασκαλίᾳ etc.; but ibid. 9 ff. ἡ ἀγάπη ἀνυπόκριτος, τῇ φιλαδελφίᾳ φιλόστοργοι, τῇ τιμῇ ἀλλήλους προηγούμενοι, τῇ σπουδῇ μὴ ὀκνηροί, because they are virtues assumed to be well known etc.). St. Paul is fond of omitting the art. with ἁμαρτία, νόμος, and occasionally with θάνατος (R. 6. 9, 8. 38, cp. supra 7), but the reason for his doing so is intelligible: R. 5. 13 ἄχρι γὰρ νόμου ἁμαρτία ἦν ἐν κόσμῳ ('before there was a law, there was sin'), ἁμαρτία δὲ οὐκ ἐλλογεῖται μὴ ὄντος νόμου, 6. 14 ἁμαρτία ('no sin,' cp. 8 θάνατος) ὑμῶν οὐ κυριεύσει· οὐ γάρ ἐστε ὑπὸ νόμον ('under any law') ἀλλὰ ὑπὸ χάριν, 3. 20 διὰ γὰρ νόμου ἐπίγνωσις ἁμαρτίας (a general statement). Σάρξ also inclines to an abstract sense (the natural state of man); hence we frequently have ἐν σαρκί and nearly always κατὰ σάρκα (τὴν is inserted as a v.l. in 2 C. 11. 18, and by nearly all MSS. in Jo. 8. 15).

9. Whereas hitherto no case has occurred where the classical usage of the article is opposed to the N.T. usage, such opposition appears in the case of a **noun which governs a genitive**, and which in Hebrew would therefore be in the construct state or would have a suffix attached to it, and in either case would be without an article; this **Semitic** usage has exercised a considerable influence on the Greek of the N.T. writers, especially where they make use of Semitic (*i.e.* Hebrew or Aramaic) originals. But as it was repugnant to the spirit of the Greek language, the article has in general only

---

[1] Also in profane writers like Polybius; there are similar classical phrases, κατ' ὀφθαλμούς, ἐν ὀφθαλμοῖς etc.

§ 46. 9-10.]   THE ARTICLE.   151

been omitted, where the whole clause was governed by a preposition (cp. supra 5-7), and the phrase has thus become a fixed formula: ἀπὸ (πρὸ) προσώπου τινός,[1] διὰ χειρός τινος, διὰ στόματός τινος, ἀπὸ ὀφθαλμῶν σου L. 19. 42, ἐν ὀφθαλμοῖς ἡμῶν Mt. 21. 42 O.T. (πρὸ ὀφθ. ὑμῶν Clem. Cor. i. 2. 1),[1] formulas which are all thoroughly Hebraic, § 40, 9 ; further instances are ἐν ἡμέραις Ἡρῴδου Mt. 2. 1, ἐν ἡμέρᾳ ὀργῆς R. 2. 5, Ph. 1. 6 ἄχρις ἡμέρας Ἰησοῦ Χριστοῦ, cp. 10, 2. 16 (ἐν τῇ ἡμ. τοῦ κυρίου 1 C. 5. 6, 2 C. 5. 14, 2 Th. 2. 2; on the other hand the art. is omitted even with the nom., ἡμέρα κυρίου 1 Th. 5. 2 [ἡ add. AKL], 2 P. 3. 10 BC [with ἡ אAKLP]); εἰς οἶκον αὐτῶν Mc. 8. 3, cp. 26 (the use with the art. largely preponderates; L. 14. 1 εἰς οἶκόν [τὸν ο. A] τινος τῶν Φαρισ. [cp. A. 18. 7, 10. 32] is excusable: τὴν κατ' οἶκον αὐτῶν ἐκκλησίαν R. 16. 5, Col. 4. 15, cp. Philem. 2, is a regular phrase and perhaps not a Hebraism); ἐκ κοιλίας μητρὸς (αὐτοῦ) Mt. 9. 12, L. 1. 15, A. 3. 2, 14. 8; ἐν βίβλῳ ζωῆς Ph. 4. 3 (but in Ap. with two articles), ἐν βίβλῳ λόγων Ἡσαΐου L. 3. 4, cp. 20. 42, A. 1. 20, 7. 42 (ἐν τῇ β. Μωϋσέως Mc. 12. 26), ἐν δακτύλῳ θεοῦ L. 11. 20, ἐν τῷ Βεελζεβοὺλ ἄρχοντι τῶν δαιμονίων Mt. 12. 24 (and a v.l. in L. 11. 15), and many more. To these must be added phrases which contain a proper name in the genitive, where the omission of the art. is not dependent on the presence of a preposition: γῆ Ἰσραήλ, Σοδόμων, Αἰγύπτου, Χαλδαίων etc., βασιλέως Αἰγύπτου A. 7. 10, εἰς πόλιν Δαυίδ L. 2. 4, cp. 11 ('the city of D.'), οἶκος Ἰσραήλ Mt. 10. 6 (23 D) etc., ἐξ οἴκου καὶ πατριᾶς Δαυίδ L. 2. 4 (but in L. 1. 33, H. 8. 8, 10 O.T., it takes the article as in the LXX.), ἐξ ἐφημερίας Ἀβία L. 1. 5. It is not often that this omission of the art. goes beyond such instances as those mentioned, as it does in Mary's song of praise in L. 1. 46 ff.: ἐν βραχίονι αὐτοῦ, διανοίᾳ καρδίας αὐτῶν, Ἰσραὴλ παιδὸς αὐτοῦ, and in that of Zacharias ibid. 68 ff.: ἐν οἴκῳ Δαυὶδ παιδὸς αὐτοῦ, ἐξ ἐχθρῶν ἡμῶν, διαθήκης ἁγίας αὐτοῦ, ὁδοὺς αὐτοῦ, διὰ σπλάγχνα ἐλέους θεοῦ ἡμῶν etc., by which means an unusually strong Hebrew colouring is here produced.[2] Cp. 2. 32 (Simeon's song of praise), Ja. 1. 26, 5. 20.

10. In the case of **proper names** the final development of the language has been that in modern Greek, when used as proper names, they take the article; in classical Greek, on the other hand, as also in the Greek of the N.T., proper names as such take no article, but may take one in virtue of a reference (anaphora) to something preceding. Thus if Luke in A. 9. 1 says ὁ δὲ Σαῦλος ἔτι ἐμπνέων κ.τ.λ., his object in using the article is to remind the reader of what he has previously narrated about the man (8. 3 Σαῦλος δέ); we are then informed that he requested ἐπιστολαὶ εἰς Δαμασκόν, and further on in verse 3, that he drew nigh to τῇ Δαμασκῷ (the place of his destina-

---

[1] Cp. supra 7 ad fin. with note [1]; writers of pure Greek do not add a genitive to expressions of this kind.
[2] 1 C. 2. 16 τίς γὰρ ἔγνω νοῦν κυρίου is a quotation, and so is 1 P. 3. 12 ὀφθαλμοὶ κυρίου, ὦτα αὐτοῦ; the LXX. abounds with instances of this kind. But in 1 Tim. 5. 10 ἁγίων πόδας, πόδας is due to assimilation to ἁγίων; in 1 C. 10. 21 τραπέζης κυρίου - τρ. δαιμονίων it is the character of the thing which is in question, cp. supra 5 (the one is a table of the Lord, the other a table of devils).

tion), the use of the article being much the same as in 20. 7 κλάσαι ἄρτον compared with 11 κλάσας τὸν ἄρτον. There is a subtle, and often untranslatable, nicety of language in this use of the article. But it is obvious that it depends in great measure on the caprice of the writer, whether in a case where frequent mention is made of the same person he chooses to express this reference to the preceding narrative or not: moreover the MSS. are frequently divided. If in Acts 1. 1 אAE al. (as opposed to BD) are right in reading ὁ Ἰησοῦς, then by this ὁ the mind is carried back to the contents of the Gospel; but such a reminder was by no means necessary. Ἰησοῦς, moreover, in the Evangelists takes the article as a rule, except where an appositional phrase with the art. is introduced; since obviously in that case either the article with the name or the phrase in apposition is superfluous. Hence Mt. 26. 69, 71 μετὰ Ἰ. τοῦ Γαλιλαίου (Ναζωραίου), 27. 17, 22 Ἰ. τὸν λεγόμενον Χριστόν, L. 2. 43 Ἰ. ὁ παῖς (2. 27 τὸ παιδίον Ἰησοῦν), cp. A. 1. 14 Μαρίᾳ τῇ μητρὶ τοῦ Ἰ., etc. (L. 3. 19 ὁ δὲ Ἡρῴδης ὁ τετραάρχης, with reference to v. 1; e omits ὁ τετρ.). Again, not only at the first mention of Jesus at all, but also in the first appearance of the risen Lord, the use of the art. is excluded, since here too there cannot well be anaphora: Mt. 28. 9 (ὁ Ἰ. DL al.), L. 24. 15 (ὁ Ἰ. DNPX al.); in John's Gospel, however, while on the one hand the anaphoric article is rendered possible at this point by the context and is actually found there (20. 14 θεωρεῖ τὸν Ἰησοῦν ἑστῶτα, after 12 τὸ σῶμα τοῦ Ἰησοῦ), on the other hand it is often omitted elsewhere (*e.g.* in 1. 50), as frequently happens in the other Evangelists in the case of other less distinguished names, such as Ἰωάνης and Πέτρος. In the Epistles, on the contrary, and in the Apocalypse (and to some extent in the Acts) the article is as a rule omitted as entirely superfluous (somewhat in the same way as is done by the Greek orators in the name of the adversary in a lawsuit); exceptions are 2 C. 4. 10 f. (but D*FG omit the art.), E. 4. 21 (anaphora to αὐτῷ), 1 Jo. 4. 3 (anaphora to 2; but א has no art.). **Χριστός** is strictly an appellative, = the Messiah, and this is made apparent in the Gospels and Acts by the frequent insertion of the article; here again the Epistles for the most part (but not always) omit it.—A special case is that of **indeclinable** proper names, with which the article, without its proper force, has occasionally to serve to determine the case of the word: Mt. 1. 2 ff. Ἀβραὰμ ἐγέννησεν τὸν Ἰσαάκ...τὸν Ἰακώβ etc. (the same form is also used in the case of declinable names, such as τὸν Ἰούδαν, and where there is a clause in apposition as in 6 τὸν Δαυὶδ τὸν βασιλέα; ibid. ἐκ τῆς τοῦ Οὐρίου) cp. A. 7. 8, 13. 21. On οἱ τοῦ Ζεβεδαίου see § 35, 2.

11. The preceding statements hold good equally for **place-names** as for personal names (the art. is anaphoric in A. 9. 3 vide supra, 9. 38 τῇ Ἰόππῃ, 42 τῆς Ἰόππης, cp. 36); τῆς Ῥώμης 18. 2 is due to τῆς Ἰταλίας in the same verse; τὴν Ῥώμην 28. 14 denotes Rome as the goal of the whole journey. Τρῳάς also, although strictly subject to an article (Ἀλεξάνδρεια ἡ Τρῳάς), only takes one in a peculiar way in 2 C. 2. 12 (without an art. in A. 16. 8, 20. 5). There is a peculiar use of the art. in the Acts in the statement of

§ 46. 11-12.] THE ARTICLE. 153

halting-places on a journey: 17. 1 τὴν Ἀμφίπολιν καὶ τὴν Ἀπολλωνίαν (the places lying on the well-known road between Philippi and Thessalonica), 20. 13, 21. 1, 3, 23. 31, but in 20. 14 ff. there is no article. Ἰερουσαλήμ, Ἱεροσόλυμα hardly ever take an art., Winer, § 18, 5 (ἐν τοῖς Ἱεροσολύμοις Jo. 10. 22 ABL, ἐν Ἱερ. the rest; the force of the article is, in the very same place which was the scene of the previous narrative.)—The case is different with names of countries, many of which being originally adjectives (sc. γῆ, χώρα) are never found without an article: ἡ Ἰουδαία[1], ἡ Γαλιλαία[2], ἡ Μεσοποταμία, ἡ Μυσία (Μύσιος adj.), ἡ Ἑλλάς A. 20. 2; for a different reason ἡ Ἀσία like ἡ Εὐρώπη (ἡ Λιβύη does not come under this head) takes the art. from early times, as one of the two divisions of the globe that are naturally opposed to each other, and keeps it even when it is used to denote the Roman province (in A. 2. 9 f. Μεσοποταμία, Ἀσία and ἡ Λιβύη ἡ κατὰ Κυρήνην are the only places with an article); only in A. 6. 9 do we find ἀπὸ Κιλικίας καὶ Ἀσ., and in 1 P. 1. 1 the names of all the countries are without the art. (but there there is no art. at all in the whole address: ἐκλεκτοῖς παρεπιδήμοις διασπορᾶς Πόντου κ.τ.λ.).[3] Also with other names of countries the article is found more frequently than it would be with names of towns: always with Ἰταλία, generally with Ἀχαΐα (without art. R. 15. 26, 2 C. 9. 2); Συρία, Κιλικία, Φρυγία, Ἀραβία are strictly adjectives, and therefore generally take the art., but A. 21. 3 εἰς Σ., Κιλ. 6. 9 (vide supra), 23. 34, Φρυγίαν καὶ Παμφυλίαν 2. 10, εἰς Ἀραβίαν G. 1. 17. Παμφυλία, although strictly on a par with the others (τὸ Παμφύλιον πέλαγος A. 27. 5 β text), yet in a majority of cases omits the art.; it has it in A. (27. 5 infra) 13. 13: εἰς Πέργην τῆς Παμφυλίας is a chorographical gen. of the whole, § 35, 4, which absolutely requires the article (A. 13. 14, 22. 3, 27. 5, cp. 16. 12, 21. 39). Αἴγυπτος never takes the art. (except in a wrong reading of אABCD in A. 7. 11, and of BC in 7. 36).—**River-names**: ὁ Ἰορδάνης ποταμός Mc. 1. 5, elsewhere ὁ Ἰορδάνης (τὸν ποταμὸν τὸν Τίβεριν Herm. Vis. i. 1. 2; classical usage is the same); **names of seas**: ὁ Ἀδρίας A. 27. 27 as in classical Greek.[4]

12. The names of **nations**, where the nation as a whole is indicated, do not require the article any more than personal names require it, and it is therefore omitted in almost every instance where Ἰουδαῖοι are referred to in St. Paul's vindications of himself against the Jews, A. 26. 2, 3, 4, 7, 21, 25. 10 (as it is in the name of the opponent in speeches in an Athenian lawsuit, supra 10), the

---

[1] For which the Hebraic γῆ Ἰούδα is also used Mt. 2. 6. (Cp. ἡ Ἰουδαία γῆ in Jo. 3. 22, and also according to D in 4. 3.)

[2] Exception L. 17. 11 μέσον Σαμαρείας καὶ Γαλιλαίας, where the omission with Σ. has produced the omission with Γ.

[3] This is not so much an enumeration of the persons addressed as a characterization of them, and the omission of the art. becomes intelligible by a comparison with 1 Tim. 1. 2 Τιμοθέῳ γνησίῳ τέκνῳ = ὃς εἰ γνήσιον τ. Cp. also Winer, § 18, 6, note 4; infra § 47, 6, note 1 on p. 159; see also 47, 10.

[4] Cp. on the article with names of countries etc. Kallenberg Philol. 49, 515 ff.

exception being 25. 8 τὸν νόμον τῶν Ἰουδαίων, where τὸν ν. Ἰουδαίων could not well be used, while τὸν ν. τὸν Ἰ. (the Attic phrase, see § 47, 7) was contrary to the predominant practice of the N.T. Also in the Pauline Epistles Ἰουδαῖοι takes no article, except in 1 C. 9. 20 ἐγενόμην τοῖς Ἰουδαίοις ὡς Ἰουδαῖος ('individual' article, those with whom I had to deal on each occasion; τοῖς ἀνόμοις etc. in the following clauses are similar); nor yet Ἕλληνες, although this comprehensive name, just because of its comprehensiveness (in opposition to βάρβαροι, cp. 11 on Ἀσία) in classical Greek regularly has the article[1]; but the point with St. Paul is never the totality of the nation, but its distinctive peculiarity (cp. supra 5 on ἥλιος etc.), consequently R. 1. 14 Ἕλλησίν τε καὶ βαρβάροις is not less classical than Demosth. viii. 67 πᾶσιν Ἕλλησι καὶ βαρβάροις (all, whether Greeks or barbarians), or σοφοῖς τε καὶ ἀνοήτοις which follows it in St. Paul, see § 47, 2. On the other hand in the narrative of the Evangelists (and to some extent in the Acts[2]) the article is rarely omitted with Ἰουδαῖοι and other names of nations (Mt. 28. 15 παρὰ Ἰουδαίοις, D inserts τοῖς: 10. 5, L. 9. 52 εἰς πόλιν Σαμαριτῶν is easily explained: in Jo. 4. 9 the clause is spurious). An instance of a national name in the masc. sing. is ὁ Ἰσραήλ; the art. is wanting in Hebraic phrases like γῆ Ἰ., ὁ λαὸς Ἰ. (υἱοὶ Ἰ.), but also not infrequently elsewhere.

§ 47. ARTICLE. II. The article with adjectives etc.; the article with connected parts of speech.

1. Every part of speech which is joined to a substantive as its attribute or in apposition to it—adjective, pronoun, participle, adverb, prepositional expression, the same case or the genitive of another substantive etc.—may in this connection, and without the substantive being actually expressed, be accompanied by the article, which in the case of the omission of the substantive often takes its place and indicates the substantive to be supplied: thus οἱ τότε sc. ἄνθρωποι, where the omission of οἱ is impossible. We deal with the latter case first, where **the additional definition stands alone without the substantive.**

The **adjective**, where it is not a predicate to a substantive, in most cases takes the article, which may be either individual or generic. **Masc. sing.**: ὁ ἀληθινός 1 Jo. 5. 20 (God), ὁ μόνος 'the only One' (God) Jo. 5. 44 B (the other MSS. insert θεός, cp. 17. 3), ὁ πονηρός 'the devil,' ὁ ἅγιος τοῦ θεοῦ L. 4. 34 (Christ), ὁ δίκαιος (Christ) A. 22. 14, in all which cases the art. is individual and denotes him who possesses this quality κατ' ἐξοχήν. Quite different is 1 P. 4. 18 ὁ δίκαιος—ὁ ἀσεβής, as we say 'the righteous—the godless,' *i.e.* one (everyone) who is righteous or godless, regarded in this capacity,

---

[1] See Rhein. Mus. xliv. 12.

[2] In this book we also find the correct classical phrases Ἀθηναῖοι πάντες 17. 21, cp. § 47, 9; πάντες Ἰουδαῖοι 26. 4 BC*E (ins. οἱ ℵAC² al.).

§ 47. 1.] THE ARTICLE. 155

where an individual is taken as a concrete instance of the genus: similarly with a substantive introduced ὁ ἀγαθὸς ἄνθρωπος Mt. 12. 35, L. 6. 45 (§ 32, 3): frequently with participles: the usage stands midway between the individual and the generic use. A third mode of using the art. may be illustrated by Ja. 2. 6 τὸν πτωχόν 'that beggar,' where it is individual and anaphoric, referring to the instance in verse 2 (§ 32, 3). The masc. plur. can also be used in this last sense, but it is more frequently generic: οἱ πλούσιοι 'the rich,' οἱ ἅγιοι a name for Christians. The fem. sing. is used elliptically, ἡ ἔρημος and the like, § 44, 1 (the art. is individual: ἡ ἔρημος χώρα opposed to inhabited country). The neut. sing. is used with individual sense of a single definite thing or action, 2 C. 8. 14 O.T. τὸ πολύ and τὸ ὀλίγον, Philem. 14 τὸ ἀγαθόν σου 'thy good deed,' but more frequently with generic sense as in L. 6. 45 ὁ ἀγαθὸς ἄνθρωπος ἐκ τοῦ ἀγαθοῦ θησαυροῦ τῆς καρδίας προφέρει τὸ ἀγαθόν (corresponding to ὁ ἀγ. ἄνθρ., vide supra), G. 6. 10 ἐργαζώμεθα τὸ ἀγαθόν, R. 13. 3 τὸ ἀγαθὸν ποίει, cp. just before τῷ ἀγαθῷ ἔργῳ = τοῖς ἀγαθοῖς ἔργοις or ἀγαθοῖς ἔργ., as Mt. 12. 35 (the parallel passage to L. 6. 45) has τά (om. B al.) ἀγαθά and πονηρά (LUΔ ins. τά) in the corresponding clause, cp. also R. 3. 8 τὰ κακά – τὰ ἀγαθά. A peculiar usage of Paul (and Hebrews) is that of the neut. sing. adjective **equivalent to an abstract noun**, usually with a genitive: R. 2. 4 τὸ χρηστὸν τοῦ θεοῦ εἰς μετάνοιάν σε ἄγει, differing from χρηστότης (which precedes), since the adjective denotes this goodness in a concrete instance; 1. 19 τὸ γνωστὸν τοῦ θεοῦ 'the fact of God's being known,' or else that part of God which is (to be) known at all, in which case φανερόν ἐστιν ἐν αὐτοῖς must be 'is evident to them,' cp. § 41, 2. The genitive would then be partitive, and the adjective would not be used for an abstract noun. It is also perhaps so used in τὸ δοκίμιον ὑμῶν τῆς πίστεως Ja. 1. 3 = 1 P. 1. 7, for δοκίμιος is = δόκιμος, see G. A. Deissmann, Neue Bibelstudien, 86 ff.; see further 1 C. 1. 25 τὸ μωρὸν τοῦ θεοῦ σοφώτερον τῶν ἀνθρώπων ἐστίν (cp. μωρία 21, 23), this divine attribute which appears as foolishness; 2 C. 4. 17 τὸ παραυτίκα ἐλαφρὸν τῆς θλίψεως ἡμῶν (opposed to βάρος ibid.), 8. 9 τὸ τῆς ὑμετέρας ἀγάπης γνήσιον, Ph. 3. 8 διὰ τὸ ὑπερέχον τῆς γνώσεως Χριστοῦ (more concrete and vivid than ὑπεροχή), 4. 5 τὸ ἐπιεικὲς ὑμῶν, R. (8. 3)¹, 9. 22, H. 6. 17, 7. 18, 1 C. 7. 35 τὸ εὔσχημον καὶ εὐπάρεδρον τῷ κυρίῳ (§ 37, 7) ἀπερισπάστως. This is the most classical idiom in the language of the N.T., and may be paralleled from the old heathen literature, from Thucydides in particular.²—The neut. sing. is also occasionally

---

¹ Here not in abstract sense, τὸ ἀδύνατον τοῦ νόμου means the one thing which the law could not do: still the genitive belongs to the same class of gen. in either case.

² Still it is not to be attributed to imitation; since the imitation must, according to the usual way with imitative writers of that period, have betrayed itself in details. Moreover, other contemporary writers avail themselves of this method of expression: Strabo 3, p. 168 τὸ εὐμεταχείριστον τῆς θήρας (Winer, § 34, 2); on Joseph. and others, see W. Schmidt de Jos. elocut. 365 ff. See also Clem. Cor. i. 19. 1, 47. 5. "Quite a current usage in the higher κοινή," W. Schmid. Atticism. iv. 608.

used collectively to denote **persons**, τὸ ἔλαττον – τοῦ κρείττονος = οἱ ἐλάττονες – τῶν κρειττόνων, § 32, 1; a peculiar instance is τὸ δωδεκάφυλον ἡμῶν 'our 12 tribes' A. 26. 7 (Paul before Agrippa), cp. Clem. Cor. i. 55. 6 τὸ δ. τοῦ Ἰσραήλ (and with the same meaning 31. 4 τὸ δωδεκάσκηπτρον τ. Ἰ.). Elsewhere the **neut. plur.** is used of **persons**, 1 C. 1. 27 f. τὰ μωρὰ τοῦ κόσμου etc., § 32, 1; also of things with the genitive, τὰ κρυπτὰ τῶν ἀνθρώπων, τοῦ σκότους, τῆς καρδίας, τῆς αἰσχύνης R. 2. 16, 1 C. 4. 5, 14. 25, 2 C. 4. 2, τὰ ἀόρατα τοῦ θεοῦ R. 1. 20, a use analogous to that of the singular (vide supra), but referring to a plurality of phenomena. Other instances like τὰ ὁρατὰ καὶ ἀόρατα Col. 1. 16 (without a genitive) need only brief mention; τὰ καλά – τὰ σαπρά of fish caught in a net (*what* is good or bad) Mt. 13. 48. Neuters of this kind are not frequent in the Gospels.

2. With the different ways of employing the adjective that have been quoted, the **article** is sometimes essential, sometimes unnecessary. In R. 1. 14 as we have Ἕλλησίν τε καὶ βαρβάροις (§ 46, 12), so also σοφοῖς τε καὶ ἀνοήτοις: Mt. 23. 34 προφήτας καὶ σοφούς, 11. 25 = L. 10. 21 ἀπὸ σοφῶν καὶ συνετῶν ... νηπίοις, where the article would be as little in place as it would be if a substantive were employed (cp. § 46, 5 on 1 C. 15. 39), Mt. 5. 45 ἐπὶ πονηροὺς καὶ ἀγαθούς, 1 C. 1. 20 ποῦ σοφός; ποῦ γραμματεύς; occasionally too it is absent with neuter words, where its presence or omission appears to be more optional: Ja. 4. 17 καλὸν ποιεῖν ('some good'), Herm. x. 2. 3 πονηρὸν ἠργάσατο, but followed in 4 by τὸ πονηρόν anaphoric: 2 C. 8. 21 προνοούμενοι καλὰ οὐ μόνον ἐνώπιον κυρίου, ἀλλὰ καὶ ἐνώπιον ἀνθρώπων, in this passage the article would have broken the connection with what follows. It is not accidental that beside ἐν τῷ φανερῷ (Mt. 6. 4 etc.) there is regularly found εἰς φανερὸν ἐλθεῖν (because the latter refers to something not yet in existence), Mc. 4. 22, L. 8. 17; usually too we have ἐν τῷ κρυπτῷ as in Mt. 6. 4, R. 2. 29, but in Jo. 7. 4, 10, 18. 20 ἐν κρυπτῷ (εἰς κρύπτην subst. L. 11. 33); the opposite to which in John is not ἐν τῷ φανερῷ, but (ἐν) παρρησίᾳ or φανερῶς. Εἰς τὸ μέσον, ἐν τῷ μέσῳ, ἐκ τοῦ μέσου are used if no genitive follows; otherwise the article is dropped, not so much on account of the Hebraic usage (§ 46, 9), as because ἐν τῷ μέσῳ ὑμῶν would be superfluously verbose in a common formula; classical Greek also leaves out the article. Instances of these phrases without a gen. and without an art. (frequent in class. Greek) are Mc. 14. 60 (ins. τὸ DM), L. 4. 35 only DΓΔ al., 'Jo.' 8. 3, 9, A. 4. 7 DEP, 2 Th. 2. 7. Cp. Mc. 13. 27 ἀπ' ἄκρου γῆς ἕως ἄκρου οὐρανοῦ, Mt. 24. 31, vide inf. 6, note 2; ἐπ' ἐσχάτου τῶν ἡμερῶν H. 1. 1, 2 P. 3. 3 (ἐσχάτων from (τὰ) ἔσχατα, as in Barn. 16. 5, Herm. Sim. ix. 12. 3), ἐπ' ἐσχάτου τῶν χρόνων 1 P. 1. 20 (τοῦ χρόνου א, cp. Jd. 18), = בְּאַחֲרִית הַיָּמִים LXX.; ἕως ἐσχάτου τῆς γῆς A. 13. 47 O.T., 1. 8; but τὰ ἔσχατα τοῦ ἀνθρώπου ἐκείνου Mt. 12. 45 = L. 11. 26, opposed to τὰ πρῶτα.

3. The **participle**, when it stands alone and does not refer to a noun or pronoun, takes the article in most cases. Thus it is often found even as **predicate** with the article, though this part of the

sentence elsewhere generally omits the article. There are, however, frequent instances where even a subst. or adj. used predicatively takes the art.: Mc. 6. 3 οὐχ οὗτός ἐστιν ὁ τέκτων; (he who is known by this designation), Mt. 5. 13 ὑμεῖς ἐστε τὸ ἅλας τῆς γῆς, cp. 14, 6. 22 ὁ λύχνος τοῦ σώματός ἐστιν ὁ ὀφθαλμός (σου), 16. 16 σὺ εἶ ὁ χριστὸς ὁ υἱὸς τοῦ θεοῦ, Mc. 15. 2 σὺ εἶ ὁ βασιλεὺς τῶν Ἰουδαίων; Jo. 1. 4, 8 etc.,[1] *i.e.* not *one* salt etc. as compared with another, but that which alone has or deserves this title; more striking are Jo. 3. 10 σὺ εἶ ὁ διδάσκαλος τοῦ Ἰσραήλ 'the (great) teacher,' 5. 35 ἐκεῖνος (John) ἦν ὁ λύχνος ὁ καιόμενος καὶ φαίνων, the light of which one speaks in proverbs; Mt. 24. 45 τίς ἄρα ἐστὶν ὁ πιστὸς δοῦλος καὶ φρόνιμος; in connection with an anarthrous noun Jo. 8. 44 ὅτι ψεύστης ἐστὶν καὶ ὁ πατὴρ αὐτοῦ (a passage which from early times was grossly misunderstood, as though ὁ πατήρ were a further subject, see Tischend.). So with an adjective Mt. 19. 17 εἷς ἐστιν ὁ ἀγαθός, cp. supra 2 ad init. This use is very frequent with participles: Mt. 7. 15 ἐκεῖνά ἐστιν τὰ κοινοῦντα τὸν ἄνθρωπον, Jo. 5. 39 ἐκεῖναί εἰσιν αἱ μαρτυροῦσαι περὶ ἐμοῦ etc., in all which cases it is taken for granted that something which produces this or that result exists, and then this given category is applied to a definite subject. A periphrasis of the verbal idea by means of εἶναι is the only case where an art. could not stand, § 14, 2.—On the other hand a participle which stands alone is occasionally found, as in classical Greek, without the art. even when it is the subject of the sentence as in Mt. 2. 6 O.T. ἡγούμενος, but in this case it must be regarded as a substantive (cp. Wilke-Grimm ἡγεῖσθαι; other exx. in § 73, 3).

4. **Adverbs or prepositional expressions** when used alone to denote persons or things require the article practically in all cases (πλησίον 'neighbour' is used as predicate without ὁ in L. 10. 29, 36); in the same way the article is found governing the genitive, although all these modes of expression are not very frequent in the N.T. οἱ ἐκεῖθεν L. 16. 26, τὰ κάτω, τα ἄνω Jo. 8. 23, Col. 3. 1 f.; οἱ περὶ αὐτόν Mc. 4. 10, L. 22. 49; Πέτρος καὶ οἱ σὺν αὐτῷ L. 9. 32; with the gen. οἱ τοῦ Ζεβεδαίου Jo. 21. 2 (§ 35, 2), τα Καίσαρος and τὰ τοῦ θεοῦ L. 20. 35, οἱ τοῦ Χριστοῦ 1 C. 15. 23; more peculiar is Ja. 4. 14 τὸ (Α τὰ) τῆς αὔριον 'the things of the morrow,' 'what happens to-morrow'; 2 P. 2. 22 τὸ τῆς ἀληθοῦς παροιμίας 'the import of the proverb,' τὰ τῆς εἰρήνης R. 14. 19, 'that which makes for peace.' Especially noticeable are the adverbial accusatives (§ 34, 7) like τὸ κατ' ἐμέ 'so far as I am concerned,' R. 1. 15 (see § 42, 2; elsewhere τὰ κατ' ἐμέ appears as subject or object, Ph. 1. 12, Col. 4. 7), τὸ ἐξ ὑμῶν R. 12. 18, τὸ κατὰ σάρκα 9. 5, where the insertion of the article puts strong emphasis on the limitation, 'so far as the material side is considered,' τὸ καθ' ἡμέραν § 34, 7, in which case the art. may be equally well used or omitted, τὸ πρωΐ (ibid.) etc.— Quite peculiar is L. 17. 4 in D: ἐὰν ἑπτάκις ἁμαρτήσῃ καὶ τὸ ἑπτάκις ἐπιστρέψῃ ('these 7 times,' cp. Syr. Sin., therefore anaphoric).

---

[1] Cp. Winer, § 18, 7.

5. On the **infinitive** with the article see § 71. The neut. sing. of the article may be prefixed, in the same way as to the infin., to **indirect interrogative sentences**, but this usage is rarely represented except in the Lucan writings: R. 8. 26 τὸ γὰρ τί προσευξώμεθα οὐκ οἴδαμεν, 1 Th. 4. 1 καθὼς παρελάβετε παρ' ἡμῶν τὸ πῶς (ὅπως without τὸ FG) δεῖ ὑμᾶς κ.τ.λ. (Herm. Sim. viii. 1. 4, Clem. Hom. i. 6); for Lucan instances see l. 62, 19. 48, 9. 46 (εἰσῆλθεν διαλογισμός, τὸ τίς ἂν εἴη κ.τ.λ.), A. 4. 21, 22. 30. No apparent distinction in meaning is caused by using or omitting the article.—The art. τό is prefixed to quotations of words and sentences as in classical Greek: τὸ ᾽Αγάρ G. 4. 25 (v.l.), τὸ ἀνέβη E. 4. 9, τὸ Οὐ φονεύσεις κ.τ.λ., Mt. 19. 18 (τὸ om. DM.), ἐν τῷ ᾽Αγαπήσεις κ.τ.λ. G. 5. 14; cp. R. 13. 9, H. 12. 27.

6. The **adjective** (or **participle**) which is not independent, but is used as an **attribute** to a substantive, must, as in classical Greek, if the substantive has the article, participate in this art. by being placed in a middle position—ὁ ἀγαθὸς ἄνθρωπος: or, if placed after the substantive, it must take an article of its own—ὁ ἄνθρωπος ὁ ἀγαθός; if it stands outside the article and the substantive without an article, then it is predicative. If it is placed between the art. and the subst. greater emphasis is laid on the adjective—ὁ ἀγαθὸς ἄνθρωπος Mt. 12. 35: if it is placed after the subst. the emphasis falls on the substantive—εἰς τὴν γῆν τὴν ἀγαθήν opposed to πέτραν etc. L. 8. 8. Examples of predicative use: Jo. 5. 35 ἔχω τὴν μαρτυρίαν μείζω=ἡ μ. ἣν ἔχω μείζων ἐστίν, Mc. 8. 17, H. 7. 24, 1 C. 11. 5 ἀκατακαλύπτῳ τῇ κεφαλῇ=ἀκατακάλυπτον ἔχουσα τὴν κεφ. (§ 38, 3), A. 14. 10 εἶπεν μεγάλῃ τῇ φωνῇ (26. 24)=ἡ δὲ φ. ᾖ εἶπεν μεγάλῃ ἦν (also expressed without an art. by φωνῇ μεγάλῃ, the adjective being placed after the noun, 8. 7 etc.). Under this head there comes also the **partitive use** of the adj., with μέσος as in classical Greek, L. 23. 45, Mt. 25. 6, A. 26. 13 (§ 36, 13), while for ἄκρος τὸ ἄκρον with the gen. and so elsewhere τὸ μέσον is used [1] (A. 27. 27 κατὰ μέσον τῆς νυκτός, for which we have κατὰ τὸ μεσονύκτιον 16. 25, never as in classical Greek περὶ μέσας νύκτας: L. 16. 24 τὸ ἄκρον τοῦ δακτύλου αὐτοῦ=τὸν δ. ἄκρον, H. 11. 21, Mc. 13. 27);[2] besides μέσος, this use in the N.T. is only found with πᾶς and ὅλος (where they are contrasted with a part), vide infra 9.—In the case of an attributive adjective it may also happen that the subst. has no article, while the adjective (participle etc.) that follows it has one, since the definiteness is only introduced with the added clause by means of the article, and was not present before. See Kühner Gr. ii.[2] 530: L. 23. 49 γυναῖκες αἱ συνακολουθοῦσαι women viz. those who etc., A. 7. 35 ἐν χειρὶ ἀγγέλου τοῦ ὀφθέντος αὐτῷ an angel viz. that one who etc.; this happens especially with a participle, which may be resolved into an equivalent relative sentence,

---

[1] Also in older Greek (Xenophon etc.), Lobeck Phryn. 537.

[2] Mt. 24. 31 ἀπ' ἄκρων οὐρανῶν ἕως (τῶν add. B) ἄκρων αὐτῶν only resembles the classical usage in appearance: the plural ἄκρα is occasioned by the plural οὐρανοί. Cp. ἔσχατον (-α) sup. 2 ad fin.

§ 47. 6–7.]   THE ARTICLE.   159

cp. § 73, 2; Jo. 14. 27 εἰρήνην ἀφίημι ὑμῖν, εἰρήνην τὴν ἐμὴν δίδωμι ὑμῖν.[1]

7. The rule which holds good for adjectives holds good in the classical language also for **defining clauses with an adverb or preposition**; to a certain degree also for **attributive genitives**: thus ὁ 'Αθηναίων δῆμος or ὁ δῆμος ὁ 'Αθηναίων, although ὁ πατήρ μου is obligatory and ὁ ἵππος τοῦ στρατηγοῦ is possible. In the N.T. genitives in a middle position are frequent, and still more so are genitives placed after the noun which they qualify, but without a repetition of the article: genitives in the later position with the article are not frequent: A. 15. 1 τῷ ἔθει τῷ Μωϋσέως (om. the 2nd τῷ DEHLP),[2] 1 C. 1. 18 ὁ λόγος ὁ τοῦ σταυροῦ,[3] Tit. 2. 10 τὴν διδασκαλίαν τὴν τοῦ σωτῆρος ἡμῶν θεοῦ.[4] Cp. § 46, 12. The **partitive** gen. *must*, as in classical Greek, stand outside the principal clause and without a repetition of the article: οἱ πρῶτοι τῶν 'Ιουδαίων (A. 28. 17 is different, τοὺς ὄντας τῶν 'Ιουδ. πρώτους). Where the defining clause is formed by a **preposition**, if the clause stands after the main clause, the article appears to be especially necessary for the sake of clearness (just as there are scarcely any instances of such a prepositional clause used as attribute to an anarthrous subst.: in 1 C. 12. 31 εἴ τι for ἔτι is read by D*F [Klostermann], whereby καθ' ὑπερβολὴν is separated from ὁδόν, sc. ζηλοῦτε), and the omission of the article in classical authors is by no means sufficiently attested; in the N.T., on the other hand, a considerable number of instances of omission are commonly supposed to exist, apart from those cases where the subst. has additional defining clauses (infra 8), 1 C. 10. 18 βλέπετε τὸν 'Ισραὴλ κατὰ σάρκα, 1 Th. 4. 16 οἱ νεκροὶ (oἱ add FG, cp. it. Vulg. *qui in Chr. sunt*) ἐν Χριστῷ, 2 C. 9. 13 (τῇ) ἁπλότητι τῆς κοινωνίας εἰς αὐτοὺς (where, however, τῇ ὑποταγῇ τῆς ὁμολογίας ὑμῶν [vide infra 8] εἰς τὸ κ.τ.λ. precedes, and ὑμῶν is also to be supplied with κοιν.), R. 6. 4 συνετάφημεν αὐτῷ διὰ τοῦ βαπτίσματος εἰς τὸν θάνατον (cp. 3 εἰς τὸν θ. αὐτοῦ ἐβαπτίσθημεν). This last instance (if our text is correct) appears conclusive; but in τὸν 'Ισραὴλ κατὰ σάρκα the repetition of the art. was quite impossible, as the sense is ὁ κατὰ σ. ὢν 'Ισρ. ('Ισρ. is **predicate**); so with οἱ κατὰ σ. κύριοι E. 6. 5 v.l. οἱ κ. κατὰ σ., Col. 3. 22 id., τὰ ἔθνη ἐν σαρκί E. 2. 11[5]; ὁ δέσμιος ἐν κυρίῳ 4. 1,

---

[1] Buttmann is not to be followed in his assertion (p. 81) that the art. had sometimes to stand before the substantive as well; Winer, § 20, 4 is here correct. L. 5. 36 ἐπίβλημα τὸ ἀπὸ τοῦ καινοῦ is a wrong reading, which is only by error found in Lachmann. A. 15. 23 ἀδελφοῖς (this is the right reading, see the author's note on that passage), τοῖς κατὰ τὴν 'Αντιόχειαν is an address, see § 46, 11, note 3.

[2] Μωϋσέως is found without an art. after the noun qualified in A. (13. 39), 15. 5, Mc. 12. 26, L. 2. 22, 24. 44 (Jo. 7. 23 ὁ νόμος ὁ Μ. א, like 6. 33 ὁ ἄρτος ὁ τοῦ θεοῦ אD), A. 28. 23, 2 C. 3. 7.

[3] In the preceding verse (17) we have ὁ σταυρὸς τοῦ Χριστοῦ; so that ὁ τοῦ στ. appears to be a kind of anaphora.

[4] Appositional clauses like Μαρία ἡ τοῦ 'Ιακώβου sc. μήτηρ do not come under this head.

[5] Hence the reading of DEFG in R. 9. 3 τῶν ἀδελφῶν μου τῶν συγγενῶν μου τῶν (om. cett.) κατὰ σάρκα is wrong.

τοῖς πλουσίοις ἐν τῷ νῦν αἰῶνι 1 Tim. 6. 17, ὁ πιστὸς ἐν ἐλαχίστῳ L. 16. 10, in all which instances the closely connected predicative clause could not be severed by the insertion of the article. With a participle (R. 15. 31 τῶν ἀπειθούντων ἐν τῇ Ἰουδαίᾳ) it is quite obvious that the article is not repeated.

8. If a single substantive has **several defining clauses** it often becomes inconvenient and clumsy to insert all of these between the article and the substantive, and there is a tendency to divide them so that some stand before the substantive and some after it. But in this case the clauses placed after the substantive do not require the repetition of the article, which on the contrary is only repeated in a case where the particular defining clause is emphasized (or implies a contrast), or else if the meaning would be in any way ambiguous. Similarly the additional article can be dispensed with if the substantive is immediately followed by a genitive, which does not require the article (supra 7), and this again is followed by a further defining clause with a preposition: E. 3. 4 τὴν σύνεσίν μου ἐν τῷ μυστηρίῳ τοῦ Χρ. (τὴν ἐν would contrast this particular σύνεσις of Paul with another),[1] G. 1. 13 τὴν ἐμὴν ἀναστροφήν ποτε ἐν τῷ Ἰουδαϊσμῷ. Exx. of repeated article: 1 Th. 1. 8 ἡ πίστις ὑμῶν ἡ πρὸς τὸν θεὸν ἐξελήλυθεν (to prevent ambiguity), 2 C. 9. 3 (ditto), R. 7. 5 (ditto), 8. 39 (emphasis). An adjective (or participle) following a genitive must take the art.: ὁ υἱός μου ὁ ἀγαπητός Mt. 3. 17; cp. 2 C. 6. 7, H. 13. 20, E. 6. 16 (τὰ om. BD*FG); if there is no art. it is a predicate: Tit. 2. 11 ἐπεφάνη ἡ χάρις τοῦ θεοῦ (ἡ add. Cᶜ al.) σωτήριος πᾶσιν ἀνθρώποις. The presence of a numeral between the art. and the noun never renders a subsequent article dispensable: Ja. 1. 1 ταῖς δώδεκα φυλαῖς ταῖς ἐν –, Jo. 6. 13, Ap. 21. 9 (since the numeral is nothing more than a nearer definition of the plural): on the other hand an adjective (or participle) in this position can exempt a subsequent adj. from the article: 1 P. 1. 18 τῆς ματαίας ὑμῶν ἀναστροφῆς πατροπαραδότου (but πατρ. ἀναστρ. is read by C Clem. Orig.), 1 C. 10. 3 τὸ αὐτὸ βρῶμα πνευματικόν? (אᶜDEFG al., but πν. stands before βρ. in א*AB al.), G. 1. 4 τοῦ ἐνεστῶτος αἰῶνος πονηροῦ (אᶜDEFG al.; του αἰ. τοῦ ἐν. π. א*AB a harsher reading; so Herm. Mand. x. 3. 2 τὸ πνεῦμα τὸ δοθὲν τῷ ἀνθρώπῳ ἱλαρόν), cp. Kühner ii.² 532; no offence is caused by ὁ πιστὸς δοῦλος καὶ φρόνιμος Mt. 24. 45, where καὶ carries over the article; on the other hand in Ap. 2. 12 τὴν ῥομφαίαν τὴν δίστομον τὴν ὀξεῖαν the repetition is necessary, as in H. 11. 12 ἡ ἄμμος ἡ παρὰ τὸ χεῖλος τῆς θαλάσσης ἡ ἀναρίθμητος. The repetition of the art. **before** the subst. is rare (more frequent in class. Greek): L. 1. 70 τῶν ἁγίων τῶν ἀπ' αἰῶνος ... προφητῶν only AC al. (cp. A. 3. 21), 1 P. 4. 14 τὸ τῆς δόξης καὶ τὸ τοῦ θεοῦ πνεῦμα; but ὁ ἄλλος, οἱ λοιποί, if not followed immediately by a noun but by a defining clause, require to be followed by an article, as in classical Greek: Jo. 19. 32 τοῦ ἄλλου τοῦ συσταυρωθέντος, Ap. 2. 24 τοῖς λοιποῖς τοῖς

---

[1] 1 C. 8. 7 τῇ συνηθείᾳ (al. συνειδήσει) ἕως ἄρτι τοῦ εἰδώλου, the ordinary position of the gen. being reversed (but τ. εἰδ. ἕ. ἄ. ALP).

ἐν Θυατείροις (since ἀλλ. and λ. do not unite with other defining clauses to form a single phrase).

9. On **οὗτος, ἐκεῖνος, αὐτός 'self' with the article** when used with a subst. see §§ 49, 4; 48, 10. Τοιοῦτος is occasionally preceded by the art. (when referring to individuals or embracing a class): Mt. 19. 14 τῶν τοιούτων (referring to the previous τὰ παιδία); but this rarely happens when a subst. follows, 2 C. 12. 3, Mc. 9. 37 ABDL (τοιούτους before τοὺς in Jo. 4. 23 is predicative). Τὸ τηλικοῦτο κῆτος Herm. Vis. iv. 1. 9. Ἔκαστος is never followed by the art. (Attic usage is different); with ὅλος and πᾶς (cp. supra 6; ἅπας is only found in Luke with any frequency)[1] the relations are more complicated. Thus, with πάντες 'all' the subst., to which it belongs, as one which must be understood in its entirety, is naturally defined by the (generic) article, although πάντες in itself does not require the art. any more than οὗτος does; hence πάντες Ἀθηναῖοι as in Attic A. 17. 21, because names of peoples do not need the art., cp. 26. 4, § 46, 12, note 2; also in (Luke and) Paul πάντες ἄνθρωποι A. 22. 15, R. 5. 12, 18, 12. 17, 18 etc. (Herm. Mand. iii. 3), often in the weakened sense of 'all the world,' 'everybody'; cp. for Attic usage Kühner ii.[2] 545 [2] (πάντες ἄγγελοι H. 1. 6 O.T.). It is just this weakening of meaning which is the cause of the omission; the words do not denote any totality as such, but the meaning approximates to that of πᾶς 'every' (vide infra), as in πᾶσιν ἀγαθοῖς G. 6. 6, 1 P. 2. 1 πάσας καταλαλιάς (πᾶσαν καταλαλιάν ℵ*), πᾶσιν ὑστερουμένοις Herm. Mand. ii. 4. But in 2 P. 3. 16 πάσαις ταῖς (τ. om. ABC) ἐπιστολαῖς, E. 3. 8 πάντων τῶν ἁγίων (τῶν ins. P. only), the art. according to classical usage can by no means be omitted; a similar violation of classical usage is seen in L. 4. 20 πάντων ἐν τῇ συναγωγῇ ('those who were in the syn.'), cp. 25.[3] Ἀμφότεροι like πάντες also takes the art., but only in L. 5. 7 (elsewhere used without a subst.). Πᾶς '**whole**' in Attic is only used of definite individual ideas, ὅλος 'whole' also of indefinite ideas, and so in Jo. 7. 23 ὅλον ἄνθρωπον 'a whole man,' A. 11. 26 ἐνιαυτὸν ὅλον, also perhaps L. 5. 5 δι' ὅλης νυκτὸς 'a whole night' (v.l. with τῆς); the latter word is also used with anarthrous city-names, A. 21. 31 ὅλη Ἱερουσαλήμ like πᾶσα (om. D) Ἱεροσόλυμα Mt. 2. 3 (§ 46, 11); elsewhere it always takes the article. Πᾶς before an anarthrous subst. means '**every**' (not every individual like ἕκαστος, but any you please): Mt. 3. 10 πᾶν δένδρον, 19. 3 κατὰ πᾶσαν αἰτίαν, etc.; πᾶσα δικαιοσύνη = πᾶν ὃ ἂν ᾖ δίκαιον (W.-Gr.) Mt. 3. 15; it is also equivalent to *summus* (W.-Gr.): μετὰ πάσης παρρησίας A. 4. 29; πάσῃ συνειδήσει ἀγαθῇ A. 23. 1 (in

---

[1] The instances besides those in Luke are Mt. 6. 32, 24. 39 (πάντας D), 28. 11 (ἅπαντα A), Mc. 8. 25 (D πάντα), 11. 32 v.l., 'Mc.' 16. 15 (om. D), G. 3. 28 ℵAB³, E. 6. 13 (all MSS.), Ja. 3. 2. The Attic distinction, that πᾶς stands after a vowel, ἅπας after a consonant (Diels Gött. Gel. Anz. 1894, 298 ff.), cannot be made in all cases even in Luke, cp. 1. 3 ἄνωθεν πᾶσιν, although ἅπας is generally found after a consonant.

[2] So Dem. 8. 5, 42.

[3] The words ἐν τῇ συναγ. are probably spurious, as they vary much in their position in different MSS.

every respect). The distinction between πᾶς with and without the art. appears in 2 C. 1. 4 (W.-Gr.): ὁ παρακαλῶν ἡμᾶς ἐπὶ πάσῃ τῇ θλίψει ἡμῶν (that which actually exists in its totality), εἰς τὸ δύνασθαι ἡμᾶς παρακαλεῖν τοὺς ἐν πάσῃ θλ. (any which may arise); so also A. 12. 11 πάσης τῆς προσδοκίας τοῦ λαοῦ τῶν Ἰουδαίων (the whole expectation actually entertained); 1 C. 13. 2 πᾶσαν τὴν γνῶσιν and π. τ. πίστιν (all that there is in its entirety). But in imitation of Hebrew we have πᾶς Ἰσραήλ R. 11. 26, the whole of I., πᾶς οἶκος Ἰσρ. A. 2. 36 (ἐξ ὅλης καρδίας αὐτῶν Herm. Sim. vii. 4), cp. § 46, 9; similar but not incorrect is πᾶσα σάρξ 'all flesh,' 'everything fleshly' = 'all men' (כָּל־בָּשָׂר) Mt. 24. 22, L. 3. 6, R. 3. 20, 1 C. 1. 29 (never otherwise), cp. sup. πάντες ἄνθρωποι; with a negative as in Mt. loc. cit. οὐκ ἂν ἐσώθη π. σ. like Hebr. כֹּל ... לֹא = 'no flesh,' § 51, 2. In other cases πᾶς ὁ and πᾶς must be carefully distinguished: Ph. 1. 3 ἐπὶ πάσῃ τῇ μνείᾳ 'the whole' (or omit τῇ with DE), R. 8. 22 πᾶσα ἡ κτίσις 'the whole creation,' πᾶσα κτ. 'every created thing' 1 P. 2. 13, Col. 1. 23 (with τῇ א°D° al.), 15 πρωτότοκος πάσης κτίσεως. A very frequent use is that of πᾶς ὁ with a participle (§ 73, 3) cp. the partic. with art. without πᾶς e.g. ὁ κλέπτων 'he who stole hitherto' E. 4. 28; without an art. Mt. 13. 19 παντὸς ἀκούοντος, L. 11. 4; so always if a subst. is interposed, Mt. 3. 10 πᾶν δένδρον μὴ ποιοῦν κ.τ.λ.—Ὁ πᾶς, οἱ πάντες contrast the whole or the totality with the part, A. 19. 7 ἦσαν οἱ πάντες ἄνδρες ('on the whole,' 'together') ὡσεὶ δώδεκα (cp. class. examples, e.g. Thuc. 1. 60), 27. 37, G. 5. 14 ὁ πᾶς νόμος ἐν ἑνὶ λόγῳ πεπλήρωται (opposed to the individual laws), A. 20. 18 τὸν πάντα χρόνον (ἀπὸ πρώτης ἡμέρας has preceded); frequently in Paul we have οἱ πάντες without a subst., 1 C. 9. 22 (a comprehensive term for the individual persons named in verses 20 ff.; also in 19 πᾶσιν has preceded), 10. 17, R. 11. 32, E. 4. 13, 2 C. 5. 10 τοὺς πάντας ἡμᾶς (not only he, of whom he had previously spoken), somewhat differently in 15 οἱ πάντες 'they all' (ὑπὲρ πάντων has preceded), cp. Ph. 2. 21; similarly τὰ πάντα in 1 C. 12. 6 (opposed to the individual thing), 19, R. 8. 32, 11. 36 (the universe), 1 C. 15. 27 f. (similarly, and with reference to πάντα preceding, etc.; also A. 17. 25 (Mc. 4. 11 v.l.). A peculiar use is 1 Tim. 1. 16 τὴν ἅπασαν (πᾶσαν) μακροθυμίαν 'the utmost (cp. supra) long-suffering which He has,' cp. Herm. Sim. ix. 24. 3 τὴν ἁπλότητα αὐτῶν καὶ πᾶσαν νηπιότητα. Like οἱ πάντες, τὰ πάντα we also have οἱ ἀμφότεροι, τὰ ἀμφότερα E. 2. 14, 16, 18 (A. 23. 8, but here there is no contrast to the individual things, so that ἀμφότερα ταῦτα would be more correct); τοὺς δύο E. 2. 15 utrumque, because οἱ ἀμφότεροι 16, 18 had to be used to express utrique.

10. A phrase in **apposition** with a **proper name** takes the article, if a well-known person has to be distinguished from another person of the same name, as Ἰωάνης ὁ βαπτιστής, Φίλιππος ὁ εὐαγγελιστής A. 21. 8, ὁ βασιλεὺς Ἡρῴδης (v.l. Ἡ. ὁ β.) 12. 1, Ἀγρίππας ὁ β. 25. 13; in that case the proper name itself must generally stand without the art., § 46, 10 (hence the reading in A. 12. 12 τῆς [אABD] Μαρίας τῆς μητρός is incorrect, cp. ibid. 25 D*); on the other hand we have Σίμωνι βυρσεῖ 10. 6, Μνάσωνί τινι Κυπρίῳ 21. 16,

Μαναὴν Ἡρῴδου τοῦ τετραάρχου σύντροφος 13. 1 (ibid. the MSS. except D* wrongly read Λούκιος ὁ Κυρηναῖος); the necessity for the person to be well known does not hold in the case of ὁ (ἐπι)καλούμενος with a surname following, or the equivalent ὁ καί, or again where a man is denoted by the name of his father or other relation by an art. and gen. (with or without υἱός etc.), § 35, 2. On Φαραὼ βασιλέως Αἰγύπτου A. 7. 10 see § 46, 9.—In the case of the anarthrous θεός (§ 46, 6) the article may be dispensed with in a clause in apposition with it, but only in more formal and ceremonious language, as in the opening of an epistle, R. 1. 7 ἀπὸ θεοῖ πατρὸς ἡμῶν καὶ κυρίου Ἰ. Χρ., 1 Th. 1. 1 ἐν θεῷ πατρὶ καὶ κυρίῳ Ἰ. Χρ., 1 Tim. 1. 1 ἀπόστολος ... κατ' ἐπιταγὴν θεοῦ σωτῆρος ἡμῶν (cp. § 46, 11, note 3); similarly κύριος (§ 46, 6) is used in apposition to Ἰησ. Χρ., though not often except in an opening clause (Ph. 3. 20).—In ὁ ἀντίδικος ὑμῶν διάβολος 1 P. 5. 8 ἀντίδ. is treated as an adjective; Jo. 8. 44 ὑμεῖς ἐκ τοῦ πατρὸς τοῦ διαβόλου ἐστέ must mean 'you are descended from your father (cp. 38) the devil'; but the first article is apparently spurious (and πατρός is predicative, supra 6). On Mt. 12. 24 see § 46, 9.

11. Where **several substantives** are **connected by καί** the article may be carried over from the first of them to the one or more substantives that follow, especially if they are of the same gender and number as the first, but occasionally too where the gender is different: Col. 2. 22 κατὰ τὰ ἐντάλματα καὶ διδασκαλίας τῶν ἀνθρώπων, L. 14. 23 εἰς τὰς ὁδοὺς καὶ φραγμούς, 1. 6, Mc. 12. 33 v.l. (Winer, § 19, 3). Inversely there are a number of instances where with the same gender and number the repetition of the article is necessary or more appropriate: A. 26. 30 ὁ βασιλεὺς καὶ ὁ ἡγεμών (different persons), 1 C. 3. 8 ὁ φυτεύων καὶ ὁ ποτίζων ἕν εἰσιν (ditto), Jo. 19. 6 οἱ ἀρχιερεῖς καὶ οἱ ὑπηρέται (whereas ἀρχ. with πρεσβύτεροι or γραμματεῖς may dispense with a repetition of the art., Mt. 16. 21 etc.), μεταξὺ τοῦ θυσιαστηρίου καὶ τοῦ οἴκου L. 11. 51 (Mt. 23. 35). Also in the case of τε καί repetition generally takes place, though in A. 14. 6 we have τῶν ἐθνῶν τε καὶ (τῶν add. D) Ἰουδαίων. There is frequently a variety of readings, but the alteration in the sense is for the most part unimportant. The article appears to be dropped, not unnaturally, between two clauses in apposition connected by καί, in Tit. 2. 13 (τὴν) ἐπιφάνειαν τῆς δόξης τοῦ μεγάλου θεοῦ καὶ σωτῆρος ἡμῶν Ἰ. Χρ., cp. 2 P. 1. 1 (but ℵ here reads κυρίου for θεοῦ, probably rightly, cp. 11, 2. 20, 3. 2, 18); however in Titus loc. cit. σωτῆρος ἡμ. Ἰ. Χρ. may be taken by itself and separated from the preceding, in which case cp. for the loss of the art. supra 10; Winer, § 19, 5, note 1.

SYNTAX OF THE PRONOUNS.

§ 48. PERSONAL, REFLEXIVE, AND POSSESSIVE PRONOUNS.

1. The **nominatives of the personal pronouns**—ἐγώ, σύ, ἡμεῖς, ὑμεῖς—are, as in classical Greek, not employed except for emphasis or contrast. Jo. 4. 10 σὺ ἂν ᾔτησας αὐτόν (not, vice versâ, I thee), A. 4. 7 ἐν ποίᾳ δυνάμει ἐποιήσατε τοῦτο ὑμεῖς; (people like *you, this* miracle), Jo. 5. 44 πῶς δύνασθε ὑμεῖς πιστεῦσαι (persons like you), 39 ὑμεῖς δοκεῖτε ἐν αὐταῖς ζωὴν αἰώνιον ἔχειν (you yourselves), 38 ὃν ἀπέστειλεν ἐκεῖνος, τούτῳ ὑμεῖς οὐ πιστεύετε (ἐκεῖνος – ὑμεῖς contrasted), 1. 30 ὑπὲρ οὗ ἐγὼ εἶπον (I myself), 42 σὺ εἶ Σίμων..., σὺ κληθήσῃ Κηφᾶς (cp. 49, this particular person as opposed to others), E. 5. 32 τὸ μυστήριον τοῦτο μέγα ἐστίν· ἐγὼ δὲ λέγω εἰς Χριστὸν καὶ εἰς τὴν ἐκκλησίαν (subject and speaker contrasted).—As an equivalent for the third person in the N.T., especially in Luke (Mt., Mc.; also LXX.), **αὐτός** is used = '*he*' with emphasis (besides ὁ in ὁ δέ, ὁ μὲν οὖν, § 46, 3)[1], L. 2. 28 (the parents bring in the child Jesus) καὶ αὐτὸς (Simeon) ἐδέξατο αὐτὸ κ.τ.λ. (in Simeon's own narration of the event it would run καὶ ἐγὼ ἐδεξάμην), 1. 22, 2. 50 (καὶ αὐτοί), 9. 36 (ditto), 11. 14 (καὶ αὐτὸ), L. 24. 21 ἠλπίζομεν ὅτι αὐτός ἐστιν ὁ μέλλων λυτροῦσθαι τὸν Ἰσραήλ (here too ἐγώ would be used if the story were told in the first person), Mc. 14. 44 ὃν ἂν φιλήσω, αὐτός ἐστιν (*he* is the man), A. 3. 10 ἐπεγίνωσκον δὲ αὐτόν, ὅτι αὐτὸς (BDEP οὗτος, cp. Jo. 9. 8 f.) ἦν ὁ ... καθήμενος (1st pers. ὅτι ἐγὼ ἤμην, cp. Jo. 9. 9), cp. Herm. Mand. vi. 2. 5 γίνωσκε ὅτι αὐτός ἐστιν ἐν σοί: Mt. 12. 50 (cp. with οὗτος Mc. 3. 35), 5. 4 ff. Also αὐτὸς δέ, Mc. 5. 40 (ὁ δὲ A), L. 4. 30, 8. 37 etc. (even where the name is added, Mt. 3. 4 αὐτὸς δὲ ὁ [ὁ om. D] Ἰωάνης, 'but he, John'; Mc. 6. 17 αὐτὸς γὰρ ὁ [ὁ om. D] Ἡρ.); the feminine of αὐτός is not so used: αὕτη should be written in L. 2. 37, 7. 12, 8. 42 καὶ αὕτη (καὶ αὐτὸς is also a wrong reading in 8. 41 BD, and in 19. 2 where D reads οὗτος without καί. Classical Greek employs sometimes οὗτος, sometimes ἐκεῖνος (ὁ), § 49, 2 and 3; in modern Greek αὐτός has become a demonstrative pronoun and dropped the meaning of 'self' (for which ὁ ἴδιος is used). Of the oblique cases, the genitive alone is used with emphasis in this way (class. ἐκείνου etc.): L. 24. 31 αὐτῶν δὲ διηνοίχθησαν οἱ ὀφθαλμοί, Mt. 5. 3, 10, cp. infra 7 (Herm. Sim. v. 7. 3 αὐτοῦ γάρ ἐστιν πᾶσα ἐξουσία, viii. 7. 1 ἄκουε καὶ περὶ αὐτῶν).

2. A prominent feature in the Greek of the N.T. (and still more in that of the LXX.) is the extraordinary **frequency** of the oblique cases of the **personal pronouns** used without emphasis. The reason for this is the dependence of the language on Semitic speech, where

---

[1] Cp. Buttmann, p. 93 ff. (Winer, § 22, note 4). The use is an old one, though foreign to Attic writers: Hom. Il. iii. 282 αὐτὸς ἔπειθ' Ἑλένην ἐχέτω ... ἡμεῖς δέ, 'he ... we.'

§ 48. 2–3.] *POSSESSIVE PRONOUNS.* 165

these pronouns are easily and conveniently attached as suffixes to substantival and verbal forms, and are therefore everywhere employed, where the full expression of the thought requires them. The case is different with classical Greek, which has separate words for them, of which some indeed are enclitic, but those for the 3rd person and for the plural are dissyllables, and therefore it expresses these words only so far as they are essential to the lucidity of the sense, while in other cases it leaves them to be understood. The tendency of the N.T., then, is to express the pronoun in each case with every verb which is joined with other verbs in a sentence, and not, according to the classical method, to write it once and leave it to be supplied in the other instances; again, the possessive genitives μου, σου, αὐτοῦ etc. are used with a quite peculiar and tiresome frequency, being employed, to take a special instance, with reference to the subject of the sentence, in which connection the simple pronoun cannot possibly stand in classical Greek, but the reflexive is used instead, vide infra 6. Still no rule can be laid down, the practice depends on the pleasure of the writer, and superfluous pronouns are often omitted by the better MSS. As in classical Greek 'my father' may be expressed at the option of the writer by ὁ πατήρ μου (ὁ ἐμὸς π.) or ὁ πατήρ, so also in John's Gospel Christ speaks of God as ὁ πατήρ μου, and more often as ὁ πατήρ, 8. 38 ἐγὼ ἃ ἑόρακα παρὰ τῷ πατρὶ (μου add. אD al.) λαλῶ, καὶ ὑμεῖς οὖν ἃ ἠκούσατε παρὰ τοῦ πατρὸς (so without ὑμῶν BLT) ποιεῖτε: Mt. 27. 24 ἀπενίψατο τὰς χεῖρας. The pronoun is omitted in other cases or connections: A. 16. 15 παρεκάλεσεν (*sc.* ἡμᾶς) λέγουσα (without ἡμῖν), 19 ἐπιλαβόμενοι τὸν Παῦλον καὶ τὸν Σιλᾶν εἵλκυσαν κ.τ.λ. (instead of ἐπιλαβ. τοῦ Π. ... εἵλκ. αὐτούς). On the other hand we have 22. 17 ἐγένετό μοι ὑποστρέψαντι—προσευχομένου μου—γενέσθαι με (§ 74, 5), 7. 21 ἐκτεθέντος δὲ αὐτοῦ, ἀνείλατο αὐτὸν—καὶ ἐξεθρέψατο αὐτόν (vide ibid.; also for combinations such as Mt. 6. 3 σοῦ ποιοῦντος ... μὴ γνώτω ἡ ἀριστερά σου, Mt. 8. 1, v.l. ἐξελθόντι αὐτῷ ... ἠκολούθησαν αὐτῷ). On the acc. and inf. instead of the inf. see § 72, 2 and 3; on αὐτοῦ etc. after the relative § 50, 4.

3. The longer and **unenclitic** forms of the **pronoun** of the **1st pers. sing.**—ἐμοῦ, ἐμοί, ἐμέ—are employed as in classical Greek to give emphasis or to mark a contrast; they are generally used after a preposition (even ἕνεκεν), except after πρός: Mt. 25. 36 (א ἐμέ), Mc. 9. 19 (do.), A. 22. 10 (do.: in 8 ἐμέ א*AB); with πρός the short forms are used even where there is a contrast, Mt. 3. 14 ἐγὼ χρείαν ἔχω ὑπὸ σοῦ βαπτισθῆναι, καὶ σὺ ἔρχῃ πρός με (where Tisch. writes πρὸς μέ; the classical language certainly knows nothing of an accented μέ); only in Jo. 6. 37 πρὸς ἐμέ is read by nearly all MSS., in the next clause πρὸς ἐμέ is read by אE al., πρός με ABD al. (we also find ἐνώπιόν μου in several MSS. in Lc. 4. 7). Cp. Kühner Gr. i.³, i. 347. It follows that in the case of the second person, the forms σοῦ etc. after prepositions other than πρός should be accented. Of the strengthened Attic forms ἔγωγε, ἔμοιγε there are no instances in the N.T.

4. There is a wide-spread tendency among Greek writers, when they speak of themselves, to say ἡμεῖς instead of ἐγώ. The same meaning is often attributed to many instances of the 1st pers. plur. in St. Paul; in his letters, however, there are usually several persons from whom, as is shown in the opening clause, the letter proceeds, and where this is not the case (Pastoral Epp.; Romans, Ephesians), no such plurals are found: cp. *e.g.* Col. 1. 3 εὐχαριστοῦμεν with E. 1. 15 κἀγὼ ... οὐ παύομαι εὐχαριστῶν. In R. 1. 5 δι' οὗ ἐλάβομεν χάριν καὶ ἀποστολὴν κ.τ.λ. while the language clearly applies to Paul himself (ἀποστ.), yet the words are not limited to him (χάριν), but the persons addressed, and indeed all Christians (cp. just before, 4 τοῦ κυρίου ἡμῶν), are fellow-partakers in the χάρις; so that ἔλαβον χάριν would not have been suitable. The author of the Epistle to the Hebrews, however (an epistle, moreover, which has no introduction at all with the name of the writer), appears really to use the plur. and sing. without distinction, 5. 11, 6. 1, 3, 9, 11 etc., 13. 18 f. (plur. – sing.), 22 f. (ἐπέστειλα, ἡμῶν): and even in those Pauline Epistles, which are indited in the name of several persons, it is not always possible appropriately to refer the plural to these different persons, *e.g.* in 2 C. 10. 11 ff. Similarly in 1 John 1. 4 γράφομεν is apparently identical in meaning with γράφω (2. 1 and elsewhere).—Quite different is such a plural as we meet with in Mc. 4. 30 πῶς ὁμοιώσωμεν τὴν βασιλείαν τοῦ θεοῦ, where in a way that is not unknown to us the audience are represented as taking part in the deliberation.

5. The pronoun of the 3rd person **αὐτοῦ** etc. is very frequently used with a **disregard to formal agreement**, where there is no noun of the same gender and number to which it may refer. The occurrence of the name of a place is sufficient ground for denoting the inhabitants of it by αὐτῶν: A. 8. 5 Φίλιππος κατελθὼν εἰς τὴν πόλιν τῆς Σαμαρείας ἐκήρυσσεν **αὐτοῖς** τὸν χριστόν, 16. 10, 20. 2, 2 C. 2. 12 f. etc.; in the same way κόσμος ... αὐτοῖς ibid. 5. 19, πᾶν ... αὐτοῖς (ℵ*αὐτῷ) Jo. 17. 2, see § 32, 1 (classical usage is similar). Further we have L. 23. 50 f. βουλευτὴς ... αὐτῶν, *i.e.* the members of the high council (the reference being understood from the preceding narrative); R. 2. 26 ἐὰν ἡ ἀκροβυστία τὰ δικαιώματα τοῦ νόμου φυλάσσῃ, *i.e.* ὁ ἀκροβυστίαν ἔχων, and therefore followed by αὐτοῦ; 1 P. 3. 14 τὸν φόβον αὐτῶν, the persecutors, who are understood from the sense and context, E. 5. 12 ὑπ' αὐτῶν, those who belong to the σκότος of verse 11, etc. To these must be added instances of *constructio ad sensum* (§ 31, 4) such as Mc. 5. 41 κρατήσας τῆς χειρὸς τοῦ παιδίου λέγει αὐτῇ, and on the other hand cases where the subject referred to is obvious without further explanation, as in Jo. 20. 15 αὐτόν, 1 Jo. 2. 12 αὐτοῦ.[1] Cp. Buttmann, p. 92 f., Winer, § 22, 3. The relative pronoun is sometimes used in a similar way: G. 4. 19 τεκνία μου, οὕς, Jo. 6. 9 παιδάριον, ὃς (v.l. ὅ), Ph. 2. 15 γενεᾶς σκολιᾶς, ἐν οἷς; also A. 15. 36 κατὰ πᾶσαν πόλιν, ἐν αἷς, 2 P. 3. 1 δευτέραν ἤδη ἐπιστολήν, ἐν αἷς (*i.e.* ταῖς δυσὶν ἐπιστ.) etc.

6. The **reflexive pronouns**—ἐμαυτοῦ, σεαυτοῦ, ἑαυτοῦ, with plural

---

[1] In Jo. 8. 44 (ὁ πατήρ) αὐτοῦ (§ 47, 3) may be referred without difficulty through ψεύστης to ὅταν λαλῇ τὸ ψεῦδος.

for 1st, 2nd, and 3rd persons ἑαυτῶν (§ 13, 1)[1]—have in the N.T. been to some extent displaced by the simple personal pronoun; but a more noticeable fact is that they have had no share at all in the extended use which the personal pronouns acquired (supra 2). When the pronoun is employed as a direct complement to the verb, referring back to the subject, no other than the reflexive form is found in all (or nearly all) authors; but if the pronoun is governed by a preposition, there are at least in Matthew numerous instances of the simple pronoun being used; finally, if a substantive governing the pronoun is interposed, and the pronoun has no emphasis at all (so that classical writers would omit it altogether, supra 2), then the reflexive form is never employed. Thus, in proportion as the number and the independent character of the words interposed between the pronoun and the subject becomes greater, the rarer becomes the use of the reflexive. (For instances of this in classical writers, Kühner ii.[2] 489, 494.) Direct complement: Mt. 6. 19 f. θησαυρίζετε ὑμῖν θησαυροὺς (instead of ἑαυτοῖς).[2] After a preposition: Mt. 5. 29 f., 18. 8 f. βάλε ἀπὸ σοῦ, 6. 2 μὴ σαλπίσῃς ἔμπροσθέν σου, 11. 29 ἄρατε τὸν ζυγόν μου ἐφ' ὑμᾶς, 13. 13 παράλαβε μετὰ σοῦ BDI (σεαυτοῦ אKLM). The simple form is still more frequent where two pronouns are connected: 18. 15 ἔλεγξον ... μεταξὺ σοῦ καὶ αὐτοῦ, 17. 27 δὸς ἀντὶ ἐμοῦ καὶ σοῦ. (In Semitic speech, where the reflexive is expressed by a periphrasis with נפשׁ[3], there can be no question of this kind of expression in these cases.) Yet even Mt. has εἶπον ἐν ἑαυτοῖς (9. 3, 21), μερισθεῖσα καθ' ἑαυτῆς (12. 25), 15. 30 ἔχοντες μεθ' ἑαυτῶν, etc.—In the case of a possessive genitive attached to a substantive, the MS. evidence is often conflicting, not however in the case of ἐμαυτοῦ or σεαυτοῦ, but only with ἑαυτοῦ. The only instance with ἐμαυτοῦ is 1 C. 10. 33 τὸ ἐμαυτοῦ συμφέρον (of σεαυτοῦ there is no example); then with ἑαυτῶν = 2nd pers. we have H. 10. 25 τὴν ἐπισυναγωγὴν ἑαυτῶν, with ἑαυτοῦ, -ῆς, -ῶν between the art. and the noun (infra 7) we have Mc. 8. 35 v.l., L. 11. 21 τὴν ἑαυτοῦ αὐλήν (D. τ. α. αὐτοῦ), 13. 34 τὴν ἑαυτῆς νοσσιάν (τὰ νοσσία αὐτῆς D), 14. 26 (ἑαυτοῦ stands after the noun in אB), 33 (αὐτοῦ D al.), also 16. 8 εἰς τὴν γενεὰν τὴν ἑαυτῶν; frequent in the Pauline Epp., e.g. R. 4. 19, 5. 8, 16. 4, 18. On the other hand, the simple pronoun is also used e.g. in A. 28. 19 τοῦ ἔθνους μου, ibid. β text τὴν ψυχήν μου, G. 1. 14 μου

---

[1] The corresponding use of ἑαυτοῦ for (ἐμαυτοῦ or) σεαυτοῦ, which is far from being established for classical prose, rests even in the N.T. on doubtful authority: Jo. 18. 34 ἀφ' ἑαυτοῦ σὺ τοῦτο λέγεις, but ἀπὸ σεαυτοῦ אBC*L: R. 13. 9 = G. 5. 14 O.T. ὡς ἑαυτόν read by FGLP and FGLN*P in the respective passages; cp. Herm. Vis. iv. 1. 5 ἠρξάμην λέγειν ἐν ἑαυτῷ (א* as; ἐμαυτ. א°), Sim. ii. 1 τί σὺ ἐν ἑαυτῷ ζητεῖς (א is wanting), ix. 2. 5: Clem. Hom. xiv. 10, xvii. 18 for ἐμαυτοῦ. Buttm. 99. On ὑμῶν αὐτῶν 1 C. 5. 13 vide infra 10.

[2] We also have ἔδοξα ἐμαυτῷ with inf. in A. 26. 9, whereas classical Greek in a case like this where no stress is laid on the reflexive, says δοκῶ μοι. On ἑαυτόν as subj. of the accus. and inf. see § 72, 2; Buttm. 236 (αὐτόν for ἑαυτὸν A. 25. 21).

[3] Hence in translating from Semitic the reflexive is interchangeable with τὴν ψυχὴν αὐτοῦ: cp. L. 9. 25 ἑαυτὸν δὲ ἀπολέσας ἢ ζημιωθείς with 24 ἀπολέσῃ τὴν ψ. αὐτοῦ. Cp. Winer § 22, 7 note 3.

bis, 16 τὸν υἱὸν αὐτοῦ, etc.; on ἐμός σός, vide infra 7.—Other instances of reflexives: Mt. 12. 45 πονηρότερα ἑαυτοῦ (DE* αυτου), Mc. 5. 26 τὰ παρ' ἑαυτῆς (αὐτῆς ABL), L. 24. 27 τὰ περὶ ἑαυτοῦ (αὐτοῦ DEL al.); on the other hand, Ph. 2. 23 ἀφίδω τὰ περὶ ἐμέ, R. 1. 15 τὸ κατ' ἐμὲ πρόθυμος sc. εἰμί (§ 42, 2). A loose but intelligible use is 1 C. 10. 29 λέγω οὐχὶ τὴν ἑαυτοῦ.—The mode of strengthening the reflexive by means of αὐτός, frequent in Attic, appears in a few instances (from the literary language): 2 C. 10. 12 αὐτοὶ ἐν ἑαυτοῖς ἑαυτοὺς μετροῦντες, 1. 9, A. 5. 36 D κατελύθη αὐτὸς δι' ἑαυτοῦ (αυτου D); but in Jo. 9. 21 the pronouns must not be connected: αὐτὸς (he himself) περὶ ἑαυτοῦ λαλήσει (cp. R. 8. 23).—On ἑαυτῶν for ἀλλήλων, vide infra 9.

7. The **possessives** ἐμός, σός, ἡμέτερος, ὑμέτερος are employed in classical Greek to represent the **emphasized** genitives ἐμοῦ, σοῦ etc., whereas if there is no emphasis on the pronoun possession is denoted by the genitives μου, σου, ἡμῶν, ὑμῶν; the position of the latter, as of the corresponding αὐτοῦ, -ῆς, -ῶν of the 3rd pers., if the subst. takes the article, is after the substantive (and the article is not repeated), or even before the article, as in Mt. 8. 8 ἵνα μου ὑπὸ τὴν στέγην, 1 Th. 3. 10 ἰδεῖν ὑμῶν τὸ πρόσωπον, 13 στηρίξαι ὑμῶν τὰς καρδίας, or lastly, if the subst. has an attribute before it, the position of the pronoun is after the attribute: 2 C. 4. 16 ὁ ἔξω ἡμῶν ἄνθρωπος, Mt. 27. 60 ἐν τῷ καινῷ αὐτοῦ μνημείῳ, 1 P. 1. 3, 2. 9, 5. 10 etc. (Buttmann, p. 101). On the other hand, the possessives take the position of the attributes, as in classical Greek is the case with emphasized genitives like ἐμαυτοῦ, σεαυτοῦ, ἑαυτοῦ, τούτου, ἐκείνου (=his). The noticeable point in the N.T. is that while ἐμοῦ and σοῦ are not used as possessives (except in connection with another gen., R. 16. 13 αὐτοῦ καὶ ἐμοῦ, 1. 12), the emphatic ὑμῶν (in the Pauline Epp., Buttmann 102) undoubtedly is so used (in the position of the attribute; cp. Soph. Oed. R. 1458 ἡ μὲν ἡμῶν μοῖρα), and hence it happens that the words ἡμέτερος and ὑμέτερος are by no means represented in all the N.T. writings (there are not ten instances of each, none at all e.g. in Mt., Mc.): 1 C. 16. 18 τὸ ἐμὸν πνεῦμα καὶ τὸ ὑμῶν, 2 C. 1. 6 ὑπὲρ τῆς ὑμῶν παρακλήσεως (object. gen., which however may equally well be expressed by the possessive: R. 11. 31 τῷ ὑμετέρῳ ἐλέει, 1 C. 11. 24 τὴν ἐμὴν ἀνάμνησιν, W. § 22, 7, cp. for class. exx. Kühner ii.[2] 486, note 11), 2 C. 9. 2 τὸ ὑμῶν (v.l. ἐξ ὑμ.) ζῆλος, 1 C. 16. 17 τὸ ὑμῶν (ὑμέτερον BCD al.) ὑστέρημα, 1 Th. 3. 7, Clem. Hom. x. 15 τῷ ὑμῶν (reflex.) παραδείγματι. Still the possessive is also found in another position in ἡμῶν γὰρ τὸ πολίτευμα Ph. 3. 20 (stronger emphasis, for which τὸ γὰρ ἡμ. πολ. was not sufficient), and there are similar exceptions in the case of reflexive genitives: τὴν ἐπισυναγωγὴν ἑαυτῶν H. 10. 25 (i.e. ὑμῶν αὐτῶν), A. 21. 11 δήσας ἑαυτοῦ τοὺς πόδας (there is a wrong reading αὐτοῦ, which would refer to Paul), G. 6. 4 τὸ ἔργον ἑαυτοῦ, ibid. 8 εἰς τὴν σάρκα ἑαυτοῦ (αὐτοῦ D*FG, cp. the v.l. in E. 4. 16, Mt. 21. 8, 23. 37; Herm. Vis. iii. 11. 3 ἑαυτῶν [2nd pers.] τὰς μερίμνας, Sim. iv. 5 τὸν κύριον ἑαυτῶν [3rd pers.], v. 4. 3; in general, according to what has been said above [see 6] αὐτοῦ deserves the preference). **Emphatic αὐτοῦ=his** is found in the position of the attribute: Tit. 3. 5 κατὰ τὸ αὐτοῦ ἔλεος (opposed to preceding ἡμεῖς; τὸ ἔλ. αὐτοῦ

§ 48. 7-9.]   POSSESSIVE PRONOUNS.   169

D*EFG), H. 2. 4 κατὰ τὴν αὐτοῦ θέλησιν, R. 11. 11 τῷ αὐτῶν παραπτώματι ἡ σωτηρία τοῖς ἔθνεσιν 3. 24, 1 Th. 2. 19, Ja. 1. 18 (v.l. ἑαυτοῦ); cp. supra 1 (in R. 3. 25 ἐν τῷ αὐτοῦ αἵματι the gen. is from αὐτός 'self').[1] For this classical Greek uses ἐκείνου (which may even have reflexive force, Kühner ii.[2] 559, 12); the latter appears in the correct position (that of the attribute), in Jo. 5. 47, 2 C. 8. 9, 14, 2 Tim. 2. 26 etc. (exception R. 6. 21 τὸ τέλος ἐκείνων); cp. with τούτου etc., R. 11. 30, 2 P. 1. 15 (but contrary to rule are A. 13. 23 τούτου ὁ θεὸς ἀπὸ τοῦ σπέρματος, cp. on Ph. 3. 20 above; Ap. 18. 15 οἱ ἔμποροι τούτων; H. 13. 11).—**Ἐμός** is very frequent in John, not very frequent in the remaining writers (σός besides its use in Gospels and Acts occurs only three times in Paul); ἐμός (like σός) is also used **reflexively** for ἐμαυτοῦ (σεαυτοῦ), Philem. 19, Mt. 7. 3 (3 Jo. 4), Herm. Sim. i. 11 τὸ σὸν ἔργον ἐργάζου (also occasionally in class. Greek, Kühner ii.[2] 494a).—The possessives are also used **predicatively** (without an art.): Mt. 20. 23 = Mc. 10. 40 οὐκ ἔστιν ἐμὸν τοῦτο δοῦναι (for which we have in the plur. ὑμῶν ἐστιν 1 C. 3. 21 f., cp. supra § 35, 2); with a subst. inserted ἐμὸν βρῶμά ἐστιν ἵνα κ.τ.λ. Jo. 4. 34, 13. 35; under other circumstances also the art. may be dropped: Ph. 3. 9 μὴ ἔχων ἐμὴν δικαιοσύνην ('a righteousness of my own') τὴν ἐκ νόμου (cp. § 47, 6), as with ἴδιος, infra 8, and with ἑαυτοῦ L. 19. 13 δέκα δούλους ἑαυτοῦ ('of his').

8. A common possessive pronoun is **ἴδιος**, which in classical Greek is opposed to κοινός or δημόσιος, while in modern Greek the new possessive ὁ ἐδικός μου, σου etc. has been fully developed (with the N.T. and LXX. use agree also Philo, Josephus, Plutarch etc., W. Schmidt Jos. elocut. 369). It is opposed to κοινός A. 4. 32 (H. 7. 27); or means 'peculiar,' 'corresponding to the particular condition' of a person or thing, 1 C. 3. 8, 7. 7 etc. (class.); but generally means simply 'own,' = ἑαυτοῦ etc. (like class. οἰκεῖος): Jo. 1. 11 εἰς τὰ ἴδια ἦλθεν, καὶ οἱ ἴδιοι αὐτὸν οὐ παρέλαβον, 42 εὑρίσκει τὸν ἀδελφὸν τὸν ἴδιον Σίμωνα, Mt. 22. 5 εἰς τὸν ἴδιον ἀγρόν (without emphasis = εἰς τ. αὐ. αὐτοῦ), 25. 14; with v.l. ἑαυτοῦ L. 2. 3. It is joined with the gen. αὐτοῦ etc. (a use which in itself is classical) in Mc. 15. 20 (v.l. without αὐτοῦ, D also omits ἴδια) A. 1. 19, 24. 23, Tit. 1. 12, 2 P. 3. 3, 16. Κατ' ἰδίαν is frequent = class. καθ' ἑαυτόν 'by Himself,' Mt. 14. 13 etc.; ἰδίᾳ ἑκάστῳ 1 C. 12. 11 is classical.—It is not surprising that the article is occasionally dropped, cp. supra 7 ad fin. (1 C. 15. 38, a v.l. inserts τό; Tit. 1. 12); in Tit. 2. 9 δούλους δεσπόταις ἰδίοις ὑποτάσσεσθαι there is a kind of assimilation to the anarthrous δούλους (somewhat as in H. 12. 7, § 46, 7); 2 P. 2. 16 ἔλεγξιν ἰδίας παρανομίας is due to Hebrew usage like παρ. αὐτοῦ (§ 46, 9).—On the periphrasis for the possess. gen. with κατά see § 42, 2.

9. Ἑαυτῶν is found (as previously in classical Greek) for the

---

[1] In H. 7. 18 διὰ τὸ αὐτῆς ἀσθενὲς καὶ ἀνωφελές there is no emphasis on the pronoun, but here there is no substantive: τὴν αὐτῆς ἀσθένειαν would scarcely be written. (Still in Herm. Mand. vi. 2. 2 we have τὰς αὐτῶν ἐνεργείας without emphasis, cp. Clem. Hom. xiv. 7, 10.)

reciprocal ἀλλήλων in 1 C. 6. 7, Col. 3. 13, 16, etc., and often in conjunction with it for the sake of variety : L. 23. 12 ἀλλήλων ... πρὸς ἑαυτούς with v.l. in אBLT πρὸς αὐτούς, a use of the simple pronoun which here appears to be inadmissible. The individual persons are kept separate in ἄλλος πρὸς ἄλλον A. 2. 12 = πρὸς ἀλλήλους; cp. εἰς τὸν ἕνα for ἀλλήλους (Semitic) § 45, 2.

10. **Αὐτός** 'self' has its classical usages (usually followed by an article, which however does not belong to αὐτός, and is therefore sometimes omitted, as in αὐτὸς Ἰησοῦς Jo. 2. 24, according to § 46, 10); it is naturally found also in connection with the personal pronoun, where it is to be sharply distinguished from the reflexive: ἐξ ὑμῶν αὐτῶν A. 20. 30, like αὐτὸς ἐγώ, αὐτοὶ ὑμεῖς (in the 3rd pers. it is of course not repeated : ἵνα αὐτοὺς ζηλοῦτε G. 4. 17, 'the men themselves'); even in 1 C. 5. 13 ἐξάρατε τὸν πονηρὸν ἐξ ὑμῶν αὐτῶν the words ὑ. α. are not reflexive, although this quotation is taken from Deut. 17. 7 ἐξαρεῖς τὸν π. ἐξ ὑμῶν αὐτῶν, where ἑαυτῶν could not be used because of the singular ἐξαρεῖς.—For αὐτὸς οὗτος (ἐκεῖνος) Luke uses αὐτός in the phrases ἐν αὐτῇ τῇ ὥρᾳ, ἡμέρᾳ L. 12. 12, 13. 31, 20. 19, A. 22. 13 etc., ἐν α. τῷ καιρῷ L. 13. 1 (cp. ἐξ αὐτῆς, § 44, 1); so also ἐν αὐτῇ τῇ οἰκίᾳ 10. 7.

§ 49. DEMONSTRATIVE PRONOUNS.

1. The demonstrative pronouns of the N.T. are : **οὗτος, ἐκεῖνος**, and **αὐτός**, which is beginning to be so used, see § 48, 1, remnants of **ὁ, ἡ, τό**, § 46, 1-3, remnants also of **ὅδε**, § 12, 2, which is not even used correctly in all cases (τάδε λέγει to introduce some information is correct in A. 21. 11, Ap. 2. 1 etc.), just because it belonged to the language of literature and not to the living language : L. 10. 39 καὶ τῇδε ἦν ἀδελφή κ.τ.λ. instead of ταύτῃ (Ja. 4. 13 πορευσόμεθα εἰς τήνδε τὴν πόλιν appears to mean 'such and such a city,' Attic τὴν καὶ τήν, as in Plat. Leg. 4. 721 B τῇ καὶ τῇ ἀτιμίᾳ[1]; the passage in James is followed by 15 ποιήσομεν τοῦτο ἢ ἐκεῖνο with the same meaning). **Τοιόσδε** for τοιαύτης (correctly introducing some information following) only occurs in 2 P. 1. 17.

2. The uses of **οὗτος** and **ἐκεῖνος** are quite clearly distinguished. Οὗτος refers to persons or things actually present : Mt. 3. 17 οὗτός ἐστιν ὁ υἱός μου etc.; to persons or things mentioned, = one who continues to be the subject of conversation, as e.g. in Mt. 3. 3 οὗτος (John, verse 1 f.) γάρ ἐστιν ὁ ῥηθεὶς κ.τ.λ., especially used after a preliminary description of a person to introduce what has to be narrated of him, Mt. 27. 57 f. ἄνθρωπος πλούσιος ἀπὸ Ἀριμαθαίας ... οὗτος προσελθὼν κ.τ.λ., L. 23. 50 ff., Ja. 3. 2, 4. 47, A. 1. 18 οὗτος μὲν οὖν κ.τ.λ., etc.; somewhat different is καὶ οὗτος in Luke in the continuation of a description, L. 2. 25 f. καὶ ἰδοὺ ἄνθρωπος ἦν ... ᾧ ὄνομα Συμεών, καὶ ὁ ἄ. οὗτος δίκαιος κ.τ.λ., cp. 17, 7. 12, 8. 41 (with a wrong reading αὐτός, see § 48, 1), 19. 2 (the same v.l.; only D has

---

[1] With this is rightly compared τήνδε τὴν ἡμέραν in Plut. Qu. conviv. i. 6. 1.

§ 49. 2–3.] DEMONSTRATIVE PRONOUNS. 171

οὗτος); cp. also καὶ τῇδε (sup. 1), 10. 39. Slight ambiguities (where several substantives precede) must be cleared up by the sense: A. 8. 26 αὕτη ἐστὶν ἔρημος, referring to ἡ ὁδός, not to Γάζα; L. 16. 1 ἄνθρωπός τις ἦν πλούσιος ὃς εἶχεν οἰκονόμον, καὶ οὗτος (referring to οἰκ.) διεβλήθη αὐτῷ (to ἄνθ. πλ.). It very commonly stands in the apodosis, referring back to the protasis: Mt. 10. 22 ὁ δὲ ὑπομείνας εἰς τέλος, οὗτος σωθήσεται, R. 7. 15 οὐ γὰρ ὃ θέλω, τοῦτο πράσσω, ἀλλ' ὃ μισῶ, τοῦτο ποιῶ; but τοῦτο is also found in the preceding principal clause, as a preliminary to a subordinate clause with ὅτι, ἵνα etc.; 1 Tim. 1. 9 εἰδὼς τοῦτο, ὅτι κ.τ.λ., 1 Jo. 2. 3 ἐν τούτῳ γινώσκομεν..., ἐὰν κ.τ.λ.; also before an infinitive or substantive, 2 C. 2. 1 ἔκρινα ἐμαυτῷ τοῦτο, τὸ μὴ πάλιν ... ἐλθεῖν, 2 C. 13. 9 τοῦτο καὶ εὐχόμεθα, τὴν ὑμῶν κατάρτισιν. St. Paul frequently also has αὐτὸ τοῦτο, just this (and nothing else), R. 9. 17 O.T., 13. 6, Ph. 1. 6 πεποιθὼς αὐτὸ τοῦτο (with reference to their endurance already emphasized in verse 5), also 2 P. 1. 5; an adverbial use (like τί) is τοῦτο αὐτό just for this reason 2 C. 2. 3, § 34, 7.[1] Another adverbial use is τοῦτο μὲν ... τοῦτο δὲ on the one hand ... on the other hand, both ... and H. 10. 33 (Attic; literary language). We further have καὶ τοῦτο *idque* 'and indeed' 1 C. 6. 8 (κ. ταῦτα CD[b]), 8 (ταῦτα L), R. 13. 11, E. 2. 8 (Att. καὶ ταῦτα, Kühner ii.[2] 791); on καὶ ταῦτα with part. 'although' H. 11. 12 etc. see § 74, 2.—Οὗτος appears to be often used in a contemptuous way (like Latin *iste*) of a person who is present: L. 15. 30 ὁ υἱός σου οὗτος, 18. 11 οὗτος ὁ τελώνης, A. 17. 18.—On οὐ μετὰ πολλὰς ταύτας ἡμέρας A. 1. 5 see § 42, 3.

3. The much rarer word ἐκεῖνος (most frequent, comparatively speaking, in St. John) may be used to denote persons who are absent, and are regarded in that light: ὑμεῖς – ἐκεῖνοι are opposed in Mt. 13. 11, Jo. 5. 39, A. 3. 13, 2 C. 8. 14, ἡμεῖς (ἐγώ) – ἐκ. in Jo. 3. 28, 30, 1 C. 9. 25, 10. 11, 15. 11; of course the conversation must have turned on the persons indicated, to make the pronoun intelligible at all.[2] It is never used in the N.T. in connection with, or in opposition to, οὗτος (Buttm. p. 91); but see Herm. Mand. iii. 5 ἐκεῖνα (the past) – ταῦτα (the present). Frequently in the N.T. ἐκείνη ἡ ἡμέρα is used of the last day, Mt. 7. 22, 2 Th. 1. 10. But it is especially used in narrative (even imaginary narrative) about something that has been previously mentioned, and that which is connected therewith. When thus used, it is distinguished from οὗτος, which refers to something which is still under immediate consideration. Thus confusion between the two pronouns is not often possible. Mt. 3. 1 ἐν δὲ ταῖς ἡμέραις ἐκείναις in the transition to a fresh narrative, cp. Mc. 1. 9, 8. 1, L. 2. 1; but Luke also uses ταύταις in this phrase, 1. 39, 6. 12 (D ἐκείναις), A. 1. 15, 6. 1 (v.l.

---

[1] 2 P. 1. 5 καὶ αὐτὸ δὲ τοῦτο (v.l. κ. α. τοῦτο δὲ) σπουδὴν πᾶσαν παρεισενέγκαντες might be a corruption of κατ' αὐτὸ δὲ τοῦτο.

[2] It is used contemptuously or invidiously of an absent person in Jo. 9. 28, cp. οὗτος, sup. 2; in A. 5. 28 D has τοῦ ἀνθρ. ἐκείνου for τ. ἀ. τούτου of the other MSS. (the latter is due to ἐπὶ τῷ ὀνόματι τούτῳ in the same verse).

ἐκείν.), 11. 27 (B αὐταῖς, cp. § 48, 1) : Mt. 7. 25, 27 τῇ οἰκίᾳ ἐκείνῃ (referring to 24 and 26 ; other subjects, namely the rain etc., have intervened), 8. 28 διὰ τῆς ὁδοῦ ἐκείνης (where the possessed persons dwelt ; the road itself has not previously been mentioned), 9. 22 ἀπὸ τῆς ὥρας ἐκείνης (when these words were spoken), 26, 31, 13. 44 τὸν ἀγρὸν ἐκεῖνον (referring to τῷ ἀγρῷ ibid., but again there has been interruption caused by other subjects intervening).[1]—In the apodosis (cp. οὗτος): Mc. 7. 20 τὸ ἐκ τοῦ ἀνθρώπου ἐκπορευόμενον, ἐκεῖνο (that *other* thing) κοινοῖ τὸν ἄνθρωπον, Jo. 10. 1 (ἐκ. opposed to the speaker), similarly R. 14. 14, 2 C. 10. 18 ; with weakened force and indefinite reference ('*he*') Jo. 14. 21 ὁ ἔχων τὰς ἐντολάς μου ..., ἐκεῖνός ἐστιν ὁ ἀγαπῶν με, cp. 6. 57, 2 C. 10. 18, Herm. Mand. vii. 5, etc.; even with reference to the speaker in Jo. 9. 37. It is not often followed by the word or clause referred to : Mt. 24. 23 ἐκεῖνο (that other thing, see 42) δὲ γινώσκετε ὅτι (R. 14. 15 ἐκεῖνον ... ὑπὲρ οὗ opposed to σύ), Jo. 13. 26 'he,' cp. supra. Its meaning is also weakened to '*he*' ('they') in Jo. 10. 6 ταύτην τὴν παροιμίαν εἶπεν αὐτοῖς ὁ Ἰησ., ἐκεῖνοι δέ (for which οἱ δέ, αὐτοὶ δέ are synonyms, §§ 46, 3 ; 48, 1), and so frequently in John in unbroken connection with the first mention, G. 9. 11, 25, 36 ; similarly 'Mc.' 16. 10 ff.[2]

4. The substantive that is connected with οὗτος or ἐκεῖνος takes the article as in classical Greek ; it is only necessary to consider whether the words are really to be connected, or whether the substantive or the pronoun forms part of the predicate : Jo. 2. 11 ταύτην (obj.) ἐποίησεν ἀρχὴν τῶν σημείων, L. 2. 1 αὕτη (subj.) ἀπογραφὴ πρώτη ἐγένετο (on the agreement in gender see § 31, 2), A. 24. 21 μιᾶς ταύτης φωνῆς ἧς ἐκέκραξα ὅτι = ἡ φωνὴ ἣ ἐγένετο ἦν μία αὕτη (predic.)—The position of the pronoun, either before the article or after the substantive, is quite optional : οὗτος (ἐκεῖνος) ὁ ἄνθρωπος or ὁ ἄ. οὗτος (ἐκεῖνος).

§ 50. RELATIVE AND INTERROGATIVE PRONOUNS.

1. The **relative** of definite reference ὅς (by the ancients called ἄρθρον ὑποτακτικόν, § 46, 1) and that of **indefinite** reference ὅστις are no longer regularly distinguished in the N.T.; and with this is connected the fact that the latter is almost entirely limited to the nominative (§ 13, 3), although in this case it is used by nearly all

---

[1] See also Jo. 1. 6 ff. ἐγένετο ἄνθρωπος ... Ἰωάνης· **οὗτος** (vide sup. 2) ἦλθεν εἰς μαρτυρίαν,—ἵνα πάντες πιστεύωσιν δι' αὐτοῦ· οὐκ ἦν **ἐκεῖνος** τὸ φῶς (the discourse passes from John to Jesus) ; 7. 45 ἦλθον οὖν οἱ ὑπηρέται πρὸς τοὺς ἀρχιερεῖς, καὶ εἶπον αὐτοῖς ἐκεῖνοι (those who were at a distance from the scene of action, and were previously mentioned in verse 32).

[2] The Johannine use of ἐκεῖνος is exhaustively discussed by Steitz and A. Buttmann in Stud. u. Kr. 1859, 497 : 1860, 505 : 1861, 267 ; see also Zeitschrift f. w. Th. 1862, 204 for the passage 19. 35 καὶ ἐκεῖνος οἶδεν κ.τ.λ. (*i.e.* the narrator, whose personality, however, is not prominently put forward, unless with Zahn we refer ἐκεῖνος to Christ). Nonnus (see his paraphrase) read κἀκείνου οἴδαμεν ὅτι ἀληθινὴ ἡ μαρτυρία ἐστίν· ἐγένετο δὲ κ.τ.λ.; the Latin codex e omits the verse, and has (like Nonnus) ἐγένετο δέ in v. 36.

writers (least of all by John). A similar case is that of ὅσος, which, except in Hebrews, is used only in the nominative and accusative. Mt. uses ὅστις correctly in general statements, 5. 39, 41, 10. 33 etc., but also ὅς 10. 14, 23. 16, 18; esp. πᾶς ὅστις 7. 24, 10. 32, 19. 29; but πᾶς ὅς occurs in L. 14. 33, A. 2. 21 O.T., G. 3. 10 O.T., παντὶ ᾧ L. 12. 48; Mt. also uses this phrase where a subst. is inserted, 12. 36 πᾶν ῥῆμα ἀργὸν ὅ, 15. 13 πᾶσα φυτεία ἣν (πᾶσα ψυχὴ ἥτις A. 3. 23 O.T.). Ὅστις is also correctly used in connection with a subst. of indefinite reference : Mt. 7. 15 τῶν ψευδοπροφητῶν οἵτινες (description follows), 24 ἀνδρὶ φρονίμῳ ὅστις etc. (but Lc. uses ὅς : 6. 48 ἀνθρώπῳ ὅς, 49 οἰκίαν ᾗ): and to denote a definite person in a case where the relative sentence expresses the general quality, Jo. 8. 53 Ἀβραάμ, ὅστις ἀπέθανεν (who was a man who died), A. 7. 53 οἵτινες ἐλάβετε κ.τ.λ. (people who); but these limits are often exceeded esp. by Luke, and οἵτινες, ἥτις are used = οἵ, ἥ: Πέτρον καὶ Ἰωάνην, οἵτινες A. 8. 15, τὴν πύλην ἥτις 12. 10, πόλιν Δαυίδ, ἥτις L. 2. 4 (particularly where a participle follows, and the meaning of οἱ, ἡ would not have been clear, A. 8. 15, 17. 10 οἵτινες παραγενόμενοι); Ap. 12. 13 τὴν γυναῖκα ἥτις ἔτεκεν τὸν ἄρσενα. This use of ὅστις for ὅς is very old in Ionic Greek, Kühner Gr. ii.² 906 (Herod. ii. 99 πόλιν ἥτις νῦν Μέμφις καλεῖται). In the Pauline Epistles this use cannot be established, since in R. 16. 3 ff. ὅς and ὅστις are alternately used, according as a mere statement of fact is made (ὅς), or a characteristic is given (7 οἵτινές εἰσιν ἐπίσημοι ἐν τοῖς ἀποστόλοις, οἳ καὶ πρὸ ἐμοῦ γέγοναν ἐν Χριστῷ); also in G. 4. 24, 26 ἥτις = ἡ τοιαύτη, cp. 1 C. 3. 17, Ph. 1. 28, 1 Tim. 3. 15.—As an instance of ὅς for ὅστις one may further note οὐδεὶς (οὐ) ... ὅς (for ὅστις) οὐ, § 75, 6.—ὅσπερ has been given up, § 13, 3.

2. The ἄρθρον ὑποτακτικόν, ὅς, ἥ, ὅ justifies this appellation chiefly in the fact that, like the article (ἄ. προτακτικόν) which follows a substantive and introduces a further definition, its case is assimilated to that of the substantive, even though in conformity with the relative sentence it should have had another case, which is generally the accusative (**Attraction** or **Assimilation** of the relative).[1] In this peculiarity of Greek the N.T. (like the LXX.) is entirely in agreement with the classical language. Exceptions occur (as in classical Greek, Thuc. ii. 70. 5) where the relative clause is more sharply divided from the rest of the sentence (through the insertion of other defining words with the noun and through the importance of the contents of the relative sentence): H. 8. 2 τῆς σκηνῆς τῆς ἀληθινῆς, ἣν ἔπηξεν ὁ κύριος, οὐκ ἄνθρωπος; but in other passages there is always a v.l., Mc. 13. 19 ἀπ' ἀρχῆς κτίσεως, ἣν (ἧς AC² al., om. ἣν ἕκτ. ὁ θ. D) ἔκτισεν ὁ θεός, Jo. 2. 22 and 4. 50 τῷ λόγῳ ὃν (ᾧ AΔX al., DΔ al.), 4. 5 χωρίον ὅ (οὗ C*D al.), 7. 39 (οὗ אDG al.), Ap. 1. 20 (ὧν B); Tit. 3. 5 οὐκ ἐξ ἔργων τῶν ἐν δικαιοσύνῃ, ἃ (ὧν Cᵇ Dᶜ al.) ἐποιήσαμεν ἡμεῖς is an instance of the case above-mentioned of separation through the insertion of defining words. (On A. 8. 32 f. see the author's commentary on that passage.) On the other hand

---

[1] Ὅστις, in N.T. as in classical Greek, is never assimilated.

it is not only the so-called accusative of the inner object (§ 34, 3) which is capable of assimilation (E. 4. 1 τῆς κλήσεως ἧς ἐκλήθητε, A. 24. 21, 26. 16, Jd. 15), but occasionally the dative is assimilated as well : A. 1. 22 ἄχρι τῆς ἡμέρας ἧς ἀνελήμφθη (cp. L. 1. 20 D, LXX. Lev. 23. 15, Bar. 1. 15), R. 4. 17 κατέναντι οὗ ἐπίστευσεν θεοῦ, i.e. κ. τοῦ θ. ᾧ ἐπ. (see below on the attraction of the substantive into the relative clause). In addition to this, the preposition which should be repeated before the relative may be omitted (class.): A. 1. 21 ἐν παντὶ χρόνῳ (sc. ἐν) ᾧ, 13. 2 εἰς τὸ ἔργον (sc. εἰς) ὅ, 39 ἀπὸ πάντων (sc. ἀφ') ὧν, Herm. Sim. ix. 7. 3 μετὰ πάντων (sc. μεθ') ὧν (but in the case of a sharper division of the relative clause, the preposition is repeated : A. 7. 4 εἰς τὴν γῆν ταύτην, εἰς ἥν, 20. 18 ἀπὸ **πρώτης** ἡμέρας, ἀφ' ἧς, Jo. 4. 53 (ἐν) **ἐκείνῃ** τῇ ὥρᾳ, ἐν ᾗ). It is readily intelligible that the Greek relative includes our demonstrative 'he' or 'that'; it is therefore used by assimilation in the case which would belong to the demonstrative : L. 9. 36 οὐδὲν ὧν = τούτων ἅ, Jo. 7. 31 πλείονα ὧν (do.), 17. 9 περὶ ὧν = περὶ τούτων οὕς; also ἀνθ' ὧν = ἀντὶ τούτων ὅτι, ἐφ' ᾧ = ἐπὶ τούτῳ ὅτι, διότι = διὰ τοῦτο ὅτι ; cp. adverbs of place § 76, 4. More noticeable is the occasional attraction of the noun into the relative clause, in which case the article belonging to the noun, being incompatible with the ἄρθρ. ὑποτ., must be left out, while the noun itself is now assimilated to the case of the relative ; of course even where there is no assimilation of the relative, a similar attraction of the noun into the relative clause, with the case of the relative, may take place (so in classical Greek, Kühner ii.[2] 922 : e.g. ᾧ ἀνδρὶ πάντες εὖνοι ἦσαν, ἀπέθανεν). But the noun is not placed immediately after the relative, except in the case of ἡμέρα : L. 1. 20 ἄχρι ἧς ἡμέρας γένηται ταῦτα, = ἅ. τῆς ἡμ. (ἐν) ᾗ cp. supra, A. 1. 1, Mt. 24. 38 (same phrase).[1] On the other hand : L. 19. 37 πασῶν ὧν εἶδον δυνάμεων, 3. 19 περὶ πάντων ὧν ἐποίησεν πονηρῶν ὁ Ἡρῴδης (τῶν πον. ὧν ℵ*), cp. A. 25. 18[2], and with no assimilation of the relative : L. 24. 1 φέρουσαι ἃ ἡτοίμασαν ἀρώματα, Jo. 6. 14 ὃ ἐποίησεν σημεῖον. The way in which the following exx. should be resolved is ambiguous : L. 1. 4 περὶ ὧν κατηχήθης λόγων, = either περὶ τῶν λ. οὓς or τῶν λόγων περὶ ὧν (in view of passages like A. 18. 25, 20. 24, 25. 26 the first is probably correct); R. 6. 17 ὑπηκούσατε εἰς ὃν παρεδόθητε τύπον διδαχῆς, probably τῷ τύπῳ εἰς ὅν ; with omission of a preposition A. 21. 16 (but not D) ἄγοντες παρ' ᾧ ξενισθῶμεν Μνάσωνι = πρὸς Μνάσωνα, ἵνα ξεν. παρ' αὐτῷ (§ 65, 8).

3. If the **noun** is not attracted into the relative clause but stands in front of it, is still occasionally **assimilated to the case of the relative**, a practice of which instances appear in classical authors (**attractio inversa**, Kühner ii.[2] 918, 4): 1 C. 10. 16 τὸν ἄρτον ὃν κλῶμεν, οὐχὶ κοινωνία ... ἐστίν ; A. 10. 36 τὸν λόγον ὃν ... οὗτός ἐστι

---

[1] The regular phrase is ἐν ἡμ. ᾗ Mt. 24. 50, L. 1. 25 (plur.), 12. 46, without the art., which is occasionally omitted in Hebrew before אֲשֶׁר, infra 3 ; without ἐν L. 17. 29 f. ᾗ ἡμέρᾳ (in 30 D reads ἐν τῇ ἡμ. - ᾗ ἀποκαλυφθῇ). Ἡμ. is separated from the rel. in Herm. Mand. iv. 4. 3 ἀφ' ἧς μοι παρεδόθης ἡμέρας.

[2] 2 C. 10. 13 κατὰ τὸ μέτρον τοῦ κανόνος, οὗ ἐμέρισεν ἡμῖν ὁ θεὸς μέτρου = τοῦ μέτρου οὗ, although in this case the appositional clause has been very loosely annexed.

§ 50. 3-5.] *INTERROGATIVE PRONOUNS.* 175

πάντων (κύριος should be removed)[1], Herm. Sim. ix. 13. 3, L. 12. 48 παντὶ ᾧ ἐδόθη πολύ, πολὺ ζητήσουσιν παρ' αὐτοῦ (in sentences of this kind the nominative is elsewhere used with anacoluthon, see § 79), Mt. 21. 42 τὸν λίθον ὃν κ.τ.λ. O.T.; peculiar is L. 1. 73 ὅρκον ὃν ὤμοσεν instead of τοῦ ὅρκου οὗ (not a case of 'protasis,' but a supplementary amplification; the passage is strongly Hebraic, § 46, 9; Hebr. מָקוֹם אֲשֶׁר Ges.-K. § 130, 3).—Attraction with a relative adverb: Mt. 25. 24 συνάγεις ὅθεν (= ἐκεῖθεν ὅπου) οὐ διεσκόρπισας, cp. Kühner ii.[2] 915, note 6.

4. One piece of careless writing, which was specially suggested by Semitic usage (Hebr. אֲשֶׁר לוֹ; Aramaic has similar expressions with דְּ), though it is not quite unknown to the classical language[2], is the **pleonastic** use of the **personal pronoun after the relative**. Mc. 7. 25 γυνή, ἧς εἶχεν τὸ θυγάτριον αὐτῆς (a. om. אD) πνεῦμα ἀκάθαρτον, 1. 7 = L. 3. 16 οὗ ... αὐτοῦ, Ap. 7. 2 οἷς ἐδόθη αὐτοῖς, 9, 3. 8, 13. 8, 20. 8, Clem. Cor. i. 21. 9 οὗ ἡ πνοὴ αὐτοῦ (frequent in LXX., Winer, § 22, 4); with these exx. the following are quite in keeping: Ap. 12. 6, 14 ὅπου ... ἐκεῖ (אֲשֶׁר שָׁם), 17. 9 ὅπου ... ἐπ' αὐτῶν, Mc. 13. 19 οἵα οὐ γέγονεν τοιαύτη (9. 3 οἷα ... οὐ δύναται οὕτως λευκᾶναι): in G. 3. 1 ἐν ὑμῖν after οἷς is merely a v.l.; but in 2. 10 ὃ καὶ ἐσπούδασα αὐτὸ τοῦτο ποιῆσαι there is a reason for the expression, since αὐτὸ in this sense ('just') cannot be joined to the relative, and therefore required to be supplemented by τοῦτο.[3]—Another quite different negligent usage, which is also unobjectionable in the classical language, is the linking on of a further subordinate clause to a relative clause by means of καὶ ... αὐτοῦ: 1 C. 8. 6 ἐξ οὗ τὰ πάντα καὶ ἡμεῖς εἰς αὐτόν (a second ex. in the same verse), Ap. 17. 2, 2 P. 2. 3 (Kühner ii.[2] 936).

5. **Relatives** and **interrogatives** become confused in Greek as in other languages. The relatives in particular, and as is only natural the indefinite ὅστις especially (but also ὅς, where it can conveniently be so used), are frequently employed in the classical language **in indirect questions** (beside the interrogatives), a usage which, however, is wanting in the N.T. (in A. 9. 6 the reading of אABC ὅτι for τί must be rejected in view of the general practice elsewhere); ὁποῖος alone is employed as an indirect interrogative: 1 C. 3. 13, G. 2. 6 (ὁποῖοί ποτε), 1 Th. 1. 9, Ja. 1. 24 (elsewhere expressed by ποῖος), cp. ὅπως L. 24. 20. The reverse use of the interrogative **τίς instead of the relative ὅστις** is Alexandrian (and dialectical), as *e.g.* in a saying of Ptolemy Euergetes ap. Athen. x. 438 fin. τίνι ἡ τύχη δίδωσι, λαβέτω.[4] In the N.T. we have A. 13. 25 τίνα με ὑπονοεῖτε εἶναι, οὐκ εἰμὶ ἐγώ,[5] cp. Mc. 14. 36 οὐ τί ἐγὼ θέλω, ἀλλὰ τί σύ (οὐχ ὃ - ἀλλ' ὃ D), L. 17. 8 ἑτοίμασον τί δειπνήσω, Ja. 3. 13 τίς σοφὸς καὶ

---

[1] See the author's edition of the Acts, and above § 35, 2.
[2] Cp. Kühner ii.[2] 937 (Hypereides Euxen. § 3 ὧν ... τούτων).
[3] So (Kühner loc. cit. note 2) ὅς ... δεύτερος οὗτος.
[4] Cp. O. Immisch Lpz. Stud. 1887, 309 ff.
[5] [W. H. txt. reads τί ἐμὲ ὑπονοεῖτε εἶναι; οὐκ εἰμὶ ἐγώ. Tr.]

ἐπιστήμων ἐν ὑμῖν, δειξάτω (or τίς ... ὑμῖν; an interrogative sentence).¹ The employment of ὅστις or even of ὅς in a **direct** question is quite incredible, except that ὅ,τι appears to be used as an abbreviation for τί ὅ,τι 'why': Mc. 9. 11 ἐπηρώτων αὐτὸν λέγοντες· ὅ,τι λέγουσιν οἱ γραμματεῖς κ.τ.λ., 28 ἐπηρώτων αὐτόν· ὅ,τι ἡμεῖς οὐκ ἠδυνήθημεν ἐκβαλεῖν αὐτό; (διατί ADKΠ), 2. 16 (τί ὅτι AC al., διατί אD): cp. LXX. 1 Chron. 17. 6 ὅ,τι = לָמָּה But Jo. 8. 25 τὴν ἀρχὴν ὅ,τι καὶ λαλῶ ὑμῖν; means according to classical usage (a meaning, it is true, which cannot be paralleled from the N.T.): you ask, why (so in classical Greek A says τίς ἐστιν; to which B replies ὅστις; sc. ἐρωτᾷς you ask who he is?) do I speak to you at all? (τὴν ἀρχὴν = ὅλως): cp. for the direct question Clem. Hom. vi. 11 τί καὶ τὴν ἀρχὴν διαλέγομαι; xix. 6 ἐπεὶ τί καὶ τὴν ἀρχὴν ζητεῖ; while in Mt. 26. 50 ἑταῖρε ἐφ᾽ ὃ πάρει, ἑταῖρε must be a corruption either of αἶρε or ἑταῖρε αἶρε: 'take what thou art come to fetch' (D has ἑταῖρε after πάρει).²

6. It has already been remarked in § 13, 5 that the interrogative **τίς** (both in direct and indirect questions, supra 5) is also used for **πότερος** 'which of two?': Mt. 21. 31 τίς ἐκ τῶν δύο, 9. 5, L. 7. 42 etc. A stereotyped phrase is πότερον ... ἤ utrum ... an in indirect double questions, but found only in Jo. 7. 17 (Herm. Sim. ix. 28. 4). Τίς is for the most part used substantivally; beside the **adjectival** τίς (τίς βασιλεύς L. 14. 31, τί σημεῖον Jo. 2. 18, τίς μετοχή etc. 2 C. 6. 14 ff.) **ποῖος** is also used with little distinction from it, as also in classical Greek—nowhere, however, in inquiries after persons, but in such phrases as ἐν ποίᾳ ἐξουσίᾳ, ποίῳ ὀνόματι (A. 4. 7), ποίᾳ ὥρᾳ, ἐκ ποίας ἐπαρχίας (A. 23. 34), διὰ ποίου νόμου (R. 3. 27), ποίῳ σώματι (the pron. having its strict sense, how constituted) 1 C. 15. 35, cp. Ja. 4. 14 ποία γὰρ ἡ (ἡ om. B) ζωὴ ὑμῶν (how miserably constituted; on the other hand it is not elsewhere found with an article, τίς being used in that case: Mc. 6. 2 τίς ἡ σοφία, whence coming, A. 10. 21 τίς ἡ αἰτία, 17. 19 etc.); with an adj. τί is always used: τί ἀγαθόν, κακόν, περισσόν. The two words are united tautologically (for emphasis) in εἰς τίνα ἢ ποῖον καιρόν 1 P. 1. 11; there is a diversity of reading in Mc. 4. 30 ἐν τίνι (ποίᾳ AC²D al.) παραβολῇ; the two are used interchangeably in A. 7. 49 ποῖον οἶκον ... ἢ τίς τόπος. In L. 24. 19 ποῖα stands by itself, referring to 18 τὰ γενόμενα. Beside ποῖος we have also the later **ποταπός** (old form ποδαπός, of what country by birth, like ἀλλοδαπός, ἡμεδαπός; for ποτ. = ποῖος Lob. Phryn. 56), the latter being used of persons as well as things: ποταπός ἐστιν οὗτος, ὃς κ.τ.λ., Mt. 8. 27 (= τίς ἄρα Mc. 4. 41, L. 8. 25), τίς καὶ ποταπὴ ἡ γυνή L. 7. 39, 2 P. 3. 11; of things Mc. 13. 1, L. 1. 29, 1 Jo. 3. 1 (how constituted, also how great or mighty; like ποῖαι = τίνες in Herm. Mand. viii. 3 ποταπαί εἰσιν αἱ πονηρίαι).

---

[1] In Mt. 26. 62 = Mc. 14. 60 οὐδὲν ἀποκρίνῃ; τί οὗτοί σου καταμαρτυροῦσιν; it is impossible to unite the words in a single sentence, because ἀποκρίνεσθαι would require a πρός, Mt. 27. 14. In the passage of James one may adduce 5. 13 in favour of separating the clauses: κακοπαθεῖ τις; προσευχέσθω, cp. § 82.

[2] [Many commentators supply ποίησον 'do that for which thou art come.' Tr.]

§ 50. 7. § 51. 1.]   *INTERROGATIVE PRONOUNS.*   177

7. The neuter τί is used as **predicate** to ταῦτα (as in class. Greek, Krüger Gr. § 61, 8, 2) in τί (ἂν) εἴη ταῦτα L. 15, 26 (τί θέλει τοῦτο εἶναι D), A. 17. 20 DEHL (v.l. τίνα), Herm. Vis. iv. 3. 1; it is necessary in Jo. 6. 9 ἀλλὰ ταῦτα τί ἐστιν (of what use are they) εἰς τοσούτους; further we have ἄνδρες, τί ταῦτα ποιεῖτε A. 14. 15, as in Demosth. 55. 5 Τεισία, τί ταῦτα ποιεῖς (what are you doing there ?), cp. with a singular demonstr. pron. L. 16. 2 τί τοῦτο ἀκούω περὶ σοῦ; (τί predic.).[1] In the passage of Acts τί might also be understood in its very common meaning of 'why ?' (class.), Mt. 6. 28, L. 2. 48 etc.; to express this meaning besides διὰ τί we have also ἵνα τί (sc. γένηται), A. 7. 25 O.T. ἵνα τί (ἱνατί) ἐφρύαξαν ἔθνη etc. (found in Attic), and τί ὅ,τι (ὅτι), written fully in τί γέγονεν ὅτι ἡμῖν μέλλεις ἐμφανίζειν σεαυτόν Jo. 14. 22 (where ὅτι = δι' ὅ,τι, just as τί = διὰ τί), A. 5. 4, 9, L. 2. 49, v.l. in Mc. 2. 16, vide supra 5 (also LXX.). A. 12. 18 τί ἄρα ὁ Πέτρος ἐγένετο, 'what was become of him,' is like Attic τί γένωμαι[2]; so L. 1. 66 τί ἄρα τὸ παιδίον ἔσται; A. 5. 24 τί ἂν γένοιτο τοῦτο, 'what would be likely to happen in the matter,' 'how it would turn out' (τί predic.); in an abbreviated form οὗτος δὲ τί Jo. 21. 21, 'what will become of him ?'   Tί 'how' = Hebr. מַה (Win. § 21, 3, note 3), Mt. 7. 14 τί στενή (v.l. ὅτι), L. 12. 49 τί θέλω (LXX.).—Τί πρὸς ἡμᾶς (sc. ἐστι), 'what does it concern us ?' Mt. 27. 4: τί πρὸς σέ Jo. 21. 22 (cp. § 30, 3; Attic has also τί ταῦτ' ἐμοί; Kühner ii.[2] 365, and so 1 C. 5. 12 τί γάρ μοι τοὺς ἔξω κρίνειν; where it takes the inf. as in Epict. Diss. ii. 17. 14, Win.); τί ἐμοὶ καὶ σοί (sc. ἐστιν, Kühner 364; but also a Hebrew phrase as in 2 Kings 3. 13) Mt. 8. 29 etc., § 30, 3; St. Paul has τί γάρ R. 3. 3, Ph. 1. 18 (what matters it ? or what difference is it ?) and τί οὖν (sc. ἐροῦμεν) R. 6. 15. The masc. is used predicatively in ἐγὼ τίς ἤμην A. 11. 17, cp. 2 Kings 8. 13.—Neut. and masc. pronouns are combined (as in class. Greek) in τίς τί ἄρῃ Mc. 15. 24, τίς τί διεπραγματεύσατο (what each man had etc., but אBDL read τί διεπραγματεύσαντο), L. 19. 15 (Herm. Vis. iii. 8. 6, Mand. vi. 1. 1).

§ 51. INDEFINITE PRONOUNS; PRONOMINAL WORDS.

1. **Τὶς, τὶ**, as in classical Greek, is both substantival and adjectival; when used in the latter way, its position is unrestricted, so that it may even stand before its substantive, so long as there is another word in front of it, καί τις ἀνήρ A. 3. 2, ἵνα τι μεταδῶ χάρισμα R. 1. 11; τινὲς stands at the beginning of the sentence in contrasts: τινὲς (μὲν) ... τ. δὲ 1 Tim. 5. 24, Ph. 1. 15 (Demosth. 9. 56), and even where there is no contrasted clause: τινὲς δὲ A. 17. 18, 19. 31, Jo. 7. 44 etc. (Demosth. 18. 44).—Special usages: Ja. 1. 18 ἀπαρχήν τινα τῶν αὐτοῦ κτισμάτων, softening the metaphorical expression ('so to

---

[1] Also Mt. 26. 62 = Mc. 14. 60 (sup. 5, note 1) τί οὗτοί σου καταμαρτυροῦσιν resolves itself into τί ἐστιν ὃ οὗτοί σ. κ.

[2] Joseph. de vita sua, § 296, οἱ εἰκοσι χρυσοῖ τί γεγόνασιν; Xenoph. Hell. ii. 3. 17 τί ἔσοιτο ἡ πολιτεία (W.-Gr.).

M

speak,' 'a kind of first fruits'); with numbers in classical Greek it has the effect of making them indefinite, 'about,' but in A. 23. 23 (cp. Herm. Vis. i. 4. 3) we have τινὰς δύο 'a certain pair' (to which corresponds εἷς τις L. 22. 50, Jo. 11. 49; cp. § 45, 2); with an adjective (frequent in class. Greek) φοβερά τις ἐκδοχή H. 10. 27, it has an intensifying force like *quidam*, Kühner ii.[2] 570 f. (ὑπερηφανία πολλή τις, Herm. Mand. vi. 2. 5); but in A. 8. 9 εἶναί τινα ἑαυτὸν μέγαν, μέγαν appears to be an interpolation, and τινα to be used emphatically, a person of importance, cp. 5. 35, Kühner 571 note 1; so εἶναί τι 'to be something important' G. 2. 6 (δοκούντων εἶναί τι, = Plat. Gorg. 472 A, Gercke), 6. 3.—Τις is used for 'each' in Herm. Sim. viii. 2. 5 καθὼς ἄξιός ἐστί τις κατοικεῖν, cp. 4. 2 (A. 15. 2 according to the Syriac).—On τις to be supplied with a partitive word see § 35, 4.

2. '**No one**,' '**nobody**' is οὐδείς or μηδείς (on -θείς, see § 6, 7 fin.; οὐθέτερος Clem. Hom. xix. 12); in addition to these we have the Hebraic οὐ (μή) ... πᾶς, where the verb becomes closely attached to the οὐ (or μή): Mt. 24. 22 οὐκ ἂν ἐσώθη πᾶσα σάρξ, like Hebr. כֹּל ... לֹא, R. 3. 20 (cp. Ps. 142. 2), L. 1. 37 οὐκ ἀδυνατήσει παρὰ τῷ θεῷ πᾶν ῥῆμα (= nothing), Ap. (7. 16, 9. 4) 21. 27, A. 10. 14 οὐδέποτε ἔφαγον πᾶν κοινόν (on the other hand οὐ πᾶς with no words intevening = 'not everyone,' as in class. Greek, Mt. 7. 21, 1 C. 15. 39); πᾶς ... οὐ (also Hebraic לֹא ... כֹּל has the same meaning, but is less harsh than the other, Ap. 18. 22, 22. 3, E. 4. 29, 5. 5, 2 P. 1. 20, 1 Jo. 2. 21, 3. 15; this use is excusable, where a positive clause with ἀλλά follows, containing the principal point of the sentence, Jo. 3. 16 ἵνα πᾶς ὁ πιστεύων μὴ ἀπόληται, ἀλλὰ ἔχῃ κ.τ.λ., 6. 39, or where such a clause is clearly to be supplied as in 12. 46.[1] Εἷς ... οὐ is stronger than οὐδείς, Mt. 10. 29 ἓν ... οὐ πεσεῖται, 5. 18, L. 11. 46 etc., as in Demosth. 30. 33 ἡ γυνὴ μίαν ἡμέραν οὐκ ἐχήρευσεν (Krüger, § 24, 2, 2); the same is true of the divided οὐδὲ εἷς A. 4. 32, Mt. 27. 14, Jo. 1. 3 (א*D οὐδέν), R. 3. 10 O.T. (οὐ ... οὐδὲ εἷς, cp. § 75, 6; ibid. 12 O.T. οὐκ ἔστιν ἕως ἑνός, Buttm. p. 106, 1).

3. The **generalizing relatives** ὁστισοῦν, ὅστις δήποτε etc. do not appear either as relatives or (with a verb to be supplied) as indefinite pronouns ('someone or other'); οἵῳ δηποτοῦν with v.l. ᾧ δήποτε (relat.) is found in an interpolated passage 'Jo.' 5. 4. In A. 19. 26 after Παῦλος D adds τις ποτε, which should be corrected to τίς ποτε = Lat. *nescio quis*; so Clem. Hom. v. 27 τίς ποτε 'Ιουδαῖος 'some Jew or other,' τί ποτε 'something' (modern Greek uses τίποτε for 'something' or 'nothing') xi. 28, xvii. 8 (τίς for ὅστις, § 50, 5[2]; cp. the adverb **ὅπως ποτέ** 'somehow' Clem. Hom. ii. 22, where ἐστί is to be supplied): Attic uses ὅστις ἐστίν or ἂν ᾖ, Eurip. Bacch. 247, Demosth. iv. 27, the latter being used by St. Paul in G. 5. 10.

4. On the **derived correlatives** οἷος, ὅσος, τοιοῦτος, τοσοῦτος etc. (§ 12, 4) the following points may be noticed. In exclamations (direct or indirect; originally indirect, 'see how,' 'I marvel how')

---

[1] On 1 C. 15. 51 οὐ πάντες, as also on οὐ πάντως, πάντως οὐ, see § 75, 7.

[2] So also τινοσοῦν (according to the ms. p) for ἡστινοσοῦν Clem. Hom. x. 20.

the forms οἷος, ὅσος, ἡλίκος should strictly be used, as in classical Greek, because some definite thing before one is indicated (so that ὁποῖος etc. are excluded); but here too we sometimes have the interrogative forms as in indirect questions: Mc. 15. 4 ἴδε πόσα κ.τ.λ., Mt. 27. 13 (B* ὅσα), A. 21. 20, 2 C. 7. 11 (direct), ἴδετε πηλίκοις κ.τ.λ. G. 6. 11, H. 7. 14; but οἷος is correctly used in 1 Th. 1. 5, 2 Tim. 3. 11 (in L. 9. 55 D is right with ποίου),[1] cp. πῶς, § 76, 3.—In correlative clauses we have τοιούτους ... ὁποῖος A. 26. 29 (qualiscunque); τοσούτῳ ... ὅσῳ H. 1. 4; but as ὅσοι = πάντες οἵ, it has frequently to be followed by οὗτοι, as in R. 8. 14; peculiar is τὸν αὐτὸν ... οἷον Ph. 1. 30.—On ὁ τοιοῦτος see § 47, 9; it is weakened into a more indefinite term for οὗτος in 2 C. 12. 2, 3, 5, 1 C. 5. 5, 2 C. 2. 6 f.—R. 9. 6 οὐχ οἷον δὲ ὅτι ἐκπέπτωκεν is to be explained (according to Lob. Phryn. 372, Buttm. 319) as for οὐ δήπου ἐκπεπτ., cp. οὐχ ὅτι, § 81.—With H. 10. 37 O.T. ἔτι μικρὸν ὅσον ὅσον (cp. LXX. Is. 26. 20) and L. 5. 3 D ἐπαναγαγεῖν ὅσον ὅσον (for ὀλίγον of the other MSS.) i.e. a trifle, compare Aristoph. Vesp. 213.

5. 'Each' ἕκαστος (without the art. § 47, 9; ibid. for the distinction between it and πᾶς; for τις 'each' supra 1) is intensified as εἷς ἕκαστος; it is added to a plural subject without affecting the construction (class.), Winer § 58, 4; Jo. 16. 32 etc. In addition to ἕκαστος there has been developed out of the distributive κατά (or ἀνά, § 45, 3) the peculiar and grossly incorrect καθ' (ἀνά) εἷς, since καθ' ἕνα ἕκαστον became stereotyped as καθένα ἕκ., and this called forth a corresponding nominative; so in modern Greek 'each' is καθένας. Still there are not many instances as yet in the N.T. of this vulgarism, and the amalgamation of the two words into one has not yet been carried out: Mc. 14. 19 εἷς κατά (καθ' AD al.) εἷς (C εἷς ἕκαστος), 'Jo.' 8. 9 εἷς καθ' εἷς, R. 12. 5 τὸ δὲ καθ' εἷς severally, with reference to each individual, Ap. 21. 21 ἀνὰ εἷς ἕκαστος. (Herm. Sim. ix. 3. 4, 6. 3 κατὰ ἕνα = ἕκαστον, forming the whole object.)

6. Ἕτερος and ἄλλος. Ἕτερος is beside ἀμφότεροι the single surviving dual pronominal word, § 13, 5; in modern Greek it likewise has disappeared, and even in the N.T. instances of its use cannot be quoted from all writers (never in Mc. [16. 12 is spurious], the Apocalypse, or Peter, never in John except in 19. 37, used principally by Lc. and to some extent by Mt. and Paul). Moreover, the way in which it is employed is no longer always correct: Mt. 16. 14 οἱ μὲν ... ἄλλοι δὲ ... ἕτεροι δὲ (in the last two clauses Mc. 8. 28, L. 9. 19 have ἄλλοι twice; ἕτεροι could have stood correctly in the second clause = a second section), L. 8. 6 ff. καὶ ἕτερον three times (D ἄλλο, as in Mt. 13. 5 ff., Mc. 4. 5 ff.), 9. 59, 61, 1 C. 12. 9 f. (ᾧ μὲν ... ἄλλῳ δὲ ... ἑτέρῳ—then four times ἄλλῳ δὲ ... ἑτέρῳ ... ἄλλῳ δὲ), H. 11. 36. The use at the close of enumerations of καὶ ἑτέρους πολλούς Mt. 15. 30 (cp. L. 3. 18, R. 8. 39, 13. 4, 1 Tim. 1. 10) may be paralleled from Attic writers (Dem. 18. 208, 219, 19. 297): others, different from those named (the latter being conceived of as a unit);

---

[1] Also passages like A. 9. 16 ὑποδείξω αὐτῷ, ὅσα δεῖ παθεῖν αὐτόν may be so taken, but the explanation of ὅσα = πάντα ἃ is more natural (so 14. 27 etc.).

but no Attic author ever said ταῖς ἑτέραις πόλεσιν, 'the remaining cities' L. 4. 3, for ὁ ἕτερος is restricted to a definite division into two parts; hence Mt. 10. 23 is also incorrect, ἐν τῇ πόλει ταύτῃ ... εἰς τὴν ἑτέραν (אB; ἄλλην CE rell., with which the article is still more unusual; no doubt 'the next city' is what is meant[1]). Ph. 2. 4 τὰ τῶν (add. D*FG) ἑτέρων opposed to τὰ ἑαυτῶν is correct, cp. 1 C. 10. 24 al.—In the case of ἄλλος the most striking encroachment on the province of ἕτερος is that ὁ ἄλλος is written where there is only a division into two parts: Mt. 5. 39 (L. 6. 29) στρέψον αὐτῷ καὶ τὴν ἄλλην (σιαγόνα), 12. 13, Jo. 18. 16, 19. 32, 20. 3 f. etc.; but also in the case of ἄλλος ἐστὶν ὁ μαρτυρῶν Jo. 5. 32 (opposed to ἐγώ) ἕτερος should have been used, whereas in Mt. 25. 16 etc. ἄλλα πέντε τάλαντα may be illustrated from classical authors (Plato Leg. v. 745 A ἄλλο τοσοῦτον μέρος).—Ἕτεροι is used pleonastically (like ἄλλοι in class. Greek, Kühner ii.[2] 245, note 1) in L. 23. 32 καὶ ἕτεροι δύο κακοῦργοι = two others besides Him, malefactors; on the other hand, ἄλλος is absent in many places where we insert 'other': A. 5. 29 Πέτρος καὶ οἱ (sc. ἄλλοι) ἀπόστολοι; 2. 14 Π. σὺν τοῖς (sc. λοιποῖς) ἕνδεκα; cp. in classical Greek Ἕκτορι καὶ Τρώεσσι Hom. Il. 17. 291.—Ἄλλοι ἄλλο (τι) are united with the meaning 'one one thing—one another' (classical) in A. 19. 32, 21. 34.[2]

SYNTAX OF THE VERB.

§ 52. THE VOICES OF THE VERB.

The system of three voices of the verb—**active (transitive), passive (intransitive),** and **middle** (*i.e.* **transitive with reference to the subject**)—remains on the whole the same in the N.T. as in the classical language. In the former, as in the latter, it frequently happens in the case of individual verbs that by a certain arbitrariness of the language this or that voice becomes the established and recognized form for a particular meaning, to the exclusion of another voice, which might perhaps appear more appropriate to this meaning. It is therefore a difficult matter to arrive at any general conception for each of the voices, which when applied to particular cases is not bound at once to become subject to limitation or even contradiction. The **active** does not in all cases denote an action, but may equally well denote a state, or even being affected in some way or other—ideas which would be more appropriately expressed by the **passive**. Χαίρω

---

[1] The fuller (and certainly original) form of expression in D al. has an additional clause: κἂν ἐν τῇ ἑτέρᾳ (ἄλλῃ D) διώκωσιν ὑμᾶς, φεύγετε εἰς τὴν ἄλλην (once more into the next).

[2] Hermas almost always uses ἕτερος for 'other,' even with the article as in Vis. iii. 7. 1, 3 τοὺς δὲ ἑτέρους (λίθους), Sim. viii. 1. 7-18; but ἄλλος καὶ ἄλλος for 'differing in each instance,' or 'in each individual,' Sim. ix. 1. 4, 10 (cp. Xenoph. Cyrop. iv. 1. 15 'always fresh').

means 'I rejoice,' but the opposite is λυποῦμαι; accordingly in the aorist ἐχάρην we actually have the passive form as in ἐλυπήθην. In θαυμάζω, 'I am astonished' (wonder), the active voice is at most only correct with the meaning 'to see with astonishment'; it has a middle future θαυμάσομαι, cp. θεῶμαι θεάσομαι; but the verb of similar meaning ἄγαμαι has ἠγάσθην and accordingly (as a verb expressing emotion) is passive, and the later language creates the corresponding forms θαυμάζομαι depon., and aor. ἐθαυμάσθην, § 20, 1. We may therefore assert that the active voice is quite unlimited in the meanings which may be attached to it, except where a passive (or middle) voice exists beside it, as in τύπτω – τύπτομαι. It must further be added that certain verbal forms unite an active formation with a passive (intransitive) meaning, particularly the 1st and 2nd aorists passive in -θην, -ην, and frequently perfects in -α, -κα (ἀπόλωλα, ἕστηκα). On the other hand, the **middle** can be only imperfectly differentiated from the passive, with which in the forms of the tenses, with the exception of aorist and future, it entirely coincides. We may adhere to the rule of giving the name of middle only to those forms which share the transitive meaning of the active, as ἵσταμαι ἐστησάμην beside ἵστημι ἔστησα; but if no active form exists, or if the meaning of the active form does not correspond to that of the passive or middle, then it is difficult to distinguish between the two last-mentioned voices. Ἀποκρίνομαι, 'answer,' is a deponent verb when it has this meaning; since it is transitive, in classical Greek it takes the forms ἀπεκρινάμην, ἀποκρινοῦμαι; the later language, however, regardless of the meaning which elsewhere attaches to aorists in -θην, regularly uses ἀπεκρίθην, ἀποκριθήσομαι. Θαυμάσομαι from θαυμάζω should be called middle, since it is transitive, and the classical language possesses the additional form θαυμασθήσομαι with a passive meaning; the same applies to τέξομαι from τίκτω and many other such futures; but ἀποθανοῦμαι from ἀποθνήσκω, θρέξομαι from τρέχω (δραμοῦμαι from ἔδραμον), being intransitive, and having no additional future forms, must certainly be classed as passives in the same category with the later θαυμασθήσομαι,[1] if the conception of the passive is extended, as it must be, so that it becomes equivalent to intransitive. It is, in fact, quite a rare occurrence for the language to draw a distinction between intransitive and passive, such as in Attic is drawn between ἔστην 'placed myself' and ἐστάθην 'was placed,' or between στήσομαι 'shall place myself' and σταθήσομαι 'shall be placed.' In the language of poetry and in the later language this distinction hardly exists at all: there ἐστάθην is equivalent to ἔστην and φαάνθην to ἐφάνην (while in Attic ἐφάνην means 'appeared,' ἐφάνθην 'was informed against' [juridical term]).

§ 53. ACTIVE VOICE.

1. Some active verbs, which were originally transitive, subsequently developed an additional intransitive (or reflexive) meaning.

[1] Ἐθαυμάσθην Ap. 13. 3, θαυμασθήσονται 17. 8 have ceased to be used transitively.

Ἄγω 'lead,' besides the stereotyped phrase ἄγε (=class.), is also used intransitively in ἄγωμεν 'let us go' Mt. 26. 46 etc.; and still more frequently in composition: thus we have ὑπάγω, a vulgar word for 'to go,' esp. common in the forms ὕπαγε, -ετε, but also found in other forms of the present stem, e.g. ὑπάγει Jo. 3. 8 (the word is most frequent in this writer), but never in other tenses, cp. § 24 (the word is previously used in classical Greek, ὑπάγεθ' ὑμεῖς τῆς ὁδοῦ Aristoph. Ran. 174, ὑπάγοιμι τἄρ' ἄν Av. 1017, but with a more clearly defined meaning); παράγειν 'to pass by'[1], Mt. 20. 30, Mc. 15. 21 etc. (cp. Polyb. v. 18, 4): met. 'to disappear' 1 C. 7. 31, for which 1 Jo. 2. 8, 17 uses παράγεται; περιάγειν Mt. 4. 23, A. 13. 11 etc. 'to go about,' with accus. of the district traversed, cp. § 34, 1 (not so in class. Greek[2]). Also προάγειν besides the meaning 'to bring before' acquires that of 'to go before anyone (τινα)' (in class. Greek we have Plat. Phaed. 90 A σοῦ προάγοντος ἐγὼ ἐφεσπόμην, but this is different to the N.T. use; the common phrase is προηγεῖσθαί τινι, which like ἡγεῖσθαι is never so used in the N.T.), Mt. 2. 9 and passim; but ἀνάγεσθαι ἀνήχθην.—Βάλλειν 'to rush' A. 27. 14 (the use can hardly be paralleled, but cp. ῥίπτειν); ἐπιβ. 'to rush upon' (as already in class. Greek) Mc. 4. 37; ibid. 14. 72 the phrase ἐπιβαλὼν ἔκλαιεν is obscure (it is explained by ἀρξάμενος; D has ἤρξατο κλαίειν; cp. A. 11. 4 ἀρξάμενος ἐξετίθετο).—Βρέχειν trans. means 'to water'; intrans. and impers. (§ 30, 4) it stands for class. ὕειν (which nowhere appears) as in modern Greek; we also have ἔβρεξε πῦρ καὶ θεῖον L. 17. 29, after Gen. 19. 24, where κύριος is inserted as the subject.—Ἔχειν 'to be in such and such circumstances' as in class. Greek; similarly ὑπερέχειν 'to excel' (also trans. 'to surpass' Ph. 4. 7); ἀπέχειν 'to be distant' (with accus. of the distance); ἐνέχειν (sc. χόλον) 'to be angry' Mc. 6. 19 (L. 11. 53); ἐπέχειν 'to observe anything' L. 14. 7 etc. (similarly in class. Greek), also 'to stay,' 'tarry' A. 19. 22 (ditto); προσέχειν 'to take heed,' 'to listen to anyone' (never with the original supplement τὸν νοῦν, which is often inserted in Attic): also with and without ἑαυτῷ =cavere (Mt. 6. 1, L. 17. 2 etc.).[3]—Ἀνακάμπτειν 'to turn round,' 'come back' as in Attic.—Κλίνειν 'to decline' of the day L. 9. 12, 24. 29 (similarly in Polyb.); ἐκκλίνειν 'to turn aside' R. 16. 17 etc. (class.).—Ῥίπτειν: ἀπορίψαντας is intrans. in A. 27. 43 (so ῥίπτ. in poetry and late writers).—Στρέφειν: the simple verb is intrans. in A. 7. 42? as is often the case with its compounds with ἐπι-, ἀπο-, ἀνα-, ὑπο-, A. 3. 19 etc., not without classical precedent; ὑποστρέφεσθαι is never found (in class. Greek it is used as well as -ειν);

---

[1] The explanation that it means discedere arises from Mt. 9. 27 παράγοντι ἐκεῖθεν, where ὑπάγοντι would be the correct word; in 9. 9 ἐκεῖθεν should probably be omitted with ℵ*L.

[2] Demosth. 42. 5 περιαγαγὼν (to lead about) τὴν ἐσχατιάν; also in Cebes Tab. 6 περιάγονται is the reading now adopted.

[3] Περιέχειν 'to contain' (of a written document) is in the first instance transitive: περιέχουσαν τάδε A. 15. 23 D: περιέχ. (ἔχουσαν ℵB) τὸν τύπον τοῦτον 23. 25; but we also have the phrases π. τὸν τρόπον τοῦτον or οὕτως, worded in this way (Joseph.), and in 1 P. 2. 6 περιέχει ἐν (τῇ) γραφῇ (ἡ γραφή C), 'stands written.'

§ 53. 1–3.] ACTIVE VOICE. 183

ἐπιστρέφειν 'to turn round,' 'be converted' (for which we have -εστράφητε in 1 P. 2. 25, but C reads -έψατε), so esp. frequent in this sense in Polybius: pass. 'to turn oneself round,' look round' (Att.); ἀναστρ. 'to turn round,' often used transitively as well (it appears intransitively in Attic as a military expression): pass. 'to live,' 'sojourn' (Att.); ἀποστρ. is intr. in A. 3. 26 (for which Att. generally has the pass.), more often trans.; pass. with τινά 'to turn away from,' 'avoid' (Att.).—Cp. ἐγείρειν, καθίζειν in § 24; and further, technical expressions like αἴρειν (sc. τὴν ναῦν ἀπὸ τῆς γῆς) 'to set sail' A. 27. 13, etc.

2. The intransitive employment of δύειν and φύειν is based upon an old variation in the usage of these words, see § 24; that of αὐξάνειν upon the usage of the Hellenistic language, ibid. Beside the deponent εὐαγγελίζεσθαι (Att.) there is also found the form -ζειν in Ap. 10. 7, 14. 6 (elsewhere the Ap. also uses -ζεσθαι), as occasionally in the LXX., 1 Sam. 31. 9 (Dio Cass. 61. 13). The new words θριαμβεύειν and μαθητεύειν in other writers are intrans. (to celebrate a triumph, to be a disciple—corresponding to the ordinary meaning of the termination -εύειν), in the N.T. they are in (nearly) all cases transitive, to lead in triumph, to make disciples, see § 34, 1.— Ἀναφάναντες τὴν Κύπρον A. 21. 3 (there is a wrong reading -έντες) means 'made it visible to ourselves,' viz. by approaching it; it must have been a nautical expression, as ἀποκρύπτειν (Lat. *abscondere*) is used to express the opposite meaning.

3. **Active for middle.**—If emphasis is laid on the reference to the subject, then the middle is never employed, but the active with a reflexive pronoun takes its place: ἀπέκτεινεν ἑαυτόν (on the other hand ἀπήγξατο is used, because ἀπάγχειν τινά, *i.e.* someone else, is unusual, the reflexive action being in this instance far the commoner of the two). So we say 'he killed himself' [tödtete sich **selbst**]. Elsewhere the reflexive reference which is suggested by the context remains unexpressed, as in the case of (κατα-)δουλοῦν (which Attic also uses beside -οῦσθαι): 2 C. 11. 20 εἴ τις ὑμᾶς καταδουλοῖ, cp. G. 2. 4 (so too ἀναφάναντες, supra 2). Inversely, the reflexive may be expressed twice over, by the middle and by a pronoun; διεμερίσαντο ἑαυτοῖς Jo. 19. 24 O.T., cp. A. 7. 21 (as in Attic). With the following verbs the use of the active instead of the middle is contrary to Attic usage: (πειράζειν for πειρᾶσθαι, see § 24); εὑρίσκειν 'to obtain' the usual form, except in H. 9. 12 (Attic uses the middle, poets have the act. as well); καθῆψεν τῆς χειρὸς αὐτοῦ A. 28. 3 instead of καθήψατο which C reads (but τόξου καθάψαι is also cited by Pollux i. 164); λῦσον τὸ ὑπόδημα τῶν ποδῶν σου A. 7. 33 O.T. (LXX. λῦσαι). For παρέχειν see § 55, 1. Ποιεῖν is used (with μονὴν Jo. 14. 23 only in AEGH al.) (with ὁδόν Mc. 2. 23, BGH have ὁδοποιεῖν), with τὴν ἐκδίκησιν L. 18. 7 f., τὸ ἔλεος μετ' αὐτοῦ a Hebraic phrase (Gen. 24. 12) L. 10. 37, 1. 72, with ἐνέδραν A. 25. 3? κοπετόν 8. 2 (-σαντο EHP), κρίσιν Jo. 5. 27, Jude 15, πόλεμον Ap. 11. 7 etc., συμβούλιον Mc. 3. 6 (BL ἐδίδουν), 15. 1 (v.l. ἑτοιμάσαντες), (with συνωμοσίαν A. 23. 13 only in HP), with συστροφήν ibid. 12; in all

which cases the active is incorrect because the ποιοῦντες are at the same time the very persons who carry out the action which is expressed by the verbal substantive. We also have elsewhere in the N.T. ποιεῖσθαι λόγον, ἀναβολήν, πορείαν, σπουδήν etc. Σπάσασθαι τὴν μάχαιραν is correctly written in Mc. 14. 47, A. 16. 27, but in Mt. 26. 51 we have ἀπέσπασεν τ. μ. αὐτοῦ, in which case Attic Greek must certainly have omitted the αὐτοῦ and expressed the reflexive force by means of the middle; similarly in 26. 65 διέρρηξεν τὰ ἱμάτια αὐτοῦ, but in this case the use of the active is also classical (Aesch. Pers. 199 πέπλους ῥήγνυσιν, cp. 1030).

§ 54. PASSIVE VOICE.

1. Even **deponent verbs** with a transitive meaning can (as in Attic) have a **passive**, the forms of which are for the most part identical with those of the deponent. Λογίζεται 'is reckoned' R. 4. 4 f. (therefore even the present of this vb. occasionally has a passive meaning: the instances of this in classical writers are not numerous, but cp. Hdt. 3. 95 λογιζόμενον). Ἰῶντο A. 5. 16 D: ἴαται perf. Mc. 5. 29; ἐργαζομένη Herm. Sim. v. 3. 8. But the passive sense is frequent in the case of the aorist, where the passive and deponent forms are distinguishable: ἐλογίσθην, ἰάθην, ἐχαρίσθην, ἐρρύσθην etc. (fut. λογισθήσομαι R. 2. 26, ἰαθήσ. Mt. 8. 8, ἀπαρνηθήσ. [§ 20, 1] L. 12. 9).

2. While in Attic Greek the **passives** of some **ordinary verbs** are regularly **represented** by the **actives** of other verbs,—*e.g.* ἀποκτείνειν takes for passive ἀποθνῄσκειν, εὖ (κακῶς) ποιεῖν pass. εὖ (κακῶς) πάσχειν, εὖ (κακ.) λέγειν pass. εὖ (κακ.) ἀκούειν, and ὑπό is used with these verbs the connecting particle as it is elsewhere with true passives—there are but few traces of this usage in the N.T. (ἐκπίπτειν A. 27. 17, 26, 29 = ἐκβάλλεσθαι, but does not take ὑπό: on the other hand ἐκβάλλεσθαι is used in Mt. 8. 12 etc., though this form is also found in Attic; πάσχειν ὑπό Mt. 17. 12, where ἐποίησαν has preceded, Mc. 5. 26, 1 Th. 2. 14); still the instances of the contrary usage are also not numerous: ἀποκτανθῆναι Mc. 9. 31 etc. The passive of ποιεῖν, with the exception of H. 12. 27 is entirely unrepresented.

3. As in Attic, a **passive** verb may have a **person for its subject** even in a case where in the **active** this person is expressed by the **genitive or dative**; the accusative of the thing remains the same with the passive as with the active verb. The N.T. instances cannot indeed be directly illustrated from the classical language, but they are perfectly analogous to the classical instances. They are **διακονηθῆναι** Mc. 10. 45 (διακονεῖν τινι); **ἐγκαλεῖσθαι** to be accused (ἐγκαλεῖν τινι) A. 19. 40 etc.; **εὐαρεστεῖσθαι** (act. with τινί) H. 3. 16 (Diod. Sic.); **κατεγνωσμένος** G. 2. 11 (act. τινός), so Diod. Sic.; **κατηγορεῖσθαι** (act. τινός) with acc. of the thing Mt. 27. 12, A. 22. 30, 25. 16 ; **μαρτυρεῖσθαι** (act. τινί) to have a (good) testimonial (late writers) A. 6. 3 etc., 1 Tim. 5. 10, H. 7. 8 etc. (but in 3 Jo. 12 Δημητρίῳ μεμαρτύρηται);

§ 54. 3-5. § 55. 1.] PASSIVE AND MIDDLE VOICES. 185

πιστεύεσθαί τι 'to have something entrusted to one' (πιστεύειν τινί τι) R. 3. 2 etc. (Polyb.): also (without an object) 'to find credit,' 1 Tim. 3. 16 ἐπιστεύθη (Χριστὸς) ἐν κόσμῳ (act. τινί or εἴς τινα), cp. 2 Th. 1. 10 (so previously in Attic); χρηματίζεσθαι 'to receive instructions' (from God; act. τινί) Mt. 2. 12 etc.: only in L. 2. 26 do we have ἦν αὐτῷ κεχρηματισμένον (D κεχρηματισμένος ἦν).—Quite distinct from this is the use of the passive with a **thing** for its subject: 2 C. 1. 11 ἵνα τὸ χάρισμα εὐχαριστηθῇ (εὐχαριστεῖν τι Herm. Sim. vii. 5; in the N.T. the act. takes ἐπί, περί etc.), and its use where an infinitive or a ὅτι clause may be regarded as the subject, ἐπιτρέπεταί σοι ... λέγειν A. 26. 1, 1 C. 14. 34, as also the impersonal passive, § 30, 4.

4. The **passives of** ὁρᾶν, γιγνώσκειν, εὑρίσκειν have a certain independent position as compared with their actives, since they assume a purely intransitive meaning, and are followed by the dative of the person concerned, instead of making use of ὑπό, see § 37, 4. A frequent instance is ὀφθῆναί τινι (an old use), *apparere, supervenire*, with the new present ὀπτάνομαι A. 1. 3 (§ 24). **Γνωσθῆναι** 'to become known' A. 9. 24 etc., cp. γιγνώσκεσθαί τινι 'to be known,' in Eur. Cycl. 567, Xenoph. Cyr. vii. 1. 44; but 'to be recognized' is expressed by the pass. with ὑπό in 1 C. 8. 3. **Εὑρεθῆναι** in R. 10. 20 O.T. (v.l. with ἐν) is used along with ἐμφανῆ γενέσθαι (on 2 P. 3. 14, see § 37, 5). **Θεαθῆναι** is used like ὀφθ. in Mt. 6. 1, 23. 5; **φαίνεσθαί** τινι dates from the earliest stage of the language.

5. The passive must occasionally be rendered by '**to let oneself**' be etc. Ἀδικεῖσθε 1 C. 6, 7 'let yourselves be wronged' (in the sense of allowing it to take place), so in the same verse ἀποστερεῖσθε. Βαπτίζεσθαι 'to let oneself be baptized' (aor. ἐβαπτίσθην, but see § 55, 2). Cp. ἀγνίζεσθαι A. 21. 24, 26, ἀπογράφεσθαι L. 2. 1, γαμίζεσθαι (§ 24), δογματίζεσθαι 'to let precepts be made for one' Col. 2. 20, περιτέμνεσθαι passim. On the other hand, 'to let' in the sense of occasioning some result is expressed by the middle voice, § 55, 2.

§ 55. MIDDLE VOICE.

1. As the active is used in place of the middle, so the **middle** often stands **for the active** which would naturally be expected. Ἀμύνεσθαι 'to assist' = the Attic ἀμύνειν in A. 7. 24 (the word occurs here only). For ἀπειλεῖσθαι see § 24. Ἀπεκδυσάμενος τὰς ἀρχάς is found in Col. 2. 15, whereas in Attic ἀποδύσασθαι is 'to undress oneself.' Ἡρμοσάμην ὑμᾶς ἀνδρί 2 C. 11. 2 'betrothed' is for ἥρμοσα (the word here only). (Ἐνεργεῖσθαι is wrongly quoted in this connection: in the following passages R. 7. 5, 2 C. 1. 6, 4. 12, G. 5. 6, E. 3. 20, Col. 1. 29, 1 Th. 2. 13, 2 Th. 2. 7, Ja. 5. 16 it is everywhere intransitive, and never applied to God, of whom the active is used; the fact that the active appears in Mt. 14. 2, Mc. 6. 14 with δυνάμεις as subject, causes ἐνεργεῖν to appear equivalent to ἐνεργεῖσθαι). (The middle ἐκλέγεσθαι is always found, meaning 'to choose out *for oneself*,' and it is only in A. 6. 5, 15. 22, 25 that it is not

absolutely necessary to mentally supply 'for oneself'). (Ἐπιδείκνυσθαι A. 9. 39 [elsewhere N.T. has the act.] may mean 'to display *on their own persons.*') **Καταλαμβάνεσθαι** 'to perceive' A. 4. 13 etc. (Att. -ειν, but Dionys. Hal. also has the middle). **Παρατηρεῖσθαι** L. 14. 1 al. (used as well as -τηρεῖν; the simple verb only takes the active form). **Πληροῦσθαι** E. 1. 23 ' to fill' is equivalent to the act. in 4. 10. **Προβλέπεσθαι** H. 11. 40 is modelled on προορᾶσθαι (βλέπειν for ὁρᾶν § 24); **περιβλέπεσθαι** is the invariable form of the verb (Polyb.; Attic uses the act.). **Τίθεσθαι** ἐν φυλακῇ and similar phrases, 'to put in prison' A. 4. 3 etc. (always the middle verb) are in accordance with classical usage (καταθησόμενος εἰς τὸ οἴκημα Demosth. 56, 4); but the middle is also used with the meaning 'to appoint as' or 'to,' ἀποστόλους 1 C. 12. 28, εἰς ὀργήν 1 Th. 5. 9 = Att. ποιῆσαι, καταστῆσαι, Ionic θεῖναι (H. 1. 2 ὃν ἔθηκεν κληρονόμον).—**Συγκαλεῖν** and -σθαι ('to call to oneself') are correctly distinguished, if συγκαλεῖται is read instead of συγκαλεῖ with DF in L. 15. 6 and with ADEG al. in verse 9.—Between **αἰτεῖν** and αἰτεῖσθαι old grammarians draw the distinction, that a man who asks for something to be given him, intending to give it back again, αἰτεῖται; but αἰτεῖσθαι is applied generally to requests in business transactions, and this is its regular use in the N.T. Mt. 27. 20, 58, Mc. 15 (6), 8, 43,[1] L. 23. 23, 25, 52, A. 3. 14, 9. 2, 12. 20, 13. 28, 25. 3, 15; the active is the usual form for requests from God, but the middle is used in A. 7. 46,[2] and there is an arbitrary interchange of mid. and act. in Ja. 4. 2 f., 1 Jo. 5. 14 f. etc.; the request of a beggar, a son etc. is naturally αἰτεῖν, A. 3. 2, Mt. 7. 9 f. (cp. A. 16. 29, 1 C. 1. 22). Ἀπαιτεῖν, παραιτεῖσθαι are the Attic forms; ἐξῃτήσατο L. 22. 31 (Attic uses both -εῖν and -εῖσθαι).—**Παρεχόμενος** σεαυτὸν τύπον Tit. 2. 7 is contrary to classical usage (παρέχων), but Col. 4. 1 τὴν ἰσότητα τοῖς δούλοις παρέχεσθε is not (C reads -ετε), nor is παρέξῃ L. 7. 4, but the active is certainly unclassical in παρεῖχον φιλανθρωπίαν A. 28. 2, ἐργασίαν 16. 16 (-ετο C; in 19. 24 A*DE read -χε, -χετο is the usual reading: the passage appears to be corrupt), although Homer uses φιλότητα παρασχεῖν.—On the whole the conclusion arrived at must be that the New Testament writers were perfectly capable of preserving the distinction between the active and middle.

2. The middle must occasionally be rendered by '**to let oneself**,' cp. § 54, 4 for the pass., in the sense of occasioning some result, not of allowing something to take place. Κείρασθαι, ξύρασθαι 1 C. 11. 6; ὄφελον καὶ ἀποκόψονται G. 5. 12 'have themselves castrated,' as in Deut. 23. 1, whereas περιτέμνεσθαι is treated as a passive (let in the sense of allow). Ἐβαπτισάμην in A. 22. 16 βάπτισαι καὶ ἀπόλουσαι (1 C. 6. 11 ἀπελούσασθε) may be explained in the sense of ' occa-

---

[1] In Mc. 6. 22 αἴτησον (א -σαι), 23 αἰτήσῃς, 24 αἰτήσωμαι, 25 ᾐτήσατο (D εἶπεν), there is a nice distinction, since the daughter of Herodias, after the king's declaration, stands in a kind of business relation towards him. Cp. Mt. 20. 20, 22, Mc. 10. 35, 38.

[2] A. 13. 21 ᾐτήσαντο βασιλέα, καὶ ἔδωκεν αὐτοῖς ὁ θεὸς κ.τ.λ. probably does not come under this head. Cp. 1 Sam. 8. 5.

sioning'; but in 1 C. 10. 2 -ισαντο of BKLP appears to be wrong and -ίσθησαν to be the only right reading. In L. 11. 38 one minuscule codex (700 Greg., 604 Scriv.) exhibits the correct ἐβαπτίσατο instead of -σθη.

§ 56. THE TENSES. PRESENT TENSE.

1. It was shown in a previous discussion in § 14, 1 that every tense has generally speaking a double function to perform, at least in the indicative: it expresses at once an **action** (continuance, completion, continuance in completion), and a **time-relation** (present, past, future), and the latter **absolutely**, *i.e.* with reference to the stand-point of the speaker or narrator, not **relatively**, *i.e.* with reference to something else which occurs in the speech or narrative. In the case of the **future**, however, the function of defining action has disappeared from the Greek of the N.T., and the **moods** of this tense (including the infinitive and participle) were originally formed to denote a **relative** time-relation (with reference to the principal action of the sentence), and only in so far as they were necessary for this purpose: hence it happens that a future conjunctive [1] and imperative never existed. The **moods**, with the exception just mentioned, are not used to express the time-relation but only the character of the action.

2. The **present** denotes therefore an action (1) as viewed in its **duration** (its progress), (2) as taking place in **present** time. In the latter case the present may be regarded as a point of time, with the addition of the time immediately preceding and succeeding it, as in γράφω 'I am writing (now),' or again the time included on either side of the present moment may be extended more and more, until it finally embraces all time, as in ὁ θεὸς ἔστιν. Again, the idea of **repetition** may be added to, or substituted for, that of duration, so that what in itself is not continuous, is yet in virtue of its repetition viewed as in a certain measure continuous: this is more clearly seen in the case of past time: ἔβαλεν 'he struck,' ἔβαλλεν 'he struck repeatedly or continuously.' A distinction between the present strictly so called, denoting something which really takes place at the present moment, and the wider use, can only be made by means of a periphrasis, τυγχάνω ὤν (this however is not found in the N.T., § 73, 4).

3. Since the opposite to duration is **completion** (expressed by the aorist), the present may be used with sufficient clearness to denote, as such, an action which has **not yet reached completion**, where we have recourse to the auxiliary verb 'will.' Jo. 10. 32 διὰ ποῖον αὐτῶν ἔργον ἐμὲ λιθάζετε ('will ye stone me?'): G. 5. 4 οἵτινες ἐν νόμῳ δικαιοῦσθε 'would be justified': Jo. 13. 6 νίπτεις. The imperfect more often has this (**conative**) meaning.

---

[1] It is true that instances of it are found in the MSS. of the N.T., *e.g.* 1 C. 13. 3 καυθήσωμαι CK.

4. Since in the case of actions viewed as completed, there exists for obvious reasons no form to express present time (equivalent to a present of the aorist), the present tense must also in certain cases take over this function as well (**aoristic present**, Burton, N.T. Moods and Tenses p. 9). If Peter in A. 9. 34 says to Aeneas ἰᾶταί σε Ἰησοῦς Χριστός, the meaning is not, 'He is engaged in healing thee,' but 'He completes the cure at this moment, as I herewith announce to thee': under the same category comes παραγγέλλω σοι κ.τ.λ. in A. 16. 18 (the expulsion of a demon), where in a similar way an action is denoted from the stand-point of the actor and speaker as being completed in the present, which the narrator from his own point of view would have expressed by the aorist as completed in the past, παρήγγειλεν.[1] With this belongs ἀσπάζεται 'sends greeting': to which the corresponding term is always ἀσπάσασθε 'greet.'

5. The present also habitually takes an aoristic meaning, where an interchange of times takes place, and it is used in lively, realistic narrative as the **historic present**. This usage is frequent, as it is in classical authors, in the New Testament writers of narrative, except in Luke's writings, where we seldom meet with it. Jo. 1. 29 τῇ ἐπαύριον βλέπει ... καὶ λέγει ...; 35 τῇ ἐπαύριον πάλιν εἱστήκει (pluperf. = impf. 'was standing')... 36 καὶ ... λέγει...; 44 τῇ ἐπαύριον ἠθέλησεν ἐξελθεῖν ... καὶ εὑρίσκει; thus the tendency appears to be for the circumstances to be denoted by past tenses, and the principal actions (which take place under the circumstances described [2]) by the present, while the final results are again expressed by the aorist, because there realistic narrative would be unnatural: 40 ἦλθαν οὖν καὶ εἶδαν ... καὶ ... ἔμειναν. Even apart from narrative the present is used in a similar way: ibid. 15 Ἰωάνης μαρτυρεῖ περὶ αὐτοῦ καὶ κέκραγεν (= κράζει).

6. Ἥκω, as is well known, has a **perfect** meaning (L. 15. 27 etc.); (πάρεισιν 'are come hither' A. 17. 6 is a present used for the perfect of *another* verb [Burton, p. 10], as ἀπέχω is used for ἀπείληφα in Mt. 6. 2). Further ἀκούω is 'I hear' in the sense of 'I have heard' (L. 9. 9, 1 C. 11. 18, 2 Th. 3. 11, as in classical Greek; an equivalent for it would be λέγεται, where the use of the present is no more remarkable than in ἀκούεται 1 C. 5. 1). Ἀδικῶ in A. 25. 11 beside ἄξιον θανάτου πέπραχά τι (and following οὐδὲν ἠδίκηκα in verse 10)[3] means 'I am guilty,' 'am a criminal' *as in Attic* (this use occurs here only; in Mt. 20. 13 the word has the ordinary meaning of the

---

[1] Burton quotes in this connection (besides A. 26. 1 ἐπιτρέπεται etc.) ἀφίενταί σου αἱ ἁμαρτίαι Mc. 2. 5, Mt. 9. 2 etc., and rightly, at least if this reading is to be trusted (cp. § 23, 7).

[2] Rodemeyer, Diss. inaug. Basel 1889 (Präs. histor. bei Herodot. u. Thukyd.) endeavours to show that the historic present expresses something which takes place at or directly after a point of time already indicated: this theory holds good up to a certain point. Mt. 2. 13 ἀναχωρησάντων αὐτῶν ἰδοὺ ἄγγελος κυρίου φαίνεται (Win.); Herm. Vis. i. 1. 3 διαβὰς ἦλθον ... καὶ τιθῶ τὰ γόνατα.

[3] Thus it appears that the perfect remains where there is a reference to particular trespasses; the present is only used of the general result.

pres.); also ὁ νικῶν in Ap. 2. 7 etc. may remind one of the Attic use of νικῶ for 'I am a conqueror,' while πράσσει in A. 26. 31 refers to Paul's whole manner of life and his Christianity in particular. Throughout these remarks we are concerned only with the special usage of individual verbs, and not with the general syntactical employment of the present.

7. Presents such as those in L. 15. 29 τοσαῦτα ἔτη δουλεύω σοι (cp. 13. 7 ἰδοὺ τρία ἔτη ἀφ' οὗ ἔρχομαι, Jo. 8. 58 εἰμί, 15. 27 ἐστέ, and many others) are by no means used for perfects : on the contrary, no other form was possible, because the continuance or the recurrence of the action in the present had to be included in the expression.

8. **Present for future.**—The classical language is also acquainted with a (lively and imaginative) present for future in the case of prophecies (*e.g.* in an oracle in Herodot. vii. 140 f.), and this present —a sort of counterpart to the historic present—is very frequent in the predictions of the N.T. It is not attached to any definite verbs, and it is purely by accident that ἔρχομαι appears with special frequency in this sense : Jo. 19. 3 ἐὰν ἑτοιμάσω τόπον ὑμῖν, πάλιν ἔρχομαι καὶ παραλήμψομαι ὑμᾶς ; so esp. ὁ ἐρχόμενος 'He who is to come' (the Messiah) Mt. 11. 3, cp. 11. 14 Ἠλίας ὁ μέλλων ἔρχεσθαι, 17. 11 Ἠλ. ἔρχεται. But we find equally well: Mc. 9. 31 ὁ υἱὸς τοῦ ἀνθρώπου παραδίδοται (= μέλλει παραδίδοσθαι Mt. 17. 22)..., καὶ ἀποκτενοῦσιν αὐτόν, Mt. 27. 63 μετὰ τρεῖς ἡμέρας ἐγείρομαι : Herm. Vis. ii. 2. 4 ἀφίενται. The present is also used without any idea of prophecy, if the matter is regarded as something that is certain to take place, so that μέλλει (ἔρχεσθαι) could have been used : *e.g.* in Jo. 4. 35 ἔτι τετράμηνός ἐστι καὶ ὁ θερισμὸς ἔρχεται, Mt. 24. 43 ποίᾳ φυλακῇ ὁ κλέπτης ἔρχεται, and repeatedly in ἕως ἔρχομαι (-εται), see § 65, 10 ; in other cases ἐλεύσομαι is necessary, Mt. 24. 5, Mc. 12. 9, 13. 6 etc. But verbs of going and coming when used in the present also have the meaning of being in course of going (or coming), in which case the arrival at the goal still lies in the future : Jo. 3. 8 πόθεν ἔρχεται καὶ ποῦ ὑπάγει, almost = is about to go, 8. 14 πόθεν ἦλθον καὶ ποῦ ὑπάγω ... πόθεν ἔρχομαι καὶ ποῦ ὑπ.; so ποῦ ὑπάγω -εις in Jo. 14. 4 f., πορεύομαι ibid. 2, 12, A. 20. 22 : ἀναβαίνομεν Mt. 20. 18, Jo. 20. 17 (but in Jo. 7. 8 οὐκ ἀναβαίνω the present is used for future).

9. **Present used to express relative time** (cp. 1).—It is a well-known fact that when the speech of another person is directly repeated the tenses refer to the points of time of the speech itself, and that in the classical language the form of oratio obliqua is frequently assimilated in this respect to that of direct speech. In the N.T. the use of oratio obliqua is certainly not favoured, and that of oratio recta predominates ; but it is noteworthy that subordinate sentences after verbs of perception and belief are assimilated to oratio recta, and the tenses therefore have a relative meaning. Thus Mt. 2. 22 ἀκούσας ὅτι Ἀρχέλαος βασιλεύει : Jo. 6. 24 εἶδεν ὁ ὄχλος ὅτι Ἰησοῦς οὐκ ἔστιν ἐκεῖ. This practice also appears in the classical language, but not as a general rule, whereas in the

N.T. the rule is so far established that the imperfect in such sentences must in most cases be rendered by the pluperfect, since it refers to an earlier time than that spoken of, § 57, 6. Still we have Jo. 16. 19 ἔγνω ὅτι ἤθελον (v.l. ἤμελλον) αὐτὸν ἐρωτᾶν, with which cp. the instances of pluperf. for the usual perf. in § 59, 6; 18. 32 ἤμελλεν after σημαίνων, cp. § 61, 2 (A. 22. 2 ἀκούσαντες ὅτι προσεφώνει, but the better reading is προσφωνεῖ DEH). The aorist however may be used: Mc. 12. 12 ἔγνωσαν ὅτι εἶπεν (Mt. 21. 45 has ὅτι λέγει = ἔλεγε).

§ 57. IMPERFECT AND AORIST INDICATIVE.

1. The distinction between continuous and completed action is most sharply marked in the case of the imperfect and aorist indicative, and moreover this distinction is observed with the same accuracy in the N.T. as in classical Greek.

2. **Repetition**, as such, is regarded as **continuous** action, and expressed by the **imperfect** (cp. § 56, 2), as also is action **left uncompleted** (Imperf. de conatu, cp. § 56, 3). Exx.: (*a*) A. 2. 45 τὰ κτήματα ἐπίπρασκον καὶ διεμέριζον αὐτὰ πᾶσιν; this frequently happened, although it is not stated that it took place or was carried into effect in every case (aorist), cp. 4. 34, 18. 8, Mc. 12. 41; (*b*) A. 7. 26 συνήλλασσεν αὐτοὺς εἰς εἰρήνην, 'sought to reconcile,' 26. 11 ἠνάγκαζον βλασφημεῖν, where however the imperf. also expresses repetition (like ἐδίωκον ibid.), L. 1. 59 ἐκάλουν αὐτὸ Ζαχαρίαν 'wished to call him Z.,' Mt. 3. 14 διεκώλυεν 'wished or tried to prevent Him' (A. 27. 41 ἐλύετο 'began to be broken up').

3. The action is further regarded as continuous if the **manner** of it is vividly portrayed. H. 11. 17 πίστει προσενήνοχεν Ἀβραὰμ τὸν Ἰσαάκ ..., καὶ τὸν μονογενῆ προσέφερεν κ.τ.λ., a supplementary characterization of the peculiar feature of this instance. A. 5. 26 ἦγεν αὐτοὺς οὐ μετὰ βίας, cp. 27 ἀγαγόντες δὲ (conclusion of the act) αὐτοὺς ἔστησαν; 41 ἐπορεύοντο χαίροντες ἀπὸ προσώπου τοῦ συνεδρίου (it was here unnecessary to denote the conclusion of the act); 15. 3 διήρχοντο ... ἐκδιηγούμενοι τὴν ἐπιστροφὴν τῶν ἐθνῶν, καὶ ἐποίουν (everywhere) χαρὰν μεγάλην ... (conclusion given in 4 παραγενόμενοι δέ); 15. 41 is similar; on the other hand, we have in 16. 6 διῆλθον δὲ τὴν Φρυγίαν (where there is no description). See also 21. 3 ἐπλέομεν εἰς Συρίαν, καὶ κατήλθομεν εἰς Τύρον, where (as in 18. 22, 21. 15) the description consists in the statement of the direction (εἰς ...); cp. 21. 30 εἷλκον ἔξω τοῦ ἱεροῦ, καὶ εὐθέως ἐκλείσθησαν αἱ θύραι (i.e. after the first action had been completed, so that there is an indirect indication of its completion), whereas in 14. 19 the reading ἔσυραν (instead of ἔσυρον) ἔξω τῆς πόλεως is preferable, as otherwise the completion of the act, which certainly was carried out, would be in no way indicated. Occasionally, however, we do find an imperfect contrasted with a subsequent verb denoting completion, where the descriptive clause has not previously been *expressed*: 21. 20 ἐδόξαζον τὸν θεόν, εἶπόν τε ('they glorified God for a long time and in various ways, till finally

they said'); 18. 19 διελέγετο τοῖς Ἰουδαίοις (D, the other MSS. wrongly read -λέξατο or -λέχθη), the conclusion is given in 20 f. (but in 17. 2 [διελέγετο HLP is the right reading, see § 20, 1] the descriptive clause is present, and repetition is also expressed by the imperf.). The most striking instance is 27. 1 f. παρεδίδουν ... ἐπιβάντες δέ, where the aorist (Lat. *tradidit*) must be considered to be required by the sense.—In the Pauline Epistles cp. 1 C. 10. 4 ἔπιον (the fact), ἔπινον γὰρ ἐκ πνευματικῆς πέτρας (the manner), 10. 11 ταῦτα τυπικῶς συνέβαινεν (manner), cp. with 6 ταῦτα τύποι ἡμῶν ἐγενήθησαν (result).

4. There are certain **verbs** in Attic, which in virtue of their **special meaning** to some extent prefer the form of incompleted action: that is to say, the action in question finds its true end and aim in the act of another person, without which it remains incomplete and without result, and the imperfect is used according as this fact requires to be noticed. To this category belong κελεύειν, ἀξιοῦν, παρακελεύεσθαι, ἐρωτᾶν, πέμπειν, ἀποστέλλειν and many others. In the N.T. κελεύειν like προστάττειν and παραγγέλλειν always denotes an authoritative command, the accomplishment of which is understood as a matter of course: hence we have ἐκέλευσεν (as in Attic in this instance) like προσέταξεν, παρήγγειλεν;[1] likewise always ἔπεμψεν, ἀπέστειλεν; on the other hand, ἠρώτα (ἐπηρ.), with the meanings 'questioned' and 'besought,' is found as well as ἠρώτησεν (ἐπηρ.), and παρεκάλει (for Att. παρεκελεύετο, which does not appear) as well as παρεκάλεσεν (παρῄνει Α. 27. 9, literary language, ἠξίου 15. 38, ditto), but used in such a way that the choice of the one tense or the other on each occasion can generally be satisfactorily accounted for. Thus in A. 10. 48 ἠρώτησαν is necessary, because the fulfilment of the request which did take place is only indicated by means of this aorist, 23. 18 is similar, whereas ἠρώτα 'besought' in 3. 3 is used quite in the manner above indicated; 'asking a question' is generally expressed by ἠρώτησεν (as it is in Attic or by ἤρετο), but in Mc. 8. 5 by ἠρώτα, 23 ἐπηρώτα, 29 ditto (which might also be employed in other places where the aorist is found, *e.g.* 9. 16); παρεκάλεσαν Mt. 8. 34 of the Gergesenes who besought Jesus to depart (L. 8. 37 has ἠρώτησαν and Mc. 5. 17 ἤρξαντο παρακαλεῖν, but D παρεκάλουν), where the fulfilment of the request necessarily followed; Mt. 18. 32 ἀφῆκά σοι, ἐπειδὴ παρεκάλεσάς με (the mere request was sufficient), 26. 53 παρακαλέσαι τὸν πατέρα (ditto), A. 8. 31 παρεκάλεσεν ἀναβάντα καθίσαι (the fulfilment is not mentioned as self-evident); on the other hand παρεκάλει appears in A. 27. 33, L. 8. 41 etc.[2] In Jo. 4. 52 ἐπύθετο is incorrectly used, and the correct form ἐπυνθάνετο has weak attestation (in 13. 24 πυθέσθαι [which should strictly be πυνθάνεσθαι] is only read by AD al., while

---

[1] Ἐκέλευον (ῥαβδίζειν) only occurs in A. 16. 22 (of magistrates), probably to express repetition and a longer continuance of the action, which also accounts for the present ῥαβδίζειν, cp. § 58, 3; the conclusion is given in 23 πολλὰς δὲ ἐπιθέντες πληγάς. For παρήγγελλεν L. 8. 29, cp. infra 5.

[2] Also in A. 16. 5 παρεκάλει might have been expected, since the issue is expressly mentioned in καὶ παρεβιάσατο ἡμᾶς. In verse 39 also the imperf. might have been used.

other MSS. have a quite different reading). On the other hand ἐπυνθάνετο is found correctly in Mt. 2. 4, L. 15. 24, 18. 36, A. 4. 7, 10. 18 (BC ἐπύθοντο), 21. 33, 23. 19 f.—(Another instance of the aorist in John's Gospel, ἀπῆλθεν εἰς τὴν Γαλιλαίαν 4. 3, is at least remarkable, since the aorist denotes the journey as completed, whereas in verses 4 ff. we have an account of what happened on the way, and the arrival in Galilee is not reached till verse 45. With this may be compared A. 28, 14 ἤλθαμεν, cp. 15, 16.)—With verbs of requesting is associated προσκυνεῖν, which when it has this meaning is used as regularly in the imperfect (Mt. 8. 2, 9. 18, 15. 25 א*BDM), as it is in the aorist with the meaning of 'to do homage' (Mt. 2. 11, 14. 33 etc.).

5. For the interchange of ἔλεγεν (-ον) and εἶπεν (-αν, -ον) the following rules may be laid down. The individual utterance of an individual person is principally denoted by the aorist; on the other hand, the utterances of an indefinite number of persons are regularly expressed by the imperfect, which may also be thought to look forward to the conclusion given by the speech of the leading person, which is subsequently appended: A. 2. 13 with which cp. 14.[1] Ἔλεγεν is sometimes used before speeches of greater length, as in L. 6. 20 before the Sermon on the Mount, after a series of descriptive clauses in the imperf. in verses 18 and 19 (Mt. 5. 2 introduces this Sermon with the words ἐδίδασκεν λέγων); again there is a tendency to link on additional remarks to the preceding narrative by means of καὶ ἔλεγεν or ἔλ. δέ, Mc. 4. 21, 24, 26, 30, 7. 9, 20, L. 5. 36, 6. 5, 9. 23 and passim, while in other passages εἶπεν is used, L. 6. 39, 15. 11 etc. The words introduced by this verb may always be looked at in two ways: they may be viewed as a sentence which has been delivered or a speech that is being delivered, and so Thucydides introduces his speeches sometimes with ἔλεγεν, sometimes with ἔλεξε. Cp. also the use of λέγων (not εἰπών), so frequently added to another *verbum dicendi*.

6. The imperfect in **statements** after **verbs of perception** (and **believing**) is generally relative in so far as it refers to a time previous to the time of perception, and must consequently be rendered by the pluperfect; synchronism (of the thing perceived and the perception of it) is similarly expressed by the present, § 56, 9. It is evident that the imperfect here still preserves its sense of continuous action. Mc. 11. 32 εἶχον τὸν Ἰωάνην ὅτι προφήτης ἦν, had been; A. 3. 10 ἐπεγίνωσκον ὅτι ἦν ὁ καθήμενος; 15. 3 ᾔδεσαν τὸν πατέρα αὐτοῦ (who was dead) ὅτι Ἕλλην ὑπῆρχεν. In Jo. 6. 22 ἰδών (v.l. εἶδον) ὅτι οὐκ ἦν and 9. 8 οἱ θεωροῦντες αὐτὸν τὸ πρότερον ὅτι προσαίτης ἦν, the words ἰδεῖν and θεωρεῖν themselves refer back to the same previous time to which the dependent clause refers; as this time remains unexpressed in the participles, it had to be expressed in the dependent clause by the imperfect.—For exceptions, see § 56, 9.

---

[1] Jo. 11. 37 τινὲς δὲ ἐξ αὐτῶν εἶπον (after ἔλεγον οἱ Ἰουδαῖοι 36; ΑΚΠ also have ἔλεγον in 37).

7. The **aorist**, which denotes completion, may also express the entering upon a state or condition, when it is known as the 'ingressive aorist'; strictly speaking, verbs of this class contain in themselves an inchoative meaning besides that denoting the state: the former meaning becomes prominent in the aorist, and the latter mainly in the present (the former meaning also, though rarely, appears in the present, as in γηράσκω 'become old' beside γηράω 'be old': in Latin these inceptive presents are wide-spread). Thus ἐσίγησεν A. 15. 12 'became silent,' ἐπτώχευσεν 2 C. 8. 9 'became poor,' R. 14. 9 ἔζησεν 'became alive.'

8. An action which the use of the aorist shows to have been completed (to have taken place), need not by any means have been a momentary action, but may have actually extended, and even be expressly stated to have extended, over any length of time, provided that it is only the **completion** and the **conclusion** of it which is emphasized, this being just the force of the aorist. Ἐβίω πολλὰ ἔτη, but then he died. Ἔτη δύο ἦρξε, but then he was deposed. It is different with κακῶς ἔζη (where the manner of life is emphasized: the conclusion is left out of consideration); and δικαίως ἦρχε (δικ. ἦρξε would be in most cases ingressive, 'he came by his office honestly'). The same explanation applies to A. 28. 30 ἔμεινεν διετίαν ὅλην ἐν ἰδίῳ μισθώματι (but then this condition of things came to an end), 14. 3 ἱκανὸν χρόνον διέτριψαν (until the end of their stay, narrated in verses 5 and 6, the length of which is summarily indicated in verse 3),[1] 18. 11 ἐκάθισεν (Paul 'sat' *i.e.* stayed in Corinth) ἐνιαυτὸν καὶ μῆνας ἕξ (until his departure). In all these cases the only reason for the aorist is to be found in the added note of the length of the stay, which necessarily suggests the end of the particular state of things; Luke even says (A. 11. 26) ἐγένετο αὐτοὺς ἐνιαυτὸν ὅλον συναχθῆναι ἐν τῇ ἐκκλησίᾳ, although συνάγεσθαι ('to assemble themselves') is certainly no continuous action, but only something repeated at regular intervals. But repeated actions, if summed up and limited to a certain number of times, may also be expressed by an aorist, as in τρὶς ἐραβδίσθην 2 C. 11. 25, and this tense may likewise be used where the separate actions of different persons are comprehended in a single word, πάντες γὰρ ἐκ τοῦ περισσεύοντος αὐτοῖς ἔβαλον Mc. 12. 44, since in a comprehensive statement of this kind the idea of the individual actions which succeed each other becomes lost (previously in 41 we have πολλοὶ πλούσιοι ἔβαλλον πολλά).—If the aorist of a verb like μένειν is used without any statement of the duration of time, then it denotes merely the fact that the stay took place, as opposed to departure: Jo. 7. 9 ἔμεινεν ἐν τῇ Γαλιλαίᾳ = οὐκ ἀνέβη εἰς Ἱεροσόλυμα, 10. 40 ἔμεινεν ἐκεῖ 'He settled down there,' without (for the present) returning to Judaea (B ἔμενεν).

9. The meaning of past time, which generally attaches itself to the aorist, is lost in the case of the so-called **gnomic aorist**, which

---

[1] On the other hand, we have in 14. 28 διέτριβον χρόνον οὐκ ὀλίγον, where there is no reference to a definite length of time; cp. 16. 12, 25. 14.

has greater emphasis in a general statement than the present which is equally possible. The latter, since it only calls attention to the repetition of an event on all occasions, neglects to express the fact of its completion: the aorist, referring to the individual case, neglects to express the general applicability of the statement to each occasion, which, however, is easily understood. This usage, however, is very rare in the N.T., and only found in comparisons or in connection with comparisons (Kühner, p. 138): Jo. 15. 6 ἐὰν μή τις μένῃ ἐν ἐμοί, ἐβλήθη ἔξω ὡς τὸ κλῆμα καὶ ἐξηράνθη, καὶ συνάγουσιν αὐτὰ καὶ εἰς τὸ πῦρ βάλλουσιν, καὶ καίεται (all that precedes the collecting and the burning is expressed by the aorist; so Hermas in a simile has Vis. iii. 12. 2 κατελείφθη ... ἐξηγέρθη ... ἐνεδύσατο ... οὐκέτι ἀνάκειται ἀλλ' ἔστηκεν κ.τ.λ.: 13. 2 ἐπελάθετο ... προσδέχεται κ.τ.λ.). We have it also in similes in Mt. 13. 48, Ja. 1. 11, 24, 1 P. 1. 24 from LXX. Is. 40. 7. (The case is different with Herm. Mand. iii. 2, v. 1. 7, Sim. ix. 26. 2, where the aorist in the first place stands for a perfect [§ 59, 3], and the latter is a more vigorous mode of expressing something still future, but certain to happen, Kühner, p. 129, 142.)

10. The aorist in **epistolary style**, referring to something simultaneous with the writing and sending of the letter, does not cease to refer to a moment of past time, as the time in question actually is past to the mind of the recipient and reader of the letter. In the N.T. the only instance of this use is ἔπεμψα in A. 23. 30, Ph. 2. 28, Col. 4. 8, Philem. 11 etc.; on the other hand we always have ἀσπάζεται and γράφω (in 1 C. 5. 11 ἔγραψα refers to an earlier letter, and in R. 15. 15 and elsewhere to an earlier portion of the same letter).

§ 58. MOODS OF THE PRESENT AND THE AORIST.

1. Between the moods (including the infinitive and participle) of the present and the aorist there exists essentially the same relation as that which prevails in the indicative between the imperfect and aorist. They have a **single** function (§ 56, 1), since they express the kind of action only and not a time-relation. As the optative is rare in the N.T., and the conjunctive, except where it is related in meaning to the imperative, does not offer any special difficulties for discussion at this point, we treat the moods in this order: Imperative (Conjunct.), Infinitive, Participle.

2. **Present and aorist imperative (pres. and aor. conj.).**—The present imperative (with which must be taken the hortatory conjunctive, 1st pers. plur.), both positive and negatived by μή, is used in **general** precepts (even to individuals) on conduct and action; on the other hand the aorist imperative (or conjunctive) is used in (the much less common) injunctions about action in **individual cases**. (1) If the aorist is used in the first case, then it must either express the entering upon a state of conduct which is in contrast with the conduct hitherto shown, or it is used comprehensively (cp. § 57, 8)

to denote conduct up to a final point, or again the general rule is specialized so as to refer to an individual case. Exx.: (a) Ja. 4. 9 ταλαιπωρήσατε καὶ πενθήσατε καὶ κλαύσατε ... μετατραφήτω ... , 10 ταπεινώθητε, 'become sorrowful' etc.[1] (b) Ja. 5. 7 μακροθυμήσατε ἕως τῆς παρουσίας τοῦ κυρίου, which however may also be referred to (a), cp. 8 μακροθυμήσατε καὶ ὑμεῖς, στηρίξατε τὰς καρδίας ὑμῶν. 1 Tim. 6. 20 (2 Tim. 1. 14) τὴν παραθήκην φύλαξον (cp. 1 Tim. 5. 21 ἵνα ταῦτα φυλάξῃς, 2 Tim. 1. 12 φυλάξαι, 1 Jo. 5. 21 φυλάξατε ἑαυτὰ ἀπὸ τῶν εἰδώλων, 1 Tim. 6. 14 τηρῆσαι ... μέχρι κ.τ.λ., 1 Th. 5. 23), 'up till the end,' to a definite point, whereas we have 1 Tim. 5. 22 σεαυτὸν ἁγνὸν τήρει (in all things, continuously), cp. Ja. 1. 27 ἄσπιλον ἑαυτὸν τηρεῖν the true mode of θρησκεία. Cp. also 2 Tim. 4. 2, 5 κήρυξον ἐπίστηθι ἔλεγξον κ.τ.λ.: κακοπάθησον ποίησον πληροφόρησον, i.e. 'up till the end,' with reference to the coming of Christ, cp. verses 1, 5, 6.[2] (c) Mt. 7. 6 μὴ δῶτε τὸ ἅγιον τοῖς κυσίν, μηδὲ βάλητε κ.τ.λ.; 6. 34 μὴ μεριμνήσητε εἰς τὴν αὔριον (but without this additional phrase we have in 25 μὴ μεριμνᾶτε, cp. 31, 10. 19, L. 11. 22, 29); 5. 39 ὅστις σε ῥαπίζει εἰς τὴν δεξιὰν σιαγόνα σου, στρέψον αὐτῷ καὶ τὴν ἄλλην, similarly in 40 and again in 42 τῷ αἰτοῦντί σε δός, καὶ τὸν θέλοντα ἀπὸ σοῦ δανείσασθαι μὴ ἀποστραφῇς. That the present is also allowable in such cases is shown by L. 6. 29 f.: τῷ τύπτοντί σε ἐπὶ τὴν σιαγόνα πάρεχε καὶ τὴν ἄλλην ... παντὶ αἰτοῦντί σε δίδου, καὶ ἀπὸ τοῦ αἴροντος τὰ σὰ μὴ ἀπαίτει.—(2) An injunction about an **individual**

[1] So also R. 13. 13 ὡς ἐν ἡμέρᾳ εὐσχημόνως περιπατήσωμεν with reference to the beginning and the entrance upon this state of things, cp. 12, 14. Περιπατεῖν (and στοιχεῖν) when used in exhortations usually appears in the present (1 C. 7. 17, G. 5. 16, E. 4. 17, 5. 2, 8, Col. 2. 6, 4. 5, 1 Th. 4. 12, G. 5. 25, Ph. 3. 16); but when the subject of discourse is the *new* life of the Christian answering to his heavenly calling, which produces a fresh beginning, then the aorist is introduced: R. 6. 4 ἵνα ἐν καινότητι ζωῆς περιπατήσωμεν, E. 2. 10, 4. 1, Col. 1. 10 (in the similar passage 1 Th. 2. 12 the readings vary between περιπατεῖν and -τῆσαι).—The force of the aorist is clear in φοβηθῶμεν οὖν τὸν θεόν (which we hitherto have not done: just before we have ὁρῶ γάρ τινας **ἀτελεῖς** τῷ πρὸς αὐτὸν φόβῳ πλεῖστα ἁμαρτάνοντας) Clem. Hom. xvii. 1 (elsewhere in that work, e.g. in chap. 11, we nearly always find φοβεῖσθαι etc.). In the N.T. cp. H. 4. 1 φοβηθῶμεν οὖν κ.τ.λ. 'let us lay hold on fear,' Ap. 14. 7; in Hermas, Mand. vii. 1 ff. φοβήθητι τὸν κύριον καὶ φύλασσε τὰς ἐντολὰς αὐτοῦ—τὸν δὲ διάβολον μὴ φοβηθῇς—φοβήθητι δὲ τὰ ἔργα τοῦ διαβόλου, the aor. in all cases being used of the fundamental position taken up: but then in 4 we have ἐὰν (so passim) θέλῃς τὸ πονηρὸν ἐργάσασθαι, φοβοῦ τὸν κύριον, and then again: φοβήθητι οὖν τὸν κύριον καὶ ζήσῃ αὐτῷ, καὶ ὅσοι ἂν φοβηθῶσιν αὐτὸν—ζήσονται; Mand. i. 2 πίστευσον αὐτῷ καὶ φοβήθητι αὐτόν, φοβηθεὶς δὲ ἐγκράτευσαι, etc.

[2] Clem. Cor. ii. 8. 4 τηρήσατε τὴν σάρκα ἁγνὴν ..., ἵνα τὴν ζωὴν ἀπολάβωμεν, cp. 4 τηρήσαντες ... λημψόμεθα ζωήν. Herm. Mand. viii. 2 has first τὸ πονηρὸν ἐγκρατεύου, then ἐγκράτευσαι ἀπὸ πονηρίας **πάσης**, comprehensively: the present again in 3 ff. up to 6 ἐγκράτευσαι ἀπὸ **πάντων** τούτων, cp. 12 ἐὰν τὸ πονηρὸν μὴ ποιῇς καὶ ἐγκρατεύσῃ ἀπ' αὐτῶν. So also ix. 12 δούλευε τῇ πίστει, καὶ ἀπὸ τῆς διψυχίας ἀπόσχου. We have the aorist of the hypothetical conjunctive in Vis. v. 7 ἐὰν αὐτὰς φυλάξητε καὶ ἐν αὐταῖς πορευθῆτε (cp. the last note on περιπατεῖν) καὶ ἐργάσησθε αὐτὰς ..., ἀπολήμψεσθε ἀπὸ τοῦ κυρίου κ.τ.λ. So too the striking uses of the aorist in 1 Peter must be explained by the instances in (a) or (b) given above: 1. 13 τελείως ἐλπίσατε 'lay hold on hope,' 22 ἀγαπήσατε 'lay hold on love'; 1. 17 ἀναστράφητε 'up to the end,' 5. 1 ποιμάνατε until Christ's appearing; 2. 17 **πάντας** τιμήσατε 'give everyone his due honour,' which is expanded in the presents following τὴν ἀδελφότητα ἀγαπᾶτε etc.

case is expressed by the present, if no definite aim or end for the action is in prospect, or if the manner or character of the action is taken into account, or again, in the case of a prohibition, if the thing forbidden is already in existence. Exx.: (*a*) Mt. 26. 38 = Mc. 14. 34 μείνατε ὧδε ('go not away,' § 57, 8) καὶ γρηγορεῖτε μετ' ἐμοῦ, L. 22. 40, 46 προσεύχεσθε μὴ εἰσελθεῖν εἰς πειρασμόν. Frequently we have ὕπαγε, or πορεύου, which indeed are often found even where the aim or end *is* stated: A. 22. 10 ἀναστὰς πορεύου ('go forth') εἰς Δαμασκόν ('as far as D.'), κἀκεῖ κ.τ.λ., cp. 8. 26, 10. 20; Mt. 25. 9 πορεύεσθε πρὸς τοὺς πωλοῦντας (in this and that direction, where you may find a seller) καὶ ἀγοράσατε (aim) ἑαυταῖς, cp. 25. 41 (where one should place a comma after κατηραμένοι); L. 5. 24 πορεύου εἰς τὸν οἶκόν σου (expressing rather direction than aim; whether he reaches his house or not, is beside the question), Jo. 20. 17. On the other hand, we have πορεύθητι in Mt. 8. 9 = L. 7. 8 (πορεύου in LDX; a general's command to his soldiers; the goal or end is omitted through abbreviation),[1] A. 9. 11, 28. 26 O.T. (*b*) 1 P. 4. 15 μή τις ὑμῶν πασχέτω ὡς φονεὺς κ.τ.λ.; 1 C. 7. 36 εἰ δέ τις ἀσχημονεῖν ... νομίζει..., ὃ θέλει ποιείτω· οὐχ ἁμαρτάνει· γαμείτωσαν, cp. in the contrasted case in 37 τηρεῖν, and 38 ὁ γαμίζων ... καλῶς ποιεῖ καὶ ὁ μὴ γαμίζων κρεῖσσον ποιήσει. In this passage the quality of the proceedings is in question: unseemly or seemly—sinful or not sinful—good, better. (*c*) L. 8. 52 ἔκλαιον ... ὁ δὲ εἶπεν· μὴ κλαίετε, Jo. 20. 17 μή μου ἅπτου (a thing which has therefore already taken place or been attempted). Frequently μὴ φοβοῦ, φοβεῖσθε, L. 5. 10, 8. 50, Mc. 5. 36, 6. 50 etc. (Mt. 1. 20 μὴ φοβηθῇς παραλαβεῖν is different, 'do not abstain from fear'); Ja. 1. 7 μὴ οἰέσθω (cp. Jo. 5. 45 μὴ δοκεῖτε; but in 2 C. 11. 16 we have μή τίς με δόξῃ, where the opinion certainly cannot yet have been entertained; cp. Mt. 3. 9, 5. 17, 10. 34 'do not let the thought arise ').[2]—Ἀσπάσασθε is the form always used in greetings (even in 3 Jo. 15 according to ℵ); the aorist is found in all the petitions of the Lord's Prayer, partly to express the desire for complete fulfilment, partly with reference to the particular occasion of the petition and the requirement for the time being: only in L. 11. 3 do we have τὸν ἄρτον ... δίδου (ℵD wrongly read δὸς as in Mt.) ἡμῖν τὸ καθ' ἡμέραν (D σήμερον as in Mt.).

3. **Present and aorist infinitive.**—In the infinitive the distinction between the two forms is on the whole easy to comprehend. Θέλειν is generally followed by the aorist infinitive, as is the corresponding

---

[1] In the corresponding passage in Mt. and Lc. ἔρχου must mean 'go with me,' not 'come hither,' which is expressed by ἐλθέ in Mt. 14. 29, Jo. 4. 16 (and in the use made of the passage Mt. 8. 9 in Clem. Hom. ix. 21): cp. Jo. 1. 47 ἔρχου καὶ ἴδε 'go with me,' 1. 40, 11. 34.

[2] A special instance is φέρε, φέρετε 'bring' (the pres. imperat. is always found with the simple verb, except in Jo. 21. 10 ἐνέγκατε), which as in classical Greek is used for the aorist as well, there being no aorist derived from this stem. But in the compound verb a distinction was made: Mt. 8. 4 προσένεγκε τὸ δῶρον (injunction as to what ought to be done), 5. 24 διαλλάγηθι ... καὶ τότε πρόσφερε τὸ δῶρόν σου (injunction as to the manner and circumstances in which it may be done).

Attic word βούλεσθαι, and naturally so, as the wish usually looks on to the fulfilment; exceptions such as θέλω εἶναι, τί θέλετε πάλιν ἀκούειν (D -οῦσαι) Jo. 9. 27 ('to hear the same thing perpetually'), are easily explained. In the same way the aorist inf. is the predominant form after δύνασθαι, δυνατός, κελεύειν etc. (ἐκέλευον ῥαβδίζειν A. 16. 22 expresses duration, cp. § 57, 4, note 1). Μέλλειν, on the other hand, in the N.T. as in classical Greek only rarely takes the aorist inf.: (A. 12. 6 AB), R. 8. 16 and G. 3. 23 μέλλουσαν ἀποκαλυφθῆναι (but ἀποκαλύπτεσθαι 1 P. 5. 1), Ap. 3. 2, 16, 12. 4, where the aorist is obviously correctly employed, while the present if used in this connection goes beyond the proper sphere of that tense. In classical Greek the most frequent construction of μέλλειν is that with the future inf., which in the active and middle voices usually has a neutral meaning so far as the kind of action is concerned; but since the vulgar language abandoned this form of expression (μέλλειν with a fut. inf. occurs only in the Acts, see § 61, 3), it allowed the present inf. to be used with the same range as the fut. inf. had previously possessed: μέλλει παραδίδοσθαι Mt. 17. 22, for which we have also merely παραδίδοται, see § 56, 8.[1]—Ἐλπίζειν in the N.T. takes the aorist inf. (instead of the fut.), correctly so far as the action is concerned; cp. § 61, 3. Elsewhere too the infinitives keep their proper force: R. 14. 21 καλὸν τὸ μὴ φαγεῖν κρέα μηδὲ πιεῖν οἶνον μηδὲ ἐν ᾧ ὁ ἀδελφός σου προσκόπτει means, 'it is a good thing *at times* not to eat meat, if offence is given thereby,' and the passage is not to be understood of continual abstinence.

4. Present and aorist participle.—A participle used in connection with a finite verb generally at first sight appears to denote relative time, namely, the aorist participle to denote a past event, and the present participle a simultaneous event, especially as the future participle (like the fut. infin. and optat.) does really express something relatively future. Actually, however, the aorist participle contains no more than the idea of completion; if therefore the participle is followed by a finite verb, the sequence of events usually is, that the first-mentioned action was accomplished when the latter took place, just as the same sequence of events is expressed, if instead of a participle and a finite verb two finite verbs connected by καί are employed. This temporal relation, however, is not necessarily implied in either case: the phrase προσευξάμενοι εἶπαν A. 1. 24 = προσεύξαντο καὶ εἶπαν = προσεύξαντο εἰπόντες (cp. Mc. 14. 39) denotes not merely simultaneous, but identical actions. If the participle stands in the second place, as in Mt. 27. 4 ἥμαρτον παραδοὺς αἷμα ἀθῷον, or Mc. 1. 31 ἤγειρεν αὐτὴν κρατήσας τῆς χειρός, it may happen, as in the second of these instances, that the true sequence of time is not expressed, though in reality it is self-evident. Still in spite of this the reading of the majority of the MSS. in Acts 25. 13 is not Greek, Ἀγρίππας καὶ Βερνίκη κατῆλθον εἰς Καισάρειαν ἀσπασάμενοι τὸν Φῆστον (since the participle always, as such, expresses an accom-

---

[1] Also in Jo. 16. 19 ἤμελλον (as ℵ has for ἤθελον) ἐρωτᾶν (D ἐπερωτῆσαι περὶ τούτου) appears to be the better reading.

panying circumstance, which in this passage, where the arrival is being narrated, cannot yet be regarded as concluded): the other reading ἀσπασόμενοι is the correct one.[1] On the other hand, the present participle is occasionally used after the main verb, since the future participle is so rarely found (see § 61, 4), to denote an action which at least in its complete fulfilment is subsequent to the action of the main verb: A. 18. 23 ἐξῆλθεν (from Antioch) διερχόμενος τὴν Γαλατικὴν χώραν (i.e. καὶ διήρχετο), 14. 21 f. ὑπέστρεψαν εἰς τὴν Λύστραν ... ἐπιστηρίζοντες τὰς ψυχὰς τῶν μαθητῶν: 21. 2 εὑρόντες πλοῖον διαπερῶν εἰς Φοινίκην, 3 ἐκεῖσε τὸ πλοῖον ἦν ἀποφορτιζόμενον τὸν γόμον. In these last two passages the pres. part. clearly takes the place of μέλλων with the inf., e.g. ἔμελλεν ἀποφορτίζεσθαι, so that they are to be compared with ὁ ἐρχόμενος = ὁ μέλλων ἔρχεσθαι and παραδίδοται = μέλλει παραδίδοσθαι § 56, 8; in the first two passages the participle is tacked on as it were to a finite verb instead of a second finite verb, to denote a subsequent action which in view of the actors' designs and preparations is regarded as already beginning to take place. In the following passages the fut. part. could have been used: A. 15. 27 ἀπεστάλκαμεν ἀπαγγέλλοντας (but cp. Thucyd. vii. 26. 9 ἔπεμψαν ἀγγέλλοντας Kühner ii.[2] 121 f.), 21. 16 συνῆλθον... ἄγοντες.—The present participle when it stands before the main verb may denote something that is already past: E. 4. 28 ὁ κλέπτων (he who stole hitherto) μηκέτι κλεπτέτω, Ap. 20. 10 ὁ πλανῶν = ὃς ἐπλάνα; also Mt. 27. 40 ὁ καταλύων ... καὶ οἰκοδομῶν = ὃς κατέλυες κ.τ.λ. ('wouldest destroy'), since it is obvious that the pres. part. like the pres. indic. may have a **conative** force (Mt. 23. 13 τοὺς εἰσερχομένους).

§ 59. THE PERFECT.

1. The **perfect** (as also the pluperfect) unites in itself as it were present and aorist, since it expresses the **continuance of completed** action: before the form καθέστᾰκα for 'I have placed' arose, this meaning was expressed by ἔχω (pres.) καταστήσας (aor.),[2] and a perfect like πεπληρώκατε in Acts 5. 28 may be resolved into ἐπληρώσατε καὶ νῦν πλήρης ἐστί. In the N.T. this form of the verb is still constantly employed, and in a manner corresponding almost entirely to its classical uses: although at a subsequent period the popular language abandoned the old perfect, and let these forms, while they still continued in existence, do duty for the aorist.

2. The **present** meaning so entirely preponderates with certain verbs (as in classical Greek), that the aoristic meaning disappears altogether: e.g. in κέκραγεν Jo. 1. 15 a word borrowed from the literary language in place of the Hellenistic κράζει, cp. § 56, 5;

---

[1] The use of the aor. in John 11. 2 is noteworthy, ἦν δὲ Μαριὰμ ἡ ἀλείψασα τὸν κύριον μύρῳ, 'who as is well known (cp. Mt. 26. 13) did (or, has done) this,' although this story belongs to a later time and is told at a later point in the narrative, 12. 1 ff.; so too Mt. 10. 4 Ἰούδας ὁ καὶ παραδοὺς αὐτόν,—ὃς καὶ παρέδωκεν αὐτόν Mc. 3. 19.

[2] Demosth. xix. 288.

§ 59. 2–3.]   PERFECT.   199

ἕστηκα (cp. 3), πέποιθα, μέμνημαι (μιμνῄσκομαι is almost unrepresented, only in H. 2. 6, 13. 3)[1]; also τέθνηκα 'I am dead,' ἤλπικα εἴς τινα Jo. 5. 45 etc. 'I have set my hope upon,' = I hope, but a stronger form than ἐλπίζω, because the continuance of the hope which has been formed is expressed by the perfect; similarly πέπεισμαι 'I am convinced' R. 8. 38 etc.; ἥγημαι 'I believe' or 'reckon' (class.) A. 26. 2 in Paul's speech before Agrippa (but in Ph. 3. 7 with its ordinary meaning 'I have reckoned').

3. Inversely, the **aoristic** meaning of the perfect may be brought into prominence and the other be made subordinate, without affecting the correctness of the employment of this tense. This happens in 2 Tim. 4. 7 τὸν καλὸν ἀγῶνα ἠγώνισμαι, τὸν δρόμον τετέλεκα, τὴν πίστιν τετήρηκα, viz. up till now, and the existing result inferred from this is stated in verse 8: λοιπὸν ἀπόκειταί μοι ὁ τῆς δικαιοσύνης στέφανος. In the well-known phrase ὃ γέγραφα γέγραφα the first perfect has more of an aoristic, the second more of a present meaning. In the following passages the aorist and perfect are clearly distinguished: A. 21. 28 Ἕλληνας εἰσήγαγεν εἰς τὸ ἱερὸν καὶ κεκοίνωκεν τὸν ἅγιον τόπον, the introduction of these persons that took place has produced a lasting effect of pollution; 1 C. 15. 3 f. ὅτι Χριστὸς ἀπέθανεν ... καὶ ὅτι ἐτάφη καὶ ὅτι ἐγήγερται τῇ ἡμέρᾳ τῇ τρίτῃ; A. 22. 15 ἔσῃ μάρτυς ... ὧν ἑώρακας καὶ ἤκουσας, the fact that Paul has seen the Lord is that which permanently gives him his consecration as an Apostle (hence Paul himself says in 1 C. 9. 1 οὐκ εἰμὶ ἀπόστολος; οὐχὶ Ἰησοῦν ... ἑώρακα;), whereas the hearing (verses 7 ff.) is far less essential.[2] Only it must be borne in mind that the perfect is not used in all cases where it might have been used, *i.e.* where there is an actually existing result at the present time: the aorist has extended its province at the expense of the perfect, and here there is certainly a distinction between the language of the New Testament and the classical language. Thus Mt. 23. 2 ἐπὶ τῆς Μωϋσέως καθέδρας ἐκάθισαν οἱ γραμματεῖς, though they still sit thereon: cp. H. 1. 3, 8. 1, 10. 12 for ἐκάθισεν: κεκάθικεν only appears in 12. 2[3]; Mc. 3. 21 ἔλεγον ὅτι ἐξέστη (he *is* beside himself), where D* has ἐξέστεται; 2 C. 5. 13 ἐξέστημεν opposed to σωφρονοῦμεν; ἕστηκα had acquired too much of a present sense to be able to lend itself still to a true perfect meaning, and it is for this reason that 'He is risen' is never expressed by ἀνέστηκεν (but by ἠγέρθη, which is another instance of aorist for perfect, and ἐγήγερται Mc. 6. 14, Paul in 1 C. 15. passim, 2 Tim. 2. 8). Cp. § 57, 9 (even classical Greek has some similar instances of the aorist for perfect, as

---

[1] Κέκτημαι does not appear in the N.T., but only κτήσασθαι and κτᾶσθαι.

[2] Also Jo. 3. 32 ὃ ἑώρακε καὶ ἤκουσε, where likewise the principal emphasis is laid on the seeing, but in 5. 37, 1 Jo. 1. 1, 3 we have ἑωράκαμεν and ἀκηκόαμεν in close connection, where the hearing is regarded as equally essential. Ἑώρακα also appears in L. 24. 23, Jo. 19. 35, 20. 18 and passim; ἀκήκοα is rare and nowhere found in Mt., Mc., or Luke.

[3] It is preceded by ὑπέμεινε σταυρόν ('Ἰησοῦς), and followed in verse 3 by ἀναλογίσασθε τὸν τοιαύτην ὑπομεμενηκότα ... ἀντιλογίαν, the perfect being due to the abiding example which He offers us.

in the saying of Euripides: τίς οἶδεν εἰ τὸ ζῆν μέν ἐστι κατθανεῖν [=τεθνάναι], τὸ κατθανεῖν δὲ ζῆν κάτω νομίζεται;).

4. The use of the **perfect instead of the aorist**, in consequence of the popular intermixture of the two tenses (vide supra 1), appears undoubtedly in the Apocalypse: 5. 7 ἦλθε καὶ εἴληφε, cp. 8. 5; 7. 14 εἴρηκα (B εἶπον), cp. 19. 3: in forms, therefore, in which the reduplication is *not* clearly marked. The following perfects have an equally certain aoristic sense: Herm. Vis. i. 1. 1 πέπρακεν, iii. 1. 2 ὦπται ℵ (as ὤφθη), Clem. Hom. ii. 53 ἐγήγερται, Gospel of Peter 23 δεδώκασιν, cp. 31. Instances in the Pauline Epistles: 2 C. 2. 13 ἔσχηκα in historical narrative, whereas 7. 5 ἔσχηκεν (B al. ἔσχεν) and 1. 9 ἐσχήκαμεν may be explained as true perfects; ἀπέσταλκα in 12. 17 does not seem right, coming as it does in the middle of nothing but aorists (ἔπεμψα is read by DE, ἀπέστειλα by some cursives): the same perfect appears in A. 7. 35 τοῦτον (Moses) ὁ θεὸς ἄρχοντα ἀπέσταλκε, most probably a wrong reading for ἀπέστειλεν of CHP al. Also in 2 C. 11. 25 νυχθήμερον ἐν τῷ βυθῷ πεποίηκα stands in connection with aorists only and without an adequate reason for the perfect. But H. 11. 28 πίστει πεποίηκεν τὸ πάσχα is explained by the abiding institution, cp. verse 3 (ἐγκεκαίνισται 9. 18), while 17 προσενήνοχεν Ἀβραὰμ τὸν Ἰσαάκ can indeed only be understood as referring to the abiding example offered to us. Lastly, γέγονεν is used for ἐγένετο in Mt. (and Apoc. Pet. 11; Burton, p. 43) in 25. 6 (B has ἐγένετο). (In 1. 22=21. 4 the perfect could be accounted for, although John uses ἐγένετο in an analogous passage, 19. 36: there is still greater reason for γέγονεν in Mt. 26. 56 of Christ's passion.)

5. In **general statements** or **imaginary examples** the perfect is only rarely used, as also in Attic it is rare in these cases. In Mt. 13. 46 πέπρακεν (ἐπώλησεν D) πάντα καὶ ἠγόρασεν αὐτόν the suspicion of an incorrect confusion with the aorist is obvious (no aorist from πιπράσκω existed), cp. Herm. Vis. i. 1. 1, supra 4; the same applies to Ja. 1. 24 κατενόησεν καὶ ἀπελήλυθεν καὶ εὐθέως ἐπελάθετο. But passages like 1 Jo. 2. 5 ὃς ἂν τηρῇ ... τετελείωται, Ja. 2. 10 ὅστις τηρήσῃ ... γέγονεν (cp. 11), R. 14. 23 etc. are perfectly correct and in accordance with classical usage (Aristoph. Lys. 545 ὁ μὲν ἥκων γάρ, κἂν ᾖ πολιός, ταχὺ ... γεγάμηκεν).

6. The perfect is used **relatively**, instead of the pluperfect, in the same way as the present is used for the imperfect after verbs of perception (cp. § 56, 9): Mc. 5. 33 εἰδυῖα ὃ γέγονεν αὐτῇ, Lc. 20. 19 D ἔγνωσαν ὅτι εἴρηκεν (al. εἶπεν=Mc. 12. 12); similarly after a verb expressing emotion in A. 10. 45 ἐξέστησαν ὅτι ἐκκέχυται. So also in L. 9. 36 we have οὐδενὶ ἀπήγγειλαν οὐδὲν ὧν ἑωράκασιν (D ἐθεάσαντο), on the analogy of the equivalent phrase οὐδ. ἀπήγγ. ὅτι ταῦτα ἑωράκασιν. Still we have Mc. 15. 10 ἐγίνωσκεν ὅτι παραδεδώκεισαν (but DHS read παρέδωκαν as in Mt. 27. 18, AE al. παρεδώκεισαν), A. 19. 32 οὐκ ᾔδεισαν τίνος ἕνεκεν συνεληλύθεισαν.

7. On the **moods of the perfect** it may be noticed that the **imperative**, apart from ἔρρωσο ἔρρωσθε (formulas in A. 15. 29, 23. 30,

but not in all the MSS.) and the periphrasis with εἰμί (§ 62, 1), only appears in the vigorous prohibition πεφίμωσο Mc. 4. 39 (cp. τέθναθι in Homer).

§ 60. PLUPERFECT.

1. The pluperfect, which naturally did not outlive the perfect in the Greek language, is still, like the perfect, a current, though not a largely employed, form with the New Testament writers; even in classical Greek, however, it is far rarer than the Latin or the German pluperfect, just because it is not used relatively as these latter are used. If an action has taken place, without leaving behind it an effect still permanent in subsequent past time, then the aorist must be employed, since the pluperfect = aorist + imperfect (cp. the perf. § 59, 1). L. 16. 20 Λάζαρος ἐβέβλητο πρὸς τὸν πυλῶνα αὐτοῦ, 'was thrown down and lay': Jo. 11. 44 ἡ ὄψις αὐτοῦ σουδαρίῳ περιεδέδετο, 9. 22 ἤδη γὰρ συνετέθειντο οἱ Ἰουδαῖοι, the stipulation even at that early date was made. Cp. also Acts 14. 23 πεπιστεύκεισαν (-ασιν D, § 59, 6), 26 ἦσαν παραδεδομένοι: but ibid. ἐπλήρωσαν, 27 ἐποίησαν = 'had fulfilled,' 'had done.'

2. The usages of the pluperfect, which vary with the particular verb and the context, correspond to those of the perfect; the aoristic meaning preponderates, e.g. in A. 4. 22 ὁ ἄνθρωπος ἐφ' ὃν γεγόνει τὸ σημεῖον, although the other meaning is present as well, and generally speaking an encroachment of the pluperfect into the province of the aorist can by no means take place.—A. 9. 21 ὧδε εἰς τοῦτο ἐληλύθει (i.e. Paul to Damascus, the words are spoken by the Jews) is explained by the fact that this intention of the Apostle had now come to an end, and therefore the perfect was no longer admissible.

§ 61. FUTURE.

1. The future, as was remarked above (§ 56, 1), is the one tense which does not express action but simply a time-relation, so that completed and continuous action are not differentiated. The synthetic future has become extinct in modern Greek; in the N.T. it is still largely used in the indicative, and is not limited to any considerable extent either by periphrasis (§ 62, 1, 2, 4) or by the use of the present (§ 56, 8). On the modal functions of the future indicative see §§ 64, 65; it is occasionally used in a gnomic sense (as in classical Greek), to express what may be expected to take place under certain circumstances, as in R. 5. 7 μόλις ὑπὲρ δικαίου τις ἀποθανεῖται, cp. 7. 3 χρηματίσει ἐὰν γένηται: so the first of these passages is an abbreviated form of ἐὰν δίκαιος ᾖ κ.τ.λ.

2. The future is used **relatively** in statements after verbs of believing, to denote a time subsequent to the time when the belief was entertained: Mt. 20. 10 ἐνόμισαν ὅτι λήψονται (= μέλλουσι λαμβάνειν); cp. the present § 56, 9: imperf. § 57, 6: perf. § 59, 6. In this case, however, another mode of expression was scarcely

possible, and the only difference in the classical language is that classical Greek uses the future infinitive, which regularly has a relative meaning, after νομίζειν, instead of ὅτι with the indicative. (After σημαίνων in Jo. 18. 32 we have ἤμελλεν ἀποθνήσκειν, instead of which μέλλει might here be expected, § 56, 9, or the fut. as in 21. 19 δοξάσει.)

3. The future **infinitive**, which like the participle and the optative of the future, expresses the time-notion relatively with reference to the principal action, has disappeared from the popular language, and is found only in the Acts and the Epistle to the Hebrews: after μέλλειν in A. 11. 28, 23. 30, 24. 15, 27. 10, after ἐλπίζειν 26. 7 B (the other MSS. have the aorist), after ὀμνύναι H. 3. 18. After μέλλειν the place of the fut. inf. is taken by the pres. inf., cp. § 58, 3, rarely by the aor. inf.; after ἐλπίζειν[1], προκαταγγέλλειν (A. 3. 18), ὀμνύναι (2. 30), προσδοκᾶν (3. 3), ὁμολογεῖν 'to promise' (Mt. 14. 7), the aorist infinitive is used, which preserves the nature of the action correctly, but surrenders the expression of the time-relation.

4. The future **participle**, used as the complement of the principal verb (to express the aim or object) is likewise rare and almost limited to the Acts: 8. 27 ἐληλύθει προσκυνήσων, 22. 5, 24. 17, H. 13. 17 ἀγρυπνοῦσιν ὡς λόγον ἀποδώσοντες; Mt. 27. 49 ἔρχεται σώσων, but ℵ* has σῶσαι, D καὶ σώσει. Its place is frequently taken by the pres. part., cp. § 58, 4; elsewhere by the infinitive (1 C. 16. 3), a relative sentence (ibid. 4. 17) or some other phrase (Viteau § 288). Scarcely more widely extended is the use of the fut. part. in a more independent position (cp. § 62, 4): 1 C. 15. 37 τὸ σῶμα τὸ γενησόμενον (also probably R. 8. 34 ὁ κατακρινῶν), A. 20. 22 τὰ συναντήσοντα, 2 P. 2. 13 κομιούμενοι μισθὸν ἀδικίας (almost certainly corrupt; ℵ*BP read ἀδικούμενοι), τίς ὁ κακώσων ὑμᾶς (= ὃς κακώσει) 1 P. 3. 13, τὸ ἐσόμενον L. 22. 49, ὁ παραδώσων Jo. 6. 64, but there D is doubtless correct in reading παραδιδούς (μέλλων παραδιδόναι ℵ, as in Jo. 12. 4), H. 3. 5 τῶν λαληθησομένων (a unique instance of the fut. part. pass.).

§ 62. PERIPHRASTIC CONJUGATION.

1. The classical language had already made use of **εἰμί with the perfect participle** as a periphrasis for the **perfect, pluperfect, and future perfect, active and passive**, which under certain circumstances was necessary, but the usage was extended far beyond the cases where that necessity existed. In the N.T. the cases where periphrasis is necessary include the future perfect and the perfect conjunctive (or optative), excluding of course οἶδα εἰδῶ; in other cases it is practically indifferent, whether one writes ἐπεγέγραπτο (A. 17. 23) or ἦν γεγραμμένον (Jo. 19. 19 f.), γέγραπται (very frequent) or γεγραμμένον ἐστί (Jo. 6. 31, 20. 30; in the next verse 31 we have

---

[1] Ἐλπίζω πεφανερῶσθαι 2 C. 5. 11 shows the deflection of the idea of 'hope' into that of 'think,' which is also in vogue in German (as in classical Greek).

§ 62. 1–2.]   *PERIPHRASTIC CONJUGATION.*   203

ταῦτα δὲ γέγραπται); cp. Herm. Sim. ix. 4. 1 ὑποδεδύκεισαν – ὑποδεδυκυῖαι ἦσαν. (Periphrasis in the active is less common, as in A. 21. 29 ἦσαν προεωρακότες.) Even where the aoristic meaning of the perfect (§ 59, 3) predominates, periphrasis may be introduced: οὐ γάρ ἐστιν ἐν γωνίᾳ πεπραγμένον τοῦτο (A. 26. 26). It occasionally serves to produce a more forcible and rhetorical expression: A. 25. 10 (א*B) ἐστὼς ἐπὶ τοῦ βήματος Καίσαρός εἰμι, which is better than ἔστηκα ἐπὶ ... or ἐπὶ τοῦ ... ἔστηκα. An example of the pluperfect is L. 2. 26 ἦν αὐτῷ κεχρηματισμένον; fut. perf. L. 12. 52 ἔσονται διαμεμερισμένοι, H. 2. 12 ἔσομαι πεποιθώς O.T.; conjunct. Jo. 16. 24 ᾖ πεπληρωμένη; imperat. L. 12. 35 ἔστωσαν περιεζωσμέναι; even the participle itself is written periphrastically in E. 4. 18, Col. 1. 21 ὄντες (-ας) ἀπηλλοτριωμένοι (-ους), here clearly to express still more forcibly the idea of persistence in the new condition of things (in the passage of Colossians καὶ ἐχθρούς is appended; cp. Aristoph. Ran. 721 οὖσιν οὐ κεκιβδηλευμένοις, ἀλλὰ καλλίστοις κ.τ.λ.). A cognate instance is ἦν κείμενος L. 23. 53, = τεθειμένος (§ 23, 6).

2. Εἰμί[1] is further used to a large extent in the N.T. in connection with the **present participle** to form a periphrasis for the **imperfect** (ἦν), the **future** (ἔσομαι), rarely the **present indic.** (εἰμί), and occasionally the **present infinitive** and **imperative** (εἶναι, ἴσθι); this use is indeed especially frequent in the narrative style of Mark and Luke, in whose writings the periphrasis mentioned in the previous paragraph (1) also finds the greatest number of instances (Buttmann p. 268). Many examples of this periphrasis may be quoted as parallels from the classical language (Kühner ii. 35, note 3), and it may be argued that this method of expression is analogous to that mentioned in 1, and that at least in the case of the future it offered the advantage of distinguishing continuous from momentary action; still, in view of the absence of an analogous development in the Hellenistic language, one cannot fail to recognize, especially in the case of the imperfect, the influence of Aramaic (W. Schmid Atticismus iii. 113 f.), since that language made an extensive use of periphrases of this kind.[2] One cannot adduce in this connection instances such as R. 3. 12 O.T. οὐκ ἔστιν ('there is no-one') ποιῶν χρηστότητα, A. 21. 23 εἰσὶν ἄνδρες ('there are persons here') εὐχὴν ἔχοντες ('who have a vow'); L. 2. 8 is also different, καὶ ποιμένες ἦσαν ... ἀγραυλοῦντες καὶ φυλάσσοντες, since the existence of these shepherds had first to be noticed, and then their occupation (cp. A. 19. 14, 24). But even after deducting all the examples, where the imperfect of the principal verb could not have been used or would not have had the

---

[1] Not ὑπάρχω, which only occurs in A. 8. 16, 19. 36 in connection with a perfect participle.

[2] In the case of the following writings—(Mt.), Mc., Luke's Gospel, and the first half of the Acts—this is no doubt due to their being direct translations from Aramaic originals. In John's Gospel in most passages (1. 9, 28, 2. 6, 3. 23) ἦν has a certain independence of its own (ὅπου ἦν – βαπτίζων, 'where he stayed and baptized'); ἦν κακὸν ποιῶν in 18. 30 seems to be a wrong reading for ἦν κακοποιός. In Mt. cp. 7. 29, 19. 22 etc.—In St. Paul, G. 1. 22 f. ἤμην ἀγνοούμενος ... ἀκούοντες ἦσαν.

same meaning, the number of instances even in the Acts is considerably large: *e.g.* 1. 10 ἀτενίζοντες ἦσαν, 13 ἦσαν καταμένοντες, 14 ἦσαν προσκαρτεροῦντες, 2. 2 ἦσαν καθήμενοι etc. A periphrastic future appears in 6. 4 D ἐσόμεθα προσκαρτεροῦντες. (But from chapter 13 of the Acts onwards the only further instances are: 16. 12 ἦμεν ἐν τῇ πόλει διατρίβοντες, cp. 14. 7, note 2 on p. 203: 18. 7 ἡ οἰκία ἦν συνομοροῦσα [an easily intelligible use]: 21. 3 ἦν ἀποφορτιζόμενον, see § 58, 4, ἀπεφορτίζετο could not have been used: 22. 19 ἤμην φυλακίζων[1]).

Instances of the pres. indic. being written periphrastically: 2 C. 9. 12 ἡ διακονία οὐ μόνον ἐστὶν προσαναπληροῦσα..., ἀλλὰ καὶ περισσεύουσα; G. 4. 24, Col. 2. 23², Ja. 1. 17, 3. 15, Herm. Vis. i. 2. 4 ἔστιν μὲν οὖν... ἡ τοιαύτη βουλὴ... ἐπιφέρουσα a periphrasis for the sake of emphasis, somewhat like Demosth. 20. 18 ἔστι δὲ... ἔχον; Mt. 27. 33 is most probably corrupt (λεγόμενος om. א*D); the phrase ὅ ἐστιν ('means') μεθερμηνευόμενον does not come under this head. The periphrases of the **impersonal verbs** must be given a place to themselves, since they are not only common in Hellenistic Greek (Schmid Atticism. iii. 114), but are also found previously in Attic (ἐστὶ προσῆκον Dem. 3. 24): A. 19. 36 δέον ἐστίν (cp. 1 P. 1. 6 δέον [ἐστί]; Clem. Cor. i. 34. 2): ἐξόν (*sc.* ἐστί) A. 2. 29, 2 C. 12. 4.—Infinitive: L. 9. 18 = 11. 1 ἐν τῷ εἶναι αὐτὸν προσευχόμενον. Imperative: Mt. 5. 25 ἴσθι εὐνοῶν (the verb is not elsewhere used in the N.T.), L. 19. 17 ἴσθι ἐξουσίαν ἔχων: Clem. Hom. Ep. ad Jac. 3 εὖ ἴσθι εἰδώς. Of the periphrastic conjunctive there is no instance.—Future expressing continuance: Mt. 10. 22 ἔσεσθε μισούμενοι, Mc. 13. 25 οἱ ἀστέρες ἔσονται πίπτοντες, L. 5. 10 ἀνθρώπους ἔσῃ ζωγρῶν, 1 C. 14. 11 ἔσεσθε εἰς ἀέρα λαλοῦντες, Herm. Mand. v. 2. 8 ἔσῃ εὑρισκόμενος, Sim. ix. 13. 2 ἔσῃ φορῶν; in these instances the reason for using the periphrasis can be recognized (cp. the periphrastic fut. perf.), see Buttmann p. 266 f.

3. Γίνομαι is also occasionally employed in an analogous way to denote the beginning of a state. 2 C. 6. 14 μὴ γίνεσθε ἑτεροζυγοῦντες ἀπίστοις ('do not give yourselves up to it'), Col. 1. 18, H. 5. 12, Ap. 3. 2, 16. 10, Mc. 9. 3 (7): the different tenses of γίνομαι are joined with the pres. or perf. participle.—The combination of εἶναι with the **aorist** participle, which is not unknown to the language of classical poetry, is only found in L. 23. 19 BLT ὅστις ἦν... βληθεὶς (om. א*, the other MSS. have βεβλημένος) ἐν τῇ φυλακῇ, where the reading is therefore quite untrustworthy.[3]

4. Another way of expressing **imminence**, besides the future, is by **μέλλω with the infinitive**, a periphrasis with which the classical

---

[1] This speech of Paul was delivered τῇ ἑβραΐδι φωνῇ. Cp. the author's edition of Luke's Gospel, p. xxi.

[2] Ἄτινά ἐστιν λόγον μὲν ἔχοντα σοφίας, cp. Demosth. 31. 11 οὐδὲ λόγον τὸ πρᾶγμ' ἔχον ἐστί and other similar passages with ἔχων (Rehdantz Ind. Demosth. ii. l'artic.).

[3] In the Gospel of Peter 23 θεασάμενος ἦν, 51 ἦν τεθείς, this combination is due to a confusion between perfect and aorist; cp. 23 δεδώκασι for ἔδωκαν. Clem. Cor. ii. 17. 7 must be emended to ἔσονται δόξαν <δι>δόντες.

§ 62. 4. § 63. 1-3.] *INDICATIVE OF UNREALITY.* 205

language is acquainted and which offers this advantage, that it presents a mode of indicating imminence in past time, *e.g.* L. 7. 2 ἤμελλε τελευτᾶν and passim; also a conjunctive can be formed in this way, Mc. 13. 4 ὅταν μέλλῃ συντελεῖσθαι; and it serves to replace the fut. inf. and the fut. part. which are going out of use, and periphrasis is therefore generally employed in these cases, *e.g.* μέλλειν πίμπρασθαι A. 28. 6, ὁ τοῦτο μέλλων πράσσειν L. 22. 36. In the case of a participle, however, the periphrastic form is of wider application than the simple form, since the latter (as a relative indication of time) can never be employed in the genitive absolute, and nowhere at all except where it is definitely connected with a finite verb: periphrasis is therefore necessary in A. 18. 14 μέλλοντος ἀνοίγειν gen. abs., 20. 3 γενομένης ἐπιβουλῆς αὐτῷ μέλλοντι ἀνάγεσθαι, Jo. 12. 4 ’Ιούδας, ὁ μέλλων αὐτὸν παραδιδόναι (but in 6. 64 τίς ἐστιν ὁ παραδώσων ABC al., cp. § 61, 4).

§ 63. THE MOODS. INDICATIVE OF UNREALITY (AND REPETITION).

1. With regard to the use of the **moods** the distinction between the language of the New Testament and the classical language is considerably greater than it is with regard to the tenses, if only for the reason that the optative which was disappearing (§ 14, 1) had to be replaced.

2. The **indicative** in Greek, besides its primary function of making assertions about real or actual events (to which in all languages is attached its use in negative or interrogative sentences), has the further function of denoting **unreality** as such, by means of the tenses expressive of past time (since the form of the verb which is used to express that which *no longer* exists acquires the general notion of non-existence). The indicative, however, is not used in this way in the principal clause without the addition of the particle ἄν, which differentiates such sentences from unqualified assertions about past time, whereas in the accompanying conditional and subordinate clauses, and in the kindred clauses expressing a wish, the indicative is used alone.

3. In the N.T. the indicative has not only kept the whole of this sphere of its use, but has also enlarged it at the expense of the optative. In the first place in **hypothetical sentences**, where unreality is expressed, the indicative is used both in the protasis and the apodosis; in the latter the insertion of ἄν is not obligatory. Jo. 15. 24 εἰ τὰ ἔργα μὴ ἐποίησα ἐν αὐτοῖς ..., ἁμαρτίαν οὐκ εἴχοσαν, cp. 19. 11 (where אA etc. have the wrong reading ἔχεις for εἶχες of B etc.), 8. 39, G. 4. 15 (ἄν is added by א°D°EKLP); on the other hand ἄν is inserted in Jo. 18. 30 εἰ μὴ ἦν ..., οὐκ ἄν σοι παρεδώκαμεν, and this is the case in the majority of instances. The position of ἄν is as near the beginning of the sentence as possible: οὐκ ἄν passim,

οἱ ὑπηρέται ἂν οἱ ἐμοὶ ἠγωνίζοντο (Jo. 18. 36).[1] The tense (imperf. or aor.; pluperf. in 1 Jo. 2. 19) keeps the ordinary meaning of its action; the imperfect in other connections is ambiguous (in the passage above quoted ἠγωνίζ. ἄν is 'would *have* fought,' which was meant to be regarded as a continuous or incomplete action, since accomplishment and result were uncertain).

4. The **imperfect indicative without ἄν** is used in classical Greek for expressions of **necessity, obligation, duty, possibility** etc., when one requires to indicate the fact that in reality the opposite is taking place or has taken place: while the present indicative asserts something about present time, as it always does, and accordingly an appeal is contained in such presents as χρή, προσήκει etc. In the former case we employ the conjunctive, it should or could be so, or where the possibility of anything happening is past, it should or could have been—a distinction which cannot be made in Greek; the indicative is logically correct, since even in the case of the verb 'should' the obligation was already an actual one in past time (cp. Latin). The N.T. keeps this usage of the imperfect, but uses it further to denote what in classical Greek is expressed by the present indicative: A. 22. 22 οὐ γὰρ καθῆκεν αὐτὸν ζῆν (καθῆκον D[2], cp. § 62, 2), they are asking for him to be put to death: Col. 3. 18 ὡς ἀνῆκεν 'as is seemly': E. 5. 4 ἃ οὐκ ἀνῆκεν (v.l. τὰ οὐκ ἀνήκοντα).[2] Elsewhere the imperfect is used correctly: ἔδει in Mt. 23. 23 ταῦτα ἔδει ποιῆσαι, κἀκεῖνα μὴ ἀφεῖναι, a frequent form of this verb (also used of course where it is merely the past necessity which is stated, οὐχὶ ταῦτα ἔδει ['was bound'] παθεῖν τὸν Χριστόν L. 24. 26): ὤφειλον in 2 C. 12. 11 ἐγὼ γὰρ ὤφειλον ὑφ' ὑμῶν συνίστασθαι, but differently used in 1 C. 5. 10 ἐπεὶ ὠφείλετε ἐκ τοῦ κόσμου ἐξελθεῖν 'must have otherwise,' where in classical Greek the insertion of ἄν is at least *admissible*, as it is in H. 9. 26 ἐπεὶ ἔδει αὐτὸν πολλάκις παθεῖν: with δύνασθαι in Mt. 26. 9 ἐδύνατο τοῦτο πραθῆναι πολλοῦ: with an impersonal expression with εἶναι, καλὸν ἦν εἰ οὐκ ἐγεννήθη Mt. 26. 24 (καλόν ἐστι 18. 8 is different; cp. 2 P. 2. 21[3]).

5. The **indicative** when used to denote an **impracticable wish** in Attic is introduced by εἴθε or εἰ γάρ, but it is more inclined to use the analytical expression εἴθε (εἰ γάρ) ὤφελον (with infinitive). From the latter phrase, through the omission of the introductory particle

---

[1] In this passage ἄν is wanting in B*, and stands after ἤγων. in אB^{mg}LX; similar fluctuation in its position is seen in 8. 19 καὶ τὸν πατέρα μου ἂν ᾔδειτε BL, ᾔδ. ἄν אΓΔ al., where perhaps ἄν should be struck out with D, as it is in verse 39 on preponderant authority. L. 19. 23 κἀγὼ ἐλθὼν σὺν τόκῳ ἂν αὐτὸ ἔπραξα contains in ἐλθών an equivalent for a (temporal) protasis. Ἄν cannot go further back in a sentence than οὐ: G. 1. 10 Χριστοῦ δοῦλος οὐκ ἂν ἤμην. —Hypothetical sentences of this kind are remarkably scarce in the Pauline Epistles; in the Acts they are wanting entirely.

[2] The Attic προσήκει does not appear in the N.T.; nor χρή except in Ja. 3. 10, nor ἔξεστι (for which ἐξόν is used, sc. ἐστι, § 62, 2), nor the verbal adj. in -τέος with ἦν etc.

[3] The Attic use of the (aorist) indicative to denote what *nearly* happened (ὀλίγου ἐδέησα with infin., ὀλίγου ἐπελαθόμην) is unattested in the N.T.

and through the auxiliary verb becoming stereotyped, there has been formed in the Hellenistic language the word ὤφελε (Callimachus) or ὤφελον ὄφελον used as a particle to introduce a wish with the indic.[1]; ὄφελον is the form which it takes in the N.T., where the particle is even used (§ 66, 1) with the future to introduce a practicable wish. 1 C. 4. 8 ὄφελον (D°EL ὤφ.) ἐβασιλεύσατε, 2 C. 11. 1 ὄφελον (ὤφ. D°EFGKL) ἀνείχεσθέ μου, Ap. 3. 15 (ὤφ. BP).—But if the idea of wishing is expressed by a particular verb, then a distinction is drawn in Attic between βουλοίμην ἄν (a practicable wish, modestly expressed) and ἐβουλόμην ἄν (impracticable), whereas in the N.T. both these meanings are combined in ἐβουλόμην or the more popular word ἤθελον (without ἄν). Thus A. 25. 22 ἐβ. ἀκοῦσαι (perfectly practicable), R. 9. 3 ηὐχόμην ἀνάθεμα εἶναι (hardly conceived of as practicable), G. 4. 20 ἤθελον (*modus irrealis*, or imperfect of unreality), Philem. 13 ἐβουλόμην ('would have liked,' cp. 14). So also Herm. Vis. iii. 8. 6, 11. 4, Clem. Hom. i. 9 ἤθελον=βουλοίμην ἄν. The classical optative is only found in A. 26. 29 (א°AB) εὐξαίμην ἄν, see § 66, 2.

6. The **indicative of unreality** in **final clauses**, which are dependent on another indicative of this class, is not found in the N.T.; on the contrary such clauses take the conjunctive, Jo. 18. 36 οἱ ὑπηρέται ἂν οἱ ἐμοὶ ἠγωνίζοντο, ἵνα μὴ παραδοθῶ τοῖς Ἰουδαίοις.

7. While the classical language expresses **indefinite repetition** in past time in principal clauses by **ἄν with the imperfect or aorist indicative**, and in subordinate clauses by the optative, in the N.T. the former method of expression has been transferred to **subordinate clauses** in place of the optative[2], while there is no instance of its use in principal clauses. The ἄν, which in this case is never dropped (ἐάν may be used, see § 26, 4), is placed as in other subordinate clauses as close as possible to the particle or the relative. Mc. 6. 56 ὅπου ἐὰν (ἄν) εἰσεπορεύετο..., ἐν ταῖς ἀγοραῖς ἐτίθεσαν τοὺς ἀσθενοῦντας: 15. 6 D ὃν ἂν ᾐτοῦντο, the correct reading, cp. § 13, 3: A. 2. 45, 4. 35 (καθότι), 1 C. 12. 2 (ὡς). The aorist is by no means excluded (cp. for a classical instance in a principal clause Dem. 18, 219 ὁ μὲν γράφων οὐκ ἂν ἐπρέσβευσεν), and so we have in Mc. 6. 56ᵇ καὶ ὅσοι ἂν ἥψαντο (אBD; ἥπτοντο AN al.) αὐτοῦ ἐσῴζοντο, LXX. Is. 55. 11 ὅσα ἂν ἠθέλησα, Herm. Sim. ix. 4. 5 ὅταν ἐτέθησαν, 17. 3³, Barn. 12. 2 ὁπόταν καθεῖλεν. Even particles compounded with ἄν, such as ὅταν, take part in this construction with the indicative: Mc. 3. 11 τὰ πνεύματα, ὅταν αὐτὸν ἐθεώρουν, προσέπιπτον, Mc. 11. 19 ὅταν (ὅτε AD al.) ὀψὲ ἐγένετο, ἐξεπορεύετο ἔξω τῆς πόλεως, where this particle also denotes custom, cp. L. 21. 37.

---

[1] So LXX., Arrian. Diss. Epict., etc., Sophocles Lexicon ὀφείλω.
[2] So also Lucian D. Mort. 9. 2 ὄντινα ἂν προσέβλεψα.
[3] With pluperfect Sim. ix. 1. 6 ὅταν ἐπικεκαύκει.

§ 64. CONJUNCTIVE AND FUTURE (OR PRESENT) INDICATIVE IN PRINCIPAL CLAUSES.

1. The **conjunctive** has apparently the primary meaning of something which **should** (or ought to) take place, and consequently its proper use is to express the will of the speaker, though in a less definite manner than the imperative, with which mood the conjunctive has close affinities. But the conjunctive, and especially the aorist conjunctive, also has close affinities with the future indicative. Not only has it to a large extent the greatest similarity of form (λύσω is the form of the 1st sing. both of the aor. conj. and the fut. ind., λύσῃ is the form of the 2nd sing. of the same tenses in the middle), but in its manner of employment it comes into the closest contact with that tense from the earliest times (Homer). The future does not assert what is about to happen merely in point of time, but frequently also what is about to happen in the intention of the speaker: βούλομαι λέγειν gives the same meaning analytically, which λέξω gives synthetically. The conjunctive, on the other hand, actually has a much wider range of employment than is contained in the primary meaning above-mentioned, and expresses that which under certain circumstances may be the outcome of the present position of affairs: from this it is at once apparent that it refers in great measure to the future, while past time lies outside its compass. In the final development of the language the future has been supplanted by θέλω ἵνα (for which modern Greek uses θά) with the present or aorist conjunctive (so that action is differentiated in future time as well as in past time); the N.T., however, is still a long way removed from this state of things, whereas the mixture of the fut. ind. and aor. conj.[1] has, in comparison with the classical language, made considerable progress.

2. The conjunctive **supplements the imperative** (as in Latin and other languages) in the 1st. pers. plur., where there is no distinction from the classical language; this also happens, but in a somewhat different way, in the 1st pers. sing., since an invitation is there made to the other person to *let* the speaker do something; in classical Greek this conjunctive is introduced by ἄγε and φέρε, also by δεῦρο, in the N.T. by ἄφες (whence ἄς in modern Greek) and δεῦρο (plural δεῦτε): Mt. 7. 4 ἄφες ἐκβάλω τὸ κάρφος, A. 7. 34 O.T. δεῦρο ἀποστείλω σε (Eurip. Bacch. 341 δευρό σου στέψω κάρα), cp. Ap. 17. 1, 21. 9. The same words may also precede the 1st pers. conj. and (δεῦτε at any rate) the 2nd pers. imp.: δεῦτε ἀποκτείνωμεν Mc. 12. 7, δεῦτε ἴδετε Mt. 28. 6; ἄφες ἴδωμεν Mt. 27. 49 (where the singular form has become stereotyped, as happens with ἄγε, φέρε etc.), Mc. 15. 36 אDV (ἄφετε ABC etc.) = our 'let us see.' Again the conj. necessarily

---

[1] On this mixture in late Greek, which for instance introduces εἴπω σοι = ἐρῶ σοι, see Sophocles Lexic. p. 45, Hatzidakis Einl. in d. neugriech. Gramm. p. 218. So in Clem. Hom. xi. 3 καὶ οὕτως ... δυνηθῇ (main clause) = δυνήσεται. But it occurs already in the LXX., *e.g.* Is. 33. 24 ἀφεθῇ γὰρ αὐτοῖς ἡ ἁμαρτία, 10. 16.

takes the place of the imperative **in the 2nd person** of the aorist after μή, as in classical Greek, and **may** do so also **in the 3rd person** (not frequently; classical Greek also uses conj. or imp.): μή τις αὐτὸν ἐξουθενήσῃ 1 C. 16. 11, cp. 2 C. 11. 16, 2 Th. 2. 3. In the N.T. such clauses are often preceded (Mt. 8. 4 al., Mc. 1. 44, 1 Th. 5. 15) by ὅρα, ὁρᾶτε, βλέπετε, as well as ἄφες etc., which do not affect the construction, see § 79, 4.—On μή expressing apprehension in independent clauses see § 65, 3 ad fin.

3. The **future indicative** takes the place of the **imperative** in the **legal language** of the O.T. (not a classical use) both in positive and negative commands (the negative being οὐ), but the N.T. language apart from O.T. quotations does not appear to have been materially affected by this use. Mt. 5. 43 O.T. ἀγαπήσεις τὸν πλησίον σου, but in the law of Christ in 44 ἀγαπᾶτε; ibid. 21 O.T. οὐ φονεύσεις etc., but the future is nowhere used in this chapter in independent precepts of Christ, since even 48 ἔσεσθε τέλειοι is modelled on Deut. 18. 13. Elsewhere however there are some isolated instances of the future (2nd and 3rd persons): 6. 5 οὐκ ἔσεσθε (the imperative ἔστε occurs nowhere in the N.T.), 21. 3 ἐάν τις ὑμῖν εἴπῃ τι, ἐρεῖτε,=εἴπατε in Mc. 11. 3, Mt. 20. 26 οὐχ οὕτως ἔσται ἐν ὑμῖν, and then ἔσται occurs twice again in 26 f. with v.l. ἔστω (Clem. Cor. i. 60. 2 καθαρεῖς). With this is connected the reverse use of the imperative for future in Mt. 10. 13 (ἐλθάτω ἡ εἰρήνη ὑμῶν ἐπ' αὐτήν [but ἔσται D] ... ἐπιστραφήτω), where the future is more natural and is actually found in L. 10. 6. On ὄφελον with the fut. ind. (in a clause expressing a wish) see § 66, 1.

4. A further **substitute** for the **imperative** is afforded by ἵνα with the conjunctive (used independently; cp. French *que*, class. ὅπως with fut.), E. 5. 33 (after ἀγαπάτω) ἡ δὲ γυνὴ ἵνα φοβῆται τὸν ἄνδρα, cp. 2 C. 8. 7, Mc. 5. 23 (see on ἵνα § 69, 1). This may be extended by θέλω: Mc. 6. 25 θέλω ἵνα δῷς (δός Mt. 14. 8). Another substitute is a question in the fut. with οὐ (as frequently in classical Greek), A. 13. 10 οὐ παύσῃ διαστρέφων, though in this passage the imperative meaning is not quite clear, and perhaps a reproach is rather intended.

5. The most definite form of a **negative assertion about the future** is that with **οὐ μή**, which also appears in classical Greek and is there also connected, as in the N.T., with both the fut. ind. and the conjunctive. But though the N.T. has this double construction of οὐ μή, still the only certain instance of its taking the fut. is Mt. 16. 22 οὐ μὴ ἔσται σοι τοῦτο, whereas in the other cases not only is there a strong similarity between the form of aor. and fut., but there is also a variety of readings, while in numerous passages the conjunctive is by its peculiar form established beyond a doubt as the correct reading. Mt. 15. 5 οὐ μὴ τιμήσει τὸν πατέρα, but τιμήσῃ is read by E*FGK al. (a quotation of a saying of the Rabbis, 'need not honour'; in the LXX. οὐ μή is also prohibitive as in Gen. 3. 1), 26. 35 οὐ μή σε ἀπαρνήσομαι (-σωμαι AEGK al.), Mc. 14. 31 ditto (-σωμαι אEFGK al.), Ap. 9. 6 οὐ μὴ εὑρήσουσιν (εὕρωσιν AP). (But Hermas has in Mand. ix. 5 οὐδὲν οὐ μὴ λήψῃ, Sim. i. 5 οὐ μὴ παραδεχθήσῃ.) On the

other hand the conj. is used *e.g.* in Ap. 2. 11 οὐ μὴ ἀδικηθῇ, L. 12. 59 οὐ μὴ ἐξέλθῃς, 13. 35 οὐ μὴ ἴδητέ με. The conj. is always that of the aorist, whereas classical Greek also uses the pres. conj. The same form is occasionally used **interrogatively** to denote an affirmation (the relation between the two uses being therefore the same as between "οὐ πράξω." and "οὐ πράξω;"): Jo. 18. 11 οὐ μὴ πίω αὐτό; L. 18. 7, Ap. 15. 4 τίς οὐ μὴ φοβηθῇ; (the classical οὐ μὴ λαλήσεις;= 'you will certainly not'='do not venture to' etc.).

6. In **questions** of **doubt** and **deliberation**, as to what **ought** to take place, classical Greek uses the conjunctive or (more rarely) the fut. ind., as in Eurip. Ion 758 εἴπωμεν; ἢ σιγῶμεν; ἢ τί δράσομεν; generally in the 1st person, rarely in the 3rd. The question is equivalent to χρή: it may be introduced by βούλει -εσθε (without a conjunction): it is negatived by μή. The N.T. in this case practically uses only the conjunctive (the fut. is a v.l. in *e.g.* A. 2. 37, 4. 16; on Ph. 1. 22 see § 65, 1), which is frequently introduced by θέλεις -ετε (βούλεσθε), and in addition to the 1st person the 2nd and 1st persons are occasionally used, where there is more of a future meaning: L. 23. 31 ἐν τῷ ξηρῷ τί γένηται (γενήσεται D); ('what will happen then?'), Mt. 23. 33 πῶς φύγητε, 'how will (or can) you escape?', 26. 54, R. 10. 14 f. πῶς οὖν ἐπικαλέσωνται (-σονται KLP) ... πῶς δὲ πιστεύσωσιν (v.l. -σουσιν) ... πῶς δὲ ἀκούσωσιν (אᶜA²B; -σουσιν L, -σονται א*D al.) ... πῶς δὲ κηρύξωσιν (the v.l. -ουσιν is hardly attested; 'how will they' or 'can they': Hermas, Sim. v. 7. 3 πῶς σωθῇ ὁ ἄνθρωπος. In these instances classical Greek must have used the future, which we have in L. 16. 11 f. τίς πιστεύσει; ... τίς δώσει; cp. 11. 11, Mt. 16. 26 τί δώσει=Mc. 8. 37 τί δοῖ (δώσει ACD al.). A peculiar instance is L. 11. 5 τίς ἐξ ὑμῶν ἕξει φίλον, καὶ πορεύσεται ... καὶ εἴπῃ (ἐρεῖ AD al.) ... 7 κἀκεῖνος εἴπῃ (ἐρεῖ D), where the thought is awkwardly expressed (§ 77, 6; Viteau p. 10), and would have been more appropriately rendered by the conditional form of sentence (ἐὰν φίλος πορευθῇ etc.), and then the future would be in its right place in the apodosis. Cp. ibid. 11 f. The fut. is used in the 1st pers. in R. 3. 5, 6. 1 τί ἐροῦμεν; (cp. Plato, Crito 50 B), which at least approximates to a deliberative sense; and this is decidedly the sense of L. 22. 49 εἰ (direct question, § 77, 2) πατάξομεν ἐν μαχαίρῃ; (-ωμεν GH al.).—Question introduced by θέλεις etc.: Mt. 13. 28 θέλεις συλλέξωμεν; Jo. 18. 39 βούλεσθε ἀπολύσω;—The question may be put analytically by the insertion of δεῖ (χρή being unusual in the N.T.), τί με δεῖ ποιεῖν A. 16. 30, or of δύνασθαι for the other sense of the future or conjunctive, Mt. 12. 34 πῶς δύνασθε λαλεῖν (Viteau p. 32).—The pres. indic. is used very rarely in a deliberative sense in place of the fut. ind. (§ 56, 8): Jo. 11. 47 (Herm. Sim. ix. 9. 1) τί ποιοῦμεν; for which there are parallels in colloquial Latin.[1]

---

[1] In 1 Jo. 3. 17 μενεῖ should be written for μένει.—Plato, Symp. 214 A πῶς ποιοῦμεν is not quite a similar case; it is not deliberative like τί ποιῶμεν ibid. B, but the present contains a gentle rebuke.

§ 65. CONJUNCTIVE AND FUTURE (OR PRESENT) INDICATIVE IN SUBORDINATE CLAUSES.

1. **Indirect interrogative sentences**, like direct, take the deliberative conjunctive, Mt. 6. 25 μὴ μεριμνᾶτε τί φάγητε: and here again the sphere of the conjunctive is extended somewhat beyond its classical limits, as in L. 12. 36 προσδεχομένοις τὸν κύριον, πότε ἀναλύσῃ (-σει GKX al.), cp. Ph. 3. 12 with εἰ 'whether' διώκω εἰ καταλάβω (cp. inf. 6): elsewhere this εἰ is followed by the fut. ind. (In Mc. 11. 13 D gives the reading ἰδεῖν ἐάν [cp. inf. 4] τί ἐστιν ἐν αὐτῇ.) In the region of past time, where the classical language according to rule employs the optative, the N.T. in this as in other cases retains the conjunctive (though not always in St. Luke, see § 66, 3): A. 4. 21 μηδὲν εὑρίσκοντες τὸ πῶς κολάσωνται αὐτούς. The use of the fut. ind. (also possible in classical Greek) in such sentences is hardly attested by Ph. 1. 22 τί αἱρήσομαι οὐ γνωρίζω, where the better punctuation is τί αἱρήσομαι; (cp. § 77, 6; B has αἱρήσωμαι).

2. **Final clauses** introduced by ἵνα, ὅπως, μή have very largely extended the range of their use in the N.T. in consequence of the infinitive being expressed by a periphrasis with ἵνα; we are here only concerned with the mood, which is in no way influenced by the character of ἵνα, whether it be a true final particle or not. This mood in the N.T. is generally the conjunctive, without regard to the right which the optative formerly possessed of expressing purpose from a past point of view, or from that of some person introduced by the narrator[1]; to a rather less extent the future indicative is also introduced, and just where in classical Greek it is *not* found, namely after ἵνα and final μή, whereas the Attic use of ὅπως and ὅπως μή in connection with the fut. ind. (after verbs of deliberating, striving, taking care) is not found in the N.T. With verbs of this class the particles used throughout the N.T. are ἵνα and for negative ἵνα μή or μή: ὅπως, in so far as it appears at all (never in the Apoc., only once in St. John's Gospel,[2] and not often in St. Paul), is limited to a purely final meaning and to its use in connection with verbs of asking (παρακαλεῖν etc.). Ὅπως has further lost, with the exception of some few passages in Luke and a quotation from the LXX., the ἄν which is often appended to it in Attic Greek; this particle was never even in Attic annexed to ἵνα and μή. On μή (μήποτε) expressing apprehension, vide inf. 3.—The fut. ind. after ἵνα occurs most frequently in the Apocalypse: 22. 14 ἵνα ἔσται ... καὶ εἰσέλθωσιν (thus the two forms are regarded as equivalent), 3. 9 ἵνα ἥξουσιν (-ωσι B) καὶ προσκυνήσουσιν (-σωσιν B) ... καὶ γνῶσιν (א reads γνώσῃ

---

[1] The supposed optat. δώῃ in E. 1. 17 is really conjunctive (§ 23, 4; B gives correctly δῷ).

[2] The passage is 11. 57, where ὅπως is evidently used for the sake of variety, since a ἵνα has occurred immediately before; the same reason applies to its use in St. Paul in 1 C. 1. 29, 2 C. 8. 14, 2 Th. 1. 12 (but not in 2 C. 8. 11, G. 1. 4, Philem. 6: ἵνα ... ἵνα occurs in G. 4. 5, 1 C. 4. 6).

not well), 8. 3 δώσει (-ῃ BP), similarly in 13. 16 (written λωϲι, from which the wrong reading δῶσι(ν) arose). See also 6. 4, 11, 9. 4, 5, 20, 13. 12, 14. 13. In St. Paul we have: 1 C. 9. 15 ἵνα τις (οὐδείς is wrong) κενώσει, 18 ἵνα θήσω, 13. 3 παραδῶ ἵνα καυθήσομαι (the readings -σωμαι CK, καυχήσωμαι אAB are wrong), G. 2. 4 καταδουλώσουσιν (אAB*CDE), Phil. 2. 11. Also probably 1 Th. 5. 10 ἵνα ζήσομεν (A; D*E have ζῶμεν; the aorist ζήσωμεν of א etc. would mean 'come to life again' as in R. 14. 9): in this passage ἄν is also omitted from an intervening clause, ἵνα εἴτε γρηγορῶμεν εἴτε καθεύδωμεν κ.τ.λ., cp. Ph. 1. 27 ἵνα εἴτε ἀκούω (conj.). Other passages are: 1 P. 3. 1 κερδηθήσονται, Jo. 17. 2 δώσει (-ῃ א°ACG al., δώσω א*, ἔχῃ D), L. 14. 10 ἐρεῖ with v.l. in AD al. εἴπῃ, 20. 10 δώσουσιν with v.l. in CD al. δῶσιν. With μή: Col. 2. 8 βλέπετε μή... ἔσται, H. 3. 12 βλέπετε μήποτε... ἔσται. A special instance is that where a conj. after ἵνα (or μή) is succeeded by a fut. linked on to the conj. by a καί to denote a further result: A. 21. 24 ἵνα ξυρήσωνται (-ονται אB*D²E al.)..., καὶ γνώσονται, for which καὶ γνῶσιν was at any rate possible; the same arrangement is used elsewhere in the N.T., and moreover in cases where the second verb should, strictly speaking, have been subordinated to the final particle; there appears therefore to be a kind of Hebraism underlying this construction, as in the LXX. this habit of writing the second verb in the future is very widely extended (Viteau, p. 81 f.). Eph. 6. 3 O.T. ἵνα... γένηται καὶ ἔσῃ, Jo. 15. 8 ἵνα καρπὸν... φέρητε καὶ γενήσεσθε (γένησθε BDL al.) ἐμοὶ μαθηταί, L. 22. 30 (with many vv.ll.), 12. 58 (μήποτε), Mt. 5. 25 (ditto), Mc. 5. 23 (according to A), Mt. 13. 15 = Jo. 12. 40 = A. 28. 27 O.T. (Is. 6. 10 μήποτε or ἵνα μή), Barn. 4. 3 ἵνα ταχύνῃ καὶ ἥξει (א for -ξῃ), Herm. Mand. vi. 2. 10, Sim. ix. 7. 6, 28. 5. There is the same construction after an **independent** conj., ἀγοράσωμεν καὶ δώσομεν Mc. 6. 37 ALΔ (-ωμεν אBD, al. δῶμεν); and in Hermas after an imperat., Vis. i. 1. 3 λάβε καὶ ἀποδώσεις μοι, Mand. ii. 1 ἄκακος γίνου καὶ ἔσῃ ὡς (esto Lat.).—Ὅπως ἄν occurs in L. 2. 35, A. 3. 19, 15. 17 O.T. (Amos 9. 12, our text has no ἄν); also in a quotation in R. 3. 4 = Ps. 51. 6.—The **present** indic. after ἵνα is of course simply due to corruption of the text.[1]

3. **Μή** after words expressing **apprehension** (φοβοῦμαι etc.) is not final, but is akin to the μή which expresses apprehension in independent sentences such as μὴ ἀγροικότερον ᾖ 'it is perhaps too rude' (Plato). Still from one point of view this μή does border on the meaning of final μή, since an apprehension of something eventually happening has for its immediate result the purpose of avoiding this thing. In the N.T. this μή of apprehension is usually strengthened by ποτε or πως: μήποτε, μήπως. On the other hand the idea of negation in the μή is so far weakened, that it is used to introduce something which is surmised, where there is no idea of warding it off: accordingly in Hellenistic Greek μήποτε in a principal clause means 'perhaps,' in a dependent clause 'if perchance,' 'if possibly':

---

[1] Jo. 5. 20 אL, G. 6. 12 ACF al., Tit. 2. 4 א*AF al. etc. But φυσιοῦσθε 1 C. 4. 6 and ζηλοῦτε G. 4. 17 are conjunctives, see § 22, 3.

(L. 3. 15 an indirect question), 2 Tim. 2. 25 μήποτε δῷ¹ αὐτοῖς ὁ θεὸς κ.τ.λ. If the thing (surmised or) feared is something negative, then the formation (as in classical Greek) is μὴ οὐ : Mt. 25. 9 μήποτε οὐκ ἀρκέσῃ אALΣ, for which BCD al. have the not impossible reading μ. οὐ μὴ ἀρκ. (ἀρκέσει D). The classical construction, if the apprehension has reference to something which is still dependent on the will, is always the conjunctive : if it refers to something which has already taken place or generally to something independent of the will, any tense of the indicative may also be used (the indicative is always used in reference to a past event). In the N.T. the phrase **φοβοῦμαι μή** is found only in Luke and Paul (Hebrews): A. 23. 10 φοβηθεὶς (HLP εὐλαβηθεὶς) μὴ διασπασθῇ, cp. 27. 17, 29, 2 C. 11. 3 (μήπως), 12. 20 (ditto), G. 4. 11 (ditto), H. 4. 1 here μήποτε δοκῇ, in G. 4. 11, with reference to something which has taken place, it takes the perf. indic. (κεκοπίακα), elsewhere the aor. conj.; clearly this construction φοβοῦμαι μή was a literary and not a popular one (Viteau, p. 83). There is a greater frequency of **dependent** clauses with **μήποτε (μήπως)**, which are attached to any verb, to express the accompanying feeling of apprehension by which the action related is influenced, the construction varying as before : G. 2. 2 ἀνεθέμην αὐτοῖς τὸ εὐαγγέλιον ..., μήπως εἰς κενὸν τρέχω (conj.) ἢ ἔδραμον, 1 Th. 3. 5 ἔπεμψα εἰς τὸ γνῶναι τὴν πίστιν ὑμῶν, μήπως ἐπείρασεν ὑμᾶς ὁ σατανᾶς καὶ εἰς κενὸν γένηται (the issue feared) ὁ κόπος ἡμῶν (L. 3. 15 with optat., see § 66, 3). There is a transition to final μή in L. 14. 8 f. μὴ κατακλιθῇς ..., μήποτε ... ᾖ κεκλημένος² (ἥξει D)..., καὶ ἐρεῖ (cp. supra 2). As in the last passage D has the fut. = conj., so we find this tense occasionally elsewhere : Mc. 14. 2 μήποτε ἔσται (Mt. 7. 6 v.l.), Herm. Sim. ix. 28. 7, Mand. x. 2. 5 (ἐντεύξεται should be read for -ηται); cp. βλέπετε μὴ (μήποτε) ἔσται Col. 2. 8, H. 3. 12, final (supra 2).—**Independent** clauses with **μή** and the conj. usually have an imperative meaning, § 64, 2 ; under this head comes 1 Th. 5. 15 ὁρᾶτε μήτις ἀποδοῖ, ἀλλὰ ... διώκετε (on ὁρᾶτε before the imperat. and conj. see §§ 64, 2 ; 79, 4). An exception to this is Mt. 25. 9 μήποτε οὐκ ἀρκέσῃ, vide supra.

4. Of **conditional sentences** the four following forms exist in classical Greek : (1) εἰ with indicative, denoting something which is simply regarded as actual ; (2) ἐάν with conjunctive, to express that which from the given stand-point of present time, the time in question being either general or a special occasion, I wish to denote as under certain circumstances actual or liable to happen ; (3) εἰ with optative, if I wish to represent anything as generally possible, without regard to the general or actual situation at the moment (hence also used with reference to a position of affairs in past time); (4) εἰ with imperfect, aorist, or pluperfect indicative, to denote that the actual state of things is the opposite to the case supposed, vide supra § 63, 2 and 3. The distinction between (1) and (2) is very slight in

---

[1] Not δῴη optat.; cp. § 23, 4 and supra 2, note 1.
[2] This perf. conj. also occurs in Jo. 17. 19, 23, 1 C. 1. 10, 2 C. 1. 9, and is in all cases easily intelligible.

the case of εἰ with the fut. indic., since ἐάν with the aor. conj. also generally refers to the future—ἐὰν πέσῃ = *si ceciderit*; the indicative, however, expresses a more definite expectation.—In the N.T. (3) is hardly represented (see § 66, 4); (1) and (2) have come into still closer contact, as is seen especially in the fact that ἐάν may also be joined with the indicative. We note at the outset that the dissyllabic form of this particle is the regular one (cp. ἑαυτοῦ, where Attic has both ἑαυτοῦ and αὑτοῦ), whereas inversely the form ἐάν for ἄν is frequently employed in relative sentences (inf. 7), § 26, 4. Still 'and if,' 'even if,' may be κἄν: Mt. 21. 21 (D καὶ ... ἐάν), L. 13. 9 (καὶ ἐάν D) etc. (see § 5, 2). Externally then the prominent distinction between (1) and (2) is that the negative used with εἰ is οὐ, while with ἐάν it is (as in all Attic conditional sentences) μή, see § 75, 3. But the internal distinction between the two forms has not been quite lost. It is only modern Greek which denotes every 'if' by ἄν; in the N.T. εἰ with the indicative is obligatory for all suppositions referring to what has already taken place: Mc. 3. 26 εἰ ὁ σατανᾶς ἀνέστη ἐφ' ἑαυτόν (which according to the speech of Christ's opponent must already have taken place), contrast ibid. 24 in an imaginary instance, ἐὰν βασιλεία ἐφ' ἑαυτὴν μερισθῇ. The same distinction holds good where the two forms occur in even closer connection, as in Jo. 13. 17 εἰ ταῦτα οἴδατε (present reality), μακάριοί ἐστε ἐὰν ποιῆτε αὐτά (future), or 1 C. 7. 36 εἰ δέ τις ἀσχημονεῖν ἐπὶ τὴν παρθένον αὐτοῦ νομίζει (reality), ἐὰν ᾖ ὑπέρακμος (future), *i.e.* the indicative is used where a supposition is made with regard to something now actually existing, and the only irregularity is that this *present* indicative is occasionally preceded by ἐάν instead of εἰ: 1 Jo. 5. 15 ἐὰν οἴδαμεν (the reading of אc ἴδωμεν is not good),[1] 1 Th. 3. 7 ἐὰν ὑμεῖς στήκετε (-ητε א*DE), whereas before the imperf. and aor. indic. the N.T. like classical Greek always uses εἰ.[2] (Inversely in 1 Th. 5. 10 εἴτε ... εἴτε takes the conjunctive, in a clause inserted in the middle of a final sentence, vide supra 2.) Εἰ with the pres. indic. is used with reference to present reality also in G. 1. 9 (8 is different); on the other hand ἐάν with pres. conj. is very rarely so used, A. 5. 38 ἐὰν ᾖ ἐξ ἀνθρώπων ἡ βουλὴ αὕτη κ.τ.λ. followed in 39 by εἰ δὲ ἐκ θεοῦ ἐστιν, where we should no doubt understand the meaning to be: 'If perchance it should be—but if, as these persons maintain, it really is' etc. That in fact is very often the meaning of this εἰ: 'if really' (as is maintained), or even 'if accordingly' (as follows from what has been said): in the latter case it approximates to the meaning of ἐπεί. Εἰ ταῦτα ποιεῖς ('really'), φανέρωσον σεαυτὸν τῷ κόσμῳ Jo. 7. 4. Εἰ τὸν χόρτον ... ὁ θεὸς οὕτως ἀμφιέννυσιν ('accordingly,' see verses 28 f.), πόσῳ μᾶλλον ὑμᾶς Mt. 6. 30. Ἐάν, on the other hand, when referring to an actually

---

[1] Not very different in meaning is 1 Jo. 2. 29 ἐὰν εἰδῆτε, where the transition from εἰ with indic. to the other, apparently less suitable, mode of expression (ἐὰν c. conj.) is quite carried out ('as' or 'as soon as you know ..., so you also know').

[2] LXX. also has ἐὰν σὺ ἦσθα Job 22. 3.

existing state of things, makes the supposition indefinite: 1 C. 4. 15 ἐὰν γὰρ μυρίους παιδαγωγοὺς ἔχητε ('even if you should have'), Jo. 5. 31 ἐὰν ἐγὼ μαρτυρῶ ('if perchance'; one might also treat μαρτυρῶ as an indic., vide supra) περὶ ἐμαυτοῦ, ἡ μαρτυρία μου οὐκ ἔστιν ἀληθής.[1] On the other hand, with reference to things which may or may not happen at any time, ἐάν with the pres. conj. is the regular construction, though indeed in the N.T. εἰ with the indic. is also found used in this way: Mt. 5. 29 εἰ ὁ ὀφθαλμός σου σκανδαλίζει σε, cp. 30, 18. 8 f. (but ἐὰν σκανδαλίζῃ Mc. 9. 43, 45, 47), L. 6. 32 εἰ ἀγαπᾶτε, but in 33 ἐὰν ἀγαθοποιῆτε (Mt. 5. 46 ἐὰν ἀγαπήσητε). Quite incorrect is Mc. 9. 42 καλόν ἐστιν αὐτῷ μᾶλλον εἰ περίκειται ... καὶ βέβληται (D is correct with περιέκειτο ... ἐβλήθη), = L. 17. 2 (περιέκειτο – ἔρ(ρ)ιπτο D). Ἐάν with the pres. conj. in other cases refers to the future: ἐὰν θέλῃς, δύνασαι[2] Mt. 8. 2 etc., ἐάν με δέῃ Mc. 14. 31, 1 Jo. 2. 3 ἐὰν τηρῶμεν (φυλάξωμεν ℵ*), cp. 1 ἵνα μὴ ἁμάρτητε and ἐάν τις ἁμάρτῃ.

5. (*Continuation:* εἰ with future, ἐάν with aor. conj. and fut.) The connection of εἰ with the fut. indic. is quite rare in the N.T., but keeps fairly well its meaning of a definite supposition: Mt. 26. 33 = Mc. 14. 29 εἰ (καὶ) πάντες σκανδαλισθήσονται (*i.e.* as you have just now said; cp. supra 4); 2 Tim. 2. 12 εἰ ἀρνησόμεθα parallel with εἰ συναπεθάνομεν ... εἰ ὑπομένομεν κ.τ.λ.; 1 P. 2. 20 twice εἰ ὑπομενεῖτε, preceded by εἰ ὑποφέρει τις 19: in this case ἐὰν ὑποφέρῃ and ἐὰν ὑπομείνητε might at least be thought to be equally possible. In L. 11. 8 εἰ καὶ οὐ δώσει is incorrect for ἐὰν καὶ μὴ δῷ; cp. the intermixture of fut. and aor. conj. ibid. 5 ff. The fut. is correct in 1 C. 9. 11 θερίσομεν (-σωμεν CDE al.) and 3. 14 f. εἰ μενεῖ ... εἰ κατακαήσεται, of a definite point of future time, the day of judgment (Ap. 13. 10 v.l.). —For ἐάν with fut. indic. there is no quite certain instance: see Mt. 18. 19 ἐὰν συμφωνήσουσιν (-ωσιν FGKM al.), a general statement; L. 19. 40 ἐὰν σιωπήσουσιν ℵAB al., σιγήσουσιν D, σιωπήσωσιν ΓΛ al., of something impending at the present moment; A. 8. 31 ἐὰν μή τις ὁδηγήσει με ℵB*CE (ditto); Ap. 2. 22 ℵA (ditto, but in 5 ἐὰν μὴ μετανοήσῃς). Cp. Herm. Mand. v. 1. 2 ἐὰν ἔσῃ (*as* pr. man. ᾖς), iv. 3. 7 ἐὰν μηκέτι προσθήσω, Vis. i. 3. 2 v.l. The bulk of the instances exhibit the aor. conj. both in general statements and in those referring to what is now impending: cp. for the latter case Mt. 21. 25 ἐὰν εἴπωμεν, Jo. 16. 7 ἐὰν μὴ ἀπέλθω ... ἐὰν δὲ πορευθῶ. It is further used (in the province of the optative, see § 66, 4) with reference to what was impending in a past state of things: ἐὰν εὕρῃ A. 9. 2. A peculiar use is that in Mc. 10. 30 οὐδείς ἐστιν ... ἐὰν (D ὃς ἄν, cp. L. 18. 30) μὴ λάβῃ 'without his receiving.'

6. **Concessive** sentences introduced by εἰ καί or ἐὰν καί 'even if' call for no special remarks, especially as there is no real distinction between them and conditional sentences. Κἄν which unites in itself

---

[1] Ibid. 8. 14 κἂν ἐγὼ μαρτυρῶ περὶ ἐμαυτοῦ, ἀληθής ἐστιν ἡ μαρτυρία μου 'even if ever.'

[2] The Hellenistic εἰ θέλεις corresponds to the French s'il vous plait, Herodas 7. 70, 8. 6 etc.; so in the N.T. Mt. 17. 4 εἰ θέλεις ποιήσω(μεν).

the meanings of 'and if,' 'if only,' 'if even' (*etsi*) does not come under this category; cp. § 78, 7.[1] But εἰ is used in a special sense to express the **expectation** attending an action, Lat. *si* (*forte*) (classical Greek uses εἰ and ἐάν thus): it is strengthened by ἄρα or ἄραγε and becomes equivalent to the εἰ in an indirect question, with which this εἰ was regarded as identical, and is also extended by the addition of πως (only found after εἰ and μή in the N.T.): A. 27. 12, R. 1. 10, 11. 14, Ph. 3. 11. This εἰ may therefore govern the conjunctive, Ph. 3. 12 διώκω εἰ καταλάβω, cp. supra 1 and (for the kindred μή, μήποτε 'whether perchance') 3, or the fut. indic. A. 8. 22 εἰ ἄρα ἀφεθήσεται. We may further note εἰ μή (class.), εἰ μή τι, ἐκτὸς εἰ μή 'except if,' 'except,' 'except that.' Of these εἰ μή is generally not followed by a verb, though we also have G. 1. 7 εἰ μή τινες εἰσὶν = πλὴν ὅτι (A. 20. 23) τ. ε. 'except that'; 1 C. 7. 17 εἰ μὴ (= πλὴν, §. 77, 13) ... περιπατείτω 'howbeit'; for this we have ἐὰν μὴ (without a verb) in Mc. 4. 22 אB, cp. § 77, 13, G. 2. 16 (also in Attic, but not frequently); εἰ μή τι ἄν (ἄν om. B) ἐκ συμφώνου 'except perhaps by agreement' 1 C. 7. 5, but with a verb in 2 C. 13. 5 εἰ μή τι ἀδόκιμοί ἐστε 'it must then be the case that,' and with a conj. in L. 9. 13 εἰ μή τι πορευθέντες ἡμεῖς ἀγοράσωμεν (all uncials), 'unless perhaps we buy'[2]; ἐκτὸς εἰ μή takes the aor. indic. in 1 C. 15. 2, the conj. in 14. 5 ἐκτὸς εἰ μὴ διερμηνεύῃ (v.l. -ων D*), and stands without a verb in 1 Tim. 5. 19. In these connections therefore εἰ and ἐάν are interchanged, and the latter is generally replaced by the former; similarly in the elliptical phrase εἰ δὲ μή (γε) 'otherwise' εἰ often stands where ἐάν would be used if the sentence were written in full, while ἐὰν δὲ μή does not appear at all (so Attic).[3] Apart from these special combinations (and apart from εἴτε ... εἴτε after ἵνα, supra 2) εἰ with the conj. is not found (the reading in Ap. 11. 5 καὶ εἰ ... θελήσῃ is quite uncertain; perhaps we should write κἄν from the KAIH of א*).

7. **Relative** sentences take the conjunctive in two ways: (1) with ἄν in the kind of hypothetical sentence such as ὅστις ἄν θέλῃ = ἐάν τις θέλῃ, (2) without ἄν, the relative having a final sense, where this construction supplants, though not entirely, the Attic future indicative. The place of ἄν is according to the popular manner of the time taken by ἐάν, the MSS. of course showing very great uncertainty about the reading[4]; the position of the particle is as in Attic immediately after the relative, unless perhaps δέ or γάρ is interposed. The negative with the conjunctive is always μή, with the indicative it is usually οὐ, even in cases where μή is used in Attic, cp. § 75, 3

---

[1] Κἄν has also become a particle meaning 'even only,' A. 5. 15, 2 C. 11. 16, Clem. Cor. ii. 7. 2, 18. 2 (Attic).

[2] Viteau, p. 114 explains the conj. as deliberative, *sc.* βούλει ('unless we should buy').

[3] Krüger, § 65, 5, 12.

[4] *Ὅς ἐάν Mt. 5. 19 (ἐάν om. D*, ἄν Dᶜ): 10. 14 ὅς ἐάν CEF al. (ἄν אBDKL): A. 7. 7 ᾧ ἐάν (ἄν BD) O.T. Also in the London papyrus of Aristotle (οἱ ἐάν col. 12, 31, chap. 30. 2). Cp. § 26, 4.

(similarly εἰ οὐ, supra 4). Now in constructions with a relative sentence, which might be replaced by hypothetical clauses, no statement is made about anything concrete and actual, but only a general statement or supposition; consequently ὅς (or ὅστις, § 50, 1) ἄν, corresponding to ἐάν, appears to be the regular phrase. So L. 8. 18 ὅς γὰρ ἄν (ἂν γὰρ ℵBLX) ἔχῃ, δοθήσεται αὐτῷ, καὶ ὃς ἂν μὴ ἔχῃ, καὶ ὃ ἔχει (no longer hypothetical, the supposition having already been made in ὃς ἂν μὴ ἔχῃ) ἀρθήσεται ἀπ' αὐτοῦ. But the same saying takes the form in Mt. (13. 12) and Mc. (4. 25) of ὃς (ὅστις) γὰρ ἔχει (ἂν ἔχῃ in Mc. AE²G al., ἂν ἔχει DE*F al.) ... ὃς οὐκ ἔχει (E*G al. οὐκ ἔχῃ). The indicative, which also appears in classical Greek, in such sentences expresses the definite assumption that such persons exist. This assumption occasionally arises directly from the circumstances: L. 9. 50 (= Mc. 9. 40) ὃς γὰρ οὐκ ἔστι καθ' ὑμῶν, ὑπὲρ ὑμῶν ἐστιν, cp. 49.—The same relation exists between the aor. conj. and the fut. ind. as between the pres. conj. and pres. ind., and the distinction here also frequently appears to be obliterated: Mt. 18. 4 (ὅστις ταπεινώσει ἑαυτόν, whereas in 23. 12 with the same sense the future tense may be purposely used with reference to the future of the disciples), 5. 39 (the reading of ℵB ῥαπίζει is not good), 41, 10. 32 ὅστις ὁμολογήσει answering to 33 ὅστις δ' ἂν ἀρνήσηται (and cp. L. 12. 8). Of course the fut. may also be equivalent to the pres. with ἄν, and the latter be equivalent to the fut. (continuous action): L. 17. 31 ὃς ἔσται ἐπὶ τοῦ δώματος. The fut. ind. is equally admissible after ὃς ἄν as it is after ἐάν, but there is a lack of certain instances of this construction: Mc. 8. 35 ἀπολέσει ℵBCD² al. (-σῃ AL al.), L. 17. 33 do. ℵAL al. (-σῃ BDE al.), 12. 8 ὁμολογήσει AB*DR al., A. 7. 7 O.T. ACD, Barn. 11. 8 ὃ ἐὰν ἐξελεύσεται ℵC¹ : while the *present* indic. ὅπου ἂν ὑπάγει Ap. 14. 4 only rests on the authority of AC and must certainly be rejected. The possibility of ἄν being omitted with ὅστις is maintained, but in no case are all the MSS. in agreement: Mt. 10. 33 (om. ἄν BL), Ja 2 10 ὅστις ... τηρήσῃ (ℵBC, σει AKLP), πταίσῃ δὲ ἐν ἑνί (ℵABC, σει KLP) ; ὅσοι without ἄν is found twice in Herm. Sim. viii. 11. 3.

8. (*Continuation*).—**Relative sentences with a final meaning** occasionally show instances of the fut. in the N.T. as in Attic: Mc. 1. 2 = Mt. 11. 10, L. 7. 27 ἀποστέλλω τὸν ἄγγελόν μου..., ὃς κατασκευάσει (O.T. Malachi 3. 1, but our LXX. has a different text), 1 C. 4. 17 (but we also say 'who shall'), but elsewhere the conj. is used, which must be explained by assimilation to sentences with ἵνα, which are elsewhere found with the same meaning. Mc. 14. 14=L. 22. 11 ποῦ ἐστιν τὸ κατάλυμα ὅπου φάγω (D in Mc. has φάγομαι), = ἵνα φάγω : A. 21. 16 ἄγοντες παρ' ᾧ ξενισθῶμεν Μνάσωνι, = πρὸς Μνάσωνα ἵνα ξεν. παρ' αὐτῷ. On the other hand we have ἵνα in 2 C. 12. 7 ἐδόθη μοι σκόλοψ ... ἄγγελος σατανᾶ, ἵνα με κολαφίζῃ (Viteau p. 134 f.).—Akin to these are the relative sentences which denote a kind of **consequence** resulting from some particular quality or state, and which in Latin

---

[1] *As ἂν συντελέσουσιν occurs in an inscription in a translation from the Latin, Viereck Sermo Graecus senatus Rom. (Gtg. 1888), p. 38. 67, 8.

take the conjunctive like final relative sentences. In this case we have the fut. in L. 7. 4 ἄξιός ἐστιν ᾧ παρέξῃ (mid.) τοῦτο, cp. Lat. *dignus qui* with conj.; on the other hand ἵνα is used in Jo. 1. 27 ἄξιος ἵνα λύσω (equivalent to ἱκανὸς λῦσαι Mc. 1. 7 etc.: classical Greek takes the inf. after ἄξιος as well).—In οὐκ ἔχω ὃ παραθήσω L. 11. 6 the future is classical, but ὅ is not, as τί must have been used (for the delib. conj. in indirect questions vide supra 1); in ἔχειν τι ὃ προσενέγκῃ H. 8. 3 (cp. Clem. Cor. i. 38. 2 ἔδωκεν δι' οὗ προσαναπληρωθῇ) the fut. would be used in classical Greek, cp. Phil. 2. 20 οὐδένα ἔχω ... ὅστις μεριμνήσει. Here again the infinitive would be possible, ἔχει τι προσενέγκαι, and that in the N.T. might be replaced by ἵνα, Jo. 5. 7, see § 69, 4.

9. **Temporal sentences** introduced by ὅτε, ὅταν (ὁπότε only in L. 6. 3 AEH al., ὅτε אBCD al.), (ἐπεί only in L. 7. 1 with v.l. ἐπειδή; elsewhere ἐπεί is causal in the N.T.), ὡς etc. (see § 78, 3), are generally only a special class of relative sentences, and exhibit the same constructions. Ὅτε is found very frequently with the aorist indicative, but according to circumstances also takes the imperfect, perfect (1 C. 13. 11 ὅτε γέγονα, but B has ἐγενόμην), present (H. 9. 17), and future. The last tense usually occurs in phrases like ἔρχεται ὥρα ὅτε προσκυνήσετε Jo. 4. 21, cp. 23, 5. 25, 28, 16. 25, L. 17. 22 (ὅτε ἐπιθυμήσετε, D τοῦ ἐπιθυμῆσαι ὑμᾶς), 2 Tim. 4. 3, which are closely related to relative phrases such as οὐδέν ἐστιν κεκαλυμμένον ὃ οὐκ ἀποκαλυφθήσεται (Mt. 10. 26),[1] (and therefore in the former as in the latter instances the place of the fut. may be taken by the infin., and that again may be replaced by ἵνα with conj., Jo. 16. 2 ἔρχεται ὥρα ἵνα δόξῃ). Hence in accordance with what was said in 8 the conj. (without ἄν) may also take the place of this fut.: L. 13. 35 ἕως ἥξει ὅτε (the time when) εἴπητε (so AD etc.; there is a v.l. ἕως ἂν εἴπητε, agreeing with Mt. 23. 39). Elsewhere ὅτε does not appear with the conj.; a further instance of its use with the fut. is R. 2. 16 ἐν ἡμέρᾳ ὅτε κρινεῖ (v.l. ἐν ᾗ ἡμ. κρινεῖ, or according to Marcion's N.T., simply κρινεῖ, cp. § 79, 7), whereas in other places ὅταν with the conj. is used in this way: Mt. 9. 15 ἐλεύσονται ἡμέραι ὅταν ἀπαρθῇ, cp. Mc. 2. 20, for which Luke uses the more awkward, but more correct construction (5. 35) ἐλεύσονται ἡμέραι, καὶ (§ 77, 6) ὅταν ἀπαρθῇ ..., τότε νηστεύσουσιν (καὶ om. אC. al.). The use of ὅταν is more justifiable in Mt. 26. 29 (Mc. 14. 25) ἕως τῆς ἡμέρας ἐκείνης ὅταν πίνω, since the phrase is a periphrasis for Attic πρὶν ἄν.—Ὅταν with the indicative denotes in the first place indefinite frequency in past time, see § 63, 7; secondly it is used quite incorrectly in Ap. 8. 1 ὅταν ἤνοιξε AC (ὅτε אP, and so this author writes elsewhere, 6. 1, 3 etc.; in modern Greek ὅταν is 'when' as ἄν is 'if'); besides this it corresponds to ἐάν with the indic. (supra 4) in L. 13. 28 ὅταν ὄψεσθε B*DX (-ησθε AB^corr. al., ἴδητε א), Mc. 11. 25 ὅταν στήκετε (cp. ἐὰν στήκετε 1 Th. 3. 7, but there there is a reason for it [see above 4], which in the passage from St. Mark is not the case) ACD al. (-ητε BG al., στῆτε א);

---

[1] For this Mc. 4. 22 has ἐὰν μὴ ἵνα φανερωθῇ, = perhaps ὥστε φανερωθῆναι or in better Attic οἷον φανερωθῆναι.

§ 65. 9-10. § 66. 1.] *IN SUBORDINATE CLAUSES.* 219

elsewhere its use is insufficiently attested (L. 11. 2 προσεύχεσθε ACH al.; Jo. 7. 27 ἔρχεται אX etc.; the evidence for ἀκούετε Mc. 13. 7 is quite insufficient). Cp. Clem. Cor. ii. 12. 1 ὅταν ἔσται (quotation), 17. 6, Barn. 15. 5 א.

10. (*Continuation*).—Temporal particles and compound expressions with the meaning 'until' ('while'), ἕως, ἕως οὗ (ὅτου), ἐν ᾧ, ἄχρι(s), ἄχρις οὗ, μέχρι(s), μέχρις οὗ (§ 78, 3) take the indicative in the regular way (the fut. ind. is rare, it is a v.l. in L. 13. 35 [see 9]; the present is used instead in ἕως ἔρχομαι Jo. 21. 22, 1 Tim. 4. 13 'until I come' [§ 56, 8] = ἐν ᾧ ἔρχομαι L. 19. 13,[1] cp. Mc. 6. 45 אBL ἕως αὐτὸς ἀπολύει, v.l. ἀπολύσῃ -σει, D αὐτὸς δὲ ἀπολύει; but here it may also mean 'while'). But where they take the conjunctive, ἕως frequently, and ἕως οὗ (ὅτου), ἄχρις (οὗ), μέχρις οὗ probably always omit the ἄν : Mc. 13. 30 μέχρις οὗ (μ. ὅτου B, μέχρι א, ἕως οὗ D) ταῦτα πάντα γένηται, 1 C. 11. 26 ἄχρι οὗ (ἂν add. א°D° al.) ἔλθῃ, E. 4. 13 μέχρι καταντήσωμεν, L. 21. 24 ἄχρι οὗ (οὗ om. A al.) πληρωθῶσιν, L. 17. 8 ἕως (ἂν add. AK al.) φάγω, Mc. 14. 32 ἕως προσεύξωμαι (D al. -ομαι), 2 Th. 2. 7 (ἕως ἂν FG); ἄν is used in Mt. 5. 26 ἕως ἂν ἀποδῷς and in all other passages (Ap. 2. 25 ἄχρι οὗ ἂν ἥξω; the fut. occurs without ἄν in 17. 17, but B reads τελεσθῶσιν as in 15. 8, 20. 3, 5). We even have ἄχρι ἧς ἡμέρας γένηται L. 1. 20. The reason for this usage of the language, which may be traced back a long way (Herodotus, Thucydides and others [2]), is probably to be found in the fact that these sentences have a certain affinity with final sentences; sentences with πρίν have this same affinity, in which the omission of ἄν is specially frequent in classical authors, but in the N.T. these have been considerably supplanted by clauses formed with ἕως etc. (πρίν with the conj. appears in L. 2. 26 πρὶν ἢ [ἢ om. B] ἂν [ἂν om. AD al.] ἴδῃ, but א* here also has ἕως ἂν ἴδῃ : 22. 34 πρὶν ἢ ἀπαρνήσῃ AΓ al., but ἕως is read by אBL, ἕως οὗ K al., ἕως ὅτου D; with the optative A. 25. 16, see § 66, 5).

§ 66. REMAINS OF THE OPTATIVE.

1. The optative in **principal sentences** to denote a **practicable** (see § 63, 5) **wish** has not yet gone out of use in the N.T.[3] (the negative is μή). Μὴ γένοιτο occurs in L. 20. 16 and frequently in Paul (to express strong aversion, LXX. has the same phrase, Hebr. חָלִילָה). 1 Th. 5. 23 ἁγιάσαι : Philem. 20 ἐγώ σου ὀναίμην : Mc. 11. 14 μηκέτι

---

[1] Viteau, p. 129 f. explains the passages in Lc. and Jo. as meaning 'while I go' or 'withdraw myself,' though this explanation cannot be applied to the passage in 1 Tim. All other explanations than that given above are completely discredited by its use in Hermas Sim. v. 2. 2, ix. 10. 5, 6, 11. 1 ἐὰν δὲ μὴ ἔλθῃ, μενεῖς μεθ' ἡμῶν ὧδε ἕως ἔρχεται until he comes (which is a *certainty*, § 56, 8). One must therefore also attribute to ἐν ᾧ L. 19. 13 with *the same* present the meaning of 'until,' = ἐς ὅ.

[2] Krüger, § 54, 17, 3 (dialekt. Synt. 54, 17, 5 and 9).

[3] There are 35 examples in all (Burton, p. 79), all with the exception of Philem. 20 in the 3rd person.

μηδεὶς φάγοι. But there is a strong inclination to use the imperative instead of the optative, not only in requests, where the imperative has a legitimate place in classical Greek as well, but also in imprecations, where it takes the place of the classical optative: ἀνάθεμα ἔστω G. 1. 6 f., cp. 1 C. 16. 22.[1] The single instance of the pres. opt. is A. 8. 20 τὸ ἀργύριόν σου εἴη εἰς ἀπωλείαν. The Attic phrases εἰ γάρ, εἴθε to introduce a wish (§ 63, 5) are not found; ὄφελον (vide ibid.) is used with a fut. ind. to express a practicable wish in G. 5. 12 ὄφελον καὶ ἀποκόψονται οἱ ἀναστατοῦντες ὑμᾶς, 'would that they would at once castrate themselves.'

2. The **optative with ἄν in principal sentences** to denote **possibility** (modus potentialis) has quite disappeared from the popular language; the unique instance of it (besides its use in questions) is A. 26. 29 (Paul before Agrippa, literary language) εὐξαίμην ἄν (cp. in class. Greek Aeschines 1. 159), whereas elsewhere ἐβουλόμην is used rather than βουλοίμην ἄν, § 63, 5, and in hypothetical sentences (infra 4) the optative (with ἄν) is at any rate never found in the principal clause. In many places where Attic could have used the potential mood, the N.T. uses the future indicative: R. 3. 6 ἐπεὶ πῶς κρινεῖ ὁ θεὸς τὸν κόσμον; 1 C. 15. 35 ἐρεῖ τις (although this future is also not unclassical, § 61, 1; Buttm. p. 188). Instances of the optative also occur in Luke in direct questions: πῶς γὰρ ἄν δυναίμην A. 8. 31 and τί ἄν θέλοι οὗτος λέγειν 17. 18, cp. infra 3 (also taken from the literary language).

3. The optative of **indirect speech** (in subordinate clauses), answering to the indicative or conjunctive of direct speech, cannot be expected to occur with any frequency in the N.T., on account of the decided preference which the language in general shows for direct expression. Luke alone uses the optative occasionally, and even he never has it after ὅτι and ὡς, and not often even in indirect questions proper (L. 22. 23 τίς ἄρα εἴη, 8. 9 τίς εἴη (εἴη om. LΞΓ); the following instances should probably all contain ἄν and the optative therefore answers to the potential mood of the direct question (supra 2)[2]: L. 1. 29 ποταπὸς ἄν (add. D) εἴη, 62 τί ἄν θέλοι καλεῖσθαι, 6. 11, 9. 46, 15. 26 (ἄν om. ℵAΓ al.; D τί θέλει τοῦτο εἶναι), 18. 32 (ἄν om. ℵABP al.), Acts (2. 12 τί θέλει τοῦτο εἶναι a direct question; E ἄν θέλοι, ℵ θέλοι, readings which in an indirect question are inadmissible after λέγοντες), 5. 24 τί ἄν γένοιτο τοῦτο, 10. 17. Besides this the optative of indirect speech is found after εἰ 'whether' (§ 65, 1 and 6) in A. 17. 27 ζητεῖν τὸν θεόν, εἰ ἄραγε ψηλαφήσειαν αὐτὸν καὶ εὕροιεν, cp. 27. 12, 39, and after μήποτε 'whether perhaps' in L. 3. 15 μήποτε εἴη infra 4, and lastly in a dependent statement of time in indirect speech, A. 25. 16 vide infra 5.

4. While no example of the optative is found in **final** sentences (on E. 1. 17 see § 65, 2, note 1: 3, note 1), there are some few

---

[1] The optative in an imprecation of ill only occurs in Mc. 11. 14, A. 8. 20. In a quotation from Ps. 109. 8, A. 1. 8 uses λαβέτω where the LXX. has λάβοι.

[2] An indirect question may also in classical Greek take every mood of the direct question, Krüger, § 54, 6, 6.

instances of it in hypothetical sentences. A. 24. 19 οὓς ἔδει ... κατηγορεῖν, εἴ τι ἔχοιεν πρὸς ἐμέ, which would certainly be more correctly expressed by εἴ τι ἔχουσι or ἐάν τι ἔχωσι: 20. 16 ἔσπευδεν γάρ, εἰ δυνατὸν εἴη αὐτῷ, ... γενέσθαι εἰς Ἱερουσαλήμ (indirect; besides εἰ may very naturally be understood as meaning 'whether,' cp. 27. 12, 39, supra 3): 1 P. 3. 14 εἰ καὶ πάσχοιτε διὰ δικαιοσύνην, μακάριοι, 17 κρεῖττον ἀγαθοποιοῦντας, εἰ θέλοι τὸ θέλημα τοῦ θεοῦ, πάσχειν ἢ κακοποιοῦντας, 'if perchance' as in Attic (literary language). Besides these we have the formula εἰ τύχοι in St. Paul, 1 C. 14. 10, 15. 37.

5. In (**relative** and) **temporal sentences** there is no further instance besides A. 25. 16 (Festus's words): ἀπεκρίθην ὅτι οὐκ ἔστιν ἔθος χαρίζεσθαι..., πρὶν ἢ ὁ κατηγορούμενος ἔχοι ... λάβοι τε, where the opt. is rightly used in indirect speech for the conj. of direct speech.

§ 67. IMPERATIVE.

1. The imperative in the N.T. keeps for the most part within the same limits as in the classical language; as in that language it by no means expresses simply a command, but also a request or a concession (Mc. 8. 32 ὑπάγετε, 2 C. 12. 6 ἔστω δέ). In the last case the imperative sentence may be equivalent to a concessive sentence: Jo. 2. 19 λύσατε τὸν ναὸν τοῦτον, καὶ ἐν τρισὶν ἡμέραις ἐγερῶ αὐτόν, = ἐὰν καὶ λύσητε; cp. in classical Greek Soph. Ant. 1168 ff. πλούτει τε γὰρ κατ' οἶκον ... ἐὰν δ' ἀπῇ τούτων τὸ χαίρειν, τἄλλ' ἐγὼ καπνοῦ σκιᾶς οὐκ ἂν πριαίμην (Kühner ii. 201). On the encroachment of the imperative into the province of the optative see § 66, 1.

2. The imperative is frequently replaced by the conjunctive, see § 64, 2, by ἵνα or θέλω ἵνα with conj., ibid. 4, or by the fut. indic., ibid. 3; cp. Viteau p. 37. On the substitution of the infinitive for it see § 69, 1.

§ 68. INFINITIVE.

1. The infinitive is another of those forms which the language at a later period gave up, in favour of a periphrasis with ἵνα (mod. Greek νά) and the conjunctive, a construction which has already been largely developed in the N.T. But the infinitive is still abundantly used beside it by all writers, so that it depends on the discretion of the writer on each separate occasion whether he employs the synthetic or the analytical expression, though the latter is not in all cases open to use. The beginnings of this development may be traced not only in the earlier Hellenistic Greek, but also previously to that in classical Greek, the only difference being that in the classical language the particle used in the periphrasis is not ἵνα but ὅπως, e.g. πειρᾶσθαι ὅπως σῳζώμεθα (Xenoph.) = πειρᾶσθαι σῴζεσθαι, whereas later ὅπως retired more into the background (§ 65, 2) and finally disappeared. Cp. also the use of *ut* in Latin which is so frequently interchangeable with the infinitive.

2. From early times there existed in Greek a second analytical expression for the infinitive, namely ὅτι (ὡς) with the **indicative**, with which cp. the Latin use of *quod* or *quia* (late Latin says *dico vobis quia unus vestrum me traditurus est*). The line of demarcation between the old ὅτι, which of course reappears in the N.T., and the new ἵνα is that the former has an indicative sense, the latter a conjunctive (or imperative) sense, while the infinitive is the ὄνομα ῥήματος (as Apollonius calls it) with a neutral meaning between the two others. To express actual facts, therefore, particularly those which belong to past time, ἵνα can never be used in the periphrasis, but only ὅτι; on the other hand things which may be regarded as a contemplated result or one likely to occur, are expressed to a wide extent by ἵνα. The intervening province, viz. that which still belongs exclusively to the infinitive, is not a large one in the N.T.: under this head, for instance, comes the rule that δύνασθαι and μέλλειν are joined exclusively with the infinitive.

3. As the ὄνομα ῥήματος the infinitive is capable of taking the neuter of the article, and this may be declined, and the cases of the infinitive so formed may be dependent on different prepositions. In this way the sphere of the infinitive has been very largely extended, so that it can also represent temporal and causal sentences. The N.T. retains this usage, and in particular employs the genitive with τοῦ in the most lavish way.

§ 69. INFINITIVE AND PERIPHRASIS WITH ἵνα.

1. The use of the infinitive in a **principal sentence** in place of a finite verb, with **imperative** sense and with the subject in the nominative[1], is extremely old and found with special frequency in Homer, while in Attic it becomes less prominent. On the other hand the later classical language (especially in legal phraseology) uses the accusative and infinitive in this sense, or the simple infinitive with no subject expressed (λέγειν 'one must say ' = λεκτέον), in which case the ideas accessory to the subject appear in the accusative.[2] At the same time Attic uses ὅπως with the fut. indic. with imperative sense. In the N.T. we find in a few passages ἵνα with the conj. used in a similar way, see § 64, 4: and the infinitive which is equivalent to it twice in St. Paul, R. 12. 15 χαίρειν μετὰ χαιρόντων, κλαίειν μετὰ κλαιόντων, Ph. 3. 16 πλὴν εἰς ὃ ἐφθάσαμεν, τῷ αὐτῷ στοιχεῖν. Where the subject has to be expressed Paul uses ἵνα: ἡ δὲ γυνὴ ἵνα φοβῆται τὸν ἄνδρα E. 5. 33. It is very easy here to supply a governing verb (a verbum dicendi or χρή, δεῖ), as it is with the (accusative and) infinitive; the infinitive χαίρειν to express a wish in epistolary style is clearly elliptical, A. 15. 23, 23. 26.

---

[1] Homer, Il. B. 75 ὑμεῖς δ᾽ ἄλλοθεν ἄλλος ἐρητύειν ἐπέεσσιν. Aristoph. Ran. 133 τόθ᾽ εἶναι καὶ σὺ σαυτόν.

[2] So in Aristotle, Bonitz Index Aristot. s. v. Infinitivus.

§ 69. 2-3.] INFINITIVE AND PERIPHRASIS WITH ἵνα. 223

2. Of equal antiquity with the last usage is the use of the infinitive to express **aim** or **object**, which in Homer has a much wider range than in Attic writers, who for the most part only employ it after verbs containing the idea of to give, appoint, present, send etc. This infinitive, which is equivalent to a final sentence, has again become widely prevalent in the N.T.: Mt. 5. 17 οὐκ ἦλθον καταλῦσαι, ἀλλὰ πληρῶσαι; 4. 1 ὁ Ἰησοῦς ἀνήχθη εἰς τὴν ἔρημον ὑπὸ τοῦ πνεύματος, πειρασθῆναι ὑπὸ τοῦ διαβόλου; L. 18. 10 ἀνέβησαν προσεύξασθαι; A. 10. 33 πάρεσμεν ἀκοῦσαι. (Attic would here use the future participle which in the N.T. is almost unused, § 61, 4.) Of course this infinitive is also found with διδόναι, ἀποστέλλειν etc. as in Attic: Mc. 3. 14 ἀποστέλλῃ κηρύσσειν (A. 5. 21 ἀπέστειλαν ἀχθῆναι αὐτούς is different, the construction being passive, and the acc. and inf. being therefore used; cp. inf. 8), Mt. 25. 35 ἐδώκατέ μοι φαγεῖν. Beside the inf. ἵνα also appears again: Mt. 27. 26 παρέδωκεν ἵνα σταυρωθῇ (= Mc. 15. 15, Jo. 19. 16), though in the case of a specially close connection of the two verbs in certain definite phrases the infinitive does not admit of being replaced by ἵνα: thus παραδιδόναι φυλάσσειν A. 12. 4, 16. 4, διδόναι (αἰτεῖν) φαγεῖν, πιεῖν *passim*, while on the other hand where the connection is not so close and the subordinate clause is of greater length, ἵνα is the natural construction: though here the infin. may also be used, as in A. 20. 28 ὑμᾶς τὸ πνεῦμα τὸ ἅγιον ἔθετο ἐπισκόπους, ποιμαίνειν τὴν ἐκκλησίαν κ.τ.λ., 1. 24 f. ἐξελέξω ... λαβεῖν κ.τ.λ. Moreover with regard to the use of ἵνα there is here and in all cases where the infinitive is in question a distinction between the different writers: John, Matthew, and Mark employ it very freely, Luke much more rarely, especially in the Acts, a work which has very few instances of the employment of this particle in an unclassical way; also in James, Peter, and the Epistle to the Hebrews it only appears as a strictly final particle.— A third construction with παραδιδόναι etc. is εἰς τὸ with the infinitive, see § 71, 5; the participle, which is also so used in the N.T., offers another alternative construction, § 74, 2, and aim or object of any kind is very frequently denoted by means of τοῦ with the infinitive, § 71, 3.

3. Akin to the infinitive of aim is the infinitive of **result**, yet so far distinguished from it, that if the result is declared to be actual, ἵνα according to what has been said has, or at least should have, no place (vide infra). The particle used to introduce this infinitive is ὥστε as in classical Greek; the alternative use of the simple ὡς is no more certainly established for the N.T. than it is for ordinary Attic.[1] Ὥστε is also used in the N.T. (as in classical Greek) to introduce independent sentences, when it takes the indicative, imperative, or hortatory conjunctive (meaning 'therefore'). It also occasionally takes the indicative where the sentence is really dependent (class.),

---

[1] In L. 9. 52 ὡς is only read by אB; A. 20. 24 ὡς τελειώσω א*(ἕως τ. אc)B, ὡς τελειῶσαι AHLP: τε has apparently fallen out before τελειῶσαι, and so E has ὥστε (ὡς τὸ C). In Josephus, however, the traditional text often has a consecutive ὡς (with infin.), Raab de Jos. elocut. (Erlangen, 1890), p. 37.

Jo. 3. 16 οὕτως γὰρ ἠγάπησεν ὁ θεὸς τὸν κόσμον, ὥστε τὸν υἱὸν τὸν μονογενῆ ἔδωκεν (cp. further G. 2. 13); but in most cases of this kind it takes the infinitive (class.), the subject being usually added in the accusative, unless it can be obviously supplied from what has preceded (cp. § 72). The construction with the infinitive has a somewhat wider range than in Attic; in a sentence like A. 15. 39 ἐγένετο παροξυσμός, ὥστε ἀποχωρισθῆναι αὐτοὺς ἀπ' ἀλλήλων, an Attic writer would rather have used the indicative, both because there was no close connection between the clauses and also on account of the importance attaching to the result. But ὥστε is by no means used (either in the N.T. or in Attic) to introduce merely the actual or the possible result, but may also introduce the contemplated result, and so the boundary-line which separates these sentences from sentences of design almost disappears.[1] In ἔδωκεν αὐτοῖς ἐξουσίαν πνευμάτων ἀκαθάρτων, ὥστε ἐκβάλλειν αὐτά (Mt. 10. 1) we still have a sentence denoting pure result, 'so that they could drive out' (there is an affinity between this construction and the simple inf. after ἐξουσίαν ἔχειν, infra 5); but L. 20. 20 ἵνα ἐπιλάβωνται αὐτοῦ λόγου, ὥστε παραδοῦναι αὐτὸν τῇ ἀρχῇ τοῦ ἡγεμόνος means 'so that they might be able' = 'in order that they might be able,' and the v.l. εἰς τὸ for ὥστε (AΓ al., cp. supra 2) is quite in accordance with the sense. Cp. further L. 4. 29 ὥστε ('in order to,' v.l. εἰς τὸ AC al.) κατακρημνίσαι αὐτόν, 9. 52 ὥστε ('in order to'; אB ὡς, see note 1 on p. 223) ἑτοιμάσαι αὐτῷ, Mt. 27. 1 συμβούλιον ἔλαβον ὥστε θανατῶσαι αὐτόν (D correctly explaining the meaning gives ἵνα θανατώσουσιν αὐτ.).[2]—The inf. without ὥστε (also with its subject in the accusative) is used in a similar way to express result: A. 5. 3 διὰ τί ἐπλήρωσεν ὁ σατανᾶς τὴν καρδίαν σου, ψεύσασθαί σε κ.τ.λ., Ap. 5. 5 ἐνίκησεν ὁ λέων... ἀνοῖξαι (B ὁ ἀνοίγων) κ.τ.λ., 16. 9 οὐ μετενόησαν δοῦναι αὐτῷ δόξαν, H. 6. 10 οὐ γὰρ ἄδικος ὁ θεός, (sc. ὥστε) ἐπιλαθέσθαι. The inf. is still more freely used in L. 1. 54 (the Magnificat) ἀντελάβετο Ἰσραὴλ παιδὸς αὐτοῦ, μνησθῆναι ἐλέους κ.τ.λ., and in 72 (the Benedictus) ποιῆσαι ἔλεος κ.τ.λ. (the clauses are joined together quite incoherently: this clause is parallel with the accusative of a noun in the preceding verse 71 σωτηρίαν ἐξ ἐχθρῶν κ.τ.λ.); cp. 78 f. (inf. after ἐπεσκέψατο).— Then again this infinitive of result may be replaced (as elsewhere in late writers [3]) by ἵνα instead of the classical ὥστε: 1 Jo. 1. 9 πιστός ἐστιν καὶ δίκαιος, ἵνα ἀφῇ τὰς ἁμαρτίας (cp. supra H. 6. 10), Ap. 9. 20 (cp. supra 16. 9) οὐδὲ μετενόησαν, ἵνα μὴ προσκυνήσουσιν, 13. 13 ποιεῖ σημεῖα μεγάλα, ἵνα καὶ πῦρ ποιῇ καταβαίνειν (cp. a similar phrase with ὥστε in Mt. 24. 24), Jo. 9. 2 τίς ἥμαρτεν..., ἵνα τυφλὸς γεννηθῇ ('so

---

[1] Ὥστε (ἐφ' ᾧτε) 'on condition that' does not appear in the N.T. (for which ἵνα is used in G. 2. 9): nor yet ὥστε after a comparative with ἤ (νεώτερος ἢ ὥστε εἰδέναι), Burton p. 150. On ἵνα in Mc. 4. 22 see § 65, 9 note.

[2] Here belongs also A. 20. 24, see note 1 on last page, 'in order to fulfil,' if ὥστε τελειῶσαι is the correct reading. Cp. for ὥστε in Josephus W. Schm d de Fl. Jos. elocut. (1893) p. 418 ff.

[3] Cp. op. cit. 420 f., where instances from Josephus are given (in all of which, however, the result is merely conceived and not actual).

§ 69. 3-4.] *PERIPHRASIS WITH* ἵνα. 225

that'), L. 9. 45 ἦν παρακεκαλυμμένον ἀπ' αὐτῶν, ἵνα μὴ αἴσθωνται αὐτό, 2 C. 1. 17, 1 Th. 5. 4: Herm. Sim. vii. 2, ix. 1. 10. In these instances the correct limits for the use of ἵνα are already exceeded. (In other passages one can quite well regard ἵνα as final, *e.g.* in the phrase ἵνα πληρωθῇ 'in order to carry out God's determinate counsel.')—The so-called infinitive **absolute** after ὡς, which is fairly frequent in Attic, only appears in ὡς ἔπος εἰπεῖν 'so to say' H. 7. 9 (literary language).

4. With the infinitive of design or result are included the well-known constructions of the infinitive with verbs meaning **to wish, strive, avoid, ask, summon, make, leave, allow, hinder, be able, have power** etc., with which in classical Greek ὥστε is often prefixed to the infinitive. An alternative Attic construction with a certain number of these verbs is that with ὅπως, though it is by no means used to the same extent in which Latin *ut* is used after verbs of this kind; at a later time ἵνα stepped into the place of ὅπως and obtained a more and more extended use, so that in the N.T. with a great number of these verbs ἵνα begins to be interchangeable with the inf., and even (especially in writers other than Luke, Paul, and the author of Hebrews) to supplant it. The subject of the inf. is often either necessarily (as with δύναμαι) or in most cases (as with θέλω) identical with that of the principal verb, elsewhere it coincides with the object of the principal verb (ἐῶ) or with the dative which follows it (προστάσσω); if it requires to be expressly stated, it stands in the **accusative.** Θέλω usually takes the (acc. and) inf.: ἵνα in Mt. 7. 12, 1 C. 14. 5 (θέλω ὑμᾶς λαλεῖν..., μᾶλλον δὲ ἵνα προφητεύητε) and elsewhere.—Βούλομαι (as a word belonging to cultured speech) only takes the (acc. and) inf., so τολμῶ takes inf. (ἀρνοῦμαι H. 11. 24; also δοκῶ in μὴ δόξητε λέγειν Mt. 3. 9 'do not let it occur to you to say': see also 1 C. 11. 16: ἔδοξέ μοι in Luke *e.g.* L. 1. 3).—Βουλεύομαι inf. and ἵνα, Jo. 11. 53 (v.l. συνεβουλ.), 12. 10 (in class. Greek inf. and ὅπως); similarly συμβουλεύομαι ἵνα Mt. 26. 4: συμβουλεύειν τινί 'to advise,' with inf. Ap. 3. 18.—Ὁρίζω inf. A. 11. 29.—Συντίθεμαι inf. and ἵνα, Jo. 9. 22; προτίθεμαι inf. R. 1. 13.—Ἐπιθυμῶ, ἐπιποθῶ only take the inf. (or acc. and inf. H. 6. 11); but we have ἠγαλλιάσατο ἵνα ἴδῃ Jo. 8. 56, where the meaning can only be 'to long with ecstasy,' 'to rejoice that he should see,' cp. the use of τοῦ and the inf. (§ 71, 3) in Herm. Vis. iii. 8. 7 περιχαρὴς ἐγενόμην τοῦ ἰδεῖν, 10. 6.—Ζητῶ (ἐπιζητ.) takes inf.: ἵνα in 1 C. 4. 2, 14. 12.—Ζηλῶ ('to strive zealously') takes ἵνα in 1 C. 14. 1.—Σπουδάζω only the (acc. and) inf. (σπεύδω acc. and inf. in Herm. Sim. ix. 3. 2; ἠγωνίζοντο ἵνα Jo. 18. 36, φιλοτιμεῖσθαι takes inf. in Paul).—Πειράζω 'to try' takes inf. (the Attic πειρῶμαι also takes ὅπως[1]).—Ἐπιχειρῶ (only in Lc.) also takes inf.: and so ἀσκῶ, only in A. 24. 16.—Βλέπετε ἵνα ('see to it that': Att. ὁρᾶτε ὅπως) occurs in 1 C. 16. 10.—Αἰσχύνομαι (ἐπαισχ.), φοβοῦμαι 'to be ashamed' or 'afraid to do something,' only the inf. (L. 16. 3 etc.); so ὀκνῶ A. 9. 38.—Φυλάσσομαι ἵνα μή 2. P. 3. 17 (Attic has μή and ὅπως

---

[1] A. 15. 10 τί πειράζετε τὸν θεόν, ἐπιθεῖναι ζυγόν must be similarly explained, unless perhaps τὸν θεόν, which is omitted in some Latin MSS., is an interpolation.

P

μή).—Δέομαι 'to request' takes ἵνα in L. 9. 40, 21. 36, 22. 32, ὅπως in Mt. 9. 38, L. 10. 2, A. 8. 24, elsewhere the inf. (Attic uses inf. and ὅπως).—Ἐρωτῶ ἵνα ('request') occurs in Mc. 7. 26 etc., ὅπως in L. 7. 3, 11. 37, A. 23. 20, elsewhere it takes inf. (and acc. of the object of ἐρ.); so ἐπερωτῶ Mt. 16. 1.—Παρακαλῶ 'to beseech,' 'exhort' similarly takes ἵνα in Mt. 14. 36 etc., ὅπως in Mt. 8. 34 (B ἵνα), A. 25. 2 (cp. Att. παρακελεύομαι with inf. and ὅπως).— Αἰτοῦμαι takes (acc. and) inf. L. 23. 23, A. 3. 14, 7. 46, 13. 28, Jo. 4. 9, E. 3. 13: ἵνα Col. 1. 9 (καὶ αἰτούμενοι om. B); in classical Greek it also takes ὅπως.—Προσεύχομαι ἵνα Mc. 14. 35 etc. (ὅπως A. 8. 15, inf. L. 22. 40; cp. τοῦ with inf. Ja. 5. 17); εὔχομαι (a more literary word) takes (acc. and) inf. A. 26. 29 etc.—Ἀξιῶ 'to ask' (Luke, literary language) only takes (acc. and) inf. A. 15. 38, 28. 22 (in class. Greek also ὅπως; ἵνα in a forged document in Demosth. 18. 155); in the sense of 'to count worthy' it also takes the inf. (cp. ἄξιος, infra 5) L. 7. 7; καταξιῶ A. 5. 41.—Παραινῶ acc. of the object and inf. (only in A. 27. 22, a literary word).—Κελεύω only takes the (acc. and) inf. (being used only by Mt. and Lc.); similarly τάσσω A. 15. 2, διατάσσω (-σομαι mid.), προστάσσω (rare), ἐπιτάσσω (rare); ἀναμιμνῄσκω 2 Tim. 1. 6, ἀπειλοῦμαι mid. A. 4. 17, νεύω A. 24. 10; παραγγέλλω also takes ἵνα Mc. 6. 8 (ἀπαγγέλλω ἵνα Mt. 28. 10); so διαμαρτύρομαι ἵνα 1 Tim. 5. 21; ἐντέλλομαι ἵνα Mc. 13. 34; κηρύσσω ἵνα Mc. 6. 12; διαστέλλομαι ἵνα Mt. 16. 20 (v.l. ἐπετίμησεν), Mc. 7. 36 etc.; ἐπιτιμῶ ἵνα Mt. 20. 31 (with the two last verbs there is no instance of the inf.; in class. Greek verbs of this class except κελεύω show a decided tendency to take ὅπως).—Χρηματίζομαι pass. 'receive a divine command' takes the inf. Mt. 2. 12, A. 10. 22 (in L. 2. 26 the inf. expresses an assertion).—Ἐξορκίζω ἵνα occurs in Mt. 26. 63 (ὁρκίζω or ἐνορκ. with acc. and inf. in 1 Th. 5. 27).—Λέγω frequently takes ἵνα, as well as the (acc. and) inf. when it expresses a command (ἵνα is used in this way in Ap. 14. 13); similarly γράφω, e.g. γέγραπται ἵνα Mc. 9. 12 (12. 19), and ἀποστέλλω ἵνα A. 16. 36, cp. supra 2.—Πείθω ἵνα Mt. 27. 20, elsewhere it takes acc. of the object and inf.—Ποιῶ ἵνα is used in Jo. 11. 37, Col. 4. 16, Ap. 3. 9 ποιήσω αὐτοὺς ἵνα ἥξουσιν, cp. 13. 12, 15 f. (in 15 ἵνα is wanting in אB); ἵνα has more of a final sense in Mc. 3. 14, cp. ἔθηκα ἵνα Jo. 15. 16 (ποιῶ τινα with inf. occurs in L. 5. 34 etc.; classical Greek has also occasionally ποιεῖν ὅπως 'to cause that'); ποιεῖν with acc. and inf. occurs in Mc. 1. 17 (Mt. 4. 19 double acc.), L. 5. 34 etc.; διδόναι (a Hebrew usage) is similarly used in A. 10. 40, 14. 3, 2. 27 O.T.—Ἀγγαρεύω ἵνα Mt. 27. 32 (no instance of the inf.; ὅστις σε ἀγγαρεύσει [D -ρεύει] μίλιον ἕν Mt. 5. 41).—Ἐῶ τινα only takes inf.; the commoner ἀφίημι 'let' also takes ἵνα, Mc. 11. 16; καταλείπω τινά takes the inf. L. 10. 40 (not so much an inf. of aim as of result, cp. Hom. Il. P. 151.—Ἐπιτρέπω τινί only takes the inf.; similarly κωλύω τινά (with this the verb Attic μή is not annexed to the *simple* inf., §§ 71, 3; 75, 4).—'To be able,' 'to understand' etc. only take the inf.: δύναμαι (δυνατῶ Paul), ἰσχύω (κατισχύω L. 21. 36 אB al., v.l. καταξιωθῆτε; ἐξισχ. E. 3. 18), ἔχω Mt. 18. 25 (in the N.T. it also has the meaning 'to have to,' 'be obliged to,' L. 12. 50 βάπτισμα ἔχω βαπτισθῆναι, cp. Clem. Hom.

i. 17, xii. 8), οἶδα Mt. 7. 11 etc., γινώσκω Mt. 16. 3; further μανθάνω 1 Tim. 5. 4 etc., παιδεύομαι pass. 1. 20; προμελετῶ L. 21. 14, διδάσκω 11. 1 (παραλαμβάνω Mc. 7. 4), δεικνύω A. 10. 28, ὑποδεικ. Mt. 3. 7. —The inf. is likewise used with ὀφείλω, μέλλω, εἴωθα, φιλῶ Mt. 6. 5 (23. 6 f.), ἄρχομαι (never with the participle in N.T., cp. § 73, 4)[1], προστίθεμαι (a Hebraism, יוֹסִיף with לְ and inf.) 'continue to do,' 'repeat' L. 20. 11, A. 12. 3 (LXX. also uses the active), κινδυνεύω A. 19. 27, 40, προσποιοῦμαι L. 24. 28, ἐπιλανθάνομαι 'forget to do' Mt. 16. 5 = Mc. 8. 14 (also in Attic), and its opposite προσέχειν (not so used in Att.) Mt. 6. 1 (with ἵνα Barn. 16. 8). The construction with the inf. is very widely extended in individual instances, and used with far greater freedom than in Attic. Thus we have διαβλέψεις ἐκβαλεῖν Mt. 7. 5, L. 6. 42; δοκιμάζω 'approve,' οὐ δοκ. 'disdain' 1 Th. 2. 4, R. 1. 28 (in Att. with inf. of opinion), εὐδοκῶ Col. 1. 19 with (acc. and) inf. (Polyb. i. 8. 4), συνευδ. with inf. 1 C. 7. 12 (acc. and inf. in Herm. Sim. v. 2. 11, ἵνα ibid. 8). H. 11. 5 οὐχ ἑαυτὸν ἐδόξασεν γενηθῆναι ἀρχιερέα, like ἀξιοῦν. A. 25. 21 τοῦ Παύλου ἐπικαλεσαμένου τηρηθῆναι αὐτόν, like verbs of asking (the β text reads differently). A. 15. 14 ἐπεσκέψατο λαβεῖν, cp. L. 1. 25 ἐπεῖδεν ἀφελεῖν. A. 14. 15 εὐαγγελιζόμενοι ὑμᾶς ἐπιστρέφειν (D is different, using ὅπως), 17. 21 εἰς οὐδὲν ἕτερον ηὐκαίρουν ἢ λέγειν τι ... καινότερον (there is no need to supply εἰς τὸ before the inf., since εὐκαιρεῖν takes the inf. in Lucian Amor. 33). R. 1. 10 εὐοδωθήσομαι ἐλθεῖν, like δύναμαι. 1 Th. 2. 2 (E. 6. 20) παρρησιάζομαι (like τολμῶ). Mc. 5. 32 περιεβλέπετο ἰδεῖν, 14. 8 προέλαβεν μυρίσαι (cp. the Attic use of φθάνω with partic. or inf., προφθάσῃ βαλεῖν Clem. Cor. ii. 8. 2). A. 16. 10 προσκέκληται ἡμᾶς εὐαγγελίσασθαι αὐτούς. H. 11. 8 ὑπήκουσεν ἐξελθεῖν. Tit. 3. 8 φροντίζωσιν προΐστασθαι. L. 12. 45 χρονίζει ἔρχεσθαι. We have the same construction with longer phrases: τιθέναι (τίθεσθαι) ἐν τῇ καρδίᾳ (τῷ πνεύματι) 'to resolve,' 'to think of' (a Hebraism) L. 21. 14, A. 19. 21, ἧς διήνοιξεν τὴν καρδίαν (a Hebraism) προσέχειν A. 16. 14 (cp. the same phrase with τοῦ and inf. in L. 24. 45); the following take ἵνα, βουλὴ ἐγένετο A. 27. 42, θέλημά ἐστιν Mt. 15. 14 etc.: ἐγένετο ὁρμή A. 14. 5 takes the inf.; cp. L. 2. 1, Jo. 13. 2, 34, A. 17. 15, E. 3. 8 etc.

5. A similar relation between the infinitive and ἵνα exists in the case of a series of **impersonal** expressions, whether they consist of a simple verb or combinations of ἐστίν with an adj., such as δεῖ, συμφέρει, ἔξεστι, ἐγένετο, δυνατόν ἐστιν, ἀρεστόν ἐστιν: also in the case of **combinations of ἐστίν with a substantive** such as ὥρα ἐστίν, καιρός ἐστιν, and in the case of adjectives like **δυνατός** ἄξιος ἱκανός ἕτοιμος used as predicates (with ἐστί) or as attributes. The infinitive might here be said to express the direction or goal. Equivalent to these are combinations like ἐξουσίαν ἔχω, χρείαν ἔχω etc. In Attic ὅπως is excluded with expressions of this kind, ὥστε is not entirely excluded (ἔστιν ὥστε 'it is possible that' Sophocles); in the N.T. ἵνα may be

---

[1] Very common in Mt., Mc., Lc., often used almost superfluously, as in Mc. 1. 45 ἤρξατο κηρύσσειν which is hardly distinguishable from ἐκήρυσσεν.

used in all cases, except where a fact is stated to have taken place, as in the common phrase ἐγένετο (cp. § 72, 5) and its classical equivalent συνέβη (only in A. 21. 35), or where the close connection of the word with the inf. has become quite established, as with δεῖ[1] and ἔξεστι (with the latter cp. ἐλευθέρα ἐστὶν γαμηθῆναι 1 C. 7. 39). **Συμφέρει** ἵνα occurs in Mt. 5. 29 f., 18. 6 etc., besides (acc. and) inf. **Ἀρκετὸν** (sc. ἐστιν) ἵνα γένηται Mt. 10. 25 (differing from ἀρκοῦσιν ἵνα Jo. 6. 7, where the result is stated, = ὥστε); on the other hand the inf. is used in 1 P. 4. 3 ἀρκετός ἐστιν ὁ παρεληλυθὼς χρόνος ... κατειργάσθαι. **Δυνατόν** ἐστι (A. 2. 24 with acc. and inf.) and δυνατός ἐστι (somewhat more frequent) only take the inf. like δύναμαι. Οὐκ εἰμὶ **ἱκανὸς** ἵνα is used in Mt. 8. 8, elsewhere the inf.[2]; οὐκ εἰμὶ **ἄξιος** ἵνα Jo. 1. 27 (often with inf.; with τοῦ and inf. 1 C. 16. 4, see § 71, 3; with a relative sentence L. 7. 4, § 65, 8). **Συνήθειά** ἐστιν ἵνα Jo. 18. 39; ἔρχεται (ἡ) **ὥρα** ἵνα Jo. 12. 23, 13. 1, 16. 2, 32 (acc. and inf. as in Attic in R. 13. 11; (ὁ) **καιρὸς** [sc. ἐστι] τοῦ ἄρξασθαι τὸ κρίμα 1 P. 4. 17; cp. § 71, 3[3]; elsewhere these words take ὅτε or ἐν ᾗ, ἔσται κ. ὅτε ... ἀνέξονται 2 Tim. 4. 3, ἔρχεται ὥρα ἐν ᾗ ... ἀκούσουσιν Jo. 5. 25, where the prediction is more definite, whereas ἵνα or the inf. states the tendency or drift of the impending event). **Χρείαν ἔχω** ἵνα Jo. 2. 25, 16. 30, 1 Jo. 2. 27; elsewhere it takes inf., Mt. 3. 14 etc., Jo. 13. 10 (with νίψασθαι, the two verbs having the same subject, while in the ἵνα passages a new subject is introduced[4]). **Ἐξουσίαν** ἔχω takes inf. H. 13. 10, Ap. 11. 6; ἐδόθη ἐξουσία inf. ibid. 13. 5 (with ὥστε Mt. 10. 1, vide sup. 3); δότε τὴν ἐξουσίαν ταύτην ἵνα A. 8. 19. With ἵνα must also be quoted 1 C. 4. 3 ἐμοὶ εἰς ἐλάχιστόν ἐστιν ἵνα. Τὸ ἐμὸν βρῶμά ἐστιν ἵνα Jo. 4. 34, cp. the passages quoted below in 6. Ἄνθρωπον οὐκ ἔχω ἵνα βάλῃ με Jo. 5. 7, instead of ὃς βαλεῖ or the Attic τὸν βαλοῦντα, cp. § 65, 8.—Again ἵνα is used after a comparative with ἤ: L. 17. 2 λυσιτελεῖ αὐτῷ εἰ περίκειται ... ἢ ἵνα σκανδαλίσῃ, 1 C. 9. 15 καλόν μοι μᾶλλον ἀποθανεῖν, ἢ τὸ καύχημά μου ἵνα τις κενώσει (א*BD* have the bad reading οὐδεὶς for ἵνα τις).—The infinitive is freely used in some special phrases such as in G. 5. 3 ὀφειλέτης ἐστὶν (= ὀφείλει) ποιῆσαι, H. 4. 1 καταλειπομένης ἐπαγγελίας εἰσελθεῖν (cp. ἀπολείπεται, ἀπόκειται with inf. in 4. 6, 9. 27): a classical use is 5. 11 λόγος δυσερμήνευτος λέγειν (like λευκὸς ἰδεῖν etc.; elsewhere not used in N.T.); another very classical use occurs in H. 9. 5 οὐκ ἔστιν νῦν λέγειν (Viteau p. 251). A peculiar use of the inf. is ὁ ἔχων ὦτα ἀκούειν ἀκουέτω Mc. 4. 9, L. 14. 35 and elsewhere (to hear, δυνάμενα ἀκούειν), cp. ὦτα τοῦ μὴ ἀκούειν R. 11. 8 such ears that they cannot hear, § 71, 3.

---

[1] Still Barn. 5. 13 has ἔδει ἵνα πάθῃ.
[2] Cp. πολλά, μικρὸν λείπει (is wanting) with ἵνα and with inf. in Herm. Vis. iii. 1. 9, Sim. ix. 9. 4.
[3] A peculiar instance is Ap. 11. 18 ἦλθεν ὁ καιρὸς τῶν νεκρῶν κριθῆναι καὶ δοῦναι κ.τ.λ., = ἵνα κριθῶσιν οἱ νεκροὶ καὶ δῷς κ.τ.λ.; cp. R. 9. 21 ἔχει ἐξουσίαν τοῦ πηλοῦ, ποιῆσαι κ.τ.λ.
[4] 1 Th. 4. 9 οὐ χρείαν ἔχομεν γράφειν ὑμῖν א°D* al., ἔχετε ... γράφειν א*AD° al. incorrectly: a third reading which is also grammatically correct is ἔχετε ... γράφεσθαι (= 5. 1) H al.

6. Closely related to some of the expressions quoted under 4 and 5 is the **explanatory** (accusative and) infinitive, preceded by a **demonstrative**; the demonstrative may also be omitted without rendering the construction with the infinitive thereby impossible. Ἵνα may here also take the place of the infinitive. Ja. 1. 27 θρησκεία καθαρὰ ... αὕτη ἐστίν, ἐπισκέπτεσθαι ὀρφανούς, A. 15. 28 μηδὲν πλέον ὑμῖν ἐπιτίθεσθαι βάρος πλὴν τούτων τῶν ἐπάναγκες, ἀπέχεσθαι κ.τ.λ., 1 Th. 4. 3 τοῦτο γάρ ἐστιν τὸ θέλημα τοῦ θεοῦ, ὁ ἁγιασμὸς ὑμῶν, ἀπέχεσθαι ὑμᾶς κ.τ.λ., E. 3. 8 (cp. without a demonstr. and with ἵνα 1 C. 16. 12). With ἵνα: L. 1. 43 καὶ πόθεν μοι τοῦτο, ἵνα ἔλθῃ ἡ μήτηρ τοῦ κυρίου μου πρὸς ἐμέ (here somewhat irregular, as the clause introduced by ἵνα is already a fact), Jo. 15. 8 ἐν τούτῳ ἐδοξάσθη ὁ πατήρ μου, ἵνα καρπὸν πολὺν φέρητε, = ἐν τῷ φέρειν ὑμᾶς (conception and wish, not actual fact), 1 Jo. 5. 3 αὕτη γάρ ἐστιν ἡ ἀγάπη τοῦ θεοῦ, ἵνα τὰς ἐντολὰς αὐτοῦ τηρῶμεν. It is specially frequent in John, see further 6. 39, 17. 3, 1 Jo. 3. 11, 23, 4. 21, 2 Jo. 6 (without a demonstr. Jo. 4. 34, supra 5); akin to this use are 1 Jo. 3. 1 (ποταπὴν ἀγάπην ... ἵνα), 1 C. 9. 18 (τίς μου ἐστὶν ὁ μισθός; ἵνα). A further noteworthy instance is Jo. 15. 13 μείζονα **ταύτης** ἀγάπην οὐδεὶς ἔχει, ἵνα τὴν ψυχὴν αὐτοῦ θῇ (= τοῦ θεῖναι), cp. 3 Jo. 4. But if the epexegetical phrase consists of facts, John uses not ἵνα but ὅτι (§ 70, 3): 1 Jo. 3. 16 ἐν τούτῳ ἐγνώκαμεν τὴν ἀγάπην, ὅτι ἐκεῖνος ... τὴν ψυχὴν αὐτοῦ ἔθηκεν, or again if the fact is only supposed to take place, ἐάν or ὅταν is used: 1 Jo. 2. 3 ἐν τούτῳ γινώσκομεν ὅτι ..., ἐὰν τηρῶμεν, 5. 2 ἐν τ. γ. ὅτι ..., ὅταν ἀγαπῶμεν.

7. The infinitive with πρίν (or πρὶν ἤ which is not such good Attic) belongs, generally speaking, to this series of infinitives, which correspond to a conjunctive and not to an indicative: although ἵνα cannot be introduced in this case, and the conjunctive, where it is used, is sharply distinguished from the infinitive, viz. the conjunctive stands after a negative principal sentence, the infinitive after a positive sentence (as in Attic).[1] Mt. 1. 18 πρὶν ἢ συνελθεῖν αὐτούς, εὑρέθη κ.τ.λ., 26. 34, 75 πρὶν (ἤ is added by A in verse 75; L. 22. 61 ἤ add. B; Mc. 14. 30 ἤ om. אD, 72 no MSS. have ἤ) ἀλέκτορα φωνῆσαι τρὶς ἀπαρνήσῃ με, Jo. 4. 49, 8. 58,[2] 14. 29, A. 2. 20 O.T., 7. 2 (never in the Epistles). In a similar way to this πρίν, πρὸ τοῦ with the inf. may also be used, e.g. in Mt. 6. 8, L. 2. 21, G. 2. 12, 3. 23, especially in the case of a fact which is regarded as really taking place at a subsequent time, though πρίν is not excluded in this case, A. 7. 2, Jo. 8. 58 (so in Attic). Πρίν with the conj. or optat. in the respective cases (for the opt. of indirect speech see § 66, 5) after a negative principal sentence is found only in Luke, see § 65, 10.

8. With regard to the **voice** of the verb, it is noticeable that after

---

[1] The conj. (without ἄν) is used after a *positive* principal sentence, and therefore incorrectly, in Herm. Sim. v. 7. 3.

[2] D has πρὶν Ἀβραάμ without the inf. γενέσθαι, so that πρίν is used as a preposition (with the gen.), like ἕως with the gen., § 40, 6. Cp. Stephanus πρίν (πρὶν ὥρας Pindar Pyth. 4, 43; often in Josephus; Arrian al.), W. Schmid de Joseph. eloc. 395.

verbs of commanding the inf. pass. is used instead of the inf. act. in a manner that is more characteristic of Latin than of classical Greek, if it is necessary to state that something is to be done to a person, without mentioning the agent.[1] Mt. 18. 25 ἐκέλευσεν αὐτὸν πραθῆναι, A. 23. 3 κελεύεις με τύπτεσθαι, and so frequently with κελεύειν in Mt. and Lc. (who alone use this verb, supra 4). On the other hand we have A. 23. 10 ἐκέλευσε τὸ στράτευμα ἁρπάσαι αὐτόν (16. 22 ἐκέλευον ῥαβδίζειν is contrary to the above rule). A. 5. 21 ἀπέστειλαν ἀχθῆναι αὐτούς, 22. 24 εἴπας μάστιξιν ἀνετάζεσθαι αὐτόν, Mc. 6. 27 ἐπέταξεν ἐνεχθῆναι (ℵBC ἐνέγκαι) τὴν κεφαλὴν αὐτοῦ (but in 6. 39 ἐπέταξεν αὐτοῖς ἀνακλῖναι πάντας), A. 24. 23 (διαταξάμενος), L. 8. 55 (διέταξεν), L. 19. 15 (εἶπεν), A. 25. 21 (ἐπικαλεσαμένου), 1 Th. 5. 27 ([ἐν]ορκίζω),[2] A. 13. 28 (ᾐτήσαντο, cp. Clem. Cor. i. 55. 4).

§ 70. INFINITIVE AND PERIPHRASIS WITH ὅτι.

1. The complement of verbs of (**perceiving**), **believing**, (**showing**), **saying**, in respect of the purport of the idea or communication in question, is in classical Greek rendered to a great extent by the infinitive, the subject of which, if identical with that of the governing verb, is not expressed, while in other cases it is placed in the accusative. The participle is an alternative construction for the infinitive, see § 73, 5; in addition to these constructions, the complement of verbs of perceiving, showing, saying (not of verbs of believing) is often formed by means of an indirect question, and a development of this use is the construction with ὅτι (strictly ὅ,τι an indirect interrogative particle), which is allowable with these same verbs (and therefore not with verbs of believing). Lastly, as a less definitely [3] analytical expression, ὡς with a finite verb is also in use with verbs of saying, hearing etc.

2. In the N.T. the infinitive has not indeed gone out of use in connection with these verbs, but it has taken quite a subordinate place, while the prevailing construction is that with ὅτι. The indirect question is kept within its proper limits, ὡς is found almost exclusively in Luke and Paul and preserves more or less clearly its proper meaning of 'how,' though it is already becoming interchangeable with πῶς, which in late Greek assumes more and more the meaning of ὅτι[4]; lastly, the unclassical combination ὡς ὅτι occurs three

---

[1] And even where the agent *is* mentioned in Herm. Sim. ix. 8. 3 ἐκέλευσε διὰ τῶν παρθένων ἀπενεχθῆναι.

[2] Buttm. 236 f., who rightly rejects the following readings, Mc. 5. 43 δοῦναι (D) instead of δοθῆναι, 6. 27 ἐνέγκαι (ℵBCΔ) instead of ἐνεχθῆναι, A. 22. 24 ἀνετάζειν (D*) instead of -εσθαι, and also in Mc. 10. 49 prefers εἶπεν αὐτὸν φωνηθῆναι (ADX al.) to εἶπεν φωνήσατε αὐτόν (ℵBCLΔ). In Mc. 8. 7 the MSS. are divided between εἶπεν (ἐκέλευσεν of D is wrong) παραθεῖναι – παρατιθέναι – παρατεθῆναι (A, cp. *apponi* vulg. it.) – παρέθηκεν (ℵ*, without εἶπεν); παρατεθῆναι is the reading commended by the usage of the language (Buttm.).

[3] Riemann Revue de philol. N.S. vi. 73.

[4] Ὡς is used in Mc. 12. 26 after ἀναγινώσκειν (v.l. πῶς), L. 6. 4 (ἀναγ.; v.l. πῶς, om. BD), L. 8. 47 (ἀπαγγέλλειν; D ὅτι), 23. 55 (θεᾶσθαι), 24. 6 (μνησθῆναι; D ὅσα),

times in Paul.[1] The point above all to be noticed is that the use, which is so largely developed in classical Greek, of the indirect form of speech with the (acc. and) infinitive, is almost entirely wanting; it may be said that Luke is the only writer who uses it at any length, and even he very quickly passes over into the direct form, see A. 25. 4 f., 1. 4.—Details : verbs of **perceiving (recognizing** and **knowing)** with the acc. and inf. Ἀκούειν Jo. 12. 18, 1 C. 11. 18 (*i.e.* to receive a communication [so in classical Greek]; elsewhere it takes the participle and more commonly ὅτι). (Θεωρεῖν and βλέπειν take ὅτι Mc. 16. 4 etc.; not the inf., but part., § 73, 5.) Γινώσκειν takes acc. and inf. in H. 10. 34 (in classical Greek only with the meaning 'to pass judgment,' which may also be adopted in this passage); the prevailing construction is ὅτι, cp. Participles § 73, 5. Εἰδέναι in L. 4. 41, 1 P. 5. 9 (Clem. Cor. i. 43. 6, 62. 3) takes acc. and inf. (as occasionally in class. Greek), elsewhere the partic. and usually ὅτι (ὡς), which is also the usual construction with ἐπίστασθαι. Καταλαμβάνεσθαι 'to recognize,' 'find' (post-classical; cp. Att. -νειν) takes acc. and inf. in A. 25. 25 ; elsewhere ὅτι (4. 13, 10. 34).—To **believe** etc. contrary to Attic usage very largely take ὅτι : **δοκεῖν** 'to think' takes (acc. and) inf. in L. 8. 18, 24. 37, A. 12. 9, Jo. 5. 39, 16. 2, 2 C. 11. 16 etc., ὅτι in Mt. 6. 7 etc. (so almost always except in Lc. and Paul; there is a second reading in Mc. 6. 49); but δοκεῖν 'to seem' only takes inf. (Lc., Paul, Hebrews; Herm. Sim. ix. 5. 1 ἐδόκει μοι impers. with acc. and inf.), similarly ἔδοξέ μοι 'it seemed good to me' (only in Lc., literary language, § 69, 4). Ἐλπίζειν takes inf. in L. 6. 34, R. 15. 24 and elsewhere in Lc. and Paul (the fut. inf. in A. 26. 7 B, elsewhere the aorist, § 61, 3), and in 2 Jo. 12, 3 Jo. 14; ὅτι in A. 24. 26, 2 C. 1. 13 and elsewhere in Lc. and Paul. Ἔχειν τινὰ ὅτι 'to reckon' (Lat. *habere*, a Latinism, cp. § 34, 5) Mc. 11. 32 (D ᾔδεισαν). Ἡγεῖσθαι takes acc. and inf. in Ph. 3. 8 (for the double acc. § 34,5). Κρίνειν, 'to decide that something is,' takes acc. and inf. in A. 16. 15, τοῦτο ὅτι in 2 C. 5. 15 ; 'to decide that something should be' ('to choose,' 'conclude') takes inf. in A. 15. 19, 1 C. 2. 2, acc. and inf. in A. 25. 25 (τοῦ with inf. in 27. 1 ; this construction like ἔδοξέ μοι belongs to the same category as βούλεσθαι, κελεύειν etc., § 69, 4). Λογίζεσθαι, 'to decide,' takes (acc. and) inf. in R. 3. 28, 14. 14, 2 C. 11. 5, Ph. 3. 13 ; ὅτι in R. 8. 18, Jo. 11. 50, H. 11. 19 (in John and Hebr. 'to reflect,' 'say to oneself,' as in 2 C. 10. 11 ; with this meaning ὅτι is not unclassical). Νοεῖν acc. and inf. H. 11. 3; ὅτι Mt. 15. 17 etc. (both unclassical). Νομίζειν takes (acc. and) inf. in L. 2. 44 and elsewhere in Lc. and Paul (ἐνόμιζον *solebant* with inf. A. 16. 13 ?); ὅτι in Mt. 5. 17 etc., A. 21. 29 (the acc. and inf.

---

24. 35 (ἐξηγεῖσθαι ; D ὅτι), A. 10. 28 (οἴδατε, ὡς ἀθέμιτον), 38 (ἐπίστασθαι ; D reads differently), 20. 20 (ἐπίστ.; πῶς is used previously in verse 18), R. 1. 9 and Ph. 1. 8 and 1 Th. 2. 10 (μάρτυς) and in a few passages elsewhere. Πῶς (Hatzidakis Einl. in d. ngr. Gramm. 19) occurs in Mt. 12. 4 after ἀναγινώσκειν, Mc. 12. 41 with ἐθεώρει, L. 14. 7 with ἐπέχων, A. 11. 13 ἀπήγγελλεν, 1 Th. 1. 9. Barn. 14. 6, Clem. Cor. i. 19. 3, 21. 3, 34. 5, 37. 2, 56. 16.

[1] 2 C. 5. 19, 11. 21, 2 Th. 2. 2. See on this late usage of the language Sophocles Lex. s.v. ὡς (Clem. Hom. i. 7).

would have been ambiguous).[1] Οἴεσθαι (acc. and) inf. Jo. 21. 25 (last verse of the Gospel), Ph. 1. 17; ὅτι Ja. 1. 7. Πείθεσθαι (acc. and) inf. L. 20. 6, A. 26. 26 (apparently with ὅτι in H. 13. 8, but the passage is probably corrupt; v.l. πεποίθαμεν); similarly the (acc. and) inf. is used with πεποιθέναι R. 2. 19, 2 C. 10. 7; ὅτι in R. 8. 38 etc.; Ph. 2. 24 etc. Πιστεύειν takes inf. in A. 15. 11, R. 14. 2 ; ὅτι passim. Προσδοκᾶν takes (acc. and) inf. A. 3. 5 (aor. inf.), 28. 6 (with μέλλειν πίμπρασθαι). Ὑποκρίνεσθαι acc. and inf. L. 20. 20. Ὑπολαμβάνειν takes ὅτι in L. 7. 43 (this is also classical, Plato Apol. 35 A). Ὑπονοεῖν acc. and inf. A. 13. 25, 27. 27. On the whole, therefore, the use of the infinitive with verbs of believing is, with some very rare exceptions, limited to Lc. and Paul (Hebrews), being 'a remnant of the literary language' (Viteau, p. 52).

3. Verbs of **saying, showing** etc. take ὅτι with a finite verb to a very large extent, as do also the equivalent expressions such as μάρτυρα ἐπικαλοῦμαι τὸν θεόν 2 C. 1. 23, αὕτη ἐστὶν ἡ μαρτυρία 1 Jo. 5. 11, ἐστὶν αὕτη ἡ ἀγγελία 1 Jo. 1. 5, ἵνα πληρωθῇ ὁ λόγος Jo. 15. 25, ἀνέβη φάσις A. 21. 31, ἐν ὀνόματι Mc. 9. 41 ('for the reason that, 'on the ground that'); further, adjectives like δῆλον (sc. ἐστί) take this construction. Special mention may be made of φάναι ὅτι 1 C. 10. 19, 15. 50 (with acc. and inf. in R. 3. 8), whereas in classical Greek this verb hardly ever takes ὅτι (any more than it takes an indirect question). Λαλεῖν ὅτι is rare, H. 11. 18, this verb never takes acc. and inf.; the commoner construction is ἐλάλησεν λέγων like ἔκραξεν λέγων, ἀπεκρίθη λέγων etc., the usual phrase formed on the model of the Hebrew (וַיְדַבֵּר לֵאמֹר), cp. § 74, 3. Κράζειν, (ἀπο)φθέγγεσθαι, φωνεῖν never take ὅτι or acc. and inf., ἀποκρίνεσθαι only in Lc. (20. 7 with inf., A. 25. 4 acc. and inf., 25. 16 ὅτι), βοᾶν only in A. 25. 24 takes the inf. Ὀμνύειν ὅτι occurs in Mt. 26. 74, Ap. 10. 6 (unclassical; it takes the aor. inf. in A. 2. 30, the fut. inf. as in class. Greek in H. 3. 18); ὅτι is also used with other expressions of asseveration such as ἐστιν ἀλήθεια τοῦ Χριστοῦ ἐν ἐμοί, ὅτι 2 C. 11. 10, cp. (Clem. Cor. i. 58. 2), G. 1. 20, R. 14. 11, 2 C. 1. 23 (vide supra). The use of the (acc. and) inf., as compared with that of ὅτι, is seldom found in writers other than Lc. and Paul: λέγειν takes acc. and inf. in Mt. 16. 13, 15, 22. 23 = Mc. 8. 27, 29, 12. 18, Jo. 12. 29 etc., κατακρίνειν in Mc. 14. 64, ἐπιμαρτυρεῖν in 1 P. 5. 12, ἐπαγγέλλεσθαι takes the inf. in Mc. 14. 11, A. 7. 5; in Lc. and Paul the following verbs also take this construction, ἀπαγγέλλειν A. 12. 14, προκαταγγέλλειν 3. 18, ἀπαρνεῖσθαι L. 22. 34, διισχυρίζεσθαι A. 12. 15, μαρτυρεῖν 10. 43, προαιτιᾶσθαι R. 3. 9, σημαίνειν A. 11. 28, χρηματίζειν to predict L. 2. 26; while the ὅτι used with παραγγέλλειν to command in 2 Th. 3. 10 is a ὅτι recitativum (infra 4).—Verbs of **showing** (which may be regarded as the causatives of verbs of perceiving) in Attic Greek, in cases where ὅτι is not used, generally express the complement by means of the

---

[1] Thuc. iii. 88 is quite wrongly adduced as an instance of νομίζειν ὅτι.

[2] R. 14. 2 πιστεύει φαγεῖν πάντα. Πιστεύειν here therefore means not 'believe,' but to have confidence and dare.

§ 70. 3–5. § 71. 1–2.] *INFINITIVE WITH ARTICLE.* 233

participle (δεικνύναι, δηλοῦν, also φανερός εἰμι etc.; occasionally also ἀπαγγέλλειν and the like). In the N.T. we find ἐπιδεικνύναι A. 18. 28 and δηλοῦν H. 9. 8 with acc. and inf. (which is not contrary to Attic usage),[1] ὑποδεικνύναι A. 20. 35 and φανεροῦσθαι pass. 2 C. 3. 3, 1 Jo. 2. 19 with ὅτι (φανεροῦν takes acc. and inf. in Barn. 5. 9); so δῆλον (πρόδηλον) ὅτι 1 C. 15. 27, G. 3. 11, H. 7. 14; instances of the use of the participle are entirely wanting.

4. By far the most ordinary form of the complement of verbs of saying is that of **direct** speech, which may be introduced by ὅτι (the so-called ὅτι recitativum), for which see § 79, 12. An indirect statement after verbs of perceiving and believing is also assimilated to the direct statement so far as the tense is concerned, see §§ 56, 9; 57, 6; 59, 6; 60, 2. Ὅτι is used quite irregularly with the acc. and inf. after θεωρῶ in A. 27. 10; in A. 14. 22 we can more readily tolerate καὶ ὅτι (equivalent to λέγοντες ὅτι) with a finite verb following παρακαλεῖν with an infinitive.

5. The very common use in the classical language of ἄν with the infinitive (= ἄν with indic. or optat. of direct speech) is entirely absent from the N.T. (ὡσάν with the inf. is not connected with this use, § 78, 1).

§ 71. INFINITIVE WITH THE ARTICLE.

1. The article with an infinitive strictly has the same (anaphoric) meaning which it has with a noun; but there is this difference between the two, that the infinitive takes no declension forms, and consequently the article has to be used, especially in all instances where the case of the infinitive requires expression, without regard to its proper meaning and merely to make the sense intelligible. The use of the infinitive accompanied by the article in all four cases, and also in dependence on the different prepositions, became more and more extended in Greek; consequently the N.T. shows a great abundance of usages of this kind, although most of them are not widely attested, and can be but very slightly illustrated outside the writings which were influenced by the literary language, namely those of Luke and Paul (James). See Viteau, p. 173. The rarest of these usages is the addition to the infinitive of an attribute in the same case (which even in classical Greek is only possible with a pronoun): the only N.T. instance is H. 2. 15 διὰ παντὸς τοῦ ζῆν.

2. The **nominative** of the infinitive **with the article**, as also the **accusative** used independently of a preposition, are found sporadically in Mt. and Mc., somewhat more frequently in Paul, and practically nowhere in the remaining writers; they are generally used in such a way that the anaphoric meaning of the article, with reference to something previously mentioned or otherwise well known, is more or less clearly marked. Mt. 15. 20 τὸ ἀνίπτοις χερσὶν φαγεῖν subj.

---

[1] On συνιστάναι with acc. and inf. in 2 C. 7. 11 (?) see § 38, 2 note.

(see verse 2) : 20, 23 τὸ καθίσαι obj. (καθίσωσιν verse 21): Mc. 9. 10 τὸ ἀναστῆναι (9 ἀναστῇ ; D has ὅταν ἐκ νεκρῶν ἀναστῇ): 12. 33 τὸ ἀγαπᾶν (see 30): A. 25. 11 θανάτου ... τὸ ἀποθανεῖν: R. 4. 13 ἡ ἐπαγγελία ... τὸ κληρονόμον αὐτὸν εἶναι (epexegetical to ἐπαγγ.: the art. in both cases denoting something well known): 7. 18 τὸ θέλειν ... τὸ κατεργάζεσθαι, ideas which have already been the subjects of discussion; cp. 2 C. 8. 10 f. (τὸ θέλειν is added as the opposite of τὸ ποιῆσαι), Ph. 2. 13 (do.), 1. 29 (do.), 1. 21 f., 24: R. 13. 8 τὸ ἀλλήλους ἀγαπᾶν (the well-known precept): 1 C. 11. 6 κειράσθω ἢ ξυράσθω ... τὸ κείρασθαι ἢ ξύρασθαι : 7. 26,[1] 14. 39, 2 C. 7. 11, Ph. 2. 6, 4. 10 τὸ ὑπὲρ ἐμοῦ φρονεῖν (which you have previously done ; but FG read τοῦ, cp. § 19, 1), H. 10. 31 (in G. 4. 18 אABC omit τὸ). The force of the article is not so clear in 2 C. 9. 1 περισσόν ἐστι τὸ γράφειν, cp. Demosth. 2. 3 τὸ διεξιέναι ... οὐχὶ καλῶς ἔχειν ἡγοῦμαι (the article denotes something obvious, which might take place), Herm. Vis. iv. 2. 6 αἱρετώτερον ἦν αὐτοῖς τὸ μὴ γεννηθῆναι. But its use is still more lax with μή in 2 C. 10. 2 δέομαι τὸ μὴ παρὼν θαρρῆσαι[2], R. 14. 13, 21, 2 C. 2. 1, and quite superfluous in 1 Th. 3. 3 τὸ (om. אABD al.) μηδένα σαίνεσθαι, 4. 6 τὸ μὴ ὑπερβαίνειν (whereas there is no art. in verses 3 f. with ἀπέχεσθαι and εἰδέναι) ; this τὸ μή (like τοῦ μή, infra 3) is equivalent to a ἵνα clause, and is found to a certain extent similarly used in classical writers after a verb of hindering (κατέχειν τὸ μὴ δακρύειν Plato, Phaedo 117 C), while δέομαι τὸ θαρρῆσαι without a μή would clearly be impossible even in Paul.[3]

3. The **genitive** of the infinitive, not dependent on a preposition, has an extensive range in Paul and still more in Luke ; it is found to a limited degree in Matthew and Mark, but is wholly, or almost wholly, absent from the other writers. According to classical usage it may either be dependent on a noun or verb which governs a genitive, or it is employed (from Thucydides onwards, but not very frequently) to denote aim or object (being equivalent to a final sentence or an inf. with ἕνεκα). Both uses occur in the N.T., but the manner of employing this inf. has been extended beyond these limits, very much in the same way that the use of ἵνα has been extended. It is found after **nouns** such as χρόνος, καιρός, ἐξουσία, ἐλπίς, χρεία : L. 1. 57, 2. 6, 1 P. 4. 17, L. 10. 19, 22. 6, A. 27. 20, 1 C. 9. 10, R. 15. 23, H. 5. 12 ; in these cases the inf. without the art. and the periphrasis with ἵνα may also be used, § 69, 5, without altering the meaning (whereas in Attic a τοῦ of this kind ordinarily keeps its proper force), and passages like L. 2. 21 ἐπλήσθησαν ἡμέραι ὀκτὼ τοῦ περιτεμεῖν αὐτόν show a very loose connection between the inf. and the substantive (almost = ὥστε περιτεμεῖν, ἵνα

---

[1] In this passage and in 2 C. 7. 11 (R. 14. 13, 2 C. 2. 1) τοῦτο precedes, but the pronoun in no way occasions the use of the art., cp. (without an art.) 1 C. 7. 37 etc., § 69, 6 (Buttm. p. 225).

[2] In A. 4. 18 παρήγγειλαν τὸ (om. א*B) καθόλου μὴ φθέγγεσθαι the article, if correctly read, should be joined with καθόλου, cp. § 34, 7, Diod. Sic. 1. 77.

[3] A parallel from the LXX. is quoted (Viteau, p. 164), viz. 2 Esdr. 6. 8 τὸ μὴ καταργηθῆναι, 'that it may not be hindered.'

§ 71. 3.] *INFINITIVE WITH ARTICLE.* 235

περιτέμωσιν). Cp. further R. 8. 12 ὀφειλέται ... τοῦ κατὰ σάρκα ζῆν, R. 1. 24 ἀκαθαρσίαν, τοῦ ἀτιμάζεσθαι, = ὥστε ἀτ.; the connection with the subst. is quite lost in 1 C. 10. 13 τὴν ἔκβασιν, τοῦ δύνασθαι ὑπενεγκεῖν, R. 11. 8 O.T. ὀφθαλμοὺς τοῦ μὴ βλέπειν καὶ ὦτα τοῦ μὴ ἀκούειν, 'such eyes that they' etc. (ibid. 10 O.T. σκοτισθήτωσαν οἱ ὀφθ. τοῦ μὴ βλ.). Also A. 14. 9 ὅτι ἔχει πίστιν τοῦ σωθῆναι, the faith necessary to salvation, = π. ὥστε σωθῆναι; Ph. 3. 21 τὴν ἐνέργειαν τοῦ δύνασθαι (the force whereby He is able), ἡ προθυμία τοῦ θέλειν 2 C. 8. 11 the zeal to will, which makes one willing. With **adjectives** we have ἄξιον τοῦ πορεύεσθαι 1 C. 16. 4 as in classical Greek; the instances with **verbs**, which in classical Greek govern the genitive, are equally few, ἐξαπορηθῆναι τοῦ ζῆν 2 C. 1. 8 (ἀπορεῖν τινος; also ἐξαπορεῖσθαί τινος Dionys. Hal.), ἔλαχεν τοῦ θυμιᾶσαι L. 1. 9 (LXX. has the same use in 1 Sam. 14. 47; but in classical Greek in spite of λαγχάνειν τινός this verb only takes the simple inf., and the τοῦ with the inf. corresponds rather to its free use in the examples given below). The construction of τοῦ μή and the inf. with verbs of hindering, ceasing etc. (Lc., but also in the LXX.) has classical precedent, *e.g.* Xen. Anab. iii. 5. 11 πᾶς ἀσκὸς δύο ἄνδρας ἕξει τοῦ μὴ καταδῦναι; but the usage is carried further, and τοῦ μή clearly has the meaning 'so that not': L. 4. 42 (κατέχειν), 24. 16 (κρατεῖσθαι), A. 10. 47 (κωλύειν), 14. 18 (καταπαύειν), 20. 20, 27 (ὑποστέλλεσθαι; D incorrectly omits the μή), also L. 17. 1 ἀνένδεκτόν ἐστι τοῦ μὴ ... (cp. from the O.T. 1 P. 3. 10 παύειν, R. 11. 10 σκοτισθῆναι, vide supra[1]). Paul however has this inf. without μή, so that its dependence on the principal verb is clear, R. 15. 22 ἐνεκοπτόμην τοῦ ἐλθεῖν. Cp. τὸ μή, supra 2.—A **final** (or **consecutive**) sense is the commonest sense in which τοῦ and τοῦ μή are used in the N.T.: Mt. 13. 3 ἐξῆλθεν ὁ σπείρων τοῦ σπείρειν, 2. 13 ζητεῖν τοῦ ἀπολέσαι, 21. 32 μετεμελήθητε τοῦ πιστεῦσαι (so as to), 3. 13, 11. 1, 24. 45 (om. τοῦ D), H. 10. 7 (O.T.), 11. 5. The simple inf. has already acquired this final sense; there is a tendency to add the τοῦ to the **second** of two infinitives of this kind for the sake of clearness: L. 1. 76 f., 78 f., 2. 22, 24, A. 26. 18. The τοῦ is then used in other cases as well, being attached in numerous instances at any rate in Luke (especially in the Acts; occasionally in James) to infinitives of any kind whatever after the example of the LXX.[2]: it is found after ἐγένετο A. 10. 25 (not in D, but this MS. has it in 2. 1), ἐκρίθη 27. 1, cp. ἐγένετο γνώμης τοῦ 20. 3 (ἀνέβη ἐπὶ τὴν καρδίαν Herm. Vis. iii. 7. 2), ἐπιστεῖλαι 15. 20, παρακαλεῖν 21. 12, ἐντέλλεσθαι L. 4. 10 O.T. (Ps. 90. 11), προσεύχεσθαι Ja. 5. 17, κατανεύειν L. 5. 7, στηρίζειν τὸ πρόσωπον 9. 51, συντίθεσθαι A. 23. 20, ποιεῖν 3. 12, ἕτοιμος 23. 15 (Herm. Sim. viii. 4. 2). The only infinitive which cannot take the τοῦ is one which may be resolved into a ὅτι clause: it is the possibility of substituting ἵνα or ὥστε for it which forms the limitation to

---

[1] The LXX. has Gen. 16. 2 συνέκλεισεν τοῦ μὴ ..., 20. 6 ἐφεισάμην σου τοῦ μὴ ... Ps. 38. 2 φυλάξω τὰς ὁδούς μου τοῦ μὴ ..., 68. 24 (= R. 11. 10). Viteau, p. 172.

[2] *E.g.* in 1 Kings 1. 35 after ἐνετειλάμην, Ezek. 21. 11 and 1 Macc. 5. 39 after ἕτοιμος. Viteau, p. 170.

its use.[1] It is especially frequent in an explanatory clause loosely appended to the main sentence: L. 24. 25 βραδεῖς τῇ καρδίᾳ, τοῦ πιστεῦσαι (in believing; τοῦ π. om. D), cp. βραδ. εἰς τὸ infra 4, A. 7. 19 ἐκάκωσεν τοὺς πατέρας, τοῦ ποιεῖν[2] (so as to make, in that he made, = ποιῶν or καὶ ἐποίει), L. 1. 73, R. 6. 6, 7. 3, Ph. 3. 10 (R. 1. 24, 1 C. 10. 13, vide supra). A quite peculiar instance is Ap. 12. 7 ἐγένετο πόλεμος ἐν τῷ οὐρανῷ, ὁ Μιχαὴλ καὶ οἱ ἄγγελοι αὐτοῦ τοῦ (τοῦ om. אB) πολεμῆσαι μετὰ τοῦ δράκοντος ('it happened ... that there fought ... ').[3]

4. The **dative** of the inf. without a preposition is found only once in Paul to denote reason: 2 C. 2. 13 οὐκ ἔσχηκα ἄνεσιν τῷ πνεύματί μου, τῷ μὴ εὑρεῖν με Τίτον (LP τὸ μὴ, א*C² τοῦ μὴ, both readings impossible; but DE perhaps correctly have ἐν τῷ μὴ, cp. inf. 6).

5. **Prepositions** with the **accusative** of the infinitive. Εἰς τὸ denotes aim or result (= ἵνα or ὥστε): Mt. 20. 19 παραδώσουσιν εἰς τὸ ἐμπαῖξαι, cp. 26. 2, 27. 31, Mc. 14. 55 (ἵνα θανατώσουσιν D), L. 5. 17 (D reads differently), A. 7. 19, Ja. 1. 18, 3. 3 (v.l. πρὸς), 1 P. 3. 7, 4. 2; very frequent in Paul (and Hebrews), R. 1. 11, 20, 3. 26, 4. 11 bis, 16, 18 etc., also used very loosely as in 2 C. 8. 6 εἰς τὸ παρακαλέσαι 'to such an extent that we exhorted'; further notable instances are 1 Th. 3. 10 δεόμενοι εἰς τὸ ἰδεῖν, = ἵνα ἴδωμεν, § 69, 4: τὴν ἐπιθυμίαν ἔχων εἰς τὸ ἀναλῦσαι Ph. 1. 23 (DEFG omit εἰς, which gives an impossible construction). (This use of εἰς is nowhere found in the Johannine writings; on the other hand it is found in the First Epistle of Clement, e.g. in 65. 1 where it is parallel with ὅπως.) It is used in another way in Ja. 1. 19 ταχὺς εἰς τὸ ἀκοῦσαι, βραδὺς εἰς τὸ λαλῆσαι, βραδὺς εἰς ὀργήν, the inf. being treated as equivalent to a substantive (Herm. Mand. i. 1 ὁ ποιήσας ἐκ τοῦ μὴ ὄντος εἰς τὸ εἶναι τὰ πάντα, like ποιεῖν εἰς ὕψος Clem. Cor. i. 59. 3).—Aim (or result) is likewise denoted by **πρὸς τὸ**, which however is nowhere very frequent: Mt. 5. 28 ὁ βλέπων γυναῖκα πρὸς τὸ ἐπιθυμῆσαι αὐτῆς, 6. 1 πρὸς τὸ θεαθῆναι αὐτοῖς, 13. 30, 23. 5, 26. 12, Mc. 13. 22, L. 18. 1 (πρὸς τὸ δεῖν προσεύχεσθαι, with reference to), A. 3. 19 אB (rell. εἰς), 2 C. 3. 13, Eph. 6. 11 (DEFG εἰς), 1 Th. 2. 9, 2 Th. 3. 8.— **Διὰ τὸ** to denote the reason is frequent in Luke: 2. 4, 8. 6 etc., A. 4. 2, 8. 11 etc.; also in Mt. 13. 5, 6, 24. 12, Mc. 4. 5, 6, 5. 4 (D is different), Jo. 2. 24 (Syr. Sin. omits the whole clause), Ja. 4. 2, Ph. 1. 7 (the solitary instance in Paul), H. 7. 23 f., 10. 2.—**Μετὰ τὸ** is used in statements of time: Mt. 26. 32, Mc. 1. 14, 14. 28 [16. 19], L. 12. 5, 22. 20, A. 1. 3, 7. 4, 10. 41, 15. 13, 19. 21, 20. 1, 1 C. 11. 25, H. 10. 15, 26.—The accus. of the inf. is nowhere found with ἐπί, κατά, παρά.

---

[1] In Hermas, however, even this limit is transgressed, Mand. xii. 4. 6 σεαυτῷ κέκρικας τοῦ μὴ δύνασθαι, = ὅτι οὐ δύνασαι.

[2] There is an exact parallel in the LXX., 1 Kings 17. 20 σὺ κεκάκωκας τοῦ θανατῶσαι τὸν υἱὸν αὐτῆς.

[3] Buttmann, p. 231; the nom. with the inf. is certainly quite a barbarism. A forced explanation, by supplying ἦσαν with πολεμῆσαι, is given by Viteau, 168.

§ 71. 6–7. § 72. 1.] INF. WITH ART. CASES WITH INF.

6. Prepositions with the **genitive** of the infinitive. Ἀντὶ τοῦ 'instead of' Ja. 4. 15. Διὰ παντὸς τοῦ ζῆν H. 2. 15 'all through life,' cp. supra 1 ad fin. Ἐκ τοῦ ἔχειν 2 C. 8. 11, probably = καθὸ ἂν ἔχῃ of verse 12 (*pro facultatibus*, Grimm). Ἕνεκεν τοῦ φανερωθῆναι 2 C. 7. 12 (formed on the model of the preceding ἕνεκεν τοῦ ἀδικήσαντος κ.τ.λ.; otherwise ἕνεκεν would be superfluous). Ἕως τοῦ ἐλθεῖν A. 8. 40 (post-classical, in the LXX. Gen. 24. 33, Viteau); the Attic use of μέχρι (ἄχρι) τοῦ with the inf. does not occur. Πρὸ τοῦ Mt. 6. 8, L. 2. 21, 22. 15, A. 23. 15, Jo. 1. 49, 13. 19, 17. 5, G. 2. 12, 3. 23. The gen. of the inf. is nowhere found with ἀπό, μετά, περί, ὑπέρ, nor yet with ἄνευ, χωρίς, χάριν etc.

7. The **preposition** ἐν is used with the **dative** of the infinitive, generally in a temporal sense = 'while': Mt. 13. 4 ἐν τῷ σπείρειν αὐτόν, = the classical σπείροντος αὐτοῦ (since Attic writers do not use ἐν τῷ in this way, as Hebrew writers certainly use בְּ, Gesen.-Kautzsch § 114, 2), 13. 25, 27. 12, Mc. 4. 4, L. 1. 8, 2. 6, 43, 5. 1 etc. (ἐγένετο ἐν τῷ is specially frequent, *e.g.* 1. 8, 2. 6), A. 2. 1, 9. 3, 19. 1 (ἐγέν. ἐν τῷ), R. 3. 4 O.T., 15. 13 (om. DEFG, the clause is probably due to dittography of εἰς τὸ περισσεύειν), G. 4. 18. This phrase generally takes the present infinitive, in Luke however it also takes the aorist inf., in which case the rendering of it is usually altered from 'while' to 'after that' (so that it stands for the aorist participle or ὅτε with the aorist): L. 2. 27 ἐν τῷ εἰσαγαγεῖν = εἰσαγαγόντων or ὅτε εἰσήγαγον, (3. 21 ἐν τῷ βαπτισθῆναι [= ὅτε ἐβαπτίσθη] ἅπαντα τὸν λαὸν καὶ Ἰησοῦ βαπτισθέντος, the two things are represented as simultaneous events), 8. 40 (ὑποστρέφειν אB), 9. 34 (simultaneous events), 36, 11. 37, 14. 1, 19. 15, 24. 30, A. 11. 15.[1] Also H. 2. 8 ἐν τῷ ὑποτάξαι, where again simultaneousness is expressed, 'in that' or 'by the fact that,' = ὑποτάξας; a similar meaning is expressed in 8. 13 by ἐν τῷ λέγειν 'in that he says,' 'by saying'; further instances of a meaning that is not purely temporal are Mc. 6. 48 βασανιζομένους ἐν τῷ ἐλαύνειν, in rowing: L. 1. 21 ἐθαύμαζον ἐν τῷ, when and that he tarried: A. 3. 26 ἐν τῷ ἀποστρέφειν, in that he turned = by turning; so 4. 30 (Herm. Vis. i. 1. 8).—The articular infinitive is never found with ἐπί or πρός.

§ 72. CASES WITH THE INFINITIVE. NOMINATIVE AND ACCUSATIVE WITH THE INFINITIVE.

1. The classical language has but few exceptions to the rule that the **subject** of the infinitive, if identical with the **subject of the main verb**, is not expressed, but is supplied from the main verb in the **nominative** (§ 70, 1); the exceptions are occasioned by the necessity for laying greater emphasis on the subject, or by assimilation to an additional contrasted subject, which must necessarily be expressed

---

[1] Accordingly one might expect in L. 10. 35 ἐν τῷ ἐπανέρχεσθαί με ἀποδώσω rather to have ἐπανελθεῖν, cp. 19. 15; but the meaning is not 'after my return' but 'on my way back.'

by the accusative. On the other hand, the interposition of a preposition governing the infinitive produces no alteration of the rule, nor again the insertion of δεῖν, χρῆναι (of which insertion there are no instances in the N.T. if we except A. 26. 9 in Paul's speech before Agrippa). The same rule applies to the N.T.; the subject of the infinitive which has already been given in or together with the main verb, in the majority of cases is not repeated with the infinitive: and if the infinitive is accompanied by a nominal predicate or an appositional phrase agreeing with its subject, the latter is nowhere and the former is not always a reason for altering the construction, in other words the appositional phrase must and the predicate may, as in classical Greek, be expressed in the nominative. 2 C. 10. 2 δέομαι τὸ μὴ παρὼν (apposition) θαρρῆσαι, R. 9. 3 ηὐχόμην ἀνάθεμα (predic.) εἶναι αὐτὸς ἐγώ, (Jo. 7. 4 where according to BD the acc. αὐτὸ should be read for αὐτὸς), R. 1. 22 φάσκοντες εἶναι σοφοί, H. 11. 4 ἐμαρτυρήθη εἶναι δίκαιος (in Ph. 4. 11 ἔμαθον αὐτάρκης εἶναι the nom. is necessary, since the acc. and inf. is out of place with μανθάνειν which in meaning is related to the verb 'to be able'). Instances of omission of subject, where there is no apposition or predicate: L. 24. 23 λέγουσαι ἑωρακέναι, Ja. 2. 14, 1 Jo. 2. 6, 9, Tit. 1. 16 (with λέγειν and ὁμολογεῖν; it is superfluous to quote instances with θέλειν, ζητεῖν etc.).

2. There are however not a few instances where, particularly if a nominal predicate is introduced, the infinitive (in a way that is familiar in Latin writers)[1] keeps the **reflexive** pronoun in the **accusative** as its **subject**, and then the predicate is made to agree with this. A. 5. 36 Θευδᾶς λέγων εἶναί τινα ἑαυτόν, 8. 9, L. 23. 3, Ap. 2. 9 and 3. 9 τῶν λεγόντων Ἰουδαίους εἶναι ἑαυτούς (in 2. 2 most MSS. omit εἶναι), L. 20. 20 ὑποκρινομένους ἑαυτοὺς δικαίους εἶναι (εἶναι om. D), R. 2. 19 πέποιθας σεαυτὸν ὁδηγὸν εἶναι, 6. 11 λογίζεσθε ἑαυτοὺς εἶναι νεκρούς. According to the usage of the classical language there would in all these cases be no sufficient reason for the insertion of the reflexive; after λεγόντων in Ap. 2. 9 Ἰουδαίων would have had to be used, but this assimilation is certainly not in the manner of the N.T., vide infra 6; in 1 C. 7. 11 συνεστήσατε ('you have proved') ἑαυτοὺς ἁγνοὺς εἶναι, classical Greek would have said ὑμᾶς αὐτοὺς ὄντας, see § 70, 3. The only instances of the reflexive being used where there is no nominal predicate are: Ph. 3. 13 ἐγὼ ἐμαυτὸν οὔπω λογίζομαι κατειληφέναι, H. 10. 34 γινώσκοντες ἔχειν ἑαυτοὺς κρείσσονα ὕπαρξιν (cp. § 70, 2), Clem. Cor. i. 39. 1 ἑαυτοὺς βουλόμενοι ἐπαίρεσθαι, = class. αὐτοί, Herm. Sim. vi. 3. 5, A. 25. 21 τοῦ Παύλου ἐπικαλεσαμένου τηρεῖσθαι αὐτόν (cp. § 69, 4): this last is the only instance (besides the reading of CD in L. 20. 7 μὴ εἰδέναι αὐτούς) where the pronoun is not reflexive (cp. E. 4. 22 ὑμᾶς, but the whole construction of that sentence is far from clear). In A. 25. 4 the reflexive is kept where there is a contrasted clause as often in classical Greek: τη-

---

[1] Also found in inscriptional translations from Latin, Viereck Sermo Graecus senatus Rom. p. 68, 12.

ρεῖσθαι τὸν Π., ἑαυτὸν δὲ μέλλειν κ.τ.λ. (in classical Greek αὐτὸς might also be used).

3. More remarkable are the instances where an infinitive dependent on a **preposition**, though its subject is identical with that of the main verb, nevertheless has an **accusative**, and moreover an accusative of the simple personal pronoun (not reflexive), attached to it as its subject. This insertion of the pronoun is a very favourite construction, if the clause with the inf. and prep. holds an independent position within the sentence. Thus it is found after μετὰ τὸ in Mt. 26. 32 = Mc. 14. 28 μετὰ τὸ ἐγερθῆναί με προάξω, A. 1. 3 παρέστησεν ἑαυτὸν ζῶντα μετὰ τὸ παθεῖν αὐτόν (19. 21 μετὰ τὸ γενέσθαι, but D adds με, Herm. Vis. ii. 1. 3, Mand. iv. 1. 7, Sim. viii. 2. 5, 6. 1). After διὰ τὸ: L. 2. 4 ἀνέβη ... διὰ τὸ εἶναι αὐτόν, 19. 11, Jo. 2. 24 διὰ τὸ αὐτὸν γινώσκειν, Ja. 4. 2 οὐκ ἔχετε διὰ τὸ μὴ αἰτεῖσθαι ὑμᾶς, H. 7. 24. Ἕως τοῦ ἐλθεῖν αὐτὸν A. 8. 40. Πρὸ τοῦ L. 22. 15. Ἐν τῷ κατηγορεῖσθαι αὐτὸν οὐδὲν ἀπεκρίνατο Mt. 27. 12, cp. L. 9. 34, 10. 35, A. 4. 30, R. 3. 4 O.T., Clem. Cor. i. 10. 1. With the simple dative of the inf. 2 C. 2. 13. This accus. is not found in the N.T. in expressions denoting aim by means of εἰς τὸ and πρὸς τὸ (though it occurs with εἰς in Clem. Cor. i. 34. 7); nor is it found in all cases with μετά etc. That the reflexive pronoun is not used is natural in view of the independent character of the clause with the infinitive and preposition. (The acc. is found after ὥστε in Clem. Cor. i. 11. 2, 46. 7, Herm. Sim. ix. 6. 3, 12. 2; after τοῦ in Clem. Cor. i. 25. 2; after πρίν in Herm. Sim. ix. 16. 3.)

4. A certain **scarcity** of the use of the **nominative with the infinitive** is seen in the fact that the personal construction with the passive voice such as λέγομαι εἶναι is by no means common in the N.T. writers (for H. 11. 4 ἐμαρτυρήθη εἶναι vide sup. 1; cp. Χριστὸς κηρύσσεται ὅτι 1 C. 15. 12, ὁ ῥηθεὶς Mt. 3. 3, ἠκούσθη ὅτι used personally Mc. 2. 1?, φανεροῦσθαι ὅτι 2 C. 3. 3, 1 Jo. 2. 19, φανεροὶ ἔσονται ὅτι Herm. Sim. iv. 4). The personal construction is used more frequently with the inf. denoting something which ought to take place (δεδοκιμάσμεθα πιστευθῆναι 1 Th. 2. 4; χρηματίζεσθαι § 69, 4; the latter verb is also found with the nom. and inf. of **assertion** in L. 2. 26 according to the reading of D), and with adjectives (§ 69, 5) such as δυνατός, ἱκανός (but ἀρκετός in 1 P. 4. 3 does not affect the inf. which has a subject of its own); so too we have ἔδοξα ἐμαυτῷ δεῖν πρᾶξαι A. 26. 9, as well as ἔδοξέ μοι L. 1. 3 etc.

5. The **accusative and infinitive** is also in comparison with its use in the classical language greatly **restricted**, by direct speech or by ἵνα and ὅτι; similarly instances of τό (nom. or acc.) with the acc. and inf. (as in R. 4. 13) are almost entirely wanting. On the other hand this construction has made some acquisitions, cp. supra 2 and 3, § 70, 2 etc.; and a certain tendency to use the fuller construction (acc. and infin.) is unmistakable. However, even in cases where the accusative *may* be inserted, it need not always be used: thus we have οὕτως ἔχειν in A. 12. 15, but in 24. 9 ταῦτα οὕτως ἔχειν; it may further be omitted with ἀνάγκη and δεῖ as in Mt. 23. 23 ἔδει ποιῆσαι

(*i.e.* ὑμᾶς), R. 13. 5 ἀνάγκη ὑποτάσσεσθαι (see § 30, 3; DE etc. read διὸ ὑποτάσσεσθε); or again if the subject of the inf. has already been mentioned in another case with the main verb, as in L. 2. 26 ἦν αὐτῷ κεχρηματισμένον μὴ ἰδεῖν (*i.e.* αὐτὸν) θάνατον, or if it may readily be supplied from a phrase in apposition with the subject, as in 1 P. 2. 11 ἀγαπητοί, παρακαλῶ (*i.e.* ὑμᾶς) ὡς παροίκους ... ἀπέχεσθαι, cp. ibid. 15, Viteau, p. 149 f. The following, therefore, are the cases where the acc. and inf. is allowable:—with verbs of perceiving, recognizing, believing, asserting, showing, § 70, 1-3, where the object of this verb and the subject of the inf. is generally not identical with the subject of the principal verb: with verbs of making and allowing, also with some verbs of commanding and bidding such as κελεύειν, where the two things are never identical: with verbs of willing, where they usually are identical (and the simple inf. is therefore the usual construction), of desiring etc.: again with impersonal expressions like δεῖ, ἐνδέχεται, ἀνάγκη, δυνατόν, ἀρεστόν (ἐστι), ὥρα (ἐστίν) etc., also ἐγένετο, συνέβη; with a certain number of these last expressions the subject of the infinitive is already expressed in the dative outside the range of the infinitive clause, while in the case of others there is a tendency to leave it unexpressed, either because it may readily be supplied as has been stated above, or in general statements because of its indefiniteness. To these instances must be added the inf. with a preposition and the article, and the inf. with πρίν, τό, τοῦ, ὥστε, if the subject is here expressed and not left to be supplied. Some details may be noticed. With verbs of perceiving, knowing etc. (also making) frequently, as in classical Greek, the accusative is present, while the infinitive is replaced by ὅτι (or ἵνα respectively) with a finite verb: A. 16. 3 ᾔδεισαν τὸν πατέρα αὐτοῦ ὅτι Ἕλλην ὑπῆρχεν, 3. 10, 4. 13, Mc. 11. 32, G. 5. 21, Ap. 3. 9 ποιήσω αὐτοὺς ἵνα ἥξουσιν; cp. supra 4 for the nom. with a personal construction with ὅτι, and 1 C. 9. 15, § 69, 5; the accus. may also be followed by an indirect question, as in Jo. 7. 27 etc.[1] We may further note the ordinary **passive** construction with verbs of **commanding**, see § 69, 8; the verb λέγειν belongs to this category, which when used to express a command, though it may take the dative of the person addressed with a simple infinitive (corresponding to an imperative of direct speech) as in Mt. 5. 34, 39, L. 12. 13, yet is also found with the acc. and inf.: A. 21. 21 λέγων (om. D) μὴ περιτέμνειν αὐτοὺς τὰ τέκνα, 22. 24 (pass.), L. 19. 15 (do.), where the ambiguity as to whether command or assertion is intended must be cleared up by the context. The dative with the inf. is also found after διατάσσειν (-εσθαι) A. 24. 23, ἐπιτάσσειν (Mc. 6. 39 etc.; also τάσσειν A. 22. 10), παραγγέλλειν, ἐντέλλεσθαι, also ἐπιτρέπειν, after impersonal and adjectival or substantival expressions like συμφέρει, ἔθος ἐστί, ἀθέμιτον, αἰσχρόν, καλόν ἐστι etc. (cp. Dative § 37, 3); to which may be added συνεφωνήθη ὑμῖν πειράσαι A. 5. 9, § 37, 6, p. 114 note 1. But the acc. and inf. is

---

[1] Even by μήπως after φοβεῖσθαι, a verb which can certainly not take acc. and inf.: G. 4. 11 φοβοῦμαι ὑμᾶς (for you), μήπως εἰκῇ κεκοπίακα εἰς ὑμᾶς, with which Soph. O.T. 760 is compared (Win. § 66, 5).

not excluded from being used with these words, being found not only with a passive construction as in A. 10. 48 προσέταξεν αὐτοὺς βαπτισθῆναι, Mc. 6. 27 ἐπέταξεν ἐνεχθῆναι (אBC have ἐνέγκαι) which is less in accordance with N.T. idiom) τὴν κεφαλήν, but also with an active (ἔταξαν ἀναβαίνειν Παῦλον A. 15. 2), and even where the person addressed is identical with the subject of the inf., 1 Tim. 6. 13 f. παραγγέλλω ... τηρῆσαί σε. Also with συμφέρει and πρέπει there is nothing to prevent the inf. from having a subject of its own, as distinct from the person interested: Jo. 18. 14 συμφέρει ἕνα ἄνθρωπον ἀποθανεῖν, 1 C. 11. 13; it is more remarkable that with καλόν ἐστι 'it is good' the interested person may be expressed by the accusative with an inf.: Mt. 17. 4 = Mc. 9. 5, L. 9. 33 καλόν ἐστιν ἡμᾶς ὧδε εἶναι, where however the accusative may be justified, the phrase being equivalent to 'I am pleased that we are here': Mc. 9. 45 καλόν ἐστίν σε εἰσελθεῖν εἰς τὴν ζωὴν χωλόν (cp. 43, 47, where the MSS. are more divided between σοι and σε; σοι is used in Mt. 18. 8 f.). So too we have R. 13. 11 ὥρα ἡμᾶς ἐγερθῆναι, where ἡμῖν would be equally good : L. 6. 4 οὓς οὐκ ἔξεστιν φαγεῖν εἰ μὴ μόνους τοὺς ἱερεῖς (D has the dat. as in Mt. 12. 4; in Mc. 2. 26 אBL have the acc., ACD etc. the dat.): L. 20. 22 ἔξεστιν ἡμᾶς ... δοῦναι אBL (ἡμῖν ACD al.). Ἐγένετο frequently takes acc. and inf.; with the dat. it means 'it befell him that he' etc. A. 20. 16, G. 6. 14; but the acc. and inf. may also be used after a dative, A. 22. 6 ἐγένετό μοι ... περιαστράψαι φῶς, even where the accusative refers to the same person as the dative, 22. 17 ἐγένετό μοι ... γενέσθαι με (a very clumsy sentence). On the indicative after ἐγένετο see § 79, 4. The person addressed is expressed by the genitive after δέομαι 'request'; if the subject of the inf. is the petitioner,[1] then we have the nom. and inf., L. 8. 38, 2 C. 10. 2 : if the person petitioned, the simple inf. is likewise used, L. 9. 38, A. 26. 3. The verbs of cognate meaning with the last take the accus. of the person addressed, namely ἐρωτῶ, παρακαλῶ, αἰτοῦμαι, also ἀξιῶ, παραινῶ; here therefore we have a case of acc. and inf., but the infinitive has a greater independence than it has in the strict cases of acc. and inf., and may accordingly in spite of the accusative which has preceded take a further accusative as its subject (especially where a passive construction is used): A. 13. 28 ᾐτήσαντο Πιλᾶτον ἀναιρεθῆναι αὐτόν, 1 Th. 5. 27 ὁρκίζω ὑμᾶς ἀναγνωσθῆναι τὴν ἐπιστολήν (here the choice of the passive is not without a reason, whereas in Acts loc. cit. D has τοῦτον μὲν σταυρῶσαι). (A. 21. 12 παρεκαλοῦμεν ... τοῦ μὴ ἀναβαίνειν αὐτόν.)

6. Since the subject of the inf. generally stands or is thought of as standing in the accusative, it is natural that **appositional clauses** and **predicates** of this subject also take the accusative case, not only where the subject itself has or would have this case if it were expressed, but also where it has already been used with the principal verb in the genitive or dative. The classical language has the

---

[1] This strikes one as an unusual construction, but it is found elsewhere, ἠρώτα λαβεῖν A. 3. 3, ᾐτήσατο εὑρεῖν 7. 46 (28. 20?); a classical instance is αἰτῶν λαβεῖν Aristoph. Plut. 240.

choice of saying συμβουλεύω σοι προθύμῳ εἶναι or πρόθυμον εἶναι ; in the case of a genitive δέομαί σου προθύμου εἶναι is given the preference (an adj.), but προστάτην γενέσθαι (a subst.; Kühner, Gr. ii.² 510 f.); appositional clauses formed by means of a participle are freely expressed by the dat. (or acc.), but not by the gen., the accusative being used instead. In the N.T. there is no instance of a predicate being expressed by gen. or dat.; appositional clauses are also for the most part placed in the accusative, as in L. 1. 73 f. τοῦ δοῦναι ἡμῖν... ῥυσθέντας λατρεύειν, H. 2. 10, A. 15. 22, 25 (in 25 ABL have ἐκλεξαμένοις) etc.; the dat. is only found in the following passages, 2 P. 2. 21 κρεῖσσον ἦν αὐτοῖς μὴ ἐπεγνωκέναι...ἢ ἐπιγνοῦσιν ἐπιστρέψαι (where however the participle belongs rather to κρεῖσσον ἦν αὐτοῖς than to the inf., as it decidedly does in A. 16. 21, where Ῥωμαίοις οὖσιν goes with ἔξεστιν ἡμῖν; so in L. 1. 3), L. 9. 59 ἐπίτρεψόν μοι πρῶτον ἀπελθόντι (but D has -τα, ΑΚΠ ἀπελθεῖν καὶ) θάψαι τὸν πατέρα μου, A. 27. 3 ἐπέτρεψεν (sc. τῷ Παύλῳ) πρὸς τοὺς φίλους πορευθέντι (אAB; -τα HLP) ἐπιμελείας τυχεῖν.

§ 73. PARTICIPLE. (I.) PARTICIPLE AS ATTRIBUTE— REPRESENTING A SUBSTANTIVE—AS PREDICATE.

1. The participles—which are declinable nouns belonging to the verb, used to express not action or being acted upon, like the infinitive, but the actor or the person acted on—have not as yet in the N.T. forfeited much of that profusion with which they appear in the classical language, since their only loss is that the future participles are less widely used (§ 61, 4); the further development of the language into modern popular Greek certainly very largely reduced the number of these verbal forms, and left none of them remaining except the (pres. and perf.) participles passive and an indeclinable gerund in place of the pres. part. act. The usages of the participle in the N.T. are also on the whole the same as in the classical language, though with certain limitations, especially with regard to the frequency with which some of them are employed.

2. Participle as **attribute** (or **in apposition**) with or without an article, equivalent to a relative sentence. Mt. 25. 34 τὴν ἡτοιμασμένην ὑμῖν βασιλείαν, = τ. β. ἣ ὑμῖν ἡτοίμασται : Mc. 3. 22 οἱ γραμματεῖς οἱ ἀπὸ Ἱεροσολύμων καταβάντες : L. 6. 48 ὅμοιός ἐστιν ἀνθρώπῳ οἰκοδομοῦντι οἰκίαν, cp. Mt. 7. 24 ἀνδρὶ ὅστις ᾠκοδόμησεν αὐτοῦ τὴν οἰκίαν : Mc. 5. 25 γυνὴ οὖσα ἐν ῥύσει αἵματος κ.τ.λ. (the participles continue for a long way; cp. L. 8. 43, where the first part. is succeeded by a relative sentence. Frequently we have ὁ λεγόμενος, καλούμενος (in Lc. also ἐπικαλ., of surnames, A. 10. 18, cp. ὃς ἐπικαλεῖται 5. 32) followed by a proper name, the art. with the participle being placed after the generic word or the original name : ὄρους τοῦ καλουμένου ἐλαιῶν A. 1. 12, Ἰησοῦς ὁ λεγόμενος Χριστός Mt. 1. 16¹ (we never find such expressions

---

¹ Jo. 5. 2 ἔστιν... ἐπὶ τῇ προβατικῇ κολυμβήθρα ἡ ἐπιλεγομένη...Βηθζαθά (D reads λεγ. without ἡ, א* τὸ λεγόμενον); in this passage the article must have been

as in Thuc. ii. 29. 3 τῆς Φωκίδος νῦν καλουμένης γῆς, or in iv. 8. 6 ἡ νῆσος ἡ Σφακτηρία καλουμένη). A point to be noticed is the separation of the participle from the word or words which further define its meaning: R. 8. 18 τὴν μέλλουσαν δόξαν ἀποκαλυφθῆναι, G. 3. 23, 1 C. 12. 22 τὰ δοκοῦντα μέλη ... ὑπάρχειν, 2 P. 3. 2, A. 13. 1 ἐν Ἀντιοχείᾳ κατὰ τὴν οὖσαν ἐκκλησίαν, 14. 13 τοῦ ὄντος Διὸς πρὸ πόλεως according to the reading of D (see Ramsay, Church in Roman Empire, p. 51 f.), 28 17. Participles as a rule do not show a tendency to dispense with the **article**, even where the preceding substantive has none; in that case (cp. § 47, 6) the added clause containing the article often gives a supplementary definition or a reference to some well-known fact : 1 P. 1. 7 χρυσίου τοῦ ἀπολλυμένου, L. 7. 32 παιδίοις τοῖς ἐν ἀγορᾷ καθημένοις, Jo. 12. 12 ὄχλος πολὺς ὁ ἐλθὼν εἰς τὴν ἑορτήν, A. 4. 12 οὐδὲ γὰρ ὄνομά ἐστιν ἕτερον τὸ δεδομένον. In these last two and in similar passages (Mc. 14. 41, A. 11. 21, where DE al. omit the art., Jd. 4, 2 Jo. 7) the presence of the article is remarkable, not because it would be better omitted—for that must have obscured the attributive character of the clause—but because according to Attic custom this attributive character should rather have been expressed by a relative sentence. The same use of the art. is found with τινές without a substantive: L. 18. 9 τινὰς τοὺς πεποιθότας ἐφ' ἑαυτοῖς, G. 1. 7 εἰ μή τινές εἰσιν οἱ ταράσσοντες ὑμᾶς, Col. 2. 8 ; the definite article here has no force, and we may compare in Isocrates εἰσί τινες οἳ μέγα φρονοῦσιν (10. 1), ε. τ. οἳ ... ἔχουσι (15. 46).[1] These constructions have therefore been caused by the fact that a relative sentence and a participle with the article have become synonymous.[2]—The participle with article is found, as in classical Greek, with a personal pronoun, Ja. 4. 12 σὺ τίς εἶ ὁ κρίνων (ὃς κρίνεις KL), 1 C. 8. 10 σὲ (om. B al.) τὸν ἔχοντα, R. 9. 20, Jo. 1. 12 etc.; also where the pronoun must be supplied from the verb, H. 4. 3 εἰσερχόμεθα ... οἱ πιστεύσαντες, 6. 18 ; it is especially frequent with an imperative, Mt. 7. 23, 27. 40 (also οὐαὶ ὑμῖν, οἱ ἐμπεπλησμένοι [= οἳ ἐμπέπλησθε] L. 6. 25, though in 24 we have οὐαὶ ὑμῖν τοῖς πλουσίοις; A. 13. 16 ἄνδρες Ἰσραηλῖται καὶ [sc. ὑμεῖς] οἱ φοβούμενοι τὸν θεόν, 2. 14 ; § 33, 4).

3. The participle when used **without a substantive** (or pronoun) and in place of one, as a rule takes the article as it does in classical Greek: ὁ παραδιδούς με Mt. 26. 46 (cp. 48 ; Ἰούδας ὁ παρ. αὐτόν 25), ὁ κλέπτων 'he who has stolen hitherto' E. 4. 28 etc. so also when used as a predicate (cp. § 47, 3), Jo. 8. 28 ἐγώ εἰμι ὁ μαρτυρῶν, 6. 63 etc. Where it is used with a general application as in E. 4. 28 loc. cit. πᾶς may be inserted: πᾶσι τοῖς κατοικοῦσιν A. 1. 19; πᾶς ὁ

omitted according to Attic usage, but may stand according to the usage of the N.T.: cp. the further instances given of this in the text. The reading τὸ λεγόμενον (and the insertion of ἡ) may be due to κολυμβήθρα being taken as a dative.

[1] In Lys. 19. 57 εἰσί τινες οἱ προαναλίσκοντες it has not unreasonably been proposed to read οἱ προαναλίσκουσι.

[2] For an instance where οἱ is omitted cp. Mc. 14. 4 ἦσάν τινες ἀγανακτοῦντες, a periphrasis for the imperfect.

ὀργιζόμενος Mt. 5. 25, cp. 28, 7. 8 etc., L. 6. 30, 47 etc., A. 10. 43, 13. 39 (πᾶς ὁ not elsewhere in Acts), R. 1. 16, 2. 1 etc., though in other cases the article cannot be used with πᾶς 'everyone,' § 47, 9. Cp. Soph. Aj. 152 πᾶς ὁ κλύων, Demosth. 23. 97 πᾶς ὁ θέμενος (Krüger, Gr. 50, 4, 1 : 11, 11). The article is omitted in Mt. 13. 19 παντὸς ἀκούοντος, L. 11. 4 παντὶ ὀφείλοντι (LX insert art.; D reads quite differently), 2 Th. 2. 4, Ap. 22. 15; and in all cases where a substantive is introduced as in Mt. 12. 25 (here again participle with art. is equivalent to a relative sentence, cp. πᾶς ὅστις Mt. 7. 24 with the part. in 26). Instances without πᾶς where the art. is omitted (occasionally found in class. Greek, Kühner ii. 525 f.): ἡγούμενος Mt. 2. 6 O.T. (see § 47, 3), φωνὴ βοῶντος Mc. 1. 3 O.T., ἔχεις ἐκεῖ κρατοῦντας Ap. 2. 14, οὐκ ἔστιν συνίων κ.τ.λ. R. 3. 11 f. O.T. (according to (A)BG, other MSS. insert art., in LXX Ps. 13. 1 f. most MSS. omit it), 'one who' or 'persons who,' though with οὐκ ἔστιν, ἔχω and similar words the article is not ordinarily omitted in Attic.— **Neuter** participle, sing. and plur.: Mt. 1. 20 τὸ ἐν αὐτῇ γεννηθέν, 2. 15 and *passim* τὸ ῥηθέν, L. 2. 27 τὸ εἰθισμένον (ἔθος D) τοῦ νόμου (cp. § 47, 1), 3. 13 τὸ διατεταγμένον ὑμῖν, 4. 16 κατὰ τὸ εἰωθὸς αὐτῷ, 8. 56 τὸ γεγονός, 9. 7 τὰ γενόμενα, Jo. 16. 13 τὰ ἐρχόμενα, 1 C. 1. 28 τὰ ἐξουθενημένα, τὰ μὴ ὄντα, τὰ ὄντα, 10. 27 **πᾶν** τὸ παρατιθέμενον, 14. 7, 9 τὸ αὐλούμενον etc., 2 C. 3. 10 f. τὸ δεδοξασμένον, τὸ καταργούμενον etc., H. 12. 10 κατὰ τὸ δοκοῦν αὐτοῖς, ἐπὶ τὸ συμφέρον, 12. 11 πρὸς τὸ παρόν etc. On the whole, as compared with the classical language, the use of the neuter is not a very frequent one: like the masculine participle it sometimes has reference to some individual thing, sometimes it generalizes; τὸ συμφέρον has also (as in Attic) become a regular substantive, if it is the correct reading, and not σύμφορον, in 1 C. 7. 35, 10. 33 τὸ ὑμῶν αὐτῶν (ἐμαυτοῦ) συμφέρον (א^c al.).—In one or two passages we also find the rare future participle used with the article without a substantive: L. 22. 49 τὸ ἐσόμενον (τὸ γενόμ. D; other MSS. omit these words altogether from the text), etc., see § 61, 1.

4. The participle stands as **part of the predicate** in the first place in the periphrastic forms of the verb, § 62 : viz. in the perfect (and fut. perf.) as in classical Greek, also according to Aramaic manner in the imperfect and future, the boundary-line between this use of the participle and its use as a clause in apposition being not very clearly drawn, ibid. 2. The finite verb used with it is εἶναι or γίνεσθαι (ibid. 3). This predicative participle is further used as the complement of a series of verbs which express a **qualified form of the verb** '**to be**' (to be continually, to be secretly etc.), and which by themselves give a quite incomplete sense; still this use of the part. as the complement of another verb has very much gone out in the N.T. and is mainly found only in Luke and Paul (Hebrews). Ὑπάρχειν (strictly 'to be beforehand,' 'to be already' so and so, though in the N.T. and elsewhere in the later language its meaning is weakened to that of εἶναι ; nowhere in the N.T. has it the sense of 'to take the lead in an action') takes a participle in A. 8. 16, 19. 36, Ja. 2. 15 γυμνοὶ ὑπάρχωσιν καὶ λειπόμενοι (ὦσιν add. ALP) τῆς ... τροφῆς; προϋπάρχειν

(which obviously contains the meaning of 'before'; a classical word) takes a part. in L. 23. 12 (D is different): but the part. is independent in A. 8. 9 προϋπῆρχεν ἐν τῇ πόλει, μαγεύων κ.τ.λ. (cp. the text of D). If the complement of this and of similar verbs is formed by an adjective or a preposition with a noun, then ὤν should be inserted; but this participle is usually omitted with this verb and the other verbs belonging to this class, cp. infra; Phrynichus 277 notes φίλος σοι τυγχάνω without ὤν as a Hellenistic construction (though instances of it are not wanting in Attic).—This verb τυγχάνω 'to be by accident' never takes a part. in N.T.; διατελεῖν 'to continue' takes an adj. without ὤν in A. 27. 33, for which we have ἐπιμένειν (cp. διαμένω λέγων Demosth. 8. 71[1]) in 'Jo.' 8. 7 ἐπέμενον ἐρωτῶντες, A. 12. 16, Clem. Cor. ii. 10. 5, and as in Attic οὐ διέλιπεν καταφιλοῦσα L. 7. 45, cp. A. 20. 27 D, Herm. Vis. i. 3. 2, iv. 3. 6, Mand. ix. 8. Ἄρχεσθαι in Attic takes a participle, if the initial *state* of anything is contrasted with its continuation or end, elsewhere the inf., which is used in all cases in the N.T.; however there is no passage where the part. would have had to be used according to the Attic rule. Παύεσθαι takes a part. in L. 5. 4, A. 5. 42, 6. 13 etc., E. 1. 16, Col. 1. 9, H. 10. 2 (where it has a part. pass. οὐκ ἂν ἐπαύσαντο προσφερόμεναι); for which we have the unclassical τελεῖν in Mt. 11. 1 ἐτέλεσεν διατάσσων (cp. D in Luke 7. 1).—Λανθάνειν only takes a part. in H. 13. 2 ἔλαθον (sc. ἑαυτοὺς) ξενίσαντες (literary language); φαίνεσθαι in Mt. 6. 18 ὅπως μὴ φανῇς τοῖς ἀνθρώποις νηστεύων, where however νηστεύων is an addition to the subject as in verse 17 σὺ δὲ νηστ. ἄλειψαι, and φανῇς τ. ἀνθρ. is an independent clause as in verse 5 (we nowhere have φαίνομαι or φανερός εἰμι, δῆλός εἰμι with a part. in the Attic manner='it is evident that'; on φανεροῦσθαι ὅτι see § 70, 3).—With verbs meaning 'to cease' or 'not to desist' may be reckoned ἐγκακεῖν which takes a part. in G. 6. 9, 2 Th. 3. 13; the Attic words κάμνειν, ἀπαγορεύειν 'to fail,' ἀνέχεσθαι, καρτερεῖν, ὑπομένειν do not appear with a participle.—Προέφθασεν αὐτὸν λέγων Mt. 17. 25 agrees with classical usage (the simple verb has almost lost the meaning of 'before'); it takes the inf. in Clem. Cor. ii. 8. 2, see § 69, 4.—Other expressions denoting action qualified in some way or other take a part.: καλῶς ποιεῖν as in Attic, καλῶς ἐποίησας παραγενόμενος A. 10. 33, cp. Ph. 4. 14, 2 P. 1. 19, 3 Jo. 6; for which we find incorrectly εὖ πράσσειν in A. 15. 29 ? To this category belongs also τί ποιεῖτε λύοντες Mc. 11. 5, cp. A. 21. 13; and again ἥμαρτον παραδούς Mt. 27. 4.—Οἴχεσθαι and the like are never found with a participle.

5. A further category of verbs which take a participle as their complement consists of those which denote **emotion**, such as χαίρειν, ὀργίζεσθαι, αἰσχύνεσθαι and the like; this usage, however, has almost disappeared in the N.T. A. 16. 34 ἠγαλλιᾶτο πεπιστευκώς is an undoubted instance of it; but Jo. 20. 20 ἐχάρησαν ἰδόντες undoubtedly means '*when* they saw Him' (the participle being an additional independent statement), as in Ph. 2. 28 ἵνα ἰδόντες αὐτὸν χαρῆτε, Mt.

---

[1] Ἐμμένειν with a part. occurs in an inscriptional letter of Augustus, Viereck Sermo Graecus senatus Rom. p. 76.

2. 10. Another instance is 2 P. 2. 20 δόξας οὐ τρέμουσιν βλασφημοῦντες 'do not shudder *at* reviling'; but in 1 C. 14. 18 εὐχαριστῶ... λαλῶν is a wrong reading (of KL; correctly λαλῶ).—The use of the participle as a complement has been better preserved in the case of verbs of **perceiving** and **apprehending**; in classical Greek the part. stands in the nominative, if the perception refers to the subject, *e.g.* ὁρῶ ἡμαρτηκώς, in the accusative (or genitive) if it refers to the object, whereas in the N.T. except with passive verbs the nominative is no longer found referring to the subject (ὅτι is used instead in Mc. 5. 29, 1 Jo. 3. 14). With verbs meaning **to see** (βλέπω, θεωρῶ, [ὁρῶ], εἶδον, ἐθεασάμην, ἑόρακα, τεθέαμαι, ὄψομαι) we have Mt. 24. 30 ὄψονται τὸν υἱὸν τοῦ ἀνθρ. ἐρχόμενον, cp. 15. 31, Mc. 5. 31, Jo. 1. 32, 38 etc.; with ὄντα A. 8. 23, 17. 16; with an ellipse of this participle (cp. supra 4; also found in classical Greek, Krüger, Gr. § 56, 7, 4) Jo. 1. 51 εἶδόν σε ὑποκάτω τῆς συκῆς, Mt. 25. 38 f. εἴδομέν σε ξένον, ἀσθενῆ (ἀσθενοῦντα BD), cp. 45, A. 17. 22 ὡς δεισιδαιμονεστέρους ὑμᾶς θεωρῶ.[1] (These verbs also take ὅτι, § 70, 2.) Occasionally with the verb 'to see' as with other verbs of this kind the participle is rather more distinct from the object and presents an additional clause, while object and verb together give a fairly complete idea: Mt. 22. 11 εἶδεν ἐκεῖ ἄνθρωπον οὐκ ἐνδεδυμένον κ.τ.λ., = ὃς οὐκ ἐνεδέδυτο, Mc. 11. 13 ἰδὼν συκῆν ἀπὸ μακρόθεν ἔχουσαν φύλλα, 'which had leaves.'— **Ἀκούειν** with a part. is no longer frequent; alternative constructions, if the substance of the thing heard is stated, are the acc. and inf. and especially ὅτι, § 70, 2; it takes the acc. and part. in L. 4. 23 ὅσα ἠκούσαμεν γενόμενα, A. 7. 12, 3 Jo. 4, 2 Th. 3. 11,[2] and incorrectly instead of the gen. in A. 9. 4, 26. 14, vide infra. The construction with a gen. and part. is also not frequent apart from the Acts: Mc. 12. 28 ἀκούσας αὐτῶν συζητούντων, 14. 58, L. 18. 36 ὄχλου διαπορευομένου, Jo. 1. 37, A. 2. 6, 6. 11 etc.; in 22. 7 and 11. 7 ἤκουσα φωνῆς λεγούσης μοι, for which in 9. 4, 26. 14 we have φωνὴν λέγουσαν (in 26. 14 E has the gen.), although φωνή refers to the speaker and not to the thing spoken. Cp. § 36, 5.—**Γινώσκειν** has this construction in L. 8. 46 ἔγνων δύναμιν ἐξεληλυθυῖαν ἀπ' ἐμοῦ, A. 19. 35, H. 13. 23; but ἐπιγιν. Mc. 5. 30 (cp. L. loc. cit.) takes an object with an **attributive** participle, ἐπιγνοὺς τὴν ἐξ αὐτοῦ δύν. ἐξελθοῦσαν.—**Εἰδέναι** is so used only in 2 C. 12. 2 οἶδα ... ἁρπαγέντα τὸν τοιοῦτον (it takes an adj. without ὄντα in Mc. 6. 20 εἰδὼς αὐτὸν ἄνδρα δίκαιον, where D inserts εἶναι); elsewhere it has the inf. and most frequently ὅτι, § 70, 2.—**Ἐπίστασθαι** in A. 24. 10 ὄντα σε κριτὴν ἐπιστάμενος, cp. 26. 3 where ℵ*BEH omit ἐπιστ.—**Εὑρίσκειν** commonly takes this construction (also classical, Thuc. ii. 6. 3), Mt. 12. 44 εὑρίσκει (sc. τὸν οἶκον, which D inserts) σχολάζοντα, 24. 46 ὃν... εὑρήσει

---

[1] No further instances occur of this use of ὡς with verbs of seeing: but cp. infra ὡς ἐχθρὸν ἡγεῖσθε 2 Th. 3. 15 'as if he were an enemy' (see also § 34, 5); the meaning therefore must be, 'so far as I see it appears as if you were' etc. (ὡς softens the reproof).

[2] The classical distinction between the inf. and the part. with this verb (the part. denoting rather the actual fact, and the inf. the hearsay report, Kühner ii.² 629) seems not to exist in the N.T.

§ 73. 5. § 74. 1-2.] *PARTICIPLE* (*I.*) *AND* (*II.*). 247

ποιοῦντα οὕτως, etc. (occasionally as with the verb 'to see,' the part. is more distinct from the object, A. 9. 2 τινὰς εὕρῃ τῆς ὁδοῦ ὄντας 'who were'); the pass. εὑρίσκεσθαι is used with the nom. of the part. (=Attic φαίνεσθαι, Viteau), εὑρέθη ἐν γαστρὶ ἔχουσα Mt. 1. 18.—Δοκιμάζειν in 2 C. 8. 22 ὃν ἐδοκιμάσαμεν ('have proved') σπουδαῖον ὄντα (used in another way it takes the inf., § 69, 4).—Instances of this construction are wanting with συνιέναι, αἰσθάνεσθαι, μεμνῆσθαι and others; μανθάνειν (class. μανθάνω διαβεβλημένος 'that I am slandered') only appears to take it in 1 Tim. 5. 13 ἅμα δὲ καὶ ἀργαὶ μανθάνουσιν περιερχόμεναι, where περιερχ. is in any case an additional statement, while ἀργαί is the predicate, with the omission (through corruption of the text) of εἶναι (μανθ. takes the inf. ibid. 4, Ph. 4. 11, Tit. 3. 14).—Verbs of **opining** strictly take an inf. or a double accusative (§ 34, 5); but in the latter case the acc. of the predicate may be a participle, ἔχε με παρῃτημένον L. 14. 18, ἀλλήλους ἡγούμενοι ὑπερέχοντας Ph. 2. 3. The participle with ὡς may also in classical Greek be used with verbs of this class (Hdt. ii. 1 ὡς δούλους πατρωίους ἐόντας ἐνόμιζε), as it is in 2 C. 10. 2 τοὺς λογιζομένους ἡμᾶς ὡς κατὰ σάρκα περιπατοῦντας, but we may equally well have εὑρεθεὶς ὡς ἄνθρωπος Ph. 2. 8, ὡς ἐχθρὸν ἡγεῖσθε 2 Th. 3. 15, so that one sees that in the first passage the participle possesses no peculiar function of its own. Cp. § 74, 6.—Ὁμολογεῖν takes a double accusative in Jo. 9. 22 (D inserts εἶναι) and R. 10. 9 ἐὰν ὁμολογήσῃς κύριον Ἰησοῦν 'confessest J. as Lord'; accordingly we have also in 1 Jo. 4. 2 Ἰησ. Χρ. ἐν σαρκὶ ἐληλυθότα, unless B is more correct in reading ἐληλυθέναι; cp. 3 with the reading of א Ἰ. κύριον ἐν σ. ἐλ., and 2 Jo. 7.—Verbs of **showing** are never found with a participle, § 70, 3.

§ 74. PARTICIPLE. (II.) AS AN ADDITIONAL CLAUSE IN THE SENTENCE.

1. The participle is found still more abundantly used as an **additional clause** in the sentence, either referring to a noun (or pronoun) employed in the same sentence and in agreement with it (the conjunctive participle), or used independently and then usually placed together with the noun, which is its subject, in the genitive (the participle absolute). In both cases there is no nearer definition inherent in the participle as such, of the relation in which it stands to the remaining assertions of the sentence; but such a definition may be given by prefixing a particle and in a definite way by the tense of the participle (the future). The same purpose may be fulfilled by the writer, if he pleases, in other ways, with greater definiteness though at the same time with greater prolixity: namely, by a prepositional expression, by a conditional, causal, or temporal sentence etc., and lastly by the use of several co-ordinated principal verbs.

2. The **conjunctive participle**.—1 Tim. 1. 13 ἀγνοῶν ἐποίησα, cp. A. 3. 17 κατὰ ἄγνοιαν ἐπράξατε, *per inscitiam*: Mt. 6. 27 (L. 12. 25) τίς μεριμνῶν δύναται προσθεῖναι κ.τ.λ., 'by taking thought,' or = ἐὰν καὶ

μεριμνᾷ. We may note the occasional **omission** of the part. ὤν: L. 4. 1 Ἰησοῦς δὲ πλήρης πνεύματος ἁγίου ὑπέστρεψεν, cp. A. 6. 8 a quite similar phrase: H. 7. 2, A. 19. 37 οὔτε ἱεροσύλους οὔτε βλασφημοῦντας (cp. Kühner ii. 659), where the part. is **concessive** or **adversative**: as in Mt. 7. 11 εἰ ὑμεῖς πονηροὶ ὄντες οἴδατε κ.τ.λ., 'although you are evil' (cp. L. 11. 13). To denote this sense more clearly classical Greek avails itself of the particle καίπερ, which is rare in the N.T.: Ph. 3. 4 καίπερ ἐγὼ ἔχων πεποίθησιν κ.τ.λ., H. 5. 8, 7. 5, 12. 17: 2 P. 1. 12 (Herm. Sim. viii. 6. 4, 11. 1); it also uses καὶ ταῦτα, which in the N.T. appears in H. 11. 12; a less classical use is καίτοι with a part., likewise only found in H. 4. 3 (before a participle absolute), and a still less classical word is καίτοιγε (in classical Greek the γε is detached and affixed to the word emphasized), which however is only found with a finite verb, and therefore with a sort of paratactical construction: Jo. 4. 2 (καίτοι C), A. 14. 17 (καίτοι ℵ°ABC*); in A. 17. 27 καίγε 'indeed' appears to be the better reading (καίτοιγε ℵ, καίτοι AE), here a participle follows. Cp. § 77, 4 and 14. —**Conditional** participle: L. 9. 25 τί ὠφελεῖται ἄνθρωπος κερδήσας τὸν κόσμον ὅλον, = Mt. 16. 26 ἐὰν κερδήσῃ. **Causal**: Mt. 1. 19 Ἰωσὴφ..., δίκαιος ὢν καὶ μὴ θέλων αὐτὴν δειγματίσαι, ἐβουλήθη κ.τ.λ., = ὅτι δίκαιος ἦν, or διὰ τὸ δίκαιος εἶναι, or (in class. Greek) ἅτε (οἷον, οἷα) δ. ὤν, particles which are no longer found in the N.T. **Final** participle: the classical use of the fut. part. in this sense in the N.T. apart from Lc. (A. 8. 27 ἐληλύθει προσκυνήσων, 22. 5, 24. 17, also 25. 13 according to the correct reading ἀσπασόμενοι, § 58, 4) occurs only in Mt. 27. 49 (ἔρχεται σώσων: but ℵ* has σῶσαι, D καὶ σώσει). More commonly this function is performed by the pres. part., § 58, 4, as in L. 7. 6 ἔπεμψεν φίλους ὁ ἑκατοντάρχης λέγων αὐτῷ, unless (Viteau, p. 186) another construction with kindred meaning is introduced, such as in Mt. 11. 2 πέμψας εἶπεν, 1 C. 4. 17 ἔπεμψα Τιμόθεον, ὃς ἀναμνήσει, or the infinitive, which is the commonest construction of all, § 69, 2.—Then the most frequent use of this participle is to state the manner in which an action takes place, its antecedents and its accompaniments, in which case it would sometimes be possible to use a temporal sentence in its place, and sometimes not, viz. if the statement is of too little importance to warrant the latter construction. For instance, in Mc. 1. 7 οὗ οὐκ εἰμὶ ἱκανὸς κύψας λῦσαι τὸν ἱμάντα, no one would have said ἐπειδὰν κύψω; nor again in A. 21. 32 ὃς παραλαβὼν στρατιώτας κατέδραμεν ἐπ' αὐτόν would anyone have used such a phrase as ἐπειδὴ παρέλαβεν, since the part. in this passage (as λαβών often does in class. Greek) corresponds to our 'with' and admits of no analysis (see also Jo. 18. 3, which Viteau compares with Mt. 26. 47, where we have μετ' αὐτοῦ; Mt. 25. 1). Similarly **φέρων** = 'with' in Jo. 19. 39; **ἔχων**, which is also very common in class. Greek, occurs in L. 2. 42 in D, besides in Mt. 15. 30 with the addition of μεθ' ἑαυτῶν (ἄγων occurs nowhere). While therefore these classical phrases with the exception of λαβών are disappearing, **λαβών** is also used in another way together with other descriptive participles, which according to Hebrew precedent become purely **pleonastic** (Viteau, p. 191): Mt. 13. 31 κόκκῳ σινάπεως, ὃν **λαβὼν** ἄνθρωπος

§ 74. 2-3.] *PARTICIPLE (II.).* 249

ἔσπειρεν, and again in 33 ζύμῃ ἣν λαβοῦσα γυνὴ ἐνέκρυψεν, 14. 19 λαβὼν τοὺς ἄρτους εὐλόγησεν, 21. 35, 39 etc.; so also **ἀναστάς** (after the Hebr. קוּם) L. 15. 18 ἀναστὰς πορεύσομαι, ibid. 20, A. 5. 17, 8. 27 etc.; Mt. 13. 46 **ἀπελθὼν** πέπρακεν (cp. 25. 18, 25), **πορευθεὶς** 25. 16 (both verbs representing the Hebr. הָלַךְ), cp. infra 3.—The classical use of ἀρχόμενος 'at the beginning,' τελευτῶν 'in conclusion,' is not found; but we find as in class. Greek **ἀρξάμενοι** ἀπὸ 'Ιερουσαλήμ L. 24. 47, ἀ. ἀπὸ τῶν πρεσβυτέρων 'Jo.' 8. 9 'beginning with,' with which in the passage of 'Jo.' we have in the ordinary text (D is different) the unclassical addition of ἕως τῶν ἐσχάτων, as also in A. 1. 22 ἀρξάμενος ἀπὸ τοῦ βαπτίσματος Ἰωάνου ἄχρι (ἕως BD) κ.τ.λ. (L. 23. 5, Mt. 20. 8). Ἀρξάμενος is used pleonastically in A. 11. 4 ἀρξάμενος Πέτρος ἐξετίθετο αὐτοῖς καθεξῆς, with a certain reference to καθεξῆς and occasioned by that word; cp. on ἤρξατο with inf. § 69, 4 note 1, on p. 227.—With προσθεὶς εἶπεν 'said further L. 19. 11, cp. προστίθεσθαι with the inf. (a Hebraism) § 69, 4.

3. Conjunctive participle and co-ordination.—The pleonastic use of λαβεῖν etc. (supra 2) does not necessarily require the participle, and the finite verb (with καί) may also be employed in this way—a construction which exactly corresponds to the Hebrew exemplar, and which in Greek would only be regarded as intolerable when continued at some length. In the LXX. we have Gen. 32. 22 ἀναστὰς δὲ τὴν νύκτα ἐκείνην, ἔλαβε τὰς δύο γυναίκας ... καὶ διέβη ..., (23) καὶ ἔλαβεν αὐτοὺς καὶ διέβη κ.τ.λ., which for the most part agrees word for word with the Hebrew, except that a perfect agreement would have also required καὶ ἀνέστη ... καὶ ἔλαβεν at the beginning, which was felt to be intolerable even by this translator. The N.T. writers have also in the case of this particular verb usually preferred the participle; co-ordination is only rarely found as in A. 8. 26 ἀνάστηθι καὶ πορεύου (here also D has ἀναστὰς πορεύθητι; the MSS. often give ἀνάστα without καὶ with asyndeton, A. 9. 11 B, 10. 13 Vulgate, 20 D* Vulg., so in 11. 7; cp. § 79, 4); L. 22. 17 λάβετε τοῦτο καὶ διαμερίσατε. In the introduction to a speech we find already in Hebrew לֵאמֹר used with a finite verb such as 'asked' or 'answered': the Greek equivalent for this is λέγων, numerous instances of which appear in the N.T. after ἀποκρίνεσθαι, λαλεῖν, κράζειν, παρακαλεῖν etc. But in Hebrew the word 'answered' is also succeeded by וַיֹּאמֶר (LXX. καὶ εἶπεν), and the same construction occurs in the N.T. e.g. Jo. 20. 28 ἀπεκρίθη Θωμᾶς καὶ εἶπεν, 14. 23, 18. 30 (so almost always in John's Gospel, unless ἀπεκρ. is used without an additional word), L. 17. 20; beside which we have ἀπεκρίθη λέγων Mc. 15. 9 (D ἀποκριθεὶς λέγει), A. 15. 13 (not in D), ἀπεκρίθησαν λέγουσαι Mt. 25. 9, cp. 37, 44 f. (Jo. 12. 23), and by far the most predominant formula except in John ἀποκριθεὶς εἶπεν (twice in the second half of the Acts 19. 15 [not in D], 25. 9). We never find ἀποκρινόμενος εἶπεν, any more than we find ἀπεκρίθη εἰπών, since the answer is reported as a fact, and therefore in the aorist, while the verb of saying which is joined with it in the participle gives the manner of the answer, and must therefore be a present participle. John (and Paul) have also the following combinations: Jo. 1. 25 καὶ ἠρώτησαν αὐτὸν καὶ εἶπον αὐτῷ (but Mt. 15. 23 ἠρώτων λέγοντες, and so John himself has ἠρώτησαν λέγ. 4. 31, 9. 2 etc.), 9. 28 ἐλοιδόρησαν αὐτὸν καὶ εἶπαν, 12. 44 ἔκραξεν καὶ εἶπεν (D ἔκραζε καὶ ἔλεγεν), cp. D in L. 8. 28 (but Mt. 8. 29 has ἔκραξαν λέγοντες, so 14. 30 etc.; κράξας λέγει Mc. 5. 7 [εἶπε D], κράξας ἔλεγε 9. 24 [λέγει a better reading in D]; ἐκραύγαζον [v.l. ἔκραζον] λέγ. Jo. 19. 12, ἐκραύγασαν λέγ. 18. 40); 13. 21 ἐμαρτύρησε καὶ εἶπε (A. 13. 22 εἶπεν μαρτυρήσας; Jo. 1. 32 ἐμαρτύρησεν λέγων); R. 10. 20 ἀποτολμᾷ καὶ λέγει; Jo. 18. 25 ἠρνήσατο καὶ εἶπε, Mt. 26. 70 etc. ἠρν. λέγων, but A. 7. 35 ὃν ἠρνήσαντο εἰπόντες.[1] The tense in the last instance εἰπόντες is occasioned by the fact that ἠρν. is not here a verbum dicendi; accordingly we find the same tense elsewhere, Jo. 11. 28 ἐφώνησεν τὴν ἀδελφὴν (called) εἰποῦσα (with the words), = καὶ εἶπεν 18. 33; A. 22. 24 ἐκέλευσεν εἰσάγεσθαι... εἴπας, 21. 14 ἡσυχάσαμεν εἰπόντες, L. 5. 13 ἥψατο εἰπών, 22. 8 ἀπέστειλεν εἰπών (Mt. inversely has πέμψας εἶπεν 'sent with the words'; 11. 3 πέμψας διὰ τῶν μαθητῶν εἶπεν is rather different 'he bade them say'). By the use of the aorist participle nothing is stated with regard to the sequence of time (cp. § 58, 4), any more than it is by the use of the equivalent co-ordination with καί: L. 15. 23 φαγόντες εὐφρανθῶμεν, = D φάγωμεν καὶ εὐφρ. With the finite verb εἶπεν we do indeed occasionally find λέγων (L. 12. 16, 20. 2; see § 24 s v. λέγειν), but other participles, which express something more than merely saying, are always aorist participles as in the instances quoted hitherto: παρρησιασάμενοι ε. A. 13. 46, προσευξάμενοι ε. 1. 24, since the two verbs, which denote one and the same action, are assimilated to each other. Between two participles of this kind a connecting copula is inserted: κράζοντες καὶ λέγοντες Mt. 9. 27, ἀποταξάμενος καὶ εἰπών A. 18. 21 (the β text is different), Paul rather harshly has χαίρων καὶ βλέπων Col. 2. 5 meaning 'since I see'; where no such close homogeneity exists between them, the participles may follow each other with asyndeton, and often are bound to do so: A. 18. 23 ἐξῆλθεν, διερχόμενος τὴν Γαλατικὴν χώραν, στηρίζων τοὺς μαθητάς, = ἐξῆλθεν καὶ διήρχετο (§ 58, 4) στηρίζων (the latter part. being subordinated as the sense requires): 19. 16 ἐφαλόμενος ὁ ἄνθρωπος ἐπ' αὐτοὺς..., κατακυριεύσας ἀμφοτέρων ἴσχυσεν κατ' αὐτῶν, = ἐφήλετο καὶ κ.τ.λ., whereas the reading καὶ κατακ. (א*HLP) connects κατακυριεύειν with ἐφαλέσθαι in a way that is not so good; in 18 22 κατελθὼν εἰς Καισάρειαν, ἀναβὰς καὶ ἀσπασάμενος τοὺς μαθητάς, κατέβη εἰς Ἀντιόχειαν a second καί before ἀναβάς would be possible but ugly: the sentence may be resolved into κατῆλθεν εἰς K., ἀναβὰς δὲ καὶ κ.τ.λ. These instances of accumulation of participles, which are not uncommon in the Acts (as distinguished from the simpler manner of

---

[1] Among remarkable instances of co-ordination belongs ἔσκαψεν καὶ ἐβάθυνεν L. 6. 48, as the meaning is 'dug deep'; βαθύνας would therefore be more appropriate. But the LXX., following the Hebrew, has the same construction, ἐτάχυνε καὶ ἔδραμεν Judges 13. 10 (Winer).—Also Jo. 8. 59 ἐκρύβη καὶ ἐξῆλθεν ἐκ τοῦ ἱεροῦ, = ἐκρύβη ἐξελθών 'withdrew from their sight.'

the Gospels[1]), are never devoid of a certain amount of stylistic refinement, which is absent from the instances of accumulation in the epistolary style of St. Paul, which consist rather of a mere stringing together of words.

4. A thoroughly un-Greek usage, though common in the LXX., is the addition to a finite verb of the **participle belonging to that verb**, in imitation of the infinitive which is so constantly introduced in Hebrew, and which in other cases is rendered in more correct Greek by the dative of the verbal substantive, § 38, 3. The N.T. only has this part. in O.T. quotations: Mt. 13. 14 βλέποντες βλέψετε, A. 7. 34 ἰδὼν εἶδον, H. 6. 14.

5. **Participle absolute.**—Of the absolute participial constructions the classical language makes the most abundant use of the genitive absolute: the use of the accusative absolute is in its way as regular, but is not found very frequently: the nominative absolute (as in Hdt. vii. 157 ἀλὴς γινομένη ἡ Ἑλλάς, χεὶρ μεγάλη συνάγεται) is antiquated and was never a common construction. The N.T. has only preserved the use of the genitive in this way; since the so-called instances of the nom. absolute to be found there are really no construction at all, but its opposite, i.e. anacoluthon (see § 79, 7). Now the use of the gen. abs. in the regular classical language is limited to the case where the noun or pronoun to which the participle refers does not appear as the subject or have any other function in the sentence; in all other cases the conjunctive participle must be used. The New Testament writers on the other hand—in the same way in which they are inclined to detach the infinitive from the structure of the sentence, and to give it a subject of its own in the accusative, even where this is already the main subject of the sentence (§ 72, 2 and 3)—show a similar tendency to give a greater independence to participial additional clauses, and adopt the absolute construction in numerous instances, even where classical writers would never have admitted it as a special license.[2] Mt. 9. 18 ταῦτα αὐτοῦ λαλοῦντος αὐτοῖς, ἰδοὺ ἄρχων ... προσεκύνει αὐτῷ; cp. 10 (where it is more excusable), 18. 24, 24. 3, 26. 6, 27. 17, in all which cases the noun which is the subject of the participle appears in the dative in the main sentence (in 5. 1 αὐτῷ is omitted in B; in 8. 1 according to ℵ*KL al. we should read καταβάντι αὐτῷ ... ἠκολούθησαν αὐτῷ, likewise grossly incorrect, cp. inf.; a similar v.l. appears ibid. 5, 28, 21. 23, but in 8. 28 ℵ* gives a correct construction reading ἐλθόντων αὐτῶν); so also Mc. 13. 1, L. 12. 36, 14. 29 (D gives a different and correct constr.), 17. 12 (BL om. αὐτῷ; D is quite different), 22. 10, Jo. 4. 51 (αὐτῷ om. d), A. 4. 1 (D om. αὐτοῖς). Again we have in Mt. 18. 25 μὴ ἔχοντος αὐτοῦ ἀποδοῦναι, ἐκέλευσεν αὐτὸν ὁ κύριος πραθῆναι (the **accusative** following); so Mc. 5. 18, 9. 28 (v.l. εἰσελθόντα αὐτὸν ... ἐπηρώτων

---

[1] Occasionally, however, it is found there as well: Mt. 14. 19 κελεύσας (ℵZ ἐκέλευσεν) ... λαβὼν ... ἀναβλέψας, 27. 48 δραμὼν ... καὶ λαβὼν ... πλήσας τε (τε om. D) ... καὶ περιθείς.
[2] On the same usage in the LXX. see Viteau, p. 199 f. (e.g. Gen. 18. 1, Ex. 5. 20).

αὐτόν), 10. 17, 11. 27 (πρὸς αὐτὸν), 13. 3, L. 9. 42, 15. 20, 18. 40, 22. 53 (ἐπ' ἐμέ), Jo. 8. 30 (εἰς αὐτόν), A. 19. 30 (αὐτὸν om. D), 21. 17 (the β text is different), 25. 7, 28. 17 (πρὸς αὐτοὺς), 2 C. 12. 21 (v.l. ἐλθόντα με, and without the second με). If the accusative is dependent on a preposition, and the participle precedes the accusative, it is of course impossible to make it into a conjunctive participle.—If the word in question follows in the **genitive**, the result is the same incorrect pleonasm of the pronoun as is seen in the case of the dative in the example quoted above from Mt. 8. 1 with the reading of א*: Mt. 6. 3 σοῦ ποιοῦντος ἐλεημοσύνην μὴ γνώτω ἡ ἀριστερά **σου** (Herm. Sim. ix. 14. 3 κατεφθαρμένων ἡμῶν ... τὴν ζωὴν ἡμῶν), cp. 5. 1 if αὐτῷ is omitted (with B, vide supra). The instance which intrinsically is the harshest, and at the same time the least common, is that where the word in question is afterwards used as the subject, as in Mt. 1. 18 μνηστευθείσης τῆς μητρὸς αὐτοῦ Μαρίας τῷ Ἰωσήφ, πρὶν ἢ συνελθεῖν αὐτοὺς εὑρέθη, an anacoluthon which after all is tolerable, and for which classical parallels may be found (Kühner ii. 666); but A. 22. 17 is an extremely clumsy sentence, ἐγένετο δέ μοι ὑποστρέψαντι εἰς Ἱερουσ., [καὶ] προσευχομένου μου ἐν τῷ ἱερῷ, γενέσθαι με ἐν ἐκστάσει (καὶ should apparently be removed, because if it is kept the connection of the dat. and gen. remains inexplicable). Cp. also L. 8. 35 D; Herm. Vis. i. 1. 3 πορευομένου μου εἰς Κούμας καὶ δοξάζοντος (ἐδόξαζον as) ..., περιπατῶν ἀφύπνωσα. The gen. abs. stands **after the subject** in H. 8. 9 O.T., cp. Viteau, p. 210 (the meaning is 'in the day when I took'); it has the same position after the **dative** in 2 C. 4. 18 ἡμῖν, μὴ σκοπούντων ἡμῶν (but D*FG read with an anacoluthon μὴ σκοποῦντες, perhaps rightly), Herm. Vis. iii. 1. 5 φρίκη μοι προσῆλθεν, μόνου μου ὄντος.—The **omission** of the **noun** or **pronoun** which agrees with the part., if it can be readily supplied, is allowable in the N.T. as in the classical language: Mt. 17. 14 אBZ (C etc. insert αὐτῶν), 26 (with many variants), L. 12. 36 ἐλθόντος καὶ κρούσαντος, A. 21. 31 ζητούντων (ibid. 10 with ἡμῶν inserted as a v.l.), etc. Another instance of the omission of a noun with the participle occurs in Attic where the participle is impersonal; this is a case for the employment of the accusative absolute, ἐξόν, ὑπάρχον, προστεταγμένον etc., followed by an infinitive. But in the N.T. ἐξόν is only used as a predicate with an ellipse of ἐστί, A. 2. 29, 2 C. 12. 4, and even Luke is so far from employing a passive part. in this way that he says very awkwardly in A. 23. 30 μηνυθείσης δέ μοι ἐπιβουλῆς εἰς τὸν ἄνδρα ἔσεσθαι, instead of μηνυθὲν ἐπιβουλὴν ἔσ. (Buttm. 273). The solitary remaining instance, rather obscured, of the acc. abs. is τυχόν 'perhaps' in 1 C. 16. 6, L. 20. 13 D, A. 12. 15 D.

6. **Particles used with a participle.**—It has already been noticed above in 2 that the particular relation in which the additional participial clause (whether absolute or conjunctive) stands to the principal sentence may be rendered perceptible by the insertion of a particle (καίπερ, καὶ ταῦτα, καίτοι). This usage is but slightly represented in the N.T.; since even of the temporal use of ἅμα to denote simultaneousness or immediate sequence (τρίβων ἅμα ἔφη 'while rubbing') it contains no real instance (A. 24. 26 ἅμα καὶ ἐλπίζων is 'withal in the

expectation,' 27. 40 ἅμα ἀνέντες 'while they at the same time also,' Col. 4. 3 προσευχόμενοι ἅμα καὶ περὶ ἡμῶν, 'at the same time for us also'; cp. ἅμα δὲ καί with imperat. in Philem. 22). A more frequent particle with a participle is the simple **ὡς** (ὥσπερ in A. 2. 2, denoting comparison; ὡσεί 'as though' R. 6. 13); however the participle is for the most part used with ὡς (as with ὡσεί in the passage of Romans) in just the same way as a noun of any kind may be used with these particles, cp. §§ 34, 5 and 78, 1, and of constructions which may really be reckoned as special participial constructions with ὡς, many are entirely or almost entirely wanting in the N.T. Thus we never find ὡς with the acc. abs. (ὡς τοὺς θεοὺς κάλλιστα εἰδότας 'in the belief that'); and again ὡς with a future participle occurs only in H. 13. 17 ἀγρυπνοῦσιν ὡς λόγον ἀποδώσοντες 'as persons who' (cp. L. 9. 52 bql *quasi paraturi* = ὡς ἑτοιμάσοντες; Mc. 11. 13 ὡς εὑρήσων Origen, minusc. 100, afq). In all these instances ὡς with a participle gives a reason on the part of the actor or speaker. The use of this construction without an acc. abs. and with a participle other than the future is more common: L. 16. 1 and 23. 14 'on the assertion that,' 'on the plea of,' so also in A. 23. 15, 20, 27. 30 (here with προφάσει prefixed); see also A. 3. 12 ἡμῖν τί ἀτενίζετε, ὡς πεποιηκόσιν 'as though we had,' 1 C. 7. 25 γνώμην δίδωμι ὡς ἠλεημένος, 'as one who,' 'in the conviction that I am one'; 2 C. 5. 20 (gen. abs.), H. 12. 27; A. 20. 13 (β text) ὡς μέλλων ... 'since he said that'; in the negative we have οὐχ ὡς 'not as if' A. 28. 19, 2 Jo. 5. We also find abbreviated expressions where the participle is dropped: Col. 3. 23 ὃ ἐὰν ποιῆτε, ἐκ ψυχῆς ἐργάζεσθε, ὡς τῷ κυρίῳ (*sc.* ἐργαζόμενοι αὐτό) καὶ οὐκ ἀνθρώποις, 1 C. 9. 26, 2 C. 2. 17, E. 6. 7, 1 P. 4. 11, R. 13. 13 ὡς ἐν ἡμέρᾳ = ἡμέρας οὔσης, 2 Th. 2. 2 δι' ἐπιστολῆς, ὡς δι' ἡμῶν, *sc.* γεγραμμένης, or rather = ὡς ἡμῶν γεγραφότων αὐτήν, G. 3. 16 etc. Classical Greek has similar phrases.—Ἄν **with the participle has quite gone out of use**,[1] as it has with the infinitive.—Where a participial clause is placed first, the principal clause which follows may be introduced by a οὕτως referring back to the previous clause; but this classical usage is found only in the Acts: 20. 11 ὁμιλήσας ..., οὕτως ἐξῆλθεν, 27. 10.

§ 75. THE NEGATIVES.

1. The distinction between the two negatives, the **objective** οὐ and the **subjective** μή, in classical Greek is to some extent rather complicated; on the other hand in the κοινή of the N.T. all instances may practically be brought under the single rule, that **οὐ** negatives the **indicative, μή** the **other moods**, including the **infinitive** and **participle**.

2. **Principal clauses with the indicative.**—The prohibitive future makes no exception to the rule just given: οὐ φονεύσεις Mt. 5. 21

---

[1] Ὡς ἄν with a gen. abs. in Barn. 6. 11 is different; cp. the modern Greek (ὠ)σάν 'as,' Hatzidakis Einl. in d. ngr. Gr. 217; infra § 78, 1.

O.T. (§ 64, 3).[1] But in an interrogative sentence both οὐ and μή are employed (as in classical Greek): οὐ (or οὐ μή, § 64, 5) if an affirmative answer is expected, μή if a negative; so in L. 6. 39 μήτι δύναται τυφλὸς τυφλὸν ὁδηγεῖν ('is it possible that... ?' Ans. Certainly not), οὐχὶ ἀμφότεροι εἰς βόθυνον ἐμπεσοῦνται (Ans. Yes, certainly). Of course the negative used depends on the answer expected and not on the actual answer given: thus in Mt. 26. 25 Judas asks like the other Apostles (22) μήτι ἐγώ εἰμι, ῥαββί ('it surely is not I?'), and receives the answer σὺ εἶπας.[2] (In L. 17. 9, according to AD al., the answer of the first speaker is appended with the words οὐ δοκῶ.) **Μήτι** instead of μή is a very favourite form in questions of this kind, just as οὐχί takes the place of οὐ in those which expect a positive answer; but the simple forms are also used. In questions introduced by μή the verb itself may also be negatived, as in classical Greek, of course with οὐ: this produces μὴ ... οὐ (and an affirmative answer is naturally now expected): R. 10. 17 μὴ οὐκ ἤκουσαν 'can it be that they have not heard it?' (Ans. Certainly they have), 1 C. 11. 22 al. (only in the Pauline Epp.).—Μήτι is further found in the elliptical μήτιγε 1 C. 6. 3 = πόσῳ γε μᾶλλον 'much more' (μή τί γε δὴ τοῖς θεοῖς Demosth. 2. 23).

3. Subordinate clauses with the indicative.—The chief point to notice here is that **εἰ with the indicative** (supposed reality) takes the negative οὐ in direct contradistinction to the classical language, as it even does in one instance where the indicative denotes something contrary to fact: Mt. 26. 24 = Mc. 14. 21 καλὸν ἦν αὐτῷ, εἰ οὐκ ἐγεννήθη ὁ ἄνθρωπος ἐκεῖνος. Elsewhere however these suppositions contrary to fact take μή: Jo. 15. 22 εἰ μὴ ἦλθον..., ἁμαρτίαν οὐκ εἴχοσαν, 24, 9. 33, 18. 30, 19. 11, Mt. 24. 22 = Mc. 13. 20, A. 26. 32, R. 7. 7, no distinction being made as to whether εἰ μή means 'apart from the case where' (nisi) or 'supposing the case that not' (si non, as in Jo. 15. 22, 24). Moreover in other cases where the meaning is nisi εἰ μή is used (cp. Kühner ii.[2] 744), viz. either where, as generally happens, no verb follows the particle, as in Mt. 5. 13 εἰς οὐδὲν εἰ μὴ βληθῆναι (and in εἰ δὲ μή γε, § 77, 4), or where a verb is used, which is generally in the pres. indic., as in εἰ μή τινές εἰσιν G. 1. 7, cp. § 65, 6. But in all other cases we find εἰ οὐ (even in L. 11. 8 εἰ καὶ οὐ δώσει for ἐὰν καὶ μὴ δῷ, § 65, 5); an abnormal instance is 1 Tim. 6. 3 εἴ τις ἑτεροδιδασκαλεῖ καὶ μὴ προσέχεται κ.τ.λ. (literary language; εἰ ... οὐ appears in 3. 5, 5. 8), and another is the additional clause in D in L. 6. 4 εἰ δὲ μὴ οἶδας.—Similar to this is the use of **οὐ** in **relative sentences with the indicative**; exceptions are (1 Jo. 4. 3 ὃ μὴ ὁμολογεῖ a wrong reading for ὃ λύει), Tit. 1. 11 διδάσκοντες ἃ μὴ δεῖ, 2 P. 1. 9 ᾧ μὴ πάρεστιν ταῦτα, τυφλός ἐστιν (literary language; there is no question here of definite persons or things, Kühner ii.[2] 745). In affirmations introduced by ὅτι (or ὡς), also in temporal and causal

---

[1] Still Clem. Hom. iii. 69 has μηδένα μισήσετε (in the middle of positive futures expressing command).

[2] Still Jo. 21. 5 μή τι προσφάγιον ἔχετε; hardly lends itself to the meaning 'certainly not I suppose' (cp. also the use of this negative in 4. 33, 7. 26).

sentences with the indicative, the general use of οὐ is a matter of course; H. 9. 17 ἐπεὶ μήποτε (or μὴ τότε) ἰσχύει, ὅτε ζῇ ὁ διαθέμενος is an interrogative sentence (Theophylact),[1] and the only exception to this rule which can be established is Jo. 3. 18 ὁ μὴ πιστεύων ἤδη κέκριται, ὅτι μὴ πεπίστευκεν εἰς τὸ ὄνομα κ.τ.λ.[2]—After μήπως or μὴ expressing apprehension, if the verb itself is negatived, an οὐ must be inserted before the conjunctive: Mt. 25. 9 μήποτε οὐκ ἀρκέσῃ (cp. the v.l. in the same passage, infra 6); φοβοῦμαι μὴ ... οὐ 2 C. 12. 20.

4. **The infinitive.**—Μή is used throughout, since in H. 7. 11 it is not the inf. but only the idea κατὰ τὴν τάξιν 'Ααρών which is negatived (cp. in class. Greek Lys. 13. 62 εἰ μὲν οὐ πολλοὶ [= ὀλίγοι] ἦσαν, Kühner ii.[2] 747 f.). We may particularly note the use of μή according to classical precedent (Kühner 761 f.) in certain instances after verbs containing a **negative idea** (a pleonastic use according to our way of thinking): L. 20. 27 οἱ ἀντιλέγοντες (AP al.; אBCDL read λέγοντες as in Mt. and Mc.) ἀνάστασιν **μὴ** εἶναι (ἀντιλέγειν here only takes an inf.), 22. 34 ἕως τρὶς ἀπαρνήσῃ μὴ εἰδέναι με (με ἀπ. εἰδ. אBLT; ἀπαρν. not elsewhere with an inf.), cp. 1 Jo. 2. 22 ὁ ἀρνούμενος ὅτι Ἰησ. οὐκ ἔστιν ὁ Χριστός (as in Demosth. 9. 54 ἀρν. ὡς οὐκ εἰσὶ τοιοῦτοι), H. 12. 19 παρῃτήσαντο μή (om. א*P) προστεθῆναι, G. 5. 7 τίς ὑμᾶς ἐνέκοψεν ἀληθείᾳ μὴ πείθεσθαι; (ἐγκόπτεσθαι takes τοῦ ἐλθεῖν in R. 15. 22, cp. Kühner 768 c.). But in H. 11. 24 we have ἠρνήσατο ('scorned') λέγεσθαι; and κωλύειν is regularly used without a subsequent μή, a construction which is also admissible in classical Greek, Kühner 767 f.; see however § 71, 2 and 3.

5. **The participle.**—Here the tendency of the later language to use μή is noticeable even in writers like Plutarch; the Attic language on the other hand lays down rules as to the particular negative required according to the meaning of the participle in individual cases. Hardly any exceptions to the N.T. usage occur in Mt. and John: Mt. 22. 11 εἶδεν ἄνθρωπον οὐκ ἐνδεδυμένον ἔνδυμα γάμου, = ὃς οὐκ ἐνεδέδυτο (Attic Greek would therefore have οὐ; but C³D have μή perhaps correctly, cp. 12), Jo. 10. 12 ὁ μισθωτὸς καὶ οὐκ ὢν ποιμήν (no definite person is referred to, therefore Attic would use μή): in this passage οὐ is no doubt a Hebraism, since in the case of a participle with the article the LXX. render לֹא by οὐ, as in G. 4. 27 O.T. ἡ οὐ τίκτουσα κ.τ.λ., R. 9. 25 (Viteau, p. 217 f.). There are more exceptions in Luke: 6. 42 αὐτὸς ... οὐ βλέπων (D is different), A. 7. 5 οὐκ ὄντος αὐτῷ τέκνου, 26. 22 οὐδὲν ἐκτὸς λέγων, 28. 17 οὐδὲν ... ποιήσας (all correct Attic Greek). Οὐχ ὁ τυχών 'no ordinary person' explains itself (it is the single idea in τυχών which is negatived, supra 4)

---

[1] Ἐπεὶ μή instead of ἐπεὶ οὐ is an established usage in Clem. Hom. (ix. 14, xviii. 6), and for many instances of ἐπεὶ μή in Philostratus see W. Schmid Atticism. iv. 93; but at any rate in the passage of Hebrews μήποτε (μὴ τότε א*D*) is clearly interrogative ('never' would be μηδέποτε or οὐδέποτε). Cp. further § 82, 2.

[2] It is said (Viteau, p. 213 f.) that the second μή is here occasioned by assimilation to the first, i.e. the use of μή is explained as a piece of carelessness, which I should rather attribute to the copyist than to the author.

A. 19. 11, 28. 2; there is a different reason for οὔ in 28. 19 (1 Th. 2. 4) οὐχ ὡς ἔχων κ.τ.λ. ('I have not done this as one who' etc.). Instances of οὔ in Paul (Hebrews and Peter): (R. 9. 25 O.T. [vide supra] τὸν οὐ λαὸν κ.τ.λ. after the Hebrew, = τὸν οὐκ ὄντα λ. in class. Greek; cp. 1 P. 2. 10), 2 C. 4. 8 f. θλιβόμενοι ἀλλ' οὐ στενοχωρούμενοι κ.τ.λ. (here again it is the single idea in στενοχ. which is negatived), Ph. 3. 3 καὶ οὐκ ἐν σαρκὶ πεποιθότες, Col. 2. 19 καὶ οὐ κρατῶν κ.τ.λ. (elsewhere καὶ μή is used, as in L. 1. 20 ἔσῃ σιωπῶν καὶ μὴ δυνάμενος λαλῆσαι)[1]: H. 11. 1 πραγμάτων οὐ βλεπομένων (= Att. ὧν ἄν τις μὴ ὁρᾷ), 35 οὐ προσδεξάμενοι (correctly): 1 P. 1. 8 ὃν οὐκ ἰδόντες ἀγαπᾶτε correctly, but the writer continues with εἰς ὃν ἄρτι μὴ ὁρῶντες πιστεύοντες δὲ, where it is artificial to wish to draw a distinction between the two negatives. With ὡς (with which Attic prefers to use οὔ, Kühner 755) we have 1 C. 9. 26 ὡς οὐκ ἀδήλως ... ὡς οὐκ ἀέρα δέρων.

6. **Combined negatives.**—For μὴ οὐ vide supra 2 and 3; for οὐ μή (frequently used) see § 64, 5, with the conj. or fut. indic.; once we find as a v.l. μήποτε οὐ μή Mt. 25. 9 BCD al., vide supra 3 ad fin.— The only examples of οὐ ... οὐ, οὐ ... μή neutralizing each other are 1 C. 12. 15 οὐ παρὰ τοῦτο οὐκ ἔστιν ἐκ τοῦ σώματος (cp. μή ... μή in L. 14. 29 D, ἵνα μήποτε ... μὴ ἰσχύσῃ), A. 4. 20 οὐ δυνάμεθα ... μὴ λαλεῖν (classical usage corresponds), apart from the instances where the second negative stands in a subordinate clause, viz. οὐδεὶς – ὃς (class. ὅστις) οὐ (but here we do not find the classical practice of directly connecting οὐδείς with, and assimilating it to, the relative, Kühner 919, 5) Mt. 10. 26, L. 12. 2, οὐ ... ὃς οὐ Mt. 24. 2 al.; the same meaning is expressed by giving an interrogative form to the principal clause and omitting the first negative (Buttmann 305), τίς ἐστιν ... ὃς οὐ A. 19. 35.—The classical combination of negatives οὐ (μή) ... οὐδείς (μηδείς) and the like, to intensify the negation, is not excessively frequent: the instances are Mc. 15. 4 οὐκ ἀποκρίνῃ οὐδέν; 5 οὐκέτι οὐδὲν ἀπεκρίθη, L. 10. 19 οὐδὲν .. οὐ μή (not in D), 23. 53 οὐκ ἦν οὐδέπω οὐδείς, A. 8. 39 οὐκ ... οὐκέτι, Mc. 11. 14 μηκέτι ... μηδείς, etc. (οὐδέποτέ μοι οὐδεὶς Herm. Mand. iii. 3); on the other hand we find (contrary to the classical rule, Kühner 758, but cp. 760, 4) οὐχ ἁρπάσει τις Jo. 10. 28, οὐ ... ὑπό τινος 1 C. 6. 12, οὐδὲ τὸν πατέρα τις ἐπιγινώσκει Mt. 11. 27, 12. 19, οὔτε ... τις A. 28. 21, οὐ δυνήσῃ ἔτι οἰκονομεῖν L. 16. 2, οὐ ... ποτέ 2 P. 1. 21.

7. **Form and position of the negative.**—The strengthened form οὐχί, besides being used in questions (supra 2), is also specially frequent where the negative is independent = 'no,' L. 1. 60, οὐχί, λέγω ὑμῖν 12. 51, 13. 3, 5 (the opposite to which is ναί [Attic never has ναιχί], λέγω ὑμῖν 7. 26; οὐ λ. ὑμῖν would not have been quite clear, though οὔ also appears elsewhere for 'no,' Mt. 13. 29 etc., and in a strengthened form οὐ οὔ like ναί ναί Mt. 5. 37[2]); the longer

---

[1] In E. 5. 4 τὰ οὐκ ἀνήκοντα is only a v.l. for ἃ οὐκ ἀνῆκεν, see § 63, 4. In 1 C. 11. 17 read οὐκ ἐπαινῶ (with a stop before it, and παραγγέλλω).

[2] So too in 2 C. 1. 17 ἵνα ᾖ παρ' ἐμοὶ τὸ ναὶ ναὶ καὶ τὸ οὒ οὔ; but in Ja. 5. 12 the words should apparently be divided, ἤτω δὲ ὑμῶν τὸ ναὶ ναί ('let your yea be a yea, and nothing more') καὶ τὸ οὒ οὔ.

form of the negative is also occasionally used elsewhere, Jo. 13. 10 f. οὐχὶ πάντες, 14. 22, 1 C. 10. 29, πῶς οὐχὶ R. 8. 32, οὐχὶ μᾶλλον 1 C. 5. 2, 6. 7, 2 C. 3. 8.—The position of the negative is as a matter of course before the thing to be negatived, especially therefore does it stand before the verb; frequently negative and verb coalesce into a single idea, as in οὐκ ἐῶ (or the more colloquial οὐκ ἀφίω) 'prevent,' A. 19. 30 etc. A separation of the negative from the verb may cause ambiguity, as in A. 7. 48 ἀλλ' οὐχ ὁ ὕψιστος ἐν χειροποιήτοις κατοικεῖ (as if the writer's intention was to state that someone else dwelt therein); Ja. 3. 1 μὴ πολλοὶ διδάσκαλοι γίνεσθε; hence the tendency is to place it immediately before the verb, ἑνὸς οὐκ ἔστιν G. 3. 20. A difficulty is caused by οὐ πάντως R. 3. 9, 1 C. 5. 10, which looks like a **partial** negation (a general negation being expressed by πάντως οὐκ ἦν θέλημα 1 C. 16. 12), but at any rate in R. 3. 9 the meaning must be 'by no means.' But in this passage οὐ π. stands by itself, and one can understand that πάντως οὔ would not be written (a final position for the negative is quite unusual, and cp. οὐ παντελῶς Herm. Sim. vii. 4); Herodotus also has οὐδὲν (οὐδέν τι) πάντως in this sense, v. 34, 65, vi. 3. In the other passage the meaning appears to be rather 'not altogether' (Winer, § 61, 5, cp. Clem. Hom. iv. 8, xix. 9, xx. 5). The meaning of the passage 1 C. 15. 51 is uncertain on critical grounds : πάντες (μὲν) οὐ κοιμηθησόμεθα, πάντες δὲ ἀλλαγησόμεθα the reading of B al. gives a quite unsatisfactory sense (unless πάντες οὐ is taken as = οὐ πάντες, as it is at any rate used in Herm. Sim. viii. 6. 2 πάντες οὐ μετενόησαν 'not all'), but there are several other readings supported by the authority of MSS. and Fathers, see Tischendorf.—The order of words in H. 11. 3 is correct in classical Greek, εἰς τὸ μὴ ἐκ φαινομένων (= ἐκ μὴ φ.) τὸ βλεπόμενον γεγονέναι (2 Macc. 7. 28 ὅτι οὐκ ἐξ ὄντων ἐποίησεν αὐτὰ ὁ θεός), since participles and adjectives used in connection with a preposition have a tendency to take any adverbial words which are in apposition with them before the preposition, as in οὐ μετὰ πολλὰς A. 1. 5, L. 15. 13 D (al. μετ' οὐ πολλὰς, as in A. 27. 14 μετ' οὐ πολύ), Demosth. 18. 133 οὐκ ἐν δέοντι 'unseasonably' (like ὡς εἰς ἐλάχιστα, οὕτω μέχρι πόρρω and many others).

§ 76. OTHER ADVERBS.

1. **Adverb as predicate.**—Adverbs like ἐγγύς and πόρρω may, as in the classical language, be joined with εἶναι as predicates, or be used as predicates with an ellipse of εἶναι, e.g. ὁ κύριος ἐγγύς Ph. 4. 5, no less than prepositions with their cases which are so abundantly used in this way, e.g. ἦν ἐν τῇ πόλει. The use of οὕτως as a predicate is less classical: Mt. 1. 18 ἡ γένεσις οὕτως ἦν (for τοιαύτη ἦν or οὕτως ἔσχεν), 19. 10 εἰ οὕτως ἐστὶν ἡ αἰτία τοῦ ἀνθρώπου κ.τ.λ., R. 4. 18 O.T., 1 P. 2. 15 (although ἔσσεται οὕτως, i.e. ὡς λέγεις, and ἔστιν οὕτως in an answer are also classical constructions); besides this use we have οὕτως ἔχει in A. 7. 1 etc. Another predicative use of οὕτως occurs in R. 9. 20 τί με ἐποίησας οὕτως, = τοιοῦτον. The phrase τὸ εἶναι ἴσα (an adverbial neut. plur.) θεῷ Ph. 2. 6 is in agreement with an old usage

of the language, cp. Thuc. iii. 14 ἴσα καὶ ἱκέται ἐσμέν, Winer, § 27, 3. With γίνεσθαι (with which verb the use of an adverb is in itself quite unobjectionable) we have 1 Th. 2. 10 ὡς ὁσίως καὶ δικαίως καὶ ἀμέμπτως ὑμῖν τοῖς πιστεύουσιν ἐγενήθημεν (beside 2. 7 ἐγενήθημεν ἤπιοι) 'we have behaved'; cp. A. 20. 18 πῶς... ἐγενόμην (D ποταπῶς ἦν).

2. There is a tendency in Greek to express certain adverbial ideas by **particular verbs**: thus 'secretly' or 'unconsciously' is expressed by λανθάνειν with a participle, § 73, 4 (H. 13. 2; elsewhere the adverb λάθρᾳ is used as also in class. Greek, Mt. 1. 19 etc.), 'continuously,' 'further,' 'incessantly' by διατελεῖν, ἐπιμένειν, οὐ διαλείπειν, vide ibid.; cp. with an infinitive φιλοῦσι προσεύχεσθαι 'gladly' (Mt. 6. 5, Winer, § 54, 4), and (with an imitation of Hebrew) προσέθετο πέμψαι L. 20. 11 f. (*not* in D) = πάλιν ἔπεμψεν in Mc. 12. 4, although (according to A. 12. 3 προσέθετο συλλαβεῖν καὶ Πέτρον) it must rather be rendered 'he proceeded to' (Hebr. וַיֹּסֶף לְ with an inf.); the same meaning is elsewhere given by the participle of προστιθέναι, προσθεὶς εἶπεν L. 19. 11, like προσθεῖσα ἔτεκεν LXX. Gen. 38. 5 'further.'

3. Of the **correlative adverbs** (§ 25, 5) the interrogative form is used instead of the relative in exclamations: πῶς δύσκολόν ἐστι Mc. 10. 23, cp. 24, L. 18. 24, πῶς συνέχομαι L. 12. 50, πῶς ἐφίλει αὐτόν (Attic ὅσον) Jo. 11. 36 (Herm. Mand. xi. 20, xii. 4. 2). Cp. the Pronouns, § 51, 4. Still in R. 10. 15 O.T. we have ὡς ὡραῖοι κ.τ.λ., 11. 33 ὡς ἀνεξερεύνητα κ.τ.λ.—Ὅπως (D ὡς) in an indirect question representing πῶς is only found in L. 24. 20 (cp. § 50, 5). On πῶς = ὡς = ὅτι see § 70, 2.—(Ὁτὲ μὲν... ὁτὲ δὲ for 'now... now,' instead of τότε μὲν... τότε δὲ, occurs in Barn. 2. 4, 5 [a Hellenistic use; cp. ὃς μὲν... ὃς δὲ, § 46, 2]; but we also find ποτὲ μὲν.. ποτὲ δὲ in Barn. 10. 7, which is classical; in the N.T. no instances of these phrases are attested).

4. Instances of **attraction with adverbs of place**, as for instance in class. Greek we have ὁ ἐκεῖθεν πόλεμος (for ὁ ἐκεῖ ὢν) δεῦρο ἥξει (Demosth. 1. 15; Buttm. p. 323), cannot be quoted from the N.T., except the passage L. 16. 26 μηδ' οἱ ἐκεῖθεν (οἱ before ἐκ. is omitted by אBD) πρὸς ὑμᾶς διαπερῶσιν, where however we might supply θέλοντες διαβῆναι from the preceding clause. Still we find a corresponding use of ἐξ instead of ἐν: L. 11. 13 ὁ πατὴρ ὁ ἐξ οὐρανοῦ δώσει πνεῦμα ἅγιον (ὁ before ἐξ om. אLX), Mt. 24. 17 μὴ καταβάτω ἆρα τὰ (D ἀραί τι = Mc. 13. 15) ἐκ τῆς οἰκίας αὐτοῦ, Col. 4. 16 τὴν ἐκ Λαοδικείας (ἐπιστολὴν) ἵνα καὶ ὑμεῖς ἀναγνῶτε, the letter which you will find there. (But in Ph. 4. 22 οἱ ἐκ τῆς Καίσαρος οἰκίας membership is denoted by ἐξ, as also in οἱ ἐκ περιτομῆς R. 4. 12, cp. § 40, 2; ἀσπάζονται ὑμᾶς οἱ ἀπὸ τῆς Ἰταλίας H. 13. 24 is ambiguous and obscure, as the place where the letter was written is unknown.)— An attraction, corresponding to that of the relative (§ 50, 2), is found in the case of an adverb in Mt. 25. 24, 26 συνάγων ὅθεν (= ἐκεῖθεν οὗ) οὐ διεσκόρπισας.

§ 77. PARTICLES (CONJUNCTIONS).

1. One part of the functions of the particles (including the conjunctions) is that they serve to give greater prominence to the **modal character** of the sentence, as is the case with the particle ἄν and the interrogative particles, but their more usual function is to express the mutual relations existing between the sentences and the clauses which compose them: membership of a single series, antithesis, relation between cause and effect, or between condition and result etc. The number of particles employed in the N.T. is considerably less than the number employed in the classical language, see § 26, 2; still in spite of this it appears excessively large in comparison with the poverty displayed by the Semitic languages in this department.

2. On the particle ἄν, cp. §§ 63; 65, 4-10; 66, 2 (70, 5; 74, 6).— **Direct interrogative sentences**, which are not introduced by an interrogative pronoun or adverb, but expect the answer 'yes' or 'no,' do not require a distinguishing particle any more than in classical Greek, since the tone in which they are uttered is a sufficient indication of their character, though it is true that when they are transmitted to writing the general sense of their context is the only thing which distinguishes them, and this in certain circumstances may be ambiguous (§ 4, 6; instances of this are Jo. 16. 31, 1 C. 1. 13, Viteau p. 23, 50). If an affirmative answer is to be intimated, this character of the sentence is marked by the insertion of οὐ, if a negative answer, by the insertion of μή (μήτι); and this is a case where a question is distinguished as such by an external symbol, since the use of μή with an indicative where the particle is in no way dependent can certainly not be found except in an interrogative sentence, cp. § 75, 2. Double questions with the distinguishing particles πότερον ... ἤ occur nowhere in the N.T. in direct speech (in indirect speech only in John 7. 17; also Barn. 19. 5); more often the first member of the sentence is left without a distinguishing particle, as in G. 1. 10 ἄρτι γὰρ ἀνθρώπους πείθω ἢ τὸν θεόν; (the simple interrogative ἤ=*an* 'or' occurs in Mt. 20. 15, 26. 53, 2 C. 11. 7, where FG have ἢ μή 'or perhaps,' a combination of particles not elsewhere attested). Still there are certain **interrogative particles**, of which may be mentioned in the first place ἆρα or ἆρά γε; this, it is true, can only be distinguished from the inferential ἄρα (γε) by the prosody, and it is moreover quite rare and only represented in Luke and Paul (therefore a literary word): L. 18. 8 ἆρα εὑρήσει τὴν πίστιν ἐπὶ τῆς γῆς; A. 8. 30 ἆρά γε γινώσκεις ἃ ἀναγινώσκεις; G. 2. 17 ἆρα Χριστὸς ἁμαρτίας διάκονος; μὴ γένοιτο (this phrase μὴ γ. in the Pauline Epp. is always an answer to a question, 66, 1: therefore ἄρα cannot be read here; still ἄρα in this passage has the meaning of 'therefore' which ἄρα elsewhere has, § 78, 5). We have a kindred use of ἄρα (as in classical Greek) after τίς in Mt. 18. 1 τίς ἄρα μείζων ἐστὶν κ.τ.λ., L. 1. 66 etc. (in indirect speech in 22. 23): after εἰ (indirect and direct) in Mc. 11. 13, A. 7. 1, 8. 22 (εἰ ἄραγε 17. 27); after μήτι in 2 C. 1. 17; it

denotes astonishment in A. 21. 38 οὐκ ἄρα σὺ εἶ ὁ Αἰγύπτιος; ('not then'), while in other cases it corresponds to our 'well' or 'then'; τίς ἄρα in Mt. 19. 25, 27 is inferential, 'now,' 'then,' cp. supra on G. 2. 17. Again the εἰ of indirect questions (§ 65, 1, cp. 6) may also be attached to a direct question: Mt. 12. 10 ἐπηρώτησαν αὐτὸν λέγοντες· Εἰ ἔξεστιν τοῖς σάββασιν θεραπεῦσαι; 19. 3 λέγοντες Εἰ ... (it introduces similar words in indirect speech in Mc. 10. 2, Viteau p. 22, 1), A. 1. 6, 7. 1 etc. (most frequently in Luke, Win. § 57, 2); the usage is unclassical, but is also found in the LXX. (Gen. 17. 17 etc., Winer loc. cit.).[1] The alternative use of the interrogative ἦ, like the use of the same word affirmatively, is entirely wanting.

3. Sentences which denote **assurance**, both direct and indirect (in the latter case the infinitive is used), are in classical Greek introduced by ἦ μήν, which in the Hellenistic and Roman period is sometimes written in the form of εἶ (accent?) μήν[2]; so in the LXX. and in a quotation from it in H. 6. 14 εἶ μὴν εὐλογῶν εὐλογήσω σε (ἦ KL*). Another corroborative word is the particle ναί = 'yea,' to which the opposite is οὐ οὐχί 'nay,' § 75, 7. Ναί is also used in the emphatic repetition of something already stated, 'yes indeed,' L. 12. 5 ναί, λέγω ὑμῖν, τοῦτον φοβήθητε, 11. 51, Ap. 1. 7, 14. 13, 16. 7; also in a repeated request Ph. 4. 3, Philem. 20 (it is a favourite word in classical Greek in formulas of asseveration and adjuration, e.g. ναὶ πρὸς τῶν γονάτων Aristoph. Pax 1113). Ναί is not the only form for expressing an affirmative answer, the statement made may also be repeated and endorsed (as in class. Greek): Mc. 14. 61 f. σὺ εἶ ...; ...ἐγώ εἰμι, cp. A. 22. 27 where the β text has εἰμί for ναί of the α text; another formula is σὺ λέγεις Mt. 27. 11, Mc. 15. 2, L. 23. 3, i.e. 'you say so yourself, not I' (§ 48, 1), which always to some extent implies that one would not have made this particular statement spontaneously if the question had not been asked; in Jo. 18. 37 we have σὺ λέγεις, ὅτι (not 'that,' but 'since,' 'for,' § 78, 6) βασιλεύς εἰμι, which is similar to L. 22. 70 ὑμεῖς λέγετε, ὅτι ἐγώ εἰμι.—A certain extenuation, and at the same time a corroboration, of a proposition made is contained in the word **δήπου** 'surely,' 'certainly' (an appeal to the knowledge possessed by the readers as well): it is only found in H. 2. 16 (a classical and literary word).

4. The particle **γε** which serves to emphasize a word (known by the old grammarians as the σύνδεσμος παραπληρωματικός) in the N.T. is almost confined to its use in connection with other conjunctions, in which case it often really sinks into being a mere unmeaning appendage. Thus we have ἄρά γε, ἄρα γε (supra 2; § 78, 5), καίτοιγε, μενοῦνγε § 77, 14; frequently εἰ δὲ μή γε with an ellipse of the verb, 'otherwise' (classical), Mt. 6. 1, 9. 17 (B omits γε), L. 5. 36 etc., 2 C. 11. 16 (on the other hand Mc., Jo., and Ap. have this phrase without γε), μήτιγε § 75, 2. Still γε keeps its proper meaning in

---

[1] It is probably a Hebraism (Viteau), being another rendering (besides μή) of the Hebrew אִם.

[2] Blass Ausspr. 33[3] n. 77; so also Berl. Aegypt. Urk. 543.

ἀλλά γε ὑμῖν εἰμι 1 C. 9. 2 'yet *at least* I am so to you,' which class. Greek would express by separating the particles ἀλλ' ὑμῖν γε (and the particles are somewhat differently used in L. 24. 21 ἀλλά γε καὶ σὺν πᾶσιν τούτοις 'but indeed'); also in καί γε ἐπὶ τοὺς δούλους A. 2. 18 O.T. (Herm. Mand. viii. 5 καί γε πολλά) '*and also*' (or 'and indeed'), where again class. Greek would separate the particles καὶ ἐπί γε, as St. Paul does in 1 C. 4. 8 καὶ ὄφελόν γε ἐβασιλεύσατε 'and I would also that ye did ...' (D*FG omit γε)[1]; and in εἴ γε *si quidem* (R. 5. 6 v.l.) 2 C. 5. 3, E. 3. 2, 4. 21, Col. 1. 23 (classical). It appears without another conjunction in L. 11. 8 διά γε τὴν ἀναίδειαν αὐτοῦ, cp. 18. 5, R. 8. 32 ὅς γε *qui quidem* '*One* who,' Herm. Vis. i. 1. 8 ἁμαρτία γέ ἐστι ('indeed it is'), καὶ μεγάλη.

5. Particles which **connect sentences or clauses** with one another or place them in a certain **relation** to each other, fall into two classes, namely those which indicate that the clauses possess an equal position in the structure of the sentence (**co-ordinating** particles), and those which subordinate and give a dependent character to the clauses introduced by them (**subordinating** particles). The former are of the most diverse origin, the latter are for the most part derived from a relative stem. They may be divided according to their meaning as follows: (only co-ordinating)—(1) copulative, (2) disjunctive, (3) adversative; (only subordinating)—(4) comparative, (5) hypothetical, (6) temporal, (7) final, (8) conjunctions used in assertions and in indirect questions; (partly co-ordinating, partly subordinating)—(9) consecutive, (10) causal, (11) concessive conjunctions.

6. The **copulative conjunctions** in use in the N.T. are καί, τε, οὔτε μήτε, οὐδὲ μηδέ. In the case of **καί** a distinction is made between its strictly copulative meaning ('and') and its adjunctive meaning ('also'). The excessive and uniform use of καί to string sentences together and combine them makes the narrative style, especially in Mark, but also in Luke as *e.g.* in A. 13. 17 ff., in many ways unpleasant and of too commonplace a character, cp. § 79, 1: whereas elsewhere in Luke as well as in John the alternative use of the particles τε, δέ, οὖν, and of asyndeton gives a greater variety to the style, apart from the fact that these writers also employ a subordinating or participial construction. Καί may be used even where a **contrast** actually exists: Mc. 12. 12 καὶ ἐζήτουν αὐτὸν κρατῆσαι, καὶ ἐφοβήθησαν τὸν ὄχλον, cp. L. 20. 19 (but D in Luke reads ἐφοβ. δέ), Jo. 1. 5. It frequently = 'and yet' (καὶ ὅμως, ὅμως δέ are not in use): Mt. 6. 26 οὐ σπείρουσιν ..., καὶ ὁ πατὴρ ὑμῶν ὁ οὐράνιος τρέφει αὐτά, 10. 29, Jo. 1. 10, 3. 11, 32 etc. (with a negative in Mt. 11. 17, A. 12. 19 etc., where this meaning is less striking), and hence the mutual relation of the several clauses is often very vaguely stated, and must be helped out with some difficulty by the interpretation

---

[1] L. 19. 42 is a difficult passage, εἰ ἔγνως καὶ σὺ καί γε ἐν τῇ ἡμέρᾳ σου ταύτῃ τὰ πρὸς εἰρήνην σου, where Eusebius has καί γε σὺ ἐν, and D καὶ σὺ ἐν (καίγε must mean 'at least,' = class. ἔν γε τῇ κ.τ.λ.); also A. 17. 27, for which cp. § 74, 2.

which is put upon the passage, e.g. in Jo. 7. 28 κάμὲ οἴδατε καὶ οἴδατε πόθεν εἰμί (as you say), καὶ ἀπ' ἐμαυτοῦ οὐκ ἐλήλυθα, ἀλλ' κ.τ.λ., i.e. 'and yet in reality I did not' etc., = classical καὶ μήν, καίτοι, or with a participle καὶ ταῦτα ἀπ' ἐμ. οὐκ ἐληλυθότα. A different use is that of the so-called **consecutive** καί, in English 'and so' or 'so': Mt. 5. 15 ἀλλ' ἐπὶ τὴν λυχνίαν (τιθέασιν), καὶ λάμπει κ.τ.λ. (= ὥστε λάμπειν; in L. 8. 16 = 11. 33 expressed by ἵνα), H. 3. 19 καὶ βλέπομεν 'and so we see,' ὁρῶμεν οὖν; this use is specially found after imperatives, Mt. 8. 8 εἰπὲ λόγῳ, καὶ (so) ἰαθήσεται, cp. L. 7. 7 where BL give a closer connection to the clauses by reading καὶ ἰαθήτω: Ja. 4. 7 ἀντίστητε τῷ διαβόλῳ, καὶ φεύξεται ἀφ' ὑμῶν (= φεύξεται γάρ, εὐθὺς γὰρ φ.); still we have a similar classical use, θέσθε... καὶ... οἴσει Soph. O.C. 1410 ff., πείθου λέγοντι, κοὐχ ἁμαρτήσῃ ποτέ El. 1207, Kühner ii.² 792, 5. On καί with a future following sentences of design with a conjunctive, to denote an ulterior result, see § 65, 2; cp. also Mt. 26. 53, H. 12. 9; further L. 11. 5 τίς ἐξ ὑμῶν ἕξει φίλον, καὶ πορεύσεται πρὸς αὐτὸν... καὶ εἴπῃ αὐτῷ—κἀκεῖνος... εἴπῃ (§ 64, 6), instead of subordinating the clauses by means of ἐάν or a gen. abs., just as the first καί might also have been avoided by writing ἔχων φίλον. Co-ordination in place of subordination occurs in statements of time: Mc. 15. 25 καὶ ἦν ὥρα τρίτη καὶ ('when' or 'that') ἐσταύρωσαν (but D ἐφύλασσον which gives a better sense) αὐτόν (the crucifixion has already been narrated in 24), which differs from L. 23. 44 καὶ ἦν ἤδη ὥρα ἕκτη, καὶ σκότος ἐγένετο, which may be paralleled from classical Greek (Plat. Sympos. 220 c, Win. § 53, 3); still even Luke has the unclassical use ἥξουσιν ἡμέραι... καὶ ('when') L. 19. 43: Mt. 26. 45, H. 8. 8 O.T. The use of καὶ with a finite verb after καὶ ἐγένετο, ἐγένετο δέ, instead of the acc. and inf. which is likewise found (§ 65, 5), is an imitation of Hebrew: L. 19. 15 καὶ ἐγένετο ἐν τῷ ἐπανελθεῖν αὐτὸν... καὶ (om. syr. latt.) εἶπεν, 9. 28 ἐγ. δὲ μετὰ τοὺς λόγους τούτους, ὡσεὶ ἡμέραι ὀκτὼ (§ 33, 2) καὶ (om. א*BH latt. syr.)... ἀνέβη, cp. A. 5. 7 (here all MSS. read καί), although in constructions of this kind the καί is more often omitted: Mc. 4. 4 καὶ ἐγένετο ἐν τῷ σπείρειν, ὃ μὲν ἔπεσεν κ.τ.λ., Mt. 7. 28 etc.; the ἐγένετο which is purely pleonastic owes its origin solely to a disinclination to begin a sentence with a statement of time (§ 80, 1). Another Hebraistic use of καί is to begin an apodosis[1]: L. 2. 21 καὶ ὅτε ἐπλήσθησαν..., καὶ (om. D) ἐκλήθη κ.τ.λ., 7. 12 ὡς δὲ ἤγγισεν... καὶ ἰδοὺ ἐξεκομίζετο κ.τ.λ., where the reading of D shows that this use is scarcely different from the use with ἐγένετο, viz. ἐγένετο δὲ ὡς ἤγγιζεν..., ἐξεκομίζετο, cp. also A. 1. 10 (καὶ ἰδού), 10. 17 (καὶ ἰδ. CD al., אAB omit καί), Ap. 3. 20 after a sentence beginning with ἐὰν (AP omit καί). But the case is different with 2 C. 2. 2 εἰ γὰρ ἐγὼ λυπῶ ὑμᾶς, καὶ τίς ὁ εὐφραίνων με, i.e. 'who then,' as Winer correctly explains it, comparing Mc. 10. 26 καὶ τίς δύναται σωθῆναι (cp. also Mc. 9. 12 D: εἰ Ἠλίας ἐλθὼν ἀποκαθιστάνει πάντα, καὶ πῶς γέγραπται... ἵνα... ἐξουθενηθῇ;), Jo. 9. 36, 14. 22 א al. (a classical use, Xenoph. Cyr. v. 4. 13 etc., Kühner ii.² 791 f.); Ph. 1. 22 should accordingly

---

[1] Found also in Homer, e.g. Il. A. 478.

§ 77. 6–8.] *PARTICLES (CONJUNCTIONS).* 263

be interpreted in the same way, εἰ δὲ τὸ ζῆν ἐν σαρκί, τοῦτό μοι καρπὸς ἔργου, καὶ τί αἱρήσομαι; οὐ γνωρίζω, συνέχομαι δὲ κ.τ.λ.[1]

7. **Καί** meaning '**and indeed**' (epexegetic καί as Winer calls it, cp. Kühner 791) appears in Jo. 1. 16 καὶ χάριν ἀντὶ χάριτος, 1 C. 3. 5, 15. 38 καὶ ἑκάστῳ; with a demonstrative it gives emphasis, καὶ τοῦτον ἐσταυρωμένον 1 C. 2. 2, καὶ τοῦτο *idque* R. 13. 11, 1 C. 6. 6, 8 (in 8 there is a v.l. καὶ ταῦτα, as in H. 11. 12 and in class. Greek, Kühner ibid.). With A. 16. 15 ὡς δὲ ἐβαπτίσθη, καὶ ὁ οἶκος αὐτῆς ('and likewise,' 'together with'; so 18. 2) cp. Aristoph. Ran. 697 f. οἳ μεθ' ὑμῶν πολλὰ δὴ χοῖ πατέρες ἐναυμάχησαν. It is used after **πολύς** before a second adjective, pleonastically according to our usage (a classical and literary use), in A. 25. 7 πολλὰ καὶ βαρέα αἰτιώματα (Tit. 1. 10?). It is *not* used as in class. Greek after ὁ αὐτός, ὁμοίως and the like (Kühner 361 note 18).—For **καί** '**also**' in and after sentences of comparison vide infra § 78, 1; it = 'even' in Mt. 5. 46 etc., and before a comparative in 11. 9, but in H. 8. 6 ὅσῳ καὶ κρείττονος κ.τ.λ. the καί is the same as that in comparative sentences; there is a tendency to use it after διό, διὰ τοῦτο to introduce the result, L. 1. 35, 11. 49. On καὶ **γάρ** see § 78, 6; a kindred use to this (καί occupying another position) is seen in H. 7. 26 τοιοῦτος γὰρ ἡμῖν καὶ ἔπρεπεν ἀρχιερεύς. In μετὰ καὶ Κλήμεντος Ph. 4. 3 it is pleonastic, cp. Clem. Cor. i. 65. 1 σὺν καὶ Φουρτυνάτῳ. On καὶ ... δέ vide infra 12. A peculiar (but classical) use of it is after an interrogative, as in τί καὶ βαπτίζονται 1 C. 15. 29, 'why at all?' (or 'even as much as'), cp. R. 8. 24, L. 13. 7, Kühner 798.

8. **Τέ** by no means appears in all writings of the N.T., and would not be represented to any very great extent at all but for the Acts, in which book alone there are more than twice as many instances of it as occur in the rest of the N.T. together (the instances are equally distributed over all parts of the Acts; next to the Acts the greatest number of instances occur in Hebrews and Romans; there are only eight instances in Luke's Gospel[2]). The use of the **simple** τέ (for τέ ... καί, τέ καί, τέ ... τέ vide infra 9) is also foreign for the most part to cultured Atticists, while the higher style of poetry uses it abundantly. In the N.T. τέ is not often used to connect single ideas (this use in classical Greek is almost confined to poetry, Kühner ii.[2] 786), as in H. 6. 5 θεοῦ ῥῆμα δυνάμεις τε μέλλοντος αἰῶνος, 9. 1, 1 C. 4. 21, cp. further infra 9; in the connection of sentences it denotes a closer connection and affinity between them: A. 2. 40 ἑτέροις τε (δέ *male* D) λόγοις πλείοσιν διεμαρτύρατο ('and likewise'), 37 κατενύγησαν τὴν

---

[1] In Ja. 4. 15 it is perfectly admissible to let the apodosis begin with καί (both) ζήσομεν instead of beginning it at καὶ ποιήσομεν, Buttm. 311 note.—Coordination with καί instead of a subordinate clause: L. 1. 49 ὁ δυνατός, καὶ ἅγιον τὸ ὄνομα αὐτοῦ (= οὗ τὸ ὄν. ἅγ.), L. 8. 12 οἱ ἀκούσαντες, εἶτα ἔρχεται, Mt. 13. 22.

[2] The simple τέ only occurs in L. 21. 11 *bis*, although here too it is followed by a καί, σεισμοί τε ('and,' τε om. AL) μεγάλοι καὶ ... λιμοὶ ... ἔσονται, φόβητρά τε ('and') καὶ σημεῖα ... ἔσται: unless this is rather a case of asyndeton, vide 9 (since τε is not a suitable word for a connecting particle). In 24. 20 for ὅπως (ὡς D) τε αὐτὸν the correct reading may be that of D ὅπως (ὡς) τοῦτον. (Still in 23. 36 D has ὄξος τε προσέφερον αὐτῷ λέγοντες.)

καρδίαν, εἶπόν τε ('and so they said'), 27. 4 f. ὑπεπλεύσαμεν τὴν Κύπρον ... τό τε πέλαγος τὸ κατὰ τὴν Κιλικίαν ... διαπλεύσαντες κ.τ.λ. (in pursuance of the course adopted).[1]

9. We find the following **correlative** combinations (meaning 'as well ... as also') καὶ ... καὶ ..., τε ... καὶ (τε καί), τε ... τε. The last (which in classical Greek is more frequent in poetry than in prose, though in prose it is commoner than a simple τε, Kühner ii.[2] 788), besides its use in οὔτε ... οὔτε etc. (inf. 10) occurs in εἴτε ... εἴτε, see § 78, 2; also in ἐάν τε ... ἐάν τε R. 14. 8 *bis*; but otherwise only in A. 26. 16 ὧν τε εἶδες ὧν τε ὀφθήσομαί σοι; the combined phrases are in this way placed side by side (often = even as ... so ...). Τε ... καί affords a closer connection than the simple καί: in Attic Greek it is generally avoided if καί would immediately follow τε, since in this case τε might appear to have no point; in the N.T. however it is found in this case as well, Mt. 22. 10 πονηρούς τε καὶ ἀγαθούς, A. 1. 1 ποιεῖν τε καὶ διδάσκειν, 2. 9 f., 4. 27, R. 1. 12 ὑμῶν τε καὶ ἐμοῦ, 3. 9 Ἰουδαίους τε καὶ Ἕλληνας, etc. The connection of Ἰουδαῖοι and Ἕλληνες is almost always made by means of τε καὶ or τε ... καί: A. 14. 1 (18. 4 ἐπειθέν τε Ἰ. καὶ Ἕλληνας, for an obvious reason), 19. 10 (without τε D), 17 (om. τε DE), 20. 21, R. 1. 16 (τε om. א*), 2. 9, 10. 12 (without τε DE), 1 C. 1. 24 (τε om. FG); but in 10. 32 we have ἀπρόσκοποι καὶ Ἰουδαίοις γίνεσθε καὶ Ἕλλησιν καὶ τῇ ἐκκλησίᾳ τοῦ θεοῦ, where the distinction of the different nationalities is kept, whereas in the other passages with τε καὶ the difference is rather removed. For καὶ ... καὶ cp. Mt. 10. 28 καὶ (not in all MSS.) ψυχὴν καὶ σῶμα, which however may mean 'even soul and body' (as is still more clearly the meaning in 8. 27 = Mc. 4. 41 = L. 8. 25 καὶ ὁ ἄνεμος καὶ ἡ θάλασσα ὑπακούουσιν αὐτῷ), L. 5. 36 καὶ τὸ καινὸν σχίσει, καὶ τῷ παλαιῷ οὐ συμφωνήσει κ.τ.λ. ('on the one hand ... on the other,' so that there is a double injury); the use is somewhat more frequent in John, ἵνα καὶ ὁ σπείρων ὁμοῦ χαίρῃ καὶ ὁ θερίζων 4. 36, where the two clauses are sharply distinguished: 7. 28 (supra 6), 11. 48 (in these two passages the particles have a less definite meaning), 12. 28, 15. 24 νῦν δὲ καὶ ἑωράκασιν καὶ ('and yet') μεμισήκασιν καὶ ἐμὲ καὶ τὸν πατέρα μου (Who appear to them to be different Persons). Paul uses a double καὶ in R. 14. 9 *bis*, 1 C. 1. 22 etc.; a peculiar instance is Ph. 4. 12 οἶδα καὶ ταπεινοῦσθαι, οἶδα καὶ περισσεύειν, where καί even in the first clause has rather the meaning of 'also.'—In longer enumerations τε (...) καὶ may be followed by a further τε, as in A. 9. 15 ἐθνῶν τε (τε om. HLP) καὶ βασιλέων υἱῶν τε Ἰσραήλ, 26. 10, Clem. Cor. i. 20. 3 (on the other hand in L. 22. 66 τὸ πρεσβυτέριον τοῦ λαοῦ, ἀρχιερεῖς τε καὶ γραμματεῖς the last words are an explanatory apposition, since otherwise the article must have been used [D καὶ ἀρχ. καὶ γρ.]); we have τε ... τε ... καὶ in H. 6. 2 (ἀναστάσεως and κρίματος being closely connected by τε ... καί), ... τε καὶ ... καὶ ... τε καὶ ... καὶ in 11. 32, an enumeration of names, where however the

---

[1] So in Clem. Cor. i. 20. 10 twice, i. 3 – ii. 1 four times. It cannot be wondered at that τε was often confused in course of transmission with δέ; thus τε is inadmissible in a parenthesis, as in A. 1. 15 אAB have ἦν τε for ἦν δὲ (infra 12).

§ 77. 9–10.] *PARTICLES (CONJUNCTIONS).* 265

first three conjunctions are wanting in אA: in this passage the τε must be taken as a connective particle and not as correlative to καί (similarly in A. 13. 1, 1 C. 1. 30), whereas in the long enumerations in A. 1. 13 and 2. 9 ff. couples are formed by means of τε καί or a simple καί, and the relation between the several couples is one of asyndeton (cp. Mt. 10. 3 f., 24. 38, R. 1. 14, 1 Tim. 1. 9, Clem. Cor. i. 3. 2, 35. 5, Herm. Mand. xii. 3. 1; in L. 6. 14 ff. there is a v.l. in אBD al. [opposed to A al.] with a *continuous* use of καί, as in the reading of all the MSS. in Mc. 3. 16 ff.).—Position of the correlative τε: where a preposition precedes which is common to the connected ideas, the τε is notwithstanding placed immediately after this preposition, A. 25. 23 σύν τε χιλιάρχοις καὶ ἀνδράσιν, 28. 23, 10. 39 (a v.l. repeats the ἐν), as also in classical Greek (Win. § 61, 6); on the other hand we have τῶν ἐθνῶν τε καὶ Ἰουδαίων A. 14. 5 (τῶν ἐ. καὶ τῶν D).

10. The use of **correlative negative clauses** with **οὔτε ... οὔτε** or **μήτε ... μήτε** respectively, and of **οὐδέ** or **μηδέ** respectively as a **connecting particle** after **negative** sentences (and of **καὶ οὐ, καὶ μή** after **positive** sentences) remains the same as in classical Greek. Therefore οὐ ..., οὔτε ... οὔτε is 'not ... neither ... nor,' Mt. 12. 32 etc.; cp. L. 9. 3 μηδὲν ..., μήτε ... μήτε κ.τ.λ. with Mt. 10. 9 f. (Winer). In 1 C. 6. 9 f. a very long enumeration which begins with οὔτε ... οὔτε etc. finally veers round to asyndeton with οὐ ... οὐ (once also in Mt. 10. 10 μή is interposed between several cases of μηδέ). Of course it often happens, as in profane writers, that οὔτε - οὐδέ, μήτε - μηδέ are confused in the MSS., as is also the case with δέ and τε (supra 8)[1]. If οὐδέ or μηδέ stands at the beginning of the whole sentence, or after an οὐ or μή within the same clause of the sentence, it then means 'not even,' 'not so much as': Mc. 8. 26 μηδὲ (μή א*) εἰς τὴν κώμην εἰσέλθῃς (with many vv.ll.; the sense requires εἴπῃς in place of εἰσέλθῃς), Mt. 6. 15 etc., Mc. 3. 20 ὥστε μὴ δύνασθαι αὐτοὺς μηδὲ (*male* μήτε אCDE al.) ἄρτον φαγεῖν.[2] The positive term corresponding to this οὐδέ is καὶ 'even,' as the positive equivalent for οὐ ..., οὐδέ etc. is a series of words strung together by καί, but the equivalent for οὔτε ... οὔτε is καὶ ... καί, or τε ... καὶ (τε): hence the reading in Mc. 14. 68 οὔτε οἶδα οὔτε ἐπίσταμαι of אBDL appears to be inadmissible, since the two perfectly synonymous words could not be connected by καὶ ... καί, τε καί, and therefore the right reading is that of AKM οὐκ ... οὐδέ (CE al. read οὐκ ... οὔτε, which seems to be the origin of the

---

[1] In L. 20. 36 οὔτε γάρ is wrongly read by אQ al. for οὐδὲ γάρ (§ 78, 6). In Ap. 9. 21 all MSS. read οὔτε several times after οὐ, as in 21. 4; in 5. 4 nearly all have οὐδεὶς .. οὔτε, but in 5. 3 they are divided: in 12. 8, 20. 4 οὐδέ preponderates (as also in Jo. 1. 25): in 7. 16, 9. 4, 21. 23 all have οὐδέ. Ja. 3. 12 is quite corrupt.

[2] The sequence οὔτε ... οὔτε ... οὔτε ... **οὐδέ** ('nor at all,' as though a *single* οὐ or οὐδαμοῦ had preceded) is perfectly admissible, A. 24. 12 f., Buttm. 315 note. But we also find μή ... μηδέ (אABCE μήτε) ... μήτε A. 23. 8, where two ideas are connected and the second is subdivided, cp. for class. exx. Kühner ii.² 829 c; accordingly in G. 1. 12 οὐδὲ γάρ ('since not even') ... παρέλαβον οὔτε ἐδιδάχθην (B al.) would be possible, though οὐδὲ ἐδ. is better attested and is more regular.

confusion). A disjunctive expression with a negative preceding may also be equivalent to οὐ..., οὐδέ, or οὐ... οὔτε... οὔτε: Mt. 5. 17 μὴ νομίσητε ὅτι ἦλθον καταλῦσαι τὸν νόμον ἢ τοὺς προφήτας = οὐκ ἢ. κατ. οὔτε τ.ν. οὔτε τ. πρ.; A. 17. 29 etc.; cp. inf. 11.—Of course a correlation of negative and positive members is allowable, though this is not a frequent construction in the N.T.: Jo. 4. 11 οὔτε ἄντλημα ἔχεις, καὶ τὸ φρέαρ ἐστὶν βαθύ (D has οὐδέ, which seems preferable), 3 Jo. 10 οὔτε αὐτὸς ἐπιδέχεται ... καὶ τοὺς βουλομένους κωλύει (in class. Greek οὔτε ... καί is very rare, Kühner ii.² 831 a). A 27. 20 μήτε... μήτε... τε (however this τε is hardly a correlative, but rather a connecting particle). Καὶ οὐ after **negative** sentences, as in Mt. 15. 32 (Jo. 5. 37 f. οὔτε ... οὔτε ... καί ... οὐ) does not imply a correlation, but an independent continuation, Buttm. p. 316. (In L. 18. 2 we have τὸν θεὸν οὐ φοβούμενος καὶ ἄνθρωπον οὐκ ἐντρεπόμενος, somewhat incorrectly, but in v. 4 אB etc. read οὐδὲ ἄνθρ. ἐντρέπομαι while AD etc. again read καί...οὐκ.)

11. The **disjunctive** particle is ἤ, also ἢ καί 'or even' (L. 18. 11 al.); correlatively ἤ...ἤ 'either...or' (for which we have the classical ἤτοι ... ἤ in R. 6. 16, Kühner ii.² 837); in addition to this we have εἴτε... εἴτε sive ... sive, which strictly introduces subordinate clauses, but in virtue of an ellipse may also (as in class. Greek) be used without a finite verb, as in 2 C. 5. 10 ἵνα κομίσηται ἕκαστος ... εἴτε ἀγαθὸν εἴτε κακόν, Ε. 6. 8, Ph. 1. 18 etc., and not solely in a disjunctive sense, but equally well (as τε is included in it) as a copula; cp. § 78, 2. Ἤ also approximates, especially in negative sentences, to the meaning of a copula: A. 1. 7 οὐ ... χρόνους ἢ καιρούς (synonymes), 11. 8 κοινὸν ἢ ἀκάθαρτον οὐδέποτε κ.τ.λ., cp. 10. 18 οὐδέποτε ἔφαγον πᾶν κοινὸν καὶ (ἢ CD al.) ἀκάθαρτον: Jo. 8. 14 οἶδα πόθεν ἦλθον καὶ ποῦ ὑπάγω· ὑμεῖς δὲ οὐκ οἴδατε πόθεν ἔρχομαι ἢ ποῦ ὑπάγω, 1 C. 11. 27 ὃς ἂν ἐσθίῃ ... ἢ πίνῃ ... ἀναξίως; similarly in interrogative sentences, which in meaning are equivalent to a negative sentence, 1 Th. 2. 10 τίς γὰρ ἡμῶν ἐλπὶς ἢ χαρὰ ἢ στέφανος (in 20 the positive statement runs ἡ δόξα καὶ ἡ χαρά). Ἤ an in interrogative sentences, vide supra 2, is sharply disjunctive ('otherwise this must be the case'). A singular instance of its use is in 1 Th. 2. 19 (vide supra) τίς γὰρ ... στέφανος; ἤ (ἤ is wanting in א*) οὐχὶ καὶ ὑμεῖς...; where ἤ has probably been foisted into the text for the sake of the τίς ('who else but'); cp. Jo. 13. 10 v.l. (and ἀλλ' ἤ inf. 13).

12. The **adversative** particles most in use are δέ and ἀλλά, the former of which has its correlative in μέν, while the latter usually refers to a preceding negative ('but on the contrary'). This reference, however, may also be expressed, though not so strongly, by δέ: A. 12. 9 οὐκ ᾔδει ... ἐδόκει δέ ('but rather'), 14, H. 4. 13, 6. 12 etc. A distinction must also be made between contradiction (ἀλλά) and antithesis (δέ): H. 2. 8 οὐδὲν ἀφῆκεν αὐτῷ ἀνυπότακτον· νῦν δὲ οὔπω ὁρῶμεν αὐτῷ τὰ πάντα ὑποτεταγμένα ('but,' 'on the other hand'). The correlation of μέν and δέ, which is so essentially characteristic of the classical Greek style, is very largely reduced in the N.T., so that μέν is wholly absent from Ap., 2 P., 1, 2 and 3 Jo.

2 Th., 1 Tim., Tit. (μέν in 1. 15 is spurious) and Philemon, and is practically unrepresented in Ja. (3. 17 πρῶτον μὲν ... ἔπειτα, an antithesis also found in classical Greek without δέ; cp. Jo. 11. 6, 1 C. 12. 28), Eph. (4. 11 τοὺς μὲν ... τοὺς δὲ), Col. (2. 23, an anacoluthon without an answering clause), and 1 Th. (2. 18 ἐγὼ μὲν Παῦλος, the antithetical clause being omitted but sufficiently intimated by μέν; classical Greek has a similar use, Hdt. iii. 3 ἐμοὶ μὲν οὐ πιθανός ['to me at least'], Kühner 813 f.); it is also comparatively rare in the Gospels as a whole, and only occurs with any frequency in Acts, Hebrews (1 Peter) and some of the Pauline epistles.[1] Moreover a large number of these instances, especially those in Luke, are instances of the resumptive μὲν οὖν, § 78, 5, where the μέν in very few cases indicates a real antithesis: other examples of anacoluthic μέν are also fairly common in Luke, where the style and structure of the sentence are more or less harshly violated, as in L. 8. 5 f. ὃ μὲν ... καὶ ἕτερον (occasioned by a development of the idea being interposed: so in Mc. 4. 4 f.), A. 1. 1, 3. 13, 21, 17. 30, 27. 21 (cp. also 2 C. 11. 4, H. 7. 11): not to mention the instances, where the omission of δέ is excusable or even classically correct, viz. πρῶτον μὲν R. 1. 8, 3. 2, 1 C. 11. 18 (perhaps 'from the very outset'), A. 28. 22 περὶ μὲν γὰρ τῆς αἱρέσεως ταύτης γνωστὸν ἡμῖν ἐστὶν κ.τ.λ. ('so much we do indeed know'), R. 10. 1 ἡ μὲν εὐδοκία κ.τ.λ. ('so far as my wishes are concerned'), 11. 13 ἐφ᾽ ὅσον μὲν οὖν εἰμι ἐγὼ ἐθνῶν ἀπόστολος κ.τ.λ., cp. Kühner 814.—In Jo. 7. 12 οἱ μὲν is followed by ἄλλοι (ἄ. δὲ BTX) with the asyndeton of which this gospel is so fond (§ 79, 4); in H. 12. 9 οὐ πολλῷ δὲ (ℵ^cD*, the other MSS. omit δὲ) is probably the correct reading; we have instances of μὲν ... ἀλλά, μὲν ... πλήν (Kühn. 812 f.) in A. 4. 16, R. 14. 20, 1 C. 14. 17: L. 22. 22 ; and a kindred use to this occurs in Mt. 17. 11 f. Ἠλίας μὲν ἔρχεται ..., λέγω δὲ ὑμῖν, with which cp. Mc. 9. 12 μὲν ... (om. DL), 13 ἀλλά ..., where μέν means 'indeed,' 'certainly,' and δέ (or ἀλλά) is an emphatic 'but.'—Δέ introduces a parenthesis in A. 12. 3 ἦσαν δὲ αἱ ἡμέραι τῶν ἀζύμων, cp. 1. 15 ἦν δὲ κ.τ.λ. (τε is wrongly read by ℵAB al.): 4. 13 ἐπεγίνωσκον δὲ (so D reads instead of τε). It introduces an explantion or a climax ('but,' 'and indeed ') in R. 3. 22 δικαιοσύνη δὲ θεοῦ, 9. 30, 1. C. 2. 6, Ph. 2. 8.—We find καὶ ... δὲ in connection with each other in A. 2. 44, 3. 24 καὶ πάντες δὲ κ.τ.λ., 'and also all,' 22. 29 καὶ ὁ χιλίαρχος δὲ, Mt. 16. 18 κἀγὼ δὲ σοὶ λέγω, Jo. 8. 16 etc. (Tisch. on 6. 51), etc.: whereas δὲ καὶ means 'but also,' A. 22. 28 etc.

13. Ἀλλά, besides its use in opposition to a preceding οὐ[2] (with which must be classed οὐ μόνον ... ἀλλὰ καὶ[3]), is also found with οὐ,

---

[1] Μέν is not unfrequently interpolated in the inferior MSS., Buttm. p. 313. Also in Clem. Cor. i. (62, 1 anacol.), Cor. ii., Barnabas (i. 2 anacol.) and Hermas it is only rarely represented.

[2] Οὐ ... ἀλλά may also mean 'not so much ... as,' Mc. 9. 37 οὐκ ἐμὲ δέχεται, ἀλλὰ τὸν ἀποστείλαντά με, Mt. 10. 20, Jo. 12. 44, A. 5. 4 etc., the first member of the sentence being not entirely negatived, but only made subordinate.

[3] Οὐ μόνον ... ἀλλά is used without a καί if the second member includes the first, A. 19. 26, 1 Jo. 5. 6, or as in Ph. 1. 12 ἀλλὰ πολλῷ μᾶλλον κ.τ.λ.

in opposition to a foregoing positive sentence ('but not'): 1 C. 10. 23 πάντα ἔξεστιν, ἀλλ' οὐ πάντα συμφέρει, ibid. 5, Mt. 24. 6; it is further used where no negative precedes or follows it, as in 1 C. 6. 11 καὶ ταῦτά τινες ἦτε, ἀλλὰ ἀπελούσασθε, ἀλλὰ ἡγιάσθητε, where one can easily supply 'but you are so no longer' and render ἀλλά by 'on the contrary': 1 C. 3. 6 ἐγὼ ἐφύτευσα, Ἀπολλῶς ἐπότισεν, ἀλλὰ ὁ θεὸς ηὔξανεν (but He Who gave the increase was not I nor he, but God), 7. 7, Jo. 16. 2. It stands at the beginning of the sentence with or without a negative: R. 10. 16 ἀλλ' οὐ πάντες ὑπήκουσαν, where the difference is more strongly marked than it would be with δέ, 10. 18 f. ἀλλὰ λέγω..., 11. 4, 1 C. 12. 24, 15. 35; similarly before commands or requests, A. 10. 20, 26. 16, Mt. 9. 18, Mc. 9. 22 etc. A similar meaning is expressed in Mt. and Lc. (not in Acts) by πλήν, 'yet,' 'howbeit' (in Acts and Mc. it is a preposition meaning 'except' as in class. Greek, § 40, 6; we also have πλὴν ὅτι [class.] 'except that' in A. 20. 23): Mt. 26. 39 (L. 22. 43) πλὴν οὐχ ὡς ἐγὼ θέλω ἀλλ' ὡς σύ,=Mc. 14. 36 ἀλλ' οὐχ κ.τ.λ.; Mt. 11. 22, 24, 26. 64 πλὴν λέγω ὑμῖν, but in Mc. 9. 13 ἀλλὰ λέγω ὑμῖν (cp. Mt. 17. 12 λέγω δὲ ὑμῖν); Mt. 18. 7 πλὴν οὐαὶ κ.τ.λ.,=L. 17. 1 οὐαὶ δὲ (πλὴν οὐαὶ δὲ אBDL); it even takes the place of an ἀλλά corresponding to a negative in L. 23. 28 μὴ κλαίετε ἐπ' ἐμέ, πλὴν ἐφ' ἑαυτὰς κλαίετε (ἀλλ' D); 12. 29, 31 (D ζητεῖτε δὲ); it is obvious that πλήν was the regular word in the vulgar language. (In Paul it has rather the meaning of 'only,'[1] 'in any case,' being used at the end of a discussion to emphasize the essential point, 1 C. 11. 11, E. 5. 33, Ph. 3. 16, 4. 14; so also in Ap. 2. 25, and there is a parallel use (?) in Ph. 1. 18 τί γάρ; πλὴν (om. B) ὅτι (om. DEKL) παντὶ τρόπῳ ... Χριστὸς καταγγέλλεται, καὶ ἐν τούτῳ χαίρω, where τί γάρ appears to mean as in R. 3. 3 'what matters it?', and πλήν, with or without ὅτι, seems to denote 'at all events,' and is moreover superfluous.)—**Ἀλλά** is used after an **oratorical question** as in class. Greek, in Jo. 12. 27 τί εἴπω; πάτερ, σῶσόν με ...; ἀλλὰ διὰ τοῦτο ἦλθον κ.τ.λ. (there are simpler sentences in 7. 49, 1 C. 10. 20); or in a succession of questions (the answer being either given in each case or suppressed), Mt. 11. 8 f.=L. 7. 24 ff. τί ἐξήλθατε...; ... ἀλλὰ τί ἐξήλθατε; κ.τ.λ. (class.). A peculiar instance is H. 3. 16 τίνες γὰρ ἀκούσαντες παρεπίκραναν; ἀλλ' οὐ πάντες οἱ ἐξελθόντες ἐξ Αἰγύπτου ... ; where however the ἀλλ' (cp. the Syriac VS.) may have only originated from a misunderstanding of the preceding τίνες as if it were τινές.[2]—**Ἀλλά** is used in the **apodosis** after εἰ, ἐάν, εἴπερ, meaning 'still,' 'at least' (class.): 1 C. 4. 15 ἐὰν μυρίους παιδαγωγοὺς ἔχητε ἐν Χριστῷ, ἀλλ' οὐ πολλοὺς πατέρας, 2 C. 4. 16, 11. 6, (13. 4 v.l.), Col. 2. 5 etc.; cp. ἀλλά γε ὑμῖν εἰμι 1 C. 9. 2 (supra 4).—Besides its use in this passage ἀλλά γε καί ... is found in L. 24. 21 (vide ibid.), introducing an accessory idea in an emphatic way,

---

[1] Cp. Aristotle's use, Bonitz Index Arist. s.v. πλήν.

[2] The use is different in L. 17. 7 f. τίς ... ἐρεῖ αὐτῷ ... ἀλλ' οὐχὶ ἐρεῖ αὐτῷ ... ; 'and not rather.' D here omits οὐχί, according to which the second half of the sentence is not interrogative.

§ 77. 13–14.]   *PARTICLES (CONJUNCTIONS).*   269

cp. ἀλλὰ καί ibid. 22, 12. 7, 16. 21, 'not only this, but also,' as in Ph. 1. 18 χαίρω, ἀλλὰ καὶ χαρήσομαι, 2 C. 11. 1 ὄφελον ἀνείχεσθε..., ἀλλὰ καὶ ἀνέχεσθε (not only will I utter the wish, but I entreat you directly); to this corresponds ἀλλ' οὐδέ in 1 C. 3. 2 οὔπω γὰρ ἐδύνασθε. ἀλλ' οὐδὲ ἔτι νῦν δύνασθε, A. 19. 2, L. 23. 15. The simple ἀλλά also has this force of introducing an accessory idea, in 2 C. 7. 11 πόσην ὑμῖν κατηργάσατο σπουδήν, ἀλλά ('and not only that, but also') ἀπολογίαν, ἀλλὰ ἀγανάκτησιν, ἀλλὰ φόβον κ.τ.λ. (ἀλλά 6 times repeated). We further have ἀλλὰ μενοῦν γε (without γε in BDF al.) καί (om. ℵ*) ἡγοῦμαι Ph. 3. 8, cp. inf. 14.—Notice must be taken of the elliptical ἀλλ' ἵνα 'on the contrary (but) this has happened (or a similar phrase) in order that,' Mc. 14. 49, Jo. 1. 8, 9. 3, 13. 18, 15. 25; but this must be distinguished from Mc. 4. 22 οὐ γὰρ ἔστιν τι κρυπτόν, ἐὰν μὴ ἵνα φανερωθῇ· οὐδὲ ἐγένετο ἀπόκρυφον, ἀλλ' ἵνα ἔλθῃ εἰς φανερόν, where ἀλλ' = εἰ μή 'save that,' and from the use of ἄλλ' (*i.e.* ἄλλο) ἤ in L. 12. 51 οὐχί, λέγω ὑμῖν, ἀλλ' ἤ (D ἀλλὰ) διαμερισμόν, 'nothing else but' (classical, Kühner ii.[2] 824, 5 and 6, 825 note 4), cp. 2 C. 1. 13 οὐ γὰρ ἄλλα ... ἀλλ' (ἄλλ' om. BFG) ἤ (om. A) ἅ (om. AD*) ἀναγινώσκετε[1] (ἀλλ' ἤ is an interpolation in 1 C. 3. 5), Clem. Cor. i. 41. 2.

14. Other **adversative** particles are **μέντοι** 'however,' οὐ(δεὶς) μέντοι Jo. 4. 27, 7. 13, 20. 5, 21. 4 (Herm. Sim. vi. 1. 6), **ὅμως μέντοι** 12. 42; this particle occurs very rarely except in John, viz. ὁ μέντοι θεμέλιος 2 Tim. 2. 19, Ja. 2. 8, Jd. 8 (in the two last passages with a weaker meaning = 'but.'). Ὅμως apart from the instance quoted occurs only again in 1 C. 14. 7, G. 3. 15, where it is used in a peculiar way: ὅμως τὰ ἄψυχα φωνὴν διδόντα ..., ἐάν διαστολὴν φθόγγου μὴ δῷ, πῶς γνωσθήσεται κ.τ.λ., and ὅμως ἀνθρώπου κεκυρωμένην διαθήκην οὐδεὶς ἀθετεῖ; the latter passage is explained (Fritzsche) as a substitution for καίπερ ἀνθρ., ὅμως οὐδεὶς ἀθ. 'if it be only a man's will, yet,' somewhat like Xenoph. Cyrop. v. 1. 26 σὺν σοὶ ὅμως καὶ ἐν τῇ πολεμίᾳ ὄντες θαρροῦμεν, Kühner p. 645; but as in both passages a comparison is introduced by it, and as οὕτως also follows in the passage of 1 Cor., it appears to be rather an instance of the old word ὁμῶς 'in like manner' being brought into play, which should accordingly be rendered simply by 'also' or 'likewise.'[2]—**Καίτοι** in classical Greek means 'and yet,' and rarely takes a participle with the meaning 'although,' cp. § 74, 2; in the N.T. it introduces a **parenthesis** in Jo. 4. 2 καίτοιγε (§ 77, 4) 'Ιησοῦς αὐτὸς οὐκ ἐβάπτιζεν κ.τ.λ. (= 'although He did not baptize'), and has a more independent character in A. 14. 17, though here also it may be rendered 'although' (on A. 17. 27 see § 74, 2; for καίτοι with a participle H. 4. 3).—**Καὶ μήν** 'and yet' (class.) does not occur in the N.T.; but Hermas uses it in Mand. iv. 1.

---

[1] Ἀλλ' is rendered pleonastic by a preceding ἄλλος, but the use is nevertheless not unclassical, Kühner 824, 6.

[2] Clem. Hom. i. 15 (= Epitom. 14) has καὶ ὁμῶς ἔμαθον καὶ τῷ πυλῶνι ἐπέστην, = ἅμα 'at the same time'; xix. 23 καὶ ὁμῶς τοιαῦτά τινα μυρία κ.τ.λ., = καὶ ὁμοίως. (In 1 C. l.c. the accentuation ὁμῶς is supported by Wilke Neut. Rhetorik p. 225.)

8, v. 1. 7, with an intensifying force in an answer, somewhat like *immo* (class., Kühner ii.² 690.—Μὲν οὖν in classical Greek is specially used in answers with heightening or corrective force, and is always so placed that the μέν here as in other cases has another word before it; but in the N.T. μενοῦν or μενοῦνγε with the same meaning stands at the beginning of a sentence: L. 11. 28 μενοῦν (ins. γε B³CD al.) μακάριοι οἱ κ.τ.λ. ('rather'), R. 9. 20 (γε is omitted by B only), 10. 18 μενοῦνγε (μενοῦνγε om. FG); we also find ἀλλὰ μενοῦν(γε) in Ph. 3. 8, vide supra 13. Cp. Phryn. Lob. 342. But the classical position of the word is seen in 1 C. 6. 4 βιωτικὰ μὲν οὖν κριτήρια κ.τ.λ., cp. 7 (οὖν om. ℵ*D*).

§ 78. PARTICLES (continued).

1. The **comparative particles** which are followed by a subordinate clause are ὡς and ὥσπερ, also frequently in nearly all writers καθώς, a Hellenistic word, see Phrynicus p. 425 Lob., who strongly disapproves of it and requires instead καθά (only in Mt. 27. 10 O.T. and L. 1. 2 according to D and Euseb., certainly the right reading, see p. 49 on παρέδοσαν) or καθό (which is found in R. 8. 26, 2 C. 8. 12, 1 P. 4. 13); the equally Attic form καθάπερ occurs only in Paul and Hebrews. The uses of ὡς are manifold, and some of them, as being too well known and commonplace, need not be discussed at all in this grammar. The **correlative** terms are ὡς (ὥσπερ, καθώς, καθάπερ) — οὕτως or οὕτως καί; or the term corresponding to ὡς may be simply καί, as in Mt. 6. 10, or again καί may be attached to ὡς and may even stand in both portions of the comparison, as in R. 1. 13 ἵνα τινὰ καρπὸν σχῶ καὶ ἐν ὑμῖν, καθὼς καὶ ἐν τοῖς λοιποῖς ἔθνεσιν, Mt. 18. 33 etc. (as in class. Greek, Kühner p. 799, 2).—When used to introduce a sentence ὡς and more particularly καθώς may also to some extent denote a reason: R. 1. 28 καθὼς οὐκ ἐδοκίμασαν τὸν θεὸν ἔχειν ἐν ἐπιγνώσει, παρέδωκεν αὐτοὺς ὁ θεὸς κ.τ.λ. ('even as'='since,' *quandoquidem*), 1 C. 1. 6, 5. 7, E. 1. 4, Ph. 1. 7 (Mt. 6. 12 ὡς καὶ ἡμεῖς ἀφήκαμεν,=L. 11. 4 καὶ γὰρ αὐτοὶ ἀφίομεν), cp. ὡς with a partic. § 74, 6.—A parable is introduced by ὡς in Mc. 13. 34, by ὥσπερ γάρ (γάρ om. D) in 25. 14, though no corresponding term follows, and there is also no close connection with the preceding words, cp. 81, 2. —Before ideas the place of ὡς is taken by ὡσεί (especially in the Gospels and Acts, also in Herm. Sim. vi. 2. 5, ix. 11. 5), with much variety of reading in the MSS.; this particle is also used before numerical ideas = 'about,' Mt. 14. 21 (D ὡς), Jo. 4. 6 (ὡς has preponderant evidence) etc. (classical); ὡσπερεί (in comparisons) only occurs in 1 C. 15. 8 (ὥσπερ D*) and as a v.l. in 4. 13; ὡσάν (ὡς ἄν) only in 2 C. 10. 9 ὡσὰν ('as it were') ἐκφοβεῖν, cp. § 70, 5. A very wide use is made of ὡς in connection with a **predicate**, whether in the nominative, Mt. 22. 30 ὡς ἄγγελοι θεοῦ εἰσιν, 18. 3 ἐὰν μὴ γένησθε ὡς τὰ παιδία, 1 C. 7. 7 ἐὰν μείνωσιν ὡς κἀγώ, or in the accusative, L. 15. 19 ποίησόν με ὡς ἕνα τῶν μισθίων σου, especially with the verbs λογίζεσθαι, ἡγεῖσθαι etc., § 34, 5 (all unclassical uses; but in the LXX. we have in Gen. 3. 5 ἔσεσθε ὡς θεοί, = class. ἰσόθεοι, or ἴσα καὶ

θεοὶ according to Thuc. iii. 14, cp. [§ 76, 1] εἶναι ἴσα θεῷ Ph. 2. 6). With τὴν ἴσην ὡς καὶ ἡμῖν A. 11. 17 cp. classical exx. in Kühner 361, note 18. Πορεύεσθαι ὡς (ἕως אABE) ἐπὶ τὴν θάλασσαν A. 17. 14 is a Hellenistic usage, ὡς ἐπὶ = *versus* in Polyb. i. 29. 1 etc., see Wetstein ad loc.; ὡς τάχιστα ibid. 15 is classical (literary language; § 44, 3). On ὡς with a partic. and in abbreviated sentences see § 74, 6. On exclamatory ὡς § 76, 3; ὡς (ὡς ὅτι) in assertions § 70, 2; on temporal ὡς infra 3; with an infinitive § 69, 3.

2. The **hypothetical** particles are **εἰ** and **ἐάν**, see § 65, 4 and 5; Paul (and 1 Pet. 2. 3, but א*AB read εἰ) also uses **εἴπερ** 'if on the other hand,' R. 3. 30 (v.l. ἐπείπερ), 8. 9, 17, 2 Th. 1. 6, referring to an alternative condition (or fact); **ἐάνπερ** is similarly used in H. 3 (6 v.l.) 14, 6. 3; but the particle is differently used in 1 C. 8. 5 καὶ γὰρ εἴπερ εἰσὶν λεγόμενοι θεοὶ..., ἀλλ᾽ ἡμῖν εἷς ὁ θεός, where it has a concessive sense, 'however true it may be that,' as in Homer (Kühner 991, note 2)[1]. **Εἴγε** is similarly used, but makes a more definite assumption (G. Hermann), § 77, 4. The correlative terms in use are **εἴτε... εἴτε** (ἐάν τε... ἐάν τε R. 14. 8 twice), only found in Paul and 1 Peter, either with a finite verb, as in 1 C. 10. 31 εἴτε οὖν ἐσθίετε εἴτε πίνετε εἴτε τι ποιεῖτε, πάντα εἰς δόξαν θεοῦ ποιεῖτε, 'whether it be that... or still more frequently without a verb by abbreviation (classical, Kühner 839), ibid. 3. 21 f. πάντα γὰρ ὑμῶν ἐστιν, εἴτε Παῦλος εἴτε Ἀπολλῶς εἴτε Κηφᾶς, where perhaps no definite verb can be supplied, but the meaning is 'whether one mentions,' 'whether it be,' 'whether one is concerned with'[2]; similarly 13. 8 εἴτε δὲ προφητεῖαι, καταργηθήσονται, εἴτε γλῶσσαι, παύσονται, εἴτε κ.τ.λ., and R. 12. 6 ff. ἔχοντες δὲ χαρίσματα... εἴτε προφητείαν (sc. ἔχοντες), κατὰ τὴν..., εἴτε διακονίαν, ἐν..., εἴτε ὁ **διδάσκων**, ἐν τῇ διδασκαλίᾳ· εἴτε ὁ παρακαλῶν, ἐν κ.τ.λ. The meaning of εἴτε... εἴτε in such passages approximates very closely to that of καί... καί, and the construction is also of the same character as that with καί; the passage R. 12. 7 like other cases of enumeration (R. 2. 17-20; § 79, 3) concludes with an asyndeton, ὁ μεταδιδοὺς ἐν ἁπλότητι κ.τ.λ.—Further correlative terms are **εἰ μέν... εἰ δέ**, as in A. 18. 14 f.; here we may note the thoroughly classical suppression of the first apodosis in L. 13. 9 κἂν μὲν ποιήσῃ καρπόν (sc. it is well)· εἰ δὲ μήγε, ἐκκόψεις αὐτήν (cp. Kühner 986). On εἰ δὲ μή, εἰ δὲ μήτε (the second protasis being abbreviated) see § 77, 4; on εἰ (ἐὰν) μή (τι) 'except,' 'except that' see §§ 65, 6 : 75, 3. In imitation of Hebrew εἰ is used after formulas of swearing (= Hebr. אִם): Mc. 8. 12 ἀμὴν λέγω ὑμῖν, εἰ ('there shall **not**') δοθήσεται τῇ γενεᾷ ταύτῃ σημεῖον (cp. Mt. 16. 4 a principal sen-

---

[1] We also have 1 C. 15. 15 ὃν (τὸν Χρ.) οὐκ ἤγειρεν, εἴπερ ἄρα νεκροὶ οὐκ ἐγείρονται, but the clause εἴπερ... ἐγείρ. is absent (through homoeoteleuton? cp. 16) in DE and other witnesses; the sense can perfectly well dispense with it, and is better without it; moreover the classical use of ἄρα ('as they say') is remarkable. Here also εἴπερ means 'if on the other hand' (as they say).

[2] For this in 2 C. 8. 23 we have εἴτε ὑπὲρ Τίτου, κοινωνὸς ἐμὸς κ.τ.λ., but here again the sentence continues in the nominative, εἴτε ἀδελφοὶ ἡμῶν, ἀπόστολοι ἐκκλησιῶν.

tence with οὐ), H. 3. 11=4. 3 O.T.—On concessive εἰ καί, ἐὰν καί etc. see § 65, 6; on εἰ in indirect and direct questions, and its use to express expectation (also expressed by εἴ πως, *si forte*) see §§ 65, 1 and 6; 77, 2.

3. The **temporal** particles, used to denote time **when**, are ὅτε, ὅταν, ὁπότε (ἐπειδή is generally causal, as is ἐπειδήπερ; ἐπειδή in temporal sense only occurs in L. 7. 1 with vv.ll. ἐπεί, ὅτε), and exceptionally in Paul ἡνίκα (a literary word, but also found in LXX. *e.g.* Exod. 1. 10, Deut. 7. 12) 2 C. 3. 15 f. from LXX. Exod. 34. 34 (a particle which strictly refers to a period of an hour or a year, but is already in Attic used interchangeably with ὅτε). Another equally rare word is ὁπότε, if it is correctly read in L. 6. 3 ὁπότε (ὅτε ℵBCDL al., as in Mt., Mc.) ἐπείνασεν. In addition to these we find ὡς not unfrequently used in the narrative of Luke (Gospel and Acts) and John: L. 1. 23 ὡς ἐπλήσθησαν αἱ ἡμέραι, Jo. 2. 9 ὡς δὲ ἐγεύσατο ὁ ἀρχιτρίκλινος κ.τ.λ. (classical; LXX. especially 1 Macc., Win.-Grimm); in Paul we have R. 15. 24 ὡς ἂν πορεύωμαι εἰς τὴν Σπανίαν 'in my approaching journey to Spain,' 1 C. 11. 34 ὡς ἂν ἔλθω 'when I come (shall come),' Ph. 2. 23 ὡς ἂν ἀφίδω—a use of ὡς ἄν which finds only distant parallels in classical Greek[1]; it takes the pres. indic. in G. 6. 10 ὡς καιρὸν ἔχομεν (*male* -ωμεν ℵB*) *cum*, 'now while' (Clem. Cor. ii. 8. 1, 9. 7), and in L. 12. 58 ὡς γὰρ ὑπάγεις ... ἐπ' ἄρχοντα, ἐν τῇ ὁδῷ (Mt. 5. 25 is differently expressed, using ἕως ὅτου; in Lc. ἕως ὑπάγεις would be tautological beside ἐν τῇ ὁδῷ).—Time **during which** is expressed, as in classical Greek, by ἕως (with a present), Jo. 9. 4 ἕως ἡμέρα ἐστίν, cp. 12. 35 f., where in 35 ABD al., and in 36 the same MSS. with ℵ, read ὡς, which after the instances of ὡς that have been quoted is not impossible, though the meaning 'as long as' appears more correct at least in verse 35[2]; see also Mc. 6. 45, Jo. 21. 22, 1 Tim. 4. 13, § 65, 10. Elsewhere for 'as long as' we have ἕως ὅτου Mt. 5. 25 (as ἕως has become a preposition, § 40, 6), or ἄχρις οὗ H. 3. 13, A. 27. 33, or ἐν ᾧ Mc. 2. 19, L. 5. 34, Jo. 5. 7. The same expressions together with ἕως οὗ, ἄχρι, μέχρι, μέχρις οὗ when used with the aor. conj. (or fut. indic.) mean '**until**,' § 65, 9 and 10.—'**Before**' is πρίν, πρίν ἤ, usually with an infinitive; also πρὸ τοῦ with an infin., ibid.

4. For the **final** particles **ἵνα, ὅπως, μή** see § 65, 2; on the extended use of ἵνα, § 69; on μή, μήπως, μήποτε after φοβεῖσθαι etc. § 65, 3.— For **assertions** with **ὅτι** (ὡς, ὡς ὅτι, πῶς), § 70; for indirect questions with εἰ (πότερον ... ἤ Jo. 7. 17), § 77, 2.

5. The **consecutive subordinating** particles are ὥστε, see § 69, 3, and ἵνα, ibid.—With a **co-ordinate** construction **οὖν** is particularly frequent, being one of the commonest of the particles in the N.T., and fairly represented in all writings, though a far larger use is made of

---

[1] Hdt. iv. 172 τῶν δὲ ὡς ἕκαστός οἱ μιχθῇ, διδοῖ δῶρον. But the LXX. has the same use, *e.g.* in Jos. 2. 14; also Herm. Vis. iii. 8. 9.

[2] In modern Greek ὥς (from ἕως) also means 'until'; but in the N.T. the two words are not elsewhere confused (ὥστε with an inf. = 'until' in 'Jo.' 8. 9 D?), and we should therefore perhaps write with ℵ in verse 35 ἕως 'as long as,' and in verse 36 ὡς *quando* 'now when.'

it in narrative than in epistolary style, and the greatest of all in John's Gospel (whereas in the Johannine Epistles it only occurs in 3 Jo. 8 [being interpolated in 1 Jo. 2. 24, 4. 19]). Of course it does not always imply a strictly causal connection, but may be used in a looser way of a temporal connection, and therefore to resume or continue the narrative. Luke is accustomed in the Acts, if the narrative sentence begins with a noun or pronoun (or a participle with the article), to emphasize the οὖν by the addition of μέν, which need not be succeeded by a contrasted clause with δέ: 1. 6 οἱ μὲν οὖν συνελθόντες κ.τ.λ., 18 οὗτος μὲν οὖν κ.τ.λ., 2. 41 οἱ μὲν οὖν ἀποδεξάμενοι, 9. 31 αἱ μὲν οὖν ἐκκλησίαι etc.; this combination of particles is used sometimes to state what further took place, sometimes to summarize the events which have been previously narrated, before passing on to something new (cp. for the class. use Kühner 711); the same use occurs in Luke's Gospel 3. 18 πολλὰ μὲν οὖν καὶ ἕτερα παρακαλῶν εὐηγγελίζετο τὸν λαόν (the only instance of μὲν οὖν in that Gospel). The simple οὖν is used after a participle in A. 10. 23 (15. 2 v.l.), 16. 11, 25. 17 (cp. 26. 22 etc.); in Luke's Gospel only in 23. 16=22; D has it also in 5. 7. Οὖν is used after parenthetical remarks to indicate a recurrence to the original subject in Jo. 4. 45, 6. 24, 1 C. 8. 4, 11. 20 (also classical; but the classical δὲ οὖν to indicate this recurrence is unrepresented). The interrogative οὐκοῦν 'therefore,' 'then' (Kühner 715 f.) occurs only in Jo. 18. 37 οὐκοῦν βασιλεὺς εἶ σύ; On μὲν οὖν, μενοῦν see § 77. 14.—Another consecutive particle is ἄρα 'therefore,' 'consequently,' especially frequent in Paul, who sometimes makes it, as in classical Greek, the second word in the sentence, R. 7. 21 εὑρίσκω ἄρα, sometimes contrary to classical usage the first, as in R. 10. 17 ἄρα (FG ἄ. οὖν) ἡ πίστις ἐξ ἀκοῆς, 1 C. 15. 18, 2 C. 7. 12 etc. (H. 4. 9); we also find the strengthened form ἄρα οὖν R. 5. 18, 7. 3, 25, 8. 12, 9. 16, 18 etc., G. 6. 10, E. 2. 19 (om. οὖν FG), 1 Th. 5. 6, 2 Th. 2. 15. It is strengthened by γε and given the first position in the sentence in Mt. 7. 20, 17. 26, A. 11. 18 EHLP, where other mss. have ἄρα as in L. 11. 48 (for which Mt. 23. 31 uses ὥστε with indic.). Also in an apodosis after a protasis with εἰ, the simple ἄρα is always used and is always the first word: Mt. 12. 28 = L. 11. 20, 2 C. 5. 14 according to אᶜC* al. (most mss. omit εἰ, but it would easily be dropped before εἶς), G. 2. 21 (ibid. 18 interrogatively, therefore ἆρα § 77, 2), 3. 25, H. 12. 8. On ἐπεὶ ἄρα in Paul cp. inf. 6; on ἄρα, ἆρα in interrogative sentences § 77, 2.—Another quite rare particle is τοιγαροῦν (classical), 1 Th. 4. 8, H. 12. 1, placed at the beginning of a sentence; and τοίνυν is not much commoner, standing as the second word (as in class. Greek) in L. 20. 25 ACP al., as the first word (unclassical[1]) in אBL, and omitted in D (as it is in Mc. 12. 17; Mt. 22. 21 has οὖν); as second word also in 1 C. 9. 26 (in Ja. 2. 24 it is spurious), as first word in H. 13. 13 (Clem. Cor. i. 15. 1).—Another particle of kindred meaning is δή, which is found (though rarely) according to classical usage in sentences containing a request, 1 C. 6. 20 δοξάσατε δή ('therefore') τὸν

---

[1] But found in other late writers, see Lob. Phryn. 342.

θεὸν κ.τ.λ. (but ℵ* and some Latin witnesses omit δή and present an asyndeton); in L. 2. 15, A. 13. 2, 15. 36 at the beginning of a speech ('come now'); a quite different and thoroughly classical use of it occurs in Mt. 13. 23 ὃς δὴ καρποφορεῖ 'who is just the man who' (for ὃς δή D has τότε, the Vulgate and others *et*).—Lastly we have the consecutive particle διό, *i.e.* δι' ὅ, and therefore strictly used to introduce a subordinate relative sentence, but its subordinating character is forgotten, Mt. 27. 8, L. 1. 35 (A* wrongly has διότι, which is often confused with διό): in the latter passage we have the combination, also a favourite one in classical Greek,[1] διὸ καί, and the corresponding διὸ οὐδέ in 7. 7; it is frequent in the Acts and Epistles; we also have διόπερ 1 C. 8. 13, 10. 14 (in 14. 13 most MSS. read διό). Ὅθεν is similarly used in Mt. 14. 7, A. 26. 19, and often in Hebrews, *e.g.* 2. 17, 3. 1, denoting a reason like our 'hence.'[2]

6. The principal **causal subordinating** particle is ὅτι 'because,' for which Luke and Paul (H., Ja., 1 P.) also use διότι (classical). But the subordination both with ὅτι and διότι is often a very loose one (cp. διό, ὅθεν, supra 5), so that it must be translated 'for': 1 C. 1. 25 ὅτι τὸ μωρὸν τοῦ θεοῦ σοφώτερον τῶν ἀνθρώπων ἐστίν κ.τ.λ., 4. 9, 10. 17 2 C. 4. 6, 7. 8, 14, with διότι R. 1. 19, 21, 3. 20, 8. 7 (ὅτι FG) etc. A similar use is made of ἐπεί, which in the N.T. is regulary a causal particle: R. 3. 6 ἐπεὶ ('for') πῶς κρινεῖ ὁ θεὸς τὸν κόσμον, where as in other passages it has the additional meaning of 'if *otherwise*' (classical, Xenoph. Cyr. ii. 2. 31 etc.), which it has in assertions in R. 11. 6 ἐπεὶ ἡ χάρις οὐκέτι γίνεται χάρις, 22 ἐπεὶ καὶ σὺ ἐκκοπήσῃ. Ἐπειδή, which is likewise a causal particle (supra 3), has not this additional meaning, though like ὅτι it implies a loose subordination: 1 C. 14. 16 (B ἐπεί), 1. 22 (FG ἐπεί). Ἐπειδήπερ occurs only in L. 1. 1 'inasmuch as already,' referring to a fact already well known, cp. εἴπερ supra 2.—On ἐφ' ᾧ cp. supra § 43, 3; on καθώς supra 1. Καθότι (only in Luke) strictly means 'according as,' 'just as,' and is so used in A. 2. 45, 4. 35; but in Hellenistic Greek it passes over to the meaning of διότι: L. 1. 7 καθότι ἦν ἡ Ἐλισαβὲτ στεῖρα, 19. 9, A. 17. 31 (διότι HLP).—The **co-ordinating** particle is γάρ, one of the commonest of the particles (least often, in comparison with the rest of the N.T., in John, especially in his Epistles; there are also not many instances of it in the Apocalypse). Its usages agree with the classical usages; it is also frequently found in questions, where we use 'then,' Mt. 27. 23 τί γὰρ κακὸν ἐποίησεν; 'what evil then has he done?', A. 8. 31 πῶς γὰρ ἂν δυναίμην; giving the reason for a denial or refusal which is left unexpressed, or for a reproach (whether expressed or not) as in Mt. 9. 5 τί γάρ ἐστιν εὐκοπώτερον κ.τ.λ., 23. 17 μωροὶ καὶ τυφλοί, τίς γὰρ κ.τ.λ., A. 19. 35 etc., unless it should be rendered literally by 'for who,' as in L. 22. 27. In answers it corroborates a statement about which a question has been raised (Kühner ii. 724), 'yes in truth,' 'indeed,' as in 1 C. 9. 10 ἢ δι' ἡμᾶς πάντως

---

[1] *E.g.* in Aristotle's Ἀθηναίων πολιτεία.
[2] Aristot. Ἀθ. πολ. 3. 2 etc.

§ 78. 6–7. § 79. 1.] *PARTICLES (CONTINUED).* 275

λέγει; (an oratorical question) δι' ἡμᾶς γὰρ ἐγράφη, 1 Th. 2. 20 (and it is similarly used where a statement is repeated, R. 15. 26 f. ηὐδόκησαν γὰρ .... ηὐδόκησαν γάρ, καὶ κ.τ.λ.); there is a somewhat different use after an indignant question in A. 16. 37 of οὐ γάρ, *non profecto* (classical; see the author's note on the passage), and a different use again in Jo. 9. 30 in the retort of the man born blind, ἐν τούτῳ γὰρ (οὖν D) τὸ θαυμαστόν ἐστιν, ὅτι κ.τ.λ., which is equivalent to an interrogative (vide supra) οὐ γὰρ ἐν τούτῳ κ.τ.λ.—**Καὶ γὰρ** is 'for also,' so that there is no closer connection between the two particles (= ἐπειδὴ καὶ); the well-known use of καὶ γὰρ for *etenim* (Kühner 855), where καί quite loses its force, is sometimes traced in passages like 1 C. 5. 7, 11. 9, 12. 13 (where οὕτως καὶ ὁ Χρ. precedes); but in reality καί keeps its meaning of 'also' in these places, though it refers not to a single idea, but to the whole sentence.[1] (There is however an instance of the classical καὶ γὰρ in L. 22. 37 [D omits γάρ], cp. Jo. 12. 39 D καὶ γὰρ instead of ὅτι.) Οὐδὲ γὰρ is similarly used in R. 8. 7 (but in Jo. 8. 42, where D reads οὐ γάρ, it rather = *neque enim*, corresponding to a positive *etenim*). In τε γὰρ R. 7. 7 τε has nothing whatever to do with γάρ: if τε and γάρ are genuine (τε is omitted by FG and the Latin MSS.), one must suppose it to be an instance of anacoluthon.

7. The **concessive subordinating** particles are εἰ καὶ, ἐὰν καὶ, § 65, 6; also κἄν meaning 'even if,' Mt. 21. 21, 26. 35, Jo. 8. 14, 10. 38; on the other hand καὶ εἰ is only found, where the reading is certain, in the sense of 'and if' (Mc. 14. 27 εἰ καὶ ℵBC al., καὶ ἐὰν or κἄν D, καὶ εἰ A al.; 2 C. 13. 4 καὶ γὰρ εἰ ℵᶜA al., which is more correct than καὶ γάρ without εἰ as read by ℵ*BD*F al.; Origen reads εἰ γὰρ καί, see Tisch.). On καίπερ, καίτοι with a participle, and καίτοι(γε) with a finite verb see § 74, 2. Καίτοι takes alternately a hypotactical or a paratactical construction, vide ibid., as it alternately has an adversative or a concessive meaning, § 77, 14.—On the use of ὅμως corresponding to classical καίπερ vide ibid.

§ 79. CONNECTION OF SENTENCES.

1. We find the methods of connecting sentences in Greek already divided in Aristotle's terminology[2] into two opposite classes, namely the **continuous** or **running** style (εἰρομένη) and the **compact** (κατεστραμμένη) or **periodic** style (ἐν περιόδοις). In the latter the whole discourse is subdivided into units consisting of coherent and well-balanced members; in the former the subsequent section is always loosely appended to the section preceding it, and there is never a definite conclusion within view of the reader. The periodic style is characteristic of artistically developed prose, the continuous style is that which we find in the oldest, and still quite unsophisticated, prose, and on the whole is that which characterizes the N.T. narrative,

[1] On 2 C. 13. 4 vide inf. 7. The classical use also appears in Herm. Sim. ix. 8. 2 καὶ γὰρ (*etenim*) καὶ ('also') οὗτοι κ.τ.λ.
[2] Arist. Rhet. iii. 9.

agreeing as it does with the manner of the Semitic models on which that narrative is based. To the idea which is given the first place and which is complete in itself there is appended a second and similar idea, the connecting link being in most cases καί = Hebrew ו, then follows a third, and so on in an unending series: this tedious character of uniformity is an especially noticeable feature of the narrative of Mark, but is also not wanting in the Gospels of Matthew, Luke and John. Another class of continuous style is that where the opening sentence is developed by appending to it a participle, or a clause introduced by ὅτι, or a relative sentence, or in some similar way, since in this case also there is no end or termination in view; this manner of writing, which is freely employed by Paul in large portions of the Epistles to the Ephesians and Colossians, is indeed still more tedious and presents still greater obscurity than the simple linking together of sentences by means of καί.

2. Besides the connection of clauses by means of a conjunction, a relative, a subordinate participle etc., there is further the unconnected or paratactical construction (known as **asyndeton**); this is on the whole repugnant to the spirit of the Greek language, both with regard to sentences and the members which compose them, as also with regard to parallel portions of a single clause, and accordingly in the N.T. also is only used to a limited extent. Those sentences are *not* to be regarded as strict cases of asyndeton, where the new sentence begins with a demonstrative pronoun or a demonstrative adverb, referring back to something which has preceded: A. 16. 3 τοῦτον (Timothy) ἠθέλησεν ὁ Παῦλος σὺν αὐτῷ ἐξελθεῖν, Jo. 5. 6 τοῦτον ἰδὼν κ.τ.λ. (ibid. 21. 21 AX al., but אBCD have τοῦτον οὖν), the person having been previously introduced and described; a quite parallel instance may be quoted *e.g.* from Demosth. 21. 58 Σαννίων ἐστιν δήπου τις ...· οὗτος ἀστρατείας ἥλω ...· τοῦτον μετὰ κ.τ.λ. An unclassical use, on the other hand, is that of τότε as a connecting particle, which is particularly characteristic of Matthew, though also occurring in Luke (esp. in the Acts), to introduce something which was subsequent in point of time, not something which happened at a definite point of time: Mt. 2. 7 τότε Ἡρῴδης κ.τ.λ., 16, 17, 3. 5, 13, 15, 4. 1, 5, 10, 11 etc., L. 14. 21 (D καὶ), 21. 10 τότε ἔλεγεν αὐτοῖς (om. D), 24. 45, A. 1. 12, 4. 8 etc. (esp. frequent in D, *e.g.* 2. 14, 37); John uses the combination τότε οὖν, 11. 14 (οὖν om. A), 19. 1, 16, 20. 8, τότε in that case having a fuller meaning 'at this time' (as opposed to previous time). Other circumstantial formulas with similar meaning, which can hardly be interpreted in their literal sense, are: Mt. 11. 25, 12. 1 ἐν ἐκείνῳ τῷ καιρῷ (14. 1, where D has ἐν ἐκ. δὲ), ἐν ἐκείνῃ τῇ ὥρᾳ Mt. 18. 7 (ἐν ἐκ. δὲ BM), ἐν ἐκείναις (δὲ add. D) ταῖς ἡμέραις Mc. 8. 1 (ἐν δὲ ταῖς ἡμ. ἐκ. Mt. 3. 1, but DE al. om. δὲ); ἐν αὐτῇ (δὲ add. D) τῇ ὥρᾳ L. 10. 21 (7. 21 v.l. ἐν ἐκείνῃ τ. ὥ.; with δὲ AD al.). Ἀπὸ τότε may also be noticed in Mt. 4. 17 (with γὰρ in D), 16. 21, L. 16. 16 (καὶ ἀ. Mt. 26. 16). Μετὰ τοῦτο (ταῦτα) without a conjunction occurs in John's Gospel, 2. 12, 3. 22, 5. 1, 14, 6. 1 etc. (in 19. 38 μετὰ δὲ τ., but δὲ is omitted by EGK al.), and the Apocalypse (4. 1, 7. 9,

§ 79. 2–3.] CONNECTION OF SENTENCES. 277

18. 1, 19. 1, 20. 3, with καί 7. 1 [καὶ om. AC], 15. 5); see also A. 18. 1 according to אAB (v.l. μετὰ δὲ ταῦτα), and the reading of nearly all Greek MSS. in L. 10. 1, 18. 4.—In the case of ἔπειτα and εἶτα Attic Greek is not fond of inserting a δέ (Krüger Gr. § 69, 24), and the N.T. usage is the same, L. 16. 7, Jo. 11. 7, Mc. 4. 17 etc. (Ja. 4. 14 ἔπ. καὶ אABK, ἔπ. δὲ καί only LP). The N.T. also uses ἔτι without a conjunction: L. 8. 49 ἔτι αὐτοῦ λαλοῦντος, A. 10. 44, Mt. 12. 46 (with δέ CE al.), cp. 26. 47 (where Latin MSS. omit the conj., and there are var. lect. καὶ ἔτι and ἔτι δέ).

3. **Asyndeton between individual words** or ideas is quite a natural occurrence for the sake of convenience in lengthy enumerations, but here there is a tendency at any rate to connect the words in pairs to avoid ambiguity, see § 77, 9, until at last even this becomes tedious to the writer, 1 Tim. 1. 9, 10; still, if the ideas are not strictly summed up, but merely enumerated, the use of asyndeton may be an actual necessity. Thus we have in 1 P. 4. 3 πεπορευμένους ἐν ἀσελγείαις, ἐπιθυμίαις, οἰνοφλυγίαις, κώμοις, πότοις καὶ ἀθεμίτοις εἰδωλολατρίαις (with the last word the adjective necessitates the insertion of καί); the use of καί in this passage would lay too great a charge against individual persons. 2 Tim. 3. 2 ἔσονται οἱ ἄνθρωποι φίλαυτοι, φιλάργυροι, ἀλαζόνες, ὑπερήφανοι, βλάσφημοι κ.τ.λ. (but the same men do not possess all these faults). If the particle is used in enumerations of this kind, the construction is known as **polysyndeton**, a figure of speech which may be used just as well as asyndeton for a rhetorical purpose, only in a different way: polysyndeton by evidently summing up the different ideas produces an impression of greatness and fulness, asyndeton, by breaking up the separate ideas and introducing them one after the other in a jerky manner, gives an impression of vivacity and excitement. Still neither asyndeton nor polysyndeton is used with a rhetorical effect in every case where they occur: L. 18. 29 (= Mt. 19. 29, Mc. 10. 29) οὐδείς ἐστιν ὃς ἀφῆκεν οἰκίαν ἢ γυναῖκα ἢ ἀδελφοὺς κ.τ.λ. cannot well be otherwise expressed; also L. 14. 21 τοὺς πτωχοὺς καὶ ἀναπείρους καὶ τυφλοὺς καὶ χωλοὺς εἰσάγαγε ὧδε is a simple and straightforward expression, no less than Jo. 5. 3 πλῆθος τῶν ἀσθενούντων, τυφλῶν χωλῶν ξηρῶν (in the latter passage καί would be superfluous, in Lc it is not so because the different persons are summed up). Where there are only two ideas N.T. (like classical) Greek is not fond of asyndeton, except where opposites are connected, as in 2 Tim. 4. 2 ἐπίστηθι εὐκαίρως ἀκαίρως, cp. ἄνω κάτω, *nolens volens*, Kühner 865 d, Win. § 58, 7[1]. But polysyndeton is used with a really rhetorical effect in R. 9. 4 ὧν ἡ υἱοθεσία καὶ ἡ δόξα καὶ αἱ διαθῆκαι καὶ ἡ νομοθεσία καὶ ἡ λατρεία καὶ αἱ ἐπαγγελίαι (cp. 2. 17 ff.), or in Ap. 5. 12 λαβεῖν τὴν δύναμιν καὶ πλοῦτον καὶ σοφίαν καὶ ἰσχὺν καὶ τιμὴν καὶ δόξαν καὶ εὐλογίαν; just as asyndeton is used in 1 C. 3. 12 εἴ τις ἐποικοδομεῖ ἐπὶ τὸν θεμέλιον χρυσίον, ἄργυρον, λίθους τιμίους,

---

[1] If the negative idea (with οὐ) is attached to the positive, καί may be inserted or omitted: 1 C. 10. 20 δαιμονίοις καὶ οὐ θεῷ, 3. 2 γάλα ..., οὐ βρῶμα (DEFG ins. καί), 7. 12 etc.

ξύλα, χόρτον, καλάμην, which should be recited in a vivid way, giving emphasis to the studied anti-climax.

4. If the connected ideas are finite verbs, this leads us at once to asyndeton between sentences; but there are certain **imperatives** which deserve a separate mention. Mt. 5. 24 ὕπαγε πρῶτον διαλλάγηθι, 8. 4 etc. (18. 15 ὕπαγε ἔλεγξον אBD, a v.l. inserts καί; similarly Mc. 6. 38; but in Ap. 16. 1 all uncials have καί), cp. the classical use of ἄγε and ἴθι (N.T. does not use ἔρχου thus, but has ἔ. καὶ ἴδε Jo. 1. 47, 11. 34, Ap. 6. 1, 3, 5, 7 [in Ap. there is a *correct* v.l., omitting καὶ ἴδε]); ἔγειρε ἆρον Mc. 2. 11 (in 9 most MSS. insert καί), but in L. 6. 8 only A has ἔγ. στῆθι, and there is preponderant evidence for καί, in Mt. 9. 6 אC al. read ἐγερθεὶς ἆρον, B reads as in Mc., D ἔγειρε καὶ ἆρον: we further have ἐγείρεσθε ἄγωμεν in Mt. 26. 46=Mc. 14. 42; also ἀνάστα is so used at least as a v.l. of D* in A. 11. 7 ἀνάστα Πέτρε θῦσον, § 74, 3. Further we have ὅρα ὁρᾶτε, βλέπετε = *cave*(*te*) (cp. § 64, 2), Mt. 9. 30 ὁρᾶτε μηδεὶς γινωσκέτω, 24. 6 ὁρᾶτε μὴ θροεῖσθε (Buttm. p. 209), and accordingly ὁρᾶτε (βλ.) μή with conjunctive in Mt., Mc., Lc. is also apparently to be regarded as an instance of asyndeton, Mt. 24. 4 βλέπετε μή τις ὑμᾶς πλανήσῃ, although in passages like Col. 2. 8 βλ. μή τις ἔσται, A. 13. 40, H. 12. 25 the μή subordinates the following clause no less than it does in βλεπέτω μὴ πέσῃ 1 C. 10. 12. On ἄφες with conj. see § 64, 2. Not far removed from these instances is σιώπα πεφίμωσο Mc. 4. 39 (σ. καὶ φιμώθητι D). The corresponding use of asyndeton with indicatives is limited to ἐγένετο with a finite verb, § 77, 6, and to the asyndeton after τοῦτο in an explanation of the preceding clause (classical, Kühner ii.² 864) L. 3. 20 προσέθηκε καὶ τοῦτο ἐπὶ πᾶσιν, κατέκλεισε κ.τ.λ. (א*BD al.); a peculiar instance is 1 C. 4. 9 δοκῶ γὰρ (ὅτι add. אᶜDᶜ al.) ὁ θεὸς ἀπέδειξεν, which should be compared with the insertion of δοκεῖτε and μαρτυρῶ inf. 7.—Again, where we have to do with really distinct clauses and sentences, a distinction must be drawn between narrative style on the one hand, and didactic and homiletic (or conversational) style on the other. In **narrative** the connecting link is generally retained, at least by Mt., Mc. and Lc., for John certainly shows a remarkable difference from them in this respect: thus in 1. 23 ἔφη, 26 ἀπεκρίθη, 29 τῇ ἐπαύριον βλέπει, similarly in 35, 37 ἤκουσαν (καὶ ἤκ. אᶜABC al.), 38 στραφεὶς (with δὲ אᵃABC al.), 40 λέγει, 41 ἦν (A al. ἦν δὲ), 42 εὑρίσκει, 43 ἤγαγεν (καὶ ἤγ. AX al.) and ἐμβλέψας αὐτῷ etc., beside which he uses the connecting particles οὖν, δέ, καί. These instances of asyndeton give the impression of ease, not so much of vividness or hurry on the part of the narrator. (Hermas has similar instances, *e.g.* Vis. iii. 10. 2 ἀποκριθεῖσά μοι λέγει, 9 ἀποκριθεὶς αὐτῇ λέγω – ἀπ. μοι λέγει, and again in 10, so that he uses asyndeton just in these formulas of narrated dialogue, where most of John's instances occur, and like John he is fond of using it with the historic present, Winer § 60, 1; he also uses it with μετὰ πολλὰ ἔτη, μ. χρόνον τινά etc., Vis. i. 1. 1 ff., cp. supra 2 ad fin.)—In the **didactic style** of the Gospels asyndeton is very commonly found between the individual precepts and utterances, *e.g.* almost throughout the whole passage Mt. 5. 3-17, and not only where there is no

§ 79. 4-6.] CONNECTION OF SENTENCES. 279

connection of thought,[1] but also in spite of such connection: ibid. 17 μὴ νομίσητε ὅτι ἦλθον καταλῦσαι ...· οὐκ ἦλθον καταλῦσαι κ.τ.λ. (instead of οὐ γάρ), L. 6. 27 ἀγαπᾶτε τοὺς ..., καλῶς ποιεῖτε τοῖς ..., προσεύχεσθε περί.... (29) τῷ τύπτοντι ..., καὶ ἀπὸ κ.τ.λ. (from this point onwards there is more connection). John also frequently employs it: 3. 6 τὸ γεγεννημένον ..., 7 μὴ θαυμάσῃς ..., 8 τὸ πνεῦμα κ.τ.λ. Here too the asyndeton is used with no rhetorical purpose, although it perhaps gives greater solemnity and weight to the discourse. The style of the exhortations and precepts in the Epistles is similar. But in the Epistles, especially the Pauline Epistles, we also find many instances, some of them brilliant instances, of rhetorical asyndeton, see § 82.

5. **New sections** in doctrinal writings of some length usually have, as in classical works, some link to connect them with the preceding section, and this is at any rate essentially requisite in a work that lays claim to careful execution. On the other hand, the epistolary style is apt to make use of asyndeton, when a further subject is started, and there are moreover numerous instances in Paul and other writers where such a fresh start is made (ἐξ ἀποστάσεως, i.e. 'with a break'), quite apart from the Epistle of James, which has the appearance of being a collection of aphorisms, and the first Epistle of John which is hardly less loosely put together. In the Epistle to the Romans there are connecting links till we reach 8. 16 αὐτὸ τὸ πνεῦμα συμμαρτυρεῖ κ.τ.λ., where one may very well speak of a *figure* of ἐξ ἀποστάσεως; the thought is so directly the outcome of the feeling (as also in 10. 1). The absence of a connecting link at the beginning of the second main section of the letter (9. 1), which is so distinct from the preceding section, may be surprising, but a mere conjunction would here be quite inadequate to produce a connection. In 1 Corinthians the ἐξ ἀποστάσεως construction is profusely and effectively employed; but new subjects are also sometimes introduced without a conjunction, as in 5. 9, 6. 1, 12, but in 7. 1, 25, 8. 1, 12. 1, 16. 1 we have περὶ δέ, in 15. 1 γνωρίζω δέ, etc. In the Epistle to the Hebrews the connection of sections is regularly preserved, except in the hortatory sections which are not connected with one another.

6. The other class of construction, the **compact** or **periodic**, has never been entirely wanting in any form of Greek literature; it is found for instance where the first-mentioned part of the thought defines the time of what follows, and this statement of time is not given in a few words (such as ἐν ἐκείναις ταῖς ἡμέραις), but at such length that a pause is required after it; thus we have a clause standing first which though it stands by itself gives a broken and incomplete meaning, and must therefore be succeeded by a second clause to complete the sense. This style is also found where the first part of the sentence is a condition etc., or where the subject of

---

[1] In this case Attic writers also employ asyndeton in admonitions, Isocrates R. i. ii. iii.: cp. his statement on this subject in xv. 67 f.

the sentence which is placed at the beginning is expanded by means of attributive words into a separate clause; there is a weaker, but still a true, connection of clauses, where two members of an antithesis, or a disjunction, or a parallelism, are set side by side, and the link between the first member and the second is expressed by a particle such as μέν, ἤ, τε or καί. Even a particle is not absolutely necessary to produce connection, so that we may even speak of periods where asyndeton is used, as in 1 C. 7. 27 δέδεσαι γυναικί· μὴ ζήτει λύσιν· λέλυσαι ἀπὸ γυναικός· μὴ ζήτει γυναῖκα, = εἰ μὲν δέδεσαι... εἰ δὲ λέλυσαι, cp. § 82, 8. *We*, it is true, are accustomed only to speak of a periodic style, where the number of clauses which combine to form a single unit and which only receive their full meaning from the last of them is far in excess of two, and we consequently fail to discover a periodic style in the N.T., since as a matter of fact there are not many sentences of this kind to be found in it. We have indeed the preface to Luke's Gospel, L. 1. 1-4 ἐπειδήπερ πολλοὶ ἐπεχείρησαν | ἀνατάξασθαι διήγησιν περὶ τῶν πεπληροφορημένων ἐν ἡμῖν πραγμάτων | καθὰ (sic D) παρέδοσαν ἡμῖν οἱ ἀπ' ἀρχῆς αὐτόπται καὶ ὑπηρέται γενόμενοι τοῦ λόγου | ἔδοξε κἀμοὶ παρηκολουθηκότι ἄνωθεν πᾶσιν ἀκριβῶς | καθεξῆς σοι γράψαι κράτιστε Θεόφιλε | ἵνα ἐπιγνῷς περὶ ὧν κατηχήθης λόγων τὴν ἀσφάλειαν, where, if the sentence is divided as above, and regard is had to the appropriate length of the clauses, erring neither on the side of excessive length or brevity, a beautiful relation is seen to exist between the protasis with its three clauses and the apodosis with its corresponding structure. Since πολλοί is answered by κἀμοί, and ἀνατ. διήγησιν by γράψαι, and the καθά clause by ἵνα ἐπιγνῷς κ.τ.λ., we see that the last clause, which is appended to a sentence already complete, is at least demanded by the correspondence which prevails throughout the whole passage. The same writer, however, in the rest of his Gospel has by no means taken the trouble to construct artistic periods, and his second work, the Acts, does not even open with a tolerably well-constructed sentence; the only similar period to be found besides in that author occurs at the beginning of the Apostolic letter, A. 15. 24 ff. The artificially-constructed sentence at the beginning of the Epistle to the Hebrews is of a different character. Πολυμερῶς καὶ πολυτρόπως πάλαι ὁ θεὸς λαλήσας τοῖς πατράσιν ἐν τοῖς προφήταις | ἐπ' ἐσχάτου τῶν ἡμερῶν τούτων ἐλάλησεν ἡμῖν ἐν υἱῷ (this according to ancient ideas is a complete period with two clauses or members, to which some looser clauses are then directly appended): ὃν ἔθηκεν κληρονόμον πάντων | δι' οὗ καὶ ἐποίησεν τοὺς αἰῶνας (with a rhetorical anaphoric use of the relative with asyndeton, § 82, 5; as in the subsequent passage) | ὃς ὢν ἀπαύγασμα τῆς δόξης καὶ χαρακτὴρ τῆς ὑποστάσεως αὐτοῦ | φέρων τε τὰ πάντα τῷ ῥήματι τῆς δυνάμεως αὐτοῦ | καθαρισμὸν τῶν ἁμαρτιῶν ποιησάμενος | ἐκάθισεν ἐν δεξιᾷ τῆς μεγαλωσύνης ἐν ὑψηλοῖς (a period with four clauses) | τοσούτῳ κρείττων γενόμενος τῶν ἀγγέλων | ὅσῳ διαφορώτερον παρ' αὐτοὺς κεκληρονόμηκεν ὄνομα (an appended period consisting of two clauses connected by τοσούτῳ ... ὅσῳ). The rest of the Epistle is composed in a similarly fluent and beautiful rhetorical style, and the whole work must, especially with regard to the composition of words and sentences, be reckoned as a piece of artistic prose, cp. § 82, 2. Paul, on the other hand, generally does not take the trouble which is required for so careful a style, and hence it happens that in spite of all his eloquence artistic periods are not to be looked for in his writings, while harsh parentheses and anacolutha abound.

7. In the case of a **parenthesis** the direct course of a sentence is interrupted by a subordinate idea being inserted into the middle of it. We also freely make use of parentheses in writing, but prevent the irregularity of the construction from interfering with the intelligibility of the passage by enclosing the interruption within brackets or dashes, unless indeed we throw the clause, which might be a parenthesis, into a foot-note. The need of a parenthesis usually arises from the fact that some idea or thought which occurs in the sentence necessitates a pause, such for instance as the introduction of a foreign word which requires explanation. In that case a sentence, which should strictly be closely joined together, is divided in two; this is done either in such a way that the whole construction still preserves its unity, as in Mt. 27. 33 εἰς ... Γολγοθά, ὅ ἐστιν Κρανίου τόπος[1], or else the insertion entirely destroys the structure of the sentence (anacoluthon), or again after the insertion, which is expressed as an independent clause, the writer returns to the original construction. In this last case we have a parenthesis. An instance of it is Mt. 24. 15 f. ὅταν ἴδητε τὸ βδέλυγμα ... (ὁ ἀναγινώσκων νοείτω), τότε οἱ κ.τ.λ. Or again an accessory but indispensable thought cannot be brought into line with the construction which has already been begun, and is thrown into the sentence just as it arises, e.g. in A. 12. 3 προσέθετο συλλαβεῖν καὶ Πέτρον—ἦσαν δὲ αἱ ἡμέραι τῶν ἀζύμων—ὃν καὶ πιάσας ἔθετο εἰς φυλακήν, where it would have been possible to bind the sentence more closely together by saying περὶ αὐτὰς τὰς ἡμέρας τὰς τῶν ἀζύμων καὶ Πέτρον συλλαβὼν εἰς φυλακὴν ἔθετο; but that would be the artistic style, not the style of the New Testament. Cp. 1. 15, 4. 13, (§ 77, 12). The parenthesis in A. 5. 14 μᾶλλον δὲ προσετίθεντο κ.τ.λ. is harsh; it is true that the sentence runs smoothly on from 13, but the return to the main sentence after the parenthesis is awkwardly executed; the clause ὥστε καὶ εἰς τὰς πλατείας κ.τ.λ. in reality expresses a result not of verse 14 but of 13, though it looks as if the former were the case. But many of the worst instances of this sort occur in the Pauline Epistles. If the thread of St. Paul's thought, when considered as a whole and in larger sections, includes many lengthy digressions (Win. § 62, 4), it is not to be wondered at that in smaller matters also the connection of clauses suffers in the same way. A parallel passage to A. 5. 14 is

---

[1] If an explanatory clause of this kind is inserted into the report of a direct speech, of which it can form no part, it must certainly be enclosed in brackets, in spite of the fact that the construction is not broken by it. Thus Mc. 7. 11 ἐὰν εἴπῃ ... κορβᾶν (ὅ ἐστιν δῶρον), Jo. 1. 39. (It is different if a scholium of this kind is *appended* to a direct speech, as in Jo. 9. 7, 1. 42 etc., Winer § 62, 2 note.)

R. 1. 13 ὅτι πολλάκις προεθέμην ἐλθεῖν πρὸς ὑμᾶς, καὶ ἐκωλύθην ἄχρι τοῦ δεῦρο, ἵνα τινὰ καρπὸν σχῶ καὶ ἐν ὑμῖν, where the ἵνα clause is to be joined with προεθέμην. As here there is a lacuna in the thought between the words δεῦρο and ἵνα, so is there in 2. 15 f. between ἀπολογουμένων and ἐν ᾗ ἡμέρᾳ, so that it might appear best to suppose that in the latter passage there is a parenthesis; but it is not till a long way back in the sentence that one reaches a definite point, to which ἐν ᾗ κ.τ.λ. may be smoothly and logically joined according to the original conception of the thought.[1] But to all appearance it is Marcion's text (which is known from some quotations) which alone affords us real help here, by omitting the ἐν ᾗ ἡμέρᾳ (or ἐν ἡμ. ᾗ, or ἐν ἡμ. ὅτε), and introducing a very expressive asyndeton, cp. 1. 22, 7. 24, 8. 16 etc. But these details are matters for the commentator to discuss as they severally arise. Another grammatical point to note is that, as in classical Greek, a finite verb is occasionally inserted in the middle of the construction (which there would be no point in isolating from the rest of the sentence by marks of parenthesis, and to do so might even give a wrong meaning): L. 13. 24 πολλοί, λέγω ὑμῖν, ζητήσουσιν κ.τ.λ. ('I tell you'), 2 C. 8. 3 ὅτι κατὰ δύναμιν, **μαρτυρῶ**, καὶ παρὰ δύναμιν κ.τ.λ., H. 10. 29 πόσῳ **δοκεῖτε** χείρονος ἀξιωθήσεται τιμωρίας (Herm. Sim. ix. 28. 8 τί δοκεῖτε ποιήσει), in all which passages it would be very easy to work the word into the construction; classical writers however have the same construction in numerous passages with οἶδα, ὁρᾷς, οἶμαι etc., Kühner ii.[2] 873 f. (Aristoph. Ach. 12 πῶς τοῦτ' ἔσεισέ μου δοκεῖς τὴν καρδίαν;). To this category belong the Pauline phrases κατὰ ἄνθρωπον λέγω R. 3. 5, ἐν ἀφροσύνῃ λέγω 2 C. 11. 21, ὡς τέκνοις λέγω 6. 13, which are epidiorthoses and prodiorthoses expressed in the concisest way. But the insertion of φασίν, ἔφη etc. does not come under this head, as this is only a case of displacement in the position of the word in the sentence: 2 C. 10. 10 ὅτι αἱ ἐπιστολαὶ μέν **φασιν** βαρεῖαι (= ὅτι φασίν· "Αἱ μέν" κ.τ.λ.), Mt. 14. 8, A. 23. 35 etc. Also proper names and temporal statements placed in the nominative in defiance of the construction (§ 33, 2) are not parenthetical, because they form an essential part of the main thought, and occur in their right place in the sentence.

8. **Anacoluthon** is due to a failure in carrying out the originally intended structure of the sentence; since the continuation and *sequence* do not correspond with what has gone before. In artistic prose instances of anacoluthon must generally be reckoned as blemishes, although they are not entirely wanting even in the prose of Isocrates; on the other hand its occurrence in writings where there is an imitation of a natural conversational tone, as in the cases where Plato has it, is quite justified, and it may therefore be considered justifiable in epistolary style as well, so long as it does not interfere with the understanding of the passage, though this limitation certainly seems not unfrequently to be transgressed by St. Paul.

---

[1] Wilke d. neutest. Rhetorik (Dresden 1843) p. 216, 228 f. makes the suggestion that verses 14 and 15 were added as a marginal note.

§ 79. 8–9.]   CONNECTION OF SENTENCES.   283

Of the very various forms of anacoluthon I give the first place to a peculiar instance, which appears in the simplest periods, consisting of two members or clauses (supra 6). Mt. 12. 36 πᾶν ῥῆμα ἀργὸν ὃ λαλήσουσιν οἱ ἄνθρωποι | ἀποδώσουσιν περὶ αὐτοῦ λόγον, 10. 32, Jo. 6. 39,[1] 17. 2, L. 12. 48, 2 C. 12. 17 μή τινα ὧν ἀπέσταλκα πρὸς ὑμᾶς | δι' αὐτοῦ ἐπλεονέκτησα ὑμᾶς; In these instances the two halves of the sentence required to be placed in opposition to each other, with a pause between them and a reference in the second half back to the first, and a certain weightiness is given to the style by treating each part of the sentence independently, instead of writing for instance ὅσα ἂν ῥήματα ἀργὰ λαλήσωσιν, περὶ πάντων (τούτων) ἀποδώσουσιν λόγον. In the passage from St. Paul τινα is obviously occasioned by ἀπέσταλκα; with this is compared 1 Jo. 2. 27 καὶ ὑμεῖς τὸ χρῖσμα ὃ ἐλάβετε ἀπ' αὐτοῦ | μένει ἐν ὑμῖν, where the pronoun occurs in both members, and in the first is to be taken with ἐλάβετε, whereas the passage might have run without anacoluthon καὶ ἐν ὑμῖν τὸ χρ. ὃ ἐλ. α. α. μένει. A similar case occurs ibid. 24 ὑμεῖς ὃ ἠκούσατε ἀπ' ἀρχῆς | ἐν ὑμῖν μενέτω[2] (μένει or μενέτω by itself was not sufficient to make a clause, and the contrast between beginning and continuance required to be sharply expressed). Other instances of anacoluthon of this or a kindred sort are: A. 7. 40 ὁ Μωϋσῆς οὗτος, ὃς ..., οὐκ οἴδαμεν τί ἐγένετο αὐτῷ (O.T. Ex. 32. 1),[3] Jo. 7. 38 ὁ πιστεύων εἰς ἐμέ ... ποταμοὶ ἐκ τῆς κοιλίας αὐτοῦ ῥεύσουσιν κ.τ.λ.[4], Mc. 9. 20 καὶ ἰδὼν αὐτόν, τὸ πνεῦμα συνεσπάραξεν αὐτόν (instead of συνεσπαράχθη ὑπὸ τοῦ πν.), A. 19. 34 ἐπιγνόντες δὲ ὅτι Ἰουδαῖός ἐστιν, φωνὴ ἐγένετο μία ἐκ πάντων (instead of ἐβόησαν ὁμοῦ πάντες, which would not conveniently suit the following words). A very awkward instance occurs in Ap. 2. 26 and 3. 12, 21 ὁ νικῶν, δώσω αὐτῷ; on the other hand in 2. 7, 17 we have τῷ νικῶντι, δώσω αὐτῷ, cp. 6. 4, Mt. 4. 16 O.T., 5. 40 (the pronoun referring back to the preceding clause, § 48, 2). Herm. Mand. iv. 5 is like an instance of nominative absolute of the old sort (§ 74, 5), ἀμφότερα τὰ πνεύματα ἐπὶ τὸ αὐτὸ κατοικοῦντα, ἀσύμφορόν ἐστιν ... ἐκείνῳ ἐν ᾧ κατοικοῦσιν.

9. Another kind of anacoluthon is found in sentences of greater length, where the interruption of the original construction by **intervening sentences** causes that construction to be forgotten, so that in the mind of the writer another is substituted for it. Thus A. 24. 6

---

[1] Here we find ἵνα πᾶν ὃ δέδωκάς μοι, μὴ ἀπολέσω ἐξ αὐτοῦ, ἀλλὰ ἀναστήσω αὐτὸ κ.τ.λ., with πᾶς ... μὴ for οὐδείς, § 47, 9, though here no doubt the negative looks on to the second positive half of the sentence, Buttmann p. 106, as in Jo. 3. 16. According to Buttm. 325 the πᾶν in all these instances is nominative ('nominative absolute,' cp. § 74, 4); as it also is according to him in Jo. 15. 2 πᾶν κλῆμα ἐν ἐμοὶ μὴ φέρον καρπόν, αἴρει αὐτό.

[2] Therefore this is not a case of the subject being thrown forward before the relative (§ 80, 4), whereas 1 C. 11. 14 ἀνὴρ μὲν ἐὰν κομᾷ, ἀτιμία αὐτῷ ἐστιν κ.τ.λ. may be so explained, as = ἐὰν μὲν ἀνήρ.

[3] In L. 21. 6 there is no reference in the second clause to the ταῦτα ἅ, and we should probably follow D in omitting ἅ.

[4] Herm. Mand. vii. 5 τῶν δὲ μὴ φυλασσόντων ... (the genitive is due to assimilation with the preceding antithetical clause), οὐδὲ ζωή ἐστιν ἐν αὐτοῖς.

(in the speech of Tertullus, which is transmitted by Luke with greater negligence than any other), εὑρόντες γὰρ τὸν ἄνδρα τοῦτον λοιμόν..., ὃς καὶ..., ὃν καὶ ἐκρατήσαμεν κ.τ.λ.; this ὃν καὶ, which is occasioned by ὃς καὶ preceding, should have been dropped, in order to make the period run correctly, whereas the writer here continues as though he had begun with εὕρομεν. The narrative portions of the N.T. do not contain many anacolutha of this kind: the passage Jo. 6. 22-24 has been transmitted with too much variation in the MSS. for us to be able to clearly recognize the hand of the author; according to the usual reading the τῇ ἐπαύριον ὁ ὄχλος at the beginning is taken up again in 24 with ὅτε οὖν εἶδεν ὁ ὄχλος, in a manner that is not unknown in classical writers, where there is no question of forgetfulness at all; cp. 1 Jo. 1. 1-3. But the Pauline Epistles (though not all to the same extent, as the care with which they were written varied considerably) contain numerous and more flagrant instances. In G. 2. 6 ἀπὸ δὲ τῶν δοκούντων εἶναί τι... ὁποῖοί ποτε ἦσαν, οὐδέν μοι διαφέρει· πρόσωπον θεὸς ἀνθρώπου οὐ λαμβάνει... ἐμοὶ γὰρ οἱ δοκοῦντες οὐδὲν προσανέθεντο, instead of ἐμοὶ οὐδὲν προσανετέθη, the author may either have forgotten his opening clause or else considered it convenient to repeat it in a new form. At all events the passage is easily understood[1]; but just before in 4 διὰ δὲ τοὺς παρεισάκτους ψευδαδέλφους... οἷς (οὐδὲ) πρὸς ὥραν εἴξαμεν κ.τ.λ., it is by no means easy to say what was the drift of St. Paul's thought in the opening clause, unless the οἷς (which is omitted by Latin MSS.) is spurious.[2] In many cases defective transmission or criticism of the text is certainly to blame: in R. 2. 17 ff. an obvious remedy is by adopting the reading ἴδε for εἰ δὲ (which can hardly be called a variant: ΕΙΔΕ – ΙΔΕ, ide – ĭde) to change what appears to be a protasis without a correct apodosis into a principal clause.[3] But in 1 Tim. 1. 3 ff. the construction which began with καθὼς παρεκάλεσά σε κ.τ.λ. through innumerable insertions and appended clauses is unmistakably reduced to utter confusion.

10. Frequent instances of anacoluthon are occasioned in St. Paul by the **free use of the participle**, which he is fond of using, and sometimes in a long series of clauses, instead of a finite verb. Thus 2 C. 7. 5 οὐδεμίαν ἔσχηκεν ἄνεσιν ἡ σὰρξ ἡμῶν, ἀλλ᾽ ἐν παντὶ **θλιβόμενοι**· ἔξωθεν μάχαι, ἔσωθεν φόβοι, where one may no doubt supply ἐσμέν in the first clause as εἰσίν in the second, though this does not do away with the harshness and the want of accurate sequence in the passage. Similarly in 5. 12 οὐ... συνιστάνομεν..., ἀλλ᾽ ἀφορμὴν **διδόντες** (sc. γράφομεν ταῦτα). So ibid. 8. 18 ff. συνεπέμψαμεν δὲ τὸν ἀδελφὸν..., οὗ

---

[1] Belser (die Selbstvertheidigung des. P. im Gal. br., Freiburg im Br. 1896, p. 69) says with regard to the attempt (of Spitta and others) to give a uniform construction to this sentence: ' A philologist, who with a sane mind proceeds to expound the verse, cannot οὐδὲ πρὸς ὥραν be in doubt as to the perverseness of the undertaking.'

[2] In any case in R. 16. 27 ᾧ should be removed (with B), not only because of the anacoluthon, but especially in order to give διὰ Ἰ. Χρ. its proper connection.

[3] Cp. Wilke (op. cit. p. 282, note 1) p. 215 f., who, it is true, decides conclusively in favour of εἰ δὲ.

ὁ ἔπαινος ... διὰ πασῶν τῶν ἐκκλησιῶν, οὐ μόνον δέ, ἀλλὰ καὶ **χειροτονηθεὶς** (instead of ἐχειροτονήθη) ὑπὸ τῶν ἐκκλησιῶν συνέκδημος ἡμῶν σὺν τῇ χάριτι τῇ διακονουμένῃ ὑφ' ἡμῶν, **στελλόμενοι** τοῦτο, μή τις ἡμᾶς μωμήσηται κ.τ.λ., where στελλ. is closely connected not so much with συνεπέμψαμεν (i.e. sent with Timothy), as with συνέκδημος ἡμῶν etc., so that it is an undoubted case of anacoluthon, the participle standing for στελλόμεθα γάρ. In E. 5. 21 there is no direct anacoluthon, but ὑποτασσόμενοι has not the same closer connection with the last finite verb πληροῦσθε 18, which λαλοῦντες etc. 19, and εὐχαριστοῦντες 20 have; the style is the same as in R. 12. 9 ff, where in the exhortations (after the style has already been entirely broken up in 6 ff., cp. § 78, 2) participles (or adjectives) are appended to each other in an unending series, with no possibility of bringing them into any construction. Thus in the opening verse 9 ἡ ἀγάπη ἀνυπόκριτος interrupts the remarks about what the Romans should be, individually (8) or collectively; after the interruption, however, he continues with ἀποστυγοῦντες ... φιλόστοργοι etc. up to διώκοντες 13; then in 14 f. there is a fresh interruption of clauses in the imperative or infinitive; in 16 we again have participles φρονοῦντες etc. and again an imperative γίνεσθε, in 17 ff. there is a continuation of the series of participles; it looks as though St. Paul regarded the descriptive participle (whether ἔστε is mentally supplied or not) as completely equivalent to the imperative. Cp. further E. 4. 20 παρακαλῶ ὑμᾶς περιπατῆσαι ... **ἀνεχόμενοι** ἀλλήλων ... σπουδάζοντες (cp. 2 P. 3. 3), 3. 18, Col. 3. 16 f. ὁ λόγος ἐνοικείτω ... διδάσκοντες κ.τ λ., where the participle follows upon imperatives and is equivalent to them as in Rom. loc. cit.; but there is a similar anacoluthon in 2 C. 9. 11 πλουτιζόμενοι after an assertion in the future tense, in 13 δοξάζοντες κ.τ.λ. there is an extension of the preceding διὰ πολλῶν εὐχαριστιῶν τῷ θεῷ (the subject of the part. being the recipients of the benefit), cp. 1. 7; participles are used without anacoluthon, but in a very long series in 2 C. 6. 3-10. The constant element in all these instances is the *nominative* of the participle, which is therefore essentially connected with this free use. Cp. λέγων, λέγοντες § 30, 6. The reverse use is occasionally found, namely the use of a finite verb in place of a participle. Col. 1. 26 τὸ μυστήριον τὸ ἀποκεκρυμμένον ..., νυνὶ δὲ ἐφανερώθη (D φανερωθέν); 2 Jo. 2 τὴν μένουσαν ἐν ἡμῖν, καὶ μεθ' ἡμῶν ἔσται, Jo. 15. 5 ὁ μένων ἐν ἐμοί, κἀγὼ (sc. μένω) ἐν αὐτῷ, οὗτος φέρει καρπόν, 5. 44 (but ℵ*e etc. regularly ζητοῦντες), 2 C. 6. 9; Ap. 3. 7; it is less harsh in 1 C. 7. 37 ὃς ἕστηκεν ... μὴ ἔχων ... ἐξουσίαν δὲ ἔχει, cp. Jo. 5. 44, 1. 32. Parallels may undoubtedly be quoted from classical writers for this use, as also for the free use of appended participles in the nominative, Kühner ii.[2] 661 ff.; it is the frequency, harshness, and awkwardness of its use in the N.T. which makes the difference; since anacolutha such as A. 15. 22 f. ἔδοξεν τοῖς ἀποστόλοις (= the Apostles determined) ... πέμψαι ..., γράψαντες might be equally well written by a classical author, as Thuc. iii. 36. 2 writes ἔδοξεν αὐτοῖς ... ἀποκτεῖναι, ἐπικαλοῦντες.[1]

---

[1] Clem. Cor. i. 11. 1 may be noticed, Λὼτ ἐσώθη ἐκ Σοδόμων, τῆς περιχώρου κριθείσης ..., πρόδηλον ποιήσας ὁ δεσπότης κ.τ.λ., as though ἔσωσεν had preceded.

11. On the absence of a particle corresponding to the particle μέν, which strictly requires a δέ corresponding to it, see § 77, 12. A unique case of anacoluthon occurs in A. 27. 10 θεωρῶ ὅτι...μέλλειν (§ 70, 4), where the ὅτι was required to prevent ambiguity, and the infinitive is due to forgetfulness (supra 8), cp. Xenoph. Hell. ii. 2. 2 etc., Winer § 44, 8, note 2. To a **relative clause** there is sometimes appended a further clause with a co-ordinating particle (such as καί), in which the relative cannot be supplied in the same form as in the first clause (classical, Kühner 936 f.): Tit. 1. 2 f. ζωῆς, ἣν ἐπηγγείλατο..., ἐφανέρωσεν δὲ νῦν τὸν λόγον αὐτοῦ, Ap. 17. 2 (also 1 C. 7. 13 with the reading ἥτις, but a better reading is εἴ τις in אD* al.), L. 17. 31. The construction is rather one of *oratio variata* than of anacoluthon in R. 2. 6 ff. ὃς ἀποδώσει ... τοῖς μὲν ... ζωήν· τοῖς δὲ ... ὀργὴ καὶ θυμός (*sc.* ἔσται ; the idea conveyed by δώσει would not admit of being supplied with these nouns), the passage continues with the same construction, but a fresh contrast is formed, θλῖψις καὶ στενοχωρία ἐπὶ πᾶσαν ψυχήν..., δόξα δὲ κ.τ.λ. Cp. 11. 22 ; G. 4. 6 f. ὅτι δέ ἐστε υἱοί, ἐξαπέστειλεν... εἰς τὰς καρδίας ἡμῶν.... Ὥστε οὐκέτι εἶ κ.τ.λ. (but ibid. 6. 1 σκοπῶν σεαυτόν κ.τ.λ. is a real case of anacoluthon).

12. **Mixture of direct and indirect speech.**—It has already been remarked that the employment of the indirect form of speech, whether with ὅτι and the optative, or with the accusative (nomin.) and infinitive, is not in the manner of the N.T. writers of narrative, as it is foreign to the style of popular narrators in general (§§ 66, 3 ; 70, 4) ; from this it follows that not only does ὅτι ordinarily take the indicative instead of the optative (a tendency which it also has in classical Greek), but it may also be followed by an accurate reproduction of the direct form of the speech, so that ὅτι thus performs the function of our inverted commas (Kühner p. 885). An example which shows this is Jo. 10. 36 (Buttm. p. 234)...ὑμεῖς λέγετε ὅτι "βλασφημεῖς," ὅτι εἶπον κ.τ.λ., instead of βλασφημεῖν, which would have linked on much better to the protasis ὃν κ.τ.λ.[1] But it is quite impossible for a N.T. writer to do what is so common in classical Greek (and Latin) writers, namely to continue the indirect form of speech for any length of time ; on the contrary they never fail to revert very soon to direct speech, a habit which is also not unusual in classical authors, Kühner p. 1062 f. Thus A. 1. 4 παρήγγειλεν...μὴ χωρίζεσθαι, ἀλλὰ περιμένειν ... ἣν ἠκούσατε, 23. 22, Mc. 6. 8 f. παρήγγειλεν ἵνα..., ἀλλ' ὑποδεδεμένους ... (as though an inf. had preceded), καὶ μὴ ἐνδύσησθε κ.τ.λ., L. 5. 14. Inversely, the direct form of speech is occasionally abandoned in favour of the indirect or a narrative form : A. 23. 23 εἶπεν· ἑτοιμάσατε ..., (24) κτήνη τε παραστῆσαι κ.τ.λ. (the β text is different and runs more smoothly), Mc. 11. 31 f. ἐὰν εἴπωμεν..., ἐρεῖ ... ἀλλὰ εἴπωμεν...; ἐφοβοῦντο τὸν λαόν κ.τ.λ. (instead of φοβούμεθα, as in Mt. 21. 26 and as D² al. read here from the passage of Matthew). A different use from this is that in Mc. 2. 10 ἵνα δὲ εἰδῆτε... (addressed to the Pharisees like the preceding words), λέγει τῷ παραλυτικῷ· "Σοὶ λέγω

---

[1] Herm. Mand. ix. 1 even uses ὅτι before a question : λέγων ὅτι πῶς δύναμαι κ.τ.λ.

§ 79. 12. § 80. 1.] *POSITION OF WORDS AND CLAUSES.* 287

κ.τ.λ." (as in L. 5. 24, while Mt. 9. 6 has τότε λέγει); the speech is related just as it was made, and the apostrophe to the sick man is indicated by the parenthetical words (the use of ἵνα etc. in this way, with an ellipse of 'I will say this,' is also classical, Krüger Gr. § 54, 8, note 14; and see § 81, 3).

§ 80. POSITION OF WORDS (POSITION OF CLAUSES).

1. The Greek language is not one of those which are fettered with regard to the position of the different parts of the sentence, and it does not act contrary to its nature in this respect in the N.T., and the tendency for it to do so was reduced by the fact that the Semitic languages also have no strict rules about the order of words. In spite of this, both in the Semitic languages, and in the Greek of the New Testament, particularly that of writers of narrative, certain tendencies and habits are apparent. In general the verb, or the substantival predicate with its copula, is placed immediately after the conjunction; then follows the subject, then the object, the complementary participle etc.; unemphatic pronouns, however, have a tendency to be placed in immediate connection with the verb, also anything else that is dependent on the verb, especially if the subject is extended.[1] The same rules hold good for infinitival and participial clauses (and for a participle placed at the head of a sentence[2]) as for clauses with a finite verb. Thus we have (Luke 1. 11) ὤφθη δὲ αὐτῷ ἄγγελος κυρίου ἑστὼς ἐκ δεξιῶν. (12) καὶ ἐταράχθη Ζαχαρίας ἰδών. (13) εἶπεν δὲ πρὸς αὐτὸν ὁ ἄγγελος. (18) καὶ εἶπεν Ζ. πρὸς τὸν ἄγγελον. (19) καὶ ἀποκριθεὶς ὁ ἄγγ. εἶπεν αὐτῷ. With a nominal predicate: Mc. 2. 28 ὥστε κύριός ἐστιν ὁ υἱὸς τοῦ ἀνθρώπου καὶ τοῦ σαββάτου (cp. L. 6. 5), for which Mt. 12. 8 has κύριος γάρ ἐστιν τοῦ σαββ. ὁ υἱὸς τοῦ ἀνθρώπου, since here the extended subject possessed more weight than the genitive, unemphasized by καί. Mt. 13. 31, 33 ὁμοία ἐστὶν ἡ βασιλεία τ. οὐρ. κόκκῳ ..., = 24 ὡμοιώθη κ.τ.λ. But the participle stands after the subject: L. 2. 33 ἦν ὁ πατὴρ αὐτοῦ καὶ ἡ μήτηρ θαυμάζοντες, A. 12. 6 ἦν ὁ Πέτρος κοιμώμενος, Mc. 1. 6, 14. 4, 40. Still in all these cases there is by no means any binding rule about the order, so that in L. 1. in the middle of the clauses quoted above we find in verse 12ᵇ καὶ φόβος ἐπέπεσεν ἐπ' αὐτόν, clearly because φόβος offers more of a parallel to ἐταράχθη in 12ᵃ than ἐπέπεσεν does: whereas in A. 19. 17 we have καὶ ἐπέπεσεν φόβος ἐπὶ πάντας αὐτούς, L. 1. 65 καὶ ἐγένετο ἐπὶ πάντας φόβος (D φόβος μέγας ἐπὶ π.) τοὺς περιοικοῦντας αὐτούς, where the reason for placing πάντας early in the sentence in the ordinary reading is to give it stress and preserve the parallelism, as the passage continues καὶ ἐν ὅλῃ τῇ ὀρεινῇ ... διελαλεῖτο πάντα τὰ ῥήματα ταῦτα, καὶ ἔθεντο **πάντες** οἱ ἀκούσαντες ἐν ταῖς καρδίαις αὐτῶν. Any emphasis whatever on any part of a sen-

---

[1] *E.g.* L. 2. 13 καὶ ἐξαίφνης ἐγένετο **σὺν τῷ ἀγγέλῳ** πλῆθος στρατιᾶς οὐρανίου αἰνούντων κ.τ.λ., A. 27. 2 ὄντος **σὺν ἡμῖν** Ἀριστάρχου Μακεδόνος Θεσσαλονικέως.

[2] For details see Gersdorf, Beiträge zur Sprachcharakteristik d. Schriftst. d. N.T., Leipzig 1816, p. 90 f., 502 ff.

tence generally tends at once to throw that part into the forefront of the sentence: ibid. 67 καὶ Ζαχαρίας ὁ πατὴρ αὐτοῦ ... (as opposed to the neighbours etc., who were the last subjects of discourse), 57 τῇ δὲ 'Ελισαβὲτ ἐπλήσθη ὁ χρόνος τοῦ τεκεῖν αὐτήν. Statements of time, which mark a transition, also have a tendency to stand at the beginning; but there too the inclination to begin a sentence with a verb occasions the introduction of a meaningless ἐγένετο, which does not in all cases affect the construction, before the temporal statement: L. 2. 1 ἐγένετο δὲ ἐν ταῖς ἡμέραις ἐκείναις ἐξῆλθεν δόγμα κ.τ.λ., cp. § 77, 6; so 1. 8 ἐγένετο δὲ ἐν τῷ ἱερατεύειν αὐτὸν ... ἔλαχε κ.τ.λ., 23 καὶ ἐγένετο ὡς ἐπλήσθησαν ... ἀπῆλθεν κ.τ.λ.

2. **Closely related parts of the sentence**, *e.g.* noun and attribute, noun and dependent genitive, several subjects or objects connected by καί etc., are usually in simple and plain discourse placed together, whereas not only in poetry, but also in discourse which has any claims to a rhetorical style, they are frequently severed from each other, in order to give greater effect to the separated words by their isolation. Thus the epistolary formula runs χάρις ὑμῖν καὶ εἰρήνη, not χάρις καὶ εἰρ. ὑμῖν, an order of words which is partly occasioned by the tendency which from early times exists in Greek as in cognate languages, to bring unemphasized (enclitic) pronouns and the like as near as possible to the beginning of the sentence (though not to put them actually at the beginning[1]); hence we find also R. 1. 11 ἵνα τι μεταδῶ χάρισμα ὑμῖν πνευματικόν, A. 26. 24 τὰ πολλά σε γράμματα εἰς μανίαν περιτρέπει, Jo. 13. 6 σύ μου νίπτεις τοὺς πόδας, 9. 6 (אBL) ἐπέχρισεν αὐτοῦ τὸν πηλὸν ἐπὶ τοὺς ὀφθαλμούς, H. 4. 11 ἵνα μὴ ἐν τῷ αὐτῷ τις ὑποδείγματι πέσῃ κ.τ.λ., 1 C. 5. 1 ὥστε γυναῖκά τινα τοῦ πατρὸς ἔχειν (also to emphasize both γυν. and πατρὸς), L. 18. 18 καὶ ἐπηρώτησέν τις αὐτὸν ἄρχων λέγων. But here again there is no obligation to use this order of words: thus we have 2 C. 11. 16 κἂν ὡς ἄφρονα δέξασθέ με, where no doubt the object was to give δέξασθε the prior position. A prior position gives emphasis, a position at the end of the sentence does so only indirectly, where the word is torn from its natural context and made independent; the later position may also be influenced by the connection with the following clause, as in 1 P. 2. 7 ὑμῖν οὖν ἡ τιμὴ τοῖς πιστεύουσιν· ἀπειθοῦσιν δὲ κ.τ λ. Sometimes the regular order of words would be too cumbrous and unpleasant: A. 4. 33 ΑΕ μεγάλῃ δυνάμει ἀπεδίδουν οἱ ἀπόστολοι τὸ μαρτύριον τῆς ἀναστάσεως 'Ιησοῦ χρ. τοῦ κυρίου, but אB etc. have a better reading τὸ μαρτ. οἱ ἀπόστολοι, and B also has τοῦ κ. 'Ιησ. τῆς ἀναστ. We even have in Ap. 3. 8 μικρὰν ἔχεις δύναμιν (cp. 4 with v.l.).—The Epistle to the Hebrews not unfrequently has a really oratorical and choice order of words: 1. 4 τοσούτῳ κρείττων γενόμενος τῶν ἀγγέλων, ὅσῳ διαφορώτερον παρ' αὐτοὺς κεκληρονόμηκεν ὄνομα (it was necessary to make ἀγγ. and ὄνομα stand out; the latter word also forms a link with the following clause), 5 τίνι γὰρ εἶπέν ποτε τῶν ἀγγέλων (for the

---

[1] See J. Wackernagel, Ueber ein Gesetz der indogerm. Wortstellung, Indogerm. Forschungen i. 333 ff.

§ 80. 2-3.] POSITION OF WORDS AND CLAUSES. 289

same reason), 11. 32 ἐπιλείψει με γὰρ (v.l. γάρ με, infra 4) διηγούμενον ὁ χρόνος περὶ Γεδεών κ.τ.λ., which offers a close parallel to Demosth. 18. 29 f. ἐπιλείψει με λέγονθ' ἡ ἡμέρα τὰ τῶν προδοτῶν ὀνόματα, 12. 1 τοσοῦτον ἔχοντες (τοσ. emphatic) περικείμενον ἡμῖν νέφος μαρτύρων, ὄγκον ἀποθέμενοι (ὅ. emphatic) πάντα καὶ τὴν εὐπερίστατον ἁμαρτίαν. But many similar instances may also be cited from Paul and 1 Peter; such is the versatility of the Greek language that lively and animated discourse everywhere gives rise to these dislocations of words.

3. With regard to the position of the adjectival **attribute**, the rule holds good that it generally stands *after* its substantive[1]; *i.e.* the principal word comes first, and then the word which defines it more closely, just in the same way that the **adverb** which gives a nearer definition of an adjective (or a verb) is given the second place: ὑψηλὸν λίαν Mt. 4. 8, ἐθυμώθη λίαν 2. 16. But we also find λίαν (om. D) πρωί Mc. 16. 2, λίαν γὰρ ἀντέστη 2 Tim. 4. 10, and in the case of an attribute δι' ἀνύδρων τόπων Mt. 12. 43 (ἀν. is the principal idea), καλὸν σπέρμα 13. 27 (κ. ditto), ἐχθρὸς ἄνθρωπος 28, καλοὺς μαργαρίτας 45 etc. The rule cannot be laid down for a substantive which is provided with an article: πνεῦμα ἅγιον is the correct phrase without an article, but with it we have both τὸ πν. τὸ ἅγ. and τὸ ἅγιον πνεῦμα as in Mt. 28. 19, A. 1. 8, which then becomes a single idea. Cp. § 47, 6; τὴν ἁγίαν πόλιν (Jerusalem) Mt. 4. 5, 27. 53 (but ἡ π. ἡ ἁγ. in Ap. 11. 2, 21. 2, 22. 19).—On the attributive genitive see § 35, 6[2]; on οὗτος and ἐκεῖνος § 49, 4.—Matthew has a habit of putting **adverbs** after **imperatives**, while he makes them precede indicatives: thus 27. 42 καταβάτω νῦν, 43 ῥυσάσθω νῦν, 3. 15 ἄφες ἄρτι, 18. 16 (ἔτι), and on the other hand 19. 20 ἔτι ὑστερῶ, 26. 65 (5. 13 ἰσχύει ἔτι, but D omits ἔτι), 9. 18 (ἄρτι; in 26. 53 before παρακαλέσαι according to AD al.), 26. 65 (νῦν).[3]—The order of words has become established by custom in certain frequently occurring combinations with καί, Winer § 61, 4, such as ἄνδρες καὶ γυναῖκες, γυν. καὶ παιδία (τέκνα), but cod. D in Mt. 14. 21 puts παιδ. first, as אD do in 15. 38; also ἐσθίειν καὶ πίνειν, οἱ πόδες καὶ αἱ χεῖρες (the reverse order in L. 24. 39, but not in א), etc.; but all these are peculiarities of a lexical rather than a grammatical nature.—The **vocative** stands either at the beginning, as in Mt. 8. 2 and often, or near the beginning of the sentence, as in ὅθεν, ἀδελφοὶ ἅγιοι H. 3. 1 etc., or in proximity to the pronoun of the second person, 1 C. 1. 10 παρακαλῶ δὲ ὑμᾶς, ἀδελφοί, or to a verbal form in the second person, Ja. 1. 2 πᾶσαν χαρὰν ἡγήσασθε, ἀδελφοί μου (this may be compared with the ordinary sequence of verb—subject; there is the same position of the voc. in Jo. 14. 9 τοσοῦτον ... καὶ οὐκ ἔγνωκάς με Φίλιππε, where Φ. could not well have stood earlier); it also stands after a 1st pers. plur. in which the persons addressed are included, H. 10. 19 ἔχοντες οὖν, ἀδελφοί, κ.τ.λ. It

---

[1] Gersdorf (op. cit. supra 1) p. 334 ff. (the rule applies to adjectives of *quality*, since those of quantity may stand first in all cases, as may also μικρός).
[2] See also op. cit. 295 ff.
[3] Op. cit. 106.

T

rarely stands at the end of the sentence: L. 5. 8, A. (2. 37), 26. 7, the last passage occurring in Paul's speech before Agrippa, in which there are other instances of the vocative being purposely given a peculiar position (verses 2 and 13).

4. To the obvious rule, that a **subordinating conjunction** stands at the beginning of the subordinate clause dependent upon it, there are some exceptions, as in classical Greek, especially in St. Paul, since emphasized portions of the subordinate sentence are placed before the conjunction: τὴν ἀγάπην ἵνα γνῶτε 2 C. 2. 4, 12. 7, 1 C. 9. 15, G. 2. 10, Col. 4. 16, A. 19. 4; βιωτικὰ μὲν οὖν κοιτήρια ἐὰν ἔχητε 1 C. 6. 4, 11. 14 (§ 79, 7 note), 14. 9, Mt. 15. 14, Jo. 10. 9; R. 12. 3 ἑκάστῳ ὡς ἐμέρισεν κ.τ.λ., 1 C. 3. 5, 7. 17 (bis); 2 Th. 2. 7 ἕως; Jo. 7. 27 ὅταν. We have further A. 13. 32 καὶ ἡμεῖς ὑμᾶς εὐαγγελιζόμεθα, τὴν πρὸς τοὺς πατέρας ἐπαγγελίαν γενομένην, ὅτι ταύτην ὁ θεὸς ἐκπεπλήρωκεν κ.τ.λ., instead of ὅτι τὴν—without ταύτην (p. 90, note 1). The same thing happens sometimes with the relative, Jo. 4. 18 νῦν ὃν ἔχεις, 1 C. 15. 36 σὺ ὃ σπείρεις, and akin to this is the habit in interrogative sentences of putting the emphasized idea before the interrogative: Jo. 1. 19 (= 8. 25, 21. 11, R. 9. 20, 14. 4, Ja. 4. 12) σὺ τίς εἶ; cp. Jo. 9. 17, 8. 25 (ὅ, τι, § 50, 5), L. 9. 20, 16. 11 f., Jo. 21. 21 οὗτος δὲ τί[1] etc., Buttmann 333 c.—Of the **co-ordinating conjunctions** some stand in the first place, such as καί, ἤ, ἀλλά, others in the second (on deviations from classical usage in this respect see §§ 77, 13; 78, 5); the latter class, however, are occasionally found also in the third, fourth, or fifth place, partly from necessity, as in 1 Jo. 2. 2 οὐ περὶ τῶν ἡμετέρων δὲ μόνον, Jo. 8. 16 καὶ ἐὰν κρίνω δὲ ἐγώ ('even if I however'), partly at the option of the writer, for instance where there is a preposition governing a case, or a noun with an attributive genitive: 2 C. 1. 19 ὁ τοῦ θεοῦ γὰρ υἱὸς אAB al., which gives greater prominence to θεοῦ than the reading of DF al. ὁ γὰρ τ. θ. υἱός, 1 C. 8. 4 περὶ τῆς βρώσεως οὖν τῶν εἰδωλοθύτων (instead of οὖν DE insert δὲ after περί): Herm. Sim. viii. 7. 6 ἐν ταῖς ἐντολαῖς δέ, ix. 21. 1 ἐπὶ τὴν καρδίαν δέ, Mand. ix. 3 οὐκ ἔστι γάρ, Vis. iii. 13. 2 ὡς ἐὰν γάρ.—On the position of τε see § 77, 9; on the position of the negative § 75, 7; on that of the secondary class of prepositions § 40, 6 (with οὗ χωρὶς H. 12. 4 cp. ὧν ἄνευ Xenoph. Hell. vii. 1. 3; χάριν is placed after its case except in 1 Jo. 3. 12 χάριν τίνος).

5. The adoption of a **hyperbaton,** *i.e.* a departure from the natural arrangement of words, is a very old expedient for the purpose of exegesis: it is at any rate found as early as Plato, who makes Socrates use it (Protagoras 343 E), in order to compel Simonides the poet to use the expression which Socrates regards as correct. It is employed in a similar way, and with scarcely more justification, by the exegetes of the N.T., see Win. § 61, 5.

6. The question of the arrangement within the **whole sentence** of the **principal** and **subordinate clauses** which compose it, is a matter

---

[1] This final position of τί is also found in Demosthenes: ταῦτα δ' ἐστὶ τί; 9. 39 etc.—Cp. also τὸ σκότος πόσον Mt. 6. 23, οἱ δὲ ἐννέα ποῦ; L. 17. 17. Wilke (op. cit. § 79, 7) p. 375.

§ 80. 6. § 81. 1.] *ELLIPSE, BRACHYLOGY, PLEONASM.* 291

rather of style than of grammar. Grammar should perhaps take note of licenses that are permitted, such as the insertion of a final sentence before its due place : Jo. 19. 28 μετὰ ταῦτα 'I. εἰδὼς ... ἵνα τελειωθῇ ἡ γραφή, λέγει Διψῶ, 19. 31, R. 9. 11. On the other hand it is a very forced explanation which makes in 1 C. 15. 2 τίνι λόγῳ εὐηγγελισάμην ὑμῖν dependent on the following εἰ κατέχετε; it appears rather that εἰ, like the reading in D* ὀφείλετε κατέχειν, is an explanatory gloss, so that we only have a protasis standing before a principal clause (κατέχετε)[1]. Jo. 10. 36 has the appearance of being an *oratorical* sentence, since the subordinate clause ὃν ὁ πατὴρ ἡγίασεν κ.τ.λ. is placed before the principal clause ὑμεῖς λέγετε ὅτι βλασφημεῖς (see § 79, 12, = βλασφημεῖν); in reality however the sentence with its defective structure (ὃν referring to βλασφημεῖς) is one of the instances of the loose formation of sentences with two members, found elsewhere in John's Gospel, § 79, 8.

§ 81. ELLIPSE (BRACHYLOGY), PLEONASM.

1. An **ellipse** is where it is left to the reader or hearer to complete for himself the thought which is incompletely expressed: not because the writer is afraid of saying something—that is the figure of aposiopesis—but because he finds any further addition superfluous. Still *every* omission of this sort is not therefore to be regarded as an ellipse. It is equally superfluous to insert what would be a mere repetition of something already stated, as for instance in the case of a preposition repeated before a second noun which is connected by καί with a previous noun, the omission or insertion of which preposition is an optional matter (see Winer § 50, 7); again the verb in the protasis sufficiently indicates the verb which should stand in the apodosis, in 2 C. 5. 13 εἴτε γὰρ ἐξέστημεν, θεῷ (*sc.* ἐξέστ.)· εἴτε σωφρονοῦμεν, ὑμῖν (*sc.* σωφρ.); this is the figure known as ἀπὸ κοινοῦ (Kühner ii.[2] 1066).[2] Moreover some slight alterations or changes in the form of the word may require to be supplied : Mc. 14. 29 εἰ πάντες σκανδαλισθήσονται, ἀλλ' οὐκ ἐγώ, *sc.* σκανδαλισθήσομαι, which is actually inserted in D and in Mt. 26. 33 (a harsher instance is G. 3. 5 ἐξ ἔργων νόμου, where ἐπιχορηγεῖ τὸ πνεῦμα καὶ ἐνεργεῖ κ.τ.λ. must be supplied from the participles). The omission becomes of a somewhat different character where positives and negatives are combined, as in 1 C. 10. 24 μηδεὶς τὸ ἑαυτοῦ ζητείτω, ἀλλὰ τὸ τοῦ ἑτέρου, *sc.* ἕκαστος (to be understood from μηδείς); and entirely different in 1 Tim. 4. 3 κωλυόντων γαμεῖν, ἀπέχεσθαι βρωμάτων *sc.* κελευόντων (a similar instance is found in Lucian Charon § 2 κωλύσει ἐνεργεῖν καὶ [*sc.* ποιήσει] ζημιοῦν, as Dr.

---

[1] Therefore a full stop should be placed after σῴζεσθε, where a fresh sentence begins which is unconnected with the last, § 79, 5.

[2] Wilke (op. cit. in § 79, 7 note) p. 121 ff.—The formula οὐ μόνον δέ, ἀλλὰ καί = 'moreover too' comes under this category, R. 5. 3, 11, 8. 23, 9. 10, 2 C. 8. 19, where an immediately preceding word or thought has to be supplied, which in 2 C. 7. 7 is actually repeated ; it is only in R. 9. 10 that the definite words to be supplied are not given in the preceding clause, cp. Win. § 64, 1 c, who compares Diogenes L. 9. 39 (Antisthenes) and οὐ μόνον γε ἀλλά in Plato.

Moulton points out), with which cp. 1 C. 3. 2 γάλα ὑμᾶς ἐπότισα, οὐ βρῶμα (sc. something like ἐψώμισα, § 34, 4): here one verb refers to two objects (or subjects), to only one of which it is applicable in its literal acceptation (the figure of **zeugma**, Kühner Gr. ii.² 1075 f.).[1] On the other hand, an **ellipse** proper may only then be supposed to exist, when the idea itself is not expressed in any shape whatever, and there is also no cognate idea which takes its place in the form required. Under these circumstances the following words may be omitted: anything which may obviously be supplied from the nature of the structure of the sentence, such as the **copula**, § 30, 3; the **subject** if it is an ordinary word (such as the thing, or men), or if it is absolutely required by the statement, § 30, 4; the **principal word**, if it is sufficiently indicated by the attribute, therefore especially feminines like ἡμέρα, ὥρα etc., § 44, 1 (also in the case of an article with an attributive genitive, § 35, 2). Omissions of this sort are **conventional**, and parallels may in some instances be found in other languages as well; a specially Greek idiom is the omission of the idea of '*other*' or '*at all*,' in Πέτρος σὺν τοῖς ἕνδεκα A. 2. 14 = σὺν τοῖς λοιποῖς τῶν ἔνδ. (ἀποστόλων), cp. 37, where א etc. read τὸν Πέτρον καὶ τοὺς λοιποὺς ἀποστόλους, while D omits λοιποὺς; 5. 29 Π. καὶ οἱ ἀπόστολοι (D is different); 1 C. 10. 31 εἴτε ἐσθίετε εἴτε πίνετε εἴτε τι (sc. ἄλλο 'besides' or 'at all') ποιεῖτε, R. 14. 21 μηδὲ sc. to do anything else, Mt. 16. 14. **Objects** are omitted with verbs like τελευτᾶν, viz. τὸν βίον, 'to die,' or διάγειν (ditto) 'to live,' Tit. 3. 3 (βίον is *inserted* in 1 Tim. 2. 2), also διατελεῖν, διατρίβειν used intransitively show a similar ellipse; we also have προσέχειν sc. τὸν νοῦν, cp. § 53, 1, etc. Γλώσσαις λαλεῖν should strictly be ἑτέραις γλ. λαλεῖν, a form which it takes in the narrative of the first appearance of the phenomenon in A. 2. 4 ('Mc.' 16. 17 γλ. καιναῖς); but in similar narratives further on in the Acts (10. 46, 19. 6) the additional word is at best only found in the β text, and in Paul it occurs nowhere (but see 1 C.14. 21). As an instance of conventional omission of a **verb** may be reckoned the omission of 'he said' in the report of a conversation, where the recurrence of the word would be superfluous and wearisome: A. 25. 22 Ἀγρίππας δὲ πρὸς τὸν Φῆστον (with ἔφη CEHLP); ibid. 9. 5, 11 the verb might be supplied from the previous clause (ἀπὸ κοινοῦ). Somewhat different is καὶ (ἰδοὺ) φωνή, sc. ἐγένετο Mt. 3. 17 etc., § 30, 3. In letters we always find χαίρειν without λέγει, § 69, 1, unless indeed even χαίρειν is omitted, as in Ap. 1. 4 and in Paul, though in his Epistles (and in the Apocalypse) its place is always taken by the Christian greeting χάρις ὑμῖν κ.τ.λ.[2] Verbs of any kind

---

[1] Wilke p. 130 (1 C. 14. 34 ἐπιτρέπεται: A. 14. 22 παρακαλοῦντες). A kindred use is that in A. 1. 21 εἰσῆλθεν καὶ ἐξῆλθεν ἐφ' ἡμᾶς, = εἰσ. ἐφ' ἡμ. καὶ ἐξ. παρ' ἡμῶν (cp. 9. 28), where the clause which more nearly defines the verb ought to be expressed twice in different forms.

[2] The formula οὐχ ὅτι = οὐ λέγω ὅτι, as we say 'not that,' occurs in Jo. 6. 46 οὐχ ὅτι τὸν πατέρα ἑόρακέν τις, 7. 22, 2 C. 1. 24, 3. 5, Ph. 4. 17, 2 Th. 3. 9; its origin has become so obscured that Paul can even say in Ph. 4. 11 οὐχ ὅτι καθ' ὑστέρησιν λέγω, Win. § 64, 6. Cp. for classical instances of it Kühner ii. 800, but in classical Greek it involves the idea of a climax (being followed by ἀλλά),

§ 81. 1-2.] ELLIPSE, BRACHYLOGY, PLEONASM. 293

are omitted in formulas and proverbs, which are apt to be expressed in an abbreviated form : Mt. 5. 38 ὀφθαλμὸν ἀντὶ ὀφθαλμοῦ κ.τ.λ. ⟨δώσει according to Ex. 21. 24), Ap. 6. 6 χοῖνιξ σίτου δηναρίου (πωλεῖται 'costs'), A. 18. 6 τὸ αἷμα ὑμῶν ἐπὶ τὴν κεφαλὴν ὑμῶν, cp. Mt. 27. 25 (sc. ἐλθέτω according to Mt. 23. 35 ; a Hebrew phrase, see LXX. 2 Sam. 1. 16), 2 P. 2. 22 ὗς λουσαμένη εἰς κύλισμα βορβόρου (classical γλαῦκ' 'Αθήναζε etc.; but in the passage from 2 Pet. ἐπιστρέψασα may be supplied from the preceding proverb, Win. § 64, 2). Ὅρα μή (sc. ποιήσῃς) must also have been a common phrase, Ap. 19. 10, 22. 9. On ἵνα τί, τί πρὸς σέ etc. see § 50, 7. Ὑμεῖς δὲ οὐχ οὕτως (should act) occurs in L. 22. 26. 'Αλλ' ἵνα, but it was, it came to pass etc. for this reason that = the Divine will was, occurs in Jo.1. 8, 9. 3, 13. 18, 15. 25, Mc. 14. 49.—Εἰ δὲ μή (γε) (§ 77, 4) 'otherwise' has become a stereotyped phrase, so that it may even stand (instead of εἰ δέ) after a negative sentence, as in L. 5. 36 (a classical use, Kühner 987); also instead of ἐὰν δὲ μή after ἐὰν μέν..., L. 10. 6, 13. 9 (in Ap. 2. 5 an explanatory clause with ἐὰν μή is tacked on at the end), see for classical instances Krüger § 65, 5. 12. Also εἰ μή, ἐὰν μή (Mc. 4. 22, G. 2. 16) 'except' were originally elliptical phrases.—In 2 Th. 1. 5 ἔνδειγμα τῆς δικαίας κρίσεως κ.τ.λ. (after ταῖς θλίψεσιν αἷς ἐνέχεσθε) stands for ὅ ἐστιν ἔνδ. κ.τ.λ. (cp. E. 3. 13, Ph. 1. 28), but may be classed with the accusative used in apposition of sentences, Kühner 243 (Buttm. p. 134), as in R. 12. 1 παρακαλῶ ὑμᾶς παραστῆσαι τὰ σώματα ὑμῶν θυσίαν..., τὴν λογικὴν λατρείαν ὑμῶν (so that this is etc.). —Jo. 7. 35 ποῦ οὗτος μέλλει πορεύεσθαι, ὅτι ἡμεῖς οὐχ εὑρήσομεν αὐτόν; is not elliptical, since ὅτι = δι' ὅ,τι as in 14. 22 (§ 50, 7), 9. 17, Mt. 8. 27, Mc. 4. 41[1]; but Mt. 16. 7 ὅτι ἄρτους οὐκ ἐλάβομεν = τοῦτ' ἐκεῖνο, ὅτι κ.τ.λ.; cp. the classical ellipses with ὅτι given in Kühner p. 889, note 4.

2. Omissions which are due to **individual style** and taste go much further, especially in letters, where the writer reckons on the knowledge which the recipient shares with himself, and also imitates ordinary speech, which is likewise full of ellipses, both conventional and such as depend more on individual caprice. Examples : 1 C. 1. 31 ἵνα καθὼς γέγραπται· Ὁ καυχώμενος κ.τ.λ. 'in order that it may come to pass,' or 'proceed as' etc.[2]: 4. 6 ἵνα ἐν ἡμῖν μάθητε τὸ μὴ ὑπὲρ ἃ γέγραπται (φρονεῖν is added by אᶜDᶜ al.) : 2 C. 8. 15 O.T. ὁ τὸ πολὺ οὐκ ἐπλεόνασεν, καὶ ὁ τὸ ὀλίγον οὐκ ἠλαττόνησεν, = Ex. 16. 18 which is based on 17 καὶ συνέλεξαν ὁ τὸ πολὺ καὶ ὁ τὸ ἔλαττον, sc.

---

which is not inherent in it in the N.T. Once Paul uses οὐχ οἷον ὅτι with a similar meaning (= 'it is not as if '), R. 9. 6 οὐχ οἷον δὲ ὅτι ἐκπέπτωκεν ὁ λόγος τοῦ θεοῦ (as Polyb. iii. 88. 5 uses οὐχ οἷον ... ἀλλά with the idea of a climax = class. οὐχ ὅτι). Cp. the elliptical μήτιγε, § 75, 2.

[1] These combinations of particles are ultimately derived from Hebrew, cp. H. 2. 6 = Ps. 8. 5 τί ἐστιν ἄνθρωπος, ὅτι μιμνήσκῃ αὐτοῦ; κ.τ.λ., where ὅτι = כִּי. So in Exod. 3. 11, 16. 7, Judges 19. 18 etc. (Gesenius-Kautzsch § 107, 4. b 3); in 1 Sam. 11. 5 the equivalent in the Greek for כִּי מַה־לָּעָם is τί ὅτι (p. 177) κλαίει ὁ λαός.

[2] Or else (Win. § 64, 7) the literal quotation takes the place of a paraphrase, which would have required the conjunctive.

therefore some word like συλλέξας (cp. Num. 11. 32)[1]: R. 13. 7 ἀπόδοτε πᾶσιν τὰς ὀφειλάς, τῷ τὸν φόρον (sc. perhaps ὀφειλόμενον ἔχοντι) τὸν φόρον, τῷ τὸ τέλος τὸ τέλος κ.τ.λ.: G. 5. 13 μόνον μὴ τὴν ἐλευθερίαν εἰς ἀφορμὴν τῇ σαρκί, sc. something like ἔχετε: in the case of this warning '(only) not' we also are inclined to use ellipse (Mt. 26. 5, Mc. 14. 2 μὴ ἐν τῇ ἑορτῇ, where however the ellipse can and must be supplied from the preceding words): Ph. 3. 14 ἓν δὲ (I do): 2 C. 9. 6 τοῦτο δέ (sc. φημι, according to 1 C. 7. 29, 15. 50), ὁ σπείρων φειδομένως φειδομένως καὶ θερίσει: 9. 7 ἕκαστος καθὼς προῄρηται, may give: G. 2. 9 δεξιὰς ἔδωκαν κοινωνίας, ἵνα ἡμεῖς μὲν εἰς τὰ ἔθνη (εὐαγγελιζώμεθα [Win.] according to 2 C. 10. 16), αὐτοὶ δὲ εἰς τὴν περιτομήν: R. 4. 9 ὁ μακαρισμὸς ἐπὶ τὴν περιτομὴν ἢ ...; (sc. λέγεται): 5. 18 ὡς δι' ἑνὸς παραπτώματος εἰς πάντας ἀνθρώπους εἰς κατάκριμα, οὕτως κ.τ.λ., which would be unintelligible without the long exposition preceding, and even so hardly admits of being supplemented by a definite word such as ἀπέβη, ἀποβήσεται; Paul once more emphasizes the correspondence between the two actions (of Adam and Christ)—their opposite cause (διά), their equal range or extent (εἰς), the opposite nature of their ultimate end (εἰς).—**Aposiopesis** (supra 1) is sometimes assumed in L. 19. 42 εἰ ἔγνως καὶ σὺ τὰ πρὸς εἰρήνην, νῦν δὲ ἐκρύβη, because the apodosis is suppressed (cp. 22. 42 where the reading is doubtful, εἰ βούλει παρενέγκαι τοῦτο τὸ ποτήριον ἀπ' ἐμοῦ, πλὴν κ.τ.λ., with v.l. παρενεγκεῖν and παρένεγκε); but since in the former passage nothing else can be supplied but 'it would be (or is) pleasing to me,' the passage should rather be compared with the classical omission of the first apodosis with εἰ μὲν ... εἰ δέ, § 78, 2. There is likewise no aposiopesis in Jo. 6. 62 ἐὰν οὖν θεωρῆτε ..., sc. what could you say then?, or in A. 23. 9 εἰ δὲ πνεῦμα αὐτῷ ἐλάλησεν, sc. what opposition can we make? (HLP interpolate μὴ θεομαχῶμεν), R. 9 22. Abbreviation in the principal clause is also found in sentences of comparison: καὶ οὐ ('and it is not so') καθάπερ Μωϋσῆς κ.τ.λ., 2 C. 3. 13, Mt. 25. 14, Mc. 13. 34, cp. § 78, 1.

3. Distinct from ellipse is what is known as **brachylogy**, where something is passed over for the sake of brevity, not so much affecting the grammatical structure as the thought: the omission may either be conventional or due to individual style. An instance of the former is to be found in ἵνα clauses which are thrown forward in a sentence, and which give the aim or object of the subsequent statement, Mt. 9. 6 ἵνα δὲ εἰδῆτε κ.τ.λ. (§ 79, 12)[2]; an instance of the latter is R. 11. 18 εἰ δὲ κατακαυχᾶσαι (you must know then that) οὐ σὺ τὴν ῥίζαν βαστάζεις, ἀλλ' ἡ ῥίζα σέ, 1 C. 11. 16, Win. § 66, 1.

4. The opposite to ellipse is **pleonasm**, which consists especially in expression being given a second time to an idea which has already been expressed in the sentence, not with any rhetorical object (such

---

[1] Winer § 64, 4 supplies ἔχων, comparing expressions in Lucian such as ὁ τὸ ξύλον sc. ἔχων 'the man with the stick.'

[2] Under this head should probaby be classed 2 C. 10. 9 ἵνα δέ (δὲ add. H vulg. al.) μὴ δόξω κ.τ.λ. (verse 10 is a parenthesis). We have a final sentence after a question (sc. 'answer') in Jo. 1. 22, 9. 36.

§ 81. 4. § 82. 1.] *ARRANGEMENT OF WORDS: FIGURES.* 295

as accounts for the emphatic reduplication of a word or sentence, § 82, 7), nor again from mere thoughtlessness, but simply in conformity to certain habits of the language. Cp. on μᾶλλον with a comparative § 44, 5, on αὐτοῦ after ὅς (Hebraic) § 50, 4; on pleonastic negatives § 75, 4 and 6, ἐκτὸς εἰ μή = εἰ μή § 65, 6; we may also reckon as pleonasms εἶπεν λέγων (§ 74, 3), ἰδὼν εἶδον (ibid. 4), θανάτῳ τελευτάτω (§ 38, 3) and other cases of Hebraistic prolixity of expression.[1] On ἀπὸ μακρόθεν and the like see § 25, 3; with which must be compared προδραμὼν (εἰς τὸ) ἔμπροσθεν L. 19. 4,[2] πάλιν ἀνακάμπτειν A. 18. 21, π. ὑποστρέφειν G. 1. 17 (π. ἐπιστρ. 4. 9), π. ἐκ δευτέρου, δεύτερον, ἄνωθεν Mt. 26. 42, 44, A. 10. 15, Jo. 4. 54, G. 4. 9[3]; ἔπειτα μετὰ τοῦτο Jo. 11. 7 (there are similar phrases in classical Greek, Kühner ii.[2] 1087 f.), L. 22. 11 τῷ οἰκοδεσπότῃ τῆς οἰκίας (without τῆς οἰκ. in Mc. 14. 14), with which one may class the classical αἰπόλια αἰγῶν and the like, Kühner ibid. 1086.

§ 82. ARRANGEMENT OF WORDS; FIGURES OF SPEECH.

1. The sophists and rhetoricians who about the end of the fifth and the beginning of the fourth centuries B.C. created the Attic **artistic prose** style, did so with a certain amount of emulation with the only artistic form of speech previously in existence, namely poetry, and accordingly they endeavoured sometimes to borrow its external charms, sometimes to replace them by others equivalent to them. We are here speaking not so much of expression, as of the **combination** (arrangement, σύνθεσις) of words, and anything else that may be regarded as connected with their arrangement. Since verse was excluded, Gorgias of Sicily, the first master of artistic prose, introduced into use as in some way equivalent to it certain **figures of speech**, which in the language of rhetoric took their name from him (Γοργίεια σχήματα). These figures consist in the artificial and formal combination of opposites (antithesis) or parallels (parison, isocolon), the charm of which was enhanced by various assonances at the end of the clauses (*i.e.* rhyme) as also at the beginning and in the middle of them (παρόμοια, parechesis etc.). There is here an obvious point of contact with that which poetry elsewhere usually regarded as its distinctive feature, and also a particularly close contact with the old Hebrew parallelism of clauses. These mannerisms of Gorgias were not free from a certain degree of pedantry and indeed of obvious affectation, and for this reason they were subsequently exploded and

---

[1] On ἄρξασθαι, ἀρξάμενος see §§ 69, 4 note; 74, 2; on ἐγένετο § 77, 6.

[2] Also in Jo. 20. 4 προέδραμεν τάχιον τοῦ Πέτρου there is a superfluity of words: ἔδραμεν was sufficient (or προέδρ. τοῦ Πέτρου), especially as καὶ ἦλθεν πρῶτος εἰς τὸ μνημεῖον follows. It is somewhat different in L. 1. 76 προπορεύσῃ πρὸ προσώπου (= πρὸ) τοῦ κυρίου; since it is a common phenomenon of the language, that if a verb compounded with a preposition has its literal meaning, the preposition is again repeated in the complement (εἰσβάλλειν εἰς), § 37, 7.

[3] But Winer § 65, 2 notes with reason that ἐκ δευτέρου etc. if it *follows* πάλιν is not superfluous, but a nearer definition.—D has εὐθέως παραχρῆμα (classical) in A. 14. 10.

went out of fashion; they were most unsuitable for *practical* speech, and for this purpose the Attic orators of the fourth century created a very different and flexible artistic style, which is based upon an imitation of lively speech, springing directly from the feelings, with its forms and figures (σχήματα). But in place of rhyme which had been carried to excess and of assonance in general, the artistic prose of the fourth century, showing herein a certain direct approximation to the style of lyric poetry, had recourse to manifold rhythms, which by their mutual accordance imparted to the language a beautifully harmonious character; it further borrowed from the poets (a practice of which the beginnings are found in Gorgias himself) a smoothness and absence of friction in the juncture of words, doing away with the harsh collision between vowels at the end and beginning of contiguous words,—the so-called **hiatus**. This avoiding of hiatus continued to be practised by Hellenistic and Atticistic writers of the following centuries with a greater or less degree of strictness.

2. The **Epistle to the Hebrews** is the only piece of writing in the N.T., which in structure of sentences and style shows the care and dexterity of an artistic writer, and so it cannot be wondered at, if it is in this work alone that the principle of avoiding **hiatus** is taken into account. But it is by no means the case that all collisions of vowels are of the same kind: those which are faulty in the strictest sense are only such as are not rendered inaudible by a pause in the thought (end of a sentence or clause), or such as cannot be effaced by elision of the first vowel (ἀλλ', δ') or crasis (κἄν), or lastly are not formed by small 'form-words' such as καί, εἰ, μή, τοῦ, ὁ, τὸ (the various forms of the article; also ὅ, οὗ etc.) in the case of which a prose-writer excuses a license which can hardly be helped. The use of hiatus with τί, τι, ὅτι, περί, πρό is also allowable, as it is previously in poetry. Elisions of ᾰ, ε, ο, however, are not readily adopted, if the words combined in this way are other than 'form-words' (cp. § 5, 1); on the other hand, the αι of verbal terminations is subject to elision (and is written with elision [1]), being also reckoned for the purpose of the accent as short or almost short. If then in the Epistle to the Hebrews one leaves out of sight in the first place all the O.T. quotations, next chapter xiii. (concluding warnings etc.), and lastly chap. 9. 2-7 (description of the tabernacle), the test of hiatus gives the following results. Hiatus is a matter of indifference where there is a pause (this includes such passages as 2. 11 | ἐξ ἑνὸς, 3. 3 οἴκου | ὁ, 6. 17 αὐτοῦ |, 7. 24 αἰῶνα |, 11. 18 | ὅτι, 25 | ἢ); hiatus with καί is also a comparatively indifferent matter. With μή there are 7 instances, with ὁ only 4 (6. 16,[2] 9. 25, 10. 23, 11. 28), with τό 14, τά 4, οἱ 5, ἡ 1, τοῦ 7, τῷ 5, τῇ 1, ὅ 1, διό 2 (10. 5, 11. 16; it is avoided by using δι' ἣν αἰτίαν in 2. 11), οὗ 2, ᾧ 1 (instances with art. and rel. amount to 47 in all [3]). With ᾰ and ε (not reckoning ἀλλά, δέ, τε, ἵνα

---

[1] *E.g.* in the Herculanean rolls of Philodemus, Kühner I.[3] i. 238.

[2] Ὁ before ὅρκος may be quite well dispensed with.

[3] In the Epistle to the Romans this number (not reckoning quotations) is already surpassed at 4. 14, in 1 Corinthians at 6. 19.

§ 82. 2–3.] FIGURES OF SPEECH. 297

and prepositions) there are 17[1] and 7 respectively; with αι of verbal terminations 17.[2] Apart from these, the harsher cases of hiatus are as follows: 1. 1 πάλαι ὁ θεός (the article can be dispensed with, § 46, 6), 2. 8 αὐτῷ ἀνυπότακτον (αὐτῷ is superfluous, as just before in the same verse it is removed by Lachm. on the authority of B etc.), οὔπω ὁρῶμεν (βλέπομεν as in 9 ?), (9 O.T. quot.), 9 θεοῦ ὑπὲρ (περὶ ? cp. 5. 3, 10. 18, 26, 13. 11. 18, § 42, 4), (14 ἐπεὶ οὖν as in 4. 6, ἐπεί as a 'form-word' may be used with hiatus also in Demosthenes), 15, 16, 3. 1, 2 (αὐτόν is superfluous; ibid. a quotation as in 5), 12 is full of instances of hiatus, two of which are harsh; (4. 7 according to א* ὁρίζει τινὰ ἡμέραν; ibid. 11 hiatus is avoided by the insertion of τις), (5. 9 read αὐτῷ πᾶσιν with KL al.), 10 θεοῦ ἀρχιερεὺς (to be reckoned as a quotation?), 6. 3 ἐπιτρέπῃ ὁ θεός (see on 1. 1), 6. 7, 10 (7. 1 O.T. quot.), 3, 14, 8. 7 πρώτη ἐκείνη ἦν, 9. 9, 12, 14, 15, 17,[3] 21, 23, 24, 25 bis, 26 (ἐπεὶ ἔδει), 10 (2 the text is uncertain[4]), 10 three instances of hiatus,[5] (13 quotation), 19, 11. 4, 5 πίστει Ἐνὼχ, similarly 21, 22, 11. 7, 8 (ποῦ, excusable), 19 (not without v.l.), (21 quot.), 22, 28. 30 two cases of hiatus with Ἰεριχώ, 31, 34, 12. 8 (the position of ἐστέ varies and the word can be dispensed with), 24 (Ἰησοῦ superfluous), 25. The attention that has been been bestowed on the avoiding of hiatus is accordingly put beyond a doubt,[6] though the different portions of the work seem not to have been executed with quite a uniform amount of care.

3. To look for **verses** and **fragments of verse** (apart from the three quotations, A. 17. 28, 1 C. 15. 33, Tit. 1. 12), *i.e.* to look for rhythm in the N.T., is on the whole a useless waste of time, and the specimens of verse which have been found are for the most part of such a quality that they are better left unmentioned (Ja. 1. 17 is a hexameter πᾶσα δόσις κ.τ.λ., but contains a tribrach in the second foot). It is somewhat different, however, with the Epistle to the Hebrews, where in 12. 13 there occurs a faultless hexameter, καὶ τροχιὰς ὀρθὰς ποιήσατε[7] τοῖς ποσὶν ὑμῶν, and immediately after in 14 f. two equally

---

[1] 3. 17 κῶλα ἔπεσεν is a quotation. This calculation includes 4. 1 ἄρα, also 11. 14 πατρίδα ἐπιζητοῦσι, where D* al. read ζητοῦσι; an additional instance is 4. 7 τινὰ ἡμ., on which see below in the text.

[2] In 12. 7 προσφέρεται ὁ θεός, ὁ can be dispensed with as in 1. 1 (see lower down in the text); 3. 18 is a quotation.

[3] The clause ἐπεὶ μήποτε ἰσχύει, ὅτε ζῇ ὁ διαθέμενος may be perfectly well dispensed with, and cp. § 75, 3.

[4] Ἐπεὶ οὐκ ἂν ἐπαύσαντο (which must be taken as a question) with v.l. omitting οὐκ; an obvious suggestion is to read κἄν.

[5] Not according to the text of Theophylact: ἐν ᾧ θελήματι **τοῦ πατρὸς** ἡγιάσθημεν οἱ διὰ τῆς προσφορᾶς τοῦ σώματος τοῦ Χρ. **τῆς** ἐφάπαξ κ.τ.λ.

[6] See also 12. 7 παιδεύει πατήρ without the article (§ 46, 7), which would have caused a hiatus; ibid. 14 οὗ χωρὶς stands for χωρὶς οὗ (where οὐδεὶς follows). Also in 1. 1 ἐν τῷ υἱῷ might have been expected.

[7] א*P have a v.l. ποιεῖτε, as ποίει is read in Prov. 4. 26 on which the passage is based, but here at any rate the present is not in keeping with the sense, as the aorist is needed to express the contrast with the state of things hitherto existing, § 58, 2. The question of rhythm in Hebrews has been specially con-

faultless trimeters in succession, οὗ χωρὶς[1] οὐδεὶς ὄψεται τὸν κύριον | ἐπισκοποῦντες μή τις ὑστερῶν ἀπὸ |. The opening of the Epistle has a similar rhythm, especially if ὁ is expunged (supra 2): πολυμερῶς καὶ πολυτρόπως πάλαι θεός, ‿ ‿ ‿ — ‿ ‿ ‿ — ‿ ‿ ‿ —, which would be a senarius if a single syllable, e.g. ὁ, were prefixed to it; then there follows another senarius ἐπ' ἐσχάτου τῶν ἡμερῶν τούτων ἐλά(λησεν); see further 4 τοσούτῳ κρείττων γενόμενος τῶν ἀγγέλων, where the metre is made correct by transposing κρείττων τοσούτῳ, 11. 27 τὸν γὰρ ἀόρατον ὡς ὁρῶν ἐκαρτέρη(σεν), 12. 2 ὃς ἀντὶ τῆς προκειμένης αὐτῷ χαρᾶς, 28 δι' ἧς λατρεύομεν (but with v.l. -ωμεν) εὐαρέστως τῷ θεῷ | μετ' εὐλαβείας καὶ δέους· καὶ γὰρ ὁ θεός |. At any rate one cannot feel quite so certain in this Epistle as elsewhere, that one is merely dealing with purely fortuitous cases of rhythm.

4. The studied employment of the so-called **Gorgian assonances** is necessarily foreign to the style of the N.T., all the more because they were comparatively foreign to the whole period; accident however of course produces occasional instances of them, and the writer often did not decline to make use of any that suggested themselves. **Paronomasia** is the name given to the recurrence of the same word or word-stem in close proximity, **parechesis** to the resemblance in sound between different contiguous words. Instances of paronomasia are: Mt. 21. 41 κακοὺς κακῶς ἀπολέσει αὐτούς (a good classical and popular combination of words[2], 2 C. 9. 8 ἐν παντὶ πάντοτε πᾶσαν αὐτάρκειαν,[3] 8. 22, A. 21. 28, 24. 3 (Herm. Mand. xi. 3 αὐτὸς γὰρ κενὸς ὢν κενῶς [MSS. κενὸς] καὶ ἀποκρίνεται κενοῖς); then there may be a contrast in the sentence, so that there is a certain subtlety and sometimes a suggestion of wit in the paronomasia: 2 C. 4. 8 ἀπορούμενοι, ἀλλ' οὐκ ἐξαπορούμενοι, 2 Th. 3. 11 μηδὲν ἐργαζομένους, ἀλλὰ περιεργαζομένους, A. 8. 30 ἆρά γε γινώσκεις ἃ ἀναγινώσκεις; (cp. 2 C. 3. 2), R. 12. 3 μὴ ὑπερφρονεῖν παρ' ὃ δεῖ **φρονεῖν**, ἀλλὰ **φρονεῖν** εἰς τὸ **σωφρονεῖν** (which might almost be called finical), 1 C. 11. 29 ff. κρίμα—διακρίνων—διεκρίνομεν—ἐκρινόμεθα—κρινόμενοι—κατακριθῶμεν (ditto), 2 C. 10. 2 f. κατὰ σάρκα—ἐν σαρκὶ—κατὰ σ.; the paronomasia is most sharply marked in Ph. 3. 2 f. βλέπετε τὴν **κατατομήν** (the Jewish circumcision), ἡμεῖς γὰρ ἐσμεν ἡ **περιτομή**,[4] where Paul in an

---

sidered by Delitzsch in his commentary, see the review by J. Köstlin in Gtg. gel. Anz. 1858, art. 84, p. 827 ff., who however is inclined to disbelieve in it.

[1] This verse is noticed by Delitzsch, the following verse is added by his reviewer. Χωρίς in this passage only stands after its case, § 80, 4; but hiatus is also avoided by this expedient, supra note 6 on p. 297.

[2] Demosth. 21. 204 εἰ κακὸς κακῶς ἀπολεῖ, Winer § 67, 1.

[3] Plato Menex. 247 A (a Gorgian assonance): διὰ παντὸς πᾶσαν πάντως προθυμίαν πειρᾶσθε ἔχειν. For the N.T. see numerous instances of the figures here discussed in Wilke p. 342 ff., 402-415.

[4] Winer § 68, 2 compares Diog. Laert. 6. 24, who says of Diogenes the Cynic τὴν μὲν Εὐκλείδου **σχολὴν** ἔλεγε **χολήν**, τὴν δὲ Πλάτωνος **διατριβὴν κατατριβήν**.— Paul does *not* make any word-play on the name of the slave Onesimus, although he uses (in this passage only) the word ὀναίμην, Philem. 20; the most that can be said is that the recipient of the letter might make for himself the obvious play of words from 'Ονήσιμον – ἄχρηστον 10 f.

oratorical manner robs his opponents of the word in which they pride themselves and turns it into a disgrace. The paronomasia in A. 23. 3 also appears to be oratorical, where Paul in answer to Ananias, who had commanded τύπτειν αὐτοῦ τὸ στόμα, replies τύπτειν σε μέλλει ὁ θεός, using the same word in another and metaphorical sense; cp. Ap. 22. 28 f., and with parechesis σχῖνος—σχίσει, πρῖνος —πρίσει LXX. Dan. Sus. 54 f., Winer § 68, 2; so that this appears to have been a common method of retort among the Jews. The practice of twisting a word that occurs in the sentence into a metaphorical sense is illustrated also by 2 C. 3. 1 ff. (ἐπιστολή): similarly L. 9. 60 (Mt. 8. 22) ἄφες τοὺς νεκροὺς θάψαι τοὺς ἑαυτῶν νεκρούς : Mt. 5. 19 (ἐλάχιστος); but Paul is particularly fond of dwelling on an idea and a word, although it does not assume different meanings and is not repeated absolutely immediately, while there is still a certain artificial and reflective manner in the repetition (known as *traductio* in Latin rhetoricians). Thus in 2 C. 3. 5 ff. we first have ἱκανοί—ἱκανότης—ἱκάνωσεν, then γράμμα (following ἐγγεγραμμένη 2 f.) three times, also πνεῦμα (which has likewise been used already in 3); διάκονος 6, διακονία 7 ff. four times; δόξα 7-11 eight times besides δεδοξάσθαι twice in 10 (οὐ δεδόξασται τὸ δεδοξασμένον, a kind of oxymoron with an apparent contradiction).—**Parechesis** is seen in the old combination of words, which became popular, L. 21. 11 λιμοὶ καὶ λοιμοὶ ἔσονται (Hesiod, W. and D. 241 λιμὸν ὁμοῦ καὶ λοιμόν); H. 5. 8 ἔμαθεν ἀφ' ὧν ἔπαθεν (the proverb πάθει μάθος occurs in Aesch. Agam. 170); Paul in enumerations combines the following words, R. 1. 29 (G. 5. 21?) φθόνου φόνου, 31 ἀσυνέτους ἀσυνθέτους; but κλάδων ἐξεκλάσθησαν 11. 17, 19 may be accidental or a kind of etymological figure (like φόβον φοβεῖσθαι).—The ὁμοιοτέλευτον in R. 12. 15 χαίρειν μετὰ χαιρόντων, κλαίειν μετὰ κλαιόντων (where there is assonance also in the first words of the two clauses, so that this is a case of ὁμοιοκάταρκτον as well) arose naturally and unsought; but in 5. 16 it may be considered as studied and deliberate, οὐχ ὡς δι' ἑνὸς ἁμαρτήσαντος τὸ δώρημα· τὸ μὲν γὰρ κρίμα ἐξ ἑνὸς εἰς κατάκριμα, τὸ δὲ χάρισμα ἐκ πολλῶν παραπτωμάτων εἰς δικαίωμα. Paul has certainly not sought after rhyme in this passage, but has no doubt (as already in 14 f.) played with the formations in -μα, which were among the *deliciae* of the Hellenistic stylist.[1]

5. **Antitheses** and **parallelisms** of all kinds are very largely developed in the N.T., not only in the Pauline Epistles, but also in the Gospels, especially those of Matthew and Luke; in the latter their occurrence is due to the gnomic character of ancient Hebrew literature (supra 1), in the former it is the outcome of the Apostle's dialectic and eloquence. With these should be reckoned a further series of **figures** (σχήματα), of which we learn in Greek and Latin rhetoricians, and for which instances are quoted from Demosthenes, Cicero etc. Antithesis and parison (supra 1), considered on their own merits, form part of these figures; but it may easily happen in

---

[1] *E.g.* of Epicurus, from whom Cleomedes περὶ μετεώρων B cap. 1 gives excerpts containing the words κατάστημα ἔλπισμα λίπασμα ἀνακραύγασμα.

cases of parallelism of this kind, that the first words are alike (**anaphora**), or the last words are alike (**antistrophe**), or the first and the last words are alike (**symploce**), and by this means the parallelism is rendered still more striking to the ear. Moreover words in the middle of the sentence may be alike or have a similar termination. Again cases frequently occur where there is a double anaphora etc., if each section of the parallelism is again subdivided, and the repetition of the word may take place not only twice, but even thrice and still more often. Thus we have in 1 C. 1. 25 ff. ὅτι τὸ μωρὸν τοῦ θεοῦ | σοφώτερόν ἐστιν τῶν ἀνθρώπων ‖ καὶ τὸ ἀσθενὲς τοῦ θεοῦ | ἰσχυρότερόν ἐστι τῶν ἀνθρώπων[1]. βλέπετε γὰρ τὴν κλῆσιν ὑμῶν ἀδελφοί | ὅτι οὐ πολλοὶ σοφοὶ κατὰ σάρκα | οὐ πολλοὶ δυνατοί | οὐ πολλοὶ εὐγενεῖς ‖ ἀλλὰ τὰ μωρὰ τοῦ κόσμου ἐξελέξατο ὁ θεός | ἵνα καταισχύνῃ τοὺς σοφούς (τὰ σοφά according to the text of Marcion, a better reading) ‖ καὶ τὰ ἀσθενῆ τοῦ κόσμου ἐξελέξατο ὁ θεός | ἵνα καταισχύνῃ τὰ ἰσχυρά ‖ καὶ τὰ ἀγενῆ τοῦ κόσμου καὶ τὰ ἐξουθενημένα ἐξελέξατο ὁ θεός | τὰ μὴ ὄντα[2] | ἵνα τὰ ὄντα καταργήσῃ | ὅπως μὴ καυχήσηται πᾶσα σὰρξ ἐνώπιον τοῦ θεοῦ. In this passage the parallelism is developed, though not quite from the beginning, into rounded periods of three sections, and the third section in the last parallelism, which gives the finish to the whole sentence, exceeds the others in the number and length of its clauses, which is just what rhetoricians require in final sections of this kind[3]; the parallelism is thus sustained throughout the whole passage with a precision as accurate as the thought admitted of, while the sharpness of the thought is not sacrificed to form. This is a point which the rhetoricians praise as a merit in Demosthenes also, that his antitheses are *not* worked out with minute accuracy. And so too St. Paul does not say ἵνα τὰ εὐγενῆ καταργήσῃ because τὰ ἀγενῆ has preceded, but the expansion of the concluding clause enables him to introduce τὰ μὴ ὄντα, which together with its opposite τὰ ὄντα, which is annexed, gives a better and much more powerful expression to the thought. No Greek orator—for one must naturally compare the passage with practical speech, and not with the quiet flow of artistic speech, in

---

[1] Ἐστι is read in both places *before* ἀνθρ. in DEFG ; ℵABC al. have σοφώτ. τ. ἀ. ἐστίν, and then ℵ°AC al. have in the corresponding clause ἰσχ. τ. ἀ. ἐστίν, but here ℵ*B omit ἐστίν. A similar termination must in any case be retained. Cp. 10. 16 (where B is wrong).

[2] The καὶ before τὰ μὴ ὄντα in Bℵ° al. is certainly an interpolation. Marcion had in his text (instead of the third τοῦ κόσμου) καὶ τὰ ἐλάχιστα, then he omits the third ἐξελέξατο ὁ θεός, and gives in the following clause ἵνα καταισχύνῃ τὰ ὄντα, a reading the whole of which seems to give additional force and beauty to the sentence.

[3] Cic. de Orat. iii. 186 (apparently following Theophrastus) : *membra si in extremo breviora sunt, infringitur ille quasi verborum ambitus* (period) ; *quare aut paria esse debent posteriora superioribus et extrema primis, aut, quod etiam est melius et iucundius, longiora.* Demetrius περὶ ἑρμηνείας 18 : ἐν ταῖς συνθέτοις περιόδοις τὸ τελευταῖον κῶλον μακρότερον χρὴ εἶναι, καὶ ὥσπερ περιέχον καὶ περιειληφὸς τἆλλα. Cp. 1 C. 15. 42 ff. σπείρεται ἐν φθορᾷ | ἐγείρεται ἐν ἀφθαρσίᾳ ‖ σπείρεται ἐν ἀτιμίᾳ | ἐγείρεται ἐν δόξῃ ‖ σπ. ἐν ἀσθενείᾳ | ἐγ. ἐν δυνάμει ‖ σπ. σῶμα ψυχικόν | ἐγείρεται σῶμα πνευματικόν (10 syllables, the longest of all these κῶλα) ; ibid. 48 f. three periods containing parallels, the last being far the longest in both portions of the comparison ; R. 8. 33 ff., 2. 21 ff.

§ 82. 5–7.] *FIGURES OF SPEECH.* 301

which everything which may be termed δὶς ταὐτὸν λέγειν is proscribed —would have regarded the eloquence of this passage with other feelings than those of the highest admiration.

6. The practice of giving a similar termination to clauses (**antistrophe**) may occasionally take a simpler form as in H. 2. 16 οὐ γὰρ δήπου ἀγγέλων ἐπιλαμβάνεται, ἀλλὰ σπέρματος Ἀβραὰμ ἐπιλαμβάνεται (more emphatic than if the verb were left to be supplied in the second clause). The same Epistle has an excessively long instance of **anaphora** in 11. 3-31 πίστει (repeated 18 times), a passage which taken together with the forcible and comprehensive conclusion (32-40) corresponds in some measure to the peroration of a speech following upon the demonstration; before (and after) this point this letter is by no means so rich in figures as some of the Pauline Epistles, but exhibits in this respect a certain classically temperate attitude. St. Paul, on the other hand, has *e.g.* in 2 C. 6. 4 ff. ἐν 19 times, followed immediately by διά 3 times, and ὡς 7.[1] (Clem. Cor. i. 36. 2 has anaphora with διὰ τούτου 5 times repeated; with ἀγάπῃ [after 1 C. 13] in 49. 4.) The speeches in the Acts, which are certainly nothing more than excerpts from speeches, for this reason alone cannot have much embellishment: anaphora occurs with ὑμεῖς ... ὑμῖν in 3. 26 f., τούτῳ ... οὗτος 4. 10 f., τοῦτον ... οὗτος 3 times in 7. 35 ff., see further 10. 42 ff., 13. 39.

7. The emphatic duplication of an impressive word (**epanadiplosis** of the rhetoricians) is not unknown in the N.T., but is nowhere to be reckoned as a rhetorical device: thus Ap. 14. 8 = 18. 2 ἔπεσεν ἔπεσεν Βαβυλὼν ἡ μεγάλη, Mt. 25. 11 κύριε κύριε, 23. 7, Mc. 14. 45 ῥαββὶ ῥαββί (some MSS.), L. 8. 24 ἐπιστάτα ἐπιστάτα, Jo. 19. 6 σταύρωσον σταύρωσον, L. 10. 41 Μάρθα Μάρθα, in all which passages we have a direct report of the actual words spoken, as is most clearly shown by A. 19. 34 μεγάλη ἡ Ἄρτεμις Ἐφεσίων, μεγάλη ἡ Ἄ. Ἐ. (so B reads), words which were in fact shouted for two hours. (On the other hand the repetition is rhetorical in Clem. Cor. i. 47. 6 αἰσχρά, ἀγαπητοί, καὶ λίαν αἰσχρὰ καὶ ἀνάξια κ.τ.λ.). Another figure in which repetition plays a part is the kind of **climax**, which consists in each clause taking up and repeating the principal word of the preceding clause; the rhetoricians found this figure already existing in Homer Il. ii. 102, where the following words occur on the subject of Agamemnon's sceptre, Ἥφαιστος μὲν δῶκε Διὶ ..., αὐτὰρ ἄρα Ζεὺς δῶκε διακτόρῳ Ἀργειφόντῃ, Ἑρμείας δὲ κ.τ.λ. So Paul has in R. 5. 3 ff. ἡ θλῖψις **ὑπομονὴν** κατεργάζεται, ἡ δὲ **ὑπομονὴ δοκιμήν**, ἡ δὲ **δοκιμὴ ἐλπίδα**, ἡ δὲ **ἐλπὶς** οὐ καταισχύνει, cp. 8. 29 f., and a decidedly artificial passage 10. 14 πῶς οὖν ἐπικαλέσωνται εἰς ὃν οὐκ **ἐπίστευσαν**; πῶς δὲ **πιστεύσωσιν** οὗ οὐκ **ἤκουσαν**; πῶς δὲ **ἀκούσωσιν** χωρὶς **κηρύσσοντος**; πῶς δὲ **κηρύξωσιν** ἐὰν μὴ ἀποσταλῶσιν; Cp. also 2 P. 1. 5 ff. ἐπιχορηγήσατε ἐν τῇ πίστει ὑμῶν τὴν ἀρετήν, ἐν δὲ τῇ ἀρετῇ τὴν γνῶσιν, ἐν δὲ κ.τ.λ. (7 clauses in all; but the object of using the figure in this passage is by no means intelligible). A further instance is Herm. Mand. v. 2. 4 ἐκ τῆς ἀφρο-

---

[1] See for further details Wilke 396 f.

σύνης γίνεται πικρία, ἐκ δὲ τῆς πικρίας θυμός, ἐκ δὲ τοῦ θυμοῦ ὀργή, ἐκ δὲ τῆς ὀργῆς μῆνις· εἶτα ἡ μῆνις κ.τ.λ.[1]

8. Asyndeton and **polysyndeton** have already been discussed in § 79, 3 ff.; here we may lay greater stress on one form of asyndeton, which is based upon the resolution of a periodic sentence, but which gives a more lively and effective expression to the thought than the periodic form of sentence would do, 1 C. 7. 27 δέδεσαι γυναικί | μὴ ζήτει λύσιν ‖ λέλυσαι ἀπὸ γυναικός | μὴ ζήτει γυναῖκα, = εἰ μὲν δέδεσαι γυν., μὴ ζ. λ., εἰ δὲ κ.τ.λ. (where there is likewise a strong instance of antistrophe, supra 5, and in λύσιν | λέλυσαι the figure called by the rhetoricians **anastrophe**, that is the end of one clause is equivalent to the beginning of the next; moreover the point of the sentence is further heightened by the brevity of the clauses). Cp. ibid. 18, 21, Ja. 5. 13 ff.; many sentences of the same kind occur in the practical writings of Greek orators. In the passages in the orators and in the N.T. the first portion of resolved sentences of this kind is ordinarily written as a question; but certainly German has analogous phrases which are not interrogative, ' bist du los, so suche ' etc. The more ordinary forms of asyndeton are occasionally employed by Paul with almost too great a profusion, so that the figure loses its force as an artistic expedient, and the whole discourse appears broken up into small fragments. The Epistle to the Hebrews shows more moderation in this respect, even in the brilliant passage where πίστει is repeated 18 times with asyndeton (supra 6); since the separate paragraphs in that passage, which are in many cases of a considerable length, are not without their own connecting links, and in the concluding summary 11. 31 ff., though twice over we have 10 or almost 10 short clauses standing without connecting links, yet a piece of connected speech is interposed between them (35 f.), and the whole chapter is rounded off by a periodic sentence in verses 39, 40.

9. Besides figures of **expression** (σχήματα λέξεως), to which those hitherto considered belong, the rhetoricians discriminate and give a separate name to an equally large number of figures of **thought** (σχ. διανοίας), with which it is not the case, as it is with the former class, that the substitution of one synonym for another, or the deletion of a word, or an alteration in the order of words causes the figure to disappear. As a general rule these figures of thought belong not so much to the earlier as to the later period of Attic oratory, since their development presupposes a certain amount of advance in the acuteness and subtlety of the language. The orator pretends to pass over something which in reality he mentions: thus ὅτι μὲν ..., παραλείπω (a figure known as **paraleipsis** or *praeteritio*); and under this figure one may of course, if one pleases, bring Paul's language in Philem. 19 ἵνα μὴ λέγω ὅτι καὶ σεαυτόν μοι προσοφείλεις.[2] Again, 2 C.

---

[1] There is a similar instance in a fragment of the comedian Epicharmus, ἐκ μὲν θυσίας θοίνα, ἐκ δὲ θοίνας πόσις ἐγένετο—ἐκ δὲ πόσιος κῶμος, ἐκ κώμου δ' ἐγένεθ' ὑανία, ἐκ δ' ὑανίας δίκα κ.τ.λ.—Cp. Wilke 398, who further adduces Ja. 1. 14 f. and 1 C. 11. 3 (in the latter passage there is no climax).

[2] Wilke p. 365 cites also passages like 1 Th. 4. 9, where however no figure

§ 82. 9-10.]   FIGURES OF SPEECH.   303

9. 4 μήποτε ... καταισχυνθῶμεν ἡμεῖς, ἵνα μὴ λέγωμεν ὑμεῖς is not a simple and straight-forward statement: the simple expression of the Apostle's thought would be καταισχυνθῆτε, but as that would pain his hearers, he appears to turn the reproach against himself, while he makes it clear that he does so by what the rhetoricians call a σχῆμα ἐπιεικές. Paul also occasionally employs **irony** (εἰρωνεία) of the sharpest kind: 1 C. 4. 8 ἤδη κεκορεσμένοι ἐστέ; ἤδη ἐπλουτήσατε; χωρὶς ἡμῶν ἐβασιλεύσατε; 2 C. 11. 19 f. ἡδέως ἀνέχεσθε τῶν ἀφρόνων, φρόνιμοι ὄντες· ἀνέχεσθε γὰρ κ.τ.λ., 12. 13[1]; he knows how to change his tone in an astonishing way, and if conscious of the offence which he is about to give or has given, he employs **prodiorthoses** as in 2 C. 11. 1 ff., 16 ff., 21 ἐν ἀφροσύνῃ λέγω, 23, or **epidiorthoses** as in 12. 11 γέγονα ἄφρων κ.τ.λ., 7. 3, R. 3. 5 κατὰ ἄνθρωπον λέγω,[2] since he everywhere puts himself in a position of the closest intercourse and liveliest sympathy with his readers.

10. Other figures of thought have more of an obviously rhetorical character, so especially the (so-called rhetorical) **question** with its various methods of employment, sometimes serving the purpose of dialectical liveliness and perspicuity, as in R. 3. 1 τί οὖν τὸ περισσὸν τοῦ Ἰουδαίου; with the answer πολὺ κατὰ πάντα τρόπον, 4. 10 πῶς οὖν ἐλογίσθη; ἐν περιτομῇ ὄντι ἢ ἐν ἀκροβυστίᾳ; οὐκ ἐν περιτομῇ κ.τ.λ. (this use is especially frequent in the Epistle to the Romans: but cp. also Jo. 12. 27), sometimes used as an expression of keen sensibility, astonishment, or unwillingness, but also of a joyful elation of spirit, as in R. 8. 31 τί οὖν ἐροῦμεν πρὸς ταῦτα; εἰ ὁ θεὸς ὑπὲρ ἡμῶν, τίς καθ' ἡμῶν; to which there is subsequently attached a pair of questions, with their subordinate answers, which are also expressed in an interrogative form (ὑποφορά, subjectio): τίς ἐγκαλέσει κατὰ ἐκλεκτῶν θεοῦ; θεὸς ὁ δικαιῶν; τίς ὁ κατακρινῶν; Χριστὸς Ἰησοῦς ὁ κ.τ.λ.[3] This is one of the brilliant oratorical passages, which are a distinguishing feature of this Epistle and the Corinthian Epistles (see further e.g. 2 C. 11. 22 Ἑβραῖοί εἰσιν; κἀγώ. Ἰσραηλῖταί εἰσιν; κἀγώ. σπέρμα Ἀβραάμ εἰσίν; κἀγώ, κ.τ.λ.), but the discussion of such passages is out of place in a grammar and can only be tolerated if briefly dwelt on and treated by way of appendix.

can be recognized (οὐ χρείαν ἔχετε), any more than in H. 11. 32, where the expression used corresponds accurately to the fact.

[1] Ibid. 356. From the Gospels, L. 13. 33 comes under this head.

[2] Ibid. 292 ff. Epidiorthosis is used in another sense in the case of a correction which enhances a previous statement: R. 8. 34 ὁ ἀποθανών, μᾶλλον δὲ ἐγερθείς, G. 4. 9.

[3] So Augustine and most modern authorities take θεὸς ὁ δικ. and Χριστὸς κ.τ.λ. as questions. It is true that Tischendorf and Wilke (p. 396) are opposed to this view; but as there is undoubtedly a question in the third place, and as θεὸς ὁ δικ. does *not* mean 'God is *here*, who' etc. (as Luther renders it), it appears better to keep the other (interrogative) interpretation throughout. The passage is oratorical rather than strictly logical.

INDEX.

I. INDEX OF SUBJECTS.

Accents 14 f.
Accusative—With transitive verbs 87 ff. With verbs compounded with κατά etc. 89. Acc. of the inner object (content) 90 f., 174. With passive verbs 93. Double acc. 91 ff. Acc. of reference 94. In apposition with the sentence 293. Adverbial acc. 94, 157. Acc. of extension etc. in space and time 94 f., 121. After prepositions 122 ff., 132 ff. Acc. of the infinitive with article 233 f. Acc. of inf. dependent on prepositions 236. Acc. with the inf. in clauses in apposition with subject 241 f.
Accusative and infinitive 239 ff. Cp. 238 f., 225 ff., 230 ff., 237 ff. (Acc. with ὅτι or ἵνα used instead of acc. and inf. 240.)
Accusative absolute 251 f.
Active 180 ff. With intransitive meaning 182 f. For middle 183 f. For passive 184.
Adjective—Inflection and degrees of comparison 32 ff. Syntax 140 ff. Feminine (masc., neut.) of adj. with ellipse of a subst. 140 f. Neuter adj. (sing. and plur.) used substantivally of persons 82, 156. Other instances of independent use of adj. without subst. (with and without article) 154 ff. Neuter adj. with genitive 155. Adj. instead of adverb 141. Adj. as attribute with article, predicative (and partitive) adj. without art. 158. Position 289.
Adjective, verbal: has (almost) disappeared 37, 64, 206 note 2.
Adverbs of manner 58. Derived from participles 58. Adverbs of place 58 f. Adv. of time 59. Correlative adverbs 59 f. Interrogative adv.

258. Adjectival and adverbial comparative of adverbs 34 f. Compounded adverbs 65 f., 69 f. Adv. with the article 157, 159. Adv. as predicate 257 f. Position of adv. 289.
Adversative particles 261, 266 ff.
Agreement 76 ff.
Anacoluthon 251, 267, 282 ff.
Anaphora 300 f.
Anastrophe (figure of speech) 302.
Antistrophe (figure of speech) 300 f.
Antithesis 295, 299 f.
Aorist, 1st and 2nd and 43 f. Middle and passive aorist 44 f. Terminations 45 f. Aorist of deponent verbs 44 f. Uses of the aorist 190 ff., 205, 207 ff., 218. Gnomic aorist 193 f. Epistolary aorist 194. Moods of the aorist: imperative 194 ff.—infinitive 196 f., 202, 231, 237—participle 197 f., 204.—conjunctive 208 ff., 211 ff. Aorist indic. with ἄν 207, cp. Indicative.
Apocalypse, solecisms in, 80 f. Other details in Ap.: 117 (instrumental ἐν frequent), 123 (εἰς not used for ἐν), 126 (ἐξ frequent), 128 (ἐνώπιον etc.), 132 (σύν never used), 135 (ὑπό with acc. never), 138 (παρά with acc. never), 152 ('Ιησοῦς without art.), 179 (ἕτερος never), 200 (perfect for aorist), 211 (ὅπως never), 211 f. (ἵνα with fut.), 266 (μέν never), 274 (γάρ).
Aposiopesis 291, 294.
Apposition with and without the article 152, 162 f. (159 note 4), 242 f. (participles). Apposition of sentences 293.
Aramaic 4 f.

304

INDEX OF SUBJECTS. 305

Arrangement of words § 82, 295 ff.
Article—ὁ ἡ τό. With crasis 18 f. Uses 145 ff. As pronoun 145 f. Individual or generic 146 ff., 155. Anaphoric sense of art. 146, 148-152, 233 (infin.), etc. Omission of art. 147 ff.: usually omitted with predicate 147, 157 f., 169: omitted with ordinal numbers 149: after the relative 174: with abstract nouns 150: with nouns governing a genitive 150 f.: before the relative 174 note 1. Art. with proper names 151 f., 95: with place-names 152 f.: names of countries 153: names of rivers and seas 153: names of nations 153 f. Art. with adjectives 154 ff., 158. With participles 156 f., 158, 242 ff. With adverbs 157, 159. With prepositional expressions 94, 157, 159 f. At the beginning of a defining clause 159. Art. governing the genitive 157, 159. Art. with several defining clauses 160. Repeated after ὁ ἄλλος, οἱ λοιποί 160 f. Art. with οὗτος, ἐκεῖνος 161, 172. With αὐτός 161, 170. With possessives (ἴδιος) 169. Not with ἕκαστος 161. With ὅλος, πᾶς (ἅπας) 161 f. With appositional phrases 162 f. Repetition of art. in the case of several connected substantives 163. Art. with infinitive 233 ff. τό prefixed to indirect questions 158: prefixed to quotations of words and sentences 158.

Article, indefinite: beginnings of (εἷς) 144.

Aspirate, doubling of the, 11.

Assertion, sentences of: with ὅτι etc. 222, 230 ff., 272. Negative οὐ 254 f.

Assertion, particles of 261, 272.

Assimilation of consonants 11 f.: in independent words 11 f. Ass. in gender of the subject (pronoun) to the predicate 77. Of ἥμισυς to the genitive which it governs 97. Of the relative: see Attraction.

Assurance, sentences denoting, 260.

Asyndeton 276 ff. (299). Between ideas 265, 277. In the case of certain imperatives 278. Between clauses and sentences (thoughts, paragraphs) 278 ff., 267, 271. Cp. 250 (participles). New subject introduced with a fresh start (ἐξ ἀποστάσεως) 279, cp. Figures of speech.

Attic declension 25. Attic future 41 f.

Attraction of the relative 173 f. Attractio inversa 174 f. Attraction in the case of a relative adverb 258.

Augment (syllabic and temporal) 37 ff. In compound verbs 39. Double augment in verbs compounded of two prepositions 39.

Brachylogy 294.

Breathing, rough and smooth, 15 f. In Semitic words 16.

Cardinal numbers 35. Used instead of ordinals 144.

Causal particles 261, 274 f.

Causal sentences 274, 254 f. (negative οὐ).

Causative verbs with a double accusative 92.

Clement of Rome, Epistle to the Corinthians 1.

Climax 301 f.

Common speech of the Hellenistic period 2 ff. Differences which may be traced in it 3 note 1, 33 note 1.

Compact (or periodic) form of speech 275, 279 f.

Comparative 33 ff. Adjectival comp. of adverbs 34 f., 58. Used instead of superlative 33, 141 f. Corresponding to English positive 142. Heightening of comp. 143. ἵνα after a comp. with ἤ 228.

Comparative particles 261, 270 f.

Comparison of adjective (and adverb) 33 ff.

Composition, proper and improper 65, cp. Word-formation.

Composition (arrangement) of words 295 ff.

Concessive particles 261, 275.

Concessive sentences 215, 248 (participial), 275.

Conditional particles 213 f., 261, 271.

Conditional sentences 205, 213 ff., 221, 271, 254 (negative οὐ and μή).

Conjugation, system of 36 f.

Conjunctions, see Particles.

Conjunctive of verbs in -όω 48. Its use in principal sentences 208 ff. Its use to supplement and take the place of the imperative 208 f. With

υ

INDEX OF SUBJECTS.

οὐ μή 209 f. In questions 210. Its use in subordinate sentences 211 ff. In indirect questions 211. In final sentences 211 f. After μή 212 f. In conditional sentences 213 ff. In concessive sentences 215 f. In relative sentences 216 ff. In temporal sentences 218 f. After ἵνα 221 ff. After πρίν 229. Conj. of the present, aorist, perfect, see Present, Aorist, Perfect.—The conj. negatived by μή 253.

Consecutive particles 261, 272 ff.

Consecutive sentences with ὥστε (ὡς) 223 f., 272. With ἵνα 224 f.

Consonants—Variable final consonants 19 f. Interchange of consonants 23 f. Orthography 10 ff. Single and double cons. 10 f. Assimilation 11 f. Rendering of Semitic cons. 12 f.: of Latin cons. 13.

Constructio ad sensum 79, 166.

Continuous style 275 f.

Contraction 22 f. In the 1st and 2nd declensions 25. In the 3rd declension 27. In verbs 47 f.

Co-ordination of finite verbs and participial expressions 249 ff.

Copulative particles 261 ff.

Correlative pronouns 36, 178 f. Correlative adverbs 59 f.

Crasis 18 f.

Dative—As the necessary complement of the verb 109 ff.│ Dat. commodi et incommodi 111. Dat. with εἰμί etc. 111 f. With the (perfect) passive 112 f. Ethic dative 113. Dat. of community 113 ff. With words compounded with prepositions 114 (σύν), 115 f. Instrumental dat. 116 f. Dat. of cause or occasion 117. Dat. of respect 117. Dat. of manner 118 f. Dat. of verbal subst. used with its cognate verb 119. Temporal dat. 119 f. Also used for duration of time 121. Periphrasis for dat. with εἰς or ἐν 109 f. 124, 131; with ἔμπροσθεν or ἐνώπιον 128. Dat. of the infinitive 236; after ἐν 237.

Demonstrative pronouns 35 f. Uses of, 170 ff. Preceding an infinitive 229. Used to connect sentences 276. Demonstrative adverbs 58 f.

Derivatives of compounds (παρασύνθετα) 65.

Design, sentences of. See Final Sentences.

Diaeresis, marks of 16 f.
Diminutives 63 f.
Disjunctive particles 261, 266.
Division of words. See Words.
Doubling of consonants 10 f. Of aspirates, 11.
Dual, disappearance of the, 3, 36, 76.
Duality no longer distinguished (or scarcely so) from plurality 3, 34, 36.

Elative 33, 143. Distinguished from superlative 33 note 1.

Elision 18. Neglected in some compound words 70. Avoids hiatus 296 f.

Ellipse § 81, 291 ff. Of the verb 'to be' 72 ff. Of other verbs 292 ff. Of the subject 75. Of a substantive (usually feminine) with an adjective etc. 140 f. Of the object 292. Cp. 180 and 292 (ἄλλος). 269 (ἀλλ' ἵνα). Absence of the apodosis 271, 294.

Epanadiplosis 301.

Epidiorthosis 282, 303.

Feminine (of the pronoun) instead of neuter 82.

Figures of speech 295 ff. Gorgian figures 295 f., 298 f. Oratorical 299 ff. Figures of thought 302 f. The figure ἐξ ἀποστάσεως 279: ἀπὸ κοινοῦ 291.

Final particles 211, 261, 272.

Final sentences 211 f., 207, 220 (223, 225 ff., 272), 291 (position).

Formation of words. See Word-formation.

Future—Only one form of the fut. in each voice 36. But by means of periphrasis a fut. perf. is formed 37, 202: and a fut. expressing continuance 204. The moods denote *relative* time 187; they are becoming obsolete 37 (cp. 211). Formation of the fut. 41 ff. Fut. of deponent verbs 44 f. Use of the fut. 201 f., 208 ff. Interchangeable with the present 189. Fut. for optative 220. For imperative 209, 253. Interchangeable with the conjunctive in principal clauses 208 ff.: with οὐ μή 209 f.: in questions 210: in subordinate clauses 211 ff. Fut. after ὅτε 218. With ὄφελον 220. Fut. infinitive (rare) 37, 202, 231. Fut. participle (rare) 37, 202.

INDEX OF SUBJECTS.

Genitive with nouns 95 ff., 159 f. (article). Gen. of origin and membership 95 f. With εἶναι and γίνεσθαι 95 f., 99. Objective gen. 96 (168). Gen. of the whole (partitive) 96 ff., 144, 159 (position): with verbs 100 ff. : as subject or object 97. Gen. of the country to define particular places 97 : with the art. 153 f. Gen. of quality etc. (gen. for adj.) 98 f. Of content 98. Of apposition 98. Several genitives connected with a single noun 99 f. Gen. with verbs 100 ff.: verbs of touching and seizing 101 f. : of attaining, desiring 102 : verbs denoting to be full, to fill 102 f.: of perception 103 : of remembering, forgetting 103 f.: of emotion 104 : of ruling, excelling 104 : of accusing etc. 104 f. Gen. of price 105. With verbs denoting separation 105 f. With compounds of κατά (ἐξ) 106. With adjectives and adverbs 106 f. (114 f.). With the comparative (and superlative) 107 f. Local and temporal gen. 108 f. With prepositions 124 ff., 132 ff., 136 ff. Periphrases for gen. with ἔμπροσθεν, ἐνώπιον 128 : with ἐξ, ἀπό 96 f., 100 f., 144, 125 f. : with κατά 133. Article with the gen. 156 f. Gen. of the infinitive 234 ff.: dependent on a preposition 237.

Genitive absolute 251 f. Without noun or pronoun 252.

Gorgian figures 295 f., 298 f.

Hebrew, its influence on the Greek of the N.T., 4 f. and passim.

Hebrews, Epistle to the. Its artistic style 1, 5, 280 f. (construction of sentences), 288 f. (position of words), 296 f. (avoidance of hiatus), 297 f. (verse), 301 (figures of speech), 279 and 302 (asyndeton). Details:—24 (πόρρω[θεν]): 52 (εἶμι): 100 : 127 (ἕως not used as a preposition): 139 note 2 (does not use παρά with dat.): 155 (neut. adj. with genitive): 166 (ἡμεῖς for ἐγώ): 202 (fut. inf.): 213 (φοβοῦμαι μή): 223 (ἵνα only used as a final particle) : 231 f. (inf. with verbs of believing) : 260 (δήπου): 263 (τε fairly frequent): 267 (also μέν) : 274 (ὅθεν, διότι).

Hellenistic language, see Common speech, Popular language.

Hexameter in the N.T. 297.

Hiatus avoided in artistic prose 296. In the Epistle to the Hebrews 296 f.

Hyperbaton 290.

Imperative—Termination -σαν 46. Uses of the imperat. 220. Present and aorist imp. 194 ff. Perf. imp. 200 f. : periphrasis for perf. imp. 201. Periphrasis for pres. imp. 203 f. Imp. supplemented or replaced by the conj. 208 f., 213: by the fut. 209: by ἵνα with conj. 209, 222: by the infin. 222. Imp. for optative 220. Imp. used with asyndeton, 278.

Imperfect—Terminations 46. Uses of the impf. 190 ff. With relative meaning, 192. Denoting unreality 205 f. Impf. of verbs denoting necessity etc. 206. Impf. (with ἄν) denoting indefinite repetition 207. Impf. with ὅτε 218. Periphrasis for the impf. 203 f.

Impersonal verbs 75. Periphrastically expressed 204. Construction 227 f., 252 (participle).

Indefinite pronouns 177 f.

Indicative 205 ff. Ind. of unreality (with and without ἄν) 205 ff. Used for expressions of necessity etc. 206. Denoting an impracticable wish 206 f. A practicable wish (fut. ind.) 220. Used instead of the optative and ἄν 207. Used with ἄν in subordinate clauses to denote indefinite repetition 207. In hypothetical sentences (ind. of reality and unreality) 205 f., 213 ff. Fut. ind. interchangeable with conjunct. in principal clauses 208 ff.: for imperative 209 : with οὐ μή 209 f.: in questions 210 (pres. ind. ibid.) : in subordinate clauses 211 ff. (Pres. ind. not used in final sentences 212. Aorist and perfect ind. after μή 213. Fut. ind. after ἐάν 215 : after ὅς ἄν 217. Ind. after ὅταν 218 f.). Negatived by οὐ (μή) 253 ff.

Indirect speech 220, 231. Mixture of direct and indirect speech 286.

Infinitive 221 ff. Periphrasis with εἶναι for pres. inf. 203 f. Inf. with μέλλω a periphrasis for fut. 204 f. Periphrasis for inf. with ἵνα 221-230: with ὅτι 222, 230 ff. Inf. for imperat. 222. Expressing a wish in epistolary style 222. Inf. absolute 225. Inf. of aim or object 223. Of result 223 ff. After verbs of

INDEX OF SUBJECTS.

wishing, striving etc. 225 ff. (after ἄρχομαι 227, 245). After impersonal expressions, adjectives etc. 227 f. Explanatory inf. 229. After πρίν 229 (πρὸ τοῦ ibid.). After verbs of (perceiving), believing, (showing), saying 230 ff. Never used with ἄν 233. Inf. pass. for inf. act. 230, 240 f. Present and aorist inf. 196 f., 202, 231, 237. Future inf. (rare) 37, 197, 202, 205, 231. Inf. with the article 233 ff.: after prepositions 236 f. Cases with the inf. (nom. and acc. with inf.) 237 ff. Inf. negatived by μή 253, 255.

Interrogative particles 259 f.

Interrogative pronouns 176 f. Confused with relatives 175 f. Used in exclamations 178 f., cp. 258 (adverbs).

Interrogative sentences, direct 259 f., 220. With οὐ and a fut. = imperative 209. With οὐ μή 210. Questions of doubt and deliberation 210. Questions with γάρ 274 f. Indirect interrog. sentences 211, 220, 230, 240. With the article τό prefixed 158.—Oratorical questions etc. 268, 274, 303.

Irony 303.

Isocolon 295.

James, Epistle of. Character of its style 279. Details: 127 (ἕως), 223 (ἵνα only used as a final particle), 233 (inf. with art.), 235 (τοῦ with inf.), 267 (μέν almost unrepresented), 274 (διότι).

John (Gospel and Epistles). Style 261, 276, 278, 279 (Epp.), 291. Details: 97, 100 (κοινωνεῖν τινι), 122 f. (εἰς for ἐν), 126 (ἐξ frequent), 127 (ἕως, μέχρι, ἄχρι absent), 128, 132 (σύν almost unrepresented), 135 (ὑπό with acc. almost unrepresented), 138 (παρά with acc. absent), 146 (ὁ δὲ not frequent), 152 ('Ιησοῦς often used without the art.), 169 (ἐμός frequent), 171 (ἐκεῖνος largely used), 173 (ὅστις rare), 179 (ἕτερος hardly ever used), 203 note 2, 211 (ὅπως hardly ever used), 223 (ἵνα freely used), 236 (εἰς τό with inf. unused), 249 f., 266 (μέν absent from the Epistles), 272 (temporal ὡς), 272 f. (οὖν), 274 (γάρ not common), 276 (τότε οὖν, μετὰ τοῦτο or ταῦτα).

Latin, its influence on the Greek of the N.T. 4, 63 (terminations in -ιανός), 76 (ἱκανόν etc.), 95 (ἀπὸ σταδίων δεκαπέντε), 126 f. (πρὸ ἓξ ἡμερῶν τοῦ πάσχα), 230? (inf. pass. for act.), 238? (acc. of the reflexive in the acc. and inf.).

Literary language 1 f., 5, and *passim*.

Luke (Gospel and Acts). Style 1, 5, 203 note 2, 250 f. (Acts), 261, 276, 278, 280, 299, 301 (speeches in the Acts). Details: 5 (ἄφιξις), 24 (πόρρω[θεν]), 37 and 211 and 220 f. (optat.), 52 (εἰμι), 74 (ὀνόματι in Acts), 100, 101 (φείδομαι), 112 note 1, 122 f. (εἰς for ἐν, esp. in Acts), 128 (ἐνώπιον), 132 (σύν), 133 (κατά with gen.), 134 (σύν and μετά, Acts), 141 (ἀνὴρ 'Ιουδαῖος), 146 (ὁ μὲν οὖν, Acts), 152 f. (Acts), 158 (τὸ prefixed to indirect questions), 161, 164 (αὐτός), 170 (καὶ οὗτος), 173 (ὅστις), 179 (ἕτερος), 188 (historic present rare), 197 (Acts, fut. inf.), 202 (fut. inf. and part.), 203 (periphrasis for imperf. etc.), 206 note 1 (Acts), 211 (ὅπως ἄν), 213 (φοβοῦμαι μή), 223 (Acts, ἵνα generally has its correct classical sense), 226 and 230 (κελεύω, ἀξιῶ), 227 note 1 (ἄρχομαι), 230 (ὡς for ὅτι), 231 (indirect speech), 231 f. (inf. with verbs of believing and saying), 233 (inf. with art.), 234 f. (gen. of the inf., Acts), 236 (διὰ τὸ with inf.), 237 (ἐν τῷ with aor. inf.), 246 (Acts), 253 (Acts), 255 f. (οὐ with part.), 259 (ἀρά[γε]), 260 (εἰ with direct questions), 260 f. (γε), 263 f. (τε, Acts), 267 and 273 (Acts, μέν, μὲν οὖν), 268 (Gosp., πλήν), 270 (ὡσεί), 272 (temporal ὡς), 274 (Acts, διό), 274 (διότι, καθότι), 276 (τότε, Acts).—Preface to the Gospel 49, 280. Distinctions between 1st and 2nd parts of the Acts 203 note 2, 116 (ἐν), 128 (ἐνώπιον), 204 (periphrasis for impf.), 249.—Speech of Paul before Agrippa (Acts xxvi.) 5, 20, and 127 (ἕνεκα), 33 (ἀκριβέστατος), 50 (ἴσασιν), 156 (τὸ δωδεκάφυλον), 199 (ἥγημαι for ἡγοῦμαι), 220 (εὐξαίμην ἄν), 238.

Mark—Style 203 note 2, 261, 276, 278. Details: 127 (ἕως), 128 (ἐνώπιον not used), 138 (παρά with acc. only in local sense), 164 (αὐτός), 179 (never ἕτερος), 203 (periphrasis for impf. etc.), 223 (free use of ἵνα), 227 note 1 (ἄρχομαι), 233 f. (nom.

INDEX OF SUBJECTS. 309

acc. and gen. of the inf. with art.), 268 (πλήν).
Matthew—Style 276, 278, 299. Details: 122 (εἰς and ἐν distinguished), 127 (ἕως), 128 (ἐνώπιον not used), 138 (παρά with acc. only in local sense), 164 (αὐτός), 173 (ὅστις), 179 (ἕτερος), 200 (γέγονεν for aorist), 223 (free use of ἵνα), 226 and 230 (κελεύω), 227 note 1 (ἄρχομαι), 233 f. (nom. acc. and gen. of the inf. with art.), 268 (πλήν), 276 (τότε).
Metaplasmus in the declensions 28 f., 32.
Middle voice 180 f. Future mid. for active verbs 42 f. Aorist (and fut.) pass. or mid. 44 f. Uses of the middle 185 ff. Active for mid. 183 f.
Mixed declension 31.
Modern Greek 2, and *passim*.
Mountains, names of, 31 f.

Negatives 253 ff., 214, 216.
Neuter plural with sing. or plur. verb 78 f. Adjectival predicate in the neuter 76 f.: use of τι and οὐδέν as predic. 76 f.: of τοῦτο 77: of τί 177. ὅ ἐστιν 77. Neuter of pronouns etc. used as acc. of the inner object 91. Neut. of the adj. (or part.) used in sing. or plur. of persons 82, 156, 244. Other uses of independent neut. adj. (or part.) 155 ff., 244.
Nominative 84 ff. Used where a proper name is introduced 84 f. Used in a parenthesis interrupting the construction (also in statements of time) 85, 282. Double nom. 85 f. Nom. for vocative 86 f. Nom. of the infinitive 233 f. Nom. absolute 251, 283 with note 1. Nom. of the participle (solecism) 81 note 1, 285.
Nominative with the infinitive 237 ff.
Numerals 35. Syntax 144 f., 160 and 162 (the article).

Optative becoming obsolete 37. Fut. opt. no longer found 37. Terminations 46 f. Remaining uses of the opt. 219 ff. Replaced by the indicative 207.
Ordinal numbers, cardinals used instead of, 144. Omission of the article with them 149.
Orthography (§ 3) 6 ff.

Paraleipsis 302 f.
Parechesis 295, 298 f.
Parenthesis 281 f. Indicated by δέ 267, 269.
Parison 295, 299.
Paromoion 295.
Paronomasia 298 f.
Participle, present and aorist 197 f., 250, 204 (aor. part. with εἶναι). Fut. part. rare 37, 202, 205, 244, 248, 253. Fut. part. pass. 202. Uses of the part. 242 ff. Part. as attribute (or in apposition) 156 f. (article), 242 f. Part. representing a substantive 157 (article), 243 f. Πᾶς (ὁ) with part. 162, 243 f. Participle as part of the predicate 37 and 202 ff. (periphrases), 244 ff. Conjunctive part. and part. absolute 247 ff. Pleonastic use with finite vb. of part. belonging to the vb. 251. Part. negatived by μή 253, 255 f. (part. with article takes οὐ by a Hebraism 255).—Perf. part. pass. with the genitive 107.—Free use of the part. 284 f. Finite verb in place of part. 285.
Particles 60 f. Uses 259 ff. Co-ordinating and subordinating particles 261. Particles used with a participle 247 f., 252 f. Position of the particle 290.
Passive 180 f., 184 f. Pass. of deponent verbs 184. Of intransitive verbs 184 f. Impersonal pass. 75 (185). Construction of the pass. with the accusative 93. With the dative 112 f., 185. Infin. pass. for act. 230, 240 f.
Paul—Style 1, 5, 251, 276 (Ephesians and Colossians), 281 (bis), 284 f., 290, 300 (1 Cor.), 301 ff. (figures), 302, 303, 303 (Rom. and Cor.). Details: 100, 101 (φείδομαι), 111 (dative), 127 (ἕως), 131 f., 134 (Philippians and Pastoral Epp.), 135 (ὑπέρ), ibid. (ὑπέρ with gen.), 155 (neut. adj. with gen.), 166 (ἡμεῖς and ἐγώ), 171 (αὐτὸ τοῦτο), 173 (ὅς and ὅστις), 179 (ἕτερος), 200 (perf. for aor.), 206 note 1, 211 (ὅπως not frequent), 213 (φοβοῦμαι μή), 230 f. (ὡς for ὅτι, ὡς ὅτι), 231 f. (verbs of believing and saying), 233 (inf. with article), 233 f. (acc. of inf., gen. of inf.), 236 (εἰς τὸ with inf.), 259 (ἄρα, ἄρά γε), 267 (μέν), 268 (πλήν), 271 (εἴπερ; εἴτε ... εἴτε), 272 (ἡνίκα; temporal ὡς), 273 (ἄρα), 274 (διότι), 279 (the figure ἐξ ἀποστάσεως), 280 f., 282 ff. (anacolu-

thon), 298 f. (paronomasia), 299 (dwelling on a word ; paromoion, antithesis).—Speech before Agrippa (Acts xxvi.), see Luke.

Perfect, periphrasis for, 37, 202 f. Terminations of the perf. 46. Uses of the perf. 198 ff. Perf. for aorist 200. In relative sense for pluperf. 200. After ὅτε 218. Moods 200 f. Perf. conjunctive 213 note 2.

Periodic (or compact) form of speech 275, 279 ff.

Periods 279 ff., 283, 300, 280 and 302 (periods where asyndeton is used).

Periphrasis of verbal forms 37, 201 (bis), 202 ff.

Personal pronouns 35. Uses 164 ff. Nom. used for emphasis 164. Frequent use of the personal pronouns 164 f. Used instead of reflexives 165, 167 f. Unenclitic forms of the pron. of the 1st pers. 165. Interchange of personal and possessive pronouns 168 f. Pleonastic pron. after the relative 175, 283.

Persons—3rd pers. plur. = ' one ' (Germ. man) 75. 1st pers. plur. for 1st pers. sing. 166.

Peter (esp. the 1st Epistle). Details: 100 (κοινωνεῖν), 101 (φείδομαι 2 Pet.), 179 (ἕτερος never used), 223 (ἵνα only used in final sense). 266 f. (μέν fairly often in 1 Pet., never in 2 Pet.), 271 (εἴπερ ; εἴτε ... εἴτε), 274 (διότι), 288 (position of words).

Place-names 31 f. With and without the article 152 f.

Play on words. See Words.

Pleonasm 294 f., 59 and 295 (ἀπ' ἄνωθεν and similar phrases), 143 and 295 (μᾶλλον with a comparative), 175 and 251 f. (pers. pronoun), 180 (ἕτεροι), 227 note 1 and 249 (ἄρχομαι), 255 (μή), 263 (πολλὰ καί), 269 note 1 (ἀλλ').

Pluperfect, periphrasis for, 37, 202 f. Augment generally wanting 37. Terminations 47. Uses of plupf. 201, 206 (unreality).

Plural used of a single person 83, 166 (ἡμεῖς). The plurals αἰῶνες, οὐρανοί etc. 83 f. Names of feasts 84. Plur. of abstract words 84. Plur. (and sing.) of verb with neut. plur. subject 78 f. Collective words 79. Plur. in the case of a complex subject 79 f.

Polysyndeton 277.

Popular language, the Hellenistic, 1 f.

Position of words. See Words.

Positive for comparative 143.

Possessive pronouns 35. Their uses 168 f. With and without the article 169.

Predicate (nominal). Agreement with the subject 76 f. Without the article 147. With the article 156 f., 243. Predicative adjective without the art. 158, 169 (possessives). Predicate with an infinitive, its case 241 f. Participle as part. of the predicate 244 ff. (202 ff.). ὡς with a predicate 270 f.

Predicate (verbal) takes its number from the nominal predicate 78 f.

Prepositions 121 ff. Prepositions proper and improper (quasi-prepositions) 121 f. With the accusative 121-124. With the genitive 124-130. With the dative 130-132. With two cases 132-135. With three cases 136-140. Prep. with the infinitive 236 f., 239. Prep. omitted in the case of assimilation of the relative 174. Prep. repeated or not repeated with several connected nouns 291.

Present—New formation of pres. tense from the perf. 40 f. Other new forms of pres. 41. Periphrasis for pres. 203 f. Uses of the pres. 187 ff. Conative pres. 187. Aoristic pres. 188. Historic pres. 188. Pres. with perfect sense 188 f. Pres. for future 189, 219. Pres. denoting relative time 189 f. Moods 194 ff. Imperative 194 ff. Infinitive 196 f. Participle 197 f. Conjunctive 208 ff., 211 ff. Pres. indic. with ὅτε 218.

Prodiorthosis 282, 303.

Pronouns 35 f. Syntax 164 ff. Pron. as predicate brought into agreement with the noun 77. Pron. as subject agreeing with the predicate 77.

Proper names, Semitic, declinable and indeclinable 29 f. Hypocoristic (abbreviated) proper names 70 f. Proper names with and without the article 151 f., 162 f. Omission of article with substantive which has a proper name dependent on it 151.

Prothetic vowel 23.

Punctuation 17.

INDEX OF SUBJECTS. 311

Reduplication 38 f. In compound verbs 39. Cf. Doubling.
Reflexive pronouns 35. Their uses 166 ff. In the acc. and inf. construction 238 f.
Relative pronouns 36. Uses 172 ff. Confusion of relatives and interrogatives 175 f.
Relative sentences equivalent to participles 242 f. Moods in relative sentences 216 ff. Negative οὐ and μή 254. Noun attracted into the relative clause 174. Clause with καὶ ... (αὐτοῦ) linked on to a relative clause 175, 286.
Rhythm 296, 297 f.
River-names 31 f., with the article 153.

Semitic words, transcription of 12 f., 16 f.
Senarii in the N.T. 298.
Sense-lines, writing in, 17.
Sentences, connexion of, 275 ff.
Singular—Collective use of the masc. sing. (of substantives and adjectives) 82. Of the neut. sing. 82, 155 f. Sing. (or plur.) used of objects which belong to several persons 83. Sing. verb with neut. plur. subject 78. Number of the verb in the case of collective words 79 : in the case of a complex subject 79 f.
Solecisms 76, 80 f.
Sound-changes, general (in the case of ει and ι adscript) 6. Sporadic (§ 6) 20 ff.
Superlative has (almost) disappeared 33 f. (58), 141 ff.

Symploce (figure of speech) 300.

Temporal particles 261, 272.
Temporal sentences 272. Moods used in them 221. Negative οὐ 254 f.

Verse in the N.T., specimens of, 297 f.
Vocative—Use 86 f. Position 289 f.

Wish, sentences expressing a, 206 f., 219 f., 222 (infin.).
Words, division of, 13 f.
Word-formation 61 ff. By composition 65 ff.
Words, play on, 298 f.
Words, position of, § 80, 287 ff. Ordinary rules 287 f. Position of enclitic words 288. Position of the governing gen. before the dependent gen. 99 f. Of the attribute (adj., gen. etc.) 158 ff., 288 f. Of the adverb 289. Of the partitive genitive 159. Of the possessives and the possessive gen. of the personal pron. 168 f., 288. Of ἐκείνου and τούτου 169. Of several defining clauses 160. Of οὗτος and ἐκεῖνος 172. Of the vocative 289 f. Of ἕνεκεν and other quasi-prepositions 127, 290. Of ἄν 205 f., 216. Of the negative 257. Of τε 265. Of ἆρα and τοίνυν 273. Of the subordinating conjunction (and the relative) 283 note 2, 290. Separation of the participle from the inf. dependent on it 243.

Zeugma 292.

II. INDEX OF GREEK WORDS.

A interchanged with ε 20 f. With ο 21. With ω 22.
-α, -ας etc. for -ον, -ες etc. in the 2nd aor. 45 f. In the impf. 46.
ἀγαθοεργέω, -ουργέω 22, 67, 70.
ἀγαθός, degrees of comparison 34.
ἀγαλλιάω, -άομαι 52. Aor. 44. Construction 118, 225, 245.
ἀγανακτέω περί τινος 135.
ἀγγαρεύω and ἐγγ. 20 f. Constr. 226.
ἀγγέλλω, aor. pass. 43, 52.
ἄγε with plur. 85 note 1.
ἅγια, τὰ 84. τὰ ἅγ. τῶν ἁγίων 84, 143.
ἀγορά without article, 148 f.
ἀγριέλαιος, ἡ 67.
ἀγρός without art. 148.
ἄγω, aor. 43, 52. Intrans. 182. ἄγει τρίτην ταύτην ἡμέραν 75.
ἀγωνίζομαι ἵνα 225.
ἀδελφός to be supplied with a genitive 95.
ἀδελφότης 63.
ᾅδης : ἐν τῷ ᾅδῃ, εἰς ᾅδην (not Ἅιδου) 96.
ἀδικέομαι 'let myself be wronged' 185. ἀδικῶ with perfect sense 188.
Ἀδρίας, ὁ 153.
ἀεί not often used, πάντοτε used instead 59.
ἄζυμα, τὰ 84.
Ἄζωτος 24.
αι interchanged with ε 9.
-αι of verbal terminations subject to elision 296 f.
-αι optat. 46 f.
Αἴγυπτος without art. 153.
-αιεν optat. 46.
Αἰλαμῖται 9.
αἵματα 84.
-αίνω aor. -ᾶνα 40.

αἱρέω aor. 45, 52 : fut. 52.
-αίρω aor. -ᾶρα 40.
αἴρω intransit. 183.
αἰσθάνομαί τι 103.
αἰσχύνομαι with ἀπό 88. With inf. 225.
αἰτέω and αἰτέομαι distinguished 186. Constr. 91, 226, 230, 241.
αἰῶνες 83.
αἰώνιος, 2 and 3 terminations 33.
Ἀκελδεμάχ 12.
ἀκολουθέω constr. 113 f.
ἀκούω fut. 42, 52. Constr. 103, 231, 239, 246. With perfect sense 188.
ἀκροβυστία 67.
ἄκρος, τὸ ἄκρον with gen. 158.
ἀκύλων aquilo 13.
ἀλάβαστρος, ὁ and ἡ 26.
ἅλα(ς), τό, for οἱ ἅλες 27.
ἀλεκτοροφωνία 68. -ας answering the question When? 109.
ἀλήθεια, ἐπ' ἀληθείας 137.
ἀλήθω for ἀλέω 52.
ἀληθῶς λέγω ὑμῖν 141 note 2.
ἁλιεύς plur. -εεῖς 22.
ἀλλά 60, 267 ff. οὐ μόνον ... ἀλλά (καί) 267. ἀλλ' οὐ 267 f. ἀλλά γε 261, 268. ἀλλὰ καί, ἀλλ' οὐδέ 269. ἀλλ' ἵνα 269, 293.
ἅλλομαι 52.
ἄλλος and ἕτερος 179 f. With article repeated 160 f. ἄλλος πρὸς ἄλλον 170. Ellipse of ἄ. 180, 292. ἀλλ' ἤ 269 with note 1.
ἅλων, ἡ, for ἅλως 29.
ἅμα 60. With dat. 115. With participle 252 f.
ἁμαρτάνω 52. Fut. and aor. 42 f. Constr. 128, 245.
ἁμαρτία without art. 150.

INDEX OF GREEK WORDS. 313

ἁμαρτωλός 64.
ἀμελέω with gen. 104.
ἀμύνεσθαι for -ειν 185.
ἀμφιάζω, -έζω 52, 20, 41.
ἀμφότεροι 36. With art. 161, 162.
-αν for -α in acc. of 3rd decl. 26.
-αν for -ασι in perf. 46.
ἄν 60, 259. With indic. 205 ff. With conjunct. 211 f., 216 f., 219. With fut. (and pres.) indic. 217. With optat. 220. Not with infin. 233. Not with part. 253. ὅπως ἄν 211 f. ὡς ἄν 272. Omission of ἄν with ὅστις? 217. With ἕως, ἄχρι, μέχρι 219.
ἄν for ἐάν 'if' 60.
ἀνά with acc. 122. Stereotyped as an adverb 122, 145, 179. ἀνὰ μέσον 122, 129.
ἀνάγαιον (ἀνώγ.) 9, 22, 67. ἀνώγεων incorrect form 25.
ἀναγινώσκω constr. 230 note 4.
ἀνάγκη without ἐστίν 73. Constr. 239 f.
ἀναθάλλω aor. -έθαλον 43, 54.
ἀνάθεμα for -ημα 62 f.
ἀνακάμπτω intrans. 182.
ἀναλόω 52.
ἀναμιμνῄσκω, -ομαι constr. 104, 226.
ἀναπαύομαι fut. and aor. 44, 56.
ἀνάπειρος for -ηρος 9.
ἀναστρέφω intrans. 182.
ἀνατίθεμαί τινι 116.
ἀνατολαί plur. 83 f. Without art. 148. ἡ ἀνατολή 'the East' 148.
ἀναφαίνω γῆν 183.
ἀνέθη. See ἀνίημι.
ἀνέλεος 66.
ἄνεμος omitted 141.
ἄνευ with gen. 127.
ἀνέχομαι augment 39, 54. Constr. 104.
ἀνῆκεν 206.
ἀνὴρ Ἰουδαῖος etc. 141. ἄνδρες καὶ γυναῖκες 289.
ἄνθρωπος : πάντες ἄνθρωποι 161.
ἀνίημι 51. ἀνέθη 38.
ἀνίστημι : pleonastic use of ἀναστάς 249 : of ἀνάστηθι (καὶ) 249, 278. ἀνέστηκε not used for 'is risen' 199.
Ἅννα 11, 30.
Ἅννας 11, 30.

ἀνοίγω 56. Augment etc. 39, 56. Aor. and fut. pass. 43.
ἀντέχομαι with gen. 102.
ἀντί with gen. 124. ἀνθ' ὧν 124. ἀντὶ τοῦ with inf. 237. Construction with compounds of ἀντί 116.
ἀντικρύς 20. With gen. 128.
ἀντιλαμβάνομαι with gen. 102.
ἀντιλέγω with μή and inf. 255.
ἀντιπέρα 7.
ἄνωθεν and ἀπ' ἄν. 59.
ἀνώτερον 35.
ἄξιος constr. 106 (gen.), 218, 228, 235.
ἀξιῶ constr. 105 (gen.), 226, 241.
ἀπαγγέλλω constr. 226, 230 note 4, 232.
ἀπαιτέω 186.
ἀπαντάω 52, fut. 42.
ἀπαρνέομαι aor. 44 f. Pass. 184. Constr. 232, 255 (μή and inf.).
ἀπάρτι 14.
ἅπας beside πᾶς 161 with note 1. With art. 161 f.
ἀπειλέομαι 52. Constr. 226.
ἀπείραστος κακῶν 106.
ἀπεκδύομαι 185.
Ἀπελλῆς beside Ἀπολλῶς -ώνιος 21, 71. Declension 31.
ἀπέναντι 14. With gen. 127 f.
ἀπέρχομαι : pleonastic use of ἀπελθών 249.
ἀπέχω, -ομαι constr. 105, 182. ἀπέχει 75. ἀπέχω = ἀπείληφα 188.
ἀπό with gen., 124 ff. For ἐξ 124 f. Denoting extraction (place of birth) 125. For partitive gen. 96, 125 : do. with verbs 100 f. For ὑπό 125 (also with passive verbs). For παρά 125, 103 (ἀκούω). For gen. of separation 105 f., 125 f. With κρύπτω 91. With φεύγω, φυλάσσομαι etc. 87 f., 126. With adjectives 106. Answering the question How far distant? 95. ἀπὸ προσώπου τινός 83, 129. ἀπὸ τ. στόματός τινός 130. ἀφ' ἧς 140. ἀπὸ μιᾶς 140 f. ἀπὸ τότε 276.
ἀπόκειται with inf. 228.
ἀποκόπτομαι 186.
ἀποκρίνομαι 55. Fut. and aor. 44, 181. Constr. 232, 249 (with λέγων ; ἀποκριθεὶς εἶπεν etc.), cp. 278.
ἀποκτείνω, -έννω 41, 55. Aor. pass. 44, 55. Use of the verb 184.

INDEX OF GREEK WORDS.

ἀπολείπεται with inf. 228.
ἀπόλλυμι 56.
'Απολλῶς, -ώνιος, 'Απελλῆς 21, 71. Declension 31.
ἀπολογέομαί τινι 110.
ἀπορέομαι constr. 88.
ἀπορίπτω intrans. 182.
ἀποστέλλω constr. 223, 226, 230.
ἀποστρέφω intrans. 182.
ἀποτάσσομαί τινι 110.
ἀποφθέγγομαι constr. 232.
ἅπτομαι with gen. 101.
'Απφία 24.
ἄρα, ἄραγε 60, 216, 259 f., 273. ἄρα οὖν 273.
ἆρα, ἆρά γε 60, 259.
'Αραβία with and without article 153.
ἀργός, -ή 32 f.
ἀργύρια 84.
ἀρέσκω constr. 110, 128.
ἀρεστόν ἐστι constr. 227, 240.
ἄρθρον προτακτικόν (ὁ ἡ τό) and ὑποτακτικόν (ὅς ἥ ὅ) 145, 172 f.
ἀριστερά sc. χείρ 140. ἐξ ἀριστερῶν 84.
ἀρκετόν (satis) 76. Constr. 228. ἀρκετός 228 and 239.
ἀρκέω constr. 228.
ἄρκος for ἄρκτος 24.
ἁρμόζομαι for -ω 185.
ἀρνέομαι aor. 44 f. Constr. 225, 255.
ἁρπάζω 40, 52. Aor. and fut. pass. 43.
ἀρραβών 10.
ἄρρην, ἄρσην 23.
ἄρτι, position of, 289.
ἀρχή : τὴν ἀρχήν 94, 176. ἀπ' ἀρχῆς etc. without art. 149.
-άρχης and -αρχος 28, 68.
ἀρχι- in composition 66.
ἀρχιερεύς 66.
ἄρχω with gen. 104. -ομαι constr. 227, 245. Often almost superfluous 227 note 1.
ἀρξάμενος 'beginning with' 249.
-ας gen. -α (and -ου) 25, 29, 31. Abbreviated names in -ας 70 f.
-ᾶσαι 2nd sing. pres. ind. pass. of verbs in -άω 47.
-ασία, substantives in, 69.
'Ασία with art. 153.
ἀσκέω with inf. 225.

ἀσπάζομαι 194. ἀσπάσασθε aor. 196.
ἀστήρ, -έρες without art. 147.
ἀστοχέω constr. 105.
ἄστρα without art. 147.
ἄτερ with gen. 127.
αὐθεντέω τινός 104.
αὔξω, -άνω 53, 183 (intrans.).
αὔρα omitted 140.
αὐτο- in composition 69, 70.
αὐτόματος 69. -μάτη 33. Adj. for adv. 141.
αὐτός 'self' 170, 168 (α. δι' ἑαυτοῦ etc.), 171 (αὐτὸ τοῦτο). 'He' (emphatic) 164, 168 f. (αὐτοῦ 'his'). ἴδιος αὐτοῦ 169. αὐτοῦ etc. used with disregard to formal agreement 166. Frequent use of αὐτοῦ etc. 164 f., 251 f., and 283. Do. (after a relative) 175. καὶ ... αὐτοῦ after a relative clause 175. ὁ αὐτός constr. 114, 179, 263. ἐπὶ τὸ αὐτό 136.
αὐτοῦ adv. 59 note 2.
ἀφαιρέω constr. 91.
ἄφες with conjunctive 208.
ἀφίημι ἀφίω 51. ἤφιεν 39. ἀφέθην 38. Constr. 226.
ἄφιξις 'departure' 5.
'Αχαΐα with and without art. 153.
ἀχρεῖος accent 14. ἀχρεῖος -εοῦν 22.
ἄχρι(ς) 20, 60. With gen. 127. ἄ. οὗ 127, 219, 272. As conjunction 219, 272.
ἄψινθος, ὁ? 26.
-άω, verbs in -άω and -έω confused 47 f.

Βαίνω 2nd aor. imperat. 50, 53.
βαλλάντιον 10 f.
βάλλω aor. 45. Intrans. 182.
βαπτίζομαι aor. 185 ff.
βάπτισμα and -σμός 61 f.
βαρέω (-ύνω) 53.
βασιλεύω constr. 104, 136 f.
βασκαίνω 53. Aor. 40. Constr. 89
βάτος, ὁ and ἡ 26.
βατταλογεῖν for -ολογεῖν 21.
βέβαιος, -αία 33.
Βηθανία 31.
βιβλαρίδιον 64.
βίβλος without art. 151.
βιόω 53 f. Aor. 43.
βλαστάνω and -άω 53. Aor. 43.

βλασφημέω constr. 88.
βλέπω for ὁρῶ 3, 56. Aor. and fut. 42, 53. Constr. 88 note 1, 126, 225, 231, 246. βλέπε(τε) 209, 278.
βοάω constr. 232.
Βοές Βοος Βοοζ 13.
βορρᾶς 25. Without art. 148.
βουλεύομαι constr. 225.
βούλομαι = θέλω 47. Augment 37 f. βούλει 47. Constr. 225. ἐβουλόμην 207. βούλεσθε with conjunct. 210.
βοῦς acc. pl. βόας 26.
βρέχει for ὕει, personal and impers. 75. Trans. and intrans. 182.

Γαζοφυλάκιον 15.
Γάϊος 16 f.
Γαλιλαία 8. With art. 153. -αῖος 8.
γαμέω -ίζω -ίσκω 53. γαμέομαι constr. 113.
γάμοι 84.
γάρ 60, 274 f.
γε 60, 260 f. Cp. ἄρα γε, ἀρά γε, καίγε, καίτοιγε, μενοῦνγε.
Γεθσημανί (-σαμανί) 7.
γελάω 53. Fut. 42.
γεμίζω constr. 102.
γέμω constr. 102.
γένημα and γέννημα distinguished 11.
Γεννησαρ, not -αρεθ -αρετ 13.
γένος : τῷ γένει 117.
γεύομαι with acc. and gen. 101.
γῆ omitted 140. Without art. 147.
γῆρας -ους -ει 26.
γίνομαι, not γιγν. 24. Aor. 44, 53. γέγονεν for ἐγένετο 200. With gen. 96, 99. With dat. 111 f. With εἰς and ἐν 85 f., 122, 124. With ἐπί 136. With adv. 258. In periphrases with participle 204, 244. ἐγένετο with inf. 75, 227 f., 235 (τοῦ with inf.), 241. With a finite verb (with and without καί) 262, 288. ἐγένετο ἐν τῷ with inf. 237. μὴ γένοιτο 219, 259. ἐγένετο omitted 74, 292.
γινώσκω, not γιγν. 24, 53. Conj. γνῶ, γνοῖ 49. Constr. 227, 231 (note 4), 238, 240, 246. Pass. with dat. 113, 185.
γλῶσσα omitted 140. γλώσσαις λαλεῖν 292.
γλωσσόκομον 68.
Γολγοθᾶ 31.

Γόμορρα, -ων 12, 31.
γονυπετέω constr. 89.
γοῦν wanting 60. Cp. note 1.
γράφω constr. 226. γρ. and ἔγραψα in letters 194.
γρηγορῶ 40 f., 53.
γυμνητεύω -ιτεύω 9.
γυνή with gen., ellipse of, 95. Without art. 150. ἄνδρες καὶ γυναῖκες, γ. καὶ παιδία 289.

Δάκρυον dat. -υσιν 29.
δαμάζομαι pass. constr. 113.
Δαυίδ (-είδ) 7.
δέ 60, 266 f. μέν ... δέ see μέν. καί... δέ, δέ... καί 267. Position 290.
δεῖ constr. 227 f., 239. For deliberative conj. 210. ἔδει 206. δέον (ἐστίν) 204.
δείκνυμι 48. Constr. 227.
τὸ δειλινόν answering the question When? 94.
δεῖπνος for -ον 28.
δεκαδύο, δεκατέσσαρες etc. 35.
Δελματία for Δαλμ. 21.
δεξιά, ἡ 140. ἐν δεξιᾷ (ἐνδέξια), ἐκ δεξιῶν etc. 84, 140.
δέομαι 53. ἐδέετο 47. Constr. 105, 226, 234, 238, 241 f.
δέσμιος τοῦ Χριστοῦ 107 note 2.
δεσμοί and -ά 28.
δεῦρο, δεῦτε with conjunctive 208.
δευτεραῖος 141.
δευτερόπρωτον σάββατον 66.
δέω 'bind,' pass. with acc. 93.
δή 60, 273 f.
δῆλον ὅτι 73, 233. δῆλός εἰμι with partic. not used 245.
δηλόω constr. 232 f.
Δημᾶς 71.
δημοσίᾳ 141.
δήπου 58, 60, 260.
διά with acc. 132. διὰ τό with inf. 236, 239. With gen. 132 f. διὰ τοῦ with inf. 237 (233). διὰ μέσου = διὰ 129. διὰ χειρός (-ῶν) τινος 83, 130, 151. διὰ στόματός τινος 83, 130, 151. Verbs compounded with διά which take the acc. 89 : do. which take the dat. 114.
διαβάλλομαι with dat. 114.
διαβλέπω constr. 227.

INDEX OF GREEK WORDS.

διάβολος without art. 148.
διάγω intrans. 292.
διαθήκαι 84.
διακονῶ 53. Augm. 39. Pass. 184.
διακρίνομαι aor. 44. Constr. 114.
διαλέγομαι 55. Aor. 44. Constr. 114.
διαλείπω with participle 245, 258.
διαμαρτύρομαι constr. 226.
διαμερίζομαι mid. 183.
διαπαρατριβή 65.
διαρρήγνυμι for mid. 184.
διαστέλλομαι constr. 226.
διάστεμα for -ημα 63.
διατάσσω, -ομαι constr. 226, 230, 240.
διατελέω with partic. 245, 258. Intrans. 292.
διατηρέω with ἐξ and ἀπό 126.
διατρίβω intrans. 292.
-διδάσκαλος in composition 68.
διδάσκω with double acc. 91. Pass. with acc. 93. With inf. 227.
δίδωμι 49 f. Conj. δῷ δοῖ (δώῃ) 49 f. Opt. δῴη 50. With inf. 223. With acc. and inf. 226.
διετής accent 14.
διισχυρίζομαι constr. 232.
δικαιόω constr. 117.
διό 60, 274. δ. καί 263, 274.
διόπερ 60, 274.
διοπετές, τό 141.
διότι 60, 274.
διπλότερον 34, 58.
διψάω contract verb in α 47, 53. Constr. 90, 102.
δίψος, τό 28.
διώκω, fut. -ξω 42, 53.
δοκέω constr. 225, 231. ἔδοξέ μοι ibid., 239. ἔδοξα ἐμαυτῷ 167 note 2, 239. δοκῶ with finite verb 278. δοκεῖτε inserted in middle of sentence 282.
δοκιμάζω constr. 227, 239.
δοξάζω constr. 227.
δραχμή omitted 140.
δύναμαι 53. Augm. 38. δύνομαι etc. 49. δύνασαι and δύνῃ 49. Fut. 45. Constr. 197, 210, 222, 225, 226. ἐδύνατο 'could have been' 206.
δυνατέω constr. 226.
δυνατόν ἐστι, δυνατός constr. 197, 227 f., 239 f.
δύο declension 35. δύο δύο 145. οἱ δύο 162.

δυσεντέριον 28.
δυσμαί 83 f. Without art. 148.
δύω 53. Intrans. 183. δύω, δύνω, ἐνδιδύσκω 53 (41). Aor. 43 (bis).
τὸ δωδεκάφυλον ἡμῶν 67, 156.

ε interchanged with α 20 f. With ο 21. With ι 21 f.
ἐάν not ἄν or ἤν 60, 214, 271. Constr. 213 ff. (with pres. ind. 214. With fut. 215). ἐὰν καί 215. ἐάν τε ... ἐάν τε 271. ἐὰν μή 'except' 216, 293.
ἐάν for ἄν 60 f., 216.
ἐάνπερ 60, 271.
ἑαυτοῦ not αὑτοῦ 35. For ἐμαυτοῦ, σεαυτοῦ 167 note 1. ἑαυτῶν for ἡμῶν αὐτῶν, ὑμῶν a. 35. For ἀλλήλων 169 f. ἑαυτοῦ and αὐτοῦ 167 f. Position of ἑ. 168. Strengthened by addition of αὐτός 168.
ἐάω constr. 226. οὐκ ἐῶ 257.
ἐγγαρεύω for ἀγγαρ. 20 f.
ἐγγίζω constr. 114.
ἔγγιστα 33.
ἔγγονα, ἔκγ. 12.
ἐγγύς with gen. (or dat.) 107. As predicate 257.
ἐγγύτερον 35.
ἐγείρω, -ομαι, forms in use 53. Aor. 44. ἠγέρθη, ἐγήγερται 'is risen' 199. ἔγειρε ἆρον, ἐγείρεσθε ἄγωμεν 278.
ἐγκαίνια 84.
ἐγκακεῖν (ἐκκ.) 67. Constr. 245.
ἐγκαλέω constr. 105, 110, 184.
ἐγκόπτω constr. 235, 255.
ἐγκρατεύομαι constr. 91.
Ἐζεκίας 8 note 1.
ἐθελο-, compounds with, 68.
ἔθνη with predicate in sing. and plur. 78. Without art. 147, 148.
εἰ = ῑ 6 f., 7 f.
ει interchanged with ε 22.
-εί, adverbs in, 69.
εἰ 60, 205, 213 ff., 271 f., 254 (οὐ and μή). 'Whether' 211, 216, 220 f. Before direct questions 260. εἰ καί 215. εἰ μή (τι) 216, 254, 293. εἰ δὲ μή (γε) 216, 260, 271, 293. εἰ ἄρα (γε) 259. εἴ γε 261, 271. εἴπως 60, 216.
εἰ μήν for ἦ μήν 9, 60, 260.

INDEX OF GREEK WORDS.

-εια interchanged with -ία 8.
-εία, substantives in, 62.
εἶδον and -α 45, 56. Cp. ὁράω.
εἰδώλιον -εῖον 15, 64.
εἰδωλολατρία (-εία) 68.
εἰκῇ 7.
εἴκοσι not -ιν 19 with note 7.
εἴκω εἶξα 38.
εἰμί, forms of, 51 f. Omission of, 72 ff., 92 (εἶναι), 245 and 246 f. (ὤν). In periphrases 37, 201, 202 ff. ε. with gen. 95 f., 99. With dat. 111 f.
εἶμι, remnants of, 52.
-ειον, -ιον, substantives in, 15, 64.
εἴπερ 60, 271.
εἶπον, -α 45, 55. εἶπεν and ἔλεγεν 192. ὡς ἔπος εἰπεῖν 225. εἰπών, καὶ εἶπεν 249 f. εἶπεν λέγων 55, 250. Cp. λέγω.
εἴπως 60, 216.
εἴρηκεν with subject unexpressed 75. For aorist 200.
εἰρήνη ὑμῖν 74. ὕπαγε εἰς εἰρήνην, ἐν εἰρήνῃ 123.
-εῖς for -έας (substantives in -εύς) 26.
εἰς with acc. 122 ff. Confused with ἐν 122 ff., 130. For ἐπί and πρός 124. εἰς τό with inf. 224, 236, 239. εἰς with ἔσομαι, γίνομαι (εἰμί) 85 f. With λογίζεσθαι (pass.) 86. With ἐγείρω, ἔχω etc. 93. Interchangeable with dat. 109 f. Compounds of εἰς, constr. 115. εἰς πρόσωπον 130. εἰς χεῖρας 130. εἰς ἐλάχιστόν ἐστι 86, 228.
εἷς as indefinite article 144. μία for πρώτη 144. εἷς τις 144, 178. εἷς οὐ 178. εἷς ἕκαστος etc. 179. ὁ εἷς ... ὁ ἕτερος 144. εἷς ... καὶ εἷς 144, 145. εἷς τὸν ἕνα 144 f. ἀπὸ μιᾶς 140 f.
-εῖσαι 2nd sing. pass. termination of verbs in -έω 47 note 2.
-εισαν in plupf. 47.
εἶτα, εἶτεν 20, 60, 277.
εἴτε 60. εἴτε ... εἴτε 212, 214, 271.
εἴωθα constr. 227.
ἐκ see ἐξ.
ἕκαστος 179. Does not take art. 161. Distinguished from πᾶς 161. With partitive gen. 97.
ἐκδιδύσκω constr. 92.
ἐκεῖ 59. Pleonastic use after ὅπου 175.
ἐκεῖθεν 59. For ἐκεῖ? 258.

ἐκεῖνος 171 f. With (or without) art. 172. ἐκείνης sc. ὁδοῦ 109, 140.
ἐκεῖσε = ἐκεῖ 59.
ἐκκλίνω intrans. 182.
ἐκλανθάνομαι constr. 104.
ἐκλέγω perf. pass. 55. ἐκλέγομαι mid. 185 f.
ἔκπαλαι 14, 66.
ἐκπερισσοῦ 66. ἐκπερισσῶς 66.
ἐκπίπτω constr. 106. Equivalent to ἐκβάλλομαι 184.
ἐκτός 58 note 1. With gen. 107. ἐκτὸς εἰ μή 216.
ἔκτοτε 14.
Ἐλαιῶν (not -ών) ὄρος 32, 64, 85.
ἐλάσσων -ττων 23. Meaning 34. Without ἤ 108.
ἐλάχιστος perexiguus 33. -ιστότερος 33, 34.
ἐλεάω for -έω 47 f., 54. Transit. 88.
ἐλ(ε)εινός 23.
ἔλεος, (ὁ and) τὸ 28.
Ἐλισαβέτ, -βέθ 7, 13, 30.
Ἐλισαῖος 8.
ἑλκόω augm. 39, 54.
ἕλκω aor. and fut. 54.
Ἑλλάς with art. 153.
Ἕλληνες, art. with, 154. Ἰουδαῖοί (τε) καὶ Ἕλληνες 264.
ἐλλογάω -έω 48.
ἐλπίζω, ἐλπίς 15 f. ἤλπικα 199. ἐλπίζω constr. 110 note 2, 136, 137, 197, 202, 231, 234 (ἐλπίς).
ἐμαυτοῦ 35, 166 f.
ἐμβλέπω constr. 115.
ἐμμένω constr. 115.
ἐμός 168 f.
ἐμπί(μ)πλημι 24. -πλάω 49. Constr. 102.
ἐμπί(μ)πρημι 24.
ἐμπνέω with gen. 103.
ἐμπορεύομαι intrans. and trans. 88.
ἔμπροσθεν 59, 107, 127 f. προδραμὼν ἔμπροσθεν 295.
ἐν with dat. 130 f. ἐν τῷ with inf. 237, 239. Confused with εἰς 122 ff., 130. Its use in periphrases for partitive gen. 96 f. Interchangeable with simple dat. 109 f., 131. For instrumental dat. 116 f., 130 f. Denoting the personal agent 130 f. With λέγει 131 note 1. Denoting the cause or motive 118, 131. ἐν

τούτῳ, ἐν ᾧ 131, 219, 272. With verbs expressing emotion 118. Denoting accompanying forces etc. 118. Of manner 118, 131. With μανθάνω, γινώσκω ('with' or 'by') 131. Of time 119 f. ἐν δεξιᾷ 140. ἐν (ἐμ) μέσῳ 12, 129. ἐν χειρί 130. ἐν Χριστῷ (κυρίῳ) 131.—Not assimilated in composition 12. Opposed to ἀ- 69. Compounds of ἐν, constr. 115.

ἔναντι with gen. 127 f.

ἐναντίος constr. 111. ἐναντίον with gen. 127 f. ἐξ ἐναντίας 140.

ἐνδιδύσκω 41, 53. Constr. 92.

ἔνδον 58 note 1.

ἕνεκεν εἵνεκεν (ἕνεκα) 20, 22. Uses of, 127. ἕν. τοῦ with inf. 237.

ἐνεργέω and -έομαι 185.

ἐνέχειν intrans. 182.

ἐνθάδε 58.

ἔνθεν 59.

ἔνι = ἐστί 51 f.

ἐνορκίζω constr. 88, 92, 226.

ἔνοχος constr. 106.

ἐντέλλομαι constr. 226, 235, 240.

ἐντεῦθεν 59.

ἐντός rare 58 note 1. With gen. 107.

ἐντρέπομαί τινα 89.

ἐντυγχάνω constr. 115.

ἐνώπιον with gen. 127 f. For dat. 113 note 4, 128.

ἐξ, ἐκ, ἐγ 12. Uses 124 ff. ἐκ τοῦ with inf. 237. In periphrases for partitive gen. 96 f. (144). Do. with verbs 100 f. With 'to fill' etc. 102, 117 note 3. With 'to sell' etc. 105, 126. With verbs denoting separation 105 f. For ὑπό 126. For ἐν (attraction) 258. ἐκ μέσου = ἐξ 129. ἐκ χειρός, ἐκ στόματος 83, 130. Compounds of ἐκ with gen. 106.

ἐξαυτῆς 14, 140.

ἔξεστιν constr. 227 f., 241. ἐξόν sc. ἔστι 73, 75, 204, 252.

ἐξολοθρεύω 21.

ἐξουσίαν ἔχω etc. constr. 227 f., 234.

ἐξορκίζω constr. 88, 133, 226.

ἐξουθενέω (-όω) 24, 61.

ἔξω 58 note 1. With gen. 107.

ἔξωθεν 59.

ἐξώτερος 35.

ἑόρακα and ἑώρακα 39, 56. Use 199 f.

-εος in 2nd declension contracted and uncontracted 25.

ἐπαγγέλλομαι constr. 232.

ἐπαισχύνομαι augm. 38.

ἐπακούω τινός 103.

ἐπακροῶμαί τινος 103.

ἐπάνω 14, 65. With gen. 107, 108, 129.

ἐπαρχία -ειος 8.

ἐπαύριον 14, 136.

Ἐπαφρόδιτος Ἐπαφρᾶς 71.

ἐπεί 60, 218, 274.

ἐπειδή 60, 218, 272, 274.

ἐπειδήπερ 60, 272, 274.

ἐπείκεια for ἐπιείκ. 23.

ἐπείπερ 60.

ἔπειτα 60, 277. ἐπ. μετὰ τοῦτο 295.

ἐπέκεινα 14, 66, 84. With gen. 107.

ἐπερωτάω constr. 226.

ἐπέχω intrans. 182.

ἐπηρεάζω τινά 89.

ἐπί with acc. 136. ἐπὶ τὸ αὐτό 136. With gen. 136 f. With dat. 137 f. ἐφ᾽ ᾧ 137. Compounds of ἐπί, constr. 115.

ἐπιβάλλω intrans. 182. Constr. 115.

ἐπιγινώσκω constr. 246.

ἐπιδείκνυμαι mid. 186. -νυμι constr. 233.

ἐπιθυμέω constr. 102, 225.

ἐπικαλέω, -ομαι constr. 92 note 1, 227, 230, 238. ὁ ἐπικαλούμενος 163.

ἐπιλαμβάνομαί τινος 101.

ἐπιλανθάνομαι constr. 104, 227.

ἐπιλησμονή 62.

ἐπιμαρτυρέω constr. 232.

ἐπιμέλομαι -έομαι 55: fut. 45: constr. 104.

ἐπιμένω with partic. 245, 258.

ἐπιούσιος 64.

ἐπιποθέω constr. 102, 225.

ἐπισκέπτομαι constr. 227.

ἐπίσταμαι constr. 231 with note 4, 246.

ἐπιστρέφω intrans. 182 f.

ἐπιτάσσω constr. 226, 230, 240 f.

ἐπιτίθημι, -εμαι constr. 115.

ἐπιτιμάω constr. 226.

ἐπιτρέπω constr. 226, 240.

ἐπιτυγχάνω constr. 102.

ἐπιχειρέω constr. 225.

INDEX OF GREEK WORDS.

ἐραυνάω for ἐρευν. 21.
ἐργάζομαι, ἠργαζόμην -σάμην, but εἴργασμαι 38 f., 54. Constr. 92, 124.
ἔρημος, accentuation of, 14. ὁ and ἡ 33. ἡ ἔρ. as subst. 140, 155.
ἔρις, plur. -ιδες and -εις 27, 84.
Ἑρμῆς 71.
ἐρρέθην for -ήθην 10, 40, 55.
ἔρρωσο, -σθε 200.
ἔρχομαι : forms in use 54. Aor. 45. ἔρχομαι, ὁ ἐρχόμενος in future sense 189, 219. ἔρχου 'come with' 196 note 1. ἔρχου καὶ ἴδε 278.
ἐρωτάω with double accus. 91. With inf. etc. 226, 241. ἠρώτων λέγοντες etc. 250. ἠρώτα and -τησεν 191.
-ες term. of 2nd pers. in perf. and 1st aor. for -ας 46.
ἐσθής in collective sense 83.
ἐσθίω, ἔσθω 54. φάγομαι 42 (-εσαι 47). Constr. 100 f. ἐσθίειν καὶ πίνειν 289.
-εσία, substantives in, 69.
ἔστακα, -ηκα (ἔστηκα?) 50 (15, 199).
ἔστε imperat. nowhere used 209.
ἔσχατος also comparative 34. ἐπ' ἐσχάτου (-των) τῶν ἡμερῶν etc. (137, 149), 156. τὰ ἔσχατα 156.
ἔσω, not εἴσω 22. Cp. 58 note 1. Not with gen. 107.
ἔσωθεν 59. Not with gen. 107.
ἐσώτερος 35.
ἑτεροδιδασκαλέω 68.
ἕτερος and ἄλλος 179 f.
ἔτι 277. Position 289. ἔτι ἄνω, κάτω for ἀνώτερον, κατώτερον 35 note 1. ἔτι μικρὸν καί 73.
ἕτοιμος 2 and 3 terminations 33. Accentuation 14. With τοῦ and inf. 235.
εὖ, καλῶς used instead of, 58. Compounds with εὖ 69, 39 (augment of verbs compounded with εὖ). εὖ ποιέω (πράσσω) constr. 89, 245.
εὐαγγελίζομαι and -ζω 39, 69, 183. Constr. 89 f., 124, 227.
εὐαγγέλιον 69. With gen. and with κατά and acc. 96, 133.
εὐαρεστέομαι with dat. 118, 184.
εὐδοκέω 69. Constr. 88, 118, 123, 227.
εὐκαιρέω constr. 227.
εὐλογητὸς ὁ θεός 74.
εὐοδοῦμαι constr. 227.
εὐπάρεδρος 69. Constr. 115.

εὐρακύλων 66.
εὑρίσκω aor. 45. Active for mid. 183. Constr. 246 f. -ομαι pass. with dat. 113 (note 2), 185.
-εύς, acc. plur. -εῖς 26.
εὐφραίνομαι constr. 118.
εὐχαριστέω constr. 137, 185 (246).
εὔχομαι augm. 38. Constr. 110, 226.
-εύω, -εύομαι, verbs in, 61.
ἐφάπαξ 14.
ἐφικνέομαί τινος 102.
ἐφιορκέω 16.
ἐφοράω constr. 227.
Ἐφραίμ 17.
ἐχθές 23.
ἔχω 'regard as' 92, 231, 247 : 'be obliged to' 226. Fut. only ἕξω 36, 54. ἔσχηκα for aor. 200. Intrans. 182. With double acc. (ὡς, εἰς) 92, 247. With relative clause 218. With inf. 226. With ὅτι 231. ἔχων 'with' 248. ἔχομαί τινος 102.
-έω, verbs in, 61. Formed from compound adjectives in -ος 67.
-έως gen. termination of adjectives in -ύς 27.
ἕως, ἡ, not in use 25.
ἕως conj. 60, 219, 272. With gen. 127. With gen. of the inf. 237, 239. ἕως οὗ, ὅτου 127, 219, 272. ἕως with adverb 127.

ζ = σδ 24.
ζάω 54. Fut. 42. Imperf. 47.
ζβ for σβ 10.
ζῆλος, ὁ and τό 28.
ζηλόω constr. 225.
ζημιόω pass. with acc. 93.
ζητέω constr. 225.
ζμ for σμ 10.
ζυγός, not -όν 28.
ζώννυμι, perf. pass. 54.
ζῷον 7.

η interchanged with ι 8 f. η interchanged with ει 8 f.
ἤ, ἦ ... ἤ 266. In questions (also ἤ μή) 259, 266. With comparatives 107 f. With positives 143.
η changed to ει in later Attic 8.
-ῃ in 2nd pers. pass. 47.
-ῃ, adverbs in, 59.

ἡγέομαι with double acc. 92, 247.
With acc. and inf. 92, 231. With
ὡς and acc. 92 f., 270, 246 note 1,
247. ἡγούμενος subst. 157, 244.
ἥγημαι with present sense 199.
ἥδιστα 'very gladly' 33.
ἡδύτερος 34 note 1.
ἥκω, inflection 54. Has perfect sense
188.
'Ηλίας 8. Declension 25.
ἥλιος without art. 147.
ἡμεῖς for ἐγώ 166.
ἡμέρα omitted 140. Without art. 149,
151. νύκτα καὶ ἡμέραν 94, 109.
ἡμέραν ἐξ ἡμέρας 94. ἡμέρας (μέσης)
109. Dat. with and without ἐν 109,
119 f., 174 note 1. ἡμέρᾳ καὶ ἡμέρᾳ
120. διὰ τῆς ἡμ. 109, 132. δι' ἡμερῶν
τεσσεράκοντα (τεσσ. ἡμ.) 109, 132.
πρὸ ἓξ ἡμ. τοῦ πάσχα 126 f. οὐ μετὰ
πολλὰς ταύτας ἡμέρας 133. (τὸ) καθ'
ἡμέραν 94, 157. ἐκείνη ἡ ἡμ. the
last day 171. ἐν αὐτῇ τῇ ἡμ. 170.
ἐν ταῖς ἡμ. ἐκείναις (ταύταις) 171 f.,
cp. 276. ἐπ' ἐσχάτου (-ων) τῶν ἡμ.
137, 149, 156.
ἥμισυς declined 27. ἥμισυ, τὰ ἡμίσεια
with gen. 97 f.
-ην for -η in acc. of 3rd decl. 26.
ἤνεγκα, ἐνεγκεῖν etc. 45, 57.
ἡνίκα 59, 272.
ἤπερ 60.
'Ηρώδης 7.
-ης in compounds from verbs in -άω,
-έω 68.
-ης, -εντος (in proper names) = Lat.
-ēns, -entis 31.
'Ησαΐας 'Ησ. 16.
ἥσσων ἥττων, ἡσσοῦμαι ἡττῶμαι etc.
23, 54. ἥσσων, ἧσσον meaning 34.
ἤτοι 60, 266.
ἦχος, ὁ 28 : gen. -ους ibid.

θ, reduplication of, 11.
θάλασσα without art. 147.
θάνατος without art. 149, 150.
θαμβέω and deponent -έομαι 44. Aor.
ibid.
θαρρέω and θάρσει 23. Intrans. 88.
Constr. 123 note 3.
θαυμάζω and dep. -ομαι 44, 54, 181.
Aor. ibid. Fut. 42. Constr. 88,
118, 135, 137.
θεά beside ἡ θεός 25.

θεάομαι defective 54 (supplemented by
θεωρέω). ἐθεάθην with dat. 113, 185.
θ. with part. 246. With ὡς 230
note 4.
θέλω, not ἐθ. 23, 54. Augm. ἠ- 37, 54.
= βούλομαι 47. Constr. 196 f., 209,
210 (θέλετε with conj.), 225. ἤθελον
'I could wish' 207.
θεμέλιον and -ος 28.
-θεν, adverbs in, 59.
θεός voc. θεός (θεέ) 25, 87. Without
art. 148, 163, 297.
θεωρέω supplemented by θεάομαι 54.
Takes place of pres. ὁράω 56. Constr.
231 with note 4, 233, 246.
θιγγάνω with gen. 101.
θλῖψις 15.
θνήσκω 7. Perf. 50, 199.
θριαμβεύω trans. 88, 183.
Θυάτειρα declined 32.
θύρα and -αι 84, 137, 149.

ι interchangeable with ε 21 f. With υ
22 (with ο 22). Shortened before ξ
15.
ι adscript (ι mute) 6 f.
-ί in demonstratives (νυνί) 35.
-ία, substantives in, 63. Do. related
to compound adjectives in -ος and
verbs in -έω 67.
-ιάζω, verbs in, 61.
-ιανός, designations ending in, of Latin
origin 63.
ἰάομαι pass. 184.
-ίας, gen. -ίου (proper names), 25, 29.
ἰδεῖν for ἰδεῖν 16.
ἴδιος for ἴδ. 16. Generally possessive
= 'own' 169. Omission of art. with
it 169. κατ' ἰδίαν, ἰδίᾳ 141, 169.
ἰδού for ἰδού 16. Without a finite
verb 74, 292. καὶ ἰδού 262. ἰδού,
ἴδε with nom. 85 note 1. ἴδε with
plural word 85 note 1.
ιει contracted into ει 23, 51.
'Ιεράπολις dat. 'Ιερᾷ πόλει 32.
'Ιεριχώ 7, 16.
'Ιεροσόλυμα 'Ιερουσαλήμ 16, 31. Fem.
32. Hardly ever takes art. 153,
cp. 161.
ἱερουργέω trans. 88.
'Ιεσσαί 17.
-ίζω, verbs in, 61.
ἵημι with compounds 51.

INDEX OF GREEK WORDS. 321

Ἰησοῦς 29. Declined 31. With and without art. 152, 170.
ἱκανός constr. 227 f. ἱκανόν satis 76.
Ἰκόνιον 8.
-ικός (-ιακός), adjectives in, 64 f. Verbal adj. in -ικός with gen. wanting 107.
ἱλάσκομαι 54. Constr. 88 note 3.
ἵλεώς σοι 25, 74.
ἱμάτιον omitted 141. ἱμάτια 84.
-ιν, -ινος for -ις, -ινος 27.
ἵνα 60, 211 f., 221, 222 ff., 209 (for imperat.), 217 f., 240. ἀλλ' ἵνα 269, 293. ἵνα δὲ 286 f.
ἱνατί 14.
-ινός, adjectives in, 65.
Ἰόππη Ἰόπη 11.
Ἰορδάνης, ὁ 153.
Ἰουδαία with art. 153.
Ἰουδαῖοι with and without art. 153 f. Ἰ. (τε) καὶ Ἕλληνες 264.
Ἰουνίας or -νία 71 note 4.
ἴσα as adverb with εἶναι 257 f. (271).
ἴσασι for οἴδασι 5, 50.
-ισία, substantives in, 69.
ἴσος constr. 114, 270 f.
Ἰσραήλ, ὁ 154. πᾶς Ἰ., πᾶς οἶκος Ἰ. 162.
-ισσα, substantives in, 63.
ἱστάνω, -άω for ἵστημι 48. ἔστην and ἐστάθην 50, 181. 2nd aor. imperat. 50. Other tenses 50.
ἰσχύω constr. 226.
Ἰταλία with art. 153.
ἰχθῦς accent 14. Acc. plur. -ύας 26.
Ἰωάννα 11, 30.
Ἰωάνης Ἰωνα(ς) etc. 11, 30.
Ἰωνάθας (-ης) 30.
Ἰωσήφ Ἰωσῆς 30. Gen. -ῆτος 31.
Ἰωσίας 8.

καθά 270.
καθάπερ 270.
καθάπτω for -ομαι 183. With gen. 101.
καθαρίζω (-ερ-) 20. For καθαίρω 54.
καθέζομαι 54 f.
καθ' εἷς 179. τὸ καθ' εἷς 94.
καθῆκεν, καθῆκον 206.
κάθημαι 52, 54 f.
καθίζω 54 f.
καθό 270.

καθόλου, τό 234 note 2.
καθότι 274.
καθώς 270.
καί 60, 261 ff. (249 f., 275 note 1). In crasis 19. At the beginning of the apodosis 262 f. In sentences of comparison 263, 270. καὶ ... καί, τε (...) καί etc. 264 f. ἀλλὰ καί 269. καὶ γάρ 275. καὶ ... δέ, δὲ καί 267. διὸ καί etc. 263. εἰ καί see εἰ. καὶ εἰ 275. ἢ καί 266. καὶ οὔ, καὶ μή 265 f. καὶ ταῦτα with particip. 248, 263. καὶ τοῦτο 171, 263. καὶ τίς 'who then?' 262 f. Cp. καίγε, καίπερ, καίτοι(γε), κἄν.
Και(α)φας 17 note 4.
καίγε 248, 261.
Καινάν 17.
καινότερος for positive 142.
καίπερ 60. With part. 248.
καιρός without art. 149. κ. (ἐστιν) constr. 223 f., 234.
καίτοι(γε) 60, 248, 260, 269 (275).
καίω aor. and fut. pass. 43, 55.
κακολογέω τινά 89.
κακοπαθία 8.
κακός, comparison of, 34. κακοὺς κακῶς 298.
καλέω fut. καλέσω 42, 55. With double acc. 92. ὁ καλούμενος 163.
καλλιέλαιος, ἡ 67.
καλόν ἐστιν constr. 112, 240 f.
καλῶς for εὖ 58. καλῶς (εὖ) ποιέω constr. 89, 245. καλῶς λέγω 89.
κάμηλος (-ιλος) 9.
κἄν 19 note 2, 214, 275.
κατά with acc. 133. In periphrases for possessive gen. 133, 169. Distributive κατά, stereotyped as an adv. 133, 145, 179. With gen. 133. κατὰ μόνας 141. κατ' ἰδίαν 141, 169. κατὰ πρόσωπον 83, 129 f. Compounds of κατά, constr. 89 (acc.), 104, 106 (gen.).
καταγινώσκομαι pass. 184.
κατάγνυμι 52.
καταδουλόω active 183.
καταδυναστεύω constr. 104.
κατακρίνω constr. 232. θανάτῳ 111.
κατακυριεύω τινός 104.
καταλαμβάνομαι mid. 186. Constr. 231.
καταλείπω constr. 226.
καταλλάσσω, -ομαι with dat. 114.

x

καταναρκάω τινός 106.
κατανύσσω, aor. pass. 43.
καταξιώ constr. 226.
καταράομαί τινα 89.
καταχράομαι with dat. 114.
κατέναντι with gen. 127 f.
κατενώπιον with gen. 127 f. Interchangeable with dat. 113 note 4.
κατηγορέομαι pass. 184.
κατήγωρ for -opos 29.
κατηχέομαι pass. with acc. 93.
κατώτερος, -έρω 35.
καυχάομαι intrans. and trans. 88. Constr. 110, 118.
Καφαρναούμ 12 f., 32.
Κεδρών 32.
κεῖμαι 52. = τέθειμαι 51. κείμενος ἦν 203.
κείρομαι 'have one's hair cut' 186.
κέκτημαι not used 199 note 1.
κέκραγα for κράζω 198.
κελεύω constr. 110, 191, 197, 226, 230, 240 (acc. and inf. pass.).
κενεμβατεύω 67.
(κεράννυμι) perf. pass. 55.
κέρας κέρατα 26.
κερδαίνω, aor. -ανα, -ησα 40, 55. Fut. pass. 55.
κῆρυξ accent 15.
κηρύσσω constr. 124, 226, 239.
Κιλικία with and without art. 153.
κινδυνεύω constr. 227.
κλαίω 55. Fut. 42. Constr. 88, 136.
κλείς acc. κλεῖδα κλεῖν 26. Plur. κλεῖδας κλεῖς 26.
κλείω κέκλεισμαι 40, 55.
κληρονομέω constr. 102.
κλίμα accent and quantity 14 f., 63.
κλίνω aor. pass. 44, 55. Intrans. 182.
κοιλία without art. 151.
κοιμάομαι fut. 45.
κοινωνέω constr. 100, 114.
κοινωνός with gen. (or dat.) 106.
κολλάομαι with dat. 114.
κολλύριον (-ούριον) 22.
Κολοσσαί Κολασσαεῖς 21.
κόλποι 84.
κόπτομαι constr. 88.
κορβανᾶς (-βαν) 32.
κορέννυμι with gen. 101.
κόσμιος, ὁ ἡ 33.

κόσμος without art. 148.
Κούαρτος 15.
κράβ[β]ατος (-αττος, -ακτος) 11.
κραζω, κρᾶζον 15. Inflection 55. Fut. 36 note 1, 43. Aor. 43. κέκραγα = κράζω 198. Constr. 232, 250.
κρατέω constr. 101. -έομαι τοῦ μὴ with inf. 235.
κράτιστε in address 33, 86.
κρέας, κρέα 26.
κρείσσων, -ττων 23. Meaning 34.
κρίμα accent and quantity 14 f., 63.
κρίνω constr. 231. -ομαι constr. 114.
Κρίσπος 15.
κρύβω for κρύπτω 41, 55. Aor. pass. 43, 55. Constr. 91.
κρυπτός : ἐν (τῷ) κρυπτῷ 156.
κτέννω (-αίνω) for -είνω 41, 55. Cp. ἀποκτ.
κτίσις without art. 148. πᾶσα (ἡ) κτ. 162.
κυέω (κύω) 55.
κυκλόθεν 59.
κυλίω 55.
Κυρήνιος, -ίνος, more correctly -ίνιος 9, 13.
κυριεύω τινός 104.
κύριος without art. 148.
κωλύω constr. 105, 226, 255.
Κῶς, acc. Κῶ 25

λαγχάνω constr. 102, 135, 235.
λάθρᾳ 7, 258.
λακέω 55.
λαλέω constr. 232.
λαμβάνω, λήμψομαι etc. 24, 55. εἴληφα with aoristic sense 200. λ. ῥαπίσμασιν 118. λαβών (ἔλαβεν καί) pleonastic 248 f.
λανθάνω constr. 245, 258.
λεγεών, -ιών 21.
λέγω defective, supplemented by εἶπον etc. 55. λέγει without subj. 75. λέγει ἐν 'Ηλίᾳ and similar phrases 131 note 1. With acc. (τινά) 89. καλῶς, κακῶς λέγω 89. With double acc. 92. With ὅτι or acc. and inf. 232, 240. With ἵνα 226. ἔλεγεν and εἶπεν 192. λέγων, -οντες 81 note 1, 232, 249 f., 285. σὺ λέγεις 260. ὁ λεγόμενος 242. λέγω ὑμῖν inserted 282. κατὰ ἄνθρωπον λέγω and similar phrases inserted 282.

INDEX OF GREEK WORDS. 323

λείπω aor. 43, 55. Alternative pres. λιμπάνω 55. λείπει τινί 112. λείπομαί τινος 105.
λειτουργός, -ία, -έω 8.
λέντιον 21.
Λευίς (-εις) declined 29.
ληνός, ἡ (ὁ) 26.
λίαν usually placed after word qualified 289.
λίθος, ὁ (not ἡ) 26.
λιμός, ὁ and ἡ 26. λιμός and λοιμός combined 299.
λογίζομαι pass. 184. Constr. with εἰς 86. With ὡς and nom. 93, 270. With (acc. and) inf. or ὅτι 231.
λοιδορέω τινά 89.
λοιπός : (τὸ) λοιπόν 94. τοῦ λοιποῦ 94, 109. Art. repeated after λ. 160 f. λ. omitted 180, 292.
Λουκᾶς 71.
λούω, λέλου(σ)μαι 40, 55.
Λύδδα, -ης (-ας) 25, 31 f. ἡ and τὰ Λ. 31 f.
λυμαίνομαί τινα 89.
λυπέομαι constr. 137.
λυσιτελέω constr. 89.
Λύστρα, -αν, -οις 32.

-μα, substantives in, 62. With short stem-vowel 14 f., 62 f. Studied accumulation of, 299.
μαθητεύω intrans. and trans. 88, 183.
μακάριος without auxiliary verb 73 f.
μακρόθεν (ἀπὸ μ.) 59.
μακροθυμέω constr. 118.
μᾶλλον, μάλιστα 33. μᾶλλον omitted 143. Pleonastic μᾶλλον 143.
μαμωνᾶς 11.
μανθάνω constr. 247, 227, 238.
μάννα 32.
Μάρθα, -ας 25, 30.
Μαριάμ, -ία 30.
Μᾶρκος 15.
μαρτυρέω constr. 111. With λέγων etc. 250. -έομαι pass. 184. μαρτυρῶ inserted 282.
μαστός, -σθός, -ζός 24.
μάταιος 2 and 3 terminations 33.
μεθύσκομαι οἴνῳ 117.
μείγνυμι (not μίγν.) 8.
μειζότερος 34.

μέλει constr. 104.
μέλλω augm. 38, 55. Constr. 197, 202, 222, 227. With inf. as periphrasis for fut. 204 f.
μέμνημαι, see μιμνήσκομαι.
μέμφομαι constr. 89.
μέν 60, 266 f. μὲν ... δὲ 266 f. μὲν ... ἀλλὰ (πλὴν) 267. μὲν οὖν 267, 270, 273.
μενοῦν γε 60, 260, 269, 270.
μέντοι 60, 269.
μένω trans. 87.
μεριμνάω constr. 104, 111.
μερίς omitted 140.
μέρος omitted 141. μέρη ' region' 84.
μεσανύκτιον for μεσον. 21.
μεσημβρία without art. 148.
μεσονύκτιον (μεσαν.) 67. Without art. 149. -ίου 109.
Μεσοποταμία with art. 153.
μέσος partitive 109, 158. τὸ μέσον 158. ἀνὰ μέσον 122, 129. ἐμ (ἐν) μέσῳ 12: with gen. 129. μέσος, μέσον adv., ἐκ μέσου, διὰ μέσου (-ον) with gen. 129, 132. Article 156.
μεστός with gen. 106.
μετά with acc. 133. μετὰ τὸ with inf. 236, 239. With gen. 133 f. Denoting manner 118. Alternating with dat. after verbs denoting community 114. μετά and σύν 132, 133 f. μετὰ καί 263.
μεταδίδωμι constr. 100.
μεταλαμβάνω with gen. 100. μεταλαβὼν καιρόν 100.
μεταλλάσσω constr. 105.
μεταμέλομαι 55. Fut. 45. Constr. 235.
μεταξύ ' between ' (with gen.), ' afterwards ' 129.
μετέχω constr. 100.
μέτοχος with gen. 106.
μετρέω ἔν τινι 117.
μετριοπαθέω τινί 110.
μέχρι(s) 20, 60. With gen. 127. μ. οὗ 127, 219, 272. Conjunction 219, 272.
μή negative 214, 216, 253 ff. Interrogative 254, 259. Before an inf. after verbs containing a negative idea 255. τὸ μὴ with inf. 234. τοῦ μὴ with inf. 235. As conjunction 211 ff.—μὴ οὐ 213, 254. οὐ μή see οὐ. μή with ellipse 293 f.—μὴ γένοιτο 219, 259.
μηδέ 60, 261, 265.

μηδείς 14, 178. μηθείς an alternative form 24.
μηθαμώς 24.
μηθείς 24.
μήν see εἶ μήν.
μήποτε 212 f., 220, 255 note 1. μήποτε οὐ μή 256.
μήπως 60, 212 f., 240 note 1, 255.
μήτε 60, 261. μήτε ... μήτε 265 f.
μήτηρ to be supplied 95.
μήτι 254, 259. μήτιγε 254.
μητρολῴας 7, 21.
-μι, verbs in, 48 ff.
μιαίνω μεμιαμμένος 40, 55.
μιμνῄσκω -όμαι 7. Constr. 103 f. μέμνημαι with present sense 199.
Μιτυλήνη for Μυτιλ. 22.
μνημονεύω constr. 104.
μνηστεύω μεμνήστευμαι? 38, 56.
μογιλάλος 24.
μόνος never more nearly defined by reference to the whole 97 note 1. μόνος and adv. μόνον 141. κατὰ μόνας 141. οὐ μόνον ... ἀλλὰ (καὶ) 267. οὐ μ. δὲ ἀ. καὶ 291 note 2.
-μός, substantives in, 61 f.
Μυσία with art. 153.
Μωϋσῆς 10. Declined 29.

ν, variable, 19.
Ναζαρετ, -εθ, -αθ 13.
ναί 256, 260. ναί, λέγω ὑμῖν 256, 260. ναὶ ναί 256.
Ναιμάν Νεεμάν etc. 17 note 2.
ναῦς in literary lang. for πλοῖον 27.
Νεάπολις Νέαν πόλιν 32.
νεκροί without art. 148.
νεομηνία νουμ. 22.
ν(ε)οσσός ν(ε)οσσιά etc. 23.
νεύω with inf. 226.
νήθω 56.
νῆστις, plur. νήστεις 27.
νικάω, ὁ νικῶν with perfect sense 189.
νῖκος, τὸ for ἡ νίκη 28 f.
νίπτω for νίζω 41, 56.
νοέω constr. 231.
νομίζω not with double acc. 92. With inf., with ὅτι 201 f., 231 f.
νόμος without art. 150.
νότος without art. 148.

νοῦς, νοός 29.
νῦν, position of, 289.
νύξ: νύκτα καὶ ἡμέραν 94, 109. (τῆς) νυκτός 109. διὰ (τῆς) ν. 109, 132, 149. μέσης ν. 109. ἐν νυκτί 119. κατὰ μέσον τῆς ν. 158.
νυχθήμερον 66 f.
νυστάζω ἐνύσταξα 40.

ξένος with gen. 106.
ξηρά, ἡ 140.
ξηραίνω ἐξηραμμένος 40.
ξυρέω forms 56. ἐξυράμην 186.

ο interchangeable with α and ε 21. With ῑ 22.
ὁ, ἡ, τό 145 ff. τὸ, τοῦ, τῳ with inf. 233 ff. ὁ μὲν ... ὁ δὲ 145 f. ὁ δὲ, ἡ δὲ, οἱ δὲ 146. ὁ μὲν οὖν 146. As article 146 ff. ὁ καί 163.
ὅδε 35 f., 170.
ὁδός, ellipse of, 108 f., 140. ὁδόν with gen. versus 94 note 1, 98, 130. ὁδῷ with πορεύομαι etc. 119.
Ὀζίας 8.
ὅθεν 59, 258 (attraction). Conjunction 274.
οἱ- often unaugmented 38.
οἶδα forms 50, 53 (cp. ἴσασιν). Constr. 227, 231, 240, 246.
οἰκοδεσπότης 66. οἰκ. τῆς οἰκίας 295.
οἰκοδομή 62.
οἶκος without art. 151, 162.
οἰκτιρμός 8, 15. -οί 83.
οἰκτίρω (-ίρμων) 8, 15, 56. Trans. 88.
-οῖν for -οῦν in inf. 48.
οἷος 36, 178 f. οὐχ οἷον ὅτι 179, 292 note 2. οἷος δήποτ' οὖν 178.
ὀλοθρεύω, -ευτής, ἐξολ. for -ε- 21.
ὅλος with art. 161.
ὁμείρομαι for ἱμ. 22. With gen. 102.
ὁμιλέω constr. 114.
(ὄμνυμι), ὀμνύω 48. Constr. 88, 123, 131, 133, 232.
ὁμοθυμαδόν 70.
ὁμοιάζω constr. 114.
ὅμοιος accent 14. 2 terminations? 33. With dat. (or gen.) 106, 114.
ὁμοιόω constr. 114.
ὁμολογέω constr. 92, 110, 131, 202, 247.
ὁμόσε = ὁμοῦ 59.

INDEX OF GREEK WORDS. 325

ὅμως 60, 269.
ὀνειδίζω τινά 89.
ὀνίναμαι with gen. 101.
ὄνομα : ᾧ ὄν., οὗ τὸ ὄν., (καὶ τὸ) ὄν. αὐτοῦ, ὀνόματι 74, 85, 118. τοὔνομα 94. ἐπιτίθημι, ἐπικαλέω τινὶ ὄν. 115. καλέω τὸ ὄν. τινος ... (acc.) 92. πιστεύω εἰς τὸ ὄν. τινος 110. ἐπὶ (ἐν) τῷ ὄν. τινος etc. 123 f.
-οος, contraction of, in 2nd decl. 25.
ὄπισθεν with gen. 107, 128.
ὀπίσω with gen. 107, 128 f.
ὁποῖος 36, 175, 179.
ὁπότε 59 f., 218, 272.
ὅπου 'where' and 'whither' 58.
ὀπτάνομαι 56. With dat. 113, 185. Cp. ὁράω.
ὅπως 60, 175, 211 f., 221, 258.
ὁράω defective, supplemented by βλέπω, θεωρῶ, εἶδον etc. 56. Perf. ἑόρακα and ἑώρ. 39. Pass. ὀπτάνομαι, ὤφθην 56, 185. Constr. 88 note 1, 126, 246. ὅρα, ὁρᾶτε μή 209, 213, 278. ορα μή elliptical 293.
ὀργίζομαι constr. 118.
ὀρέγομαι with gen. 102.
ὀρεινή, ἡ 140.
ὀρθοποδέω 67.
ὁρίζω constr. 225.
ὁρκίζω constr. 88, 92, 133, 241.
ὄρνιξ, ὄρνεον 27.
ὁροθεσία, ἡ, or -έσια, τὰ 69.
ὀρύσσω aor. pass. 44.
ὅς, ἥ, ὅ 36. Uses 173 ff., 216 ff. Confused with ὅστις 172 f. Not used for τίς 176 (but see also 218). Used with disregard to formal agreement 166. Attraction 173 ff. ὃς μὲν ... ὃς δὲ 145 f. ἀφ' ἧς 140. ὅ ἐστι 77, 204. ἐν ᾧ see ἐν. ἐφ' ᾧ see ἐπί.
-οσία, substantives in, 69.
ὅσιος, ὁ, ἡ 33.
ὅσος 36, 178 f. ὅσον ὅσον 179.
ὅσπερ not in use 36, 173.
ὀστέον -οῦν 25.
ὅστις (almost) confined to the nom. 36. Uses 172 f., 216 ff. With conj. without ἄν? 217. Not used in indirect questions 175, but cp. 176. ὅ,τι in direct questions 176 : = δι' ὅ,τι 177. ὅστις ἄν ᾖ 178.
ὅταν 60, 218 f., 272.
ὅτε 60, 218, 228, 272. ὁτὲ μὲν ... ὁτὲ δὲ 258.

ὅτι 60, 222, 229, 230 ff., 240 (272) 286. Before direct speech 233, 286. 'Because' 274. οὐχ (οἷον) ὅτι 179, 292 note 2.
ὅτου in ἕως ὅτου, μέχρι ὅτ. 36, 127, 219.
-οῦ, adverbs in, 58 f.
οὐ, 253 ff., 214, 216 f. οὐ ... ἀλλὰ (δὲ) 266, 267. οὐ μόνον ... ἀλλὰ (καὶ) 267. οὐ μ. δὲ ἀ. καὶ 291 note 2. οὐ in questions 254, 259, 209 f. οὐ ... οὐ (μὴ) neutralizing each other 256. οὐ ... οὐδείς etc. intensifying the negation 256. οὐ οὔ (ditto) 256. οὐ μή with conj. (or fut.) 209 f. οὐ πάντως and similar phrases 257. οὐχ ὅτι 292 note 2. οὐχ οἷον ὅτι 179, 292 note 2. οὐ γάρ 275.
οὗ 'where' and 'whither' 58.
οὐαί, ἡ 32. With dat. 112.
οὐδέ 60, 261, 265 f. ἀλλ' οὐδὲ 269. οὐδὲ γὰρ 275.
οὐδείς 14. Also οὐθείς 24. οὐδείς, οὐδὲ εἷς 178. οὐδ. ὃς οὐ 173, 256. οὐδέν 'nothing worth' 76. οὐχ ὀλίγος 16.
οὐθέτερος 178.
οὐκοῦν 60, 273.
οὖν 60, 272 f. ἄρα οὖν 273. μὲν οὖν see μὲν.
οὐράνιος, ὁ, ἡ 33.
οὐρανός and -οί 83. Without art. 147 f.
Οὐρίας 8.
-οῦσαι 2nd pers. pass. in verbs in -όω 47 note 2.
οὔτε 60, 261. οὔτε ... οὔτε (καὶ) 265 f.
οὗτος 35. Uses 170 ff. With and without art. 172. Referring to a subsequent clause with ὅτι, ἵνα, or inf. 171, 229. τοῦτο μὲν .. τοῦτο δὲ 171. καὶ τοῦτο idque 171, 263. καὶ ταῦτα with part. 171, 248, 263. οὗτος with anaphora 301.
οὕτω(ς) 19 f. After a participle 253. As predicate 257. ὡς ... οὕτως (καὶ) 270.
οὐχί 254, 256 f. οὐχί, λέγω ὑμῖν 256.
ὀφειλέτης εἰμί constr. 111.
ὀφείλω : ὤφειλον 206. Constr. 227.
ὄφελον particle to introduce a wish 206 f., 220.
ὀφθαλμοδουλία (-εία) 68.
ὀφθαλμός without art. 151 with note 2.
ὀψία, ἡ 140.
-όω, verbs in, new forms of, 61.

παιδεύομαι constr. 227.
(ἐκ) παιδιόθεν 59.
παίζω 56, 40. Fut. 43.
πάλιν ἀνακάμπτειν and similar phrases 295.
παμπληθεί 8, 69.
Παμφυλία, with and without art. 153.
πανδοκεῖον, -χεῖον 24.
πανοικεί 8, 69.
πανταχῇ, πάντῃ 7.
πάντοτε for ἀεί 59.
πάντως οὐ and οὐ πάντως 257.
παρά with acc. 138. With comparative 108 : cp. 138 (with positive 143). With gen. 138. With dat. 138 f. Compounds of παρά transitive 89 : with dat. etc. 115.
παραγγέλλω constr. 226, 232, 240 f.
παράγω intrans. 182.
παραδίδωμι constr. 223, 236.
παραθαλάσσιος, -ία 33.
παραινέω constr. 90, 226, 241.
παραιτέομαι with μή and inf. 255.
παρακαλέω constr. 226, 233, 235, 241, 249. παρεκάλει, -εσεν 191.
παραλαμβάνω constr. 227. παραλαβών 248.
παράλιος, ὁ, ἡ 33.
παρατηρέω, -έομαι 186.
πάρειμι, -εῖναι constr. 115.
παρέχω, -ομαι 186. Constr. 115.
παρρησία 10.
παρρησιάζομαι constr. 227.
πᾶς with art. 161 f. πᾶς ἐξ 97. ὁ πᾶς, οἱ πάντες, τὰ πάντα 162. πᾶς ὅστις, ὅς 173 (244). πᾶς ὁ with part. 243 f. πᾶν τό with part. 244. πᾶς ... οὐ, οὐ ... πᾶς = οὐδείς 162, 178, 283 note 1. πάντες οὐ 257. πάντων a stereotyped form with πρώτη 108.
πάσχα (φάσκα) 12, 32.
πάσχω ὑπό 184.
Πάταρα (-ερα) 20.
πατρολῴας 7, 21, 68.
παύω ἐπάην 44, 56. -ομαι constr. 105, 245.
πεζῇ 7.
πειθός non-existent 64.
πείθω 56. πείθω and -ομαι constr. 226, 232. Cp. πέποιθα.
πεῖν for πιεῖν 23, 56.

πεινάω contract verb in ᾱ instead of η 47, 56. Tenses 40, 56. Constr. 90, 102.
πειράζω, meanings of, 56. Constr. 225.
πεισμονή 62.
πενθέω intrans. and trans. 88.
πέποιθα with present sense 199. Constr. 110, 123, 136, 137, 232.
περ in combinations like καίπερ 60.
πέρᾳ 7.
πέραν with gen. 107.
περί with acc. 134. οἱ περὶ αὐτόν, Παῦλον 134, 157. With gen. 134 f. : confused with ὑπέρ 134 f. Compounds of περί transitive 89 : with dat. etc. 115 f.
περιάγω intrans. 182.
περιβάλλω constr. 92, 115 f. -ομαι mid. constr. 93 with note 2.
περιβλέπομαι mid. 186. Constr. 227.
περιέχω 182 note 3.
περίκειμαι with acc. 93. With dat. etc. 116.
περιούσιος 64.
περιπατέω with dat. 119.
περιπίπτω constr. 116.
περισσός, -ότερος, -ῶς, -οτέρως for πλείων, μᾶλλον etc. 33 note 4, 58, 143. περισσός with gen. 108.
περιτέμνομαι pass. 185.
περίχωρος, ἡ 140.
πέρυσι (πέρσυ, πέρισυ), not -ιν 19.
πηλίκος 36. For ἡλίκος 179.
πῆχυς, -ῶν 27.
πιάζω, -έξω 20, 56. πιάζω constr. 101.
πίεσαι. See πίνω.
πιμπλάω for -ημι 49. Constr. 102.
πίνω 56. πεῖν or πῖν for πιεῖν 23. πίεσαι 47. πίνω constr. 100.
πιπράσκω 56 f. Perf. 200.
πιστεύω constr. 110, 123, 136, 137, 232. -ομαι pass. 93, 185.
πιστικός 64.
πίστις constr. 123, 136.
πιστός constr. 110 f., 143. τὸ πλεῖστον 'at most' 94.
πλεῖστος 33.
πλείων, neut. πλεῖον πλέον 22. οἱ πλείονες, meanings of, 142 f. πλείων before numerical statements without ἤ 108.
πληγή omitted 140.

INDEX OF GREEK WORDS. 327

πλήν 127. 'Yet' (=ἀλλά) 268. 'Only' 268.
πλήρης used indeclinably 81. Constr. 106.
πληρόω and -όομαι mid. 186. Constr. 102, 117. Pass. with acc. 93.
πλησίον with gen. 107. (ὁ) πλ. 157.
πλοῦς, πλοός 25, 29.
πλοῦτος, ὁ and τὸ 28.
πνεῦμα without art. 149.
ποθέω 40, 57.
ποιέω, -έομαι constr. 91 f., 124, 134, 135. καλῶς (εὖ) π. 89: (with part. 245). With ἵνα or inf. 226, 235, 240. ποιέω for -έομαι mid. 183 f. Pass. almost unrepresented 184.
ποῖος 36, 176, 179. ποίας sc. ὁδοῦ 108, 140.
πόλις with gen. of the name 98.
πολύς followed by καί 263. οἱ πολλοί 143. πολλὰς δέρεσθαι 91, 140. πολύ, πολλῷ with comparative 143.
πορεύομαι ὁδῷ etc. 119. πορεύου and -θητι 196, 249. πορευθείς 249.
πόρρω (in literary language) = μακράν 24. As predicate 257.
πόρρωθεν 59. = μακρόθεν 24.
πορρωτέρω (-ον) 35.
πόσος 36, 179.
ποταμοφόρητος 68.
ποταπός 36, 176, 229.
ποτέ 59 f., 212 f. (μήποτε).
πότερον..., ἤ 176, 259.
ποτίζω with double acc. 92. Pass. with acc. 93.
Ποτίολοι 22.
ποῦ 'where' and 'whither' 58.
που (rare) 58.
πρᾶος, πρᾷος 7.
πράσσω: εὖ πράσσω for καλῶς ποιῶ? 245.
πρέπει constr. 241.
πρίν 60. Constr. 219, 229, 240, 272. πρὶν ἤ 218 f., 229, 272. Prepos. with gen. 229 note 2.
Πρίσκα, Πρίσκιλλα 15 note 1.
πρό with gen. 126 f. πρὸ προσώπου τινός 129. πρὸ τοῦ with inf. 229, 237.
προάγω intrans. 182.
προαιτιάομαι constr. 232.
προβλέπομαι mid. 186.
πρόδηλον ὅτι 233.

πρόϊμος—πρώϊμος 22.
προκαταγγέλλω constr. 202, 232.
προλαμβάνω with inf. 227.
προμελετάω with inf. 227.
προνοέομαί τινος 104.
προοράω : προορώμην? 37.
πρός with acc. 139 : for παρά τινι (τινα) 139 : interchangeable with dat. 110 f., 114 f., 116. τί πρὸς ἡμᾶς 139. πρὸς τί 139. πρός με 165. πρὸς τὸ with inf. 236.—With gen. and dat. 140.—Compounds of πρός, constr. 116.
προσανατίθεμαί τινι 116.
προσέρχομαι constr. 116.
προσεύχομαί τινι 110. With ἵνα etc. 226, 235.
προσέχω intrans. 182, 292. Constr. 88 note 1, 116, 126. With inf. (or ἵνα) 227.
προσδέομαι with gen. 105.
προσδοκῶ constr. 202, 232.
προσήκει wanting in N.T. 206 note 2.
προσήλυτος 69.
προσκαλέομαι constr. 227.
προσκυνέω constr. 89, 110. Imperf. and aor. distinguished 192.
προσλαμβάνομαι constr. 100.
προσπίπτω constr. 116.
προσποιέομαι with inf. 227.
προστάσσω constr. 226.
προστίθημι constr. 116. -εμαι 'continue to' etc. with inf. 227, 258. προσθεὶς εἶπεν and similar phrases 249, 258.
προσφάγιον 69.
προσφωνέω constr. 116.
πρόσωπον without art. 150 f. In periphrases 83, 129 f., 151. πρόσωπον λαμβάνω 4 (προσωπολήμπτης etc. 68).
πρότερος -ον 34.
προτίθεμαι constr. 225.
προϋπάρχω with part. 244 f.
προφητεύω augm. 39.
προφθάνω constr. 245.
πρωΐ, τὸ answering the question When? 94, 157.
πρωΐα, ἡ 140.
πρώϊμος. See πρόϊμος.
πρῷρα 7.
πρῶτος for πρότερος 34. 'First of all' 141. πρῶτον μέν 267.

πυκνότερον 142 note 1.
πύλη and -αι 84. πύλη omitted 140.
πυνθάνομαι constr. 103.
πῶς 258. For ὡς or ὅτι 230.
πως 60, 212f. (εἴπως, μήπως).

ρ, -ρρ 10. Reduplication with ῥ- 38.
-ρᾶ 1st declens. gen. -ρης 25.
ῥαίδη 9.
Ῥαχάβ, Ῥαάβ 12.
ῥεραντισμένος 38, 57.
ῥεριμμένος 38, 57.
ῥέω fut. 43, 57.
ῥήγνυμι ῥήσσω (ῥάσσω) 57.
ῥίπτω -έω 57. ῥῖψαν 15. Perf. pass. 38.
-ρσ-, -ρρ- 2, 23.
ῥύομαι 57.

σ, variable, 19 f.
σάββατον 13. Dat. plur. -ασιν 29. (ἐν) τοῖς σ., τῷ σ. etc. 120. δὶς τοῦ σ. 97, 109. ὀψὲ σαββάτων 97.
Σαλαμίν, -ίνη 32.
σαλπίζω, ἐσάλπισα etc. 40, 57. σαλπίσει 75.
Σαλώμη 30.
Σαμάρεια, -ίτης 8.
-σαν for -ν in the imperat. 46. In the impf. 46. In the optat. 46 f.
Σάπφιρα 7. 11. -ης 25.
σαρδ(ι)όνυξ 66.
Σάρεπτα, -φθα 13, 32.
σαρκικός, -ινος 65.
σάρξ without art. 150. πᾶσα σ. 162. τὸ κατὰ σάρκα 94, 157. κατὰ σ. with Ἰσραήλ, κύριος etc. 159.
Σαρωνα 32.
σατανᾶς, σατάν 32. Without art. 148.
σεαυτοῦ not σαυτοῦ 35.
Σεκοῦνδος, Σέκ. 15.
σελήνη without art. 147.
σημαίνω, ἐσήμᾱνα, 40, 57. Constr. 232.
σήμερον (not τήμ.) 23.
σίκερα 32.
Σιλουανός, Σιλᾶς 71.
Σιλωάμ, ὁ 32.
σιμικίνθιον 9.

Σίμων for Συμεών 30.
Σινᾶ 8, 32.
σιρικόν 9.
-σις, substantives in, 62.
σῖτος plur. -α 28.
Σιών 8.
σιώπα πεφίμωσο 278.
σκάνδαλον 4.
σκέπτομαι, σκοπέω 57.
Σκευᾶς 12.
σκληροκαρδία, -κάρδιος 67.
σκότος, τὸ (not ὁ) 28.
Σόδομα, -ων 32.
Σολομών, -ῶνος and -μῶν, -μῶντος 29.
σπάω and -ομαι mid. 184.
σπίλος not σπῖλος 15.
σπλαγχνίζομαι 61. Constr. 104, 135, 136.
σπόγγος, σφόγγος 24.
σπουδάζω 57. Fut. 43. Constr. 225.
σπυρίς, σφυρίς 24.
-σσ-, -ττ- 2, 23.
στάδιον plur. -οι and -α 28.
στάμνος, ἡ 26.
στάνω for ἵστημι 48.
Στεφανᾶς 71.
στήκω for ἕστηκα 41.
στηρίζω, formation of tenses of, 40, 42, 57. στ. τὸ πρόσωπον τοῦ with inf. 235.
στοιχέω with dat. 119.
στόμα without art. 151. In periphrases 83, 103, 129 f., 137, 151.
στρατεία, στρατιά 8.
στρέφω intrans.? 182.
στρωννύω 48, 57.
συγγενής dat. plur. -εῦσι 27. Fem. -ίς 33.
συγκαλέω and -έομαι mid. 186.
συκομορέα 9.
συλλέγω 55.
συμβαίνω : συνέβη 228, 240.
συμβουλεύω, -ομαι constr. 225.
σύμμορφος with gen. 106. With dat. 114.
συμφέρει constr. 110, 227 f., 240 f. συμφέρον as subst. 244.
σύμφορον (-ερον) with gen. 110.
συμφωνέω pass. constr. 114 note 1, 240.

INDEX OF GREEK WORDS. 329

σύν in composition not assimilated 12. Its uses in comparison with those of μετά with gen. 132, 133 f. Verbs (and adjectives) compounded with σύν, constr. with dat. 114 f.
συναντάω fut. 43, 52.
συνέρχομαί τινι 'go with anyone' 114.
συνευδοκώ constr. 227.
-σύνη, substantives in, 63.
συνήθειά ἐστιν constr. 228.
συνίημι, συνίω 51.
συνίστημι constr. 118 note 1 (233 note 1, 238).
συντίθεμαι constr. 225, 235.
Συρία with and without art. 153.
Συροφοινίκισσα, -φοίνισσα 63, 66.
σφυδρόν for σφυρόν 24.
ᾤζω, σώσω etc., ἐσώθην σέσωται 7, 57.

ταμεῖον 23.
τάσσω aor. and fut. pass. 43 f., 57. Constr. 240 f.
τάχιον for θᾶσσον 34. Meaning 142.
τε 261, 263 f. τε (...) καί, τε ... τε etc. 264 f.
τέκνον, τεκνίον with μου 113.
τελευτάω intrans. 292.
τελέω, τελέσω 42, 57. With part. 245.
-τέον, verbal adjectives in, 37 (206 note 2).
τέρας, plur. τέρατα 26.
τέσσαρες, -αρα (-ερα?) 20. Acc. -αρες? 20, 26.
τεσσαρεσκαιδέκατος 35.
τεσσεράκοντα 20.
τεσσερακονταέτης 70.
τετραάρχης 70.
τετράμηνος, ἡ 140.
τηλαυγής 68.
τηλικοῦτος, neut. -ον and -ο 36. ὁ τηλ. 161.
τηρέω constr. 126.
-τήριον, substantives in, 62, 64.
-της, nouns denoting the agent in, 62. In compound words 68.
τί. See τίς.
τίθημι forms 49, 51. Act. and mid. 186. Constr. 226 f.
τίκτω aor. pass. 44, 57.
τίνω τείσω etc. 8.

τίς 36. Uses of, 175 f. Position 290. For πότερος 36, 176. For ὅστις 175 f. With partitive gen. and ἐξ (ἐν) 97. τίς ἤμην κ.τ.λ. 177. τί as predicate to ταῦτα 77, 177. τί (predic.) ἐγένετο 77, 177. τί 'why?' 177. τί ὅτι (τί γέγονεν ὅτι), ἵνα τί 177. τί 'how' 177. τί πρὸς ἡμᾶς, σέ 73, 139, 177. τί ἐμοὶ (ἡμῖν) καὶ σοί 73 (cp. 74), 177. τί γάρ μοι- 73. τί γάρ; 177, 274. τί οὖν; 177.
τις indefinite pron. 36, 177 f. With partitive gen. and ἐξ (ἐν) 97. εἷς τις 144, 178. τι 'something special' (predic.) 76 f.: similar use of τις 77. οὐ ... τις 256. τινὲς οἱ with part. 243. Position of τις 288, 297.
τίς ποτε 'someone or other' 178.
τοι only found in combinations 60.
τοιγαροῦν 273.
τοίνυν 273.
τοιόσδε 36, 170.
τοιοῦτος, neut. -ο and -ον 36. ὁ τ. 161, 179. τοιαύτη pleonastically used after οἷα 175.
τολμάω constr. 225.
-τος (verbal adj.) 37, 64. In compound words 68. Constr. with gen. 107.
τοσοῦτος, neut. -ο and -ον 36.
τότε 276.
τουτέστι, τοῦτ' ἔστι 14, 18, 77.
τρέμω with part. 246.
τρίβω, συντετρίφθαι 15.
τρίμηνος, ἡ 140.
τρίτον τοῦτο 'now for the third time' 91, 145. (τὸ) τρ. 'for the third time' 145. ἐκ τρίτου 145.
τρόπος: ὃν τρόπον etc., καθ' ὃν τρ., παντὶ τρόπῳ 94, 118.
Τρῳάς, article 152.
Τρωγίλιον, -υλία etc. 22.
τρώγω for ἐσθίω 54.
τυγχάνω forms 57. Constr. 102. εἰ τύχοι 221. τυχόν 252. οὐχ ὁ τυχών 255 f.
τύπτω defective 57.

υ shortened before ξ 15. Interchangeable with ι 22. = Lat. ŭ 13. κῦ = Lat. -qui- 13.
ὕαλος, ὁ for ἡ 26.
ὑγιής acc. -ιῆ 27.
ὕδωρ omitted 141.

ὑετός omitted 141.
υι changed into ῦ 9 f.
-υῖα 1st decl. gen. -υίης 25.
υἱός to be supplied with a gen. 95. In metaphorical sense 95 f.
ὑμῶν for ὑμέτερος 168. ὑ. αὐτῶν 'your selves' (not reflexive) 170.
-ύνω, new verb formed in, 61.
ὑπάγω 'go' 57, 182. Pres. not used in future sense 189. ὕπαγε 196, 278.
ὑπακούω with dat. 103. With inf. 227.
ὑπάρχω not employed for periphrases 203 note 1. With part. ibid. and 244.
ὑπέρ with acc. 135. With comparative 108. With gen. 135. Confused with περί with gen. 134, 135. Used adverbially (in conjunction with adv. etc.) 14, 65 f., 135.—Verb compounded with ὑπέρ transitive 89.
ὑπεράνω 65.
ὑπερβάλλω constr. 104.
ὑπερέκεινα 14, 66.
ὑπερεκπερισσοῦ, -ῶς 14 with note 1, 66, 135. With gen. 108.
ὑπερέχω constr. 89, 104.
ὑπερλίαν, ὑπὲρ λίαν 14, 66, 135.
ὑπό with acc. and gen. 135. ὑπὸ χεῖρα 135 note 2. Compounds with ὑπό, constr. 116.
ὑποδείκνυμι constr. 233.
ὑποκάτω 14, 65. With gen. 107, 129, 135 note 1.
ὑποκρίνομαι aor. 44. Constr. 232.
ὑπολαμβάνω not used with double acc. 92. With ὅτι 232.
ὑπομένω transit. 87.
ὑπομιμνήσκω, -ομαι constr. 104.
ὑπονοέω constr. 232.
ὑποστέλλομαι constr. 235.
-υσία, substantives in, 69.
ὑστερέω constr. 88 f., 91, 105, 112.
ὕστερος -ον also used in superlative sense 34 f.

φ, reduplication of, 11.
φάγομαι 42, 54. φάγεσαι 47, 54.
φαιλόνης 9.
φαίνω ἔφᾶνα 40, 57. φαίνομαί τινι 185. With part.? 245.
φανερόομαι constr. 233, 239.

φανερός: ἐν τῷ φ., εἰς φ. 156.
Φαρῖσαῖοι 8.
φαύσκω, φώσκω 57.
φείδομαι with gen. 101. φειδομένως 58.
φέρω 57. φέρε, φέρετε 196 note 2. φέρων 248.
φεύγω trans. and with ἀπό 87.
Φῆλιξ 15.
φημί 50. φησίν without subj. 75. φημὶ ὅτι 232. ἔφη omitted 292. φημί omitted 294.
φθάνω 57, 245.
φιλέω constr. 227. Used to express 'gladly' 258.
φιλόνικος not -εικος 8.
φίλος with gen. (εἰμί φ. with dat.) 112.
φοβέομαι fut. 45, 58. Trans. and with ἀπό 88. With μή 212 f., 240 note 1. With inf. 225.
φόβηθρον for -τρον 24.
φορέω, formation of tenses of, 40, 58.
φορτίζω with double acc. 92.
φρεναπάτης, -άω 68, 70.
φροντίζω constr. 227.
Φρυγία with and without art. 153.
Φύγελ(λ)ος 11.
φυλακή: τετάρτῃ φ. etc. 120.
-φύλαξ in composition 68.
φυλάσσω ἀπό 88. -ομαι trans. and with ἀπό 87 f. φυλάσσω φυλακάς 90. φυλάσσομαι ἵνα μή 225.
φύω ἐφύην 43, 58.

χαίρω, fut. 43, 58. Constr. 118, 137 (245). χαρᾷ χ. 119. χαίρειν sc. λέγει 222, 292.
χάριν and χάριτα 26. χάριν with gen. 127. Position 290. χάρις ὑμῖν καὶ εἰρήνη 288.
χειμάρρου from -ρρος (-άρρους) 25.
χείρ omitted 140. χ. in periphrases 83, 130, 151. ὑπὸ χεῖρα 135 note 2. χεῖρες καὶ πόδες 289.
χέω. See χύν(ν)ω. χεῶ ibid.
χλιαρός, -ερός 20.
χορτάζω, -ομαι constr. 101.
χράομαι, contract forms of, 47. Constr. 90, 114.
χρείαν ἔχω constr. 227 f. χρεία τοῦ with inf. 234.
χρεοφειλέτης (χρεωφ.) 22, 68.
χρή almost entirely absent 206 note 2.

INDEX OF GREEK WORDS.   331

χρῄζω constr. 105.
χρηματίζω, -ομαι (pass.) constr. 226, 232, 239 f.
Χρηστιανός not Χριστ. 63.
χρῖσμα 15.
Χριστός without art. 152.
χρίω constr. 92.
χρονίζω constr. 227.
χύ(ν)νω for χέω 41, 58. Fut. χεῶ 42, 58.
χωρίς with gen. 107, 127, 290 and 297 f. notes 6 and 1 (position).

ψεύδομαι constr. 110.
ψύχω fut. pass. 44, 58.
ψωμίζω constr. 92.

ω interchanged with α 22.
ὦ before the vocative 86.
ὧδε 'here' ('hither') 58 f.
ὠθέω ὦσα 37, 58.
-ών, substantives in, 64.
-ων (comparat.) -ονες (-ους) etc. 27.

ὠνέομαι ὠνούμην 37, 58.
ὥρα omitted 140, 149. Without art. 149. ὥρα sc. ἐστίν 73 : constr. 227 f., 240 f. ὥραν ἑβδόμην etc. (question When?) 94. Simple dat. and dat. with ἐν 120. ἐν αὐτῇ τῇ ὥρᾳ 170, 276.
-ως, adverbs in, 58.
ὡς 60, 270 f. Comparative particle 270 f. With predicate 92 f., 270. ὡς ἐπί versus 271. ὡς τάχιστα 142, 271. With participle etc. 246 f., 253. οὐχ ὡς 253. ὡς οὐ 256. In exclamations 258. ὡς, ὡς ὅτι in assertions 230 f. Temporal ὡς 218, 272. With inf. 225. With inf. for ὥστε? 223.
ὡσάν (ὡς ἄν) 233, 253 note 1, 270.
ὡσεί 253, 270.
ὥσπερ 60, 253, 270.
ὡσπερεί 270.
ὥστε 60, 223 f., 240 (272 with note 2).
ὠτίον (ὠτάριον) beside οὖς 63.
ὠφέλεια -ελία 8.
ὠφελέω constr. 89, 90.
ὤφθην apparui 56, 185 ; cp. ὁράω.

III. INDEX OF NEW TESTAMENT PASSAGES.

MATTHEW.

1. 2 ff.	152.	11. 20	143.	24. 12	143.
1. 18	252, 257.	11. 22, 24	268.	24. 15 f.	281.
1. 19	248.	12. 8	287.	24. 17	258.
1. 22	200.	12. 21	19 n. 3, 110 n. 2.	24. 22	178.
2. 6	157, 244.	12. 28	273.	24. 31	99 f., 158 note 2.
3. 4	164.	12. 32	265.	24. 43	172, 189.
3. 14	165, 190.	12. 36	283.	24. 45	157, 160.
3. 16 f.	83.	12. 41	124.	25. 6	200.
3. 17	292.	13. 12	217.	25. 9	196, 213, 255.
4. 15	94 note 1, 98, 130, 147.	13. 23	146, 274.	25. 11	301.
		13. 30	90.	25. 14	270.
5. 1	251.	13. 44	172.	25. 24, 26	175, 258.
5. 17	266.	13. 46	200.	25. 41	196.
5. 19	299.	14. 6	120 note 3.	26. 5	294.
5. 20	108.	14. 19	251 note 1.	26. 24	254.
5. 28	102.	15. 5	209.	26. 25	254.
5. 38	293.	15. 20	233.	26. 28	134.
5. 39 ff.	195, 217.	15. 32	85, 266.	26. 29	218.
5. 43 f.	209.	16. 6	88 note 1.	26. 33	215.
6. 3	252.	16. 7	293.	26. 38	196.
6. 18	245.	16. 21	125.	26. 39	268.
6. 30	214.	16. 22	209.	26. 50	176.
6. 34	104, 195.	17. 4	215 note 2.	26. 53	191.
7. 15	173.	17. 11 f.	267.	26. 62	106, 176 n. 1.
7. 24	173.	18. 4	217.	26. 64	268.
7. 25, 27	172.	18. 19	215.	27. 1	224.
8. 1	251 f.	18. 22	145.	27. 11	260.
8. 2	215.	18. 25	251.	27. 25	293.
8. 9	196.	18. 27	104.	27. 33	77, 281.
8. 27	293.	18. 32	191.	27. 38	145.
8. 28	172, 251.	19. 10	257.	27. 40	198.
8. 34	191.	19. 25, 27	260.	27. 48	251 note 1.
9. 2	51, 188 note 1.	19. 29	277.	27. 49	202, 208, 248.
9. 6	294.	20. 2	94, 105.	28. 1	97.
9. 9	182 note 1.	20. 18	111.	28. 9	152.
9. 15	218.	20. 23	234.		
9. 18	251.	21. 4	200.		MARK.
9. 22	172.	21. 5	113.	1. 23	131.
9. 27	182 note 1.	21. 8	143.	1. 31	197.
9. 30	278.	21. 25 f.	147.	1. 45	227 note 1.
10. 1	224.	21. 41	298.	2. 1	239.
10. 4	198 note 1.	22. 11	255.	2. 5	51.
10. 13	209.	22. 36	143.	2. 10	286.
10. 23	180.	23. 12	217.	2. 13	124.
10. 28	264.	23. 25 f.	107 note 1.	2. 28	284.
10. 32, 33	217.	23. 33	210.	3. 7	124.
11. 8 f.	268.	24. 4	278.	3. 11	207.
		24. 6	278.	3. 14	226.

INDEX OF N.T. PASSAGES. 333

3. 20	265.	14. 21	254.	5. 36	159 note 1, 264, 293.
3. 21	138.	14. 24	134.	6. 3	272.
3. 26	214.	14. 27	275.	6. 4	241, 254.
4. 9	228.	14. 29	215, 251, 291.	6. 8	279.
4. 20	146.	14. 34	196.	6. 14 ff.	263.
4. 22	216, 218 note 1, 269.	14. 36	175, 268.	6. 25	87 note 2.
		14. 44	164.	6. 29 f.	105, 195.
4. 25	217.	14. 60	176 note 1, 177 note 1.	6. 48	250 note 1.
4. 30	166.	14. 65	118.	7. 4	218.
4. 41	293.	14. 68	265.	7. 6	248.
5. 2	131.	14. 72	182.	7. 8	196.
5. 41	166.	15. 2	260.	7. 12	164, 262.
5. 43	230 note 2.	15. 6	36, 207.	7. 17	130.
6. 2	143, 176.	15. 10	200.	7. 24 ff.	268.
6. 7	145.	15. 25	262.	8. 5 f.	267.
6. 8 f.	286.	16. 2	120.	8. 18	217.
6. 22 ff.	186 note 1.	[Mc.] 16. 9	144.	8. 24	301.
6. 27	230.	[Mc.] 16. 10 ff.	172.	8. 27, 29	121.
6. 37	212.			8. 40	237.
6. 39 f.	145, 230.	LUKE.		8. 41 f.	164.
6. 45	219.	1. 1	274.	8. 52	196.
6. 48	237.	1. 1-4	280.	9. 3	265.
6. 56	207.	1. 4	174.	9. 7	108.
7. 11	281 note 1.	1. 7	274.	9. 13	216.
7. 20	172.	1. 8	288.	9. 24 f.	167 note 3.
7. 25	175.	1. 9	102, 235.	9. 25	248.
7. 31	124.	1. 12	287.	9. 28	85, 262.
8. 7	230 note 2.	1. 17	130.	9. 33	241.
8. 15	88 note 1.	1. 20	174, 219.	9. 34	237.
8. 23	101.	1. 21	237.	9. 36	200.
8. 26	265.	1. 23	288.	9. 45	225.
8. 32	133.	1. 37	178.	9. 46	130.
8. 35	217.	1. 43	229.	9. 49 f.	217.
9. 10	234.	1. 45	138.	9. 52	224.
9. 13	267 f.	1. 46 ff.	151.	9. 59	242.
9. 20	283.	1. 54	224.	9. 60	299.
9. 26	143.	1. 59	190.	10. 6	293.
9. 28	176, 251.	1. 65 ff.	287.	10. 35	237 note 1.
9. 37	267 note 2.	1. 68 ff.	151.	10. 37	134.
9. 40	217.	1. 70	160.	10. 39	170.
9. 43	215.	1. 71, 72	224.	10. 41	301.
9. 45	241.	1. 73	175.	11. 2	219.
10. 29	277.	1. 76	295 note 2.	11. 3	196.
10. 30	215.	2. 1	171, 288.	11. 5	210, 262.
10. 33	111.	2. 8	203.	11. 6	218.
10. 49	230 note 2.	2. 21	234, 262.	11. 8	215, 254.
11. 19	207.	2. 26	185, 219.	11. 13	258.
11. 25	218.	2. 27	107, 135, 237.	11. 28	270.
11. 30 f.	148.	2. 28	164.	12. 8	217.
11. 31 f.	286.	2. 37	164.	12. 15	88 note 1.
11. 32	192.	3. 18	273.	12. 36	211.
12. 4	61.	3. 21	237.	12. 48	175.
12. 28	108.	4. 1	248.	12. 51	269.
12. 33	234.	4. 16	112.	12. 58	272.
12. 41, 44	193.	4. 20, 25	161.	13. 9	271, 293.
13. 7	219.	4. 29	224.	13. 13	38.
13. 19	173, 175.	5. 3	179.	13. 16	85.
13. 34	270.	5. 7	138.	13. 24	282.
14. 2	294.	5. 19	108, 140.	13. 28	218.
14. 3	106.	5. 24	196, 286.	13. 33	303 note 1.
14. 9	124.	5. 35	218.	13. 35	218.
14. 14	217.				

INDEX OF N.T. PASSAGES.

14. 8 f.	213.	23. 31	210.	6. 39	283 with note 1.
14. 21	277.	23. 33	145.	6. 46	292 note 2.
14. 35	228.	23. 36	263 note 2.	6. 62	294.
15. 6	186.	23. 44	262.	6. 64	37, 202, 205.
15. 16	19 note 3, 101.	23. 50 f.	166.	7. 4	214, 238.
15. 22	124 note 2.	23. 53	203.	7. 8	189.
15. 26	177, 220.	24. 20	258, 263 note 2.	7. 9	193.
15. 30	171.	24. 13	95.	7. 12	267.
16. 1	171, 253.	24. 15	152.	7. 28	262, 264.
16. 2	177.	24. 21	164.	7. 35	293.
16. 4	105 f.	24. 25	236.	7. 38	283.
16. 20	39.	24. 27	38.	7. 40	97.
16. 24	103.	24. 47	81, 249.	7. 45	172 note 1.
16. 26	258.	24. 50	139 note 4.	[Jo.] 8. 9	249, 272 note 2.
17. 2	182, 215, 228.			8. 14	189, 215 note 1, 266.
17. 4	157.		JOHN.	8. 16	290.
17. 7 f.	268 note 2.	1. 6 ff.	172 note 1.	8. 19	206 note 1.
17. 8	175.	1. 13	84.	8. 25	176.
17. 11	132, 153 note 2.	1. 14	81.	8. 38	165.
17. 22	218.	1. 15	128, 198.	8. 42	275.
17. 31	217.	1. 16	124.	8. 44	157, 163, 166 n. 1.
17. 33	217.	1. 22	294 note 2.	8. 53	173.
18. 1	236.	1. 24	19 note 3.	8. 58	229.
18. 7	19 note 3.	1. 27	218.	8. 59	250 note 1.
18. 11	171.	1. 30	128, 164.	9. 2	224.
18. 14	108, 143.	1. 39	281 note 1.	9. 6	103, 288.
18. 18	288.	1. 42	164.	9. 7	123 n. 1, 281 n. 1.
18. 29	277.	2. 19	221.	9. 8	192.
19. 2	164.	3. 8	189.	9. 17	293.
19. 4	109, 140, 295.	3. 10	157.	9. 21	168.
19. 8	97.	3. 15	110 note 1.	9. 28	171 note 2.
19. 11	249, 258.	3. 18	255.	9. 30	275.
19. 13	169, 219.	3. 25	97.	9. 36	294.
19. 15	262.	3. 32	199 note 2.	10. 6	172.
19. 40	215.	3. 35	130.	10. 12	255.
19. 42	261 note 1, 294.	4. 2	269.	10. 32	187.
19. 43	262.	4. 9	114.	10. 36	286, 291.
20. 4 f.	148.	4. 10	164.	10. 40	193.
20. 11 f.	258.	4. 11	266.	11. 2	198 note 1.
20. 19	200.	4. 18	141.	11. 19	134.
20. 20	224, 238.	4. 27	138.	11. 47	210.
20. 22	241.	4. 34	228.	11. 48	264.
20. 27	255.	4. 36	264.	11. 57	211 note 2.
20. 36	265 note 1.	5. 2	242 note 1.	12. 1	126.
21. 6	283 note 3.	5. 3	277.	12. 4	205.
21. 11	263 note 2, 299.	[Jo.] 5. 4	130, 178.	12. 12	243.
21. 16	97.	5. 7	228.	12. 27	268, 303.
22. 11	217, 295.	5. 11	146 note 2.	12. 28	264.
22. 26	293.	5. 31	215.	12. 35 f.	272.
22. 34	219, 255.	5. 35	157.	12. 43	60, 108.
22. 40, 46	196.	5. 36	108.	13. 6	187, 288.
22. 42	294.	5. 37 f.	266.	13. 13	85.
22. 43	268.	5. 38	164.	13. 17	214.
22. 49	210, 244.	5. 39	164.	13. 27	142.
22. 66	264.	5. 44	154, 164.	14. 9	121, 289.
22. 70	260.	6. 2	37.	14. 21	172.
23. 3	260.	6. 9	166, 177.	14. 22	177, 293.
23. 12	170.	6. 13	102 with note 3.	15. 2	283 note 1.
23. 14	253.	6. 18	38.	15. 5	285.
23. 15	112.	6. 19	136.	15. 6	194.
23. 19	204.	6. 22	192.	15. 8	212, 229.
23. 28	264.	6. 22 ff.	284.	15. 13	229.

INDEX OF N.T. PASSAGES. 335

15. 22	254.	5. 7	85, 267.	11. 26	193.
15. 24	205, 264.	5. 9	114 note 1, 240.	12. 1	125.
16. 17	97.	5. 14 f.	281.	12. 3	76, 258, 267, 281.
16. 19	197 note 1.	5. 21	135, 230.	12. 12	162.
17. 2	82, 166.	5. 24	177, 220.	13. 1	163.
18. 34	167 note 1.	5. 26 f.	190.	13. 13	134.
18. 36	206, 207.	5. 28	119, 171 note 2.	13. 20	121.
18. 37	260, 273.	5. 29	292.	13. 21	186 note 2.
19. 6	301.	5. 36	168.	13. 24	129.
19. 11	205.	5. 38 f.	214.	13. 25	175.
19. 13	54.	5. 41	190.	13. 32	90 note 1, 290.
19. 17	77 note 1.	6. 3	81.	13. 42	129.
19. 24	131.	6. 5	81.	14. 3	137, 193.
19. 28	291.	6. 8	248.	14. 9	235.
19. 35	172 note 2.	6. 9	153.	14. 10	158, 295 note 3.
20. 4	295 note 2.	7. 7	217.	14. 13	243.
20. 14	152.	7. 13	113 note 1.	14. 15	177.
20. 17	196.	7. 19	236.	14. 17	269.
20. 20	245.	7. 20	113.	14. 19	190.
21. 5	254 note 2.	7. 21	165.	14. 21 f.	198.
21. 21	177, 290.	7. 24	185.	14. 22	233, 292 note 1.
21. 22	177, 214.	7. 26	190.	14. 28	193 note 1.
21. 25	232.	7. 29	131.	15. 1	117.
		7. 33	183.	15. 3 f.	190.
	ACTS.	7. 34	208.	15. 3	192.
1. 1	152.	7. 35	158, 200.	15. 10	225 note 1.
1. 3	109, 185.	7. 35 ff.	301.	15. 22 f.	285.
1. 4	286.	7. 40	283.	15. 23	159 n. 1, 182 n. 3.
1. 5	133.	7. 43	84, 107.	15. 27	198.
1. 6	146.	7. 46	186, 241 note 1.	15. 36	166.
1. 12	32, 85, 95.	7. 53	123.	15. 39	224.
1. 13	265.	8. 4	146.	16. 12	97, 193 n. 1, 204.
1. 15	264 note 1, 267.	8. 5	166.	16. 14	98.
1. 20	220 note 1.	8. 9	178.	16. 15	165, 191 n. 2, 263.
1. 21	174, 292 note 1.	8. 26	171, 249.	16. 18	188.
1. 22	174, 249.	8. 30	259, 298.	16. 21	242.
1. 24 f.	197, 223.	8. 31	215, 191.	16. 22 f.	191 n. 1, 197, 230.
2. 4	292.	8. 32	173.	16. 34	245.
2. 9 f.	153.	8. 40	237.	16. 37	275.
2. 9 ff.	265.	9. 1	103, 151.	16. 39	125, 133, 191 n. 2.
2. 12	220.	9. 3	151 (152).	17. 1	153.
2. 14	292.	9. 4	246.	17. 2	112, 191.
2. 25	38.	9. 5	292.	17. 7	128.
2. 37	263, 292.	9. 6	175.	17. 18	171.
2. 39	112.	9. 11	292.	17. 21	142, 154 n. 2, 161.
2. 40	143, 263.	9. 15	264.	17. 22	142.
2. 45	190.	9. 16	179 note 1.	17. 26	69.
2. 47	116 note 1.	9. 21	201.	17. 31	274.
3. 3	191, 241 note 1.	9. 27	101 note 5.	18. 2	152.
3. 10	164, 192.	9. 28	292 note 1.	18. 6	293.
3. 12	253.	9. 34	188.	18. 11	193.
3. 26	237.	9. 38, 42	152.	18. 15	133.
3. 26 f.	301.	10. 14	178.	18. 17	104.
4. 7	164.	10. 33	223.	18. 19 ff.	191.
4. 10 f.	301.	10. 36	96, 174.	18. 21	295.
4. 12	243.	10. 37	81.	18. 22	250.
4. 13	267.	10. 46	292.	18. 23	198, 250.
4. 20	256.	10. 48	191.	18. 24	21.
4. 17	119.	11. 4	249.	19. 1	21.
4. 18	234 note 2.	11. 7	246.	19. 6	292.
4. 33	288.	11. 17	177.	19. 7	162.
5. 3	224.	11. 24	116 note 1.	19. 16	250.

19. 24	186.	26. 5	33.	2. 7	288.
19. 26	127, 178.	26. 7	290.	2. 13	162.
19. 27	106 note 1.	26. 9	167 note 2, 238.	2. 17	195 note 2.
19. 32	200.	26. 11	190.	2. 19 f.	215.
19. 34	283, 301.	26. 13	290.	3. 12	151 note 2.
19. 37	248.	26. 16	264.	3. 14	166, 221.
20. 7	152.	26. 21	20, 127.	3. 20	123 note 2.
20. 11	152.	26. 24	143, 158, 288.	4. 3	277.
20. 13	153, 253.	26. 29	116 note 3, 207.	4. 5	148.
20. 16	221.	27. 1 f.	191.	4. 15	196.
20. 24	92, 223 note 1.	27. 3	242.	4. 18	154.
20. 28	223.	27. 4 f.	264.	5. 1	195 note 2.
20. 30	170.	27. 10	233, 286.	5. 8	163.
21. 1	153.	27. 13	34, 142.	5. 12	123.
21. 2 f.	198.	27. 15	141.		
21. 3	40, 93, 153, 183, 190, 204.	27. 20	147, 266.		2 PETER.
		27. 30	253.	1. 1	163.
21. 11	168.	27. 33	94.	1. 5	171.
21. 16	97, 174, 217.	27. 34	140.	1. 5 ff.	301.
21. 20	190.	27. 40	140, 253.	1. 9	254.
21. 21	240.	27. 41	190.	2. 5	145.
21. 23	203.	28. 3	183.	2. 6	111.
21. 24	212.	28. 14	152.	2. 10	246.
21. 28	199, 298.	28. 17	159.	2. 12	88 note 2.
21. 30	190.	28. 19	256.	2. 13	202.
21. 38	260.	28. 22	267.	2. 16	169.
22. 1	103.	28. 30	193.	2. 19	113.
22. 2	190.			2. 21	242.
22. 5	19 note 3.		JAMES.	2. 22	157, 293.
22. 6	241.	1. 14 f.	302 note 1.	3. 1	166.
22. 7	246.	1. 17	297.	3. 2	99.
22. 10	196.	1. 18	177.	3. 3	137, 156.
22. 15	199.	1. 19	236.	3. 5	147.
22. 16	186.	1. 24	200.	3. 9	105.
22. 17	165, 252.	1. 27	195.	3. 14	113.
22. 22	206.	2. 6	104, 155.	3. 16	161.
22. 24	230 note 2.	2. 10	200, 217.		
23. 3	299.	3. 7	113.		1 JOHN.
23. 8	162, 265 note 2.	3. 8	81.	1. 4	166.
23. 9	294.	3. 12	265 note 1.	1. 9	224.
23. 23	178, 286.	3. 13	175.	2. 2	290.
23. 25	182 note 3.	3. 18	113 note 3.	2. 3	215, 229.
23. 30	252.	4. 9 f.	195.	2. 5	200.
23. 31	153.	4. 13	170.	2. 22	255.
24. 3	298.	4. 14	157, 176.	2. 24	273, 283.
24. 6	283 f.	4. 15	263 note 1.	2. 27	283.
24. 12	265 note 2.	5. 7	141.	2. 29	214 note 1.
24. 19	221.	5. 7 f.	195.	3. 1	229.
24. 21	172.	5. 12	256 note 2.	3. 16	229.
24. 22	142.	5. 13 ff.	302.	3. 17	210 note 1.
24. 26	252.	5. 16	185.	4. 2	247.
25. 4	238.			4. 3	152, 254.
25. 8	154.		1 PETER.	4. 9	131.
25. 10	142, 203.	1. 1	153.	4. 19	273.
25. 10 f.	188.	1. 8	256.	5. 2	229.
25. 11	234, 292.	1. 13	195 note 2.	5. 3	229.
25. 13	197.	1. 17	195 note 2.	5. 15	214.
25. 16	220.	1. 18	160.		
25. 21	238.	1. 20	156.		2 JOHN.
25. 22	207, 292.	1. 22	195 note 2.		
26. 2	199, 290.	2. 6	182 note 3.	2	285.
26. 4	50.				

INDEX OF N.T. PASSAGES.

3 JOHN.
2	135.
10	266.

ROMANS.
1. 5	166.
1. 6	107.
1. 7	163.
1. 8	267.
1. 13	270, 282.
1. 14	154.
1. 15	74 note 1, 133, 157.
1. 19	155.
1. 24	235.
1. 28	270.
1. 29	299.
1. 31	299.
2. 4	155.
2. 6 ff.	286.
2. 15 f.	282.
2. 16	156, 218.
2. 17 ff.	284.
2. 19	238.
2. 21 ff.	300 note 3.
2. 26	166.
2. 27	132.
3. 1	303.
3. 2	267.
3. 5	210, 282, 303.
3. 6	220, 274.
3. 9	257.
3. 12	203.
3. 20	150.
3. 25	169.
3. 29 f.	148.
4. 9	294.
4. 10	303.
4. 13	234.
4. 17	174.
5. 3 ff.	301.
5. 7	201.
5. 13	150.
5. 16	299.
5. 18	294.
6. 1	210.
6. 4	195 note 1, 159.
6. 5	114.
6. 10 f.	91, 111.
6. 14	150.
6. 17	174.
7. 3	201.
7. 3 f.	111.
7. 5	160, 185.
7. 7	275.
7. 14	65.
7. 18	234.
8. 3	155.
8. 7	275.
8. 9	131.
8. 12	235.
8. 16	279.
8. 22	162.
8. 29 f.	301.
8. 31 ff.	303.
8. 33 ff.	303 note 3.
8. 34	303 note 2.
8. 39	160.
9. 1	279.
9. 3	207, 159 note 5.
9. 4	277.
9. 6	179, 292 note 2.
9. 21	228 note 3.
10. 1	267, 279.
10. 9	247.
10. 14 f.	210, 301.
10. 16	268.
11. 6	274.
11. 8	235.
11. 13	267.
11. 17, 19	299.
11. 18	294.
11. 22	274.
11. 36	132.
12. 1	293.
12. 3	298.
12. 6 ff.	271.
12. 7 ff.	150.
12. 9 ff.	285.
12. 12	120.
12. 15	222, 299.
13. 3	23 note 1.
13. 5	73, 240.
13. 7	294.
13. 9	167 note 1.
13. 11	241.
13. 13	195 note 1, 253.
14. 2	232 note 2.
14. 4	111.
14. 7 f.	111.
14. 11	111.
14. 19	157.
14. 21	197, 292.
15. 24	272.
15. 26 f.	115, 275.
16. 3 ff.	173.
16. 7	71 note 4.
16. 27	284 note 2.

1 CORINTHIANS.
1. 13	134.
1. 18	159.
1. 25 ff.	155, 274, 300.
1. 27 f.	82, 156.
1. 31	293.
2. 4	100 note 2.
2. 7	131.
2. 13	107.
2. 16	151 note 2.
3. 1	65.
3. 2	269, 292.
3. 3	65.
3. 5	269.
3. 6	268.
3. 12	277.
3. 14 f.	215.
3. 21	271.
4. 3	228.
4. 6	48, 144, 211 note 1, 293.
4. 8	207, 302.
4. 9	278.
4. 15	215, 268.
5. 1	288.
5. 7	275.
5. 10	206, 257.
5. 13	170.
6. 4	270, 290.
6. 5	82.
6. 9 f.	265.
6. 11	268.
6. 20	273.
7. 5	216.
7. 11	238.
7. 13	286.
7. 17	216.
7. 25	253.
7. 26	234.
7. 27	280, 302.
7. 35	115, 155, 244.
7. 36	214.
7. 36 ff.	196.
7. 37	285.
8. 4	290.
8. 5	271.
8. 6	132, 175.
8. 7	160 note 1.
9. 1	199.
9. 10	274 f.
9. 11	215.
9. 15	112, 228.
9. 18	229.
9. 19	142.
9. 20	154.
9. 21	106.
9. 22	162.
10. 2	187.
10. 3	160.
10. 4	191.
10. 6	191.
10. 11	78.
10. 13	235.
10. 16	174.
10. 18	159.
10. 21	151 note 2.
10. 24	291.
10. 31	271, 292.
10. 32	264.
10. 33	244.
11. 3	302 note 1.
11. 4	133.
11. 5	77, 158.
11. 6	186, 234.
11. 9	275.
11. 14	283 note 2.
11. 17	256 note 1.
11. 18	267.

11. 24	168.	7. 5	200, 284.	1. 17	295.
11. 27	266.	7. 7	142.	2. 2	213.
11. 29 ff.	298.	7. 11	118 n.1, 233 n.1,	2. 4	212, 284.
11. 34	272.		234, 269.	2. 6	284.
12. 13	275.	7. 12	237.	2. 9	294.
12. 15 f.	138, 256.	8. 1	131.	2. 10	175.
12. 31	159.	8. 2	133.	2. 18	273.
13. 2	162.	8. 3	282.	3. 1	175.
13. 3	187 note 1, 212.	8. 6	236.	3. 5	291.
13. 8	271.	8. 9	155.	3. 14	124.
13. 13	150.	8. 10 f.	234.	3. 15	269.
14. 5	216.	8. 11	235, 237.	4. 6 f.	286.
14. 7	269.	8. 15	293.	4. 9	295, 303 note 2.
14. 11	131.	8. 17	142.	4. 11	213, 240 note 1.
14. 18	246.	8. 18 ff.	284.	4. 13	133.
14. 20	150.	8. 21	156.	4. 15	205.
15. 2	216, 291.	8. 23	271 note 2.	4. 17	48, 212 note 1.
15. 3 f.	199.	9. 1	234.	4. 18	234.
15. 6	142.	9. 2	142, 168.	4. 19	166.
15. 15	271 note 1.	9. 3	160.	4. 20	207.
15. 35	176, 220.	9. 4	303.	4. 24	173.
15. 41	147.	9. 6	294.	4. 26	173.
15. 42 ff.	300 note 3.	9. 7	294.	5. 4	187.
15. 47	147.	9. 8	298.	5. 6	185.
15. 48 f.	300 note 3.	9. 11 ff.	285.	5. 12	186.
15. 51	257.	9. 13	159.	5. 13	294.
		10. 2	234.	5. 14	167 note 1, 162.
2 CORINTHIANS.		10. 2 f.	298.	5. 21	299.
1. 4	162.	10. 9	270, 294 note 2.	6. 1	286.
1. 6	185.	10. 10	75, 282.	6. 10	272.
1. 9	200.	10. 11 ff.	166.		
1. 13	269.	10. 12	168.	EPHESIANS.	
1. 17	256 note 2.	10. 13	174 note 2.	1. 15	133.
1. 19	290.	11. 1	207, 269.	1. 17	49, 211 note 1.
2. 2	262.	11. 1 ff.	303.	1. 23	186.
2. 3	171.	11. 10	232.	2. 11	160.
2. 6	76, 142.	11. 16	196.	2. 15	162.
2. 13	200, 236.	11. 16 ff.	288, 303.	3. 1	107 note 2.
3. 1 ff.	299.	11. 19 f.	303.	3. 4	160.
3. 3	65.	11. 21	282, 303.	3. 8	161.
3. 5-11	299.	11. 22	303.	3. 20	185.
3. 13	294.	11. 23	135, 303.	4. 9	98.
3. 18	93, 100.	11. 24	138.	4. 18	203.
4. 3	131.	11. 25	193, 200.	4. 20	285.
4. 8	298.	11. 26	147.	4. 22	238.
4. 10 f.	152.	11. 28	116.	4. 28	162, 198, 243.
4. 12	185.	12. 7	217.	5. 4	206, 256 note 1.
4. 15	142.	12. 9	143.	5. 12	166.
4. 16	107.	12. 11	206, 303.	5. 21	285.
4. 17	155.	12. 13	303.	5. 32	164.
4. 18	252.	12. 17	200, 283.	5. 33	222.
5. 10	162, 266.	12. 20	255.	6. 3	212.
5. 11	202 note 1.	12. 21	252.	6. 5	159.
5. 12	284.	13. 4	275.	6. 16	160.
5. 13	111, 199, 291.	13. 5	216.		
5. 14	162, 273.			PHILIPPIANS.	
5. 19	166.	GALATIANS.		1. 3	162.
6. 3-10	285.	1. 4	160.	1. 6	91, 171.
6. 4 ff.	295.	1. 7	216, 254.	1. 11	93, 102.
6. 13	91, 93, 282.	1. 12	265 note 2.	1. 14	142.
6. 14	114, 204.	1. 13	160.	1. 18	268.
7. 3	303.	1. 16	131.	1. 22	211, 262.

INDEX OF N.T. PASSAGES.   339

1. 23	236.	5. 11	144.	2. 16	301.
1. 27	212.	5. 27	241.	3. 6	80.
2. 1	81.			3. 12	98.
2. 4	180.		2 THESSALONIANS.	3. 16	268.
2. 6	257, 271.	1. 5	293.	4. 1	195 note 1.
2. 8	247.	2. 2	253.	4. 2	114.
2. 13	135, 234.	2. 7	185.	4. 7	297.
2. 15	166.	2. 12	215.	4. 11	288, 297.
2. 20	218.	3. 10	232.	5. 3	134.
2. 23	168, 272.	3. 11	298.	5. 7	126 note 1.
3. 2 f.	88, note 1, 298.			5. 8	299.
3. 7	199.		1 TIMOTHY.	5. 9	297.
3. 8	155, 269, 270.	1. 1	163.	5. 11	228.
3. 9	169.	1. 3 ff.	284.	6. 2	100, 264.
3. 12 ·	138, 216.	1. 4	108 note 1.	6. 3	297.
3. 14	294.	1. 10	277.	6. 10	224.
3. 16	222, 268.	1. 16	162.	6. 14	260.
3. 20	163, 168.	4. 3	291.	6. 16	296.
3. 21	235.	4. 13	219.	7. 9	225.
4. 5	155.	5. 9	108 with note 4.	7. 11	255.
4. 10	43, 138, 234.	5. 10	151 note 2.	7. 15	33 f. note 4.
4. 11	292 note 2.	5. 13	247.	7. 16	65.
4. 12	264.	5. 19	216.	7. 20 f.	146.
4. 22	258.	5. 22	195.	7. 23 f.	146.
		6. 3	254.	7. 26	263.
	COLOSSIANS.	6. 5	105.	8. 2	173.
1. 15	162.	6. 13 f.	241.	8. 3	218.
1. 21	203.	6. 20	195.	8. 6	263.
1. 23	162.			8. 9	252.
1. 26	285.		2 TIMOTHY.	8. 13	237.
1. 29	185.	1. 16	38.	9. 9	80.
2. 5	250.	1. 18	142.	9. 17	218, 255, 297 n. 3.
2. 8	213.	2. 25	213.	10. 2	297.
2. 10	77 note 2, 102.	3. 2	277.	10. 10	297 note 5.
2. 15	185.	4. 2	277.	10. 25	168.
2. 17	77 note 2.	4. 2 f.	195.	10. 27	178.
2. 23	204, 267.	4. 3	118.	10. 28	138.
3. 5	77 note 2, 150.	4. 7 f.	199.	10. 29	282.
3. 14	77 note 2.			10. 33	171.
3. 16 f.	285.		TITUS.	10. 37	73, 179.
4. 3	253.	1. 2 f.	286.	11. 3	257.
4. 16	258.	1. 11	254.	11. 3-31	301.
		2. 9	169.	11. 12	160.
	1 THESSALONIANS.	2. 11	160.	11. 17	190, 200.
1. 1	163.	2. 13	163.	11. 27	298.
1. 3	96, 99.	3. 5	168, 173.	11. 28	200.
1. 8	160.			11. 32	264, 289, 302 f. note 2.
2. 10	258.		PHILEMON.		
2. 12	195 note 1.	13	207.	11. 32-40	301.
2. 13	185.	19	302.	12. 1	289.
2. 18	267.	20	298 note 4.	12. 2 f.	199 note 3, 298.
2. 19	266.			12. 7	149, 297 note 6.
3. 3	234.		HEBREWS.	12. 8	297.
3. 5	213.	1. 1	137, 156, 297, 297 note 6, 298.	12. 9	267.
3. 7	214.			12. 10	146.
3. 10	236.	1. 1 ff.	280.	12. 13 ff.	297 f.
4. 1	158.	1. 4	288, 298.	12. 14	297 note 6.
4. 6	234.	1. 5	288.	12. 15	98.
4. 9	228 note 4, 302 note 2.	2. 8	237, 266, 297.	12. 24	297.
		2. 9	297.	12. 28	298.
4. 16	159.	2. 10	132.	13. 17	253.
5. 10	212, 214.	2. 15	233. 237.	13. 18	232.

13. 19	142.	5. 13	103.	12. 14	175.	
13. 23	142.	6. 1	81, 278.	13. 3	44, 118 note 3.	
13. 24	258.	6. 3	278.	13. 13	224.	
		6. 4	283.	13. 15	226.	
APOCALYPSE.		6. 5	278.	13. 16	212.	
1. 5	80.	6. 6	293.	14. 4	217.	
2. 5	113, 293.	6. 7	278.	14. 8	99, 301.	
2. 7	283.	7. 2	175.	14. 12	81.	
2. 9	238.	7. 4	81.	14. 19	80.	
2. 12	160.	7. 9	81.	15. 2	126.	
2. 14	90 note 2.	7. 14	200.	16. 1	41.	
2. 17	100 note 3, 283.	8. 1	218.	16. 9	224.	
2. 20	81.	8. 3	212.	16. 19	99.	
2. 22	215.	8. 5	200.	17. 8	44.	
2. 26	283.	9. 10	114 note 2.	18. 2	301.	
3. 9	211, 226, 240.	9. 11	85.	18. 3	99.	
3. 12	81, 283.	9. 20	224.	19. 3	200.	
3. 17	91 note 1.	9. 21	265 note 1.	19. 10	293.	
3. 18	92.	11. 4	80.	20. 4	265 note 1.	
3. 21	283.	11. 5	216.	20. 10	198.	
5. 3	265 note 1.	11. 11	130.	21. 4	265 note 1.	
5. 4	265 note 1.	11. 18	228 note 3.	21. 17	99 note 1.	
5. 5	224.	12. 5	80.	21. 21	122.	
5. 7	200.	12. 6	175.	22. 9	293.	
5. 11 f.	81.	12. 7	236.	22. 14	211.	
5. 12	277.	12. 8	265 note 1.	22. 28 f.	299.	

www.ingramcontent.com/pod-product-compliance
Lightning Source LLC
Chambersburg PA
CBHW050835230426
43667CB00012B/2014